THE RATIONALIZATION MOVEMENT IN GERMAN INDUSTRY

A Study in the Evolution of Economic Planning

BY
ROBERT A. BRADY

UNIVERSITY OF CALIFORNIA PRESS
BERKELEY, CALIFORNIA
1933

SALES REPRESENTATIVES:
UNIVERSITY OF CALIFORNIA PRESS
BERKELEY, CALIFORNIA

CAMBRIDGE UNIVERSITY PRESS
LONDON, ENGLAND
For orders originating in Great Britain only

PRINTED IN THE UNITED STATES OF AMERICA

TO

THE MEMORY

OF

RICHARD FREDERICK SCHOLZ

CONTENTS

PREFACE

IN THE INTERVAL between the completion and the publication of this study, German economic, political, and cultural life has seemingly undergone a kaleidoscopic transformation. On the contrary, its strongly established structure has scarcely even been disturbed. In order to understand what has really happened, it must be realized that the present superficial events are merely external adjustments to fundamental alterations, already accomplished, which are a peculiar blend of two converging developments. These developments had their historical origin long before the World War, and were of course vitally affected by that war.

First to appear were the coalescent forces—of coordination and integration—which began to destroy the foundations of laissez faire as early as the late seventies of the past century. The early and crude vehicles of these forces were cartels, trade federations, syndicates, financial consortiums, chambers of commerce and industry, trade unions, and cooperative societies. The World War added the central war coordination boards. In these boards, and in certain of the attempts at nationalization of basic industries under socialist influence following the Weimar Constitution, the hand of the central political authority is clearly seen. This period ended with the spectacular breakdown of the summer of 1931. At that time the center of gravity in economic affairs shifted to the state, where it has since remained.

The second development represents the presence of forces compelling a gradual but thorough interweaving of economic, political, social, and cultural issues. There is indicated here a significant admixture of the medieval concept of the corporatively organized society. Clearly, realization of any one of the basic economic objectives—high level of productivity, economic stability, individual security, and "equitable" distribution of income—can no longer be considered possible in Germany except by a frontal attack on each of the others. Moreover, no one of them is realizable, either in theory or in practice, solely by economic means.

Long before the recent upheavals were foreshadowed to the public, the accomplished evolution of the more or less formal rationalization movement had demonstrated how closely and vitally the most narrow and technical problems were bound up with social issues. Recognition of this truth sharpened, clarified, and lent direction to the course of events. The primary emphasis of the movement was, at the outset, technical. In a multiplicity of ways it helped to lay bare the engineering and organizational limitations of, as well as the paradoxes inherent in, the post-war German economic system. But, very soon, a need for the arts of organization became manifest, and thence it was an easy, if inescapable, step to consideration of larger questions of social policy. Thus throughout the entire range of rationalization activities there are to be found the directing concepts of plan, order, system, foresight, control, and rational guidance. In detail and at large *rationalization is planning,* and planning calls for the full mobilization of all scientific information and the rational utilization of unscientific criteria as to means.

But means to what end? If rationalization takes as its guiding principle the free and full cooperation of all vitally affected interests—and this principle has never been contested in any discussion of the subject—then how reconcile the divergent interests of capital and labor, industry and agriculture, producers and consumers? In particular, how reconcile these interests in a society whose very basis of organization holds within it fundamental conflicts of interest?

Organizationally, rationalization implied that the Manchesterian economic system was at an end in Germany. As Professor Bonn has made clear in his brilliant essays, the business interests of Germany, take them by and large, will probably be the last to want it back. Can capitalism, shorn thereby of so many of its assumed economic functions, long continue to exist? Wiedenfeld's penetrating tract, *Kapitalismus und Beamtentum,* shows this to be very doubtful, and the current drift of events in Europe makes it highly improbable. In transition, the newly established régime has provided the compromise answer: dictatorship by joint action of the middle class and "big business" as the economic, political, and cultural expression of an emergent (decadent?) age of monopoly capitalism.

If this view can stand the test of criticism and future history, then the surface changes, dictated by the exigencies of economic strategy and political maneuver, will serve rather as confirmation of the theses which have emerged from the following study than as occasion for significant revision at any particular point.

The acknowledgments due are many. The author is especially indebted to the Social Science Research Council, whose original donation of funds made possible the field work for this study. The aid given by numerous persons in Germany was invaluable. In particular should be mentioned Herr Gramenz and Herr Goebbels of the *Deutscher Normenausschuss,* Herr Schaeffer of the *Reichskuratorium für Wirtschaftlichkeit,* Dr. Feilen of the *Institut für Konjunkturforschung,* Dr. Wedemeyer of the *Nordwestliche Gruppe Deutscher Eisen- und Stahlindustrieller,* and Doctors Jürgen and Marguerite Kuczynski of *Finanzpolitische Korrespondenz.* Major Urwick, Director of the International Management Institute at Geneva, has been particularly helpful with numerous suggestions and criticisms. An even greater obligation is owed to Professors James W. Angell and J. M. Clark of Columbia University, Dr. Agnew and Mr. Gaillard of the American Standards Association, and Dr. Person of the Taylor Society for complete reading of the manuscript, and to Professor Wesley C. Mitchell and Dr. Harry Laidler of the National Bureau of Economic Research for perusal of special sections. Mr. Gaillard made many of the technical translations from the German. Dorothy Stahl Brady gave invaluable aid in the gathering, assembling, and assorting of the original material; her subsequent aid and intelligent criticism have been invaluable. An especial obligation is owed to Professor Felix Flügel, of the University of California, who at the expense of considerable time and effort has checked all the German translations. Valuable advice and assistance was received on special sections from numerous persons; in particular should be mentioned Professor Walter Smith of Williams College, Professor A. B. Wolfe of Ohio State University, Professor M. M. Knight of the University of California, and Mr. Irving Kaplan.

ROBERT A. BRADY

University of California
August 10, 1933

INTRODUCTION

THE PERIOD 1924–1929 stands out in recent German history as one of relative prosperity between two prolonged and disastrous depressions. In those five short years Germany managed to recover from a condition which experts believed would cripple the country for half a century. By the end of 1928 most of the significant production indices stood on a par with or above those of 1913; wages and the standard of living of the bulk of the laboring population were on or above the pre-war level. The future prosperity of the country seemed assured.

Yet the beginning of 1929 was marked by indications of a coming business depression, and through the subsequent three years the decline continued unabated. At times the recession was gradual and more or less orderly. At other times it was precipitate and chaotic. As the depression continued, with its rising totals of unemployed and part time workers, public unrest increased. The cumulative force of this national disaster brought upon the country the financial crisis of the summer of 1931. A temporary dictatorship (since given semipermanent status) was found imperative in order to prevent the financial crisis from degenerating into a general economic panic and to avert the growing threat of revolution. There is little in the picture to make the near future look more promising; at the time of writing (autumn of 1932) that future looks cloudy indeed.

The questions arise: Why did the prosperity of the period 1924–1929 come to such an unhappy close with the latter date? What set of forces brought on this disaster, the sudden appearance of which on the historical landscape so closely resembles the visitation of some unknown and dreadful plague? Are the causally efficient factors accidental and fortuitous in character, and is their diagnosis, with its accompanying prescriptive antidote, beyond the range of human capacity? Or does the depression appear merely as the inevitable if unusually severe product of the working of business-cycle processes, which fatalistically decree a taste of disaster as grim payment for previous enjoyment of national prosperity? Is the explanation to be sought in the trends of international events, or must analysis run primarily in terms of German national economy? Is fault to be found with events of the passing years, or must an indictment be laid against the entire capitalistically organized economic system?

For these questions complete answers will probably not be found for many generations, if ever. Yet it will be necessary to turn to them at frequent intervals in the following attempt to assess the bearing of the rationalization movement upon developments throughout the prosperous years of 1924–1929. For however highminded and blameless the proponents of rationalization, or however worthy and desirable the measures introduced under that rubric may have been, there are not lacking critics to lay upon that movement a large share of the responsibility for the depression which ensued. In examining the rationalization movement with the depression as a background, it may not be necessary to decide in all cases whether rationalization as such was at fault; whether it was carried too far, or not far enough. But that rationalization, *as carried out,* must bear a considerable share of the responsibility for the debâcle, is beyond question.

The post-war processes of technological, financial, and economic organization and reorganization, to which the term rationalization (*Rationalisierung*) was very early attached, passed through a series of phases and became invested with a number of meanings. The first phase—sometimes called the "negative phase"—involved the process of "rationing" production in the over-expanded heavy industries at the beginning of the reconstruction following the inflation and the Ruhr invasion. This soon led to plans for drastic reorganization of physical plant and business organization, including realignment of technically related industrial units, increased plant specialization, closing down of badly located and poorly equipped plants, mines, and business offices (*Stillegung*), the scrapping of old buildings, equipment, and machinery (*Reinigung*), and allied changes.[1] It was then a natural transition to what later became known as "positive" rationalization, that is, the systematic introduction of scientific techniques, methods, equipment, and attitudes into all phases and aspects of production, distribution, and consumption.

These latter developments showed considerable shift in emphasis. The earlier phase was largely taken up with problems of retrenchment which involved elimination of the worst features of the industrial and organizational heritage from the war, revolution, and inflation periods. Hence, in its first expression rationalization resembled a series of major operations. In its latter phase, however, it became a sort of national movement designed, according to its various proponents, to perfect the productive equipment, quicken the pace of output, and heighten the national prosperity. While, descriptively, the movement was centered around ways and means of systematically introducing standardization, utilizing the fruits of cooperative research, promoting scientific management, and coordinating and integrating activities of entire industries, it soon became apparent that in its larger implications rationalization inevitably reached out into and seriously conditioned activities in nearly every phase of national life.

But the development of rationalization was seriously conditioned by the forces which it was organized to guide, control, remake, and—in some circumstances—combat. Emphasizing, as it came shortly to do, a general "revolution" in points of view and attitudes of mind, rationalization was handicapped throughout by the general psychological, social, and political instability of the times. This was,

[1] See the "Enquete Ausschuss zur Untersuchung der Erzeugungs- und Absatzbedingungen der deutschen Wirtschaft," *Gesamtbericht* (Berlin, 1931): p. 141. (Hereafter referred to as: E. A., *Gesamtbericht*.)

in large part, the natural heritage from the disastrous years that preceded. Defeat in war was followed by a rapid succession of national catastrophes. The turn for the better did not come until the stabilization of the currency in the spring of 1924, six years after the disastrous close of the war. During the intervening period, revolution, bitter disappointment with the crushing terms of the Versailles treaty, inflation, and finally the French invasion had destroyed the foundations for political stability, had eliminated all incentives to improve and modernize plant and equipment, and had discouraged lifelong habits of thrift and work. As the old culture-conserving virtues became suspect, there was a tendency for the formerly stolid, patient, and hard-working German to become a faddist, a subscriber to almost any passing dogma, creed, or shibboleth. The older generation ceased to save and plan for a ripening future; the younger generation turned its back on the umbrageous past but found little in the prevailing chaos out of which to mold a new culture and fashion a new way of life. As in the case of the confused figures in Wasserman's *Etzel Andergast* and *Maurizius Case,* life for both old and young seemed to have become a complex of problems whose difficulty and insolubility increased with analysis, and an approach to whose answers spelled chaos. Philosophically the outlook was no brighter. For a time Spengler became almost a best seller. His brooding forecast of the decay and disintegration of western civilization was born of the same tired confusion and hopelessness which dominated Remarque's homeward bound and prematurely aged war veteran.

A by-product of these chaotic years was the undermining of the pre-war economic system. The two most conservatively minded and significant stabilizing factors in modern capitalism were here in process of rapid liquidation. The first of these, the middle class, had in large part lost its economic foundations in the period of inflation.[2] The second class, made up of farmers and peasants, had gained somewhat in the war and inflationary periods. Inflation largely wiped out the heavy mortgage indebtedness of the smaller peasant holders. Stabilization, however, brought a new alignment. Placed at a disadvantage because of the partial depletion of soil through earlier neglect, using obsolete farming methods and equipped with old-fashioned tools and machinery, forced to compete with highly specialized and low-cost outside agricultural areas, and compelled to purchase all needed supplies on high-price markets, the German farmer was nevertheless able to hold his own until new indebtedness began to accumulate.[3] From that point on, circumstances have gradually reduced the peasant population to a state of desperate poverty. Agriculture, unable to ally itself with organized labor because of its strong traditions and the nature of its class and property interests, has joined the disaffected middle class in a steady drift to-

[2] See M. J. Bonn, *Das Schicksal des deutschen Kapitalismus* (neue erweiterte Ausgabe; Berlin, 1931), Chap. II.

[3] See Chap. XI.

wards the right. It only required the final blow of the crisis of 1929 and the succeeding depression to unite these classes under the banner of extreme reaction and militant nationalism.

Meanwhile, a large percentage of the working classes, convinced of the utter bankruptcy of the capitalistic system, and encouraged by the first successes of Russian Communism and the subsequent launching of the first Five Year Plan, drifted towards the extreme left. The high level of unemployment, never dropping below 1,000,000 throughout the entire post-stabilization period, enormously accelerated trends in this direction.

The significance of these two movements lies in the fact that rationalization was begun, and largely carried through, at a time when forces were converging to undermine the institutional framework of German capitalism. As the rationalization movement developed, it became increasingly clear that its progress was to be conditioned by the solution of numerous issues directly related to the radical and far-reaching changes that were taking place in the political, economic, and social institutions of the country. The drift to the two extreme wings, and the politicization of nearly the whole range of economic problems, meant that these issues were to be resolved, if at all, in an atmosphere of bitterness, struggle, and drawn compromise.

Furthermore, when stabilization came, the new start had to be made on a much smaller foundation of natural and industrial resources. The Treaty of Versailles deprived Germany of 13 per cent of her territory (European), 13 per cent of her population, and 14.3 per cent of her arable land. In terms of her 1913 production, Germany surrendered 19 per cent of her coke, 74.5 per cent of her iron ore, 26.6 per cent of her blast furnaces, 19.2 per cent of her raw iron and steel, 15.8 per cent of her rolling mills, 68.5 per cent of her zinc foundries, 12 per cent of her livestock, her entire ocean-going merchant marine, 5,000 locomotives, 40,000 box cars, and other miscellaneous equipment.[4] More serious still, the treaty, and the subsequent decision of the League of Nations following the Polish Upper Silesian Plebiscite of 1921, split wide open two of the three major industrial centers of Germany, the Lorraine-Rhine-Westphalian and the Upper Silesian districts.[5] In the former and more important of these two centers, one section was placed under a temporary French mandate pending a plebiscite at a later date (the Saar),[6] another section was removed entirely from the German customs union (Luxemburg), two small sections were given to Belgium (Eupen and Malmedy), and a final and highly important section (Lorraine) was ceded out-

[4] Compare J. W. Angell, *The Recovery of Germany* (New Haven, 1929), Appendix B, table 7.

[5] The third district, the so-called Middle German industrial region, centers around Leipzig and Halle, and extends from Hanover on the north to Dresden and Chemnitz on the south.

[6] There is some question whether the Saar should be included as an integral portion of the Lorraine-Rhine-Westphalian district. It was closely associated industrially before the war, but it is, of course, some distance removed geographically.

right to France. The principal losses were coal (Saar and Upper Silesia) and, especially, iron ore. Lorraine ore had supplied about 75 per cent of the needs of the Ruhr iron and steel industry before the war. In Upper Silesia practically all the iron ore and about 75 per cent of the coal were transferred to Poland. In both areas the treaty settlements destroyed the whole internal balance of the heavy industries remaining under German control. Coal pits were separated from cokeries, cokeries from blast furnaces and steel mills, steel mills from rolling mills, and so forth.

Nor were the financial conditions particularly favorable for far-reaching changes. Stabilization, it is true, restored the monetary conditions required for the reorganization that was shortly to take place; but it could not supply the necessary funds, which could only come from internal accumulations or foreign borrowing. While the revolution and the subsequent inflation had greatly reduced, and in many cases entirely eliminated, both public and private indebtedness, it also left the funds available for investment and credit uses plainly inadequate. Consequently, a large portion of the money necessary for both ordinary operating expenses and for reorganization purposes had to be supplied by outside interests. Extensive as these interests were, the loans extended were never sufficient to meet the demand, with the result that interest rates on both long- and short-time capital were constantly at very high levels.

Interest rates were further kept high by shortage of foreign capital because of doubt as to the political stability of Germany, and because of the general hesitancy of German business men to surrender any portion of their business control to foreigners in guaranty that debts contracted would be promptly discharged upon maturity. And high interest rates not only increased the cost of doing business and the expenses of reorganization, but also fostered the practice of using short-term funds for financial and investment purposes. This practice tended to increase financial instability, and, in so doing, to push interest charges yet higher.

At the same time the socialistically inclined government lent its aid in support of labor union demands for higher wages, shorter hours, and social insurance legislation. Accession to these demands materially increased the direct current expenses of most branches of industry by adding a burden which was particularly onerous to industries forced to compete on international markets with foreign producers exempt from the demands of militant labor unions.

Taxation charges, the burden of which was in most cases ultimately to be borne by industry and commerce, likewise mounted steadily throughout the period under consideration. While the actual per capita taxation load in Germany was no higher than that of several others of the former belligerent powers, the real tax burden, if the amount of the national income be taken into consideration, was higher there than elsewhere. By 1928 taxation absorbed no less than 27 per cent of the national income. In contrast to the situation obtaining in various foreign countries, a substantial portion of the funds collected as taxes did not flow back into the German national economy. Reparations payments exacted a tribute, which, considering the already impoverished state of the country,[7] Germany could ill afford to pay. Had the creditor countries, however, been willing to receive reparations payments in kind, the obligations, severe as they were under the Dawes and Young plans, might have been borne. But payments in kind represented a real threat to competitive industries in the receiving countries. Tariff walls and the growing demand abroad that payments be made through the ordinary channels of international exchange made the problem of transfer acute.[8] In reality, the problem has been "solved" from year to year by the floating of private and public loans of one sort or another. Thus the demand for foreign credit has steadily increased from year to year, while at the same time private interests have been forced to compete with the government for funds with which to pay the cumulating interest and amortization charges on such loans.

The increased costs incurred on these and other accounts might easily have been borne, had it been possible to operate rehabilitated and reorganized plants to capacity. Since most of the manufacturing industries were largely dependent upon foreign markets, these became the key to low-cost operation. And here German manufacturers stumbled upon one of the most vexatious problems of the post-war period. In the first place, all contact with the most important foreign markets had been lost in the prosecution of the war. Foreign branches had been

[7] Certain experts have placed the losses of Germany through war, treaty obligations, invasion, etc., at no less than 33–45 per cent of her pre-war national wealth. See Angell, *op. cit.*, p. 15.

[8] It is frequently forgotten by critics of Germany that the problem of *transfer through the exchanges* is an entirely separate problem from that of collection in Germany. The sums exacted might be collected in Germany in the form of goods, these to be delivered directly to the creditor powers or sold abroad by the German government and the receipts credited to their account. Since the Allies would not permit either practice, with the exception of certain minor payments, it was easier to collect the sums in money through taxation and move the funds through the regular exchange channels. But since this required a favorable balance of trade, "visible" and "invisible" items included, recourse had to be taken to methods of creating such balances. The bulk of favorable "invisible" items are normally made up of income from foreign investments, shipping services, and foreign banking. Before the war these sums credited to Germany approximated about $500,000,000 annually. But the war and the Versailles treaty deprived Germany of her entire ocean-going merchant marine and her foreign banking connections, and reduced her foreign investments of nearly $7,000,000,000 to about one-tenth that amount. When it is considered that the adverse commodity trade balance, offset by those receipts, averaged approximately $370,000,000 for the five-year period 1909–1913, that Germany had to import an even larger percentage of her raw materials and foodstuffs after the war on account of the cessions of territory, and that these favorable "invisible" credit items were almost entirely lacking after 1918, it is not hard to see why recourse was had to the only other alternative offered: foreign borrowing. Since, in addition, funds were required for purposes of industrial reorganization, German borrowing (since 1924) has been considerably in excess of total reparations payments. German *net* foreign borrowings from 1924 to 1930 on long time were approximately $2,167,000,000, and on short time (1924–1929) approximately $1,476,000,000, or a total of $3,643,000,000. At the same time, total reparations payments amounted to $2,453,000,000, or $1,190,000,000 less than the total amount borrowed abroad. See J. M. Keynes, *The Economic Consequences of the Peace* (London, 1919):189, 206, and James Harvey Rogers, *America Weighs Her Gold* (New Haven, 1931):232–233.

closed, and their property confiscated in most cases. Surrender of the German colonial possessions meant, for a time, practically complete loss of formerly monopolized markets. Sequestration of foreign properties usually carried with it confiscation of all trade secrets and patent rights. Revolution in Russia and the rise of the Bolsheviki to power temporarily closed another important and rapidly growing market for German goods. Even when the U. S. S. R. became an important export market, it was often compelled to ask for long-run credits which German manufacturers could ill afford to extend. A similar situation obtained with respect to the southern and central areas of Europe. The peace treaties had effectively Balkanized all Europe to the south and east of the German frontiers. The general lack of economic balance within the new political boundaries of countries there, the poverty of their populations, political and social unrest, and racial and other antagonisms have been conducive to dictatorships, outbursts of extreme nationalism, persecution of racial minorities, and terrorism. These countries, encouraged by their territorial gains from Germany and the two leading states of the Dual Monarchy,[9] and by the right given to certain of them[10] to repudiate payment of loans received from Germany in the war, have attempted to build up water-tight national systems after the model of the late eighteenth and early nineteenth centuries. One aspect of this reactionary nationalism has been continued and bitter anti-Germanism in many quarters.[11] Another aspect has been the erection of tariff walls so high that foreign goods, German or otherwise, could be hoisted over them only with the greatest difficulty. A third aspect is the encouragement, for military reasons or for the purpose of solving domestic unemployment problems, of inefficient and badly located national industries. This policy has not only curtailed the capacity of these countries to export goods with which to pay for purchases abroad, but it has also increased the excess capacity of German industries which had been expanded to supply the whole of central Europe.[12]

Even had the problem of markets not been serious on account of such difficulties, the German dilemma would still have been complicated by the tremendous growth of foreign manufacturing capacity in the war and post-war periods. A development of this character, provided the international adjustments were such that this expansion of productive capacity was paralleled by increase in consumption and standards of living, should normally react favorably upon the economic welfare of all exporting and importing nations. But the bulk of German exports have long fallen into the very categories in which excess plant capacity has been most serious, as, for example, in those of coal, heavy chemicals, products

[9] Lithuania, Czechoslovakia, Poland, Jugoslavia, and Roumania.

[10] Bulgaria, Turkey, Hungary, Austria, and Jugoslavia.

[11] This has been particularly marked in the two border countries of Poland and Czechoslovakia.

[12] See, in particular, E. A., *Gesamtbericht*, pp. 185–196.

of the iron and steel industry, textiles, shoes, woodworking, ceramics, toys, and machinery.[13] Furthermore, in certain countries, principally the United States and Japan, comparative isolation from the arena and the burdens of the war had promoted rapid technical improvements in industrial equipment and methods. The improvements enabled the manufacturers in those countries, even with higher wage rates (as in the United States), to undersell competitors on international markets. Territory ceded to France, Belgium, and Poland contained many of the best and most modern iron and steel plants of pre-war Germany. Companies controlling these plants since the Treaty of Versailles have been able to produce and sell much more cheaply than their German competitors.[14]

It should further be borne in mind that the treaty, in addition to breaking up the internal units of the heavy industries in the Upper Silesian and Rhineland areas, had compelled the complete readaptation of important war-supply industries to entirely new types of output.[15] In turning to the manufacture of agricultural machinery, cash registers, automobiles, specialized small internal combustion motors, household machinery, and similar products, these companies had to face the competition of foreign, particularly American, concerns whose costs were extraordinarily low on account of extensive use of mass production methods. Finally, it should be noted that manufacture for export in Germany presupposes in many cases previous import of raw materials. Some of these are staple products, imported because they are not produced in Germany, or are produced there in insufficient quantities.[16] Others are imported because the quality of the foreign materials cannot be duplicated from German sources.[17] Several of the industrial raw materials are monopolistically or semi-monopolistically held, and their prices to German producers are consequently higher than they would be if domestic resources could be drawn upon.[18]

The comparative prosperity of the period 1924–1929 served to liquidate temporarily some of the more important of the various "intangible" handicaps of the preceding years and to strengthen German industry to the point where it could meet on an even footing the challenge of foreign competitors. From the vantage point of 1932, however, it can easily be seen that many of the achievements recorded were pyramided on slender foundations based on shifting sands. Throughout the period the ground was being prepared for the advance of the Hitler-Hugenberg right and the Communist left at the expense of the more moderate

---

13 Compare E. A., *Gesamtbericht*, p. 93.

14 This advantage has been due in part to lower wage rates obtaining in those countries.

15 The case of Krupp is the best example. See Chap. VI, pp. 124–125.

16 Various types of wood, iron, manganese, and other ores, petroleum, rubber, cotton, silk, wool, electric power, tobacco, hides, oil seeds, etc. See E. A., *Gesamtbericht*, p. 14.

17 E.g., Kaoline (porcelain clay) from Czechoslovakia, vegetable tanning extracts, English gas-coal, gluten-rich wheat, Scandinavian feldspar.

18 Swedish iron ores, Chilean nitrates, tin, nickel, aluminum, etc.

and compromising centrist groups. German economists and politicians correctly argued that the reparations charges demanded under the treaty, and the subsequent Dawes and Young plans, could not be paid without hopelessly ruining Germany and disorganizing the whole structure of international trade. The trend of events has borne out the prophecy, made by J. M. Keynes in 1919, that Germany could and would pay only by advance borrowing. The crisis of the summer of 1931 was "in the making" throughout the preceding years. Meanwhile the general European atmosphere was showing but little improvement. Dictatorships were increasing in number and growing in strength.[19] The problems of political frontiers, irridentas, disarmaments, tariff walls, and the general impoverishment of the European agricultural populations were growing worse rather than better. The power and prestige of the League of Nations were making but little headway. In the East the success of the Soviet cast a serious doubt over the entire future of capitalism, if not of western European culture.

Yet it was with such a heritage, and under handicaps of such a nature, that the economic rehabilitation of Germany was begun and carried through. The relatively high level of prosperity attained by the end of 1929—a level which compared quite favorably on the whole with the pre-war period—was due in no small measure to the drastic overhauling and systematization of processes and entire industries which preceded. The sensational collapse of the unwieldy Stinnes concern in 1925 paved the way for the reorganization of the heavy industries. The result of the initial and most spectacular "shake-up" was the emergence of several new and powerful combines, most important of which were the *I. G. Farbenindustrie A. G.* in heavy chemicals and the *Vereinigte Stahlwerke A. G.* in the steel industry. The same reorganization process soon became apparent in other industries. The *Reichsbahn* and *Reichspost* were reorganized and modernized. The two most important ocean shipping concerns, *Nord-Deutscher Lloyd* and the *Hamburg-Amerika Linie,* began the construction of a new fleet of freight steamers and passenger liners, the operation and management of which shortly brought them into a very close working agreement. The coal, lignite, and potash mining industries were modernized, the controlling firms regrouped, and the production, inter-industry, inter-corporate, and marketing relations placed on a more systematic and orderly footing. The development of new long-distance power transmission systems brought about a significant realignment of the electric power industry, and forced through geographic redistribution and drastic alterations in the organization of various types of plants utilizing purchased current.[20]

This "rationalization" process gradually reached out into nearly every phase of production, physical distribution, marketing, and finally even into consump-

---

[19] Poland, Hungary, Roumania, Jugoslavia, Italy, Greece, Turkey, the U.S.R.R., Spain.

[20] See E. A., *Gesamtbericht,* p. 145.

tion of ultimate-consumer goods. With expansion beyond the confines of old plant and equipment, the movement began to collect a host of commentators, critics, proponents, and enthusiastic propagandists. To its proponents, rationalization soon became "science in industry and economics." Organizations of one sort or another were called into existence to systematize the process of introducing the warp of science into the weft of the industrial and economic order. From an organizational program, rationalization, under one interpretation or another, developed into an industrial and economic faith, and finally into a credo. Discussion of rationalization found its way into the popular magazines and daily newspapers. Its enthusiastic apostles, sometimes with tongues in cheeks, urged its thaumaturgic properties upon business men, manufacturers, laborers, consumers, and the state. Rationalized production was to be followed by rationalized distribution, and this by rational consumption. Rationalization was somehow to supply the "efficiency" key to orderly social and individual life; subscription and adherence to its working codes would free the round of productive and leisure activities from lag, leak, and friction, from waste and confusion, and from the gravamen of social maladjustment or personal contumely. This new *Aufklärung* possessed many of the mystical, juvenile, and naïve properties of the recent "new economic" era in the United States.

The deflation and secularization of rationalization following the year 1929 have been almost as drastic as its previous apotheosis was spectacular and inspiring. Disappointment with the new formula is now almost as great as were the former high hopes of its success. But here, as in the first instance, the misunderstanding of the cross-sectional nature, the organizational interrelationships, and the broader implications of the process is quite pronounced. An attempt to discover the real meaning of rationalization, and thereby to obtain a sure foundation for evaluation of fact and fancy, provides the *raison d'être* for the present study.

Careful study has lent convincing force to the proposition that the meaning of rationalization is to be found in the historical congruence of certain fundamental tendencies in machine production and capitalistic economic organization. Hence, Part One will be an attempt to elucidate the character of these basic forces, and to supplement such analysis with outlines sketching the functions of German institutional equipment established to give direction and coherence to these factors.[21] The procedure will then be to examine, in Part Two, the descriptive details of the rationalization movement as they have evolved and been applied in German industry during the period in view. Here the analysis will be to some extent comparative. Certain industries, notably the so-called "heavy industries,"

[21] It is not feasible to compress "rationalization" within the walls of any rigid definition, however carefully it may be phrased. Like every major "ground swell" movement in human history, characterization by definition is more apt to be misleading than clarifying. For a summary of the various definitions currently used, see Robert A. Brady, "The Meaning of Rationalization: An Analysis of the Literature," *Quart. Jour. Econ.*, 46:526–540 (May, 1932).

and the transportation and communication services offer examples of conspicuous, though in some respects narrowly limited, success. Textiles, distribution, and agriculture are, on the contrary, fields in which rationalization has thus far made little real headway. In all cases the intention will be to show as clearly as possible, in the space available, the character of the forces making for acceleration and those making for retardation of rationalization. Here it will be of moment to learn how far these antithetical factors are of a transient or permanent character, technological or economic in their emphasis, national or international in their scope and implications, and natural (beyond the power of human beings to foresee, alter, or control) or institutional in their setting.

With this as a background, Part Three will proceed to an analysis of the incidence of rationalization upon (*a*) general economic stability, (*b*) the status and differential advantages of various special and general interest groups (capital, labor, consumers, the state), and (*c*) the facts and course of social and cultural evolution. Here also the method will be that of comparison and contrast. Rationalization *de facto*—as it was actually carried out in Germany during 1924–1929—will be compared with the logical and historical implications of rationalization as analyzed in Part One.

The reader should be warned that the following pages do not provide either a comprehensive survey of the rehabilitation of Germany during the period 1924–1929, nor a definitive answer to the problem of the causally efficient forces of the disastrous collapse which so shortly followed. They are concerned, primarily, with analysis of those peculiar developments during the recovery period which can fairly be subsumed under the head of rationalization, and with their rôles in the concatenation of events which brought recovery to an end late in 1929.

It is likewise proper to admit that the book has something in the nature of a thesis. That thesis, slowly shaped by the persuasive force of accumulated evidence, is this: that the development of rationalization in Germany has shown more or less clearly the possibilities and the directional drives inherent in the movement, and that, among men intimately acquainted with its history, there is sufficient appreciation of the shortcomings of rationalization *as carried out* to justify the rather significant sub-title of this study, "A Study in the Evolution of Economic Planning."

PART ONE

The Elements and Organization of the German Rationalization Movement

CHAPTER I

SCIENCE IN INDUSTRY, TRADE, AND COMMERCE

SCIENCE lies at the heart of the whole rationalization movement; for, "as an attitude," rationalization "records the belief that a more rational control of world economic life through the application of scientific method is possible and desirable. As a process it implies the application of the methods of science to all problems arising in the organization and conduct of production, distribution, and consumption."[1] This view is so widely accepted, and is supported by so much authority, that it seems idle to question either substance or belief. In it is reflected the persistent notion that only that is "rational" which is brought into being by the full and free use of scientific methods and techniques, and carried into effect in a scientifically impersonal and detached spirit. A rationalization *movement* could only arise when this view had become so far popularized that it could be consciously accepted by a large number of persons endowed with real discretionary power, and made the point of departure in programs systematically carried through by the aid of the cooperative effort of directly and indirectly interested persons, groups, and institutions.

With such a broad definition as a background, there is a certain poetic license involved in speaking of the "post-war rationalization movement" in Germany, for during the post-war period neither the spirit nor the techniques of science crept into all phases and portions of the round of economic activities in any particular field. It was a rare occurrence when all directly and indirectly interested persons and parties actively took part in the deliberations preceding, and wholeheartedly cooperated in efforts leading to a systematic introduction of scientific measures into any industrial and commercial sector. Further, many industries have remained almost wholly immune to the changes which rationalization would have implied.

Yet when stabilization came, interest in the changes made and in prospect was so widespread, and emphasis upon the scientific aspect of reorganization was so great, that it seems almost possible to speak of a *national effort* to introduce science into industry and commerce, even though there was a great deal of working to cross purposes. Rationalization as *science in industry* was endorsed by labor and capital, industrialists and agriculturists, producers and consumers, private traders and the state. There might not always be agreement on the ques-

[1] L. Urwick, *The Meaning of Rationalisation* (London, 1929):27.

tion whether a particular change, method, or technique *was scientific,* but there was no quarrel with the assertion that these *should be scientific.* For the emergence of this popular fixation, promoted by various special interest groups with almost apostolic fervor,[2] there are a number of reasons, both historical and logical.

I. THE IMPORTANCE OF SCIENCE FOR POST-WAR GERMAN INDUSTRY

(*a*) The need for drastic reorganization and overhauling of plants, equipment, and methods at the time of the stabilization of the currency has been sufficiently emphasized in the Introduction. It was but natural that efforts should proceed in accordance with the latest and most approved technical and scientific information. In borrowing such information from abroad, in particular from the United States, German industrial leaders and business men were in a sense reverting to an old and successfully employed practice. After 1870, the country's industrial and commercial development had been enormously accelerated by the consistent habit of borrowing from abroad or improving at home and putting directly into practice the latest and most scientific methods, organization forms, machinery, and equipment.[3] In 1924 it was possible to begin rebuilding, not where the country left off at the time of the outbreak of the war, but at the technical level made possible by the accumulated experience of those countries in which technical and organizational changes had scarcely been affected by that calamitous interval.

(*b*) Of even greater importance was the problem of natural resources. Living in a densely populated country, the Germans had long been accustomed to frugal employment of the available resources, but it required the war experience with general shortage of supplies to drive home the lesson of economy. Resources in ores, coal, water power, and land were definitely limited. The population had been growing rapidly. The demands made upon the productive facilities of the country were constantly increasing. The added demands of war time brought the problem of conservation into bold relief, and the Treaty of Versailles made the solution of this problem critically important to the future of the country.

At this juncture only the resources of human ingenuity and science seemed unlimited. Since the country was shorn by the treaty of many of its most important deposits of ore and fuel, and since the remaining domestic supplies of many important raw materials were rapidly dwindling, emphasis upon conservation became a matter of national concern. Ways must be found of substituting new supplies for the old; methods must be devised for eliminating waste, and of extracting the maximum use from every lump of coal, ton of ore, stack of wood, and acre of land. The secrets of almost all these new methods and tech-

---

[2] See, for example, the elaborate adumbration of Gottl-Ottlillienfeld, *Vom Sinn der Rationalisierung* (Berlin, 1929).

[3] This point has been dealt with at some length by Thorstein Veblen, *Imperial Germany and the Industrial Revolution* (New York, 1915).

niques were locked up in the storehouse of science. The Germans were compelled to draw ever more extensively upon this basic resource, a resource, fortunately, free from all formal restriction, treaty, boundary, or other.

(*c*) To this elevation of the rôle of science, another far more subtle and organically significant factor has lent its compelling support. This is the long-run tendency observable within most individual industries, whether new or old, towards a slowing down in the rate of technical change. Each new improvement is on the average of less importance than its predecessors for the industry as a whole. As each industry approaches a certain stage of technical maturity, the problems to be solved become increasingly complicated and abstract, and their solutions are won at a greater expense of time and effort. The amount of training required for handling the newer problems is greater, the necessary laboratory equipment is more elaborate and costly, and each succeeding set of results is on the average of less relative significance. This generalization holds in a broad way for the newer industries as well as the older. The "running-down" process is observable in the technical progress of the electrical, radio, automobile, airplane, and heavy chemicals industries as well as in metallurgy, textiles, and the building industries.[4]

In Germany, as indicated in the preceding paragraph, the handicaps which science faced were aggravated by the general shortage of basic resources. Furthermore, in that country, as elsewhere, industrialization had meant the early exhaustion of the better and more valuable raw materials. The virgin forests had been largely depleted of their better timber; the better coal seams had been worked first; the higher grade and closer ore deposits had been exploited at an early date. Other things remaining the same, raw materials must be won at a greater cost with each ensuing year. The natural fertility of the soil having long been exhausted, increasing quantities of artificial fertilizers and more expensive farming methods must be used if output is to be further increased. As in the past, so in the future, hydro-electric power must be generated from ever more distant waterfalls or more expensive water development projects. The coal seams will steadily go deeper, the earth pressure will become greater, and the working hazards will become more difficult to manage.

The burden of industrial improvement is thus laid on science at a time when, historically speaking, industry is faced with a sort of technical "scissors crisis." Industrial advance must at least keep pace with this basic technical handicap if costs of production, measured in terms of time and energy, are not to increase. Whether these costs increase or decrease per unit of output will depend more and more upon systematic and carefully planned research into both practical and theoretical possibilities of raw materials and the available productive and distributive equipment.

---

[4] Compare Simon Kuznets, *Secular Movements in Production and Prices* (New York, 1930), particularly Chap. I, on the "Retardation of Industrial Growth."

(*d*) A parallel factor is to be found (1) in the advance of technological methods. Their continuous refinement calls for ever more elaborate control and testing apparatus. Ultimately these are to be supplied, kept in order, and improved only with the ceaseless aid of experimental and testing laboratories.

It is a characteristic of modern technology that this process of unceasing refinement in equipment and methods never comes to rest. Each change suggests still further changes. Each improvement brings about alterations in the sequence of operations with which the improved method is quasi-organically connected. Though these refinements tend in each industry to be less and less revolutionary, they tend likewise to be more numerous, and more "secular" in character. That is to say, they tend to flow less from sudden inspiration and the chance observation of relatively untutored persons, and more from systematic application of scientific principles and the exhaustive research of highly specialized experts.

The stimuli for such continuous refinements may come (2) from the outside in the form of consumer demand for better quality goods, or for cheaper priced goods of given qualities. This drive has been particularly noteworthy in post-war Germany, where changes in consumption habits and relatively higher standards of living for the mass of the people coincided with a national tendency, in partial contrast to the contemporary tendency in America, to insist upon greater variety and conformity to individual taste.[5]

(*e*) There is another and curiously Germanic aspect to this attempt to make all industry and commerce scientific. It is in science that the notorious German penchant for order, system, and arrangement finds at once its most perfect and its most fruitful expression. But the light of science is essentially toneless and secular, while the Germans are perhaps the most philosophically minded of all the occidental peoples. Hence, science has been knit by them into a system—or, perhaps better, a series of interacting systems—having both metaphysical significance and something in the nature of a basic and irreducible pattern of interdependencies and interrelationships.

Generalizations here are extremely hazardous, and were it not that in Germany rationalization has become a sort of popular cult among the people and a type of scientific philosophy among the experts, further discussion of this kind would be entirely out of place in this study. But somewhat of an explanation of the German view is necessary, since it served to unite emphasis upon science with insistence upon cooperative activity more clearly than this was done in any other country in the world—excepting Soviet Russia alone. And it is the union of these two ideas—*universal application of scientific methods and techniques*, and *cooperative effort in all phases of investigation, production, and distribution*—which, given social direction, constitutes the new, the original, and the revolutionary contribution of rationalization to the *organization* of the economic

---

[5] See Chap. XV.

Paternalism

and social world. It is no accident that both Marxian socialism and the *concept* of rationalization first came to light and thrived on German soil.

This concept of rationalization may be said to be the product of the confluence of two streams of ideas, flowing from two distinct sources: (1) the growth of the concentration movement in industry and commerce, and (2) the elaboration of unifying ideas in the scientific world. Since we shall have occasion to return later for detailed consideration of the first of these two sources, it will suffice here merely to indicate that the concentration movement, considered from both the *organizational* and the *control* viewpoints, is everywhere observable in industry, trade, and commerce. In Germany it has proceeded at a pace faster than the usual, because laissez faire principles have never gained a substantial foothold in that country. Capital has always been protectionist and monopolistically inclined. Labor, dominated largely by some form or other of socialist thought, has never had either theoretical objections to, or practical programs for waging war upon combines, cartels, and syndicates as such. The government was paternalistic in the Bismarckian sense before the war, and in the Rathenau sense after that period. Experiments in war control rather accelerated than retarded the pace of unification. Unifying and concentrating forces were thus allowed to progress unhampered except when one line of concentration in one field engendered conflict with similar tendencies in the same or other fields.

Hence, throughout pre-war, war, and post-war periods, and within more and more industries and branches of industries, habits of cooperation were being acquired, and ideas relating to mutuality of interests were becoming increasingly common and axiomatic. The single unified system, however narrow the range of the functions might be to which it was confined, was becoming the prototype towards which intra- and inter-enterprise organization was rapidly tending. In more and more ways the legal and organizational "water-tight compartments" within the business and industrial world were breaking down; in their place was coming the "associational economy" or "corporational (*Korporative*) economy" which represents almost the complete antithesis of unrestricted English nineteenth-century laissez faire.[6]

The same unifying trend is to be observed in the field of science itself. (*a*) At one time physics, chemistry, mathematics, biology, and (in large part) psychology, geology, astronomy, and other "lesser sciences," were regarded as more or less self-contained disciplines. Within these various fields there tended to exist a rather sharp bifurcation between problems relating to organic and inorganic matter. Inorganic matter obeyed the mechanistic rules formulated by Spinoza, Descartes, and Newton; organic matter followed a group of "life" principles; psychological and social phenomena were subsumed under a series of generalizations of a "spiritual," emotional, intellectual, and, generally speaking, transcendental character.

---

[6] See Chap. XIV.

With the passage of time these water-tight compartments have been broken down. The view is now widely held that there exists a certain basic unity in the entire field of organic, inorganic, psychological, and perhaps social, phenomena.[7] Mathematics has become less of a formal and experimentally disembodied logical tool, and more of a shorthand method of expressing known or supposed physical relationships. The development of the ionic theory has bridged the gap between physics and chemistry, if, indeed, the gap had not been previously spanned. The growth of bio-chemistry and, more recently, bio-physics, has served to break down the wall separating biology and the related fields of physics and chemistry. Bacteriology and micro-cellular research, operating under the drive of the Darwinian hypothesis, have broken down the barrier between plant and animal organic matter. Behavioristic psychology has brought psychological phenomena into the biological and general experimental field. Social psychology and anthropological research are closing the gap between group social phenomena and individual response to appropriate stimuli. The field theory of Einstein subsumes matter and energy under a common theoretical head.

(*b*) Throughout this development there has gone on a steady process of mutual borrowing of ideas. Of peculiar interest in the present connection has been the gradual seepage of the organismic concept of functional relationships, most clearly expressed in the fields of biology and psychology, into almost every phase and aspect of scientific thought. If, as the above argument maintains, science, particularly in conjunction with technology, is the most significant force conditioning the point of view of contemporary man, and is and will be the most decisive single stimulating factor in present and future economic and industrial progress, then this trend cannot be too strongly emphasized.

The drift of opinion in the scientific world, out of which the organismic conception of natural phenomena in general has arisen, cannot be traced to any single source for its inspiration, nor has it anywhere received analysis at the hands of those best equipped to follow the trend back to its genesis. The concept, however, appears to be part and parcel of a view of the nature of the physical world which, when stated in its less sophisticated form, approximates very closely the notion which dominated the thinking of eighteenth-century science. In both views the entire universe, from the mightiest solar systems to the almost infinitely small atoms constructed of positive and negative electrical charges, from the complicated organic structure of man to the simplest micro-organisms, is united in a single and mighty system of coherent natural "law" (interdependencies). Within this system there exists a complicated hierarchy of more or less self-contained systems and sub-systems, the behavior and analysis of which are

[7] One of the greatest and most respected German engineers of the post-war period gave it as his confidential opinion (to the author) that the most serious shortcoming in the training and entire outlook of the average engineer is his lack of understanding of biology and psychology, and of their theoretical and methodological relationship to physical science and engineering.

described and elucidated by the various respective and appropriate disciplines. These are, however, but parts of the larger unity. The delicate balance of forces and factors required within each system, from the simplest to the most complex, calls for the running functional adjustment of part to part, and of force to force, both temporally and spatially. The entire universe thus becomes a single immensely elaborated and almost infinitely intricate and life-like machine. The "metabolism" of this functioning complex requires a running dynamic adjustment in every part through the uninterrupted and harmonious convergence of more or less self-equilibrating masses and forces. Like plant and animal life, the solar system, the earth, and the atom all originate out of a peculiar drift in an interlocking energy balance, which is forced to pass through a cycle of more or less turbulent and ultimately exhausting activity (for each system) and is ended in the dissolution and chemical transformation (disruption) of the system.

(*c*) This notion of functional dependence and interdependence in the more abstract reaches of science is paralleled by a similar point of view in the fields of applied science and engineering. These developments, mutually reinforcing each other, have exercised a powerful influence upon the way in which the problems subsumed under the head of industrial rationalization have been shaped. The term *function* has crept into the *patois* of the movement, and the concept of *functional* organization and interdependence has colored programs for organizing and reorganizing both shops and entire industries. One reads and hears much of *functional foremen, functionally organized* plants, *functional organizations* for maintaining control and fixing responsibility, *functionally* organized industries, and, more recently, of *functionally organized economic systems.* The parts and separate processes are required to be highly specialized at the same time that that specialization is regarded as necessarily subservient to the working demands of the larger entity, the existence and operation of which—*functioning*—is dependent in turn upon the harmonious coordination and integration of such separate parts and processes.

(*d*) To the biological contribution of *functionally* constructed and interdependent parts,[8] and the engineering notion of efficiency as the *sine qua non* in the utilization of materials and energy, the "pure scientist" adds the concept of *law* (relatively fixed interdependencies). Scientific law, though sometimes used elliptically and provisionally (hypotheses *about* and theories *of,* rather than definite statements), generally implies, as indicated above, something in the nature of an approximation to a basic ground plan in the scheme of nature. This scheme

[8] The biological concept of function must not be confused with (*a*) the mathematical expression which concerns relationships between one or more independent and one or more dependent variables in a rectangular, polar, multiple-extension, or other type of coordinate system, which are (theoretically at least) capable of expression in appropriate mathematical equations, and (*b*) the notion of a properly organized economic and social order purposely constructed, in the light of a pre-selected, self-sufficient ethical ideal, to "function" in accordance with self-validating criteria, irrespective of the drift of contemporary events.

or pattern is commonly held to possess a certain final and residual validity which the passage of time and evolution of scientific thought either cannot or probably will not completely dissolve. Numerous additions and subtractions, new interpretations, and more complete explanations may somewhat alter the basic pattern here and there, and from time to time, but on the whole there is a working hypothesis that the broad outlines will remain substantially as at present conceived. In technology this notion of a conceptually irreducible and temporally unalterable body of scientific principles is frequently expressed in the active sense as the "one best way." Scientific research and technical ingenuity, the concept argues, shall establish "once and for all" the "one best way," the "one best method," the "one best" device, the "one best" use. Rationalization literature, particularly that portion which flows from the pens of scientists and engineers, is replete with the notion of, and at times redundant with the expression, "the one best way."[9]

2. THE INDUSTRIAL ORIENTATION OF SCIENCE

This growing dependence of German technology and business enterprise upon scientific laboratory work and systematic research has raised the question of the influence of scientific methods and preconceptions upon rationalization as carried out in the contemporary German capitalistic economic order. For, as in the case of technology before the advent of the industrial revolution, her business men have become interested in science precisely at the time when it is, in the fullest and most complete sense of the term, a free, non-privately owned cultural heritage of the greatest significance both economically and technologically.

In rather sharp contrast to the shrewd and grasping codes of the business world, convention among most scientists brooks but few violations of the following general rules concerning hypotheses and discoveries: (1) Results, methods used, and deductions drawn are immediately published. (2) The fullest criticism is invited from every competent source, and is expected to develop as any weaknesses in the original statement are uncovered. (3) Proof or disproof consists in verification or lack of verification upon further experimentation under precisely the same control conditions. (4) There is no "patenting" of ideas. As a scientist the experimenter is presumably not interested in reaping other personal advantage from his discoveries than that which accrues from the personal esteem of his fellows. "Idle curiosity" and emulation are, presumably and more or less observably, the basic driving forces. As with the technologist, the scientist is typically motivated by the desire to show a workmanlike and theoretically or practically useful result. Even more than with the engineer, all suggestion of "commercial-

[9] This notion is particularly emphasized in the various articles appearing on this aspect of rationalization in such journals as the *Bulletin* of the Taylor Society, RKW *Nachrichten*, *Bulletin* of the International Management Institute, etc.

ization" of discoveries to the personal advantage of the scientist meets with the disapproval of the republic of his peers.[10]

Up to the time of the advent of business enterprise into the management of research, the professional attitude of the scientist was essentially workmanlike, disinterested, and social. Even with the rise of laboratories run for profit, there has persisted a substantial residue of the old professional point of view. Within the fraternity there has survived a curious, naïve, almost "other-worldly" neglect of the ordinary canons of good and evil, of class, race, national, and craft distinctions and invidious comparisons, of personal beliefs, prides, prejudices, and hatreds, of jockeying for personal or group advantage. The criteria of excellence have been essentially abstract, impersonal, and non-moral. Agreement has not been conditioned by "race, color, or previous condition of servitude," but solely by willingness to accept proof by demonstration according to the degree of congruence between working hypothesis and experimentally controlled results. All who have been able to study and experiment are permitted to agree; all who have accepted the working rules have been free to believe.

In part this attitude has been conditioned, heretofore, by the nature of the findings of the scientist, and in part by the character of the institutions which have provided domicile for scientific work. The farther one goes back into the history of modern science, the more general, abstract (technologically speaking), and "impractical" the subject matter has been.[11] The nearer one approaches the modern epoch the closer becomes the congruence and interdependence between the subject matter and the results of scientific research and technological developments. Before this mutual encroachment began to take place the scientist had but little occasion to notice the advantages which flowed to any particular individual, group, or vested interest as the result of practical application of his results to the industrial world. His hypotheses and conclusions were looked upon as additions to the body of intellectually useful knowledge, not as props whereby an enterprise might wring larger differential incomes from the general community.

Further, until the rise of the corporation laboratory, the institutional equipment placed at the disposal of scientists, whether publicly owned or privately

---

[10] Exceptions do not need to be made of such persons as Thomas Edison and Werner Siemens, neither of whom were scientists in the canonical sense. As technicians, however, they are very much the exception to the rule that these people are not typically motivated by desires to make fortunes from their discoveries.

[11] This statement will not bear rigid construction. There are many and notable exceptions, particularly in the early history of biology and chemistry. But while a certain portion of chemistry may owe its origin to alchemical search after hidden riches, this incentive was comparatively short-lived. On the whole, science, in particular the more mathematical and physical branches, is an epistemological offspring of the more abstract reaches of philosophy and theology, and has found its expression in the search for general, consistent, and self-validating laws. There appears, more recently, to be a tendency for scientific speculation to return to the earlier task. Even among those fields in which the "practical" applications were early evident, notably biology, it is interesting that the results of discoveries were widely disseminated and used, rather than kept secret for the private gain of small cliques.

endowed, was of an essentially public character. Use of such laboratories for non-professional gain to experimenters would at all times have been regarded as a serious violation of professional etiquette. Absorption in the experimental work at hand has usually been accompanied by an assurance of income from institutional sources large enough to care for ordinary needs. The temptation to commercialize thus largely forestalled, research has been happily combined with work of a professorial capacity where immediate and impartial dissemination of the available fund of scientific information has been the prevailing rule.

With the rise of the corporation and special interest laboratory and special research institutes, the prevalence and persistence of the scientific attitude, as sketched above, have introduced powerful leavening forces into the interstices of the business enterprise. While science has become increasingly the indispensable prerequisite to technical advance in industry and commerce, it has been enjoying a certain popular apotheosis. Correlated historically with the secularization of material values has been a secularization of intellectual and emotional values. The "rationale" of science and the machine, however naïvely conceived, has been woven into the popular complex of settled habits and beliefs. In the business world the coercive influence of this scientific leaven has meant an increasing willingness to submit all technical questions to the judgment of qualified experts, and to incorporate into the run of the technical processes all suggestions, discoveries, and improvements which promise an increase in general efficiency; provided, of course, that such alterations promise to justify themselves by improving the profit-making prospects of the enterprise in question.[12]

With the secular increase in the range of problems submitted to more or less dispassionate scientific analysis, and with the growing dependence of the capitalistically organized business enterprise upon scientific research and expert technical counsel, there has arisen a tendency to entrust an increasing portion of the technical managerial work to scientifically trained engineers and specialists. The trend in this direction has been somewhat reinforced, with growth in the size and complexity of business enterprises, by the difference in attitude and outlook of the general managerial staff and the body of shareholders and investors. The interests of the managerial staff are bound up with the long-run improvement in the status of the enterprise. The interests of investors are attached to return upon shares and bonds in the form of dividend and interest payments, and the chance to profit by fluctuations in the market values of such securities. Not infrequently the difference of interest brings these two groups into rather sharp conflict.[13] When these differences arise, there appears to be a pronounced tend-

[12] Doubtless there is a counter-reaction in the effect of business enterprise on scientific thought. Our present concern, however, is with the former drift as indicated above.

[13] Occasionally this difference of opinion becomes sufficiently great, and the disputes arising therefrom sufficiently acrimonious, to lead to court action. See the expert testimony of Dr. Vögler of the Vereinigte Stahlwerke (pp. 386–388), Herr Deutsch of A. E. G. (pp. 399–400),

ency for management to identify itself more with a position generally conducive to technical efficiency—long-run technical improvement, willingness to "write off" a larger amount of the value of plant and equipment because of technical development, stability of output and sales, stability in wages, salary, and dividend disbursements—than to quick speculative gains.

3. TYPES OF TECHNOLOGICAL AND ECONOMIC RESEARCH

Before turning to sketch the organization and work of some of the more important German agencies engaged in the labor of coordinating, planning, and promoting cooperative research, it may be useful to indicate the main divisions into which such institutional activities more or less naturally group themselves. These may be summarized under the following heads:

(*a*) Research relating to new methods, processes, material utilization, etc. Typical are the development of the rayon industry, the discovery of the Bergius process of coal liquefaction, experimentation with new metal alloys (aluminum, duralumin, chromium steel, "Electron," etc.), new types of artificial fertilizers, and projects for utilizing wind, solar, and oceanic energy. The order here is: systematic search for possibilities, verification of theories, and solution of known manufacturing difficulties by linking laboratories directly with productive processes (chemicals in particular). Frequently the initiative comes from the management, which turns over to the laboratory technicians the problem of finding out how to achieve some particular desired result, such as television perfection or the problem of automatic airplane stabilizers.

(*b*) Research directed towards (1) the recovery of waste materials known to exist, and (2) the task of finding uses for by-product materials recovered, or recoverable.

(*c*) Researches into problems of factory efficiency: comparative efficiencies of different power, heating, and lighting systems, different types of prime movers and methods of power transmission, arrangement of machinery and systems of internal transportation, shop, factory, and office organization, etc. Research of an organizational character prepares the way for the introduction of scientific management.

(*d*) Study of the human factor: (1) Physiological and psychological (psychotechnical) peculiarities and aptitudes of various types of workers as a basis for scientific job analysis, personnel selection, and training. Study of the causes of industrial fatigue, effect of different working postures, pace and monotony of work, lighting, heating, ventilation, number and length of rest pauses, etc. (2) Methods of combating and controlling industrial disease. (3) Design and con-

---

and Herr Bosch of I. G. Farbenindustrie A. G. (pp. 443–444) in *Verhandlungen und Berichte des Unterausschusses für allgemeine Wirtschaftsstruktur,* I. "Unterausschuss," 3. "Arbeitsgruppe," Erster Teil (Berlin, 1928).

struction of machinery and equipment in order to facilitate safety in operation. Elimination of explosion and choke-damp hazards in mining; methods of rescue and resuscitation, etc. (4) Time and motion studies.

Paralleling this more purely technological research are a series of fields of investigations in which the technical equipment for objective analysis, the sources of information, and the methods of approach are of but a quasi-scientific nature. Business or commercial research is concerned with such problems as the causes, behavior, and possible cures of cyclical fluctuations, the development of satisfactory cost-accounting and budgeting systems, methods of distribution, and the determinants of market demand. There is some question whether the methods of analysis followed in the more exact disciplines will ever be, or in fact can be, applied to problems of such a character; but whether they can or no, the organizations working with such methods, both private and public, have increased quite rapidly in the past few years. Likewise, there is observable in the larger and older of these institutions a tendency to give the technical staff professional standing, to adopt methods of procedure similar or analogous to those in physical and chemical laboratories, and to couch results of research in the same guarded, generalized, and dispassionate textual setting which has so long been the earmark of scientific discussion.

4. GERMAN INSTITUTIONS ENGAGED IN THE MOBILIZATION AND PLANNING OF SCIENTIFIC RESEARCH

The rapid rise of German industry before the war in large part resulted from the long-established habit of linking laboratories very closely with manufacturing processes. Since the war, this linkage has been still closer in Germany, as, indeed, throughout the industrial world. However large the sums of money spent on research by the industries of other countries,[14] it remains true, in the post-war as well as in the earlier period, that German achievement has been by far the most notable.

Where the link-up between laboratory and plant has been particularly close because of the peculiarities of the industry, the burden of promoting research work has been taken up directly by the interested corporations. Usually, because of the expense attached to establishment and maintenance of suitable facilities, private laboratories have been built up only by the larger corporations, such as the dye trust (*I. G. Farbenindustrie A. G.*), the two big electrical concerns, *Siemens & Halske-Siemens & Schuckertwerke* and *A. E. G.* (*Allgemeine Elektrizitäts-Gesellschaft*), and the big steel combines, *Vereinigte Stahlwerke* and *Krupp*. A good many smaller firms, specializing on some particular product, have been able to man their staffs with a small number of highly paid scientists and engi-

[14] Maurice Holland has estimated the annual sum spent for industrial research in the United States at $100,000,000. "Research, the Prime Mover of Industry," *Sci. Monthly* (April, 1926).

neers who may either use facilities provided by the companies in question, or may carry their problems to some special research institute for solution. Frequently, medium-sized and small concerns pay regular fees to scientists or engineers, whose main occupation may be teaching or research in some university or special institute, to aid in the solution of vexing problems as these arise in the course of production.

Where the technical problems affect an entire industry, where no one concern has a dominating importance, and where cooperative organizations, such as Cartels, Communities of Interest, Trade Associations, and special Societies (*Fachverbände*) already exist, laboratories are frequently established, the maintenance and support of which comes from the entire industry. Good examples of this type of cooperative research are to be found in the laboratories of the German textile industry located at Krefeld, Sorau, and Dresden. Generally speaking, the smaller the size of the average plant the more necessary it is to conduct research cooperatively.

It would be difficult to say how much exchange of methods and results there is between and among the various corporation and trade association laboratories. A great number of papers relating to more general scientific and engineering problems are published from such sources. Presumably, no discoveries and improvements bearing directly upon manufacturing processes, particularly those of a patentable character, are given out to the general scientific and engineering public. Almost every indication, however, points to a growing interdependence between the scientific and technical problems raised in these special-interest laboratories, and in the congresses and conventions of the specialists representing these institutions. Not only are the problems becoming general throughout the range of each separate industry, but they are also becoming common to technically related industries considered as groups. Research on cotton fiber treatment leads to study of fiber types, and thence back to agricultural research relating to plant types, methods of growing and cropping, soil and climatic conditioning factors, etc. Study of methods of dyeing fabrics and securing dye fastness brings textile research into direct contact with the dye and chemical industry. Study of the effects of certain mechanical methods of processing brings textile research into direct contact with the machine industry. The growth of electro-chemistry and ferro-chemistry have made available many of the more significant research findings in these fields for the entire electric, chemical, and metallurgical industries.

As one of the most important reasons given for the tendency towards large-scale enterprise and amalgamations has been the advantages to be derived from a pooling of scientific and technical resources, so the increasingly intimate relations between entire industries have encouraged the promotion of research work of more general significance. As early as 1911 an effort was made in Germany to establish an institution whose function it would be to correlate and integrate scientific research work of value to the economic life of the entire country. This institution, the *Kaiser Wilhelm-Gesellschaft,* was modeled in part after the Rockefeller and Carnegie Institutes in the United States, the Nobel Institute in Sweden, and the Pasteur Institute in Paris. It was believed that this institution should provide laboratory facilities and stipends for research workers in fields hitherto more or less neglected, and for scientists overburdened with academic teaching loads. The various affiliated institutes built up by the Society, now some thirty in number, are planned on a somewhat broader basis than those of foreign countries. Beginning with the more abstract problems in the more exact disciplines, institutes were established to "supplement the theoretic sciences of chemistry, physics, zoology, botany, and medicine."[15] For the purpose of federating the various branches as closely as possible, another group of institutes was established to conduct research in problems relating to economy and efficiency in various branches of applied science. Laboratories were established in various places in the Reich to deal with coal chemistry and coal technology, metallurgy, india rubber, production and treatment of light metals, textile fibers, leather and leather tanning, aerodynamic-experimentation, current (electric) and hydraulic power, and psycho-technics. Support comes from the Reich, the various states, and from donations of private individuals. The connection with private enterprise is often very close, as when research is made into coal, iron and non-ferrous metals, and rubber.

Although cooperating very closely with private industry, the Society has attempted to maintain its administrative independence from both governmental and private control.[16] A senate, consisting of "eminent men of science, delegates from the directors and scientific members of the institutes, and representatives of economy and politics, irrespective of any political considerations,"[17] elects the various administrative functionaries. A scientific council, made up of directors of the various institutes, guides the general course of research. The council is divided into three groups: biological and medicinal technique, chemical physics, and mental science. In expanding the activities of the institutes more recently to take in research lying in the fields of history, public law, international law, and anthropology, the motive is maintained to be the same, viz., with due regard

---

[15] Dr. Friedrich Glum, *The Kaiser Wilhelm-Gesellschaft for the Promotion of Science* (pamphlet). See also the *Handbuch der Kaiser Wilhelm-Gesellschaft zur Förderung der Wissenschaften* (Berlin, 1928).

[16] "The independence of science from economics is a life necessity for both. The work of the Kaiser Wilhelm Institutes must, in the first instance, always receive its driving impulses only from science itself. Only then can science be of use to economics. The economic world is always faced with the danger of technical stagnation. It will always be the rôle of science to provide it with new stimuli. These stimuli are perhaps at first of a very impractical nature. But it is precisely in the carrying over of scientific ideas into economically useful processes that the strength of German industry always existed. That economics on its side can be a stimulating force is to be taken for granted. Only it must not demand from the scientists its solution of technical problems in which it (industry) has a peculiar vested interest, and under this point of view attempt to set the objectives and control the work of the Institutes."—*Handbuch,* p. 31.

[17] Glum, *op. cit.*

to specialization, to federate as closely as possible, and, while maintaining the greatest possible freedom and elasticity, "to organize the division and coadjunction of activities over more widespread areas." Suggesting that the ultimate objective was to plan and integrate scientific research nationally within all fields of pure and applied science, Glum writes: "Thus we perceive the principal aim of the various institutes founded by the Society to be that of promoting all new departures in science; at the same time we recognize the sub-structure of a broadly conceived system still awaiting its final completion."[18]

To meet the general shortage of funds for purposes of carrying forward scientific research in the post-war period, and the herculean task of economic rehabilitation in which science would have to play an exceedingly important rôle, in 1920 another organization was set up, the Emergency Society for German Science (*Notgemeinschaft der Deutschen Wissenschaft*), charged with the task of finding means of supporting scientific research in general, and in particular with "the support of great scientific libraries in the purchase of foreign literature, the care of the younger generation of scientists, finding funds for the publication of journals and important monographs, and financing of individual research projects through supplying of apparatus and travel funds."[19] Cooperating in the establishment of the German Research Society were the *Kaiser Wilhelm-Gesellschaft,* the Federation of Colleges (*Hochschulverbände*), the technical colleges, special research institutes (not attached to the *Hochschule*) and the Federation of Technical-Scientific Societies (*Verband Technisch-Wissenschaftlicher Vereine*). The purpose of the Research Society, like that of the *Kaiser Wilhelm-Gesellschaft,* was declared to be that of promoting, through the medium of an independent non-party organization, scientific research for the economic and cultural improvement of the country. Here also, while maintaining that the ultimate objective shall be to promote technology, commerce, and the well-being of the nation, it is insisted that science should be permitted to specialize on particular problems regardless of the immediate special interests of industry, while at the same time an attempt should be made to coordinate and integrate, in a word, to "plan," research.

Although the Research Society is somewhat less interested than the Kaiser Wilhelm Institute in biological and psychological research, both societies have devoted considerable attention to these fields, the former by the subsidizing of special studies, and the latter by the establishment of special institutions, most important of which is the *Kaiser Wilhelm Institut für Arbeitsphysiologie,* in Dortmund. This latter institution, under the direction of Atzler, and in fairly close touch with the industry on the one hand, and the various academic physio-

---

18 *Ibid.*

19 *Neunter Bericht der Notgemeinschaft der deutschen Wissenschaft* (Berlin, 1930):21. The survey contains a very condensed but quite complete statement of subsidized work completed and under way, including works published.

logical and psychological laboratories on the other, has acquired an international reputation for its experimental work in the physiology and psychology of work. Particularly noteworthy is the work carried on by Atzler himself in the study of fatigue and alterations in methods of work designed to avoid exhaustion in heavy and routine labor. Research in this field and that of psycho-technics proper, carried out in the Dortmund institute and elsewhere, is designed, among other things, to provide a theoretical foundation for personnel selection and training.[20] Many of the larger corporations have established laboratories where the work is exclusively concerned with carrying into practice principles of selection and training, whether developed by the more purely research institutions or by their own trial-and-error methods.[21]

Another comprehensive organization has arisen in Germany for the purpose of pooling ideas and centralizing institutional effort on the more purely engineering side of applied science. This organization, known as the Association of German Engineers (*Verein Deutscher Ingenieure*—abbreviated *VDI*) was founded as early as 1856, and has now expanded until it is quite the most significant organization of its kind in the world. It has as its principal objective "the encouragement, assistance and prosecution of research work, and the promotion of post-graduate courses of study for engineers." For this purpose it has a very extensive organization of scientific departments and committees, and a plan of work which shows a most expansive view of the scope, methods of work, and objectives of pure and applied science. Here, as in the case of the societies reviewed above, an attempt is being made to integrate horizontally the work of the various engineering professions, and vertically the work of scientific research, directly with technology and education.[22] The society is associated quite closely with the various special engineering societies, from whose ranks its membership, now about 31,000, is drawn. As a service to its membership and the engineering and scientific public, it publishes at regular intervals nine different periodicals. Some of these are of interest to the general public, such as Engineering and Economics (*Technik und Wirtschaft*), and some of them are of interest to specialists in one field only (e.g., *Zeitschrift für Metallkunde*). Its interest in promoting scien-

---

20 *Handbuch,* pp. 131–136. For a comparatively complete cross-section of German research into the physiology and psychology of labor, consult the *Handbuch der Arbeitswissenschaft,* various volumes of which have appeared from time to time. See in particular Part II, "Biologie der Arbeit," and Part III, "Technologie der Arbeit."

21 E.g., A. E. G., Siemens & Halske, Ludwig Loewe, Vereinigte Stahlwerke, the Reichsbahn.

22 *Verein Deutscher Ingenieure* (pamphlet), p. 27. "From the very first moment of its existence, the Verein Deutscher Ingenieure has never restricted itself merely to advancing technical and scientific knowledge by the indirect means afforded by the publication of technical literature. It has also considered it its duty to deal at first hand with all problems connected with engineering and to analyse the technical achievements so far realised, and to prepare the ground for further progress, thus identifying itself in the closest manner with all creative work with a view to inspiring and furthering future development. As a spiritual center of scientific and engineering activity, it is especially called upon to coordinate theory and practice and to collect all data for ensuring cooperation on the widest and most useful basis possible."

tific research, along with the advancement of engineering studies, is paralleled by its interest in the educational needs of the younger generation. For this latter purpose it cooperates very closely with the Institute for Engineering and Scientific Instructional Material (*Technisch-Wissenschaftliche Lehrmittelzentrale*), and the German Committee for Technical Education and Training (*Deutscher Ausschuss für Technisches Schulwesen—DATSCH*).

On the more purely economic side, two research institutions are of particular interest, the Institute for Business Cycle Research (*Institut für Konjunkturforschung*) and the Institute for World Economics and Oceanic Trade (*Institut für Weltwirtschaft und Seeverkehr*). The dominating idea has been the same in both, viz., to combine detailed and specialized study with a comprehensive survey of current economic conditions, and to bring the products of such work to bear directly on the fortunes of the national economic system. The former, located in Berlin, is primarily interested in the study of business fluctuations of one sort or another, and for this purpose has built up a large staff of statisticians and research workers who cooperate very closely with various government departments, particularly the Federal Statistical Office, and with organizations representative of business and industry. The latter, attached to the University of Kiel, has been more generally interested in foreign markets and world economic conditions, although its director, Professor Harms, acted in an advisory capacity to, and its staff conducted a large portion of the research work connected with, the monumental *Enquete* Committee reports.[23]

5. SUMMARY

Scientific research has increased in importance with the slowing down of the rate of technical progress, the growing complexity and increase in the scale of manufacturing and distributing processes, and the gradual exhaustion of the better raw materials resources. It holds the key to the technical, if not to the entire economic development of the future. In Germany the loss of territory and resources through the Treaty of Versailles, the rapid exhaustion of certain important mineral deposits, population increase, and growth in the national standard of living, have combined to emphasize the importance of science in industry.

In the course of its genesis and exfoliation, science has built up certain methods of work and ways of regarding the nature and objects of research which have a tremendous significance for technology and commerce. Most important of these are (1) its social orientation, (2) the method of dispassionate and objective analysis, (3) the notion that scientific methods are universally applicable, (4) the concept of functional interdependence and functional balance, and (5) the concept of a theoretically perfect and technically possible "one best way."

[23] For a more complete description of the various scientific institutions mentioned above, see Appendix A.

Post-war industrial rationalization, in calling for mobilization of all the available productive means, is necessarily conditioned by these peculiarities of modern scientific development. Before the advent of the "rationalization movement," a number of scientific institutions had been established in which the preconceptions of the scientific world had been fairly definitely expressed. In these institutions, rigorous specialized research has been joined rather closely with a carefully integrated general and national scientific program. At the same time that they have maintained their administrative independence, they have associated themselves rather closely with both industry and government. The link-up of scientific research with engineering and commerce, on the one hand, and with education and academic problems on the other has become more intimate. The concept of *plan,* of which scientific research is the very essence, appears to have expanded gradually until it now includes integration and coordination of research on a national scale. Always without interfering with the actual conduct of research, cooperative scientific work means rather the strengthening of this tendency than the reverse.

Still, with the exception of the U. S. S. R., science has unfolded its activities within the confines of capitalistically and nationalistically organized industrial countries. Science and technology, being a social heritage of industrialism, have never been national property. Not until recently have most aspects of science been submitted to the profit-making drive of the capitalistically functioning business enterprise. It remains to be seen to what extent capitalism will retard and hold back scientific progress, and to what extent science is a corrosive and disintegrating force in the interstices of the capitalistic system, which, in these days of privately owned corporation laboratories, it appears to be meekly serving.

CHAPTER II

STANDARDIZATION

RESEARCH represents the dynamic elements of change, variety, and progress; standardization represents the conserving elements of order, arrangement, and selection. Planning of research means systematic and cooperative attack upon unsolved and interrelated problems; planning of standards means the weaving of a balanced and internally consistent system of dimensional, quality, and processing rules and ratios capable (1) of theoretical justification, and (2) of promoting efficiency of output. Both research and standardization are brought into the compass of the rationalization movement under precisely the same conditions: (1) the theoretical and practical aspects of the relevant problems have sprung the boundaries of the individual unit (process, factory, business enterprise, or industrial grouping); and (2) systematic effort has been carried to the point where special institutional equipment is required to integrate, to coordinate, and, in a word, to plan procedure, on a comprehensive basis. Both require the use of exacting scientific criteria; neither is possible (in the rationalization sense) without the maximum possible usage of the cooperative effort of all directly interested and specially skilled persons. In theory and practical application, research and standardization represent the two halves of an internally balanced and scientific whole.

It was in standardization that the German rationalization movement found one of its principal contributory streams. This was but natural, since, like cooperative research, standardization as a group activity can become of crucial importance only in a ripened industrial system. As in all other countries, the elaboration and industrial permeation of standards has served to bring out and magnify a thousandfold the potentialities and limitations of the available productive equipment. This holds, in particular, for machinery. The machine, in turn, is but an embodiment and an exaggeration of methods and habits of work which had been slowly perfecting themselves throughout the history of human technology.

1. STANDARDIZATION AND MACHINE INDUSTRY

What the machine adds to technology, and in still later times—"rationalization" times—to economic processes, is absolute regularity, uniformity, and accuracy within the limits of its construction and the rules guiding its operation.

It performs to the best advantage when permitted to operate in this way. The refinement and generalization of its field of operation is the history of modern industrialism.

From the earliest times the machine has operated most efficiently and to the best net advantage (highest ratio of output to materials and energy input) when certain basic conditions are fulfilled: (1) The material and energy input is timed to come as an even and continuous flow—i.e., there are no significant changes in timing and rhythm and the flow is uni-directional. (2) The task to be performed is extremely simple, or, if complex, has been broken up into simple and elementary parts, each, or a portion, of which has been turned over to a machine which can then specialize, singly and solely, upon the performance of these simple and elementary tasks, endlessly and without change. (3) The material used is (relatively) standard, uniform, and constant in size and shape; chemical and physical properties are relatively invariable; the output is constant or standard as to size, shape, and variety within the tolerance limits laid down by the construction of the machine. (4) The machine is continuously operated to capacity (but never over), and the capacity factor (percentage of use to total time usable) is 100 per cent or as near 100 per cent as breakdowns, repairs, and general working conditions permit. This holds good for the entire life of the machine.

Modern technology has witnessed the partial or complete domination of machines and machine methods in nearly every branch of the productive and distributive system. Coming into the shop originally as a specialist, the machine has gradually forced the organization of the entire round of productive operations into channels conforming with its own maintenance and operating requirements. Even those preceding and following ancillary operations not subject to direct mechanical manipulation have nevertheless become, in the main, mechanized. That is, the temporal and spatial rhythm has become machine-like in the sense that a high degree of specialization, routinization, and regularity of unitary and assembly processing and output has been forced through, whether machines have been permitted to take over the whole or but a small part of the entire concert of productive activities. Even the factory handworker, with but few exceptions, specializes upon a comparatively simple routine of operations from which he is not permitted to depart. His rôle in the larger entity is that of a cog in a tireless and relentlessly persisting machine.

The growth of the modern large-scale factory has compelled it to adapt its spatial and processing configuration to the structural peculiarities and operating laws of its prototype, the machine. There must be a most intimate and thorough interweaving and dovetailing of machine to machine, process to process, shop to shop, and material to material. *Simultation,* as this temporal and spatial running adjustment has been recently termed in American management literature, graduates the factory into the class of the more or less completely automatic and self-regulating mechanism.

Somewhat the same process is observable in the industrial system at large. Growth of large-scale productive enterprises has brought increasing industrial interdependence. The smooth and uninterrupted flow of the various raw materials through the various stages of manufacture and into the hands of consumers has gradually forced horizontal and vertical integration and coordination. Interdependence of materials, processes, energy types, and transportation and communication services has transformed the entire round of productive and distributive operations into something analogous to the flow through a mechanically regulated and impersonalized complex. As early as 1904 Veblen could write, "By virtue of this concatenation of processes the modern industrial system at large bears the character of a comprehensive, balanced mechanical process."[1]

The machine has been from the very start a mass-production, that is to say, a *standardizing* device. It has always claimed as its field of jurisdiction simple, uniform, repetitive, standardized tasks. The simpler and more standardized the operation, the easier it is to invent a machine to perform it. The more standard the routine of operation, the more standard and uniform the raw materials fed into the machine, the more standard and invariable the type of output, the greater is the productive efficiency[2] of the apparatus. Organizing a factory for the purposes of mass production means, with due regard to the requirements for adaptation to technical change and improvement, increasing the number, range, and importance of standards and standardized procedure. The importance of standardization is still further magnified when entire industries are placed on, and national economies are adapted to, mass production. The more widely any particular raw material, semi-manufactured good, component part (bolts, nuts, screws, hand-wheels, etc.) or type product is used, the greater the net advantage of mechanization and mass production; hence, of standardization. Standards of value to a particular machine frequently become of value to an entire plant, an integrated industry, and a systematized national or international economy.

---

1 Thorstein Veblen, *Theory of the Business Enterprise* (New York, 1904):16.

2 The engineering concept of efficiency enters into the picture as an extraneous element. With or without standards, the notion of efficient production implies the elimination of "waste" where the adjective "avoidable" may be applied. An illustration may be useful. Suppose the "potential" thermal capacity of a unit of coal of a given grade to be 100 per cent. Methods and equipment in current use for extracting and converting this latent heat into energy may operate so as to utilize 25 per cent of the theoretical total. Newer devices may have been developed capable of raising this percentage to 35 per cent. One hundred per cent is then ideal or theoretical efficiency; 25 per cent is current efficiency; and 35 per cent is realizable efficiency. The difference between the latter efficiencies, expressed as a percentage with the former as base, is then a measure of inefficiency, or "waste" incident to failure to employ the new equipment (due regard being taken of the costs incident to the change). Technical and scientific progress might heighten efficiency, or, perhaps, entirely reshape the problem (as in the case of new scientific discoveries concerning the atomic structure of material which served to heighten the theoretical possibilities of exploitation).

2. TYPES OF INDUSTRIAL STANDARDS

The more general the field of application of any particular standard, the greater is the necessity for establishing a single and universally valid norm. Certain materials, practices, and processes, however, remain unique to particular industries. A general basis for classification lies, consequently, in the scope of the field of application of standards. Thus standards may be divided into general and technical basic standards (*Grundnormen*) on the one hand, and special industry standards (*Fachnormen*) on the other.[3] The former group includes standards of general value throughout all industry, and the latter the standards of importance to a particular industry or group of special industries.[4]

Cutting across this general classification is the division into standards relating to materials, unitary products and component parts, and type standards. Type standardization (*Typisierung*) relates to assembled commodities and equipment where many of the assembled parts have previously been standardized. Examples of this latter type of standardization are to be found in industries making locomotives, wagons, box cars, automobiles, apartment houses and office buildings, office furniture, and gas and electric motors.

It is possible, again, to classify standards as they concern materials, parts, and assembled products on the one hand, and processes and standard practices on the other. Practices may be standardized where the character of the manufacturing processes, as in parts of the chemical, textile, leather, metallurgical, and agricultural industries, either permits or requires a high degree of uniformity as a condition to satisfactory results, or where the laying down of certain rather rigid rules more or less arbitrarily delineated may prove of definite advantage to all parties concerned. In this latter class belong such coded practices as safety rules, accounting methods, standard correspondence references, methods of filing, and first-aid rules.

More recently there has been a tendency to set up a body of commercial codes and practices which are parallel to but distinct from technological or industrial standards. Examples of this type are standard terms and conditions of delivery,

---

[3] "General basic standards (Grundnormen) concern themselves with units, weights and measures, nomenclature, formats, patterns, pictures, signs and symbols, graphic representation, and (letter) type, and the technical basic standards of bolts, screws, nuts, etc. Special standards (Fachnormen) are established for the general machine industry, mining, the electro-technical industry, domestic economy, health and hospital service, clothing, agriculture, land, water, and air transport, housing and settlements, accident prevention, and many others."—"Stand der Normung," *Bergbau-, Kali- und verwandte Salze* (October 15, 1928).

[4] In the hospital field, for example, the following have been, or are being standardized in Germany: "hospital furniture, medical and surgical instruments, bed linen, underlinen and clothing, ambulances, disinfection and cleaning, electrical and medical apparatus, appliances for sick nursing, first-aid boxes, bandaging material, printed forms, the construction of isolation huts, the equipment of staff quarters, food supplies, feeding and kitchen utensils and devices for the transport of meals, and special requirements for sanatoria and nursing homes."—B. I. M. I., 4:132 (June, 1930).

standard marking, methods of packing, forwarding, billing, and paying, and standard quality and trade-mark designation.[5] It is possible, further, to differentiate between producer and consumer standards, industrial and agricultural standards, and national and international standards.

Whatever the type or the field of application, the evolution of the practice and theory of standardization has produced a number of fairly definite rules of procedure. In the first place, the general condition has been set up that technical change for the particular practice, material, part, type, or process, has either ended or can be ended without prejudice to productive efficiency. ". . . . it had to become quite clear that conscious, rational standardization did not mean a uniformity deadening to the personal and emotional equation, but rather that unification shall take place only where technical development has come to an end and where the factor of personal taste is not of decisive importance."[6]

As a companion to this rule, experience has demonstrated in the second place the wisdom of keeping standards as flexible as possible. Adaptability to the requirements of technical change is a most essential condition in a standards system. "Freedom and order," Hellmich writes, "are the two poles between which every controlled development must run. Innate human creative and formative powers crave a condition of freedom; reflective and systematizing reason demands order. Both have their justification; only the unfettered interaction between these two coercive forces will give salutary results. Standardization becomes dangerous and harmful when it immoderately narrows the effective range of creative fancy and thereby crushes the most powerful driving force to progress. It dare, consequently, be extended only into realms where development has practically run its course and where the methods and the knowledge, providing a basis for rational ordering and control, lie readily at hand. . . . . Standardization must, under all circumstances, leave the way open for technical development. It must be limited, therefore, essentially to the fixation of elements, which, technically speaking, have ripened so far that it is humanly impossible to foresee further significant improvements within the calculable future."[7]

However important this condition of adaptability may be for individual products and component parts, it is held absolutely imperative for typified products. While many of the individual parts of an electric motor, automobile, or locomotive may be standardized and held invariable over a considerable period of time to the advantage of productive efficiency, the assembled product cannot be thus rigidly cast without the imminent danger of rapid technical obsolescence.[8]

---

[5] See p. 27.

[6] *Die deutsche Normung, 1927* (Deutscher Normenausschuss; Berlin, 1927):19–20.

[7] M. Hellmich, *DIN, 1917–1927* (Deutscher Normenausschuss; Berlin, 1927): 21–22.

[8] "To what extent standardization has actually been carried through is shown by the fact that out of 5,424 various parts for the passenger locomotives of Type IcI-H2 (tender and locomotive) there are 1,451 standard and 2,842 type parts; that is, single parts which will find

But the flexibility which standards must possess is relative. Contrasted with the dynamic, revolutionary, stimulating power of science and technological change, they represent stability, order, routine, and regularity. Standards lose their value with the necessity of change. While they should be established in keeping with the dictates of scientific development, still theirs is the empire of the relatively fixed and changeless in a technically regimentized world.

This implies, however, a high degree of order and system in the more stable sectors of the industrial system. Standardization rests upon and enforces specialization on the one hand and mass production on the other. Specialization is impossible, whether under machine or handicraft régimes, without a high degree of interdependence, coordination, and integration. Standards have no very great function to perform without such coordination, while such systematization and interweaving require and depend upon a system of more or less inherently consistent standards. The third requirement, then, is that standards shall partake of, conform with, and promote the possibilities inherent in the technical "ground plan" of industry.

Standards, as a precipitate of scientific experimentation and industrial practice, are consequently required to possess a high degree of internal consistency. That is what is meant by a *system of standards.* The more basic the standards, the wider the industrial and geographic range of application, the more significant the requirement that each new standard shall be drafted in keeping with the nature of the previous body of norms. Standardization has sometimes been dubbed "the rationalization of the product." The analogy is useful, since it implies that the general rules underlying factory and industrial rationalization are applicable and necessary in the development of standards. The world of technology is thus regarded as a functioning system into the warp and woof of which standards are only to be woven with considerable skill and cunning.

This objective, the fourth requirement, can only be realized when the process of standardization is made as scientific as possible. Otherwise it is quite probable (1) that given standards will clash with standards already established, (2) that standards established may not be readily adjusted to technical changes, and (3) that certain standards will not promote the maximum of industrial efficiency. Hence it is important that the standardization process be not fortuitous, haphazard, accidental, and ruled by chance, but, rather, be careful, deliberate, and selective. To insure this it is necessary that all interested opinion, not of choice but of necessity, be brought to bear upon the problem of establishing appropriate standards. ". . . . it is a fundamental principle in German standards work," Hellmich writes, "that all norms established shall be the product of the freely pooled labor of producer, consumer, and commercial interests, acting with the

---

application in locomotive construction, while 1,131 parts are left unstandardized."—A. Meckel, "Die deutsche Lokomotivnormung 1918 bis 1927," VDI *Nachrichten,* Nr. 43:9 (October 26, 1927).

aid and cooperation of the government and of science."[9] The first three must see that the standard proposed is technologically feasible and efficient, pecuniarily profitable (in capitalistic industries), and, generally speaking, useful. The interest of the government lies in the application of the standards to industrial processes owned, operated, and regulated by it, and in the relation of the norm to the general prosperity, security, and well-being of the entire community for which it is the general spokesman. To science and engineering is delegated the task of preventing all standardization which might cramp future technical development, while at the same time they must see that standards proposed shall be scientifically the best possible, all factors included. If the field of application of the standard proposed is entirely localized and industrially limited, then only a limited number of persons need be consulted in the work. If the field is international (as with weights and measures and their conversion ratios, and with nomenclature, fits and gauges, etc.), then the legislating body must be international.

3. INTEGRATION AND PLANNING OF STANDARDS

"The norm is a logical product of the common human urge for order. It originates through choice. In so far as the choice is consciously made (technical), interdependence requires that the standard be consistent with underlying scientific law."[10] As technology approaches maturity, this interdependence requires ever closer planned dovetailing and integration within the interstices of the system of standards. In view of this there can be, consequently, no such thing as an isolated standard. "All standards are dependent upon one another. Out of this simple principle has grown the recognition that the products of the labor of unification can be successfully applied to the national economic system only when standardization work has been brought together in one place. Consequently there can be but one German Standards Committee. The attempt to proceed independently with standardization in any field of national economic life must inevitably be accompanied by heavy national sacrifices."[11]

On this broad foundation the German Standards Committee (*Deutscher Normenausschuss*) has been built. While its history does not go back very far,[12] the committee has been constructed on much the broadest lines of any of the numerous national standards associations.[13] Excepting standardization on purely a factory basis, and certain special norms involved in terms and conditions of delivery and sale which have been turned over to the Committee for Conditions and Terms of Delivery (*Ausschuss für Lieferbedingungen*), all standards work in Germany is under the control of the central Standards Committee. Basic

---

[9] Hellmich, *op. cit.*, p. 17. [10] *Ibid.*, p. 29. [11] *Ibid.*, pp. 13–14.

[12] The Deutscher Normenausschuss was organized in 1917 as the Normenausschuss der deutschen Industrie. For a brief sketch of its history see Appendix A, pp. 422–423.

[13] These have been organized in nearly every major industrial country, the first being the British Engineering Standards Association, organized in 1901.

standards, which are presumably of importance to all industries and the entire national economic system, are brought directly under the supervision of the committee as a whole. Special industrial standards, of interest to a single branch of industry, or to a number of related industries, are developed by special industrial standards committees under a procedure requiring the consultation of all interested and vitally affected groups in exactly the same way as in the case of the basic standards.

The rules established to carry out the procedure indicated above have been most rigorously adhered to. The greatest care is taken to guarantee that the standard, once it has been officially approved as a German Standard (*DIN* Standard), will prove of sufficient value to merit ready and universal introduction into practice. In order that this shall be the practically certain result, occasional checks are made upon subsequent introduction into practice. From time to time special meetings are held in various parts of the country to ascertain the degree to which specific recommended standards have been introduced into practice. In these meetings it has been possible also to evaluate directly (1) the various objections raised to specific standards hitherto established, (2) arguments for changing of such standards, and (3) proposals for new standards.[14]

Of even greater importance is the direct connection between the Standards Committee and the National Board for Economy and Efficiency (*Reichskuratorium für Wirtschaftlichkeit*—abbreviated to *RKW*).[15] As a member of the *RKW*, the committee is brought into direct contact with the Committee for Conditions and Terms of Delivery, the German Committee for Technical Education and Training (*DATSCH*),[16] and other special agencies dealing with various aspects of rationalization. *DATSCH* is engaged in the rather interesting attempt to use *DIN* standards as the basis for a uniform system of technical training in all privately and public owned and operated schools.

As indicated, the Standards Committee is brought through its institutional affiliations into direct contact with all the various agencies and special committees dealing with different phases of rationalization. Through its membership and its connection with the Federation of German Engineers, for example, the committee is assured the advantage of direct engineering experience and the cooperation of and constant linkage with scientific thought and development. As a result of its association with the *RKW* it is enabled to integrate better its standards on a national basis and at the same time to dovetail more readily its specialized functions with the larger rationalization movement. An excellent example of the advantage to the standards movement from membership in the *RKW* is to be found in the case of *DATSCH* mentioned above. Through this

---

[14] See the various reports of the Deutscher Normenausschuss on its meetings on the Introduction of Standards into Practice (Einführung der Normen in die Praxis) held at Chemnitz, Kiel, Magdeburg, Stuttgart, Saarbrücken, etc.

[15] See Appendix A, p. 422. [16] See Appendix A, p. 424.

organization the Standards Committee is assured that its numerous standards will be made the basis for the education and training of the entire younger generation which is being technically trained for industry, commerce, and the teaching of technical subjects in schools.

The foundation work of the Standards Committee has been almost as broad as the plan implied in its working rules and its organizational interrelationships. Once the necessary conditions were fulfilled for systematic work, the committee turned to the task of developing a system of basic standards (*Grundnormen*). These standards, relating to scientific and engineering nomenclature, weights and measures, signs and symbols, etc., were needed (1) to provide the basis for accurate description and control in ordering supplies and equipment, (2) to facilitate works and production planning, (3) to codify and simplify instructions to workmen and staff, and (4) to supply the general groundwork without which modern machine processes would of necessity become quite chaotic. With these basic standards as a foundation, standard fits and gauges and other precision instruments can be constructed which make it possible to manufacture to close tolerance limits[17] and to place more rigid manufacturing requirements upon the mechanical equipment.

On the basic standards is also built a system of materials specifications which permits and enforces increasing uniformity and invariability in size, shape, weight, chemical and physical properties of raw, semi-finished, and finished materials and component parts.[18] This standardization and unification of materials and energy input makes possible continued refinement of tools and mechanical equipment, and methods of handling, and opens up new fields for the application of machines and mechanical processing methods. Every such development calls in turn for widening the range and increasing the rigor (narrowing the range of tolerated deviations from standard, and expanding the number) of materials standards. The circle here is: materials standards, specialization of machines, mechanization of a larger percentage of the round of operations, more delicate and precise machinery, more exacting and more numerous materials standards.

This process is impossible, of course, unless the articles produced are also standardized or typified. When commodities produced have been standardized, it is possible to use highly specialized machinery to keep operating exclusively upon a single job. Stoppages and startings can thus be reduced to a minimum, and continuous operation can be achieved. The flow of production throughout the factory can be made to approximate the flow of materials through the individual machine. Under such conditions, serial production and "flow work" (*Fliessarbeit*—with or without endless belts and other continuously operated

[17] Meaning: the standard is fixed in dimension or quality terms, plus or minus a *tolerated* deviation (bi-lateral tolerances) or a tolerated deviation in one direction from the established standard (uni-lateral tolerances).

[18] See the list of DIN standards, Appendix B, pp. 428–430.

conveyor systems) become genuine possibilities.[19] These, in turn, nearly always require a new arrangement of shops, departments, buildings, machines, and equipment. Column and floor spacing, systems of internal transport and conveyance, and the whole miscellany of semi-mechanical, mechanical, and the auxiliary hand processes must then be arranged and ordered to fit the pattern of the new configuration.

It is further true that nearly every change made in the larger organization of industry tends to increase emphasis upon standardized production methods and standardized or typified output. This is certainly true of nearly all those efforts to increase plant specialization which involve plans for either horizontal or vertical integration. The same generalization holds for every step in the direction of closer coordination of independently managed but technologically and industrially interdependent processes. For example, the growing technological interdependence of the German coal mining, coking, iron, steel, heavy machinery, heavy chemical, long-distance gas supply, and electric power industries has been accompanied, step by step, by greater insistence upon more numerous and more carefully drawn systems of inter-industry standards.

Somewhat the same picture holds for the German industrial system taken at large. In this system the various transportation networks have come to play the rôle, figuratively speaking, of endless belts which connect each and every plant, process, and operative. The communication networks play the rôle of the coordinating nerve systems. The two serve as the connecting links which cause the national industrial system to take on some of the characteristics of a technologically balanced and managerially integrated whole. Flow through the various stages and processes of the industrial system has come to resemble somewhat the flow through the machine. In order to function most smoothly and to the best advantage, such an industrial "machine" must have its processing methods regulated by a coherent, internally consistent, and continuously flexible *system* of standards.

Whether we have reference to standards within the individual shop, or within the industrial system taken at large, there is a tendency to permit change only when due attention has been paid to the probable effects upon the existing system of standards. Variation from accepted practices is typically permitted when improvement in the individual process is not outweighed by interference with other and related processes. When advantage to the whole complex can be demonstrated, a new standard or system of standards has then to be developed. That is to say, with growing standardization of materials, products, and processing methods, there goes a steady increase in the importance of careful supervision and planning of the standards themselves.

---

[19] It is interesting to note that serial and flow work, and the devices of endless belts and special (mechanically operated) conveyor systems are only to be found in industries producing a highly standardized or typified commodity, e.g., Ford cards, Bata shoes, Singer sewing machines, electrical fixtures and small motors, and lumber mills.

The conditions which promote standardization, and are forced into prominence by it are, consequently, those in which the problem of organization has become of great importance. Standardization is thus not only an integral part of Scientific Management, but also in a certain sense it lies at the foundations of that movement. As in scientific research, so in both standardization and the various phases of Scientific Management the underlying problem has become that of how best to promote and increase specialization, and at the same time to increase the emphasis upon closer coordination and integration. Generalized, the solution of this problem, in both its larger and its more intimate and practical applications, might be regarded as the central task of the whole rationalization movement. Historically, the movement in Germany has been characterized by emphasis upon organization. The technological and coded foundation for all systematic organization is to be found in some system of standards. Since standardization is the central key to the smooth functioning of mechanically regulated and mass-output methods in the modern industrial system, it occupies an unusually important position in the *sanctum sanctorum* of economic and industrial planning.

4. SUMMARY

The function of standards is to facilitate mass production. They do this by paving the way for greater specialization of plant and machinery, and by providing the necessary conditions for continuous operation. Both specialization and continuous production call for increasingly careful integration and coordination of technically and industrially interrelated processes. Every change requires increased emphasis upon more schematic arrangement of interlocking processes and more careful and comprehensive planning. Hence the standards appropriate to such processes must themselves be integrated and coordinated into a series of schematically balanced systems.

In order to find widespread use, standards must be drawn so as (1) to fit into the existing system of standards, and so as (2) to be readily adaptable to changes in technology and in demand. These conditions are fully satisfied only (1) when standards are developed by the aid of, and with constant reference to, scientific criteria, and (2) when all directly and indirectly interested parties have a hand in the deliberations leading to the drafting of standards. Standardization is essentially a cooperative activity. It is stultifying and technologically retrogressive when not linked directly to the dynamics of science.

These rules, evolved out of long practice, hold for every appropriate field of application. Certain standards apply only within the individual plant; others affect only the business enterprise; some are of significance to an entire industry; still others can be applied throughout all branches and types of industries. Those having only local significance may or may not be correlated with others having more general application. Where not so correlated, standards are usually employed by business enterprise as a competitive device. Nearly all such practices are demonstrably wasteful of time, materials, plant, and machinery. Hence their competitive justification is at the same time their rationalization indictment. So used, standards made, not for greater order and higher efficiency in the industrial system, but for waste of national resources and duplication of facilities.[20]

Hence the German Standards Committee has denied competitively used coded practices and norms the status of national standards. The view which has been formally adopted, although perhaps not always entirely realized, is that national standards must not be established which redound to the competitive advantage of any particular group in the community. Rather must national economic prosperity serve as the leitmotif. The "nature of the German Standards Committee is best characterized as a 'special purpose institution' in which all have the same aims, and none possesses a balance of power. The discipline necessary, in order to obtain the cooperative character of such a special institution, is secured by enforcing the rule that its work can and must be oriented in terms of objective criteria, and that the importance or ambition of no one person or economic branch be permitted to exercise undue influence. As the idea and planning of the German Standards Committee sprang from no one head, and as the fruits of its work cannot be written down to the exclusive advantage of any particular person or corporation, so it cannot afford to provide a place for the promotion of particular or personal influence."[21] "It is fundamentally characteristic of standardization that it is not the concern of individuals; it is much more than a matter of personal preference whether or not the individual adapt himself to standardization .... [it] is more than that. It is a national economic necessity in the process of which every individual has the right to participate, and in the carrying out of which every individual has a duty to perform."[22]

The official position of the German Standards Committee is clear. Standards must be cooperatively developed, scientifically correct, and socially oriented. Not only must standards be carefully planned, but also it is imperative that this aspect of reorganization be integrated with other phases of the rationalization movement. Hence the intimate linkage with the National Board for Efficiency and Economy, and the Federation of German Engineers.

How far practice corresponds with theory remains to be seen.

---

[20] The wastes involved in excessive variety are especially great in the finishing industries. The Solingen steel goods industry produces 20,000 varieties of finished goods. Other figures are: lock and clasp, 10,000 types; enameled ware industries, 300 different articles in 10 to 12 sizes in from 20 to 30 colors. "Many thousand types in the machine tool, screw, and roller bearing industries. Sewing needle industry, 250 types in 50 different strengths and each strength in many qualities. Leather goods industry, yearly about 5,000 new patterns. One thousand types in the purse and in the sewing and manicure goods industries. One thousand thirty types and sorts of alarm clocks, 375 of grandfather clocks, 390 of wall and table clocks."—E. A., *Gesamtbericht,* p. 41.

[21] Hellmich, *op. cit.,* p. 15.

[22] Griessmann, "Werksleitung und Normung," in minutes of the Magdeburg meeting of the Deutscher Normenausschuss on the Introduction of Standards into Practice, April 29, 1928.

CHAPTER III

SCIENTIFIC MANAGEMENT

SCIENTIFIC MANAGEMENT means science *in* management. Since management is the coordinating and guiding force in every economic unit, its alliance with science provides the rationalizing force in all phases of organization. In detail this means the systematic employment of scientific criteria in (1) the location and organization of factories and offices of all types and descriptions; (2) the selection, training, and organization of personnel, the determination of relations between master and men, and the location and fixation of responsibility; (3) the utilization of the best possible equipment and methods so as to achieve the maximum efficiency of every part of the running adjustment, and to proportion these so that, with due regard to factors of best size, high efficiency will be coexistent with low cost; and (4) to harmonize all conflicting interests in the cooperative pursuit of a clearly defined objective or set of objectives.

It is the fourth aspect of scientific management which prevents that movement from being accepted as conceptually or descriptively synonymous with rationalization. Scientific management is concerned primarily—one might almost say exclusively—with systematic employment of scientific methods and techniques. Its ultimate task is to order, arrange, and harmonize all elements required to achieve any given goal. But it cannot set the goal, because there are no scientifically indefeasible objectives.

It is with this modification that we can readily accept Person's differentiation. Scientific management, he says, should be defined as ". . . . a technique of organization and management of an enterprise, a group of enterprises, an integrated industry, or all industry for the accomplishment of common purposes with a minimum expenditure of energies, a minimum of disutilities, and a maximum of human welfare [*sic!*]." But rationalization means ". . . . a doctrine of industrial economy, involving socially-controlled integration and coordination of industries self-governed in detail management, without any implications of the technique of organization and management of the industries rationalized." Thus, ". . . . in other words, rationalization should be conceived as connoting one goal of industrial economy; Scientific Management as a means to whatever goal of industrial economy."[1]

[1] H. S. Person, "Rationalization and Scientific Management," meeting of the New York Metropolitan Section of the Taylor Society (October 9, 1930; unpublished).

Scientific management might, accordingly, be employed for achieving social or anti-social goals. Wars can be scientifically managed; labor can be scientifically exploited; resources can be scientifically wasted; consumers can be scientifically cheated of their money. In the broader sense, what rationalization adds thereto is a certain directional bent. It implies that the systematic application of science and the maximum extension of cooperative habits require a certain balance and coordination which is not conformable with exploitation of resources for the exclusive benefit of a selected few. Most writers on the subject of rationalization either openly or by implication insist upon this view. Those who do not, define rationalization so that it is indistinguishable *per se* from scientific management.[2]

Thus scientific management *may* be an element in the rationalization movement. Whether it is or not depends entirely upon the objectives which it pursues. On the other hand, the balance and coordination which rationalization necessitates requires *a* system of scientific management, and it is thus relevant to the subject in hand to examine the anatomy and physiology of existing technical development in that field. In so doing, it will be necessary to generalize rather broadly. But it should not be forgotten that, while scientific management as a movement is directly traceable to the American, Frederick Winslow Taylor, it grew as a conscious program out of problems common to all modern industry, and that, consequently, German industrialists were employing various scientific management techniques long before they ever heard of the American movement. Even in the post-war period there was far less conscious borrowing than many observers have been led to believe.

We may now turn to a brief discussion of the techniques which have been evolved in the development of the scientific management movement.

1. FACTORY ORGANIZATION

Once the site has been chosen, with due regard to all important variables—nearness of market, supply and quality of raw materials and equipment, labor supply, means of transport, climatic factors, etc.—and the factory objective has been determined, the next step is to forecast the future in terms of the "blue-print." The "blue-print" is a basic organizational plan. The merits of any such plan grow as the pattern approaches the ideal. In the ideal "blue-print" nothing is left to chance. Every wheel and pinion, every floor and partition, every shop and sub-division, every mechanical and chemical process, and the tasks of every machine and operative are pre-arranged and pre-planned. The "blue-print" is an elaborate specification the completeness and content of which depends upon the knowledge, the technical and other preconceptions, and the general perspicacity of the engineering and architectural planning staff. There exists a tend-

[2] E.g., J. Gerhardt, "Rationalisierung," *Handwörterbuch der Staatswissenschaften* (Vierte Auflage, Ergänzungsband): 709, and R. V. Holzer, *Systematische Fabriksrationalisierung* (Berlin, 1928):1.

ency at the present time to carry this technique of the "blue-print" into all phases and aspects of managerial and pecuniary organization of the modern enterprise. Everything must be schematically arranged and calculated in advance. Individual initiative is more and more confined to the perfection of the original plan, and, after its adoption, to the rigorous fulfillment of every requirement down to the most minute detail. It may be, and usually is, a part of the original pattern that it shall allow for alterations after its adoption, but the probable importance and direction of these are likewise subject to estimation in advance. Greater alterations than these become major operations, and constitute evidence of shortcomings in the original plan.

In order that these shortcomings, due to gaps in the information and preconceptions of the planning staff, may be reduced to a minimum, it becomes increasingly necessary that the element of personal judgment be eliminated as far as possible. Hence the need for "objective" criteria, which it has become the function of scientific research to provide. With these serving as guides, the advantages of the good, and the disadvantages of the bad plan become greater as (1) the degree of plant and business specialization increases, (2) as pecuniary and technical interdependencies become more pronounced, and (3) as the interweaving of technical and commercial processes grows more intimate. Thus, it is the task of technical engineering and economic research to subsume all present scientific and quasi-scientific information under a set of more or less inherently consistent general principles, while at the same time plumbing as far as possible into the unknown in order that these principles themselves may not have to be altered in the calculable future. These efforts may concern physical and chemical properties of material, techniques of regaining by-products, organizational devices, the supply of raw materials, the nature of product and market competition, the growth of population, price stability, political stability, and any and all other key factors. The principles evolved provide criteria according to which the planning staff may hew a straight and consistent line.

Aside from more purely market and commercial considerations, the factory plan, or reorganization scheme, will have to be drafted in terms of considerations more or less common to all productive enterprises. The degree of flexibility in the ground plan will be determined by the relative stability in technology. Given this, the next and most difficult task is to ascertain the best size of plant in view of the requirement for the best proportioning of productive factors. It may not be possible to obtain the best size without sacrificing some of the advantages of best proportioning of factors. The like holds good not only for the factory taken as a whole, but also for the various machines, processes, shops, and departments going to make up the larger complex.[3] Sometimes the solution of this problem lies in the direction of smaller units; usually, the reverse.

---

[3] Wiedenfeld offers the following schematic example: "If in any stage of a manufacturing process machine A is used with a capacity of 100 units in a definite time interval, and in an-

The plan must then proceed to sketch building, layout,[4] and equipment with a view to taking advantage of all the possibilities which promise the best compromise solution to the above problem. It will not be feasible to lay out machines, shops, and departments in advance unless the kinds and types of machinery, equipment, raw materials, heating and power systems, and the specific processing methods are likewise determinable in advance. Decisions here will call for examination of raw and semi-finished materials in terms of their uniformity, chemical purity, physical properties, ease of substitution, amount and type of by-product flowing from their use, ease and regularity of acquisition, amount of waste in handling and treating, the necessity of constant quality testing and control, and other similar variable factors. Machinery will have to be selected with a view to use of energy source available, probable continuous or intermittent use, capacity adjustment to the volumetric flow of materials through preceding and following operations, general mechanical efficiency, hazards in use and operation, etc. Similar considerations will govern the type of power used. Although electric power is generally superior to all other energy types, the question of source will depend upon a number of factors. Private and independent plants must be constructed if it is difficult to obtain outside current at reasonable prices and in sufficient quantities, and if a local unit can be built where the load and power factors will guarantee efficient utilization. The presence of considerable quantities of unused by-product energy, such as coke-oven and blast-furnace gas, is an added incentive to the construction of private power plants. Yet it may be preferable to sell the by-product gas and purchase outside electricity because of the relative advantage inherent in the large-scale production and distribution of the supply system.

---

other stage [of production] machine B is able to deliver 700 units in the same period of time, then the best aggregate is to be found with 7 machines of type A, and 10 of type B. But if a third machine, C, is required, whose efficiency is placed at 600 units, then the best proportioning would be found with 21 machines of type A, 30 machines of type B, and 35 machines of type C. Such careful reckoning would not be found in actual practice since the possibility of interruptions must be counted upon. The solution would probably be found with 2 A, 3 B, and 4 C machines, but absolute equalization will always remain the ideal."—*Gewerbepolitik* (Berlin, 1927):19.

[4] How far study along such lines may go, and how significant certain frequently neglected variable factors may be in the general plant and office set-up, is shown by the results of recent American examination into the subject of amounts used and required of floor space per person in various types of industries. The results were as follows:*

Business	Standard required (in square feet)	Average actual standard (in square feet)
Manufacturing	50	93
Wholesale	50	70
Fire insurance	60	102
Life insurance	60	176
Banks	60	117
Financial companies	79	50
Railroads, public utilities	60	94
Merchandising	56	99

* Source: *System* (New York, April, 1930).

Solution of such problems as those of heat and fuel economy may determine the degree to which various processes will be spatially and temporally integrated. For example, the desire to utilize coking and blast-furnace gas, and to avoid the energy loss involved in reheating cooled raw iron and steel billets for further manufacture, has led to more or less complete reorganization and regrouping of iron and steel manufacturing processes in the Ruhr district. Similar realignments may be brought about by expanding the radius of control (1) over parts used in assembly production of such commodities as automobiles and radios, and (2) over joint products from some one or more raw materials, e.g., by-products utilization in the coking and steel industries.

But the central problem will always be the same, viz., how to integrate specialized equipment and processes in order to obtain maximum results in terms of smooth, even, and continuous flow throughout the factory. Given proper layout of plant, the general solution is usually increased mechanization, the establishment of efficient internal transportation systems, and the introduction of serial and flow work by means of endless belts, roller, and other types of conveyor systems. Mechanization and such "straight line loading" more or less of necessity go hand in hand. Closer juxtaposition of processes makes it possible to break down complex operations into their constituent parts. These can then be taken over by automatic or semi-automatic machinery. Such connecting of machinery and hand labor into a continuous chain of operations has the effect of mechanizing the entire factory, and of elevating it into a single, semi-automatic and homogeneous functioning unit.

Interruptions under this arrangement must be reduced to the absolute minimum. A break at one stage of the process has the effect of disorganizing the entire concert. It is as though the machine were suddenly to lose its interlocking gears, or its source of power. The closer this mechanical dovetailing, the greater is the hazard of a stoppage at any stage. Likewise, the new configuration calls for a minimum of materials accumulated at any point. Ideally the materials should come into the factory in a smooth and even flow, pass through the concert of manufacturing operations without stopping or being accumulated at any point, and leave the factory without the necessity of more than temporary storage. As each machine must be temporally and spatially adjusted to every other machine, so must every shop and department be timed and adjusted in the rate and intervals at which it contributes its lot to the main stream. This functional integration, "simultation," has come to play an increasingly significant rôle where the assembly and fabrication of comparatively complicated products occupy the center of the stage, as in the manufacture of automobiles, all types of household, industrial, and agricultural machinery, shoes, certain types of chemicals and textiles, and many other commodities.[5] Just as the machines and processes re-

[5] An interesting example is to be found in Kempinski's new restaurant, located in Berlin, where a considerable portion of the round of operations has been simultaneously mechanized.

quire and depend for their existence upon standards, so the inevitable result of mass output is a high degree of standardization of simple or unit products and a tendency towards increased typification of complicated (assembled or fabricated) products.

2. OFFICE ORGANIZATION

Until comparatively recent times systematization and mechanization of office equipment and routines had made but little headway. However, the growth of gigantic productive and distributive institutions with an interest in standardization and typification of materials on the one hand and cost reduction on the other, has paved the way for an attack on this phase of "rationalization."

The process of mechanization, following the introduction of the first commercially salable typewriter in 1875, has gone forward rapidly. It is now possible to plan office layout, floor spacing, filing equipment, and other details with the expectation that practically all the routine work can be mechanized. Whether mechanization is desirable depends on several things. "Only when there is a sufficient number of similar cases to be handled after a common scheme, and with the utilization of uniform data, do expensive special machines pay for themselves, because it is irrational to rebuild machines to cope with new labor processes or to employ machinery where it would be but infrequently used."[6] In other words, the same conditions that make possible and advantageous the mechanization of factory operations serve to prepare the way for the introduction of machines into office work. Particularly is this true in the case of accounting. "All these factors: volume, uniformity, steady flow of materials to be accounted for, frequent repetition of the same data, and the necessity for daily accounts and balances make accounting a suitable field for the introduction of machines to take over the more mechanical and routine parts of the work."[7]

The development of typewriters and cash registers, of multigraphing, addressing, filing, counting, tabulating, and other types of semi-automatic or automatic office machinery, has been paralleled by the attempt to introduce measures designed to reduce the amount and eliminate the duplication of handling and checking such things as receipts, bills, mail, accounts, inventories, and other office details. A number of devices have been perfected for eliminating errors and for speeding up the flow of work through offices. These include standard letter and filing size and format, the use of simple internal mechanical checks to accuracy, simplified routing systems, the use of standard codes and symbols

---

Washing dishes, lifting dishes from floor to floor, moving dishes from room to room, carrying dishes from kitchens to the dining rooms, etc., have been entirely mechanized by the use of (mostly) automatic machinery, lifts, moving belts, etc.—VDI *Zeitschrift* (December 22, 1928).

[6] W. Kalveram, *Handwörterbuch der Staatswissenschaften* (Vierte Auflage, Ergänzungsband):796.

[7] *Ibid.*, p. 798.

for firms, dates, places, commodities, departments, personnel, and similar items. Here, as in the factory, specialization, mass production, mechanization, standardization, routinization, and schematization necessarily go hand in hand. This implies more adequate planning in advance. If the running adjustment is to be maintained, the division of the work, the number of employees, and the mechanical equipment of the various office departments must be temporally and spatially planned with considerable care.

3. PERSONNEL SELECTION, ORGANIZATION, AND TRAINING

But when all the problems of organization of factory and office have received a satisfactory answer, the most difficult problem of all remains to be solved: how to fit the worker and the manager into this system so that each will be efficient and relatively satisfied with the rôle which he must play. For mechanization tends to divide still more sharply the unskilled and skilled workers, and the rank and file of the workers from the owners of the enterprise. Usually the unskilled man requires less skill than before. His job can be learned more quickly; therefore he can be more easily displaced. Being more easily displaced he loses his relative importance; from a living, human individual he becomes a datum in the mechanical complex of productive forces. While the range of discretion tends to increase in the managerial group (within certain limitations) the call for the exercise of judgment, skill, and personality among the rank and file ceases almost entirely as mechanization progresses.

That is to say, the same conditions which call for careful ordering and arranging of machines and processes along scientific lines require the "rationalizing" of the work of the human agents in production. The tasks of the routine worker tend to become highly standardized. Specialization usually implies that the routine of labor for the ordinary employee shall be more repetitive, regular, uniform, and unchangeable than before. Adjustment of machine to machine is paralleled by adjustment of task to task, and labor to machine. With flow work and mechanization of entire shops and factories, this adjustment becomes more or less uni-directional; the tempo, the timing, and the structural peculiarities of the mechanical equipment tend to become decisive. When the worker is fitted into a more rigid pattern, his efficiency rises as he merges himself into the rhythm which it sets up. Such a functioning, mechanically-integrated entity promotes and compels self-effacement of the worker and he tends to become an object for scientific and "objective" analysis and scrutiny. For like the failure of any other link in the mechanically interdependent concert, a human breakdown or failure to function properly tends to bring the entire process to a standstill. The subordinate rôle of any particular machine or worker in the process is in inverse ratio to its or his capacity for damage. The more continuous the flow the greater the mechanization, the easier it becomes for any weak link to bring all links to a standstill, or to act as a catalytic agent in creating chaos out of order.[8]

But however desirable it may be from a purely technical point of view to mechanize workers, success is always bound to be tardy. Human beings differ markedly from machines. They tire quickly. The rhythm of working activity at best approximates that of machines in a very rough and inadequate way. Workers have faiths, hopes, desires and ambitions. They have likes and dislikes, friends and enemies, discouragements and incentives. Pride in work and a sense of workmanship, on the one hand, and the desire to produce or earn so that goods may be utilized and enjoyed in consumption, on the other, drive workers to perform efficiently and well. Unlike the machine, however hard it may be for many persons to agree, man does not "live by bread alone." He is not desirous of exhausting his life activity at the earliest possible date. He does not produce for the mere purpose of producing, but partly out of habit and partly out of desire to accomplish some chosen end. He cannot be forced to work, mechanized, or speeded up, except under conditions amounting to slavery, without at least his tacit consent. He cannot be forced beyond a certain point without being exhausted or without attempting retaliation, or both. Whatever, therefore, is the larger object in "rationalizing" the human equation, such efforts will meet with but little success which do not take these variables into consideration from the start.

Sabotage and bureaucracy are not new phenomena. They become serious problems whenever and wherever a productive, distributive, or other social organization has achieved a considerable measure of complexity and impersonality. The former, indeed, is as old as hired or forced labor. Taylor found "soldiering on the job" a well-nigh universal phenomenon. It becomes, however, much more serious with complex systems, for the damage of careless or maliciously bad work is greater here than elsewhere. In the more highly integrated and mechanized plants, sabotage becomes not only more dangerous to efficiency, but also (within limitations) more difficult to detect and counteract. Bureaucracy, on the other hand, is coterminous with settled, patterned, ritualized behavior. It does not arise from ill will, but from behavior which has become routinized and frozen to its mold. As found in industry and commerce, bureaucracy represents the dead hand of the past, *mortmain,* on the living present. It represents human inertia coupled with custom and taboo and frozen into a routine of perfunctory performance of formal duties. It is to be found in all human behavior; it becomes more marked, more noticeable, more decisive, and more dangerous the older and

[8] The failure, for example, to supply in sufficient quantities and of the proper quality any part of the Ford car, the Bata shoe, the Mazda lamp, etc., does more than bring production to the level of that weakest link. It destroys the whole rhythm of production at every stage of the process in the manufacture of every part. The need of readjusting every machine, operative, and process to this one breakdown, the necessary spoilage and loss of materials in certain stages of manufacture, etc., mean losses out of all proportion to the temporary curtailment of production.

the more complex the institutional setting in which it is found. Every factory and office[9] has had to cope with bureaucracy from the very beginning, whether the leading personnel realized it or not. The larger and more complex the factory and office, the greater the hazard of bureaucracy, since it makes adjustment to change difficult and perhaps impossible. When it is associated with sabotage, the inevitable result is loss of efficiency, retrogression, and ultimate dissolution.

The problem of "rationalizing" personnel is, consequently, somewhat broader, more subtly complex, and more difficult than that of obtaining mere mechanical efficiency. Taking the longer and more radical view that production improvement cannot be won at the cost of the workers, the problems of greater human efficiency in industry can be broken up under three main headings: (*a*) organization and improvement of the processes of work and the working environment; (*b*) personnel selection and training; and (*c*) incentives.

(*a*) Mechanization, specialization, and standardization mean the further division and transfer of automatic and semi-automatic operations to machines. Labor-saving devices and machinery make it possible to relieve workers of heavy and exhausting toil. Both automatization of processes and the elimination of unduly fatiguing labor tend to adjust the pace and rhythm of human labor to that of the machine. Whether the worker is engaged at some intermediate hand work, or directly as attendant on a machine, the adjustment must be the same. The set-up, in either case, most conducive to efficiency provides (1) that the materials to be worked are placed where they can be reached without extra movements, (2) that the standing or sitting place has been adjusted to the height, weight, and posture of the operative, and (3) that the auxiliary tools, equipment, or machinery are so adapted and arranged as to simplify work and economize the effort of the worker as much as possible. Physiological and psychological requirements involve paying considerable attention to proper lighting, heating, and ventilation. Breaks in shifts of ten to fifteen minutes at fairly regular intervals have proved their worth in many manufacturing industries. Short rest periods permit phyiscal and emotional relaxation, increase the efficiency of work, and postpone fatigue. Additional auxiliary aids, sometimes calling for very careful and systematic organization of personnel, must usually be provided. Machinery and tools should be made as safe and "fool-proof" as possible. Safety equipment, first-aid and hospital service, and instructions for the handling of dangerous materials and machinery should be provided for.

(*b*) When the working environment has been properly planned and arranged, it is then necessary to develop methods for most readily (1) selecting the workers best adapted to the different types of work to be performed, and (2) training

[9] It has been the favorite practice in the past to attribute bureaucracy to employment in government service. Every large manufacturer and business man, however, knows that this is not the exclusive monopoly of the government, and that only the utmost vigilance can prevent the spread of *inefficient bureaucracy* in his own establishment.

them in the most efficient methods of handling and working the materials and machines. The first problem calls for knowledge of the general social and industrial background, and the psychological and the physiological peculiarities, capabilities, and limitations of each applicant. Under the first of these, it will be desirable to know the candidate's technical, turnover, and general attitude record. The technical record will give some check upon the general training, skill, and efficiency of the applicant. The turnover record should give some check on how long he has held jobs, and why he has lost them. This in turn provides a clue to the general attitude of the worker.

Reasoning along this line is seldom clear-cut, but it is usually to the point. A docile, contented, cheerful, loyal, and hard-working laborer is usually efficient. In capitalistic society such a complement of virtues calls for a specific social and cultural background. Training in religious piety, military habits of uncomplaining obedience, patriotic loyalty, and devotion to the domestic gods of hearth and home serve to promote an attitude acceptable to employers. It is customary, therefore, to eliminate as completely as possible hostile, suspicious, bitter, dour, and rebellious types. But regardless of whether labor be "exploited" for capitalistic or other purposes, the demands for uninterrupted and smooth flow of production through the various stages and processes require "harmony" and cooperation of the entire personnel. Hence, for all industrial societies the training and background of every worker, and the nature and color of his ambitions, beliefs, and values must be carefully examined.

No less important are the physiological and psychological capabilities and limitations of the worker. On the physiological side examination will be made into such factors as age, sex, general health, conditions of the limbs and various body organs, normality and keenness of the senses, strength, and habits of exercise. The psychological problem is somewhat more complex. In the first place, psychological proclivities are closely bound up with, and in large part conditioned by physical constitution. In the second place, it appears to be more or less impossible to differentiate between "innate" and acquired proclivities. In the third place, the methods of test are of necessity much more complex, and the results of much less definitive value, than when physiological variables are dealt with. Finally, it is very difficult to approximate actual working conditions in the laboratories where the testing must take place. Yet the number and expense of such laboratories and testing stations, corporate and non-corporate alike, attest the currency of the belief that the results obtained, by and large, do and must justify the necessary expenditure in time and money.[10]

The factors stressed in psycho-technical examinations depend largely upon the methods employed, the personal equations of the examining staff, and the

---

[10] An immense descriptive and analytic literature has grown up on this subject during the past few years. Of particular value are, Giese, *Handbuch psychotechnischer Eignungsprüfungen* (Halle, 1925); Baumgarten, *Die Berufseignungsprüfungen: Theorie und Praxis* (München-Berlin, 1928).

purposes for which the tests are made. In some laboratories the primary stress is laid upon such things as nervous coordination, visual retentiveness, memory, rapidity of response to given stimuli, ability to solve elementary problems related to work applied for, immunity to distracting influences, and general resourcefulness. In other laboratories attempts are made to reach further into the complex of innate and acquired proclivities and limitations. Results of practical value as these broader problems are attacked are difficult to demonstrate, and the tendency is for the smaller laboratories, especially those directly attached to individual corporations or industries, to neglect these for the more definite and narrower testing. But work in the larger field is resulting in a more intimate tie-up with physiological research in the fields of fatigue, and the science of work, on the one hand, and the more purely psychological research of universities and special institutes on the other.

This linking of practical working problems with physiological and psychological research appears to be gradually laying a stable foundation for a science of work and for methods of personnel training. Where the former has made considerable headway, and the tasks to be performed are relatively simple, uniform, and repetitive, little special training is required. Many of the jobs in such plants as those of *Ford, Bata,* and *Osram,* can be learned in a very few days; many of them in a few hours. And, of course, the percentage of such routine jobs tends to increase with standardization, mechanization, and closer and more highly schematized factory organization.

The objectives of personnel selection and training, if one can believe the numerous writers and experimenters in the field, are somewhat larger. To the extent that it is possible, theoretically or practically, to bring out and estimate the natural endowment of the individual, it becomes feasible to determine more or less exactly the type of work for which each is fitted by nature. More definitive findings along this line would make possible a more satisfactory regimenting of the personnel. But up to the present time—with certain broad exceptions—results along this line have not been very promising. Psychology as a science has not been able as yet to build up any considerable body of more or less undisputed and definitive information. At best, psycho-technical testing appears as a pseudoscientific procedure in which rule-of-thumb methods and guess play a considerable, if not a dominating, rôle. Even that portion of the training designed to acquaint workers with energy, movement, and time economy, formed on rather painstaking time and motion studies, seems to have been considerably overestimated in the past.

In the main, two objectives appear to dominate: (1) the desire to build up a corps of workers, technically dexterous and consciously aware of the peculiar problems of the particular industry, and (2) the desire to attach a considerable corps of workers and overseers to the special interests and points of view of the management. Both call for a type of systematic training which should logically begin with the younger generation of workers. Nearly every large factory in Germany has, in fact, its apprentice school, in which training in the technique of work is combined with far-reaching propaganda campaigns designed to attach the younger generation to the interests of the respective companies. It is from these groups, very carefully selected and rigorously trained, and made up in large part of children of employees, that management expects to recruit its more skilled workmen and portions of its supervisory and executive staffs.

(*c*) It is with this group in particular that incentives assume a dominating rôle. The problem is easy to state, but difficult to answer. The question is this: How can the worker be persuaded to give his best in a factory or office (1) which he does not own or control and in which he may have but little direct personal interest, (2) in which the job is characteristically routinized and mechanized, (3) in which the pace of work is usually set not by the worker but by the interlocking and continuously operating mechanical or quasi-mechanical processes—processes which fit workers like cogs into a gigantic, impersonal, and inhuman machine, (4) in which the opportunity for the play of imagination, personality, and craftsmanlike skill is reduced to the minimum, and (5) in which the worker has little if any opportunity or incentive to visualize the concert of operations as a whole or to cooperate in promoting efficiency other than that demanded by the exigencies of his narrow and specialized job?

It has not usually been appreciated that there is a high element of paradox in the problem. Experience with attempted solutions makes it extremely doutful whether a thoroughgoing and satisfactory answer can be had under the capitalistic system. The problem as stated seems insoluble so far as enduring and active cooperation of workers is concerned under the existing economic order, and the problem of efficiency cannot be solved until such cooperation is assured. Nevertheless, the problem has been busily attacked, and a measure of success has been achieved in several of its more important aspects. Among methods, schemes, and devices being utilized in order to increase interest in the job and the company are the following: introduction of piece-work and bonus systems, and employee stock ownership; supply of rest rooms, lunch rooms, gymnasiums, athletic fields, and special forms of amusement; printing of factory and company newspapers and periodicals; provision of special disability and old-age insurance schemes, and special hospital, park and recreational facilities; establishment of works-councils; offering of rewards and prizes for exceptionally good work; promotion of competitions between individuals, shops, factories, and offices for record performances; provision of special housing facilities; making of special allowances for coal, heating, and other domestic requirements; and the building up of special employee loan funds. Nearly all these are makeshifts, and, as employed at present, usually combine a curious naïveté with a certain hardboiled cynicism. While there is doubtless often a considerable degree of genuine interest and altruistic spirit diffused through such schemes, the primary capitalistic objective is simple and direct: how to increase profits by increasing efficiency, and thereby to hold down costs (relatively).[11] The greater number of these plans, accordingly, now look towards counteracting organized or unorganized labor attacks and prevention of criticism and further attempts at social control on the part of public bodies. Within limitations, considerable success in certain branches has attended such efforts, under the disarming guise of desire to foster in workers a sense of self-respect, pride in work, feeling of responsibility, and other self-evident virtues. That is to say, emotional and intellectual objectives and points of view have been attacked with the deliberate intention of bringing them into the service of special vested interests.[12]

4. THE ORGANIZATION OF MANAGEMENT

Sabotage becomes of less, bureaucracy of greater importance as one proceeds from the simple workman up through the managerial ranks. The greater the element of discretion required, the greater the danger of judgment being exercised according to purely rule-of-thumb methods. Aside from the attempt to keep supervisory and managerial staffs as small as possible, most discussion centered about simplification and reorganization of management has been primarily concerned with methods of counteracting the corroding influence of bureaucracy and ways of fixing duties and responsibilities so as to eliminate rule of thumb as far as possible.

Experimentation has evolved two general principles as guides in the organization of management: decentralization and functional division of work. The two more or less of necessity go together. The purpose of decentralization is to allow the maximum of individual initiative while at the same time making it possible

---

[11] This point is of decisive importance for an understanding of the drive of rationalization in capitalistically organized countries. Gerhardt, one of the most gifted and versatile German writers on the subject, summarizes as follows: "Production takes place in privately owned factories. The factory is the material-technical foundation of the business enterprise; in it are assembled the various material productive factors for the purpose of producing goods in the most rational fashion. This productive purpose is subservient to the business objective of achieving the maximum profit. Hence the productive processes in the factory must be so organized as to reduce to the minimum all expenditures featured in the cost of the individual product, while at the same time constructing a commodity which meets with the requirements of demand. The productive processes in the factory must be organized, having due regard to the configuration of demand, to lower costs, and all *rationalization consists singly and solely in the elimination of costs,* in the steady narrowing of the 'specific expenditure' upon the individual product." Hence, "the *immediate purpose of rationalization* . . . . in *a competitive economy is not to increase the production of goods, to produce them cheaper and to better their quality, but to increase profits.*" (Italics mine.)—"Rationalisierung," *Handwörterbuch der Staatswissenschaften* (Vierte Auflage, Ergänzungsband):709. Holzer, in his *Systematische Fabriksrationalisierung* (Berlin, 1928), expatiates: "The purpose of every private undertaking is profit, and every action undertaken, and every forward step which the entrepreneur will make, has the sole purpose of maintaining or increasing profits. If here and there social and ethical considerations appear as the basis for decisions and policies, so these must soon drop into the background. . . . . Singly and solely to increase dividends should be the purpose of every larger measure, and consequently must be the basis for the rationalization of every enterprise."

[12] See the comments on DINTA below, p. 82, and in Appendix A, p. 424.

to fix definitely the responsibility for successes or failures at their source. The object of functional organization is to permit the maximum of specialization of the managerial staff and to promote integration and coordination of specialized operations and tasks in the interest of the best functioning of the establishment as a whole. Decentralization and specialization promote in management—as they do in science, technology, and standardization—functional organization; without functional organization decentralization and specialization lead to chaos.

This relationship was very early recognized in management practice and theory. Attempts to lend body and principle to the idea have given to management literature its curiously abstract character, which is the direct opposite of the extremely practical results to which application has led. Principles and rules evolved have been carried out in some industries in a most thoroughgoing fashion. Functional organization of plant, division of the duties of all workers, salaried employees, and executives, and methods of fixing responsibility and assessing success and blame have been carried into all or nearly all phases of the productive and commercial activities of various concerns. The larger application of these principles is best exemplified in the American Telephone and Telegraph Company and the General Motors Corporation, in the United States, and in the organization of the *Vereinigte Stahlwerke A. G.* and the *I. G. Farbenindustrie A. G.* in Germany. Functional organization, carried through with varying degrees of thoroughness, is to be found in hundreds of small and medium-sized, as well as large, concerns, in nearly every major industrial country at the present time. It has served to quicken the pace of industrial change, and to introduce a larger element of flexibility into organizations always threatened by a tendency to rigidity and unbending regimentation. It has paved the way for, and fixed attention upon, the growing necessity for more comprehensive and far-sighted budgeting systems and for more rigorous and scientific cost-accounting methods.

5. SCIENTIFIC COST-ACCOUNTING AND BUDGETING

Mass production and mechanization have shifted the ratio of overhead to variable costs. A growing portion of the costs tends to stay relatively constant regardless of the degree to which capacity is utilized. Consequently, the more managerial interest is concentrated on operation to capacity, the greater is the preponderance of such costs. When the capacity factor is 100 per cent, overhead expenses will be distributed over the maximum product; production expenses, on this account, will tend to be at a minimum per unit of output. When, on the other hand, shrinkage in production becomes marked, the point will soon be reached where unit costs will mount out of all proportion to price. When the capacity factor approaches the vanishing point, income will disappear but overhead expenses will remain.

Mass production requires mass distribution and mass consumption. Mass selling means low prices. Generally speaking, the larger the market the lower the price must be. Realizing the potentialities of mass production must mean selling at lower prices. Lower prices require decreasing the unit cost of production. These, to repeat, are at a minimum when capacity is utilized to the full. The closer production comes to capacity, the narrower may be, and usually is the profit margin. Since profits are computed as a percentage return upon invested capital, the margin of profit on individual sales can shrink steadily as long as the quantity of output more than makes up for the narrower margin. But at the same time, the chance has increased that relatively moderate fluctuation in either prices or costs might completely eliminate the profit margin. Since price lies largely outside the control of any particular enterprise, the result has been to concentrate attention on costs. Up to capacity, the possible gains or losses from cost manipulation steadily increase with output.

But while cost control grows in importance with mass production, the problem of locating the source of losses or gains becomes more difficult as overhead expenses increase. The more intimate the dovetailing and interleaving of the contributory factors the more difficult it is to allocate costs without the use of rather arbitrary criteria. Is one machine more important than another? Is the motive power of the machine more important than the machine? the meshing gears more important than the machine frame into which they are fitted? the wheels upon which they are mounted? or the locks and pinions which hold them into place? How apportion depreciation, managerial, and other general expenses upon joint products made from the same raw materials? How allocate the cost responsibilities for processes, materials, and persons contributing to an assembled commodity?

If the problem has appeared formidable, the assault upon it has been no less determined. The problem has been considerably simplified by the standardization of raw materials, machinery and equipment, processes, routine operations, and final products. Specialization, decentralization, and functional organization have made it possible to trace cost fluctuations to their approximate source with greater exactitude. The way having been prepared, important refinements in cost-accounting methods have been achieved. Some of these are of a tangible, and some of a theoretical character. Standardization of order and requisition blanks and methods of entry, books and ledgers, letter, account, and business instrument format, terminology, symbols and abbreviations, schemes of summary, instruction, and information, have been paralleled by comparative cost studies, systems of cost classification and analysis, and methods of cost supervision.

Control of a multiplicity of detailed but highly interdependent cost variables in mass production processes, where continuous and uninterrupted flow is the necessary condition to any considerable degree of manufacturing efficiency, requires, in addition to precision in the allocating of costs, accounting methods which permit a balance to be struck for the whole or any individual process upon short notice. The time factor grows in importance in accounting as it becomes decisive in the interstitial adjustment and the completed technological round of operations. Weekly, daily, and at times hourly reports are becoming more and more important. The necessity for closer and more continuous supervision of cost variables grows with every expansion in the scale of operations, every intensification of the tempo of production, and every advance in the relative importance of overhead costs.

And that is tantamount to the declaration that these dynamic changes compel, as the alternative to cost chaos, ever more careful and far-sighted cost-planning. The budget is the inevitable counterpart to cost-accounting. In it is expressed expert opinion as to just what is possible under given conditions. The costs of individual operations must be estimated, adjusted to, and interwoven with all other operations. The enforcing plan must become at once more comprehensive and more far-sighted as complexity and scale of operations increase. Here also specialization and decentralization imply ever closer integration and coordination. The basis for the more comprehensive plan is provided by the detailed matter contained in sales budgets, expense budgets, capital budgets, capital-expenditures budgets, and other types of budgets.

Budgets, consequently, are statistical statements of policies.[13] Production policies, wages policies, price policies, market policies, dividend policies—are expressed in, and work themselves out through appropriate budgets. Furthermore, preparation of and adherence to budgets demands and assumes the active and intelligent cooperation of the entire managerial staff, and, to a certain extent, of all employees. Consequently, they must be able to visualize the underlying problems and be willing to cooperate in the formation and promotion of policies. The desire and willingness to cooperate are requisites to any workable plan. Accounting, budgets, policies, system, plan, objectives, incentives, and cooperation go together. These rest upon, promote, and make possible specialization, mechanization (to a considerable degree), integration of interlocking processes, mass production, and functional organization.

6. COORDINATING, PLANNING, AND PROMOTING MANAGEMENT PRINCIPLES AND PROCEDURE

The technical and organizational problems of production and distribution, whether regarded from the more purely technological or the commercial angle, are, in one sense, as manifold as there are numbers of separate enterprises. Yet the greater number of the basic issues, problems, and principles are more or less common to all. The attempt at systematic investigation of these common problems, and to approach solution with the methods and detachment of science, has frequently fallen wide of its mark. Many of the issues at stake are highly con-

[13] "A budget properly conceived is a statement of policies expressed in the tangible form of statistical data."—James O. McKinsey, "The Relation of Budgets to Policies," International Discussion Conference on Budgetary Control, *Final Report* (I. M. I., Geneva, 1930), vol. 3.

troversial. Almost without exception objectives play a significant rôle in the formulation and solution of the problems. It is obvious that objectives and policies are not matters which subject themselves to judgment by the use of scientific and objective criteria. They are matters of social philosophy and vested interest. Some type of social philosophy lies at the very heart of all comprehensive and thoroughgoing planning. Group conflict over the gains to be achieved from actualization of large or small plans is inevitable as long as human society is divided into vested and special interest groups.

Quite aside from difficulties indicated above, however, a serious complication arises from the character of the analytical techniques for dealing with the problems at hand. Contrasted with physics and chemistry, biology is a comparatively crude and primitive science as yet. Contrasted with biology, psychology is still in its swaddling clothes. Contrasted with psychology, the "science of organization" has only begun to take on the appearance of maturity. Yet it is with these techniques derived from these sciences that "scientific" management is primarily concerned. Small wonder, then, that science, pseudo-science, witch-hunting, and casuistry are frequently brewed in the kettles of vested interests under the guise of search for scientific principles.

Yet, though promotion, back slapping, and guile play important rôles in institutional work and literature devoted to the various fields reviewed above, they appear to be gradually giving way to the more solid and substantial achievements of practical experimentation and theoretical excogitation. The alliance with science and engineering, at least on the more purely technological and organizational side, has necessarily become much closer with the passage of time. Standardization, mechanization, and the increase of inter-process and inter-enterprise dependencies have made at once more possible and more necessitous common answers to more or less common problems.

As with industrial research and standardization reviewed in chapters 1 and 2, the post-war development in Germany has provided the organization and institutional equipment for handling problems of management on a national and comprehensive scale. At the center of this institutional web stands the National Board for Economy and Efficiency (*Reichskuratorium für Wirtschaftlichkeit*), organized in 1921 at the initiative of private and governmental forces. It has gradually expanded its activities until it now acts as the central informational, promotional, and coordinating agency for the various phases of scientific management and rationalization for the entire Reich. The activities of the various organizations, for which it is the central clearing house, embrace standardization, scientific management and organization, study of the technical problems of special industries, time and motion studies, and numerous other problems concerning industry and agriculture, private and governmental enterprise.[14]

[14] For a more complete summary of the work of the Reichskuratorium, see Appendix A, p. 422.

The *RKW* has from the first taken a most expansive view of its duties and functions. Defining rationalization in terms of general industrial and economic efficiency,[15] it has taken upon itself the task of promoting and integrating all organized effort leading directly or indirectly to a higher state of (capitalistic?) well-being in the nation. It argues that, "In any economic epoch, but more particularly since the development of the capitalist system, rationalization assumes three forms: technical, commercial, and politico-economic."[16] Under the first form are to be subsumed all those "measures calculated to improve a working process" of a purely technical character, such as flow work, use of card-index systems, packing devices, better conditions of labor, mechanization, etc., which are, on the whole, confined to comparatively small areas. Under the second form, which is held to include the first also, are to be found all those measures, closely related to the technical operations of the industrial or business processes, of an organizational character looking towards the internal coordination of business and the scientific organization of systems of management. This form, the emphasis of which is placed implicitly upon the profitability of business enterprise, may involve agreements, fusions, combinations both vertical and horizontal, cartelization measures, and other developments of a more strictly business character. The third form concerns the matter of policy, which is declared to be that of forwarding national prosperity by way of bringing the well-being of society and the striving of entrepreneurs after profits into conformity with each other.

In effect, the *RKW* limits itself rather definitely to the first and second types of rationalization. Under the second heading, although it apparently cooperates rather closely with the National Federation of German Industries (*Reichsverband der Deutschen Industrie*), it has paid but little attention to industrial mergers, combinations, pooling of interests, cartels, etc. But within the range of the work in which it is interested, the basic drive has professedly been promotion of the national well-being. That general objective has called for systematization and simplification of institutional work, clarification and scientific examination within the various fields of activity, specialization of institutional work as a condition to accelerating study and promotion of principles of organization in individual fields, and coordination and integration on a national scale of all efforts devoted to the common end.[17]

---

15 "Rationalization is the adoption and employment of all the means of increasing efficiency which are furnished by technical science and systematic organization. Its aim is to raise the general level of prosperity by cheaper, more plentiful, and better quality goods."—*Reichskuratorium für Wirtschaftlichkeit* (Selbstverlag; Berlin, 1927):3.

16 *Handbuch der Rationalisierung* (Zweite Auflage; Berlin, 1930):3–4.

17 The common end is, naturally, visualized as the heightening of prosperity by bettering the profits prospects for business enterprise. Naïveté, honesty, and cynicism make queer partners at all times; there is no particular reason for believing that the Germans are so simple as to take this contention as self-evident truth. At least, if the business leaders are of this opinion, there can be no doubt that labor and organized consumer groups have serious misgivings on this score.

RKW vole

7. SUMMARY

Scientific management is concerned with the systematic introduction of scientific methods and techniques into all phases and aspects of management. It presupposes (1) the existence of a considerable body of scientific facts and techniques applicable to these more purely organizational problems, and (2) the existence of an elaborate series of theoretically valid standards and codes. The problems germane to scientific management, taken in the narrower sense—as scientific organization and administration of individual business units—can be summarized under the following heads: (1) location of plants and (in integrated concerns) determination of the nature and degree of plan specialization; (2) planning factory and office layout; (3) selecting of the type and extent of mechanical equipment, power supply, use of conveyor systems, etc.; (4) provision for maximum utilization and continuous output, while allowing for the probable necessity for adaptation to changed technology and demand for goods produced; (5) establishment of rules for scientific selection and training of workers; (6) introduction of incentive and special wage systems in order (*a*) to secure the maximum of cooperation, and (*b*) to counteract sabotage and bureaucracy; (7) provision for constant contact with latest scientific developments, and for fairly regular checks on efficiency through job study, special investigations, and periodical audits; (8) installation of standard cost-accounting systems, checked against detailed and systematically planned budgets; and (9) organization of the management so as to secure the maximum of individual initiative of every worker and supervisor which is consistent with centralized coordination and control.

Scientific management can be brought under the caption of rationalization when, in addition to its emphasis upon science and cooperation, its techniques are applied within a framework which has significance beyond the confines of the individual business enterprise. The *RKW* has been the central coordinating body for the scientific management movement in Germany. As with the detailed aspects of scientific management itself, that central coordination necessarily involves a system of policies and an implied objective or set of objectives. Although the work of the *RKW* has been primarily directed towards improving the profitability of German business enterprise, it is more than a mere service institution to unbridled capitalistic enterprise. In its centralizing, coordinating, and systematizing labors, the *RKW* has, willy-nilly, thrown the weight of its influence on the side of more careful planning throughout all phases of German industry and commerce. In so doing, it has created an exceedingly useful bit of machinery, and has helped to scatter widely seminal ideas. Time may dragoon these into the service of more adequate social control, and necessity may conscript them to aid in the drafting of more definitely social and more economically inclusive national plans.

CHAPTER IV

TOWARDS ECONOMIC PLANNING

THE LOGICAL and historically necessary product of rationalization trends seems obviously to be economic and social planning. Many writers concede this point openly; others do so by implication. Yet the German situation has been greatly complicated by a number of factors. Many of these are of non-industrial and non-economic origin; most of them are traceable to the war and pre-stabilization periods. Their presence makes analysis of rationalization factors unusually difficult, and generalization about trends of uncertain value.

As has frequently been pointed out, however, the break with pre-war conditions in German national life has been much less striking than might at first be supposed,[1] and the political and cyclical disturbances which cloud the picture so badly at times are themselves in large part traceable to the factors of growth and change which we wish to isolate here for separate treatment. In many respects these apparently extraneous happenings have served to accelerate enormously the very trends which have introduced the subjects of "industrial," "national," and "economic" planning into so much current literature, both technical and popular. The development of the Soviet Five Year Plan, the rise of the Italian Syndicalist State, and the events of the more recent depression might be cited as particularly striking examples.

Broadly speaking, the various factors making for centralized integration and coordination have not ceased to make their influence felt, nor have they at any important point changed their course, regardless of apparently non-economic complications. These centralizing forces have worked along (1) industrial, (2) inter-industrial, (3) national, and (4) international lines. In most cases they have been faced with countervailing forces of decentralization. Both trends in Germany have been notably influenced by peculiarities of cultural background.

1. THE GERMAN BACKGROUND FOR CENTRALIZATION

A voluminous literature exists to support Professor Bonn's statement that Germany passed almost immediately from a semifeudal mercantilistic state to one dominated by large-scale capitalistic enterprise without the intermediation of the Manchesterian type of laissez faire.[2] In this respect her industrial history

[1] See Alvin Harvey Hansen, *Economic Stabilization in an Unbalanced World* (New York, 1932).

[2] M. J. Bonn, *Das Schicksal des deutschen Kapitalismus* (Berlin, 1930).

differs markedly from that of the other two great industrial nations, England and the United States. England was the home of laissez faire. Her early industrial supremacy was rooted in the universal application of that doctrine to the processes of production, commerce, and finance within her own borders. The towering financial power which she subsequently developed was founded on the (temporary) world-wide adoption of that system of economic organization. The United States began its separate existence in the year that the bible of laissez faire capitalism, *The Wealth of Nations,* was published. The country completely lacked any background of opposites; its economic life from the day of the Declaration of Independence was dominated by an almost Simon-pure laissez faire capitalism. Its subsequent development has never, not even in the days of gigantic combinations and national trade associations, lost that original stamp.

But in Germany a number of factors have combined to prevent the liquidation of the mercantilistic-feudalistic point of view on the part of either the government or private enterprise. Among the most important of these have been the following: (*a*) The long domination of non-capitalistic economic forms imbued the German peoples with settled habits of thought, codes of ethics, and underlying value systems which have never been brought into complete harmony with laissez faire doctrines. These cultural peculiarities have found expression in legal systems, theories of political sovereignty and state control, disciplined habits of cooperation, and a national folklore. They are reflected in a singularly Germanic, but extraordinarily rich, profuse, and philosophically-minded literary and artistic tradition. These traditions belong to another age; they have been carried over into the modern period but have never become reconciled with the "pure" capitalistic doctrines.

(*b*) Germany's position in central Europe led, by easy steps, to an apotheosis of the state. During the long period of eighteenth- and nineteenth-century nationalistic wars, England's insularity and America's isolation reduced the rôle of government in those states to that of efficient policeman. But Germany was surrounded on every side by belligerent powers, each of which had definite territorial ambitions. On the east was the menace of Russian Pan-Slavism, and the constant threat of Polish insurgency. On the south was the Dual Monarchy interested in the dismemberment of Prussian-led Germany to the advantage of Austrian hegemony over the South German states. To the west was France, and the problem of Alsace-Lorraine. Each of the menacing political forces had aggressive imperialistic traditions. Russia was dominated by the drive, initiated by Peter the Great, towards open-water Baltic ports and by a newly acquired Pan-Slavism. Poles dreamed of a revival of the Polish state to rival that Polish empire which, under the Jagello dynasty and in alliance with Lithuania, stretched from the Baltic to the Black Sea. The Dual Monarchy had behind it the tradition of the Holy Roman Empire, while France long labored under the chauvinism of the Napoleons.

Within Germany, on the other hand, there long existed important disintegrating forces. Many decades after religious liberty had been established in England and America, Protestant northern Germany was pitted against Catholic southern Germany in a bitter feud that split the country into two more or less uncompromising camps. The old cleavage is still observable in the organization of political parties, trade unions, and employers' groupings. Furthermore, East Prussia was always dominated by a semifeudal landed aristocracy—the "Junkers" who dictated the policies of both the Hohenzollern dynasty and the von Papen "monocle" cabinet of 1932—while the west was primarily industrial and commercial.

Opposed alike to outside pressure and internal disunity, the one supreme cohesive force was the state. Without the state Germany was a geographical expression. With the state she had balance, unity, order. Hence the state was elevated to the rôle of a super-organism; by Houston Stewart Chamberlain in the name of racial purity; by von Treitschke in the name of Prussian Junkerdom; by Hegel on philosophical grounds; by Marx and La Salle in the interests of the rising industrial proletariat. For all groups the state towered above all social, racial, and economic cleavages as the supreme, socially oriented, central, cohesive, and integrative power.

(*c*) By the time German industry was able to compete with English producers, imperialistic expansion, with the exceptions of parts of Africa and eastern Asia, could only take place in economic terms. From political preemption of territory, expansion was shifted to economic domination of special markets and market areas. This method of gaining a "place in the sun" required powerful fighting organizations. These were found in huge industrial combines, market-controlling cartels, export and shipping unions, financial consortiums, and other compact and unified economic organizations. The pre-war German state never failed to encourage such alliances. Up to the time of the war they had been almost universally successful. Hence the pre-war tradition has always appeared fundamentally sound.

(*d*) Both before and after 1870 a considerable number of the larger industrial enterprises were linked directly with the state through supply of goods to the army and navy. This was particularly the case with steel, chemicals, and shipbuilding. The transportation and communication services were, likewise, regarded as instruments for offense and defense. The prominence of these industries in the German national system caused them more or less to set the pace for all domestic economic affairs. The state was the paterfamilias, and their dependence upon it freed them from many of the conditions which control in a pure capitalistic economy. The same attitude was fostered in labor by the paternalistic policies of Bismarck and his successors—policies resulting in the various and comprehensive social legislation measures which caused pre-war Germany to appear as the true workers' paradise. A product of this posture of affairs was the steady growth of a new quasi-political bureaucracy which, added to the old bureaucracy inherited directly from the pre-industrial era, modeled its rules, routines, habits of work, and objectives along lines definitely antithetical to those obtaining where free private enterprise existed as the core of practice and belief.

(*e*) Of perhaps greatest importance was the time factor. In addition to (*c*) above, Germany came on the industrial stage (1) when technology was rapidly becoming large scale, and (2) at the beginning of the concentration movement in older capitalistic countries. As with all newly industrialized countries, she did not expand her industrial system by recapitulation of the process of growth in the older countries. Instead she started with an enormous favorable odds. The tendency was to take over the latest and most advanced technological and organizational methods. Many of her most important industrial units were large scale almost at the outset.

To this fact Veblen has added the generalization that Germany's rapid industrialization meant that a very large percentage of her industrial labor staff was recruited from ranks which, by virtue of their complete unfamiliarity with large-scale factory conditions, were not obsessed with preconceptions nor hampered by workmanlike habits growing out of a definitely related but less advanced technology. He cites the English workman as a contrary case, where long familiarity with a particular process or machine method has engendered a sort of technological conservatism and resistance to change for which the English, despite their time lead in the field, have become notorious.[3] Both the Liberal Report[4] and the extensive Reports of the Balfour Committee on Industry and Trade[5] offer splendid documentary proof of the existence of this conservatism among all classes of English employers and employees.

The existence of a contrary point of view among German employers and workers, if it could be said to have existed at all after 1870,[6] would have been favorable to the rise and expansion of large-scale and highly centralized industrial activity. Such an habitual point of view may have been reenforced by two other factors: (1) direct carry-over of the feudal concept of workmanship, and (2) the common German belief in the universal efficacy of science. As regards the first, there can be no doubt about the general absence among workmen in Germany of either the spirit or the practice of "sabotage" as it has been known in Italy, France, and the United States, or "ca' canny"—"soldiering on the job"—as it has been known in England. The typical German workman seems to labor under the drive of a curious notion of duty and loyalty. He is a corporate creature. His life and work is bound up with the activities and ruling codes of the group

[3] Thorstein Veblen, *Imperial Germany and the Industrial Revolution* (New York, 1915).

[4] *Britain's Industrial Future* (London, 1928).

[5] Various reports, seven in number (London, 1927 and 1928).

[6] The E. A., *Gesamtbericht* is replete with complaints of the conservatism of employing the commercial classes in various branches of the German economic system. It is impossible to say whether this conservatism is of recent origin.

with which he has identified himself. When the group acts, he will act. Always he will exhibit something like the medieval attitude towards the task at hand.

As far as the second factor mentioned is concerned, generalization is risky, to say the least. Yet on the whole two such generalizations appear justified. (1) The average German workman is, and has been, better acquainted with the scientific significance for, and the bearing of science upon the immediate job at hand than have workmen of other industrial countries. (2) The philosophical turn of mind typical of all classes in Germany seems to have found a technologically useful precipitate in systematic scientific research precisely at the time when (*a*) science is compelled to shoulder the burden of technical and organizational change, when (*b*) the naïve scientific "millenialism" so typical of pre-war America and of practically all nineteenth-century England was giving way to more mature conceptions, when (*c*) the interdependencies between and among the various scientific disciplines, both in methods of approach and in the body of theoretical propositions, were beginning to receive great emphasis, and when (4) the progress of science in some of its more abstract reaches was beginning to trench on problems having, at some remove, definite human value implications.

All these factors carry back to and help explain the attitude of the German worker, and, within certain limtiations, of the German public at large towards working disciplines, the rise of corporational groupings, and the trends towards centralization.

(*f*) Experience in war control greatly strengthened the centralizing forces. The "lessons" of the war favored the pooling of patents and manufacturing information, elimination of trade marks and trade secrets, and the formation of cartels, trade associations, and gigantic combines for the purpose of controlling production, prices, conditions and terms of delivery, and markets. German manufacturers submitted to governmental control with less friction and in a fashion which promoted a more efficient conduct of the war than was the result of similar attempts in the allied countries. They likewise emerged from such control with a keener appreciation of the advantages of centralized coordination than seems elsewhere to have been acquired.[7]

(*g*) Post-war developments tended to lay even greater emphasis upon such coordination. Three features of the pre-stabilization period were of peculiar importance in this respect. (1) The socialists were in control, and German socialism was a variant of Marxian doctrine. Their programs were collectivist on the social side and cohesive on the organizational side. But for their temerity and lack of

[7] This generalization should be weighted against the well-known secretiveness of the German manufacturer and tradesman. A partial explanation of the paradox is provided by the generalization that the German manufacturer seems willing to surrender his business secrets only to a centralized organization in which all such information is freely pooled by all participants to the advantage of each.

strong leaders, the socialists probably would have introduced something roughly approximating the semi-autonomous but all-inclusive industrial, transportation, trading, and financial trusts of Soviet Russia. The "forced cartels" in coal and potash, the establishment of the National Economic Council, and the encouragement of the big combines and cartels under strict government supervision, may be taken as indications of what they might have done had their power been more secure and their leadership more vigorous. (2) The inflation wiped out the bonded indebtedness of the big industrial combines, caused the accumulation of huge properties in a few hands by the process of borrowing and immediately converting into property funds later to be repaid at depreciated values, and the general pauperization of the middle class. The net result was that the balance of economic power fell into the hands of a few powerful industrial leaders. This power has been more or less consistently used since that time to cement their control over existing properties, and to widen the range of their influence. Today Germany appears to be ruled as a semi-feudal state by a number of great industrial magnates. The revaluation law of 1925 which settled domestic war claims to the advantage of the holders of real property, and to the disadvantage of holders of government bonds, savings-account depositors, and holders of other intangible property claims, further strengthened their control. (3) The various reparations settlements, including original deliveries under the Versailles settlement, abrogated for the first time in modern history the doctrine that private property rights in peace times were immune from seizure in payment of government obligations, recognized or unrecognized by the debtor government. Thus a precedent, of which all German circles are keenly aware, has been established for disregarding those bundles of private rights in property which stand in the way of achieving objectives dictated by the exigencies of pressure politics. The big industrial and financial interests on the one hand, and the socialists on the other, are ready to use similar measures to further their respective policies. The partial or complete success of either group would mean further abrogation of rights which stand in the way of the exercise of more centralized power and authority.

It would carry the present discussion entirely too far afield to add further to the background factors favorable to the concentration movement in Germany. Hence, except so far as the following chapters provide the necessary ammunition, the thesis must go undefended that Germany, by virtue of her cultural, political, and economic background, was better prepared than any other capitalistic country to experiment with economic control on a national basis and to make the transition, depending upon the proper drift of events, to a more highly centralized state (Fascist or Socialist?).

2. SOME INHERENT STRUCTURAL WEAKNESSES IN THE GERMAN NATIONAL SYSTEM

Economic planning in Germany, regardless of the constitution or purposes of the planning group or groups, is faced with certain apparently insurmountable difficulties. Nearly all these center in the simple fact that Germany is one of those countries which is not in any real sense of the term a balanced economic unit. Such national units, indeed, are rare. They are to be found only in the United States, the U. S. S. R., and (to a certain extent) Australia and China. Of these four nations, if any one of them can be called a nation at all, only the United States and Russia possess anything near the ideal balance of necessary raw materials, capital resources, and manufacturing equipment. Since Russia's balance is more of a potential than an actual one, only the United States possesses the ideal combination. And even in the United States various highly important raw materials must be imported if the economic system is to be kept in balance. Manganese, rubber, silk, spices, and tropical fruits, and numerous other less important supplies must be acquired from foreign countries.

Naturally, attempts to systematize and stabilize whole industries or relatively specialized national economies meet with many and more formidable obstacles when the significant unit is much larger than that segment over which effective control can be exercised because of the limitations of national boundaries. Internally controlled and stabilized industrial systems, for example, are simply unthinkable in such countries as post-war Hungary, Poland, Austria, Czechoslovakia, the various Balkan states, and several of the South American republics, except at costs far out of line with all advantages accruing from such schemes. Stabilization of the various staple agricultural industries (e.g., wheat, cotton, rubber, silk, cattle), certain of the heavy industries (e.g., coal, coke, pig iron, heavy chemicals, textiles, automobiles, electro-technical products), and industries catering to all other industries (e.g., electric power, shipping, telephone and telegraph, banking) is simply out of the question except on an international basis. The same is true of industries in which the various stages of production are divided between and among different politically sovereign groups, such as textiles, rubber, petroleum, and, to a certain extent, iron and steel products. The raw material and extractive industries are to be found in certain countries, the manufacturing and refining industries in others, and the markets and distributive agencies in still other politically bounded areas. Vertical integration, except by international agreement, has narrowed limits where such a situation prevails. Nor are the possibilities of horizontal integration, under conditions of such a character, always more promising. A super-power network built out of interconnection of water and steam power sources (a necessary condition to an efficient system) would be impossible in Central Europe except on an international basis.[8]

---

[8] See Chap. IX, pp. 222–223.

National, or even *industrial* planning, consequently, becomes impossible and undesirable in many places in the world the very instant that the resource and organizational implications of thoroughgoing and consistently articulated plans are fully visualized. Plans which would have definite meaning and possible practicality in the United States and Russia would be utterly preposterous in many other countries simply because the functioning unit is too small. A scheme modeled after the Five Year Plan of the U. S. S. R. would have real significance for Europe as a geographic and economic entity, but very little justification for most of the smaller countries, and not any too much for the larger ones such as England, France, and Germany. Hence, attempts to build up rounded-out and self-sufficient economic systems—which involve a species of national planning, whether it be convenient for local politicians and business men to admit it or not—where the necessary resources, equipment, and markets are lacking, are bound to encourage inefficient production, high costs of manufacture, low standards of living, and, perhaps, ultimate economic disaster.

3. INTRA- AND INTER-INDUSTRY COORDINATION

In Germany, however, considerable progress has been made along lines of industrial integration and control despite the international handicaps under which many of her industries must operate. In fact, among capitalistically organized countries, and with the single exception of the United States (but not in all respects), the process has gone much further in Germany than elsewhere.

As indicated above, the post-war process of industrial coordination and integration involved no innovations in the German national scheme. Policies and programs under way in the pre-war period were merely expanded and driven forward in the post-war years under the whip of national necessity, the inspiration of war experience derived from extensive cooperation and coordination, and the impetus provided by a radical political shift to the left. Gigantic combines such as the *Vereinigte Stahlwerke A. G.* and the *I. G. Farbenindustrie A. G.,* closer working agreements such as that between the *Nord-Deutscher Lloyd A. G.* and the *Hamburg-Amerika Linie G. m. b. H.,* communities of interest, cartels, mixed private and governmental enterprises (commonly found in electric power development) became quite the order of the day in the reconstruction period of 1924–1929. The record of developments as followed, for example, in the chronicles of *Die Wirtschaftskurve,*[9] leave no room for doubt that but for the recent depression the process would have continued indefinitely.

In certain fields this larger integration has reached, or almost reached, the limits of its possibilities. The railroads, telephone and telegraph systems, as before the war, are single networks covering the entire Reich. Ocean shipping has been

[9] Quarterly publication of the *Frankfurter Zeitung.*

brought under the almost exclusive domination of the working combination of the *Nord-Deutscher Lloyd* and *Hamburg-Amerika Linie*. Radio has been largely monopolized by the government and attached to other communication services. The electro-technical industry is dominated by the *Siemens Concern* (*Siemens & Halske,* and *Siemens & Schuckertwerke*), and the *A. E. G.* (*Allgemeine Elektrizitäts Gesellschaft*). The *I. G. Farbenindustrie A. G.* has almost a monopoly in the heavy chemicals industry, and a controlling influence in the lighter chemical field. Two or three of the larger concerns control the major electric-power transmission system of the country. *Ruhrgas* and another concern practically monopolize long-distance gas transmission. *Vereinigte Stahlwerke, Krupp, Gutehoffnungshütte, Mannesmann,* and a few other large concerns practically monopolize the iron and steel industry and are able to exercise considerable influence over the coal-mining and coke industries. Potash has become the monopolized product of two or three large concerns. The three larger commercial banks (*Danat-Dresdnerbank,* the *Deutsche Bank und Disconto Gesellschaft,* and the *Commerz und Privatbank*) in collaboration with the *Reichsbank* almost completely dominate the banking and credit structure of the country. Chain-store distribution, the rise of chain department systems such as *Leonard Tietz, Karstadt* and *Wertheim,* and the increased strength of the larger cooperative systems, have begun to make over the distribution field.

These larger combines, supplemented by an elaborate system of cartels and communities of interest (*Interessengemeinschaften*), have been able, as far as the domestic system is concerned, to introduce an element of order and stability into German heavy industry. In the lighter industries and in distribution, trade associations (*Verbände*) and the quite recent development of "Exchange-of-experiences" conferences and congresses have made some progress along similar lines. In agriculture the ground for future development has been broken by cooperative producing and marketing organizations, and recent experimentation in types of collective farming.[10]

Between certain industries, located primarily in the Ruhr, Upper Silesia, and Middle-German industrial fields, a fairly high degree of inter-process integration has taken place. This is what is meant, of course, by vertical integration. When combined, however, with horizontal integration, this process means a gradual arrogation of national economic power and control to the expanding group. In the Ruhr district, for example, the tendency during the post-war period has been to combine coal mining, coking, by-products utilization (heavy chemicals and gas), iron smelting, steel production, production of machinery, and electric power systems into close working communities of interest. In a few cases nearly all these have been brought under the corporate domination of a small group of compactly organized firms. In some cases, as in exploitation of long-distance gas supply (*Gasfernversorgung*), and utilization of by-product gas and

[10] See Chap. XI.

coal for electric-power production, control, while vested in the same small group, has nominally been exercised by independent corporations specially set up for the purpose.

While the trend towards closer cooperation and interweaving of technically related industrial processes was accompanied by a good deal of working to cross purposes, friction, and, at times, bitter personal and corporate animosity, it was making steady progress up to the time of the recent crisis. Occasionally, when the personal or competitive difficulties seemed unsurmountable, the government has intervened to force systematic organization of the industry as a unit. It did so in requiring the so-called "forced cartels" (*Zwangskartelle*) in the bituminous coal, lignite, and potash industries.[11] It has not, however, taken steps towards forcing any considerable inter-industry integration during this latter period. Whether or not the possibility of state interference has proved an added incentive for private attempts to force through great systematization between interdependent industries, is a moot point. But there can be no doubt that the various dominating corporate groups in the heavy industries were drawing more and more closely together with the passage of time. While no apparent plan to integrate horizontally and vertically on the scale of the (more or less haphazardly constructed) defunct Stinnes concern has been developed, still it seems apparent that the trend of past developments points to the evolution of analogous superorganizations in the future. Prior to 1929, at any rate, business and industrial leaders did not long hesitate to accept the organizational implications of the combination movement when expansion into new fields, or closer relations with hitherto technically independent industries, appeared to be called for. Refining, assembling, manufacturing, transportation, marketing, and banking affiliations have been made as readily as the exigencies of private resources and corporate policies have permitted.

4. THE MACHINERY FOR NATIONAL PLANNING

Any group capable of developing and carrying through a national economic plan in Germany would find much of the necessary machinery already available for use. The Kaiser Wilhelm Society and the Institute for Business Cycle Research would be able to centralize and coordinate scientific research on a national basis. The German Standards Committee could easily expand its activities to include the elaboration of a complete body of national standards and coded practices. The various committees of the National Board for Economy and Efficiency would shortly be able to supply guiding rules for the internal organization of all phases of management in all the various branches of industry and commerce. The National Association of German Industry (*Reichsverband der Deutschen Industrie*) possesses a machinery which could be readily adapted for the purpose

[11] See Chap XI.

of centralizing policy-forming powers for the major industries. Similar adaptations could be made of existing central organizations in agriculture, retail and wholesale trade, banking and finance, shipping, trucking, and railroad transportation, communication, handicrafts, and other fields.[12]

Whatever the purpose of national planning might be, the methods of organization and the techniques of control would most probably not be very much different from those now used by existing central organizations. As has been pointed out in the three preceding chapters, centralized control, so far as it exists among the various institutions reviewed, has been based upon the principle that integration and coordination should be paralleled by the maximum of decentralization of responsibility and management. The Kaiser Wilhelm Society and the various committees of the National Board for Economy and Efficiency have been as insistent as the large cartels, combines, and communities of interest that neither centralization nor decentralization should be sacrificed to the advantage of the other. The guiding principles in centralization are: (1) Maximum emphasis should be laid upon cooperation of all technically equipped persons and representatives of special interests. (2) No problem, whether of organization or policy, should be remanded to the next higher authority which can be solved at the place and within the sphere of origin. (3) In general, the central controlling power should confine itself to sketching general policies applicable uniformly to all personnel and all the subsidiary plants, enterprises and institutions, and to organizing intergroup relations so that there is a minimum of overlapping of functions, duplication of facilities, and working to cross purposes. (4) All information required for fulfilling its functions should be freely pooled, and be in such a standard, simplified, and understandable form as to make quick decisions a genuine possibility at all times. (5) Every effort should be made to prevent any phase or aspect of the organizational complex from becoming rigid and inflexible.

The rules, evolved from practice, for guiding decentralization might likewise be stated as follows: (1) Provision must be made in all plants, offices, shops, laboratories, and other places for the maximum of individual initiative and personal enterprise. (2) Adjustments should be made so that every individual will fit into that niche for which he or she is best qualified by training, background, health, and general interest. (3) At no time should motives of personal aggrandizement be allowed to expand any activities beyond the bounds set (at that time) by the relationship of any sub-process to the other processes with which it is organically associated. (4) Adjustibility to technical and other changes should be constantly emphasized. (5) Maximum economy of time, energy, materials, machinery, equipment, and expense should be practiced at all times.

It would be almost impossible to keep a perfect balance between these two sets of complementary rules. Yet appreciation of the need for such balance seems to

[12] See Chap. XI.

have grown steadily in Germany as the rationalization movement advanced, and appears, in the main, to have found expression in actual practice as the various types of central units felt called upon to face the organizational implications of the changes which they were bringing about.

Should the unifying tendency, so notable in recent German economic history, be carried into all fields of productive, distributive, and financial activity, the principles of organization evolved by the rationalization movement would grow steadily in importance. If these principles should then be carried uniformly into practice the final and "completely rationalized" economic system—from the organizational point of view—would probably consist of a number of semi-autonomous, nationally organized, and independently managed trusts. Each trust would control either an entire industry—such as coal, iron, cotton textiles—or some specialized economic function such as management of export and long-term credit extension, or promulgation of industrial standards. These national trusts might then be brought together in councils for purposes of regulating inter-trust relations. Thus there might be a national metals council, a national textile council, a national agricultural council, a national banking council, and so forth. These national councils might once more be brought together in a national economic cabinet for purposes of inter-council integration and coordination.

Approximation to such national trusts are to be found in Germany in the following industries: coal, potash, the railroads, the telephone and telegraph services, certain branches of the steel industry, oceanic shipping, and banking. Examples where organization follows functional lines are to be found in the above-mentioned discussions of standards, scientific research, and scientific management. Examples where organization follows special-interest lines are to be found in the central trade-union federations and the national employers' association. With the possible exception of the various groupings under the *Reichsverband der Deutschen Industrie,* no approximation to the type of inter-trust councils is to be found in German industry. Along functional lines the National Board for Economy and Efficiency, taken as a whole, might be said to fit that pattern in a rather crude way. Nothing approximating a national economic cabinet has thus far been set up. Certainly the National Economic Council, established by the Weimar Constitution, cannot be said to fill that rôle. It is possible that the various ministries of the Reich might be able in a relatively short time to construct a national economic cabinet.

Whatever be the outcome of present trends towards centralization, two generalizations can be safely made: (1) Among all the capitalistic industrial nations the centralizing tendency has gone furthest in post-war Germany, the background in that country is the most favorable for continued advance, and the German sentiment in favor of centralization seems to be increasing rather than decreasing in almost every economically significant activity. (2) Much of the machinery for a completely integrated and coordinated national system has already been developed, and the principles of organization which would be necessary to make any set of national plans workable have already been evolved by the rationalization movement.

5. SOCIAL CRITERIA FOR A NATIONAL PLAN

All plans mean planning *for* something. That is to say, they imply the prior existence of objectives. While no proper set of objectives can be scientifically determined, it does seem certain that no national plan today stands much chance of success unless it can at least promise a reasonably satisfactory answer to four primary issues: (1) a high level of productivity, (2) general economic stability, (3) distribution of income, and (4) personal security. The first is a problem of efficiency, the second of eliminating economic—in particular, cyclical—fluctuations, the third of social class structure, and the fourth of individual risks.

How far trends in the rationalization of branches of German industry have provided the information necessary to solution of, or have in actual practice solved, each of these problems it will be one of the principal tasks of the remaining chapters of this book to show.

PART TWO

Evolution and Problems of the German Rationalization Movement in Selected Industries, 1924–1929

CHAPTER V

COAL, LIGNITE, AND COKE

In many respects these industries were ideally adapted in 1924 for experimentation along rationalization lines. Capacity had been expanded far beyond market requirements during the preceding decade. Because of the unusual conditions which had prevailed, many small and inefficiently operated mines were able to compete on even terms with the larger and better-managed establishments. The general technical level of the industries was low. In certain operations mechanization had stopped at the pre-war stage, or had even declined. In other operations scarcely the first steps had been taken in this direction. The equipment in use was in most cases technically obsolete, and in a state of disrepair. Electrification had been carried through in only a limited number of plants. Because of technical backwardness and the general lack of labor discipline, these industries were greatly overmanned, accident rates were unusually high, and individual efficiency was at low ebb. Equipment and plant for by-product utilization were quite generally lacking—a situation which was particularly noticeable in the coke industry. The market was flooded with miscellaneous qualities of coal, offered on numerous occasions at cut-throat prices, and distributed through the medium of a marketing system that was as chaotic as it was inefficient and costly. Foreign competition from England on the north, Poland on the east, and France and Belgium in the west, was, at the same time, becoming increasingly severe.

In these fields, nevertheless, the institutional setting for cooperative and far-reaching action was particularly favorable. The industry had long been accustomed to a considerable measure of price, market, and production control. The history of the largest of the syndicates, the *Rheinisch-Westfälisches Kohlensyndikat,* went back as far as 1893. Meanwhile, the cartel and combination movement had made rapid strides in the country at large, and the idea of cartel-controlled industries had secured wide adoption in business and governmental circles. The rigid control exercised by the government during the latter part of the war helped to promote, rather than to retard, developments along those lines. At the same time, it provided a suitable background for the *Kohlenwirtschaftsgesetz* of 1919, in which the radically inclined faction then dominant attempted to incorporate its dicta that coal was "ripe for socialization."

In the original law, coal and lignite were declared to be industries affected with a public interest; hence, they were brought under direct governmental supervision. The coal industry of the country was divided into ten special districts, each of which was placed under the control of a special syndicate.[1] These were then combined into a national cartel, called the *A. G. Reichskohlenverband,* endowed with power, "(1) to accept, reject, or modify the recommendations of the regional cartels concerning production, sale, and prices of fuel; (2) to fix maximum prices and to determine the amount to be produced by members of the syndicates for their own consumption; (3) to assign production quotas to the cartels and to divide market territories among them; (4) to regulate the granting of rebates and discounts and to inspect business books and correspondence of the cartel members."[2] Supplementing the *Reichskohlenverband* was a sort of coal parliament, known as the *Reichskohlenrat,* made up of representatives of mine owners, consumers, and technical experts. While this latter body was originally endowed with but little real authority, its power has been somewhat enhanced by assumption of the price-regulation functions formerly belonging to the *Reichskohlenverband.* Extensive veto and some initiatory powers (through emergency interpretation) were entrusted to the Federal Ministry of Economy (*Reichswirtschaftsministerium*).

Here, then, was a herculean task to be performed, and there was machinery available and apparently adequate to meet the task. Although there was considerable opposition to the stringency of the governmental control proposed, most of the leaders in the coal and coking industries were agreed on the character of the problems with which they were faced and the necessity for a thoroughgoing reorganization of whole existing systems. They were prevented from reorganizing until the stabilization of the currency and the withdrawal of French troops from the Ruhr district had established more normal conditions. It is the present task to trace in the following pages the measures that were taken to rationalize these industries after that time and to evaluate the results of the changes made as they stood at the beginning of the 1929 depression.

It will first be useful to present a few of the more important facts relating to the size, interrelationships, and geographic distribution of the three industries under review.

---

[1] Rheinisch-Westfälisches Kohlensyndikat
Oberschlesisches Steinkohlensyndikat
Niederschlesisches Kohlensyndikat
Sächsisches Steinkohlensyndikat
Niedersächsisches Steinkohlensyndikat
Kohlensyndikat für das rechtsrheinische Bayern
Aachener Steinkohlensyndikat
Rheinisches Braunkohlensyndikat
Mitteldeutsches Braunkohlensyndikat
Ostelbisches Braunkohlensyndikat

In addition a Gaskokssyndikat was organized.

[2] V. Trivanovitsch, *The Rationalization of German Industry* (National Industrial Conference Board, New York, 1930):65–66.

I. SUPPLY AND DISTRIBUTION OF COAL AND LIGNITE

The available supply of German coal and lignite,[3] taken together,[4] would be sufficient, at the rate of exploitation current in 1928 (147,500,000 tons) to satisfy the needs of the nation's industries for about 1,350 more years. The coal deposits are much the more extensive of the two; at the present rate of exploitation, German resources of lignite will be exhausted in another fifty-five to sixty years. The estimated reserves for the future (250 billion tons) amount to about 64 per cent of the pre-war supply which would now be available were it not for the cessions required by the Versailles treaty. The principal losses to Germany were associated with the (temporary) loss of the Saar and about two-thirds of the Upper Silesian deposits.[5]

Although coal is found quite widely scattered over the central and southern sections of the country, the major portion of the workable deposits is found in the Rhineland[6] and in Upper Silesia.[7] The former district is much the more important, both in deposits[8] and in present productive capacity.

Lignite is somewhat better distributed in terms of the requirements of German industry at large. Particularly favorable is the fact that the bulk of the lignite deposits are to be found in the central district where there is a distinct shortage

---

[3] This sum equals about 3 per cent of the estimated world supply of some 7,000 to 8,000 billion tons. It does not include "worthless" and unreclaimable coal, which probably amounts to 40 to 50 billion tons.

[4] Lignite (*Braunkohle*) is added to coal; 9 tons of lignite is considered equivalent to 2 tons of coal.

[5] Of the 5,600 qkm. (square kilometers) included in the Upper Silesian coal basin, about 3,000 qkm. belonged to Germany before the war. Of this area she was permitted by the treaty to retain but 575 qkm.

[6] The "Rhineland" is here used rather loosely to include the Ruhr district and the adjoining areas around Krefeld, Cologne, and Aachen.

[7] Meisner has summarized the statistics in the following table, showing the probable supply, in millions of tons, by districts and for various depths:*

	To 1,000 meters	To 2,000 meters	To 1,500 meters
West Upper Silesia	10,900	52,000	
Lower Silesia	1,240	2,944	
Ruhr district	55,100	213,600	
North-Krefeld	7,100		around 235,000
Brüggen-Erkelenz	1,746	10,500	
Aachen	1,567		
Other districts	472	472	
Total	78,125	279,516	235,000

*Source: *Die deutsche Bergwirtschaft der Gegenwart* (Berlin, 1928): 9.

[8] Estimates of Ruhr coal resources vary considerably. One has placed the supply at no less than 283 billion tons.—Meisner, *idem.*

of coal for industrial and domestic heating purposes.[9] This geographic feature, coupled with the peculiar technical problems of extraction and preparation for use, is responsible for the fact that lignite is much used for production of electric current and household fuel, while coal, largely in the form of coke, is used primarily for industrial purposes.[10] It has only been in recent years, however, that lignite has played such an important rôle in the German fuel and power supply.[11] German lignite production at present makes up about 80 per cent of the world's total annual output.

The quality of the coal and lignite mined in various sections of the country varies a great deal. Good coking coal in considerable quantity is found only in the Ruhr and Aachen districts. The Ruhr district has the additional advantage of possessing a fairly good supply of the various qualities and types of coal.[12] A single exception is that no genuine anthracite is found here (or anywhere else in Germany). Central German lignite has an advantage over that found in other fields in that it is rich in bitumen, making it especially valuable for the making of briquets and the extraction of motor fuels, of which the country has a natural shortage on account of the absence of petroleum deposits.

Geological and geographic features have seriously conditioned the rate of exploitation and the methods of rationalization applied in various fields. In the Ruhr district the depth and pitch of the workable seams increase from the south towards the north. Twenty-two per cent of the total output in 1929 was mined at depths ranging between 401 and 500 meters; thirty-eight per cent at depths

---

9 Lignite resources are distributed as follows:*

	Million tons
Central Germany	10,611
East Elbe district	6,749
Rhineland	3,697
Bavaria and the Palatinate	369
Oder district	471
Total	21,897

* Source: Same as for coal.

10 Sixty per cent of Central German lignite goes into electric power and chemical refining. The percentage used for electric-power production in the Rhineland is much larger; for chemical refining, practically nil. In 1928, 33.3 per cent of Rhine-Westphalian, 27.4 per cent of Aachen, 22.6 per cent of Lower Silesian, 9.7 per cent of Upper Silesian, and 7.5 per cent of Saxon coal were used for coke production.—*Enquete Ausschuss*, III (1929):27.

11 In 1913, 87,233,100 tons of lignite were mined; in 1928 output has risen to 165,588,100 tons. See Appendix B, table 5.

12 The average We (calories) per ton of the various types of German coal and lignite are given in the following table:*

Rhine-Westphalian bituminous coal:	
Fettkohle (high volatile coal)	7,600
Magerkohle (non-caking coal)	7,500
Gaskohle (gas coal)	6,800
Schlammkohle (coal slimes)	5,000
Saxon bituminous coal	6,500
Central German lignite	2,300

* Source: *Handwörterbuch der Staatswissenschaften* (Vierte Auflage), 5:757.

ranging between 501 and 700 meters.[13] With increase in depth and in the slope of the seams the problems of mechanization grow more complicated. Likewise, the presence of choke damp and water seepage, the relative frequency of geological faults, and the amount of time required for going to and from the face of the pit, tend to complicate matters as the depth of mining operations increases.

Most lignite deposits lie close to the surface; therefore it is possible to mine it from open pits under circumstances in which a high degree of mechanization is practicable.[14] The seams are usually quite thick, ranging from 8 meters in sections of the Eastern Elbe to no less than 100 meters in places in the Rhine district. Where the seams run under 8 meters in thickness they are usually found at depths where underground shafts are necessary.

Nearness of fields to rivers and canals has been an important factor in the development of coal and lignite in certain areas. Thus the Rhine and adjoining canals have given the local coal producers a decided freight advantage over southern and eastern competitors (especially those of Upper and Lower Silesia) in the foreign markets and in all areas bordering the waterways in question. Likewise, the central lignite fields have enjoyed a differential advantage over their competitors in the home district because through the waterway connection afforded by the Elbe, Spree, and tributary river and canal systems, the principal producing fields are in easy communication with the neighboring cities and industrial centers, and with those which lie in the north (Berlin, Leipzig, etc.).[15]

2. REORGANIZATION: CONCENTRATION OF PRODUCTION AND OWNERSHIP

During the war period the number of mining establishments and pits had steadily increased, while the production per operating unit and per employee had as steadily declined. By 1919 output per worker had dropped to 176 tons annual production, a figure that was but 26 tons above the average output per worker in 1800. In 1923 the lowest point was reached with an average output of but 78 tons per person. When the reorganization began in 1924, this problem was attacked with the greatest vigor. A considerable number of the smaller, badly located, and technically out-of-date mines, together with numerous pits working

[13] E. Jüngst, "Die bergbauliche Gewinnung im niederrheinisch-westfälischen Bergbaubezirk im Jahre 1929," *Glückauf* (November, 1930):1514. The decline in the modal depth in 1929 was due to temporary closing down of several of the deeper pits; the average depth (A.M.), however, increased from 591 m. in 1928 to 600 m. in 1929. The average annual increase in depth in the Ruhr district is about 17 feet.

[14] About 84 per cent of the present lignite production is mined in open pits. The ratio of surface cover to thickness of seam ordinarily cannot exceed 2:1, and at the outside 4:1 if open-pit extraction is to be used.

[15] The ratio of water transport to railroad costs ranges, for bulky commodities, such as coal and coke, from 1:2 to 1:3.

TABLE I

COAL PRODUCTION, ACCORDING TO SIZE, OF THE RHINELAND-WESTPHALIAN DISTRICT

Annual output (in tons)	Number of independently operated mines in production					Share of total production (percentage)					
	1850	1900	1913	1926	1927	1850	1900	1913	1926	1927	1928
1– 9,999	136	15	8	12	13	20.0	0.07	0.03	0.03	0.02	0.02
10,000– 99,999	54	20	9	13	9	80.0	2.0	0.5	0.7	0.4	0.3
100,000–499,999	....	155	121	96	81	....	70.8	36.1	31.6	26.0	23.4
500,000–599,999	....	13	24	30	30	....	12.0	11.1	14.6	13.8	16.0
600,000–699,999	....	3	30	18	29	....	3.2	16.7	10.3	16.0	13.7
700,000–799,999	....	4	10	19	14	....	6.1	6.5	12.8	9.1	11.9
800,000–899,999	....	3	9	14	17	....	4.3	5.8	10.5	12.2	12.0
900,000–999,999	....	1	10	5	9	....	1.6	7.5	4.2	7.2	6.6
500,000–999,999	....	24	83	86	99	....	27.2	47.6	52.4	58.3	60.3
Over 1,000,000	....	....	13	14	14	....	....	15.8	15.3	15.3	16.0
Total	190	214	234	221	216	100	100	100	100	100	100

seams of thin and low-quality coal were closed down. From 1924 to 1927 some 91 pits, normally employing about 58,000 men, were closed in the Ruhr district alone.[16]

Parallel to the closing of many pits were the processes of combining two or more shafts working close together and on the same levels, cessation of exploitation of thin and low-quality seams at various levels, decreasing the number of points of operation on the face of the seams, and the closing down of unnecessary mine openings and pit-heads.[17] The immediate effect of these changes was to increase very markedly the size of the effective operating units, as is indicated by table 1 (p. 72) for the division of production according to size for the Rhineland-Westphalian district:[18]

Equally significant has been the trend towards concentration of production and ownership of coal in the hands of a few large concerns. Table 2 (p. 74) shows production, number of employees, and square meters of coal fields owned by various large concerns in the Ruhr district in 1929.[19]

The five largest producing concerns produced 49.28 per cent of the total output and employed 48.2 per cent of the workers; the ten largest, 68.98 per cent and 67.88 per cent, respectively. The five largest coal deposit owners (not the same five, however) held 49.55 per cent of the coal-bearing area; the ten largest, 68.52 per cent.

The concentration movement in lignite mining has been equally marked, the number of establishments having decreased from 464 in 1913 to 293 in 1929, while output per establishment had increased from 187,991 tons per annum to 595,406 tons or by 316 per cent during the same period.[20] In the central field 38 works produced 46 million tons in 1913, while 43 were able to mine 102 million

---

[16] E. Wedekind, *Die Rationalisierung im Ruhrbergbau und ihre ökonomischen und sozialen Auswirkungen* (Düren, Rhineland, 1930):16.

[17] Kupczyk has summarized the facts in the following table:*

COLLIERIES CLOSED DOWN IN THE RUHR DISTRICT

Year	Completely closed collieries		Only above-ground works closed	
	Number	Production in tons	Number	Production in tons
1924	23	579,171	1	170,409
1925	31	5,020,360	1	119,132
1926	5	1,676,233	5	995,969
1927	5	85,613	1	397,856
1928	12	3,876,928	10	3,656,513

* Source: Edwin Kupczyk, "Die Konzentrationsbewegung im Ruhrkohlenbergbau," *Wirtschaftsdienst*, Heft 23 (June 6, 1930): 962.

[18] According to Kupczyk, *op. cit.*, the average production per work has increased in the Ruhr district as follows: 1850, 10,796 tons; 1900, 280,932 tons; 1913, 488,144 tons; 1924, 356,544 tons; 1925, 419,034 tons; 1926, 507,657 tons; 1927, 546,399 tons; 1928, 553,462 tons.

[19] Jüngst, in *Glückauf, op. cit.*, p. 1516.

[20] See Appendix B, table 5.

tons in 1928.[21] Corporate ownership has followed a trend similar to that noted in the case of bituminous coal.

"The results of these amalgamations," the *Enquete* Committee finds, "are extraordinarily varied. They provide, in general, all those advantages which are to be expected from concentration of establishments and business undertakings: more systematic planning on the part of the entrepreneurial group, a better planning of all extensions and new construction, a better relation between the technical and commercial management and the individual establishment, and at the same time greater efficiency in management, better equalization factors, and a better utilization of otherwise waste materials."[22]

TABLE 2

Trust or Company	Production		Employees		Ownership	
	Tons	Percentage of total	Number	Percentage of total	In square meters	Percentage of total
Vereinigte Stahlwerke	28,563,430	23.11	85,100	22.65	496,144,776	10.11
Prussian State	10,070,691	8.15	29,509	7.85	844,270,604	17.21
Krupp	8,245,341	6.67	25,231	6.72	125,790,970	2.56
Harpen	8,044,096	6.51	22,464	5.98	176,682,498	3.60
Köln-Neuessen-Hoesch	5,982,871	4.84	18,790	5.00	140,194,470	2.86
Gelsenkirchen	5,672,980	4.59	17,288	4.60	362,293,412	7.38
Rheinstahl	5,439,280	4.40	17,633	4.69	94,428,726	1.92
Gutehoffnungshütte	4,447,109	3.60	13,650	3.63	119,656,309	2.44
Stinnes	4,407,250	3.57	12,860	3.42	352,493,482	7.18
Kloeckner	4,373,816	3.54	12,542	3.34	123,286,640	2.51
Total	85,246,864	68.98	255,067	67.88	2,835,241,887	57.77
All others	38,322,839	31.02	120,644	32.12	2,071,048,951	42.23
Total	123,569,703	100	375,711	100	4,906,290,838	100

3. MECHANIZATION

The concentration movement, accompanied as it was by a process of combining many small units into large-scale operating systems, and by the closing down or abandonment of many pits, has been frequently termed "negative rationalization." Of even greater significance, from the point of view of technical efficiency, was the more positive program of general mechanization. This process had proceeded so rapidly that by 1929 about 80 per cent of all the coal, and an even

[21] *Enquete Ausschuss,* III:21. [22] *Ibid.,* p. 22.

larger percentage of all the lignite, was extracted by the use of mechanical equipment. Before the war somewhat less than 2 per cent of the coal was raised by this means.

As a preliminary and necessary condition to such mechanization, a special standardization committee was established for the mining industry (*Faberg: Fachnormenausschuss für Bergbau*), charged with the duty of simplifying, standardizing, and reducing the number of types of tools, machine parts, miscellaneous and accessory equipment. Results of a significant and far-reaching character have been achieved. The number of types of rails, for example, has been reduced from 110 to 8; of picks from 100 to 2; of coal cars from 175 to 3. Equally drastic has been the reduction of machine parts and equipment in the lignite industry. There are now three standard track gauges, one for open-pit work, one for underground work, and one for surface work where formerly there were 16, 25, and 22 respectively.[23] It is impossible even to estimate the quantitative importance of these standards in the cost structure of the mining industry. One company, mining about 3.3 per cent of the Ruhr output, estimated its saving from the use of standardized compressed-air rubber tubing to be 30,000 RM. annually.[24] A proportionate saving for the entire Ruhr district would approximate a million marks annually. Another company estimated a saving of "1½ pfennigs per ton of coal raised by the use of standardized tools, not to speak of the savings attained by reduction and cheapening of inventories. In the opinion of an expert, a saving of about 10 pfennigs per ton might be effected by a thorough standardization of tools."[25]

With standardization as a basis, the progress of mechanization has proceeded apace. The increase of various types of machines used in Prussian coal mining is shown in table 3:[26]

TABLE 3

	Numbers			
	1913	1925	1926	1927
Drill hammers	12,317	43,165	39,159	39,779
Rotary rock drills	40	3,366	2,618	2,173
Pillar coal cutters	294	1,103	841	773
Coal separating plant	....	447	340	345
High power coal cutting machine	17	809	733	638
Pneumatic mining hammers	264	44,993	50,821	70,145
Shaking-through motors	2,200	9,398	8,399	8,612

[23] H. Hirz, "Stand der Normung im Braunkohlenbergbau," *Neue Deutsche Bergbau-Zeitung*, Nr. 24:9.

[24] "Die Normung im Bergbau," *Normblattverzeichnis* (Berlin, December, 1929):4.

[25] *Statist*, 115:696 (April 19, 1930). [26] *Idem*.

Combined figures for the five major coal districts show similar results for the years 1927, 1928, and 1929. In 1927, 72.2 per cent; in 1928, 77.7 per cent, and in 1929, 83 per cent of the coal raised in these districts (Upper and Lower Silesia, Lower Rhine, the Ruhr, and Aachen) was mined with the help of the machines listed (heavy and light drill hammers, pneumatic mining hammers, undercutting machines, coal hewers, and chain and pillar coal cutters).[27] Some of the larger establishments have almost completely mechanized such operations. Thus the *"Zeche Monopol"* of the *Gelsenkirchener Bergwerks-Aktien-Gesellschaft* produced 93.2 per cent of its total output with the aid of drill hammers in 1927.[28]

Mechanization at the face of the coal seams has been accompanied, particularly where the scale of operations is large, by installation of improved and mechanically operated under- and above-ground transportation facilities, sorting and screening machinery, automatic and power-driven loading and unloading equipment, etc. Horses have almost entirely disappeared in certain districts,[29] electric locomotives and hoisting equipment have been installed, larger coal cars of the self-dumping type have come into general use, and boring, water-pumping, ventilation, and compressed-air systems have been placed on a high level of mechanical efficiency. Early mistakes involved in the attempt to apply certain types of mechanical equipment developed in the United States and other places where operating conditions and geological factors were different, have been rectified. Numerous factors have made mechanization both difficult and prohibitively expensive. Examples are choke damp and other noxious gases, the presence of water, frequent geological faults, excessive slope of the seams, the problem of "sit" and "creeps," thin seams, and presence of considerable quantities of slate.

In lignite mining, the characteristic of thick seams and closeness to the surface has made it possible to mechanize, almost completely, nearly the entire round of mining and refining operations. The result has been an increase of better than 60 per cent in the production of lignite, whereas the output of coal has decreased, since 1914, by about 4 per cent. The typical lignite mine is one in which the surface soil is ripped off by huge dredge-like bucket steam shovels and transported by the use of movable overhead bridges—sometimes reaching lengths of 300 meters—to the opposite side of the pit, where it is dumped in such a fashion that the soil will shortly become once more available for agricultural purposes.[30] The face of the lignite seam is then worked by endless-chain cutters or steam shovels of the ordinary type, which dump the lignite directly into cars moved from the pit by electrically driven cog-wheel locomotives. The lignite is usually

[27] "Nachweisungen der im Bergbau Preussens am Ende des Kalenderjahres 1929 im Betriebe befindlichen Machinen," *Zeitschrift für das Berg-, Hütten-, und Salinenwesen,* 78 (1930):29.

[28] *Statist* (April 26, 1930):749.

[29] In the Dortmund district 8,042 horses were in use in the mines in 1913; by 1920 this number had decreased to 3,712, and by 1927 to 2,024.—*Glückauf* (December 28, 1929):1789.

[30] These overhead bridges move on a double set of tracks on both sides of the pit. Some of this equipment is capable of handling 200 cubic meters per hour.

sent immediately to treating plants where the water content is reduced from about 60 per cent to about 15–17 per cent. The raw coal is then either chemically broken up for by-product utilization or made into briquets for industrial and household heating purposes. From beginning to end the human element appears in the rôles of overseer and operative. Even such things as track work have been almost completely mechanized, a rail-shifting machine having been devised which does the same work in three hours with four men that previously required 100 men working ten hours.

The extent of mechanization is shown perhaps even more clearly by the increase in horsepower employed. For all German mining (of which the overwhelming proportion is coal and lignite mining) the use of primary horsepower increased by 291 per cent from 1907 to 1925, while installed electric horsepower increased by 986.8 per cent, giving an aggregate increase of over 500 per cent.[31] In 1929 there were 238,045 power-driven machines with an average capacity of 15.2 HP in use in Prussian bituminous coal mining, while the lignite industry utilized some 30,587 machines with an average capacity of 38.9 HP.[32]

The resulting increases in productivity, so far as they can be traced directly to mechanization,[33] have been remarkable. Output per worker increased from 359 tons in Upper Silesia in 1913 to 436 tons in 1929. During the same period the increase in output per worker in Lower Silesia was from 213 to 266 tons; in Dortmund from 309 to 394 tons; on the Lower Rhine from 282 to 398 tons; in the Lower Rhine-Westphalian district from 296 to 395 tons; in the Aachen district from 243 to 296 tons. The increases seem to have been fairly steady over the intervening years (excepting the later, the post-war, and inflationary years) and the distribution of increased efficiency ratios to have been fairly general for the various classes of under- and above-ground workers in the several districts.[34] For the entire Reich the increase was from 287 to 315 tons per worker in coal mining from 1913 to 1929. In lignite the gain was from an average of 1,479 to 2,370 tons, or an increase of 60 per cent for the same period.[35]

[31] *Statistisches Jahrbuch* (1930):89.

[32] *Zeitschrift für das Berg- Hütten- und Salinenwesen, loc. cit.* This and vol. 76 for 1928 present most exhaustive statistical summaries of the progress of mechanization in the German mining industry. On page 448 of the latter publication it is stated that, "The yearly increase in mechanization . . . . for the period 1913–1926 lay between 5 and 31 per cent; on the average the increase in number of machines was around 30 per cent, and for machine capacity around 6 per cent."

[33] Increase in productivity cannot be separated, of course, by contributing factors, and of these mechanization is but one, albeit the most important in the long run. Aside from the fact that results attributable to mechanization cannot be separated directly from those due to concentration and systematization of plant, mine, and management, speeding up of workers, etc., gross productivity should not be confused with net. So long as, given careful and honest cost-accounting, costs stay the same there has been no increase in productivity of the enterprise to the individual business nor, excepting labor costs, to the general community. See pp. 95 ff.

[34] *Zeitschrift für das Berg- Hütten- und Salinenwesen* (Dritte stat. Lieferung, 1930).

[35] *Stat. Jahrbuch* (1930):104. Unless otherwise stated, figures given for 1913 will always refer to present boundaries. The figures given by the *Jahrbuch* for 1929 are official estimates.

For individual enterprises the increase has been even more striking. In the case of the *"Zeche Monopol"* mentioned above, output per man increased over 40 per cent in five years, as table 4 shows:[36]

TABLE 4

	Daily output (tons)	Number of miners	Output per man (kg.)
1924–25	3,299	3,786	941
1925–26	3,298	3,119	1,147
1926–27	3,934	3,847	1,161
1927–28	3,947	4,009	1,216
1928–29	4,332	3,866	1,321

Equally remarkable is the record of the lignite concern, *Ilse Bergbau A. G.*[37]

TABLE 5

	Lignite output (tons)	Briquets (tons)	Workmen
1924	8,689,004	2,639,046	6,942
1925	9,254,231	2,905,093	6,126
1926	9,179,033	2,910,292	5,194
1927	9,594,562	3,067,926	4,815
1928	10,843,669	3,265,394	5,287
1929	12,285,186	3,452,213	5,694
Percentage increase or decrease 1924–1929	+41	+31	−18

While mechanization in lignite extraction has been carried about as far as present technical knowledge and equipment permit, coal mining is not in such a fortunate condition. The retarding factors here are varied in character, the more decisive being the continued presence of many small individually operated mines, the conservative temperament of many of the mine owners, problems of market, labor, and transport, and other similar details. On the whole, the costs of mechanization have been fairly low. The purchase of mechanical equipment used directly in extraction represents a comparatively low percentage of the total new investment. A very large portion of the total (44 million marks out of 64 million marks invested in the lignite industry, 1924–1928) seems to have been

---

36 *Statist, loc. cit.*

37 *Ibid.* Statistics available for the Rheinische A. G. für Braunkohlenbergbau show the following for 1928–1929 over 1924–1925; increase in lignite output of 37 per cent, in briquet output of 39 per cent, and a decrease in working staff of 5 per cent.

applied to purchase of reserve fields, purchase and closing down of small mines,[38] and expansion of refining plant and equipment. Operating costs and overhead expenses attributable to mechanization have been on the whole fairly low.[39] For the machines listed on page 75, the total expense, for example, was only 49,422,-249 marks for the Ruhr district in 1927 when the coal output was 117,993,995 tons, or but 41.9 pfennigs ($.0997) per ton.[40]

4. INTRODUCTION OF SCIENTIFIC MANAGEMENT

It is impossible to say—as no comprehensive studies have been made on the subject—how far combination and mechanization have been accompanied by scientific organization of works, office, and personnel. If the results obtained through individual studies are at all representative of conditions generally to be found in the industry, the opportunities for further improvement are certainly very great. A study made of an unnamed mine by the Michel Institute in Berlin,

[38] It has been estimated that about 40 per cent of the total capital investment of the Harpener Bergbau A. G. during the five years preceding 1929 was absorbed by mines and works purchased and then closed down.—*Magazin der Wirtschaft* (May 30, 1929). See also the *Vierteljahreshefte zur Konjunkturforschung, Kapitalbildung und Investitionen in der deutschen Volkswirtschaft,* 1924 bis 1928, Sonderheft 22:42–43.

[39] The amount of invested capital per ton produced sinks, likewise, as the scale of operations increases in fully mechanized mines, as is indicated by the following table on capital expenses per ton annual ouput for collieries of various production capacities:*

AVERAGE CAPITAL EXPENSE IN MARKS PER TON FOR VARYING ANNUAL COLLIERY PRODUCTION TOTALS

Class of capital expense	1 million tons production	1.5 million tons production	2 million tons production	2.5 million tons production	3 million tons production
a. Above-ground works:					
Boilers	2.30	2.08	1.90	1.76	1.65
Compressed-air production	0.90	0.80	0.71	0.65	0.62
Current production	1.56	1.45	1.34	1.25	1.20
	1.74	1.58	1.47	1.40	1.35
Washing, sorting	3.90	3.65	3.33	3.12	3.00
Office buildings	3.00	2.70	2.45	2.24	2.10
Miscellaneous	4.60	4.05	3.65	3.30	3.10
Total *a*	18.00	16.31	14.85	13.72	13.02
b. Shaft	11.50	19.00	7.45	6.50	6.00
c. Underground structures	9.50	8.20	7.00	6.35	5.00
Totals, *a*, *b*, and *c*	39.00	33.51	29.30	26.57	24.82

* Source, *Glückauf*, Nr. 52 (December 27, 1930): 1789–1794.

[40] The total is made up as follows:*

	Marks	Percentage
Interest and amortization	7,758,605	15.6
Compressed air (estimated)	28,695,405	58.3
Grease and lubrication	888,787	1.8
Maintenance and repairs	3,642,742	7.3
Tools and implements	5,525,556	11.1
Hose and tubing	2,911,154	5.9
Total	49,422,249	100.0

* Source: *Glückauf*, Nr. 6 (1929): 199.

for example, showed considerable duplication of plant and mechanical equipment, an antiquated and unduly extensive internal transport system, and practically no centralized control over the ordering, requisitioning, and use of tools, materials, and equipment. In consequence unduly large stocks of materials, much of which were of the wrong type and dimensions, were kept. Inspection and maintenance of equipment were haphazard, "interest charges and wastage of material were particularly high and machinery for cutting and separating was not available in the vicinity of the stores. Additional transport to the work-shop machines was thus constantly required." Supplies were purchased from the outside which could be produced more easily and cheaply on the premises, possible savings in a few cases running as high as 50 per cent. Selection, training, and supervision of personnel was decentralized and inadequate. There appeared to be no semblance of functional organization and nothing even approximating a planning and control department. Several workshops were overmanned, the cost-accounting system was scarcely deserving of the name, and there was general lack of system and coordination throughout the works.[41]

Backward though the internal organization of individual mines may be, however, important steps have been taken by the industry as a whole. A great deal of work has been done along experimental and scientific lines. The coal industry has cooperated very closely with the various committees, partly under the jurisdiction of the *RKW,* engaged in the study of heat economy.[42] Valuable work has been done in coal research in coöperation with the chemical industry in the two coal research institutes of the *Kaiser Wilhelm-Gesellschaft* in Mülheim-Ruhr and Breslau.[43] Technical research institutions, equipped to carry on experiments under actual operating conditions, have been established in Beuthen, Derne, and the Hibernia colliery by Gelsenkirchen to study methods of com-

[41] B. I. M. I. (September, 1930):197.

[42] Various technical changes have produced extraordinary results—results which it would take a great deal of space to detail and evaluate. Typical of these results are those reported by Gaertner and Schneider on the effect of modern electric-light installations in the Wenceslaus pit: As regards total output, "under the new system 78,270 tons were produced in 32,878 shifts in fifteen months, disregarding the abnormal months. With the old lighting plant and the same number of shifts only 61,600 tons could have been produced. This shows therefore that, with only the same number of gangs, including repair gangs, the installation of the new electrical plant has effected an increase in output of 16,670 tons. Together with this increased output there has been an increase of about 5 Pf. per ton in the costs of lighting, including repairs, depreciation, and interest. The decrease of mineral alloy from 9.4 per cent to 4.45 per cent has resulted in a saving of 3,900 tons in the weight to be carried during the fifteen months, and if it is remembered that the waste has to be carried down into the mine again for 'gobbing' purposes, the saving in carriage will be found to be 7,800 tons. Since, thanks to the improved lighting, the number of miners in a shift can be increased, the workings have become less scattered. This makes the adoption of intensive methods possible, enabling both the tramways and the entire machinery of the mine to be turned to the best account, and considerably reducing the cost of upkeep for both."—B. I. M. I. (October, 1931):194.

[43] *Handbuch der Kaiser Wilhelm-Gesellschaft* (Berlin, 1928): 54–63.

bating explosion hazards from choke damp, coal dust, and the use of chemical explosives. A special testing station for wire cable has been established in Bochum.[44]

The need for special training of skilled workmen and supervisory staff in the peculiar problems of mining technique was early recognized in the history of the industry. The first school for this purpose was established in Freiburg in 1767. At present there are fifteen in the states of Saxony and Prussia with a total enrollment (summer of 1927) of 1,323 students. The majority of the students are preparing to be general supervisors and mine or machine overseers. By decrees issued in 1921 and 1927, these schools have been brought within the control of the state. The students in most cases work either a full or a half-shift in the mines, and are said to come about 50 per cent from the laboring class.[45]

Skilled workmen, such as hewers and machine tenders, must be apprenticed for from two to four years, and must possess special permits before being admitted to the skilled classification. Engineers and the higher technical staff must be graduated from one of the special mining schools attached to several of the larger universities (Freiberg, Berlin, Breslau, etc.).

From the point of view of management, miners in Germany have long been a more or less intractable group. Incentive programs have, in large part—particularly in the post-war period—been taken out of the hands of the individual mining enterprise because of pressure of the labor unions, the interference of the state, and the constant threat of socialization. Hours, wages, and working conditions (especially in the matter of safety measures) have been in large part regulated from above.[46] The efforts of the mine owners to speed up work, to obtain the good will and loyalty of laborers, and to better the conditions within the industry which lead to friction have been mostly confined to the introduction of piece-work wage rates, bonus schemes, the supply of special housing facilities, and various attempts to inculcate a favorable attitude of mind in the younger workers. By 1927 there were some 157,024 dwellings provided for miners in the Ruhr district alone. These are mostly of the single-family type, although more recently multiple-family houses and apartment buildings have come into the picture.[47]

---

44 *Die deutsche Bergwirtschaft der Gegenwart,* p. 259.

45 *Ibid.,* pp. 260–280.

46 See pp. 376 ff.

47 *Die deutsche Bergwirtschaft der Gegenwart,* pp. 221–244. Schwenger, following a long, closely organized, and adroitly worded discussion of the social service activities of the Ruhr coal mining industry, has come to the conclusion that these may be regarded as model for the industry in nearly every respect. Serious doubts, however, are expressed as to the desirable effects of the greatly increased social insurance burdens—a fourfold increase for employers and more than fivefold for workers since 1914—upon worker-capitalist antagonisms in the industry. Industrial peace is held to stand in an inverse ratio to the volume of the expenditures by the industry for social purposes. This is taken by the author as an occasion for chiding workers for lack of a sense of responsibility and duty, and not, unfortunately, for a thoroughgoing analysis of the revolutionary changes which brought the new worker viewpoint into existence, nor for

Of all the attempts to influence the workers, perhaps the most extensive, and certainly the boldest, is that of *DINTA* (*Deutsches Institut für Technische Arbeitsschulung*).[48] Its purpose is that of "utilizing human motive force to the best advantage" of the owners of productive equipment. For this purpose it selects only the younger workers—those under twenty years of age—whose conduct, proclivities, habits, and family background, upon examination, are judged suitable for the training and indoctrination to be given them. The technical training in the mining industry "consists of a two years' course in the training shop, followed by two years' practical work underground in a training pit."[49] Meanwhile they are given technical information in mine schools. These, as in the case of the practical work, are run in a military fashion, strict discipline being enforced at all times. An attempt is made to secure loyalty through careful selection of the men trained, company propaganda through publication of special periodicals and newspapers, provision of playgrounds and amusement facilities, and the offering of special wage and advancement incentives. The object is to bring about a recrudescence of the typically German economic virtues of the pre-war period. Duty and loyalty are to be inculcated by use of strict military discipline; piety, faithful performance, and a "higher view of life" are to be promoted through close cooperation with the church; ambition and hard work are to be stimulated by emphasizing the virtues of family life, and by romantically limning the sagas of successful business men and industrialists. These policies, the promoters of *DINTA* hope, will develop a solid corps of workers who will be loyal to the management and deaf to the arguments of unionists and the heresies of radical doctrine. It is expected that these workers will see the "reason" and the "logic" in longer hours and lower wages, and, in so doing, will appreciate that there are purposes and objectives "higher in life" than mere material rewards. This will help to bring "sound" and "profitable" conditions back into industry, and thus will help to lift "Germany" back to the road of economic recovery and prosperity.[50] More than half of the Rhine-Westphalian coal fields have introduced this euphemistically termed "system of vocational training."

5. COKE: AN INTERMEDIARY INDUSTRY

Coke is produced either as a by-product of plants—usually local in character—supplying gas for sale for light, heat, or power purposes, or as the main product of works attached directly to collieries and iron and steel mills. In the mills, gas and chemicals produced are either discarded or refined and sold as by-products. These latter grouped together (as *Zechenkokereien*) are much the more impor-

a discussion of the far-reaching implications of the attitude of labor towards such expenditures.—Rudolf Schwenger, "Die betriebliche Sozialpolitik im Ruhrkohlenbergbau," *Schriften des Vereins für Sozialpolitik*, 186:1.

48 See p. 353 and Appendix A.

49 B. I. M. I. (August–September, 1928):163.

50 See *Das DINTA dient der Wirtschaft*, the regular publication, *Arbeitsschulung*, and other material printed by DINTA.

tant, their production in 1928 being about 88 per cent of the total. Contrasted with the pre-war period they have gained somewhat in importance, the corresponding percentage for 1913 being 85.4.[51]

Most German coke—about 85 per cent of the total—is produced in the Ruhr district because of the abundance of good coking coal, the nearness of the iron and steel industry, the closeness of foreign markets, and the presence of extensive water transportation facilities. Here the industry has undergone a remarkable transformation during the period under review. Works have been concentrated, enlarged, and mechanized, or newly built on an efficiency level far above that of pre-war days. By-product utilization methods are more commonly employed now than formerly. Through the coking industry the ties that bind coal mining directly to the iron, steel, gas, chemical, and power industries, and indirectly to the machine, electro-technical, transport, and textile industries have become steadily closer and more rigid.

The first step towards systematization in the coke industry came with the establishment of central cokeries, favorably located with respect to coal sources, to interrelated technical processes, and to rivers and canals. While before the war nearly every mine producing good coking coal possessed a cokery, by 1928 over 50 per cent of the coke was turned out by the centrally located *Zentralkokereien.* These are usually placed at the mouth of the mine itself, and frequently in close contact with blast-furnace works. Many of the old ovens (usually *Abhitzöfen*—roughly similar to the old "beehive coke oven") have been discarded, and new ovens, combined in large batteries and almost completely mechanized, have been built in their stead. Filling and discharging of the ovens, and the loading and transport of the coal at one end and the coke at the other, are entirely mechanical. The newer ovens are several times as efficient as the old and are usually operated on a 24-hour basis. Where the old Chamotte oven produced an average of 5.15 tons of coke per 24-hour day, three of the large newer type ovens produced 17.5, 20.2, and 27.8 tons, or a capacity increase of 340, 398, and 540 per cent, respectively. The relative importance of the four principal types of coke ovens in use in the Ruhr is shown in the data given by table 6 for 1929:

TABLE 6

Oven type	Number in operation	Percentage of total number in operation	Aggregate production (million tons)	Percentage of total production	Production per oven (tons)
Waste heat	3,121	23.9	4.85	14.84	1,554
Regenerator	7,237	55.1	16.65	50.95	2,301
Compound	2,716	20.7	11.04	33.80	4,066
Recuperator	40	.3	.136	.51	3,412

[51] Unless otherwise stated, the material on coke is taken from the *Enquete Ausschuss, III, Glückauf,* and the *Zeitschrift für das Berg-, Hütten-, und Salinenwesen,* all previously cited.

Nine of the newer cokeries, put in operation in 1928, were equipped with 1,045 ovens, and produced (in that year) a total of 5,647,816 tons, or an average of 5,414 tons per oven—a figure that is over three times as large as the average output of the old-type ovens listed above. Angell estimated in 1928, mostly upon the basis of data gathered on the regenerative type of oven, that "the new cokeries get a yield of 40 tons or more per man per shift, as against about 5 before the war, have a capacity of up to 40 tons per oven against 6 before," aside from their greater usefulness from the point of view of by-products utilization.[52] Similar data for 1929 would show still further increase in capacity.

Concentration of production in the large *Zentralkokereien* is more significant in the Ruhr district than for the Reich at large. In 1929, 27 cokeries, each producing 400,000 or more tons of coke, were credited with approximately 50 per cent of the output. Three of them had an annual output of more than 1,000,000 tons. Ownership would appear to be even more highly concentrated, though it is impossible to secure thoroughly reliable and comprehensive data on the industry at large.

6. COAL AND COKE, AND THEIR RELATION TO THE IRON AND STEEL INDUSTRY

The relationships between the coal, iron, and steel industries in the Ruhr district have always been unusually intimate because of their nearness to one another. The ties have been strengthened in the post-war period by the conservation called for on account of (1) the loss of Lorraine ore to the iron and steel industry, (2) the need for fuel economy in smelting and reworking costly foreign ores, in order to be able to compete in domestic and foreign markets, and (3) the attempts of the coal industry—partly as a result of governmental pressure—to stabilize output and prices. The larger steel concerns, such as *Vereinigte Stahlwerke, Krupp, Gutehoffnungshütte,* and *Mannesmann,* have thus acquired large coal holdings and coking plants or have entered into special contracts (sometimes involving a partial exchange of shares) with large independent concerns in these industries, or have done both things. As table 2 shows, the first three companies mentioned produced 37.93 per cent of the Ruhr coal output in 1929. In the business year 1928–1929 the *Vereinigte Stahlwerke* produced 22.53 per cent of the Ruhr coal output and 30.10 per cent of its coke. The coke percentages of the other large steel companies roughly approximate their coal percentages. Some idea of the extent to which the larger steel concerns are involved in the coke, lignite, and coal industries may be gained by glancing over the charts published by *Die Wirtschaftskurve* of the organization and affiliations of the *Vereinigte Stahlwerke*[53] and the *Preussische Berg- und Hüttenwerke.*[54]

[52] *Angell, op. cit.,* pp. 102–103.

[53] Heft 4 (1926).

[54] Heft 1 (1927).

But no statement of the percentages of coal[55] and coke produced and consumed by the iron and steel industry could serve to convey adequately a picture of the true nature of the relationships existing between these industries. As developed in the Ruhr, and to a lesser extent in the Upper Silesian districts, the ties that bind them together are of an organic, functional, and interprocess character. In the *August Thyssenhütte* of the *Vereinigte Stahlwerke*, for example, coal mining, coking, smelting, steel making, and by-products utilization are brought together into a single compactly organized, neatly proportioned, and functionally interdependent operating unit, in which dovetailing of interrelated processes, both temporally and spatially, and mechanization, have been carried out, and all excess storage, all stoppage and starting, and all isolatable wastes have been reduced with ruthless thoroughness to the minimum consistent with present engineering knowledge. Conditions obtaining in this plant are reflected in trends affecting relationships between the industries; in a sense it is a prototype for the district at large.

7. BY-PRODUCT UTILIZATION: GAS

With the construction and operation of the newer large-scale central coking systems, the problems of fuel economy and by-product utilization were brought to the fore. Not that these problems were at all new. But the losses in resources experienced as a result of the Draconian terms of the Versailles treaty, the natural shortages in crude petroleum and water power, and the rapid rate at which coal, and particularly lignite, resources were being exhausted, gave post-war discussion and planning in regard to conservation and fuel economy an especial importance in Germany. The popular as well as the technical point of view was summarized by a writer in *Die Wirtschaftskurve* in the motto: "Not a calorie nor a molecule must any longer be wasted."[56]

In coal and lignite this program has been reflected in the attempt to find ways of utilizing all classes and types of colliery products in the most efficient and economical manner. With the exception of the remarkable growth of coal-dust

---

[55] In 1928 the consumption of coal in Germany was divided as follows:

	Percentage
Domestic, agriculture, small industry	27.7
Metal production and refining	20.7
Chemical industry	6.5
Electric power	6.8
Transportation (railroads and shipping)	12.1
Gas and water works	5.2
Building materials	6.9
Textile industry	3.2
Food products industries	3.5
Paper and cellulose products	2.8
Miscellaneous industries	4.1
	100.0

[56] Heft 4 (1928):396.

firing during the years 1925–1927,[57] the trend has been towards chemical treatment of an increasing percentage of total output. The time will come, some engineers and industrialists hold, when direct firing of coal will be completely eliminated and all coal will be broken down into its constituent chemical elements to be delivered and used as electric power, and in gas, coke, tar, ammonia, naphtha, phosphorus, and other chemical forms. By 1927–1928 nearly 60 per cent of the German output, including coal sold in the form of briquets and coal dust, was thus chemically broken up.[58]

Of the two methods in general use for chemically treating coal, "coking" processes (with by-product extraction plant) and hydrogenation, the former is as yet much the more important. And of all the by-products, perhaps gas is the most important. With the construction of the newer type of coke ovens, the heavy industries, particularly in the Ruhr district, found themselves unable to make use directly of the tremendous quantities of valuable coking gas made available.[59] While there was an increased need for gas because of its substitution in the place of direct firing, the available supply increased still more rapidly because of improvements in heat economy and the substitution of hitherto non-marketable, and consequently waste, blast-furnace for coking gas as a power source throughout the iron and steel industries. The problem thus arose of the disposal of the surplus product in a market already well supplied with fuel and energy. The solution offered—construction of long-distance gas supply systems—called for the cooperation of the coal mining, coking, iron and steel, and all other industries directly interested in the production of gas on the one hand, and in a cheap and efficient fuel and power supply on the other. It brought up the prob-

[57] Of the newly built steam boilers in Germany for the four years 1924–1927, inclusive, the following percentages of total heating surface (the first percentage for each year), and number of boilers (the second percentage for each year), were constructed for coal-dust firing: 3 per cent and 3.5 per cent; 27.1 per cent and 12.4 per cent; 30.2 per cent and 16.7 per cent; 16.4 per cent and 10.7 per cent.—*Ibid.*, p. 398.

[58] Of the total German coal consumption, the following percentages were "refined" during the typical pre-war and post-war periods:*

Refining method	1913–1914	1927–1928
Briquetting	12.8	17.4
Grinding to dust	....	2.4
Coking	28.4	28.0
Gas extraction	4.8	5.1
Distillation	0.2	0.3
Hydrogenation	....	0.1
Electricity production	1.8	6.2
Together	48.0	59.5

* Source: *Ibid.*, p. 399.

[59] A modern coke works of 260 or more ovens, with an average coal consumption of 4,000 tons of coal per day, will produce from 400 to 500 million cubic meters per year, or approximately the equivalent of the gas consumption of a city the size of Berlin. The total amount of gas produced in Germany in 1928 was 18,600,000,000 cbm., of which 14.9 billion came from colliery coke plants, and 3.7 billion came from especially constructed (local) gas plants. Of the former, but .5 billion cbm. was sold on the market through long-distance gas-main systems.—*Enquete Ausschuss,* III:38.

lems of centralized versus locally operated and controlled gas plants, private ownership versus public ownership,[60] and a host of related issues, the implications of many of which have proved to be far-reaching.

The answer to the problem as found by the interested industries visualized the issues in their broadest interpretation. The *A. G. für Kohlenverwertung* shortly after its foundation published a statement of the objectives for which it would strive. Its plan was to have the various coal and lignite districts pool their gas supply and deliver it into a single gigantic interconnected system of pipe lines which would cover the entire Reich. Where gas systems had been built up locally, old plant would be scrapped, and the local distribution net would be fed from the central mains. Where gas distribution systems had not been constructed, these would be supplied by the central system. The heating quality and chemical purity of the gas would be controlled at the source, pressure would be kept at a uniform level by a system of pumping stations and special methods of line and storage control, and rates would be adjusted to fit the needs of various consumer groups.

The idea of such a gas-supply system was not, of course, altogether new. Interconnected mains and distribution networks had become rather common in the United States before the war in districts where natural gas was to be found in abundance. Long-distance gas-main networks were known even in Germany in the pre-war period. The *Rheinisch-Westfälisches Elektrizitätswerk* and the Thyssen-controlled *Gas- und Wasserwerke G. m. b. H.* had been delivering gas on a district basis since 1910. These were, however, strictly regional organizations. Nothing of the modern sort had been either planned or visualized.

In 1928 the *A. G. für Kohlenverwertung* was reorganized as the *Ruhrgas A. G.* Between that year and 1930 the new company increased its gas delivery from 122 million cubic meters to 710 million cubic meters and its pipe system from 329 to 803 kilometers in length. The division of its gas delivery between public

60 According to data supplied by the Deutscher Verein für Gas- und Wasserfachmänner e. V. there were 1,209 establishments engaged in the supply of gas to the German public in the year 1928. These have been grouped as follows:*

Amount of production in cubic meters (annual)	Number of works			Share of the total gas produtcion in per cent
	Producing their own gas	Purchasing gas from coking plants	Total	
Over 1,000,000	45	8	53	65.5
400,000–1,000,000	41	9	50	11.4
80,000 – 400,000	269	31	300	15.7
Under 80,000	774	32	806	7.4
	1,129	80	1,209	100.0

* Source: *Enquete Ausschuss*, III: 39,40.

Most of these plants are publicly owned and operated: 981 are communal plants, and produce (1928) 84.5 per cent of the total public supply; 78 are "mixed" (owned partly by the public and partly by private individuals), and produce 12 per cent of the total; the remaining 3.5 per cent is divided among 150 purely private enterprises. The industry has invested capital to the amount of about 1.45 billion marks and employed 59,500 workers in 1927.

and private consumers illustrates the purposes which it was hoped the system would fulfil. One of the weightiest arguments in favor of such an interconnected network was that it would provide a common carrier which individual companies could use to provide distant plants with a fuel which was a surplus and otherwise "waste" by-product at its point of origin. About 330 million cubic meters were thus "transported" by *Ruhrgas* in 1930. The remainder sent through the pipes was purchased outright from coking plants and delivered as commercial product, about 135 million cubic meters being sold to cities and regional distribution nets,[61] and about 245 million cubic meters being sold to industrial plants.

The major technical problems have been solved with unusual success as they have arisen. The problem of participation was practically solved at the start when 91 per cent of the coal companies—including most of the large ones—of the Rhine-Westphalian industrial district joined in the enterprise. The danger of duplicating facilities by competitive systems has been handled by the drafting of special regional agreements with potential competitors.[62] The problem of finding an industrial market appears to be working out with the gradual transformation of industrial heating and power systems from a coal basis to gas. The more difficult and delicate conflict of locally owned and operated municipal gas-producing works versus supply from a central system seems to be in process of solution with the conclusion of agreements with cities like Cologne, Düsseldorf, Hanover, and Duisberg.

But there remain several important issues to be faced in the future. Among these, the general relationship to the electrical-power industry, particularly with the growth and expansion of interconnected super-power systems, will be of paramount importance. Competition and consequent duplication of facilities may, as some observers are convinced they already do, run all the way through the two industries—competition for raw materials (coal or gas), duplication of transmission and distribution networks, competition for lighting, heating, household consumption markets, etc. Railroads, water transportation systems, wholesale and retail coal dealers, and many other special-interest groups may find their services and functions partly or completely dispensed with as the system expands.

The strategic importance of such a system in time of war or in case of an industrial dispute is bound to strengthen political interest in the conditions governing its operation. Once the economic life of the country is built around such a system, it would be relatively easy for a body-blow to be delivered at the entire

---

[61] For this purpose the company has made special gas-delivery contracts with the Westfälisches Ferngas A. G., Dortmund, the Vereinigte Elektrizitätswerke G. m. b. H., Dortmund, the Rheinisch-Westfälisches Elektrizitätswerk A. G., Essen, and a number of cities, including such large places as Duisburg, Düsseldorf, Gelsenkirchen, Hanover, Krefeld, Cologne, Solingen, etc. See Ruhrgas A. G., "*Geschäftsbericht über das Jahr 1930.*"

[62] In addition to those mentioned before, these include the Thyssensche Gas- und Wasserwerke G. m. b. H., Hamborn, and the Vereinigte Gaswerke Westfalen G. m. b. H., Dortmund.

national economy.[63] The advantages of such a network from the point of view of economy are fully equaled by the hazards that would attend an interruption in the service which the system provides. The whole system would be thrown out of gear if the cokeries should fail to produce enough gas to provide the proper pressure, if the main lines should for any reason fail to deliver, or if consumption should suddenly rise or fall. The danger of disorganization becomes greater the larger the percentage of the total fuel and power requirements of industry and domestic economy supplied by gas. A major difficulty is that reserves cannot be accumulated to take care of emergencies. Coal can be mined in quantities far in excess of consumption for considerable periods of time, since it can be heaped up in piles and stored indefinitely without great loss in value. Gas, like electricity, must be produced as it is used; it can be stored for only a few hours at best. Coal reserves can be accumulated locally and can be set aside to meet unforeseen contingencies, such as interruption of railroad and other transport services and cessation in production because of wars, strikes, and lockouts. Nothing of this sort is at all possible with gas supply. A centralized supply system does away with even those measures which might be applied locally in case of a breakdown in service. Furthermore, the general expense and the technical problems involved in transforming heating and power systems from a coal to a gas basis would forbid in many, if not in most cases, meeting such emergencies by falling back upon coal.

Such arguments do not show, and should not be used to prove, that the net advantages claimed for the new system are very considerably less than its proponents have claimed. But they do illustrate the very important point that no party or industry, directly or indirectly dependent upon the proper functioning of such a system, will hesitate to take whatever action is necessary in order to guarantee continuous and uninterrupted service. From past experience with railroads and other public-utility enterprises, we know that such action will be taken regardless of the conflicting special interests of other parties and industries, including the service enterprises themselves. In its very nature, the gas industry in its present stage of development is directly affected with a public interest, and it is inconceivable that it will be allowed to function solely as the business discretion of its managerial staff may dictate whenever decisions affecting the quality or the price of the service are at stake. It has become, in other words, a key service industry in every factory and household using gas under circumstances in which every addition to or subtraction from the common pool concerns all participating parties. The importance of gas as a by-product will unquestionably mean in the future, if it does not mean already, that failure of this market will reduce income below cost of production for cokeries. The importance of gas as a fuel to all other industries will mean that failure at the source of

[63] See Chaps. IV, XII, XIII, and XIV.

supply will force cessation of all manufacturing activities relying upon its delivery. The gas industry thus takes on a service character in which continuous, uninterrupted, and highly regular flow become of direct and prime importance to producer, distributor, and consumer. Like the steam in the pipes or the power in the electric wires circulating throughout the factory, a break in the service is apt to cripple seriously the whole intricate and carefully integrated complex, or, at the worst, to bring it to a complete and disastrous halt.[64]

8. BY-PRODUCT UTILIZATION: CHEMICALS

No less significant for the future of the coal industry are its relationships to the chemical field. Here, as in the case of gas, the advantages accruing from full utilization of all by-products become more important as the percentage of total coal output subjected to chemical treatment makes the industry more sensitive to the conditions governing exploitation of any raw material contributing to joint products. Price adjustments in the course of time make practically certain that the sale of no one product will be sufficient to guarantee income high enough to maintain the industry, while, at the same time, the failure to find a steady market for any one of the more important joint products is apt to necessitate taking a loss until the condition can be remedied. The importance of chemical by-products to the German coal and lignite industries is indicated by tables 7 and 8:[65]

TABLE 7

BY-PRODUCTS OF THE GERMAN COAL INDUSTRY

(in 1,000 tons)

Year	Bituminous coal			Lignite	
	Tar and tar concentrates	Benzol	Sulphur, ammonia and ammonia compounds	Tar	By-products
1913	1,026	176	421	78.7	2.4
1925	982	248	401	74.3	6.0
1926	966	245	380	78.3	5.4
1927	1,187	307	458	83.6	5.3

64 "It has been pointed out by specialists that with long-distance gas supply large areas will be dependent upon the business fortunes of a particular branch of industry or even of a single plant, and that such business prospects can be destroyed as readily from factors peculiar to that industry as through general economic and political occurrences. The opponents of long-distance gas supply have especially referred to the possibility of such stoppages through labor struggles..... *If a long-distance gas-supply system is to exist, it seems to the Committee that, in view of its crucial importance to the general welfare, the problem of its functioning free from interruptions and labor struggles is a matter not only of economic but also of political security.*" —*Enquete Ausschuss,* III:57. (Italics mine.)

65 *Enquete Ausschuss,* III:59.

TABLE 8

VALUE OF THE BY-PRODUCTS OF THE GERMAN COAL INDUSTRY
(in million marks)

Year	Bituminous coal			Lignite	
	Tar and tar concentrates	Benzol	Sulphur, ammonia and ammonia compounds	Tar	By-products
1913	24.1	29.1	107.2	4.0	0.5
1925	42.9	78.8	77.8	4.3	0.5
1926	58.8	80.6	69.7	5.5	1.0
1927	92.5	85.1	80.2	7.2	1.0

The methods of extracting and refining the various by-products fall broadly into three categories: (1) the coking, or so-called "dry distillation" process; (2) distillation (or "semi-coking"); and (3) the hydrogenation process. By-products arising from the first of these processes are primarily incident to the demand for coke in the iron and steel industry, and are, consequently, extracted from high-grade coking coal. The distillation process, developed originally with an eye to making use of cheap and low-grade types of fuel, has not met with any considerable success in the bituminous coal industry. It is, however, the foundation upon which rest the extensive by-product industries in the lignite field. Hydrogenation is still more or less in the experimental stage. The three most promising processes—Bergius, Fischer-Tropsch, and the polymerization and condensation—differ only in the chemical methods whereby the coal is directly transferred into a refinable fluid. It is hoped that these hydrogenation methods, when perfected, will solve the problem of marketing low-grade coal.

For present purposes the coking and distillation processes can be taken together, the latter occupying a position of importance in the lignite industry roughly analogous to that of the former in the bituminous coal industry. All the new coke ovens have been equipped to extract by-products. From 1913 to 1928 the number of coke ovens not so equipped diminished from 3,328 to 87, and by 1930 had disappeared entirely from certain districts, among which was the Ruhr.[66] The most important by-products of the coking industry are ammonia (containing nitrogen), benzol and its homologs, and tar. The first of these is refined and used primarily for fertilizer; the second is broken up into its chemical constituents, the most important of which is benzol for use in internal combustion engines; tar is likewise treated, from it being extracted a large number of chemicals, most important of which are pitch (used as a binding medium in the making of briquets, and for street pavement) and impregnating oils (*Im-*

[66] *Ibid.*, p. 31.

pragnieröle), used mainly as a railroad fuel. The increase in production of nitrogen, crude tar, and light oil by the coking industry of the Ruhr district during the post-war years is shown in table 9:[67]

TABLE 9

Year	Nitrogen		Crude tar		Light oil	
	Tons	Percentage increase over 1925	Tons	Percentage increase over 1925	Tons	Percentage increase over 1925
1925	66,026	....	775,920	....	200,258	....
1926	66,075	.07	791,058	1.9	207,759	3.7
1927	79,313	20.0	977,338	25.9	255,460	27.6
1928	81,118	22.9	1,030,672	31.4	268,292	33.5
1929	92,442	40.0	1,202,399	54.7	313,215	55.9

The new methods now in the experimental stage and the perfection of the different hydrogenation processes will probably alter the relative importance of the by-products as the percentage of coal chemically treated increases. The development of nitrogen fixation from the atmosphere has completely overshadowed by-product nitrogen in the post-war period. While production of the latter for the Reich increased from 75,231 to 105,000 tons between 1921 and 1929, the corresponding increase for nitrogen taken from the air was from 1,267 to 650,000 tons. More significant would be the results from general substitution of the hydrogenation for the distillation process, as the new methods make possible the extraction of a much larger percentage of the available high-quality oils and chemicals.[68]

Chemical treatment of coal has not only provided a partial solution of the problems of general overproduction[69] and the disposal of unmarketable grades,

[67] *Glückauf* (November, 1930):1548.

[68] A typical example is to be found in the following percentages of gas-flame coal (*Gasflammkohle*) transferred into various chemicals by the two processes.*

	Hydrogenation percentage	Distillation percentage
Light oil (Leichtöl)	15	1.5
Fuel and impregnating oils (Treib- und Tränköl)	15	3.0
Fuel oil (Heizöl)	20	4.0
Gas	20	15.0
Coke (Schwelkoks)	....	61.0
Residue coal	11.5	....
Water	8	5.0
Ashes	10	10.0

* Source: *Die deutsche Bergwirtschaft der Gegenwart,* p. 148.

[69] Developments in heat economy, resulting from scarcity of coal during and immediately after the war, and by-product utilization, emphasized in the years following the stabilization largely because of excess coal production, have both, curiously enough, promoted chemical treatment and refinement of coal.

but it has also had the effect of bringing the coal and chemical industries into very close relationship with each other. In fact, it may be said that in certain districts the coal and chemical industries are in effect operating as unified and compactly organized industrial complexes at the present time. If the ideal is achieved at some future time, and all coal is broken down into its chemical constituents before being used, the fusion between the two industries will be complete. That is to say, coal and lignite production will be more and more tied into a continuous process, in which the original extraction will be but a technical stage in what is literally and descriptively an unbroken sequence of interlocking mechanical and chemical operations which end only with refinement and delivery of the component parts to the final private and industrial users. The interstitial adjustments necessary to maintain, temporally and volumetrically, a smooth and even flow throughout the concert of interwoven processes will not only resemble but in reality will become, in the most unambiguous engineering sense of the term, a balanced mechanical-chemical system.

Corporate growth in this borderline field has been very interesting, and is probably instructive for the future. The chemical concerns, particularly the *I. G. Farbenindustrie A. G.* in the lignite field and the *Oberkoks-Konzern, Ruhr-Chemie A. G.,* and the *Rütgers-Konzern* in the bituminous industry, have, like the great steel concerns, acquired extensive mining properties, and have steadily increased their control over large sections of the coal and lignite industries. This trend has brought these companies into very close touch with the iron and steel industry, and has further strengthened the relationships already existing between them. *Ruhr-Chemie A. G.,* in fact, appears to have been established largely at the initiative of the steel people for the purpose of handling the chemical by-product problem in the same way that *Ruhrgas A. G.* handles the problem of excess gas. Coal mine operators and chemical concerns appear to have cooperated quite readily in this venture.

The bearing of this trend upon the larger problem of inter-industry integration and rationalization must be passed over at this point.[70] It suffices here to point out that the development has been so rapid during the post-war years that one might well feel justified in assuming, so far as purely technological and organizational factors are concerned and in the absence of disturbing factors, that the future will show the two industries fused into a single, functionally integrated, administratively decentralized, and centrally coordinated system.

9. RELATION TO THE POWER INDUSTRY

Even closer is the technical interdependence of coal, lignite, and power. And here, as in the industries mentioned above, the technical interrelations are slowly compelling a general realignment of ownership, management, and control. If

[70] See Chaps. IV, XII, XIII, and XIV.

the possibilities of rationalization are to be realized in full, these must be brought to the point where the best proportioning of factors between the various interlocking processes is the certain result of organizational configuration and managerial policy.

The power industry rests, in the main, upon three energy sources: water power, coal, and lignite. Of these the latter two are much the more important, having supplied in recent years about 70 to 75 per cent of the electric energy produced. Coal figures are somewhat larger in this percentage than lignite, although the bulk of the increase in steam-generated current during the post-war period is attributable to lignite. The total coal consumption, however, is not large; electric concerns used but 6.8 per cent of the combined coal and lignite output in 1928.[71]

Before the war, when power production was, like gas production, almost exclusively on a small local basis, coal was the dominating fuel. The general scarcity of fuel, and the fact that the principal coal producing districts, both east and west, were in constant threat of invasion, led to sudden expansion in the lignite fields. Because of high water content, ranging usually between 48 and 60 per cent of its gross weight, and its relatively low heat value per ton, crude lignite proved an expensive fuel to ship long distances. In the process of perfecting methods of reducing the water content and preparing the crude fuel for industrial and domestic consumption, it soon became apparent that lignite could compete with coal as an electric-power fuel if used close to the pits from which it was extracted. Thus mining, refining, and power consumption could be combined with the advantages which accrue to integrated large-scale operation, at the same time that a phase, at least, of the transport problem could be solved through electric transmission. A difficulty, however, was encountered in the fact that most of the large lignite fields were some distance removed from the principal markets for electric current. Hence, it was necessary that the lignite power industry be born a giant equipped with immense power plants and high-tension transmission systems as a condition to existence, or not be born at all.

Post-war conditions were particularly favorable for development of the lignite industry. Reparations deliveries created a general shortage in the fuel markets. Because of antiquated and inefficient mining methods and high transport costs, coal was expensive. In the disorganized fuel and energy markets, the advantages of lignite as a power source were easily demonstrated. The way was further smoothed by technical improvements in long-distance transmission, by reduction of fuel costs per kilowatt hour through improved methods of refining and treating the crude fuel, and by the integration of the large power plants into a single technical and economic entity.

---

[71] *ETZ,* Heft 24:848 (June 12, 1930).

As the capacity of the operating power plants has increased,[72] and the network of interconnected transmission systems has spread, the rôle of lignite has increased in importance. A type of vertical integration appears to be in process here, similar to that which is taking place between coal and lignite, on the one hand, and steel, gas, and chemicals on the other. At the same time, integration between the various branches of the end-product "service" appears to foreshadow a time when the entire power industry will be woven into a single nation-wide system. Consolidation of ownership among the larger power distribution systems shows conformity with the logic of technical events. Here again, the analogy to the gas supply situation outlined above is obvious. The local plant is pitted against the economies of the efficient and centrally operated inter-district and inter-municipal system. Success of the central system raises the same questions of supply and the same problems of technical reorganization that are incident to increased consumption by industrial and domestic users of a cheap substitute fuel and energy supply.[73]

10. PROBLEMS OF DISTRIBUTION: THE COAL SYNDICATE

As pointed out at the beginning of this chapter, the Coal Law and subsequent legislation created a national agency for the purpose of centralizing and coordinating the economic activities of the entire coal, lignite, and coke industries. The law, however, has been mainly a paper achievement. A certain amount of genuine regulatory power has drifted into the hands of the Ministry of Economics. For the most part, however, such power as is centrally exercised lies exclusively in the hands of the various syndicates. Of these the *Rheinisch-Westfälisches Kohlensyndikat* is by all odds the most important, and its history may be taken as representative of the whole experiment.

By a forceful and far-sighted policy, the machinery of the syndicates would seem, at first, to be ideally adapted for the fulfillment of the purposes for which they were organized. The experience gained by the *Rheinisch-Westfälisches Kohlensyndikat* since its foundation as a private cartel in 1893 should have provided an adequate background for effective control and regulation of the industry as premeditated in the law of 1919. Aside from the fact that the conditions of scarcity obtaining during the war and first few post-war years were shortly fol-

[72] Capacities of a few of the larger plants are as follows:*

	Kilowatts
Goldenberg Werk (Lower Rhine district)	290,000
Golpa-Zschornewitz (Middle German district)	230,000
Sächsische Werke (Saxony)	200,000
Hirschfelde (Saxony)	110,000
Trattendorf (East Elbe district)	90,000
Finkenheerd (Oder district)	90,000
Lauta (East Elbe district)	88,000

* Source: *Die deutsche Bergwirtschaft der Gegenwart*, pp. 164–171.

[73] Compare Chap. IX.

lowed by the problem of excess capacity and output, the new arrangement was carried out under circumstances long familiar to the industry. And, while competition on both domestic and international markets was probably more acute in the latter period, the industry could fall back on its pre-war experience in grappling with the problem of overproduction.

The specific objectives of the syndicates were said to be regulation of production, self-consumption, and marketing, or, in other words, regulation and equalization of supply and demand. Nominally, production and marketing are completely under the control of the syndicates. All coal produced for the market, subject to certain minor exceptions, must be sold through agencies under their (nominal) control. All coal produced within integrated concerns for their own use, except under quota restrictions (when 35 per cent of the quota restriction applies to the mining works of such integrated concerns), is independent of cartel control. The remainder, subject directly to syndicate marketing regulation, is in part delivered directly to certain large consumers such as the *Reichsbahn*, gas works, and electric power plants. Much the larger percentage (70 to 75 per cent in the Ruhr) is sold through existing commercial channels. These are three in number, (1) special commercial companies belonging on a fixed ownership basis to the members of the syndicate (*Syndikatshandelsgesellschaften*), (2) companies owned and controlled by individual collieries (*Zechenhandelsgesellschaften*), and (3) independent enterprises (*freie Händler*).[74]

It is this separation between production and consumption, plus the problem of quotas, which has proved the undoing of the syndicates. Quotas have been based upon capacity, reckoned as the highest output achieved by each mine for a full quarter-year at any time during a number of preceding years. Reorganization leading to increased capacity would affect the quota of the mine only after the syndicate had formally passed upon requests for quota enlargement. Quotas could be purchased only through exchange of mine ownership, direct purchase being forbidden from the start.

The result of this arrangement has been a struggle for quotas. The more capacity outran production, the more severe the struggle. The more severe the struggle, the greater the tendency to enlarge capacity as a basis upon which to

[74] The division of the inland market of the *Rheinisch-Westfälisches Kohlensyndikat* among these agencies for the year 1928 was as follows:*

	Coal, coke, and briquets, percentage
Immediate delivery by syndicate	26.81
Syndikatshandelsgesellschaften	60.52
Zechenhandelsgesellschaften	12.01
Freie Händler	0.66
	100.0

* Source: *Enquete Ausschuss*, III:91.

claim an increased quota. The effect has been to increase quotas, i.e., capacity,[75] much more rapidly than production, as table 10, based upon data relating to the *Rheinisch-Westfälisches Kohlensyndikat,* clearly shows:[76]

TABLE 10

(In million tons)

Year	Production	Quotas (total for district)	Marketed	Marketed through the syndicate	Special exempt deliveries	Self-consumption
1913	101.6	84.1	82.3	57.4	2.7	22.2
1925–26	101.3	130.8	72.6	51.3	4.0	17.3
1926–27	117.1	135.4	91.6	66.5	3.6	21.5
1927–28	117.4	136.5	82.2	58.2	3.5	20.5
1928–29	111.8	137.3	77.4	52.1	3.5	21.8

A second difficulty was met in the exemption of the mixed enterprises—principally iron and steel—from the quota restrictions of the syndicate. As indicated above, a compromise was finally reached in which 35 per cent of such restriction was assessed on production not for sale. On the whole, however, this compromise has not met the real complaint of the pure mines, which was that during periods of coal shortage the mixed collieries would neither shorten their consumption nor make available to the market those types of coal in great demand, while in periods of superfluity they would insist on placing their excess in an already saturated market. Hence, it was argued, the burden of cyclical fluctuations was shouldered onto the pure mines, which have been, financially and industrially, the weaker of the two groups. Both quota problems have, however, found a partial solution in the process of amalgamation; in the first case by purchase in order to secure the economies of large-scale enterprise and larger quotas, and in the second case by further integration by the iron, steel, and chemical industries in order to secure certain supplies of fuel for the future, and to avoid the restrictions and control of the syndicates. But even such a partial and unsatisfactory solution, on the whole, seems to have been denied the marketing problem.

In the first place, the very existence of the syndicates does not appear to be at all secure despite the compulsory character which they were given at the outset. The cartel agreements of the *Rheinisch-Westfälisches Kohlensyndikat,* for example, were renewed, only after the greatest difficulty, in 1920, 1922, 1923,

---

75 This statement is not entirely correct. (1) *Capacity* may have been increased after quotas had been established, (2) and maximum output may never have reached real capacity. Real capacity, then, should usually, and perhaps in all cases, be rated considerably above the quotas.

76 *Enquete Ausschuss,* III:90.

1924, and 1925.[77] As long as the continued existence of the syndicate was in doubt, it followed that each colliery, disposing of its output through the cooperative enterprise, would be placed at a disadvantage in competition with collieries possessing their own outlets in the event of a breakdown of the syndicate. Hence arose the competition among collieries to obtain their own outlets, either by acquiring full ownership rights in existing organizations or by establishment of new marketing agencies. While this struggle does not appear to have brought about an increase in the number of such distributing companies, this is largely because of the fact that amalgamation of mining properties has been accompanied by fusion of marketing organizations. But that the number of these companies has not appreciably decreased is sufficient evidence of the inability of the present syndicate organization to solve the most important problem with which the industry was faced in 1919.[78]

Another factor has seriously limited the success of the system. The division of the country into separate coal districts did not provide for a division of markets. The *Rheinisch-Westfälisches Kohlensyndikat,* for example, discriminates between "contested" and "uncontested" markets. "While in uncontested (non-competitive) fields the Syndicate delivers coal only to Syndicate companies for purposes of resale, in contested (competitive) districts, independent and colliery-owned companies have the right to delivery immediately from the Syndicate, although they have no claim to delivery from a definite colliery. The wish of individual mining companies to be represented in the competitive markets has resulted, accordingly, in their taking over the greater number of the independent marketing concerns. While the independents have decreased, the total number of firms has increased, and these, in addition to facing foreign competition, are engaged in the sharpest competition amongst themselves."[79] In the domestic markets the product has been duplication of wholesale and retail facilities, resort to price competition through special discounts, rebates, tying contracts, and delivery and payment terms, and general confusion of distribution channels. In foreign markets competition of German firms has at times resulted in price cutting to the point where coal and coke were practically dumped for whatever they would bring.[80]

Meanwhile, important areas in the domestic market were lost to foreign competitors. Polish coal in the east and English coal on the north have made impor-

---

[77] The most recent negotiations have broken down and the syndicate is, at the time of writing, extinct.

[78] And this marketing problem, as indicated before, was in no way new. It has dominated the entire history of the cartel. See Michels, *Cartels, Combines and Trusts in Post-War Germany* (New York, 1928):67–82.

[79] *Enquete Ausschuss,* III:97–98.

[80] This led at one time to price levels so low as to encourage the French to demand lower prices for coal delivered on reparations account. See Michels, *op. cit.,* p. 80. Rapidly expanding markets have exempted the lignite industry from the difficulties indicated.

tant gains. Practically the entire North Sea and Baltic littorals, and the larger towns in the immediate interior tapped by navigable waterways, have become English coal markets. Partly to make it possible for German producers to meet this competition, and partly to answer complaints made by consumers of different districts that transport charges were discriminatory, the railroads put through a freight tariff system which was rather markedly scaled downwards for long distances, and for full-car and trainload shipments. While such a tariff system seems to have been considered useful, and, in fact, unavoidable, it appears to have satisfied nobody. Every district complains of discrimination on account of the new tariff as before it complained of the absence of such a rate schedule. In effect, the new schedule has tended to increase the competition between members of the different syndicates.

Nor have the syndicates been any more successful in the matter of price. While the *Reichswirtschaftsminister* and the *Reichskohlenverband,* in cooperation with the *Reichskohlenrat* nominally, and under the law, legally establish coal prices, the actual determination of prices "is preeminently a matter of competitive conditions obtaining in free markets."[81]

Certain minor activities of the *Reichskohlenrat* appear to have been accompanied with a somewhat larger measure of success. Two sub-committees, (1) the Technical-Economic Experts Committee for Bituminous Coal Mining and (2) the Technical-Economic Experts Committee for Fuel Utilization, are said to have promoted materially the technical development and exploitation of processes in the field of fuel economy such as coal-dust firing, fuel refining, and heat economy.

II. SUMMARY

A mass of detail is available for the purpose, were it deemed necessary to fill in the interstices of the broad outline sketched above. But, for present purposes at least, it does not seem important that these facts be marshaled here. For, unless the majority of the better informed German writers on the subject, and the report of the official governmental Committee of Inquiry (*Enquete Ausschuss*), are seriously in error as to the body of underlying facts, the more recent history and configuration of the German coal industry is about as delineated.

The facts show that the pivotal rôle of coal in modern industrial civilization is not only of more vital significance in Germany than in almost all other industrialized countries (excepting England), but also that this situation is and has been more fully appreciated there than elsewhere. Under these circumstances, it was but natural that the problem of rationalizing the coal industry should be vigorously attacked as soon as an opportunity was presented for correcting the

[81] *Enquete Ausschuss,* III:156.

disorganization and demoralization that prevailed prior to the stabilization, and that the programs for change, once launched, should attract the lively interest of the entire nation.

The time seemed ripe for the changes contemplated. The pre-war historical background was, on the whole, propitious. The experiences with war control deepened appreciation of the advantages of cooperation and unified control. The establishment of the compulsory coal, lignite, and coke cartels apparently provided the necessary machinery for effective and far-reaching reorganization.

The advantages of a balanced view of the possibilities of reorganization, of a definite set of objectives, and of a clearly formulated plan of procedure would certainly have been very great at this juncture. Yet in retrospect it is clear that these were entirely lacking. The central control organ, the *Reichskohlenverband,* and its various subsidiary regional cartels were lacking in the necessary authority to reconcile the divergent interests of capital, labor, government, and consumers. The machinery of control set up proved wholly inadequate to the task of adjusting capacity to current requirements, coordinating production and marketing, or forcing through the technological and organizational changes necessary in order to guarantee economical exploitation and use of the nation's most important fuel resources. Such rationalization measures as were attempted were, hence, "muddled through." Individual enterprise did what it could to place its business affairs on a profit-making basis; if this involved promotion of any rationalization technique, so much the better.

As the foregoing pages have shown, important changes along rationalization lines were made in the German coal industries under this half centralized, half "free-enterprise" régime. Many old and badly equipped mines and refining plants have been closed down and their machinery scrapped. Mining operations under and above ground have often been combined. Mechanization has made important strides. Machinery has been simplified and typified, and the component parts standardized. Safety devices have been improved, and better provisions have been made for eliminating choke-damp hazards and for improving lighting, heating, and ventilation. More coal is now being broken up chemically than heretofore, and the methods of extracting and utilizing its numerous by-products have been thoroughly overhauled. The relationships between the different concerns and the various industries associated with coal extraction and refinement have been somewhat simplified, and there has been some improvement in the systems of horizontal and vertical combination.

Yet it seems impossible to avoid the conclusion that a great deal of what has been accomplished, including much that has been called "rationalization," is really not rationalization at all. Excess plant capacity prevails in coal mining, coke production, gas production, and in the output of many of the more important by-products. The syndicates have been unable either to equate supply to current needs or to bring any degree of order out of the existing marketing chaos.

Duplicate wholesale and retail selling agencies, duplicate railroad switches, yards, bunkers, offices, trucks, and other marketing equipment, are the rule, not the exception, in every section of the country. Taking the industry as a whole, it is probable that this duplication would sum to a total from 50 to 100 per cent in excess of the requirements which a planned and efficient organization would have stipulated.[82] While no worse than the case of the same industries in England and the United States, one may doubt whether the coal situation in Germany has been helped at all because of the existence of the *Reichskohlenverband*.

Even on the more purely technological side, the German picture is far from uniform. Technically obsolete mines still operate, thanks to capital "write-offs," side by side with those which have been modernized. Technically obsolete methods and equipment are used in many mines where all other operations have been brought strictly up to date. In general, little if any attention has been paid to the human factor. What labor has gained has been at the cost of bitter and protracted struggle or through the instrumentality of the government, and has had little to do with factors of efficiency or attempts to better morale. Aside from the vicious and anti-social attempt of the *DINTA* organization, the labor problem has been handled in much the same way as the problems of mechanization and technical reorganization have been treated; that is to say, in a piecemeal and disorderly fashion, without regard to or understanding of the numerous cost, efficiency, and human variables involved, and without any notion of the bearing of changes made in any one sector upon the solution of problems affecting the industry as a whole.

What has been achieved in more rational integration and coordination of interdependent industrial processes for the industry as a whole may be taken as the product more of trial and error than of careful planning. Planning, where it has appeared at all, has been entirely of a corporate and intercorporate character. In many respects these plans have served to improve immensely the relationships existing between technologically and chemically related industries. Such is the case with respect to steel processing, coal mining, coke production, long-distance gas distribution, and by-products utilization. But even these improvements have been nullified largely, if not entirely, by failure to realize and act upon some of the more important organizational implications of the steps taken. Thus, in elaborating the long-distance gas-supply system, no general solution has been found for the problem of displaced local gas systems. No examination has

[82] This excess capacity is to be found in practically every branch of the coal and coal-products industry, and in every district in the Reich. Thus the Enquete Ausschuss estimated that the coking industry of the Rhine-Westphalian district was capable of producing 40 to 42 million tons of coke in the fiscal year 1928–1929. Actual production in that year—the highest output ever recorded for the district—was but 28.6 million tons. In the same year it was estimated that most of the gas works had an excess capacity of at least 20 per cent. In the distribution field the excess capacity must certainly be greater than in any of the production branches.—*Enquete Ausschuss,* III:32, 33 ff.

been made of the extent to which gas duplicates electric-energy systems, dispenses with rail and other transportation networks as carrier of fuel, or renders superfluous coal and other fuel distribution agencies.

Taking the industry as a whole, perhaps no better example could be offered of the danger of attempting to mix two more or less antithetical theories of control and organization. If laissez faire was to be abandoned, the logical alternative was reorganization of all phases of the industry in terms of a comprehensive and closely integrated plan which would necessitate hewing to some well-defined set of social objectives. If laissez faire was to be kept, no more mistaken piece of legislation than the *Reichskohlengesetz* could be imagined, and a more foolish policy than official toleration of the big combines and cartels could scarcely have been pursued. The compromise policy adopted has not worked well in the past; there is no reason for believing that it will work much better in the future.

CHAPTER VI

THE IRON AND STEEL INDUSTRY

1. THE PEACE TREATY AND THE PROBLEMS OF REORGANIZATION

THE DISASTROUS EFFECTS of the Versailles settlement upon the German national system were probably felt more acutely in the iron and steel industries than in other economic sectors. The Allies, in compelling the disarmament of Germany, forced her iron and steel industries to undergo complete reorganization. In many cases this meant not only revamping and regrouping of plants, but also complete reorientation. In the case of Krupp, for example, the change from almost exclusive refining and manufacture for war purposes to production of such commodities as agricultural machinery, trucks, omnibuses, cash registers, household equipment, and structural steel, practically called for a rebuilding of the enterprise from top to bottom.

The problems which faced the industry when stabilization came were many and complex. While the exigencies of war had left the German plants in a state of relative technical obsolescence, several foreign countries—the United States in particular—had been able to expand greatly, and to increase the efficiency of their steel industries. Further, the treaty presented to Germany's former war enemies and peace-time competitors large percentages of her most modern equipment for iron and steel production. Inclusive of Luxemburg and the Saar in the west, and ceded sections in Upper Silesia, Germany lost (judged by output) 43.4 per cent of her pig iron, 36.3 per cent of her crude "fluid-process" steel (*Flussstahl*), 53.9 per cent of her steel bloom (for market purposes), and 30.5 per cent of her finished rolling-mill pre-war productive capacity. Aside from the fact that these plants in the ceded western territory were the best and most modern, and that their loss immensely strengthened the French, Belgian, and Polish steel interests in the competition for foreign markets, the new alignment destroyed the whole closely knit organic unity of the German iron and steel industry. Blast furnaces and steel mills had been located in Lorraine and Luxemburg in order to take advantage of geographical specialization, and to save on shipping costs. Crude iron and steel produced in these areas were shipped eastward to rolling mills, foundries, tube and wire plants, etc., located nearer domestic markets for their finished products. Transportation costs were less for pig iron and steel billets than for iron ore, because of the larger tonnage involved in shipping ore. Further, cars traveling eastward with crude iron and steel products were assured of a return load of coke needed for the mills in the west, thus making possible a better transportation load factor, and consequently lower shipping expenses.

Not only was the German steel industry deprived of these economies, but it also lost well over half of its Bessemer iron, and nearly half of its Bessemer steel capacity[1] under circumstances in which iron mills were separated from steel plants, steel mills from rolling mills, rolling mills from machine manufacturing establishments, the bulk of the western (now French and Belgian) steel industry from its coal and coke supply, and the eastern (German) industry from its principal ore supply. Nowhere in the world had an industrial region developed on a similar scale an organic, interdependent, unified, and technically balanced system comparable to that which the Allies proceeded to split wide open in the Rhineland area. Nowhere and at no time in modern history has the technical and commercial folly of economic nationalism demonstrated itself on such an impressive scale as in this settlement. The splitting up of the Ruhr and Upper Silesian districts temporarily ruined the most important key industry of Germany; it has been among the causally significant factors which brought the country to its knees in 1920, 1924, and 1929, and it has played an important though little understood rôle in the present world-wide depression. In the face of general political instability and shortage of capital, the German iron and steel industry presented under these circumstances a problem in rationalization of major proportions, and, at the same time, of vital significance to the economic life of Germany and the future of Europe.

2. THE PROBLEM OF ORE SUPPLY

The task of reorganizing the German iron and steel industry in conformity with the needs and requirements of the post-war period was complicated to an unusual extent by the loss of the most important ore resources. The Versailles treaty deprived Germany of 72 per cent of her iron ore reserves. Whereas about 60 per cent of the 1913 pig iron production came from domestic ores, these were able to supply but 18 per cent of the total in 1925, and 11.8 per cent[2] in 1927. Since ore costs amount to about one-third of the expenses of rolled steel products,

[1] The loss of Bessemer iron and steel productive capacity, coupled with cession of Lorraine ore, temporarily increased the relative importance of the open-hearth (Siemens-Martin) process in Germany. A larger percentage of open-hearth capacity remained. In addition the process is more readily adapted to use of scrap of varying qualities, or of mixtures of scrap and ore of varying proportions, and to temporary interruptions in operation than the Bessemer process. The decline in scrap supply, however, and the conclusion of delivery arrangements for foreign, principally Swedish, ores, has reversed this trend more recently.

[2] *Enquete Ausschuss,* "Die Rohstoffversorgung der deutschen eisenerzeugenden Industrie" (III, "Unterausschuss"; 1928). This volume will be referred to as E. A., III (1) to differentiate it from the second volume relating to the iron and steel industry, "Die deutsche eisenerzeugende

and from 55 to 60 per cent of the production cost of Bessemer pig iron, the importance of these losses to the iron and steel industry, and to the entire German national economic system, can scarcely be overestimated.

The principal loss was that of the Minette ore of the Lorraine district. Although this ore had a comparatively low iron content (34 per cent approximately) and was fairly rich in phosphorus, it was used extensively because shipping expenses were low. After the war, Germany was unable to make extensive use of these resources for a number of reasons. Aside from the fact that ownership passed into the hands of French and Belgian steel interests, and that the French invasion and occupation made difficult, and at first impossible, the reestablishment of normal business relations with western ore producers, the rapid expansion of iron and steel production in France and Belgium absorbed the bulk of the domestic ore output.

For this development pre-war conditions were in part responsible. Prior to 1914 progress in fuel economy, making it necessary to use less and less coke per ton of steel produced, and the desire to be near the most important foreign steel markets, had resulted in the gradual shift in the location of the new iron and steel works away from coal and towards ore, or from the Ruhr area over towards Luxemburg and Lorraine. The result was that the cession of Lorraine to France and of Luxemburg to Belgium, meant a loss of 48.2 per cent of western German pre-war iron ore, and about 19 per cent of iron and steel capacity (1913 production taken as base). The iron and steel works built in these areas were the newest, best, and most modern existing in Germany. Their acquisition by Belgium and France endowed these countries with productive equipment capable of absorbing most of the domestic ore output.

The bulk of the imported ores now come from Sweden,[3] Germany taking 82 per cent of Swedish output in 1926. Increased freight charges incident to the greater shipping distance are largely offset by the higher iron content of Swedish ores, the percentage (by weight) averaging well over 60 per cent. The same holds true for most of the other imported ores, the Brazilian in particular averaging

Industrie," hereafter (in this chapter) referred to as E. A., III (2). The figures given above do not check exactly with other data available, but this is largely because of differences in methods of reckoning pure iron content.

[3] German importation of iron ore (reduced to terms of pure iron content) by countries for various years, in units of 1,000 tons, was as follows:*

Year	France	Belgium, Luxemburg	Sweden, Norway	Total (three) preceding columns	Other countries
Average 1909–1913	870.8	113.7	2,225.5	3,210,0	2,428.3
1913	1,410.0	63.6	2,934.6	4,408.2	2,651.9
1925	408.8	109.5	4,475.7	4,994.0	275.4
1926	537.2	86.9	3,566.3	4,186.4	872.2
1927	966.8	87.9	5,361.1	6,415.8	2,288.6

* Source: E. A., III (1): 10.

over 67 per cent.[4] Some of these ores are lacking in phosphorus, an essential ingredient in the smelting process. But a method has been discovered whereby phosphorus in the form of a chalk can be introduced directly into the furnaces in order to make up for any deficiency in the ore on this account.

The problem of manganese supply is not serious. The increased use of scrap was largely responsible for the fact that while the iron and steel output in 1925 was well over two-thirds of the 1913 total, the quantity of ore containing more than 30 per cent pure manganese had shrunk from 700,000 to 250,000 tons. Over half of the current supply comes from domestic sources, Siegerland ore containing manganese ranging from 6 to 9 per cent pure. The remainder comes from the Caucasus or Brazil.

Most of the domestic ores come from three districts, Siegerland, Lahn-Dill, and Ilsede. As indicated before, however, the total reserves are not large,[5] and their pure iron content is comparatively low as is shown by the fact that while they supplied 13.6 per cent of the ore in 1925, they contributed only 11.8 per cent of the iron produced.[6]

More important than the ore supply from the domestic point of view is the increased use of scrap iron and steel. Low-quality scrap is used in the making of iron and high-quality scrap in the production of steel without the interpolation of the pig iron stage. About one-third of the scrap supply in the first few

[4] The iron content of the various imported ores is as follows:*

	Percentage
French Minette	33 to 37
Normandy	45 (approx.)
Algeria-Tunis	58
Brazil	67 to 72
Sweden	58 to 72
Norway	40 to 50
Krivoj-Rog	55 to 69
Poland	27 to 39

* Source: *ibid.*, p. 47.

The percentage of pure manganese in Caucasian and Brazilian manganese ores ranges around 50 per cent, with the Brazilian somewhat the lower of the two.

[5] Ore resources of the more important European countries are as follows:*

Country	Ore	Metallic content	Percentage of European total	Percentage of world supply
	In million tons		In iron-metal content	
France	9,763.5	3,320.0	50.4	18.2
Great Britain	2,929.3	862.2	13.0	4.7
Sweden	1,335.3	845.0	12.8	4.6
Germany	1,117.6	391.2	6.0	2.1
Spain	711.0	349.0	5.3	1.9
Russia	830.9	376.4	5.7	2.0
All other	1,232.6	448.5	6.8	2.5
Totals	17,920.2	6,592.3	100.0	36.0

* Source: *ibid.*, p. 55.

[6] Of the pure iron-ore tonnage (in units of 1,000 tons) Siegerland produced, in 1929, 7.5 per cent, Lahn-Dill 1.3 per cent, and Ilsede 1.3 per cent of German iron supply.—Source: *ibid.*, p. 56.

years after stabilization was by-product in origin, coming from blooming, rolling and pipe mills, machine shops, etc. The ratio of such "new scrap" to the raw materials from which it is a by-product is relatively constant, and this metal source affords a fairly dependable supply. "Old scrap" was particularly important during the first few post-war years, largely because of the wrecking of old plants involved in reorganization of the steel works, and because of the large supply of war materials available for this purpose. Because of these facts, the percentage of scrap to total metallic input had risen from 32 per cent in 1913 to 44 per cent in 1924. The subsequent decline in the use of scrap resulted largely from exhaustion of the more important post-war sources of supply. Although it is impossible to gauge the future supply of old scrap,[7] there can be no doubt that its relative importance as a raw material source will be much greater than it was in the pre-war period.[8]

3. CORPORATE REORGANIZATION AND CONCENTRATION OF OWNERSHIP

In indemnifying the steel concerns for property lost by cession of territory to the Allies under the Versailles treaty, the German government stipulated that the funds should be used for reorganizing old and constructing new plant and equipment. The agreement had to be discharged, however, at a time when the steel industry was faced with a general shortage of both coal and metalliferous supplies. The result was that every company in the field attempted first to secure its own coal and ore reserves, and then to acquire, build, or enlarge its coking plants and iron and steel works. The coal and ore shortage problem being shortly overcome, competition with foreign interests soon showed the existence of excess plant capacity as gauged by existing markets. This led the steel companies to reach out in the other direction for rolling, tube, and wire mills, machine manufacturing plants, and special marketing facilities. Dominant tendencies in the direction of vertical integration were further enhanced by the inflation, and were only brought to an end with the stabilization in 1924.

With the inauguration of the Dawes plan, conditions in the steel industry showed clearly for the first time the need for fundamental and thoroughgoing reorganization. The crash of the huge and unwieldy Stinnes-controlled *Siemens-Rhein-Elbe-Schuckert-Union* in 1925 paved the way for a new alignment.

[7] See the ingenious attempts by Karl Lange, Peterson, Reichert, and others to estimate the scrap supply for the future—*ibid.*, pp. 285–327. The immediate supply has been somewhat lessened by several developments, among which the increased life of various manufactured steel products because of new methods of treatment, and the increased use of enameled goods, metal-lic alloys, new types of metals, and reinforced concrete may be taken as typical. Increased use of steel in relatively perishable objects, however, somewhat offsets these factors.

[8] Coke, limestone, and power supplies are not serious problems for the German iron and steel industries. These are available in great abundance in the districts in which the heavy industries are domiciled.

Once reorganization was begun, the obstacles to be overcome in the corporate realignment were not so serious as might at first have been supposed. The industry had long been dominated by a small group of large concerns working in close harmony with each other. After the leaders of these concerns had been convinced that reorganization was inevitable, the program moved with great rapidity. Following extensive negotiation, a series of new combines moved into the picture, the most important of which was the *Vereinigte Stahlwerke A. G.*, formed by the union of the principal properties of four of the largest steel companies in Germany, the *Rhein-Elbe-Union, Thyssen, Phoenix,* and the *Rheinische Stahlwerke*. In the east a similar move towards horizontal combination resulted in the founding of the *Vereinigte Oberschlesische Hüttenwerke A. G.*, controlled by the reorganized *Mitteldeutsche Stahlwerke A. G.* This latter company is, in turn, under the control of the *Vereinigte Stahlwerke A. G.* Thus, while the *Vereinigte Stahlwerke A. G.*, founded with a capital of 800,000,000 marks and normally employing about 200,000 persons, takes its place as the largest steel concern in Europe, and the third largest corporation in Germany, following the *Reichsbahn* and the *I. G. Farbenindustrie*, its effective power is much greater than these facts would indicate.

The *Krupp* concern, after taking part in the negotiations leading up to the founding of the *Vereinigte Stahlwerke*, decided not to enter the combine. Five other large concerns, *Kloeckner, Hoesch, Gutehoffnungshütte, Mannesmann,* and *Stumm*, refused invitations to enter into the negotiations at all. A substantial interest in *Stumm* has subsequently been acquired by the new trust.

The extent to which the German steel industry has been centralized from a corporate and managerial point of view is indicated by the facts that three concerns with outputs of 1,000,000 tons or over produced, in 1929, 68.8 per cent of the total pig iron output; four others were responsible for 68.3 per cent of crude steel output; four concerns with outputs of 20,000 tons or over produced 39.8 per cent of steel castings; three concerns with 150,000 tons output or over produced 79.6 per cent of semi-finished steel; three concerns with 700,000 tons output or over produced 55.8 per cent of finished rolling-mill output.[9]

The dominating position of the *Vereinigte Stahlwerke* is shown by the fact that in recent years it has produced about 50 per cent of the pig iron, 43 per cent

[9] E. A., III (2):36–39. Production of pig iron and crude steel in the years 1928–1929 for the larger concerns was as follows:*

	Pig iron (tons)		Crude steel (tons)	
	1929	1928	1929	1928
Vereinigte Stahlwerke	6,007,953	6,518,682	6,419,796	6,945,186
Krupp	1,292,440	1,359,417	1,587,332	1,722,854
Gutehoffnungshütte	923,805	1,001,524	1,066,340	1,127,551
Kloeckner-Werke	732,047	777,172	876,072	885,431
Hoesch	670,823	752,044	890,642	971,869
Oberhütten	180,733	203,636	432,306	427,261
Mitteldeutsche Stahlwerke	....	....	538,167	477,511

* Source: *Das Spezial Archiv*, "Die deutsche Eisen und Stahl-Industrie" (1930): 24. Note that the last two concerns might be grouped under the Vereinigte Stahlwerke, as indicated above.

of the crude steel, and 40 per cent of the rolling-mill output, and by the quota shares, shown in table 11, in the various iron and steel associations:[10]

TABLE 11

Association	Quota as of September 30, 1929, in percentage of total
Pig iron:	
Association participation	38.445
Consumption	55.585
Crude steel	38.298
"A"—Products	40.023
Bar iron	30.724
Band iron, inland and foreign	38.955
Thick sheet	39.742
Rolled wire	29.161
Wire	22.224
Pipes	50.613

Had the depression not set in during 1928, there is no reason for believing the process of horizontal and vertical integration would have ceased. Records currently compiled by *Die Wirtschaftskurve* and other publications have shown steady expansion of all the larger concerns, the *Vereinigte Stahlwerke* in particular, since 1926. Evidence of close cooperation between these combines is everywhere at hand. The eventual establishment of a single all-embracing combine or effective combination of interest for the iron and steel industry seems to be clearly indicated by the trend of events.

4. INTERNAL SYSTEMATIZATION

Amalgamation made it possible for each of the larger concerns to carry through systematic internal reorganization under quite favorable conditions. Aided by foreign loans, and encouraged by the prospect of general world-wide economic

[10] E. A., III (2):32. *Die Wirtschaftskurve*, Heft 4 (1926):448, offered the following table comparing the Vereinigte Stahlwerke with the United States Steel Corporation for the year in which the former was founded (1926).*

	United States Steel	Vereinigte Stahlwerke
Coal production	27 million tons	30 million tons
Pig iron production	13 million tons	4.8 million tons
Steel production	17 million tons	5.0 million tons
(National production)	(46.1)	(12.1)
Blast-furnace plants	123	87
Foundries	25	14
Locomotives	1,483	411
Employees	247,000	146,000
Capital (marks)	3,648 million	925 million
Bonds	1,474 million	424.9 million

* NOTE: These data do not check in all particulars with others available.

recovery from the disastrous conditions of the war and immediate post-war years, they made attempts to regroup and modernize technical plant and equipment and marketing facilities on a most comprehensive scale. Plants technically obsolete, and badly located with respect to raw materials, markets, or other plants with which they were closely related in the technique of production, were either completely reorganized or closed down permanently. The *Vereinigte Stahlwerke,* for example, had by 1930 in large part carried through plans for closing down completely 7 smelting works equipped with 19 blast furnaces, and 8 steel plants equipped with 39 open-hearth furnaces.

With this policy went the plan for concentrating the manufacture of particular products in a few specially equipped and favorably located plants. Whereas previously iron and steel products of nearly all types had been produced in every large works, each plant was now compelled to specialize upon one or a small number of similar products. In the case of the *Vereinigte Stahlwerke,* once more, "production is now so regulated that production for export—inclusive of indirect export—comprising from 40 to 50 per cent of the entire market, is concentrated on the Rhine. The Groups *Hörde* and *Dortmund* now export workshop products only; they no longer export any rolled materials. Rail production, formerly divided among nine different plants, is now confined to a single plant in which 80 to 90 per cent of permanent-way steel is produced. Semi-finished output has been confined to two or three plants, and bar iron production has already been so concentrated that the *Rhine* Group produces about 75 per cent of the total output."[11] Plants located on the Rhine or its tributaries, canals, or other navigable waterways specialize on heavy crude products. Plants located in the interior—as in the case of nearly all the plants of the *Mitteldeutsche Stahlwerke*—specialize in more highly refined products and those which cost less to transport.

Perhaps even more important was the opportunity to rectify the prevailing bad proportioning of plant capacities in various stages of the steel production process. It was possible, within the confines of the bigger concerns at least, to adjust iron smelting to steel production, steel production to rolling-mill capacity, coal ouput to coking requirements, coke output to the consumption of the steel industry, etc., under conditions in which capacity at any one stage could be neatly adjusted to requirements in every other stage. Where there was a shortage of blast furnaces on account of treaty concessions, new plants could be built without the hazard (within the individual concern) that the new capacity would overshoot the consumptive power of steel and rolling mills. Or where these were to be found in excess, the more poorly equipped and badly located plants could be scrapped in whole or in part. That is to say, amalgamation made possible systematic planning within the limits set by the scope of the owned properties and communities of interest of the individual enterprise.

[11] E. A., III (2):131–132.

Engineering considerations quite early showed the advantage of combining hitherto separate plants into single compactly organized units. Considerable progress had been made before the war in this direction. During the reorganization period plants combining most or all of the stages from extraction of raw materials through to refinishing processes became the rule rather than the exception. Pure rolling mills, for example, are now practically non-existent. Steel plants are nearly always attached directly to iron smelting works, and these in turn to coal mines, coking ovens, and, where possible (Siegerland), to iron ore extraction. Steel and rolling mills are usually combined with pipe, wire, bar iron, special alloy, heavy machinery, and other special works.

Perhaps the most powerful impetus behind this technical integration has been development in the field of fuel economy. Special coal washeries, and sorting and mixing plants have made possible delivery to the blast furnaces of a more standard and better quality coke. More careful selections of ores, the construction of special ore pre-treating plants, larger and more efficient blast furnaces, more exact control over furnaces in blast, and numerous other changes have served to lower the amount of coke required per ton of pig iron produced. One thousand tons of pig iron in 1913 required the consumption of 1,115 tons of coke; by 1924 this had fallen to 1,079, and by 1929 to 1,015.[12]

Instead of casting the molten metal in pigs, it is now taken immediately to the converters; from the converters it is poured into molds where it is allowed to harden only enough to make it possible, after reheating to obtain uniform temperature, to send the ingots immediately to the rolling mills, where the metal is turned directly into bars, wire, rails, beams, etc. The fuel saving by this process of integration has been enormous. Perfection of the process has had the result that but 6 million thermal units are now required per ton of crude steel as contrasted to 15 million in 1900. At the 1928 rate of steel production, this would have amounted to a saving of 23 million tons of coal over that which would have been required in 1900.[13]

Perhaps even greater economies have been effected by reorganization of the heating and power systems. As mentioned above,[14] the new coke ovens have been built with a view to maximum utilization of all by-products. Most important of these has been coke-oven gas. The old coke batteries, relatively inefficient though they were, had supplied enough gas to meet the bulk of the fuel needs of the iron and steel plants to which they were attached. Blast-furnace gas, con-

---

[12] E. A., III (2):26. The fact that iron ores now commonly in use in Germany have a much higher iron content may be responsible for the major economy here. Ore with 55–60 per cent pure iron content now requires but 0.9 ton of coke, while Minette ore, with a corresponding iron content of approximately 35 per cent, requires 1.1 tons of coke. The average for the Saar and Lorraine in 1913, however, was 1.8 tons of coke with ore which probably did not exceed 35 per cent pure iron content.

[13] Hans J. Schneider, *Der Wiederaufbau der Grosseisenindustrie an Rhein und Ruhr* (Berlin, 1930):67.

[14] See pp. 83–84.

siderably lower in quality, had been allowed to go to waste. The new technical plans called for utilizing blast-furnace gas as far as possible, and setting free the much larger quantity of coke-oven gas for use in neighboring plants or for sale to the public. If sufficient coke is produced on the premises to meet the requirements of the iron and steel plant, the amount of coke-oven gas that must be disposed of will be quite large, inasmuch as the blast-furnace gas will usually suffice for all local fuel and power needs.

As new plants were acquired or constructed in the immediate neighborhood, gas firing could be introduced at a considerable saving. Interconnecting pipe systems have been built by all the big plants, the *Vereinigte Stahlwerke* alone having constructed over 30 kilometers of such lines. Common fuel supply, however, becomes impossible for plants some distance apart unless a long-distance gas system can be constructed. It was to meet this need that the *Ruhrgas* system previously described was developed. The initiative was taken by the steel concerns, Vögler, chairman of the *Vereinigte Stahlwerke,* being also chairman of the new gas company. Nearly all the company's new finishing mills located to the east of the Ruhr district proper are supplied through the mains of *Ruhrgas,* although the gas fed into the system by the cokeries to the west is still considerably greater than these branches can absorb.[15] The remainder is sold directly to *Ruhrgas* for general distribution purposes.

5. STANDARDIZATION AND MECHANIZATION

If the full economies of mass production were to be realized, it was necessary for concentration of production of particular products in particular plants to be accompanied by a considerable degree of standardization in materials and processes. Here the industry has stumbled on one of its most perplexing problems. Economy in production encouraged simplification of steel types, shapes, and varieties as far as possible. Yet, because the iron and steel industry acts as feeder of a basic raw material to many different types of industries, producing many different types of goods and, consequently, having highly specialized demands, and because metallurgical research has opened up the prospect of an almost unlimited variety of steel alloys, there has been a tendency steadily to increase types of product. Without standards a high degree of mechanization is not possible, and without increased mechanization steel prices must remain prohibitively high. Many people feared, however, that standardization would render technical change impossible except within narrow limits, and that standards

[15] "The total consumption of our works via the western main of the Ruhrgas A. G. exceeded 50 million cubic meters during the business year; a total of 31.7 million cubic meters of long-distance gas was taken by way of the South Westphalian main. Our production of coking-plant gas amounted to 3,673 billion cubic meters. By this expansion of our gas activities, almost all flare losses were obviated."—Vereinigte Stahlwerke A. G., *Viertes Geschäftsjahr,* 1928–1929, p. 14.

would in general strangle progress, not only in the steel industry itself, but also in all industries directly or indirectly dependent upon it for metallic products.

Aside from simplification in sizes, shapes, and varieties, the problem of standardization was further complicated by the general lack of adequate scientific and engineering criteria of a quantitative character. Neither chemical analysis nor mechanical tests have thus far been able to give numerical and exhaustive information about the trustworthiness of performance. Standards of productive methods, the general smelting procedure, the degree of deoxidation, the uniformity of chemical composition, the amount of non-metallic ingredients, and other factors are important but not exact and conclusive for gauging the probable performance of a steel product. For refined steels, in particular, the number of chemical and physical variables has rendered the problem of standards extremely difficult of solution.[16] Even then, methods were frequently patented, and special types of steel were trade marked under circumstances in which standardization was practically impossible.

Nevertheless, important work has been done in this field. The first standard specifications for boiler-plate were written in Wurzburg as early as 1881, and international standards have been in use in this field since 1888.[17] Before the war various sections of the machine industry, the railroads, shipbuilding, the army and navy, and numerous other special-interest groups had established standards for iron and steel products. Subsequently the *Deutscher Normenausschuss* has been able through its various special committees to push the work of iron and steel standardization with considerable success. In cooperation with special consumer groups in various branches of the machine, electro-technical, railroad, and other industries, standards have been established for sizes, shapes, varieties, technical nomenclature, methods of processing and testing, physical and chemical properties of pure and alloyed steels, etc. On the whole, however, standardization in the steel industry is still in its infancy. Progress along this line will be slowed down as long as there are in existence large numbers of small-scale producers of specialty iron and steel goods, and where the disposition, and often the opportunity, to standardize is lacking.

German writers are inclined—with considerable justice—to ascribe the relatively high efficiency of American steel production to the ability to specialize because of the existence of a large free market for highly standardized goods. Rolls do not need to be changed so often, highly specialized plant, machinery, and equipment can be utilized to advantage, quality control becomes easier and more automatic, the task of supervision is less complicated, and numerous other advantages accrue to standardized mass production.

---

[16] Compare "Entwicklung der Normung der legierten Stähle und augenblicklicher Stand der Arbeiten," a paper submitted to the Magdeburg meeting of the Deutscher Normenausschuss, April 28, 1928.

[17] This standards work formed the basis for later legislation designed to lower boiler-explosion hazards. There is an immense literature on the subject.

Strenuous efforts have been made since the stabilization to standardize and specialize after the American fashion. With plant specialization went a systematic attempt to limit the variety of output of the particular product. With success along this line mechanization has proceeded apace. Rolling-mill ways have been lengthened, almost all rolling, handling, transport, trimming, and miscellaneous operations, the preparation and hoisting of ores and coke, all coke-oven and blast-furnace work, and the bulk of the miscellaneous heavy and routine work has been mechanized. Wherever possible, electrically driven machinery has been substituted for steam driven machinery and prime movers. Turbines have been substituted for reciprocating engines in the air and gas compression systems; numerous changes have been made in the mechanical equipment which have brought almost unbelievable economies. One change in the air pre-heating system resulted in a decrease in gas consumption of 38 per cent. Mechanization, standardization, and continuous processing in fine plate rolling mills have resulted in wage savings (via personnel reduction) of 80 per cent, in a decline of about one-third in power consumption, and in a reduction in the losses resulting from corrosion and scrap by about one-half, without, at the same time, the investment in plant being materially increased.[18]

These changes have made it possible to overhaul radically the key operating units in the iron and steel stages. Table 12, showing the number of furnaces in blast and the average output per furnace, indicates pretty well the extent to which the smelting process has been overhauled.[19]

TABLE 12

Year	Number of establishments	Number of blast furnaces		Total number of weeks in operation	Average capacity duration of operation per furnace in weeks	Average production per furnace and week in tons	Total production, 1,000 tons
		Existing at end of year	In operation				
1913	70	216	204	9,687	47.5	1,127	10,916
1924	55	193	138	4,783	34.3	1,655	6,267
1925	56	200	141	5,408	38.4	1,866	7,914
1926	51	183	127	4,456	35.1	2,162	7,769
1927	48	172	134	5,811	43.4	2,252	10,337
1928	46	170	125	5,140	41.1	2,296	11,804
1929	45	165	115	5,153	44.8	2,567	13,240

The average increase of well over 100 per cent in blast-furnace capacity since 1913 becomes even more significant when it is compared with English and American figures. In 1925 average annual output per furnace in blast was 138,000

18 "Die Rationalisierung der eisenschaffenden Industrie," *Magazin der Wirtschaft* (October 3, 1930):1846–1851.

19 E. A., III (2):33.

tons in the United States, 96,000 tons in Germany, and 41,354 tons in England. By 1928 German figures for the Rhineland-Westphalian district were beginning to approximate American output in production per blast furnace; the increase being from 1,491 tons per week in 1913, 3,207 tons per week in 1928, with annual output in the latter year slightly in excess of 127,000 tons. By 1929 the annual output had increased to 130,000 tons.

Similar results are shown by changes in steel production in table 13 (p. 116).[20] The output is thus shown to have increased by some 40 per cent per Bessemer oven and 35 per cent per open-hearth oven in the period from 1913 to 1929. As contrasted with England, where average annual steel output per oven was approximately 15,000 tons in 1927, the German ovens were producing 27,000 tons.

Similar increases could be shown for the various effective operating units in the different stages of iron and steel production. All these changes are promoted and accompanied by, at the same time that they in turn encourage and require, increased mechanization. Every change in one direction—further specialization, standardization of products and processes, mechanization, more efficient power and fuel systems, or increased blast furnace, steel oven or rolling mill capacity—encourages and shows the way towards further improvements in other parts of the interlocking sequence of productive operations. When changes are systematically planned and carried through, and when plans are guided and motivated by technical considerations alone, the possibilities have proved themselves to be much greater than even the most optimistic had expected. In but a very limited number of plants—the *August Thyssenhütte* alone of the *Vereinigte Stahlwerke* plants—has the technical reorganization been more or less completely rounded out. Drastic and far-reaching as the technical changes have been in many segments, the reorganization of the steel industry as a whole in these respects is far from complete; in many places it has scarcely begun.

6. BY-PRODUCTS UTILIZATION

Reorganization along the lines previously mentioned required the investment of large sums of money. While it is very difficult to estimate the amounts so utilized on account of complicating factors surrounding the pre-stabilization period, their total is certainly very great. The *Vereinigte Stahlwerke* alone reports a total expenditure of 363 million marks for depreciation, and a somewhat smaller sum for purposes of plant reorganization and new construction for the first five years of its corporate existence.[21]

Now, such heavy investment, with the consequent shifting in the ratio of overhead to variable costs, has necessitated paying unusually close attention to reduction of all miscellaneous costs and to the exploitation of all possible income

[20] *Ibid.*, p. 35.

[21] Vereinigte Stahlwerke, *Bericht über das fünfte Geschäftsjahr* (Düsseldorf, 1931).

TABLE 13

STEEL PRODUCTS BY TYPE OF PROCESS (1913–1929)

Year	Fluid process steel works					Steel ingot production						
	Number of plants	Number of			Total steel ovens*	Total from			Per furnace			Total per plant†
		Bessemer ovens	Open-hearth ovens	Electric and crucible steel ovens		Bessemer ovens	Open-hearth ovens	Electric and crucible steel ovens	Bessemer ovens	Open-hearth ovens	Electric and crucible steel ovens	
						1,000 tons						
1913	85	59	362	129	563	5,166	6,147	125	87.7	16.9	0.9	138.4
1924	103	60	466	137	674	3,990	5,462	90	66.5	11.7	0.6	94.2
1925	106	62	470	156	705	5,111	6,607	126	82.4	14.1	0.8	113.7
1926	97	63	430	137	641	5,453	6,582	66	86.6	15.3	0.5	126.1
1927	87	62	377	144	590	6,906	8,879	151	111.4	23.6	1.1	185.3
1928	85	62	372	139	580	6,542	7,490	136	105.5	20.0	0.9	168.4
1929	80	68	359	109	547	7,390	8,232	140	108.7	22.9	1.3	199.0
FOR THE RHINELAND-WESTPHALIAN DISTRICT ALONE												
1913	57	47	271	117	435	4,636	4,726	124	98.7	17.4	1.1	171.9
1925	74	50	346	139	535	4,505	5,038	115	90.1	14.3	0.8	132.7
1927	60	48	274	132	454	6,114	6,515	142	127.4	23.8	1.1	215.1
1929	....	....	......	......	......	....	....	......	....	....	......	....

* Includes Bessemer ovens.

† Includes steel castings.

sources. While by-products utilization has not, in some respects at least, played quite such a dominating rôle in the iron and steel industry as in the case of coal and lignite, its importance has been fully recognized and its possibilities have been looked into with considerable care.

The most fruitful field for work in this direction has already been examined in the chapter dealing with the coal industry. The steel companies have been the leaders in the reorganization of mining operations and the chemical treatment and refining of various types of coals, and have taken the initiative in the development of the new central cokeries and long-distance gas-supply systems. The extent to which the steel industry has taken advantage of these opportunities is indicated by the productive record of the *Vereinigte Stahlwerke* for the last two reported business years[22] and is shown in table 14.

TABLE 14

	1928–1929 (tons)	1929–1930 (tons)
Coal	27,241,990	25,722,500
Coke	9,627,304	9,338,172
Crude tar	356,640	347,285
Ammonia	129,143	128,951
Crude benzol	90,888	92,435
Refined benzol	78,902	81,711
Tar distillation products	127,505	124,515
Lubricants	4,383	4,121

The large quantities of coke-oven gas available for transmission through long-distance mains and for sale to the general public result mainly from utilization of the former waste blast-furnace gas and its substitution for the coke-oven product.[23] This change has made it possible to recover the very considerable quantities of dust, containing on the average about 30 per cent pure iron, which formerly passed off with the gas, and to return it to the furnace in the form of briquets. Slag, which was formerly piled up in huge mounds as a waste product, is now utilized almost entirely in the form of cement and special building-stone compounds. Portions of it are used as railroad bed and in public road construction; it is also used as an ingredient in concrete and mortar preparations. From the Bessemer (Thomas) steel furnaces very considerable quantities of slag high in phosphorus are recovered and ground into a meal (*Thomasmehl*) to be sold as a valuable fertilizer. The domestic production of Thomas meal is very great; in 1928 over 436,000 tons of this fertilizer were sold abroad.

[22] *Ibid.*, pp. 12–13, and report for previous year, p. 14.

[23] Approximately 1,500 cubic meters more gas is available per ton of pig iron produced than before the war. See the testimony of Dr. Peterson, E. A., III (2):154.

Mention should also be made here of the considerable decrease in certain peculiar types of by-products as a result of technical reorganization. Specialization, research in metallurgical methods, and standardization have made it possible to increase materially the rigidity of quality control and hence to eliminate completely "waste batches" at any stage of the process, and to cut down on the percentage of new scrap due to trimming and other causes.

In no other place are the advantages of large-scale operation, continuous production, vertical organization, and unified control more amply demonstrated than in by-product utilization. Without blast furnaces it is impossible for steel plants to take advantage of the economy involved in substitution of blast-furnace for coke-oven gas. Without large-scale production it would scarcely pay to attempt recovery of chemicals, Thomas meal, cement or other by-products. Without integration the contributions made to the industry by way of by-product exploitation would be largely lost, and the consequent expenses of operation would be much higher than they are at present. Without fairly continuous operation it would not be feasible to attempt recovery of certain by-products, such as gas, except to a very limited extent.

7. RESEARCH AND SCIENTIFIC MANAGEMENT

In all stages and processes of the reorganization which has been undertaken in the German steel industry, research has played a most unusual rôle. Whether attention is fixed upon cost reduction, quality improvement, standardization, by-product utilization, or other phases of the industry, systematization and technical progress are based and dependent upon careful, exhaustive, continuous, cooperative, and integrated research. Comparative and experimental research work ranges, in the steel industry, all the way from the most abstruse problems of physics and chemistry to the matter of planned organization of internal and external productive and commercial processes. It is neither possible nor necessary, in the present connection, to go into the maze of detail to which the study of research in the steel industry would lead, were one to venture even a rough descriptive outline. Suffice it to say that the various large steel companies have developed a keen appreciation of the importance of research in the industrial processes under their command, and that they have often made provision for some systematic work. Here as elsewhere, the larger the corporate entity, the larger and better equipped, usually, are the laboratory facilities at the disposal of the research staff, and the more systematic and thorough the effort to place every phase of the round of extractive, manufacturing, and commercial processes and activities upon a thoroughly scientific basis. As in other phases of rationalization in the steel industry, the *Vereinigte Stahlwerke* has led the way.

"Through the founding of the *Vereinigte Stahlwerke* it was possible to assemble and make common use of the long experience of the founder works, and hence to acquire a very great technical advantage. In the 'Research Division,' located in Düsseldorf, has been created an agency by means of which specialists in every field—steel, rolling mills, zinc plating, etc.—can be brought together at regular [short] intervals for the purpose of exchanging the results of their experience and progress and in order to acquaint themselves with literature dealing with development in their own special fields. For the latter purpose the Research Division regularly compiles data from foreign and domestic literature and from the discoveries made within the confines of the *Vereinigte Stahlwerke,* which it publishes in a journal for circulation among all engineers of the concern in order to keep them informed on current developments.

"As a result of these conferences, held for exchange of practical experiences, there is maintained a constant stimulus to test the practicability of all findings, first in the laboratory, and then in the actual processes of production in the various plants of the corporation. The possibility of producing and comparing results of one and the same product in various works of the *Vereinigte Stahlwerke* permits the Research Division to plan and carry through investigation of manufacturing processes most conducive to high quality work.

"For the purpose of carrying through research immediately connected with the various plants, the *Vereinigte Stahlwerke* has a large number of experiment institutions and laboratories, employing about 1,500 workers. All raw materials are regularly tested in these institutions in order that uniformity may be maintained. An indication of the care applied here is shown in the fact that for every 1,000 tons of iron produced as a finished rolled commodity, no less than 1,500 single tests have been made in the process of manufacture.

"In addition the *Vereinigte Stahlwerke* has established in Dortmund a special research institute whose function is to devote its labors solely to further development of steel types and methods of iron and steel production, unencumbered by the labor of testing for control purposes. In this research institute the chemical laboratory carries through investigations in the field of ferro-chemistry. . . . . The physical-chemistry laboratory works over problems of iron and steel metallurgy and the development and peculiarities of iron and steel alloys. In the coal-chemistry laboratory, experimentation is devoted to coal and its distillation products, coke and gas. In the physical laboratory the most important research relates to magnetic and electric problems of peculiar importance to iron and steel. The technological laboratory carries on research into the reworking (*Bearbeitung*) of iron and the testing of materials. Finally, there is a laboratory for silicate chemistry (problems in the fields of fire-resistant stone and slag), and a special section devoted to photography and films."[24]

In addition to the above-mentioned institutes, the *Vereinigte Stahlwerke* has established, on the proposal of Professors Wallichs and Poppelreuter, "a center for research in the psycho-physiology of 'heavy work.' This research center is directly attached to the shops and will thus be in closer touch with actual work-

[24] *Das Spezial Archiv, op. cit.,* pp. 30, 32.

ing conditions than the average psycho-technical laboratory. At first the research, which is directed by Dr. Fraenkel, an engineer, bore mainly on the psycho-physiological aspects of production. Subsequently, management problems were also dealt with. For this purpose, young engineers are taken on as research workers and trained in Dr. Fraenkel's department. The course of training includes instruction in the latest methods of time and motion study and the use of the Poppelreuter stop-watch. The newly trained research workers are then sent to firms which have applied to the department for assistance and advice."[25]

In all problems of a more general character, the *Vereinigte Stahlwerke, Krupp,* and the other large steel concerns cooperate very closely with the various special research institutes of the *Kaiser Wilhelm-Gesellschaft* devoted to coal, iron, and steel physical and chemical research.[26] There has been a disposition in recent years to withdraw from active cooperation with the Kaiser Wilhelm Institute for Labor Physiology, located in Dortmund-Münster and presided over by the distinguished Dr. Atzler, on the grounds that work carried on there has been too theoretical for practical application and lacking in sympathy with the viewpoint of the employers. It was partly for this reason that the steel concerns organized *DINTA,* Herr Vögler, chairman of the *Vereinigte Stahlwerke,* being also the general director of this organization.[27]

Much of the research work undertaken would seem, on first acquaintance at least, of little immediate value. "Experience always shows," the writer in *Das Spezial Archiv* continues, "that a sound theoretical foundation must be laid first if genuine progress is to be made. The cooperative work of special research divisions, manufacturing experience, and research institutes, made possible by the organization of the concern, has created the theoretical foundation which shortly leads to significant results. These are expressed in better control possibilities, better training of employees, and, through mechanization of production processes, an improved and progressive cheapening of production . . . ."[28] Likewise with management research. An attempt was made, to cite an example, to secure maximum efficiency in filling blast furnaces "as well as in the transport equipment used from the mixing of the ores to the tunnel-hole." The procedure called for "intensive plant observation, motion and time studies with the Poppelreuter time-registering device, and investigation of time schedules of the equipment for handling materials. It was found possible to increase output to the extent of about 20 per cent by introducing buffers at various points in the plant." The management has apparently realized—and the same holds good within

---

[25] B. I. M. I. (December, 1928):235.

[26] In particular the institutes for Physical and Electrical Chemistry (Berlin-Dahlem), Coal Research (Mülheim a. Ruhr and Breslau), Iron Research (Düsseldorf), Metal Research (Berlin-Dahlem), Silicate Research (Berlin-Dahlem), and Labor Physiology (Dortmund-Münster).

[27] The DINTA technical school at the Schalker Verein coal and steel plant in Gelsenkirchen is regarded as a model.

[28] *Idem.*

limitations for all the big steel concerns—that while much of the research and many of the organizational plans carried through may show immediate and direct returns, their principal importance is to be realized only in the long run. Even then, in the absence of a proper background for comparison, it may be impossible to weigh their importance directly in tonnage and pecuniary terms. Yet the advantages of efforts along these lines are beyond question.

This is true to an unusual degree of the most important organizational innovation of the *Vereinigte Stahlwerke,* that of centralized administration with decentralized management. The managerial pattern was frankly borrowed from the *I. G. Farbenindustrie,* which in turn was modeled after the system laid down in the organization of the General Motors Corporation and the American Telephone and Telegraph Company. Along with a high degree of plant specialization, designed to take maximum advantage of economies of standardized mass production, railroad and waterway tariff schedules, and other related economies, went a structural scheme which made each plant or each regionally homogeneous complex a separate managerial unit.[29] Usually, though not necessarily, the feature emphasized was horizontal alignment, which brings every managerial incentive to bear upon internal improvement promoting mass production. Consequently, while the concern is organized vertically, the principle guiding decentralized management is horizontal integration. The advantages of this arrangement are twofold. On the one hand, it makes it easy to avoid duplication of facilities and to prevent undue expansion along any particular line within any individual plant, while it facilitates coordination of works schedules of different plants so as to combat price-cutting competition. On the other hand, it offers a basis for securing maximum flexibility and individual initiative in the management of the separate plants. The same principle has been carried as far as possible into the management of departments and shops. Simultaneously, improvements made at any stage or process have become the common property of the entire concern, and any adjustments made necessary by expansion or contraction of output in any detailed or plant operation can be carried out with the greatest speed and thoroughness regardless of the range which they may cover within the concern. While the internal organization of *Krupp* and the other large steel concerns more closely approximates the military type of organization found in the Ford concern, a considerable measure of decentralization has been effected in the details of operation within the various plants, departments, and shops.[30]

[29] Thus all the plants owned by the company in the Siegerland district are brought under the control of Charlottenhütte A. G.; in central Germany the managerial unit is the Mitteldeutsche Stahlwerke A. G., and in Upper Silesia the Vereinigte Oberschlesische Hüttenwerke A. G. The machinery department of the Thyssen concern was separated from the trust and merged with the Deutsche Maschinenfabrik A. G. High-grade steels were brought under the control of the Deutsche Edelstahlwerke A. G.

[30] This point will be taken up later (see Chap. XIV) in connection with a consideration of the bearing of the principles of organization worked out upon all-inclusive monopolies, whether under state or private control.

8. EFFICIENCY OF PRODUCTION

The results of the numerous rationalization measures sketched above should normally be subject to fairly precise quantitative evaluation. Several factors serve to make any such estimations of doubtful value. The major changes made in the industry after the inauguration of the Dawes plan did not begin to show their effects for a considerable period. The more important corporate realignments which led up to the founding of the *Vereinigte Stahlwerke* and other large concerns had run their course by the end of 1926. Circumstances were complicated in that year by the greatly expanded output of the coal industry—incident to the English general strike—in which the steel companies were so heavily interested. The expansion which followed was brought to a close two years later, however, by the great depression, which began to affect the steel industry in late 1928, and all business by the middle of 1929. Inasmuch as the technical reorganization necessarily required some years to be carried through and rounded out, even with continuation of prosperity, an increase in net efficiency for the steel industry as a whole could scarcely be expected to show by now. Excluding by-product utilization, previously mentioned, the records of the two largest companies are shown in tables 15 and 16 (p. 123).[31]

While output had increased in the aggregate during 1926–1928 and the number of workers had either fallen (*Vereinigte Stahlwerke*) or increased but slightly (*Krupp*), the average output per worker did not increase a great deal. Within individual processes, however, output per worker increased at an extraordinary rate. Dr. Vögler, speaking before the *Enquete* Committee, cited the following examples of the "end-effect of the rationalization process":[32] "The *August Thyssenhütte* formerly produced 75,000 tons of steel with 10,000 workers; today it employs 9,900 men and produces 170,000 tons of steel. The *Hörder Union* formerly produced 40,000 tons of steel and employed 4,600 men; today 5,700 men produce 85,000 to 90,000 tons. The *Dortmund Union* has increased its steel output from 60,000 to 85,000 tons, while the number of employees in the steel and rolling mills has stayed the same. *Rheinstahl* and *Phoenix* have increased their output from 110,000 to 150,000 tons and decreased the number of workmen from 11,000 to 9,600. Turnover, all factors included, has increased by 70 per cent; the supervisory staff of 10,000 in the steel mills has stayed the same. The capital charges of the principal rolled products, excluding all special expense levies, have been reduced by from 15 to 16 marks per ton. Where rationalization has been particularly successful the savings have been as high as 21 marks [per ton]; in the less successful cases they have ranged around 4 to 5 marks."

---

[31] *Das Spezial Archiv, op. cit.,* excepting the production figures for the Vereinigte Stahlwerke, which are taken from the annual reports.

[32] E. A., III (2):157–158.

TABLE 15

VEREINIGTE STAHLWERKE: OUTPUT (TONS) AND NUMBER OF EMPLOYEES

	1926–1927	1927–1928	1928–1929	1929–1930
Coal	26,081,321	26,454,510	27,241,990	25,722,500
Coke	8,204,878	9,414,848	9,627,304	9,338,172
Pig iron	6,350,649	6,518,682	6,007,953	5,296,970
Crude steel	6,837,644	6,945,186	6,419,796	5,538,395
Rolled products	4,992,452	5,113,996	4,708,731	4,051,870
Wage earners	183,179	172,595	176,716	134,708
Office workers	15,740	15,394	15,331	16,359

TABLE 16

KRUPP: OUTPUT (TONS) AND NUMBER OF EMPLOYEES

	1913–1914	1926–1927	1927–1928	1928–1929
Coal	7,599,234	7,546,375	7,907,299	8,001,543
Coke	2,307,366	2,522,491	2,613,287	2,500,658
Pig iron	1,285,172	1,376,120	1,359,417	1,292,440
Crude steel	1,493,608	1,786,863	1,722,854	1,587,332
Rolled products	833,970	1,274,595	1,262,876	1,159,524
Wage earners	79,100	66,327	69,989	68,062
Salaried workers	....	19,500	22,400	21,700

Increased tonnage output per man may not, however, be a good criterion of technical efficiency. With the possible exception of heavy chemicals there has been no basic industry in which qualitative changes have played such an important rôle as in iron and steel products. Much of the range of output is, of course, highly standardized. This is particularly true of the earlier stages in the progress of the metal towards the finishing mills. Yet even here qualitative changes have been made, if only by the introduction of control methods which make possible the production of pig iron and crude steel where deviations from specified physico-chemical standards are kept within much narrower limits than before. But in the later stages of steel production, research and experimentation has resulted in the development of new steel types, special amalgams, and processing methods which enormously increase the value of the resultant product. Degrees of hardness, tensile strength, corrosion resistance, malleability and weight-carrying capacity, etc., have been achieved for various purposes which increase the value and the life of the product by percentages ranging in some cases as high as 400 to 500.

Utilization of by-products renders efficiency ratios expressed in terms of weight still less reliable. In the integrated plant the total output must, on the whole, be set off against the total man-power employed. Within the interstices of the plant it may be possible to increase man-power efficiency markedly at any particular point, and by reorganization of the whole system to increase aggregate output, but it is nearly impossible to combine joint products expressed in different measurement units in order to obtain a quantitatively expressed average efficiency ratio.

Even were such a measurement possible there would still remain the difficulty that failure to utilize plant and equipment to capacity might give such a bad proportioning of factors that the actual efficiency, as expressed in output ratios, would fall. More extensive changes might, further, be in prospect immediately upon improvement in general market conditions. Plans looking towards increased efficiency may be held in abeyance because of high capital requirements necessary in order to put them into execution, or by doubts as to the capacity of the existing market to absorb the increased output without reducing prices below cost of production. All this would suggest that changes in the efficiency of production can be expressed only in the universal common denominator, money. But for reasons too well known to merit discussion here, monetary cost comparisons are not much more satisfactory than those expressed in weight and tale. If total costs are included, the problem becomes in large part one of distribution of income shares, and not efficiency, as far as wages, salaries, and dividends are concerned. The current dispute over new investment, and amounts which are and should be charged on depreciation account against costs as a result of reorganization, show how risky it is to take overhead expenses indicated at their face value.

The negative aspect of the problem of efficiency is somewhat easier. To the individual company, and in a more special sense to the general community, excess plant capacity represents a source of inefficiency and waste. To the company it represents general inability to operate under favorable cost circumstances unless the unused capacity is exclusively made up of small, badly located, and relatively inefficient reserve plant and equipment. To the community it means that joint effort has been expended for the preparation of productive equipment which is forced to stand idle when it might be turning out the goods and services for which it was presumably intended.

Excess capacity in the steel industry as a source of national inefficiency, economic waste, and misappropriated capital funds (*Kapitalfehlleitung*), has been the subject of widespread discussion and bitter dispute in German financial, governmental, and labor circles. The *Enquete* Committee issued a statement condemning the industry for over-expansion, badily planned investment, and faulty structural organization. In its concluding statement the Committee declared that, "The difficult conditions under which a large part of the German iron industry is laboring are fixed, not by cyclical fluctuations in business, but by the structural upbuilding of the industry, and are therefore determined by permanent factors."[33]

The report of the Committee was attacked with the greatest vigor by the Association of Iron and Steel Producers. In that part of the report which related to excess capacity they quoted the Committee against itself to the effect that capacity had been utilized to the full from 1927 to 1929,[34] and sharply attacked the basis upon which capacity had been reckoned as being "greater in present Germany than that existing in the larger pre-war territory of the country."[35] It was further insisted that the Committee had not been at all consistent and at no time precise in its use of the expression, "excess capacity,"[36] and that examination of the facts would not bear out the contention that the industry was at fault for such difficulties as it was facing at the time the report was issued.

It is not necessary to go into the merits of the controversy here. There were various reasons why the industry had been greatly expanded before 1925. Among these were (1) the attempt to round out the works following the loss of key plants by territorial cessions, (2) the insistence of the government that indemnity money be used by the companies for rebuilding purposes, (3) the fact (*a*) that the general rebuilding of German industry, (*b*) the rehabilitation of the railroads, (*c*) the substitution of new locomotives and box cars for those ceded to the allies (5,000 locomotives and 150,000 box cars), and (*d*) the necessity of supplying equipment for the rebuilding of destroyed plants in the war areas, required a tremendous increase in steel production. But when the more important of these demands had been met, the market situation for the German steel industry became acute. In addition to the fact that the generally weakened condition of the country made it difficult for industries to expand with the vigor characteristic of the pre-war period, the German steel market was further curtailed by the treaty ruling which prevented the rebuilding of the ceded navy, and required almost complete military disarmament. Supply of the army and navy constituted a large percentage of the business of several of the larger steel companies—Krupp in particular—during and before the war.

The treaty further weakened the German steel industry by providing that Germany should not impose protective tariffs for such classes of products in

---

[33] E. A., III (2):122. [34] *Ibid.*, pp. 21, 62, 72, 74, and 79.

[35] Steel capacity, according to the steel people, was 22,377,000 tons in 1914 and 17,800,000 tons in 1927–1929, judged on a basis of highest output of the constituent plants. This represents a decline in daily capacity of about 15,000 tons. See Dr. J. W. Reichert, "Die Leistungsfähigkeit der deutschen Stahlindustrie," *Stahl und Eisen,* 50 (1930).

[36] *Ibid.* The Committee, they complain, has committed the sin of underwriting popular misconceptions by confusing "over-capacity," "over-dimensioning," "over-rationalization," "misuse of capital," "over-investment," "over-capitalization," and other common catchwords with the real root of the difficulty, which, they say, results from a combination of unnecessary governmental interference and certain international dislocations arising from the treaty, and is quite beyond their control.

defense of her internal markets from foreign competition. Meanwhile several new steel-producing countries had been added to the list of competitors, Poland and Czechoslovakia being the most important. Many foreign markets had been lost to foreign competitors on account of the war, and on account of the rise of the world-wide phenomenon of high protective tariff walls. In the interim the steel productive capacity of the world had been enormously increased.[37] Important markets in the two Americas had been lost to steel interests in the United States; Africa and the Orient were brought under the domination of British and American producers. In Europe France had, by the annexation of Alsace-Lorraine and the temporary control of the Saar district, increased its pig iron capacity by 102 per cent, its crude steel capacity by 92 per cent, and its rolling-mill capacity by 99 per cent. Inclusion of Luxemburg in the Belgian customs union had increased Belgian pig iron capacity 102 per cent, crude steel capacity 54 per cent, and rolling-mill capacity 26 per cent.[38] Aside from the new competition of Poland and Czechoslovakia, Balkanization of Europe meant that an increased percentage of continental steel production must move in international channels.[39] Belgium, the Saar, France, Poland, and Czechoslovakia are the out-

[37] The following table of world production of important iron and steel products (in millions of tons) indicates the quantitative importance of the increase noted.*

Year	Pig iron	Crude steel (including welded steel)	Rolling-mill products
1909	61	59	44
1913	80	80	60
1919	53	61	44
1922	56	70	53
1924	68	80	60
1925	77	92	69
1926	79	94	70
1927	87	104	75
1928	89	112	90
1929	99	122	98

* Source: E. A., III (2): 3.

[38] Increase in crude steel production of the more important countries since 1913 is shown as follows (in 1,000 tons):*

Country	1913	1929
United States	31,800	55,000
German Tariff Union	18,900	16,250
Great Britain	7,800	9,800
French Tariff Union	4,700	11,800
Belgian Tariff Union	2,500	6,800

* Source: Schneider, *op. cit.*, p. 8.

[39] The E. A., III(2):98, gives the following indexes for the export from Germany, France, Belgium, Luxemburg, and Great Britain of semi-finished and rolling-mill steel products for the years 1925–1929, with 1913 as base:

Year	Continental production fields	Great Britain	Total fields
1925	129	83	113
1926	158	69*	127
1927	182	93	151
1928	181	99	152
1929	183	96	153

* Strike in coal mining.

standing examples of newly created steel districts lacking in facilities for absorbing any considerable percentage of the new productive capacity in their own domestic markets. Of the increased European crude steel capacity of 8.3 million tons (1929 over 1913) better than 5 million tons were exported from the country of origin. When it is realized that about one-third of German output of such semi-finished steel products as rolled plate—practically the entirety of the increased production since 1925—is exported, the seriousness of the new alignment for the German steel industry may be easily seen.

All this suggests that the problem of excess plant capacity is patently European and not merely German in scope. Except under conditions of constantly and rapidly expanding markets, excess capacity in particular branches of the steel industry at all times,[40] and in all branches at particular times, is certain to be the rule. Both the matter of structural adjustment within the industry iself and the problem of adjusting capacity and output to the demand for steel products are now definitely, unmistakably, and unalterably international in scope. Bottled up within its own frontiers, at least one-third of Germany's iron and steel capacity would automatically become excess even in the best times, and other countries would either have to forego the use of iron and steel products entirely or develop domestic industries by the costly procedures of erecting prohibitive tariff walls, special governmental subventions, etc.[41]

However efficient or inefficient the routine processes of steel production may be in detail, the greater losses are now unquestionably incident to the lack of this larger national and international integration. German industrialists have been more keenly aware of this fact than other European producers and have taken the initiative in attempts at its solution. The internal problem of adjustment of capacity to demand has been attacked by two principal routes: (1) bringing as many stages of raw materials, iron and steel production, and industries consuming by-products and steel products as possible into compactly organized corporate units or under the control of inclusive and cooperative organizations, thus making a managerial out of a former market problem, and (2) establishment of cartels, trade associations, or special trade agreements designed to regulate and coordinate production and consumption among the various companies and within the various branches of the industry. The external, or international, problem has been met, where met at all, by expansion of these methods beyond national boundaries.

---

[40] Dr. Bierwes, of the Mannesmannröhren-Werke, for example, testified before the Enquete Committee that his company (the largest tube producer in Europe) was operating in 1929 to but 45 per cent of capacity.—E. A., III (2):254.

[41] As is the case, at the present time, in Italy, Hungary, Jugoslavia, and others of the smaller Balkan states.

9. INTER-INDUSTRY INTEGRATION AND AFFILIATIONS

Mention has already been made of the degree of concentration which has taken place in the heavy branches of the steel industry during the post-war period, and the method whereby horizontal and vertical features are combined in the new configuration has been briefly outlined. Some of the inter-industrial affiliations have also been sketched. The picture should be somewhat enlarged, however, to show the extent to which the technical facts of steel's key position in the whole vast web of the modern industrial system have been decisive in the logic of organizational change.

As shown above, steel's interest in fuel reaches to the very heart of, and exercises a controlling influence upon the entire coal industry. The facts that German steel companies produce outright or control indirectly from one-third to one-half of the domestic bituminous coal output, and that the iron and steel producing segments alone consume about 15 per cent of the current coal supply, do not indicate the full importance of the relationships existing between these two key industries. The steel interests have taken the initiative in the preliminary reorganization, and have often been directly responsible for such developments as the establishment of giant central cokeries, the system of long-distance gas supply, and (in cooperation with the chemical industry) for the whole movement towards complete chemical transformation of coal and its by-product utilization. The relationship has passed beyond a purely economic and commercial stage. It has become a matter of close and immediate technical interdependence, so binding and coercive that the coal, steel, chemical, and power segments of the particular corporation must be handled as integrated parts of compactly organized and quasi-mechanical systems. Somewhat the same situation is becoming significant for the same industries taken at large.

With respect to the other basic raw materials, the rôle of the steel industry has been somewhat different. The exigencies of post-war development have made it impossible for German steel interests to regain their former foothold in the more important neighboring ore-producing fields. Output of controlled Siegerland and Lahn-Dill deposits, and ore delivered under special agreements with French and Belgian Minette producers account for but a minor proportion of the total supply. Although Germany takes about 80 per cent of Swedish ore production, the dominating position of the semi-monopolistic and partly state-controlled Swedish company, the *Trafikaktiebolaget Grängesberg-Oxelösund,* has made it impossible for German interests to gain an effective foothold in this area. Their Swedish holdings do not exceed 20 million tons, and the annual output from this source of some 300,000 tons constitutes less than 5 per cent of Swedish ore shipments to Germany. German-controlled firms in Spain produce about 200,000 tons annually, and have extensive holdings in the as yet undeveloped fields of Portugal, Chile, and Brazil. As in the Lorraine district, deposits in Norway, North America (principally in Newfoundland), North Africa (principally in Morocco), Asia (Caucasus, India, and China), and other places are practically closed to German ownership because of preemption by other interests or because of political considerations. The only solution has been the negotiation of long-term contracts, a procedure which has the disadvantage that it tends to destroy the managerial unity and organizational—proportioning—flexibility of more closely knit entities. Under capitalistic enterprise, ownership is the indispensable prerequisite to full realization of the advantages of the organic integration dictated by technical and engineering considerations. The steel industry, however, absorbs about one-third of the domestic limestone production and exercises an effective control over its supply.

Although control becomes a questionable term, the technical interweaving of the steel and related industries appears to be even closer and more coercive as one passes from the raw materials on through the various manufacturing processes. While the desire to find a market for tubing probably entered into the considerations leading to the launching of long-distance gas-supply systems, it is more probable that decisive importance was attached to the recovery of great quantities of hitherto waste fuel, and to the supply of related plants and processes with economical fuel and power. Necessary product that this was of the technical overhauling of coke-oven and blast-furnace equipment, it bound these tightly to all manufacturing, distributing, and consuming processes—henceforth dependent upon long-distance gas-supply systems for fuel and power—into a continuous, unbroken, and organically functioning system. No part dare stop or start, slow or speed up, without either the necessity of balancing up in some or all other parts of the system, or without destroying that nice balance—in terms of quantity and evenness of flow, uniform quality, constant pressure, etc.—which is the alpha and omega of such an organic complex, and without which the whole concert disintegrates into a costly and disorderly chaos.

Equally significant has been the effect of the subtle changes in coal chemistry and metallurgical processes in binding together the steel and chemical industries. The steel interests, through their development of coal chemistry, coking processes, and by-products utilization, have become important producers of raw and finished chemical products. Of perhaps even greater importance for the tie-up between the two industries is the fact that steel metallurgy has gradually developed steel making into a species of chemical disintegration and chemical synthesis. While, on the one hand, an increasing range of the problems in the chemical field have come to involve direct physical—i.e., "physico-chemical"—analysis, on the other hand, growing importance is attached in steel metallurgy to "ferro-chemistry" and related problems in physical chemistry. There is, therefore, a significant sense in which the whole steel industry has become a "chemical" industry.

It would be surprising if these increasingly close theoretical and practical contacts did not result in drawing the two industries together in managerial and corporate ways. The Dye Trust (*I. G. Farbenindustrie*) is made up of a number of concerns which have been long accustomed to cooperating very closely with the coal, iron, and steel interests. The trust has never given up its interest in *Rheinstahl,* one of the important member companies of *Vereinigte Stahlwerke.* On the other hand, the steel companies have banded together, as noted above, to found two companies, *Ruhr-Chemie,* and the *Gesellschaft für Teerverwertung,* for the purpose of centralizing the recovery of their more important chemical by-products. How far direct and indirect inter-corporate ownership, special agreements, and effective communities of interest between steel and chemical interests have gone, it is impossible to say. There is plenty of evidence, however, of substantial agreement as to division of labor, cooperation in technically related problems, and general corporate policies.

It is also impossible to state how far the steel concerns are tied up with the resident electric power companies, the *Rheinisch-Westfälische Elektrizitätswerke* and the *Vereinigte Elektrizitätswerke Westfalens,* but there can be no doubt that mutual cooperation is effectively guaranteed in meeting common, inter-process, and inter-corporate problems. Thus the former of the two power companies mentioned ceded to the *Ruhrgas* 302 km. of gas pipe-line and the entirety of its gas-producing system when the long-distance gas-supply system was inaugurated by the steel companies. Contracts were concluded giving *Ruhrgas* effective control of the gas systems of the other power company. While, as will be outlined later, there appears to be considerable competition between the gas and electric-power industries for fuel and power markets, there seems to have been no great difficulty experienced in bringing the power companies to agree to this functional division of labor. Yet the steel companies, both as important power consumers and as large-scale contributors of coal and by-product gas for electric-current production, are almost as closely tied up with the power systems as with gas distribution.

One of the more interesting trends in the steel industry has been expansion into the fields of finished steel manufacture, steel construction, and production of industrial equipment—including machine and machine-tool building. Here likewise it is impossible to trace at all clearly the developments in detail with sufficient certainty to be able to show just how far this trend has promoted re-grouping, functional specialization, and organizational systematization. It seems but natural, however, for steel to expand in this direction as long as it must take the initiative in market control and industrial stability.

A very large percentage of steel construction and of heavy machine and machine-tool industries is bound up directly with the maintenance and expansion of the steel industry and with mining and the miscellaneous industries controlled by it. Thus the *Institut für Konjunkturforschung* has estimated that 18 per cent of the inland market for mechanical conveyor equipment, trucks, and mechanical preparation machinery is made up of the demands of blast-furnace, steel, and rolling-mill works. Practically all the big steel companies, consequently, have gone into the machine-producing business. *Hoesch* owns a machine plant producing machine tools, switches, lathes, traverse tables, and cranes. *Krupp* controls plants producing a large variety of machinery and machine equipment—all types of marine engines, turbines, diesel motors, steam boilers, marine and stationary motors, all types of small workshop, office machines—cash registers, typewriters, etc.—household and agricultural machinery, machinery especially adapted to tropical conditions, grain-mill machinery, cranes, lifts and hoists, etc. This firm produces several types of high-grade finished steel compounds and manufactures them into knives, forks, kitchen utensils and similar equipment, operates a shipbuilding plant, drydock and marine repair plant, etc. *Vereinigte Stahlwerke* controls several machine, boiler, heavy engineering and construction plants and companies. Through affiliations it is also interested in locomotive and box car works. *Gutehoffnungshütte* owns or controls plants manufacturing locomotives, bridge materials, cranes, signal apparatus, heavy mining machinery, printing presses, internal-combustion motors, and similar equipment.

Krupp probably represents the ideal combination. It owns or controls plants at every stage of the process from the extraction of raw materials to the retailing of the finished machinery and equipment made from its own steel products. The entire gigantic manufacturing complex which it dominates is an almost completely balanced and self-contained entity and offers an excellent example of nearly ideal combination of horizontal and vertical integration.

While the withdrawal of the Siemens interests from the defunct Stinnes concern severed all formal ownership relations between that concern and the steel industry, there is a wealth of evidence showing continued close cooperation between the various steel concerns and the electro-technical combines, *Siemens & Halske-Siemens & Schuckertwerke* and the *A. E. G.* (*Allgemeine Elektrizitäts-Gesellschaft*). Here, as noted in long-distance gas supply and heavy chemicals (and, within limitations, in coal, coking, and the machine industry), corporate individuality is coming more and more to take on the nature of effective operating and managerial separateness—representing the principle of centralized coordination with the maximum of managerial flexibility through decentralization of function—rather than the maintenance of a series of independent and watertight productive entities. Were a single controlling board to be set up for all these industries, there is little reason for supposing that the major principles dictating the present organizational configuration among them would be entirely altered. Overlapping and duplication unquestionably exist, but the lines of force have already clearly delineated the structural outlines of that higher integration if and when it does come about. Nevertheless, these inter-industry plans do not exist, and there is no prospect that such plans will be developed in the near future.

10. MARKETING AND DISTRIBUTION ORGANIZATION

As usual, the picture is less clear when we turn to distribution. Elaborate as the machinery for handling the marketing of steel products has become, and old as experience and experimentation in Germany has been along this line, there is scarcely a single respect in which the systems set up can be judged satisfactory from an organizational point of view. At no point do the present controlling interests appear to be fully satisfied. The cartels, selling syndicates, special agreements, and communities of interest have effectively fulfilled the basic rôles assigned to them for but short periods of time, and then but to a limited extent. These, depending upon the type of organization set up, have been designed to perform one or more of the following functions: production control, price control, market allocation and control, and control of the conditions and terms of delivery.

Among the organizations established, the cartels, many of them of pre-war origin, are by all odds the most important. Among the 73 iron and steel cartels mentioned by Metzner,[42] the following appear to be the more important:

Roheisen-Verband	(Pig Iron Cartel)
Stahlwerks-Verband	(Steel Works Cartel)—including:
Rohstahlgemeinschaft	(Steel Ingot Cartel)
A-Produkteverband	("A" Products Cartel)
Stabeisen-Verband	(Bar Steel Cartel)
Grobblech-Verband	(Steel Plate Cartel)
Bandeisen-Vereinigung	(Steel Strip Cartel)
Röhren-Verband	(Pipe and Tubing Cartel)
Schweissröhr-Verband	(Welded Pipe and Tubing Cartel)
Deutsche Stahlgemeinschaft	(German Steel Association)
Deutsche Drahtwalzwerke	(German Wire Mills)

In addition to these, German steel producers are members of a number of international cartels, of which the more important are:

Continental Steel Ingot Cartel
International Railmakers Association
International Pipe Cartel

In most cases the cartel consists of an agreement binding the members to sell through the instrumentality of a central cartel office all the steel produced for the market and falling under the classifications covered in the agreement. With the exception of the pig iron cartel, which, because of the large consumption by the producers themselves, covers but 20 per cent of total output, these cartels exercise effective monopolistic powers as far as production of member companies is concerned. Quotas are usually determined either in terms of quantities marketed prior to the agreement or in terms of previous high production for some fixed period. The long duration and strict discipline of some of the more powerful cartels have made it unnecessary to institute, or possible to dispense with, special monetary penalties for exceeding quotas established.

[42] *Op. cit.*, p. 13.

As stated above, cartels are based on agreements binding members to pursue common policies along one or more lines. They may be primarily sales organizations, may involve attempts to allocate definite market areas, may be aimed at production control, or may be agents for enforcing certain common rules concerning conditions and terms of delivery. All these functions may be confined in one. Most of the cartels listed above are sales organizations having as their stated or implied objective production and price control. Among the international cartels partial or complete monopoly of domestic markets has always been a cardinal principle. In the domestic market, attempts along this line, except such practices as routing orders for export to plants favorably located along waterways and near the country placing the order, have made on the whole but little headway. Most of the steel cartels now also enforce definite rules governing conditions and terms of delivery—standard order and billing blanks, standard specifications (as far as possible), methods of loading and routing, dates and terms of payment, etc.

Cartel agreements, further, cover only certain specified types of material and are usually made for comparatively short periods. Companies such as *Vereinigte Stahlwerke* and *Krupp,* producing a wide range of steel materials, belong to nearly all the cartels. For many steel products no syndicate agreements exist at all. About 11 per cent, or 1,700,000 tons of the 1927 crude steel output, for example, was disposed of by the steel companies under the form of tin plate, highly refined steels of all sorts, and miscellaneous products, without the intermediation of cartels.

Orders for steel covered by cartel agreements are routed by the cartel office to its member companies, an attempt being made to send orders to firms most advantageously situated for the purpose of the particular requisition and to keep all companies equally well occupied. Quota restrictions usually apply on a percentage basis equally to the output of all members, excepting those quantities produced and consumed within the confines of the individual plant, or works controlled by the individual company. Control usually means ownership of at least 51 per cent of the voting stock. Where cartel agreements include price control, prices established must be observed in all cases, subject to special rebates that may be allowed to wholesalers and large consumers receiving deliveries direct from the plant.

Steel delivered directly to large consumers may at times constitute a large percentage of the totals subject to cartel control. Thus a random example showed that 47 per cent of the bar iron and 52 per cent of the figured bar iron produced in the month of October, 1927, was delivered direct. The remainder is sold by the cartel to the wholesale trade. The wholesale establishments are of three types, Cartel Dealers (*Verbandshändler*), Works Dealers (*Werkshändler*), and "Independent" Dealers (*Freie Händler*). The first and second types are almost always identical; the companies belong to the various steel concerns and function as distributing agencies. Usually they work under special contract with the cartel office.

The independent wholesalers are financially and otherwise independent of the producing companies and usually, though not always, purchase and sell on a much smaller basis than the works companies. Export sales usually go through the same sort of machinery.

The works and cartel wholesale companies are, again, organized in wholesale distributing cartels. The most important of these are the Cartel of the Rhine-Westphalian Iron Wholesalers (*Verband Rheinisch-Westfälischer Eisengrosshändler G. m. b. H.*) and the Union of Rhine-Westphalian Pipe and Tubing Wholesalers (*Rheinisch-Westfälische Röhrengrosshändler-Vereinigung G. m. b. H.*). The former cartel is a central cartel, or "cartel of cartels," similar to the steel works cartel in the producing field. It is made up of ten large companies, separately organized with respect to particular products, and associated directly with the large concerns. These companies purchase directly from the producing cartels, and retail to large consumers, or to district and local retail concerns. The independents, on the contrary, must purchase from the cartel or works wholesalers. To defend better their interests against these latter, the independents have in turn organized themselves into an Economic Association of Independent Dealers (*Wirtschaftliche Vereinigung des freien Handels e. V.*).

These wholesale cartels are more in the nature of the typical American trade association, and less of the specifically cartel type, in that they are primarily concerned with problems of group solidarity, defense of general group interests, and the supply of special-interest information. The special accounting functions and the task of supervising legally enforceable agreements, which constitute normal functions of most cartels, play minor rôles in the wholesale associations.

Dissatisfaction with the prevailing cartel and general distributive systems is widespread. Cartels are generally looked upon as "children of necessity," and at the best as transitional institutions. They are thought of as being preparatory, and, to the extent to which they are successful, as leading logically and more or less of necessity to Communities of Interest (*Interessengemeinschaften*) and eventually to formal combination. As organized they suffer from a number of serious defects. Chief among these is their inability to prevent the rise and expansion of outside competition. Just as in the case of the coal cartels previously discussed, no machinery exists compelling new companies to join the cartels. Nor can the companies be prevented from taking advantage of cartel price, market, and production regulation while dispensing with the costs and burdens attached to such association. In the face of this situation, the steel cartels have not been able long to exercise effective monopolistic powers, and every approach in this direction appears to have had the effect of encouraging enough outside competition to negate much of the advance made.

This situation is an important source of friction within the cartel membership and between the cartels and the general public. Cartel members, realizing the general inflexibility of such a type of organization, and aware of the imminent danger of failure to renew cartel agreements because of both internal and external stresses, are loath to surrender corporate rights and prerogatives, and are more or less of necessity forced to maintain (and, if possible, to expand) their marketing contacts and distributive machinery. There is, consequently, small reason for believing that the cartels have materially aided simplification and systematization of marketing machinery, or that they have been able to slow down the tendency towards duplication of warehouses, office facilities, selling agencies, bunker, trucking and terminal facilities, personnel, and other factors incident to separate distribution by each producing system.

Failure to secure monopolistic control has sometimes been used by the cartels to prove that their members have the same competitive pressures towards increased efficiency brought to bear upon them as in non-cartelized fields. This position is scarcely consistent with the other contention that cartels by virtue of their superior organization are able to promote technical efficiency more rapidly and more easily than more competitive units. If, as the facts appear to prove, the steel industry is constantly menaced, if not always faced, with the problem of excess capacity, and if, as is universally contended, the primary function of the cartels is the adjustment of supply to demand under price conditions which would assure the industry of capacity to expand at need, then the efforts of the cartels can be written down as largely wasted.

Nor has the distribution machinery operated much more effectively. The consensus of experts before the *Enquete* Committee[43] was that circumstances should have permitted a fair division of labor between works companies and the independents, but that developments along this line had been rather disappointing. Combination, both horizontal and vertical, had made it possible for the larger concerns to simplify, concentrate, and systematize the warehousing, shipping, and marketing facilities of their constituent plants and companies. Works companies thus appear to have shared in the general overhauling incident to the larger rationalization of the respective enterprises of which they are members. They usually specialized exclusively upon storage and sale of steel types produced only by the controlling company. Deliveries from works warehouses are usually made in large lots only, leaving to the independent wholesalers the problem of distributing small lot orders to smaller consumers and dealers. The fear of further expansion of the works companies, and the desire to compensate for the disadvantage attached to small-scale purchase in the form of denial of rebate privileges, has led the independents in many cases to enter the field against the former. It is charged by the large steel concerns that this situation has resulted in overexpansion of marketing facilities, despite the reorganization of their own companies, and in practically complete failure by the independents to carry through systematically any significant rationalization measures.[44]

[43] E. A., III (2): 248–380.

[44] See in particular the testimony of Dr. Thyssen of the Vereinigte Stahlwerke and Toyka, *ibid.*, pp. 314–322.

The problem of steel produced for self-consumption purposes seems to have provided another stumbling block in the path of the cartels. The position of the larger concerns that such production be exempted from cartel control has, in the main, been successfully maintained. While thus enjoying whatever advantages may accrue to cartel control of special types of steel produced for the market, they have been able by more complete integration and by expansion into construction, shipping, machine, and miscellaneous industries, to turn increasing percentages of their output into non-cartelized, i.e., finishing, fields, where their type of organization has made possible competition on a very favorable basis. This process has made it possible for the *Krupp* company to control its output for certain specialized lines all the way from extraction of raw materials to delivery of the finished product to ultimate consumers.

The cartels are not, however, entirely without their economic justification either to their member companies or to the general public. German producers have long been accustomed to cooperation, and have doubtless been able to better their own business prospects by such efforts towards production, price, and market stabilization. If these results, to the extent to which they contain body and substance, can be said in any wise to bring order and stability into the German national system, their general economic justification is so far secured. Even were this not the case, if they clear the ground and prepare the way for the larger and more systematic integration of the future, they can be admitted as training schools to that end.

On the whole, however, they appear to have failed in the steel industry—as in coal and lignite—to introduce into either national or international productive or marketing phases any considerable measure of order, simplification, or system. What has been accomplished of a rationalization character has been brought about in the main fields beyond their province and control.

II. SUMMARY

Rationalization achievements within the confines of the larger steel concerns have been extensive and of great importance in raising the general level of productive efficiency in the industry. Shortage of ores has been compensated by drawing of long-term contracts with foreign producers, importation of ores of higher metal content, increased use of both new and old scrap, and by improved refining methods which improve the quality of the various steels produced. Fuel costs have been lowered by improvements in fuel economy such as continuous and single heat processing, the utilization of former waste fuel gases, and improvements in coking processes. The new large by-product central cokeries have made it possible to make use of former waste materials such as coke-oven tar and its various derivatives, and coke-oven gas for distribution over long-distance distribution networks. Individual plant efficiency has been generally raised by installation of larger and more economical refining, transporting, and processing equipment, by the utilization of better types of machinery, and by the employment of more power per ton of steel produced and per man employed. Electrification has become general, and direct drive has been widely substituted for central prime movers and their auxiliary shafting and belting apparatus.

These changes within individual plants have been accompanied by increased emphasis upon systematic technological and processing research, by general change in the layout of buildings, shops, and equipment, and by reorganization of personnel relationships and systems of management. Laboratories have been established; raw materials, processing methods, and in some cases finished products have been standardized and simplified; technologically related processes have been brought into direct contact with each other so as to facilitate continuous flow of production and the utilization of conveyor and new-type internal transport mechanisms. Time and motion studies have been made, and improved techniques have been used for selecting the right man for each job. Changes in the managerial organization have generally emphasized greater individual initiative through decentralization of responsibility, while at the same time they have provided for more continuous, far-reaching, and systematic coordination of the various parts of each functioning complex.

The relative degree of order and efficiency which the changes indicated have brought into the separate factories have been imperfectly reflected in the inter-factory and inter-industrial relationships of the various producers. All that has been accomplished along these lines is the work of the large combines, and the product of the efficacy which intra- and inter-corporate relationships, resting upon personal or other foundations, have possessed in forcing realignment where economic and technical factors have been predominant. Within their own corporate properties, such concerns as the *Vereinigte Stahlwerke, Krupp,* and *Gutehoffnungshütte* have been highly successful in many aspects of their various efforts to proportion and integrate productive operations. Large central by-product cokeries have been substituted for the scattered and wasteful *Abhitzöfen* which prevailed before; in contrast to earlier procedure these have been brought into close juxtaposition to smelting and steel works instead of being directly attached to separate coal mines. Technically obsolete mines, coke ovens, smelters, steel works, and auxiliary refining and manufacturing plants have been closed down and in some cases scrapped entirely. Those remaining have been remodeled to specialize on the output of a small range of products, orders coming in to the central office being routed to the specialized plants. In determining the types of products to be turned out at each plant, attention was paid to factors of transportation, raw-materials costs, and nearness and type of markets.

The principal weaknesses of the German steel industry seem to be the following: (1) The relationships between the steel producers and the coal mining industry are still unsatisfactory. There is an overlapping here which seriously affects the stability of the coal industry; it has apparently resulted in considerable increase in coal mining capacity beyond the requirements of the market and much working to cross purposes between the two industries. (2) The rationalization period has left the marketing of iron and steel products in what might be called an almost chaotic condition. While the various cartels have brought about improvements in the marketing of the more standard types of steel products, they have been unable to prevent costly duplication of warehouses, offices, and miscellaneous equipment. (3) There is considerable evidence that the German steel industry is overbuilt. Figures are not available for determination of the exact extent of over-investment and over-capacity. In the main, expansion seems to have occurred without regard to permanent shifts in world demand resulting from industrialization of outlying areas and the expansion of foreign steel industries. (4) There is no very clear evidence that expansion of the steel industry into *(a)* long-distance gas transmission, *(b)* heavy chemicals refining, and *(c)* machine production has been preceded by adequate information on and careful estimation of the dangers of duplicating facilities, of the capacity of respective markets to absorb, and the advantages of planning in view of long-run considerations. (5) Scientific information has at no time been pooled within the industry; the industry is characterized by a multiplicity of secret methods and processes and plagued by an excess of patents, trade-marks, and trade secrets. (6) The steel companies do not have the cooperation of the most of their workmen. The "science of work" movement has been restricted to elaboration of the *DINTA* organization, which is dedicated to the task of building up company morale by striking at the foundation of trade-union sentiment.

There has been, in short, much careful planning and integration within individual enterprises, a measure of coordination between technologically interdependent enterprises, but no such thing as planning for the industry. Taking the industry as a whole, its major rationalization achievements have been along the line of improvements in the efficiency *potentialities* of its various types of technical equipment. Increase in efficiency, in "economic effectiveness," is impossible to measure except with such large margins of error as to vitiate comparison. But the improvement is there. The industry has not been able to stabilize its production or its markets, although it has achieved, through cartel organization, a certain degree of price stability for certain specified commodities. Nor has it improved one iota the personal security of either workers or salaried staff. Quite the reverse. Finally, the problem of income distribution has not even been faced. The steel industry in Germany is organized first, last, and always for the sake of the stock and bond holders, and the upper salaried managerial brackets. Capital takes all it can get. Labor uses every weapon at its disposal to achieve a similar objective. As an industry it is without plan, systematic organization, or group objectives other than those common to all narrowly organized capitalistic enterprises.

CHAPTER VII

THE MACHINE INDUSTRY

A GLANCE at table 17 shows why rationalization was of paramount importance to the German machine industry:[1]

TABLE 17

PRODUCTION, CAPACITY, AND DEGREE OF UTILIZATION OF THE GERMAN MACHINE INDUSTRY
(in millions of marks)

	1925	1926	1927	1928	1929
Production	1,933	2,500	3,400	4,000	4,200
Capacity	3,359	4,940	5,350	5,500	5,650
Per cent production was of capacity	72.4	50.6	63.5	73.0	74.0
Excess capacity	27.6	49.4	36.5	27.0	26.0

But what such a table cannot show is the meaning of this state of affairs for the whole German industrial system. The fortunes of the machine industry have a peculiar importance for any economic system where the great number of productive activities are centered around machine processes. The machine-producing industry supplies the machinery and equipment which keeps the whole vast interconnected network functioning in detail and at large. The more highly mechanized an industrial system becomes, the greater the pivotal rôle of the machine-producing industry, hence the more far-reaching and disastrous the effects of a breakdown in this field.

Rationalization of the machine-producing industry is, therefore, a matter of deep concern not only to producers in that field but also to all machine-using industries. Upon the machine industry are laid three principal obligations: (1) production of cheap, efficient, and high-quality machinery; (2) promotion of technical progress; and (3) design of machinery which will facilitate the maximum employment of mass-output methods wherever machinery may be used. Balancing of these three sometimes contradictory functions, and general promotion of each without damage to the others, forms the subject matter of rationalization within the machine industry.

---

[1] *Statistisches Handbuch für die deutsche Maschinenindustrie* (published by the VDMA; Berlin, 1930):57.

1. IMPORTANCE OF THE MACHINE INDUSTRY IN THE GERMAN NATIONAL SYSTEM

The importance of the machine industry in the German rationalization movement is further increased by the commanding position which it occupies in the output of the German national system.The 1925 census of occupations showed 839,005 persons employed in the "pure" machine industry. The census of establishments, taken at the same time and based on a somewhat different classification, showed the machine industry to be made up of 17,500 establishments, employing some 790,000 persons. Estimates made by the Federation of German Machine Builders' Associations (*Verein Deutscher Maschinenbau-Anstalten*—abbreviated *VDMA*) showed these numbers to have decreased to 15,700 establishments employing 620,000 persons in 1930.[2] Extended to include auxiliary industries, the machine and vehicle building industries employed 862,000 persons in 1926, 1,080,000 persons in 1927, and 1,112,000 persons in 1928. The figure for 1928 contrasts with 690,000 persons employed in that year in mining, 379,000 persons in the iron and steel industry, 652,000 in the industries producing iron and steel goods, and 1,131,000 in the textile industry.[3]

The value of output of the German machine industry had increased from 2.8 billion marks in 1913, and 2.5 billion marks in 1926 to 4.2 billion marks in 1929.[4] By 1925 Germany's share of world machine production, rated in value of output, had fallen from 20.7 per cent in 1913 to 13.1 per cent.[5] While complete figures are not available for the last two or three years, there is evidence that subsequent increases in output have brought the German percentage up to the pre-war level.

---

[2] *Handbuch*, pp. 50–51. [3] *Ibid.*, p. 12.

[4] German production, foreign trade, and consumption of machines, valued in millions of marks, for the period 1913–1929, were as follows:*

	1913	1926	1927	1928	1929
Production	2,800	2,500	3,400	4,000	4,200
Internal market	2,050	1,660	2,440	2,830	2,770
Percentage of production	73	66	72	71	66
Foreign market	750	840	960	1,170	1,430
Percentage of production	27	34	28	29	34
Import	100	90	170	200	170
Percentage of export	13	11	18	17	12
Export surplus (export-import)	650	750	790	970	1,260
Consumpton (domestic market plus import)	2,150	1,750	2,610	3,030	2,940
Imports in percentage of domestic use	4.7	5.1	6.5	6.5	5.8

* Source: *ibid.*, p. 59.

[5] The post-war shift in the machine production of the more important countries was as follows:*

Country	1913		1925		
	Given value	Percentage of world production	Pre-war value	Given value	Percentage of world production
United States	6,775	50.0	8,465	12,697	57.5
Great Britain	1,607	11.8	2,007	3,010	13.6
Germany	2,800	20.7	1,933	2,900	13.1
All others	2,378	17.6	2,300	3,452	15.7

* Source: "Die Maschinenindustrie der Welt" published by the VDMA (Berlin, 1926): 3.

At any rate, such is the case with exports, Germany's share of the world's total being 29 per cent in 1930.[6] Although textile exports are greater than those of machinery, machinery contributes more to the net commodity export because of the high level of textile imports.[7] Even in the bad year of 1930 the machine industry contributed 13 per cent of the total exports of manufactures and 18 per cent of the export surplus. In the same year chemicals contributed 11 per cent to the export surplus; textiles 10.5 per cent; the electro-technical industry 7 per cent; and the iron and steel industry 5.6 per cent.[8]

Differences in the available figures relating to number of employed persons, value of output, percentage of export, and other details result in large part from differences in the types of industries included. The machine industry, of course, has many branches and covers a wide range of products. The *VDMA* classification of the industry, together with percentages of the number of workers employed and share of total machine exports accounted for by the various branches of the industry organized in special trade associations belonging to the *VDMA*,[9] are given in table 18 (p. 142). To this listing might be added several other categories, such as bridges, automobiles, and internal combustion engines.

The complexity of the industry is further increased by the fact that many of the larger and some of the smaller companies produce several different types of machinery and machine parts. "One makes both locomotives and fine machine tools, another milling machinery and trucks, and at the same time builds bridges, and so on."[10] Shops, sometimes established as independent plants and producing machinery and machine parts, are maintained by several industries not directly classified among the machine-producing companies. Among these are the chemical, steel manufacturing, and electro-technical industries. For convenience, the

[6] See *Maschinenbau* (1931), vol. 4. Figures for the preceding years were as follows:‡

	1913		1927		1928		1929*	
Exporting country	Million marks	Percentage of world production	Million marks	Percentage of world production	Million marks	Percentage of world production	Million marks	Percentage of world production
United States**	680.6	26.8	1,442.6	34.4	1,684.3	34.2	2,022.7	35.8
Germany	738.4	29.1	†959.8	22.9	1,168.8	23.7	†1,428.0	25.2
Great Britain	721.3	28.4	919.5	21.9	1,065.8	21.6	1,105.0	19.6
All others	396.9	15.7	862.1	20.8	1,013.8	20.5	1,099.5	19.4
Totals	2;537.2	100.0	4,184.0	100.0	4,932.7	100.0	5,655.2	100.0

* Preliminary totals.
** Fiscal year ending June 30, 1913.
† Includes reparations deliveries.
‡ Source: *Handbuch*. p 62.

[7] The machinery export surplus was 787,000,000 M. in 1927, 972,000,000 M. in 1928, and 1,255,000,000 M. in 1929. In the last-named year the export surplus for chemicals was 899,-000,000 M., textiles, 827,000,000 M., and electro-technical products, 528,000,000.—*Ibid.*, p. 38.

[8] Quoted in *Vorwärts* (March 4, 1931).

[9] *Handbuch*, p. 90. These special associations, for which the VDMA is the central organization, included, in 1930, 2,150 firms employing 430,000 persons.

[10] Angell, *op. cit.*, p. 140.

electro-technical industry is usually segregated from the machine industry, but it is nevertheless an important producer of electrical and electrically driven machinery.

TABLE 18

VDMA Classification and Trade Association Group	Percentage share of the group	
	Employees*	Exports (1929)
I. Machine tools	14	14.7
II. Textile machinery	12	19.4
III. Agricultural machinery	9	6.4
IV. Locomotives	5	1.8
V. Power machinery	8	12.5
VI. Operator machinery	6	5.4
VII. Blast furnace, steel, and rolling-mill equipment and machinery	2	†
VIII. Mechanical conveyers	7	4.7
IX. Machinery for paper and graphic arts industry	7	7.9
X. Machinery for foodstuffs, luxury, and chemical industries	8	2.2
XI. Pulverizing and ore-dressing machinery	2	2.5
XII. Special machinery and machine parts	16	22.5
XIII. Special apparatus	4	†
Totals	100.0	100.0

* On the basis of the industrial census of 1925.

† Foreign trade figures cannot be determined, inasmuch as the products are listed in the figures of other special associations, whose products cannot be classed under this heading.

2. CONCENTRATION IN THE MACHINE INDUSTRY

For a number of reasons the combination movement in the machine industry has made but little headway, and the rationalization movement, except in certain technical details, cannot be said to have made any considerable progress in any of its many branches. Amongst these reasons, the following may be taken as perhaps the more important: (1) geographically limited markets; (2) low purchasing power of the general population; (3) wide variety of manufactured products; (4) relative ease with which new competitors can come into fields where machinery has been typified and where standardized processing methods are well known; (5) secret character and importance of patents in many of the newer branches; (6) tendency to cater to highly specialized markets; and (7) the spirit of independence among many of the smaller and older firms.

In many branches of the industry the average number of concerns ranges between 50 and 100, with the different types of products manufactured per plant numbering usually from 20 to 100 or more. Including all establishments listed in the industrial census of 1925, the average plant employed but 45.5 persons; in 1930 this number had fallen to 39.5.[11] The average number of workers per establishment employing more than 25 persons had also declined from 184.2 in 1925 to 142.8 in 1930. Of the larger concerns, those associated with the *VDMA* directly or through member bodies numbered 2,150 and employed 430,000 persons in 1930, or an average of 200 persons per establishment. Companies associated directly with the *VDMA* numbered 1,424, employed 359,000 persons, and had an average of 252.1 persons per establishment.

Schulz-Mehrin, in a very compact summary of the combination movement in the machine industry, has differentiated three types:[12] (1) vertical integration of raw materials and manufacturing, of manufacturing and marketing, or of all three; (2) horizontal combination of highly specialized branches of the same industry; (3) horizontal-vertical integration combining some or all of the features of (1) and (2). He classifies these further under the head of (1) fusions or communities of interest, with primary emphasis upon production control and cost reduction, and (2) special long-term contracts, loose agreements, or cartels, with special emphasis upon market-determined costs and price control. Combinations of any of the three types may be of the fusion or cartel character.

(*a*) Initiative in organizing combinations of the vertical type usually comes from the raw-materials industries and from companies operating on a large scale. Examples are offered in the expansion of *Gutehoffnungshütte,*[13] *Kloeckner,*[14] and *Krupp* (coal, iron and steel). Examples where the initiative is taken by concerns primarily of the manufacturing type are found in the expansion of *Siemens-Schuckert* (electro-technical), *Neckersulmer Fahrzeugwerke* (motor vehicles and equipment), and *Ford*. Expansion of the finishing industries into the machine field is shown by *Zeiss* (optical, scientific, and medical instruments), *Osram* (incandescent lamps), and the *I. G. Farbenindustrie* (dyes and chemicals). Schulz-Mehrin estimates that the cost of raw materials could be reduced through combinations eliminating intermediate profits and unnecessary freight shipments by as much as 50 per cent. Further advantages are to be had in the opportunity to control manufacture to specifications and in the assurance of punctual delivery.

While the advantages of vertical combinations in the machine industry lie principally in the field of materials economy, the emphasis in horizontal com-

[11] The 1925 figures of 17,500 establishments, employing 790,000 persons, included the following groups: Repair shops, 7,260 establishments with 41,331 employees; machine-manufacturing plants with from 1–10 employees, 4,198 establishments with 22,061 employees; 11–25 employees (estimated), 2,240 establishments with 32,600 employees; over 25 employees, 3,800 establishments with 700,000 employees—or an average of 184.2 employees per establishment.—*Handbuch, op. cit.,* p. 51.

[12] Schulz-Mehrin, "Produktionswirtschaftliche Zusammenschlüsse im Maschinenbau und verwandten Zweigen," VDMA (October, 1927).

[13] Union with the machine plants, Augsburg-Nuremberg and Esslingen.

[14] Union with the machine plants, Humboldt, and the motor plant, Deutz.

binations is upon reduction of unit manufacturing and selling costs, primarily by way of increased factory specialization and the economies of continuous standardized production. This means reduction in the number of types of machinery and equipment produced, standardization or typification of output and manufacturing processes, plant specialization, and the substitution of serial or "flow" production—endless belts, automatic and semi-automatic conveyor systems—for single production. The advantages of serial or "flow" production are well known. The *VDMA* has given the following figures on unit cost for a typical example:[15]

	Unit cost in marks
Special production of a single unit	1,760
Serial production of three units	1,232
Serial production of ten units	953
Serial production of thirty units	885

To illustrate the advantages of combination which would make possible specialization and serial production, Schulz-Mehrin supposes the following examples:

BEFORE SPECIALIZATION

Firm	Type of product			Total production
	A	B	C	
I	3	2	2	7
II	2	4	2	8
III	1	3	3	7
	Production			22

AFTER SPECIALIZATION

Firm	Type of product			Total production
	A	B	C	
I	6	....	....	6
II	....	9	....	9
III	....	....	7	7
	Production			22

[15] Schulz-Mehrin, *op. cit.*, p. 2.

Thus, without altering the quantity of output, combinations or intercorporate understandings making possible plant specialization thereby open the way immediately for securing some of the economies of mass production. In addition such specialization has a tendency to eliminate the worst features of competitive production, and, if carried through with due consideration of all the significant factors—geographic, market, raw materials, etc.—to bring with it a host of individually minor, but collectively significant, advantages of great importance to the machine industry.[16]

(*b*) Schulz-Mehrin submits a number of examples of horizontal combinations or agreements where one or more of the advantages of a high degree of specialization have been realized. Four drilling-machine companies have concluded a compact making possible plant specialization by limiting factory production to particular products while permitting sale to be made as formerly by the individual companies. Similar agreements have been made by two transport-equipment producers, seven companies manufacturing envelope machinery, three electrical-machinery producers, fourteen textile-machinery companies, etc. In the case of the textile companies, the larger plans and policies are worked out in a single common central office. Five drilling-machine, four foundry-machine, and three automobile companies have combined sales in their respective fields in the hands of central sales companies, taking the legal form of limited-liability companies (*G. m. b. H.—Gesellschaft mit beschränkter Haftung*). About fifty machine-tool[17] producers have agreed to let a leading company, one of their number, act as a central sales office for the whole group. Two pump-machinery companies have agreed to specialize on certain types of equipment, to route all orders to that company most favorably located from point of view of shipping costs, and each to act as sales agent for the other in the field left to its jurisdiction. Five milling-machinery and building companies organized first in the form of a community of interests, and then merged into a single compact unit for the purpose of plant specialization, and the carrying through of comprehensive cooperative production plans. The *Demag* concern, manufacturing various types of machinery, is a pure horizontal concern, organized for the purpose of carrying through works specialization. Some shipbuilding concerns have fused for the purpose of carrying out various rationalization programs.

[16] These are listed as follows: I. Materials supply (centralized purchase, and opportunity for exchange of materials); II. Manufacture (serial production through limitation of type of product and plant specialization, establishment of common standards, pooling of patents, research works schools, construction of offices, equalization of factory loads, exchange of experience, unification of costs and cost-accounting systems, etc.); III. Sale and marketing (pooled advertising, sales offices, sales representatives, catalogues, trade expositions, study of market areas—particularly foreign—central sales); IV. Profit equalization through partial or complete pooling of profits and distribution according to some formula as a counterweight to increased risks from specialization.—*Ibid.*, p. 3.

[17] Lathes, planing, milling, drilling, and grinding tools and variations.

Combinations or contractual agreements of the horizontal type, Schulz-Mehrin classifies as follows: (1) Combinations which lead to the construction of a compact and homogeneous entity. Examples of this type are foundries, which combine iron construction, lifting machinery, smelting equipment, hydraulic moulding machine (*Form-machinen*), hand moulding machine (*Form-machinen*), sand-blast blowers, and ore-dressing machinery. (2) Combinations which produce machinery for a common market, as in the case of agricultural-machinery plants producing plows and chopping, sowing, mowing, threshing and other agricultural machines. (3) Combinations which concentrate on the production of some particular type of factory-used machinery. An example is had in plants manufacturing heavy capacity trucks, light delivery trucks, and large and small passenger cars. (4) Combinations which bring together production of various sizes of some special type of equipment, as in the case of fusion of plants producing small, medium-sized, and large forge hammers. (5) Combinations bringing together production of various component parts of some finished products, as in the case of motor-vehicle works producing their own supplies of chassis, motors, transmission, upholstery, spark plugs and other parts and accessories.

(*c*) There are several examples of the third general horizontal-vertical type of combination in the German machine industry. The *Krupp* concern, as indicated above, is of this type. The raw-materials stage includes coal mines, ore mines, graphite works, nickel and copper mining establishments; the intermediate stage includes blast furnace and steel works, non-ferrous metal refining and foundry works; the semi-manufactured stage includes cast steel foundry, rolled bar iron, rolled plate, and wire works; the finishing stage includes rolled wire nail and tack, shipbuilding, locomotive and car construction, machinery, and appliance works. The *Kloeckner, Henschel,* and *Gutehoffnungshütte* are similarly organized. Another example is that of the *Siemens-Schuckert* concern, which, as a horizontally organized electro-technical combine dividing the manufacturing field with *Siemens & Halske,* is also vertically tied up with wire works, porcelain, glazed board, machine-tool, and cable works, on the one hand, and with electric power companies on the other. Through *Siemens & Halske* it is tied up with the *Osram* company, producing incandescent lamps, which is also both vertically and horizontally organized. *Osram* combines coal mines, clay pits, glass works, and machinery plants with its raw-materials supply system, while its affiliations with its founder companies, the *Auer, Siemens & Halske,* and *A. E. G.,* complete its vertical system in the other direction.

Concerns combining both horizontal and vertical features are usually large-scale undertakings, and, as the vertical feature would indicate, usually include machine production either as an intermediate or an auxiliary industry. This is frequently the case with large concerns manufacturing highly specialized products. Thus the match trust possesses plants making match-producing machinery. The *Bemberg* (rayon) concern has an interest in the *Bermer Maschinenfabrik*

A. G., which supplies its machinery. Similar relationships, on an ownership or strong participation basis, exist between machine-producing plants and most textile plants, cigarette manufacturers, breweries, etc. Sometimes control is exercised from the marketing end. The great consumers' cooperative systems possess numerous factories (producing textiles, shoes, soap, matches, etc.) and machine plants. So do numerous warehousing and commercial distributing concerns.[18]

On the whole, the combination movement in the machine industry proper has made but little headway, although more recently there has been observable a tendency towards speeding up this particular phase of reorganization within the industry. ". . . . the number of combinations in the German mechanical industry amounted to 65 in 1928 and the first quarter of 1929 as against 50 in 1927. Of these, 42 took place in mechanical engineering proper (locomotives, boilers, railway carriages, and machine tools), 1 in the shipbuilding industry, 1 in the automobile and aeroplane industry, 4 in the electrical engineering industry, and 11 in other iron and metal working trades. In 32 cases, combinations took the form of 'financial communities of interest,' and in 23 of mergers. The tendency of the agreements was towards limiting production programs, exchanging orders, and closing down works."[19]

Although the situation is still far from satisfactory, combination in the automobile industry has been responsible for a considerable simplification and systematization. "Thus between 1924 and 1929 the number of motor factories in the country was reduced, by the elimination of the weaker units, from 86 to 17, and the number of types produced from 146 to 40. The following groups, which include branch works of four foreign companies, are now the principal groups in the industry, their production of vehicles in 1929 being given in parentheses: *Adler* (8,000); *Brennabor* (3,250); *B.M.W.* (6,300); *D.K.W.* (2,250); *Daimler* (6,800); *Hannomag* (3,250); *Horsch* (2,500); *Opel* (25,800); *General Motors* (8,150); *Ford* (6,700); *Fiat* (3,000); *Citroen* (2,200)." Here, as frequently elsewhere in the machine industry, "experience of various groups and sales syndicates has shown that only amalgamations prove successful. The most representative German company, the *Daimler-Benz A. G.*, Berlin, formed by fusion of the *Daimler Motoren-Gesellschaft* and *Benz Rheinische Automobil- und Motorenfabrik A. G.*, was able to maintain its production in 1929 and at the same time reduce the number of workmen by 2,500. The *Nationale Automobil-Gesellschaft (N. A. G.)* of Berlin has taken over the *Protos-* and *Prestowerke*. The most important recent transactions to be reported are the elimination of *Durrkopp* from the German motor car factories, the arrangement arrived at between *Wanderer* and the *N. S. U. Vereinigte Fahrzeugwerke A. G.*, and the interest taken by the *Fiat* Company, Turin, in the last-mentioned factory.

[18] The foregoing material was nearly all taken from Schulz-Mehrin, *op. cit.*

[19] B. I. M. I. (July, 1929):143. Taken from Schulz-Mehrin in *Maschinenbau* (Berlin, May 16, 1929).

"Notwithstanding this concentration, the number and capacity of the German motor-car companies are still in excess of demand. For several years efforts have been made to form a trust comprising all big German works, but for various reasons attempts have failed. The ideal solution would perhaps be an amalgamation of the 'Big Four,' i.e., *Daimler-Benz, Adler, Horsch,* and *B. M. W.*"[20]

In general the situation obtaining in the automotive branch is typical of the entire German machine industry, though the probabliity is that the combination movement has made even greater headway here than elsewhere. The difficulties are numerous. Among the factors making for localism, particularism, small-scale and inefficient production methods are (1) excess plant capacity, (2) the necessity or the custom of producing a large and varied number of types, (3) small-scale output which necessitates performance of many operations on a custom and handicraft basis, and (4) an excessive spirit of individualism. As indicated at the beginning of this chapter, the overwhelming importance of the industry in the German national system requires that this situation be rectified as soon as possible.

3. MACHINE STANDARDS

As previously indicated, the most important impetus given to the whole modern elaborate standardization movement came from the machine industry. While production by the use of power-driven machinery has meant, from the very beginning of the "Industrial Revolution," mass output of standardized commodities, or continuous performance of standardized operations, it was only with the development of serial or "flow" production on the one hand and of high-precision requirements on the other that the problem of standards in the machine-producing industry became of decisive importance. Serial or "flow" production usually required a high degree of neat mechanical adjustment in a round of mechanically integrated and automatically or semi-automatically regulated routine processes. Advancement along these lines usually meant, also, utilization of pairs, series, or special groupings of similar or identical machines and mechanical equipment performing similar or identical operations. Under these circumstances integration of mechanically continuous processes, coupled with the necessity for simple maintenance and rapid repair, quickly showed the tremendous advantage adhering to machinery having standard dimensions, equipment, methods of operation, and component parts.

While flow production required a higher element of precision in the adjustment of machine types and component parts, it was also attached to the general movement emphasizing economy of production by the use of mass-output methods. It was one of the first principles—and always later the cardinal one—of this general "rationalization" movement, that investment in buildings, equipment,

20 *Statist, loc. cit.*

and machinery should be reduced to the minimum consistent with the capacity decided upon. As the number of industries using the new methods increased in number the burden of technical innovation was thrown back on the machine industry. The latter was required to supply highly uniform, relatively simple, mechanically precise, technically efficient, and typically cheap mechanical equipment of the various new types on a mass-output basis. The machine industry was compelled, in short, to employ in its various branches the same mass—serial and "flow"—production methods that were in use elsewhere in the production of machinery meeting the new specifications.

Previous to the standardization movement, machinery of the same type and capacity purchased from different concerns would frequently be radically different in design, methods of operation, and in the number, size, shape, and placing of component parts. Frequently the same generalization would hold for the same type and capacity of machinery ordered at frequent intervals from the same plant. Often such machinery was badly adapted to the working requirements of the ordinary operative. Shafting, gears, and other moving parts would be exposed unnecessarily, thus hazarding life and limb of the workman. Frequently the height or the width of the table would be badly adapted to the ordinary worker. Controls, handwheels, tool racks, raw-materials feed and finished-materials tables or bins, etc., lacked safety controls, were badly located, required many unnecessary steps and movements, or lacked certain commonly accepted automatic features, etc. It was not a rare experience, for example, to find handwheels turning from right to left on one machine, and from left to right on another. Cases are known where handwheels turning in different directions were found on the same machines.

The major objection brought against early attempts at machine standardization was that standards would throttle technical development. War-time conditions swept this objection aside under the stress of the need for quantity output at whatever cost. However, experience during this period served in the main to show that standards, if intelligently carried through, not only would not hold back, but usually would aid the advancement of technical improvement. How long and how far this would be true, it has been shown, largely depends upon the nature and general flexibility of the system of standards developed.

Technical interdependence between plants manufacturing various types of machinery, particularly in respect of certain common component parts—screws, bolts, nuts, gears, roller bearings, handwheels, etc.—required that standardization should be on an inter-plant and inter-industrial basis. Standards established within individual plants, or within specialized branches of the industry—and there were many such standards, some of them of long standing—could only be applied to a very limited number of parts and processes. They might very easily, and frequently did, conflict with standards established for similar parts in other plants and other industries and industrial branches.

The various factors listed above which account for the small-scale production methods of the various branches of the German machine industry also show clearly why it was that no national standards movement was inaugurated in this field until after the outbreak of the war. The first attempts resulted in the founding of the Royal Production Bureau *(Königliches Fabrikationsbüro)* for the purpose of unifying and standardizing war supplies. It was soon realized, however, that this involved standardization of the basic elements of the entire machine-construction industry. Hence, the Standards Committee for the General Machine Industry (*Normalienausschuss für den allgemeinen Maschinenbau*) was founded in 1917, charged with the task of standardizing and simplifying component parts. When it was realized that this involved the further cooperation of practically all branches of the machine-using industry, this body shortly gave way to the more comprehensive German Industrial Standards Committee *(Normenausschuss der Deutschen Industrie),* subsequently reorganized as the German Standards Committee *(Deutscher Normenausschuss)*.[21]

Statistics of the committee show that the machine industry has absorbed from the beginning the principal attention of its standards work.[22] Although the large producers attacked the problem with almost religious fervor, various checks showed that many companies, particularly those operating on a small scale, had failed to make effective use of the general basic and special standards established. This situation led the *VDMA* in 1929 to begin the circulation of a series of Standards Instruction Letters *(Normen-Lehrbrief),* designed to acquaint all branches of the industry with the work of the Standards Committee, and having the object of explaining, "in brief, clear, and easily comprehensible terms the technical and, in particular, the economic effects of the practical introduction of the most important machine-building standards."[23] These letters, very widely circularized, and sold in quantities of two or more for the nominal price of 0.50 marks, are remarkable for their compactness (4 pages), clarity, and comprehensiveness. The first of the series sounded the keynote as indicated in its title, "The effects of standardization upon capital, costs, and profits of the enterprise," and purported to submit (as did the letters to follow) evidence of the "advantages of standardization as shown by actual quantitative data at hand." It was here shown that, in a typical case, introduction of standards had the effect of reducing the necessary invested capital from 500,000 to 473,000 marks, and the circulating capital from 550,000 to 455,000 marks, making a total net capital saving of 122,000 marks, while keeping production constant. In the case cited, capital tied up in machine tools, patterns, raw materials, warehousing, goods in process of manufacture, and fluid capital declined by considerable amounts, while small increases were

---

[21] DIN, "Die deutsche Normung, Stand der Arbeiten, Frühjahr 1927," *Deutscher Normenausschuss* (Berlin, 1927):6–7.

[22] See Appendix B.

[23] VDMA, "Rundschreiben," Reihe I, Nr. 17.

recorded for tools, jigs, fixtures, fits and gauges, and miscellaneous control instruments incident to the change. The decrease of total wages and overhead expenses lowered the cost of production per unit from 1,000 to 975 marks with an output of 1,000, and shifted the profit ratio (a higher absolute amount expressed as a percentage of a lower capital sum) from 4.75 to 8.1 per cent.

Running comment was introduced to show how the detailed advantages of standardization in the various phases and aspects of the machine-manufacturing processes could be realized in the special cases covered by the letters that followed. The first of these referred to an extremely complicated field, the importance of which it is difficult for the layman to understand, but absolutely basic for the machine industry, the so-called General Basic Standards (*Grundnormen*). These divide themselves into the following groups:[24]

Group	Content of the Individual Groups
General standards (Allgemeine Normen)	Units (Einheiten), symbols for formulas (Formelzeichen), nomenclature (Benennungen), format (Papier-formate).
Drawings, etc. (Zeichnungen, usw)	Format (Formate), pre-prints (Vordrucke), arrangement and execution (Anordnung und Ausführung), pictures (Bilder), graphic explanations (Graphische Darstellungen), lettering, kinds of (Schriften), symbols for drawing (Sinnbilder).
Basic technical standards (Technische Grundnormen)	Preferred numbers (Normenzahlen), standard diameters (Normaldurchmesser), rounded corners and fillets (Rundungen), bolt holes (Durchgangslöcher), tapers (Kegel), conduits (Rohrleitungen), wrench openings (Schlüsselweiten).
Screws (Gewinde)	Whitworth screws, metric screws, round threads (Rundgewinde), acme threads (Trapezgewinde), buttress threads (Sägengewinde).
Fits and gauges and tolerances (Passungen und Toleranzen)	Reference temperature (Bezugstemperatur), definitions (Grundbegriffe), basic shaft (Einheitswelle), basic hole (Einheitsbohrung), large clearances (Grosse Spiele), limits of working gauges (Abmasse der Arbeits-Lehren), grinding allowances (Schleifzugaben), etc.
Work materials (Werkstoffe)	Steel, iron, non-ferrous metals, testing materials.
Industrial standards (Betriebsnormen)	Diameters and speeds under loads of transmission shaft (Durchmesser und Lastdrehzahlen für Transmissionwellen), identification colors and symbols for pipe lines (Kennfarben und Sinnbilder für Rohrleitungen), basic standards for tools and machine tools, etc.

The next letter gave instructions and advice for the establishment of works Standards Bureaus (*Normenstelle*). It is here emphasized that every factory, no matter how small, has a direct interest in the establishment of a special standards bureau. This bureau can be very small and can be brought under the aegis of the fabricating or construction departments. It must, however, be of a permanent character and should be placed directly under the control of the factory manager. Having an independent staff position, it must be able to pass upon all matters

[24] VDMA, "Die Normenstelle," *Normen-Lehrbrief.*

relating to manufacture according to, or change in, standards in use in the plant. Drawings, blue prints, patterns, all specifications for materials, basic jigs, fixtures, fits and gauges, control over tolerance systems and limits, basic component parts such as screws, bolts, and nuts, and other standards details should pass under its review and should be subject to its control. These standards will inevitably divide into three groups, German National Standards *(Dinormen)*, Special Industry Standards *(Din-Fachnormen)*, and Works Standards *(Werksnormen)*. These are to be preferred in the order stated, it being a guiding principle that the "*DIN* standards are to be applied in the standards office, in the construction office, and in the warehouse, as near as possible according to the original."

It is also the task of the standards bureau to maintain a complete file of all the standards used. If the scale of operations justifies, every plant is advised to maintain a complete file of all German Standards Committee standards. If not, it is deemed advisable to keep a complete set of all those standards applying to the special industry of which the plant is a member. As keeper of the standards in vogue, the bureau is advised to utilize the standards sheets provided by the German Standards Committee, and to keep them filed in the standards portfolio furnished by that same body. There follows advice relating to the method of filing, with due regard to division according to basic standards groups, *DIN* and factory number systems, extent to which taken over, etc. On, or accompanying the *DIN* standards sheets, are full instructions for the use and application of the standard in question. The standards office has the task of instructing workmen in their use, checking up on the results, aiding in cost-accounting studies, and reporting ways and means of bettering, if possible, the standards utilized.

The other letters that followed elaborated in some detail the more important standards groups. These covered the following fields: tools and machine tools, limits, fits and gauges, bolts and nuts, raw and semi-manufactured materials, machine elements, jigs, fixtures and gauges *(Vorrichtungen und Lehren)*, purchase and warehousing, special industry standards. In all cases emphasis has been placed upon use of standard signs, symbols, and nomenclature, materials and parts specifications, precision instruments, interchangeability of component parts, and other details incident to reorganizing, simplifying, and systematizing factory routines, and in perfecting production methods and end products so as to fulfil the requirements of mass production.

Parallel with standardization of materials, parts, processes, and finished commodities has gone considerable emphasis throughout the industry upon "typification" *(Typisierung)* of assembled or fabricated products. Perhaps the best examples are found in machine plants engaged in the production of parts and assembled automobiles, airplanes, locomotives, and railway cars. With the reduction in the number of factories from 22 in 1928 to 14 in 1930 went a corresponding reduction in the number of motor-truck models from 56 to 41. Similar results have been achieved in other branches of the automotive industry. As in the case of parts standardization, monetary savings from typification can scarcely be separated from all those resulting from the other changes of an organic character which more or less necessarily accompany such programs.

There are no data available which would make possible a precise summary of the extent to which standardization has been carried into practice in the German machine industry. The various meetings of the German Standards Committee on the "Introduction of Standards into Practice" are largely taken up with problems relating directly to the machine industry. Roughly, three-quarters of the time taken up by these meetings has been devoted to this field. It was found that the difficulties of standardization in the machine industry were more numerous and perplexing than at first supposed.

One speaker at the Saarbrücken meeting, May 22, 1930, was of the belief that many manufacturers were either wholly ignorant of the existence of *DIN* standards or completely indifferent to all organized standards work. Many greeted all standards proposed or promulgated with distrust and suspicion. Without rather full explanations and illustrations from practice it seemed impossible to convince many managers of rather obvious advantages accruing to the use of specified standards. Frequently *DIN* standards conflicted with carefully worked out and systematically applied works standards under conditions in which it was difficult to convince the company or companies in question of the value of the change. Certain standards, such as those for stationery and standard office forms, were either not stocked by companies supplying these items, or were stocked under the protest that these only added additional sizes to those already cluttering up the shelves. At times suppliers of raw materials either would not be in possession of standards sheets relating to certain types of raw materials or would be manufacturing in compliance with some superseded *DIN* or preliminary *DIN* standard. In other cases the standards in question had not developed far enough to be free from controversy as to their technical merits. The fact that Germany imported and exported large quantities of various types of machines and machine parts opened up another difficulty. Foreign parts, standardized or unstandardized, might not—some kinds usually would not—fit German machinery, standardized or unstandardized, and vice versa. The tendency of bordering states to establish their own standards without reference to those prevailing in Germany was a source of constant difficulty. When to this is added the fact that many firms, both domestic and foreign, demanded deviation from some basic standard in filling special orders for what were at times wholly capricious reasons,[25] the difficulties faced by standards proposals in certain fields seemed at times overwhelmingly great.[26]

---

[25] An example is offered of a "Russian firm" which specified a non-standard thread for an order of incandescent lamps in order that theft might be discouraged.

[26] DIN, *Arbeitsausschuss, Einführung der Normen in die Praxis* (Saarbrücken, May 22–24, 1930; DIN, Berlin, 1930).

While most of the objections raised are easily met, and most of the difficulties presented are of an ephemeral sort, nevertheless the picture is still one of considerable chaos. Despite the emphasis upon "free" participation, "open" discussion, and non-compulsory cooperation, the view seems to be gaining ground that a drastic overhauling of the various branches of the industry must be a condition to the more rapid development of economically necessary and technically unobjectionable standards. The triumphs of capitalistically organized industry along this line have been largely conditioned by the extent to which it has abandoned the organizational implications of laissez faire economy and taken on the form of cartels, special associations, monopolistic or semi-monopolistic combinations, etc. Just as this movement leads to the more rapid advancement of standardization, so standardization prepares the way and promotes the larger integration.

The problems of basic standards, for example, are common not only to the machine industry, but to all industry in the widest sense of the term. Upon them is built the system of interchangeable parts and the methods of mass production in every field. These, in turn, call for regrouping of entire industries, further specialization of plant, and the establishment of a higher command capable of forcing through standards and changes of unquestionable engineering and economic value. Solution of the mass of detailed technical problems, in other words, is tied up with questions of scientific and orderly industrial organization, and these larger problems can only find adequate solutions when the technical foundation has been carefully laid. There is no real question of priority; both phases of rationalization must go hand in hand. Otherwise only partial answers can be found to even the most pressing problems.

4. ORGANIZATION OF PLANT AND MANAGEMENT

Paper achievements in the German machine industry along organizational and managerial lines have been extensive. A survey of the various publications of the Society of German Engineers *(VDI)*, or of the publications of the *RKW*, including the contents of its monumental handbook, will show that the machine industry as the planning, arrangement, and construction of factory and office and factory work similar to that which it has in the standards work. An immense literature has been developed which deals with such problems of the machine industry as the planning, arrangement, and construction of factory and office buildings; floor spacing; assembly equipment; lines and directions of factory flow; linkage between the main assembly and auxiliary feeder lines; auxiliary transportation systems; choice of the type of conveyor systems; integration of works, shops, machines, warehouses, etc.; volume and timing of flow of main and feeder lines; layout of yards and switching apparatus. It is not possible, nor is it desirable, to attempt here even a rough sketch of the technical details and problems surrounding the machine industry on this head.

Solution of many, if not most, of these problems would give results of direct value to nearly all branches of the machine industry. While application of various types of machinery and different methods of layout and organization naturally differ from plant to plant, the underlying principles are everywhere about the same. Because this is true, it follows as a descriptive fact that improvements along such purely technical lines are nearly always paralleled by changes leading to ever closer, more far-sighted, more skillful dovetailing of factory routines and schedules with the industrial system at large. Thus, to cite an obvious example, the type of conveyor system used will depend in part upon the scale of output. This in turn will depend upon the degree of specialization of plant, and organization for mass-production purposes. Plant specialization will depend in part upon factors of location, extent to which each plant is integrated with other technically interrelated plants and shops, size of market, and so forth. Mass output depends upon existence of standardized raw materials, processing methods, and systems of interchangeable parts on the one hand, and upon the internal layout of plants and machines on the other. It is almost an organic necessity that development along any one line be accompanied by adjustments in nearly all phases and aspects of production and the general organization of all phases of the plant or the industry affected by such innovations.

Yet the general character of the German machine industry, roughly sketched above, has rendered it almost as difficult to introduce "scientific management" as it has been to convince its members of the merits of the more basic standards proposals. The fact, for example, that most German manufacturing operations are carried out on a relatively small scale has greatly complicated many of the most important problems of reorganization. Serial or flow production has scarcely any meaning for a firm employing less than 100 men unless the work is highly specialized. As pointed out above, the average size of the larger companies associated with the *VDMA* in 1925 was only 184.2 persons per establishment. Excluding repair shops, there were 6,438 establishments employing 54,661 persons in the two classes employing less than 25 persons. In other words, 63 per cent of the establishments employed slightly over 7 per cent of all workers in the machine industry (excluding repair works). The average for the firms employing more than 25 persons was not large, the 37 per cent of the establishments employing 93 per cent of the workers having an average of but 184.2 employees in that same year. The same general grouping showed five years later an average decline of 40 workers per establishment.

This situation seems to have been greatly aggravated by the fact that the industry has been plagued throughout the post-war period by excess plant capacity. The extent of plant capacity utilization during the period 1925–1929 is shown in the table reproduced at the beginning of this chapter. How evenly this excess capacity is spread over the various branches of the machine industry it is impossible to say. In certain branches it has been high, an estimate showing, for example, that productive capacity in the locomotive making industry was probably twenty times actual output. The per cent of utilization has, of course, become much lower since 1929, the figure given by the Institute for Business Cycle Research for the industry as a whole in 1930 being 59.7 per cent according to one system of reckoning and 54.2 according to another. By July, 1931, these two figures had dropped to 47.6 per cent and 42.1 per cent, respectively.[27]

Nevertheless, important steps have been taken in certain branches of the industry along lines of internal reorganization and introduction of scientific management methods. In general, all those branches of the machine industry which have been taken over or which have been brought under the control of the large vertically organized combinations, have been systematically reorganized and rationalized. Companies so controlled usually specialize upon a narrow range of output, their raw materials, processes, and output are usually highly standardized, and their plants and offices have usually been organized on a fairly modern basis. Such seems also to be the case with respect to the larger concerns, especially those automobile companies owned or controlled by foreign interests, such as *Ford, General Motors, Opel,* and *Citroen.* The heavy truck, omnibus, and motor-tractive industries, largely owned and controlled by domestic producers, have introduced flow-production, assembly lines, and most of the changes incident to maximum utilization of these new methods.[28] A manufacturer of gas stoves has shown in some detail methods whereby unbroken continuity in the mass production of standard parts can be attained, application of these methods bringing him increases in productivity over 1914 practice of 350 per cent in the manufacture of burners, 310 per cent in making partitions, and 180 per cent in making taps. "At the end of 1922, 58 workers, working an 8-hour day, produced 800 gas taps daily; at present 32 workers, working on an unbroken continuity plan, however, for 9 hours a day under a foreman, produce 2,100 taps per day."[29] Similar figures can be obtained for many different companies[30] in various branches of the machine industry.

One of the most interesting cases is that of the reorganization of the railway car building industry. Although this industry lies rather on the fringe of the

---

27 I. K. F., *op. cit., Vierteljahreshefte* (1931), II (*b*): 19. The first figure is capacity rated in terms of numbers of workers' positions occupied; the second, to number of working hours utilized.

28 See, e.g., W. Scholz, "Rationalisierung in der Lastkraftwagenindustrie," *Verkehrswesen,* 5:68–71 (January, 1930).

29 Cited in B. I. M. I., I (August, 1927).

30 "Rationalization in the (automotive) industry has been expressed in reduced prices and increased output per worker. In 1924 the selling price of a motor car in Germany was 125.2 per cent of the pre-war figure, but in 1929 only 61.4 per cent; the corresponding figures for motor trucks were 101 per cent and 65.8 per cent as against an index of about 140 per cent for other machines. In 1927 the share in production of each workman, compared with 1925, had risen from 1.46 to 2.82 cars, i.e., by about 90 per cent. The comparison has since become still more favorable."—*Statist, op. cit.*

machine-producing field, and should perhaps be classified as an "engineering industry," the reorganization which it has undergone illustrates fairly well the problems common to the entire machine field. The case shows quite clearly, also, the tremendous advantages to be derived from an introduction of some of the more elementary principles of organization, and at the same time the hazards and disastrous results of failure to carry through the more important logical implications of the new configuration.[31]

In December, 1926, the National Railways *(Reichsbahn)* concluded with the Association of German Railway Car Builders *(Deutsche Wagenbau Vereinigung)*, organized to include nearly all the more important railway-car builders in the country, an agreement in which it pledged itself to place, for a five-year period, at least 90 per cent of all its orders with members of the association in return for the assurance that the industry would undertake a drastic program of reorganization. Although there were 69 concerns in the railway-car-producing business at the time the contract was made, the companies included in the association comprised all but two of the more important producers.

The association agreed, among other things, to attempt to reduce the number of plants as far as possible. The short period covered by the contract, and the spirit of independence common to many of the companies, made this a difficult task; yet by 1930 two plants had been entirely closed down, others partly so, and plans were being made for still further reduction. This problem was one of the most difficult with which the industry was faced. Before the war about 50 companies had been engaged in the industry; by 1919 this number had increased to 100. Post-war demands for railway renewals and reparations deliveries soon fell off, however, and the number quickly fell to 54 in 1925. With general economic recovery the number increased to 69 by the time the agreement with the association was concluded. Among these companies combinations and communities of interest had set up a number of powerful groups, the most important of which included 8 companies and worked as a single unit in its relations with the National Railways. After the formation of the association, two new groups were set up, the Federated West-German Car Manufacturing Company *(Vereinigte Westdeutsche Waggonfabrik A. G.)* and the *Linke-Hofman-Busch-Werke A. G.* These companies have made an attempt to centralize, specialize, and coordinate production within their own plants.

But to return to the contract with the association, an obvious need existed for reduction in the number of types of railway cars produced and for the placing of these orders in such a way that each plant should be able to specialize upon a particular standard type. This latter task was carried to practical completion with great energy and thoroughness. Paralleling this process the association, in co-operation with the National Railways, undertook to reduce the number of types

---

[31] The following data on the railway-car-building industry are mostly taken from the *Handbuch* of the RKW, pp. 1092–1123.

produced in the various plants. Previously, every plant had been equipped to produce, largely on a "tailor-made" basis, nearly every type required by the railroad. It became possible through the efforts of the association for each plant to specialize upon one or a narrowly limited number of types and then to introduce methods designed to place their production on a mass-output basis. Contrary to previous practice, for example, the order for the new cars of the Berlin Municipal Railways was divided among six plants; likewise the order for heavy capacity freight cars was divided between two firms.

The way was then prepared for standardization of single and component parts. The coupler and bumper equipment, doors, wooden and steel beams and bracing, bolts, nuts and screws, brakes, and numerous miscellaneous parts were standardized, although in some cases only after very careful, protracted, and painstaking investigation and analysis. Manufacture of component parts called immediately for standard specifications for parts, the construction of a set of limits, fits, and gauges in order that parts be kept within the tolerance limits necessary to insure interchangeability and close cooperation with companies supplying materials not manufactured by the car-building companies. In cooperation with raw-materials supply companies, for example, a set of standard steel profiles was established. These could be supplied by the rolling-mills at an unusually low price, for the simple reason that they could be rolled in large numbers, and the expense attached to frequent heatings, change of rolls, storage of many little-used types of beams, and rolls and special equipment for handling these and other details involved in manufacture to special order, could be eliminated. At the same time builders would save on storage expenses, and the knowledge that standard materials would be supplied as needed made it possible for both rolling-mills and car builders to dispense almost entirely with storage of even the standard types. Centralization of purchase by the association, and the placing of large orders for standard types, made it possible for individual firms to dispense with elaborate accounting and requisitioning files, while supply companies were thereby enabled to fill large orders on an efficient mass-production basis under circumstances in which such production could be dovetailed and planned with respect to other output schedules.

Utilization of standard parts and car types practically eliminated the former designing and drafting departments, and the use of simple but precise gauges and other control instruments had a tendency to reduce the necessary supervisory and highly skilled working classes. While flow production in the sense of continuously moving belts and conveyor systems did not, because of the character of the work, commend itself to the industry, yet a type of continuous production was introduced for parts and main assembly. This consisted of conveyor systems which moved the parts, came to a stop for a definite interval of time sufficiently long to permit the necessary operations, and once more moved on. The mounting of the trucks, framework, floor, and other heavy parts now takes place as the car moves through the shop, instead of their being fitted, as before, by being brought to a single spot where the car was built complete. The various parts may then be fed into the assembly schedule by the use of the type of conveyor system mentioned, without the further use of internal transportation systems or the undue accumulation of materials or parts at any point. Flow to the assembly line, being now made up almost entirely of standard parts, eliminates all special cutting and fitting on the one hand and makes possible the use of expensive lathe, joining, cutting, planing, and other machinery on the feed lines on the other. Most of this work has been subdivided to the point where a high degree of precision and finish can be obtained by unskilled workmen without any more training than the ability to read and follow simple instructions relating to the highly routinized tasks to be performed. Skilled workmen are then either graduated into the engineering, supervisory, and planning staff—all three branches of which can frequently be reduced in number—dispensed with, or reduced to the status of the unskilled.

In many cases the changes made altered almost the entire layout of the plant. Auxiliary and spatially separated shops could be joined to the main works directly or dispensed with almost entirely. In most cases nearly the entire range of operations was concentrated under a single roof, nearly all internal transportation except the belt systems was eliminated, and that which remained was mechanized by the use of electric or motor trucks, carriers, traveling cranes, and other similar equipment. Important reductions were made in the total amount of space in use, in the materials necessary in raw, semi-finished, or completed shape, and in the time required for car production. While the added expense for certain types of automatic machinery offsets measurably some of the savings attached to the changes, the net advantages have been striking. Operations which formerly required three hours have been reduced to half that time in some cases, and to 20 minutes or less in others. Freight-car types that formerly required 24 days to make by unit production can be turned out in 15½ days by the introduction of plant and personnel systematization, and in 8½ days by the addition of flow-production methods. Certain types can be produced in five days which formerly required 24 days, and changes in prospect forecast further reductions still.

Many of the changes made were carried out at a time when general financial conditions were very bad both for the car-building industry and for the railroad company. The success of the rationalization measures under way and in prospect inspired enough confidence in the industry, however, to cause a banking consortium to guarantee, in 1929, credit on order to the car-building industry to the amount of 100 million marks. Meanwhile other difficulties were encountered. Shortage of funds, making it hard for the railroad to plan its purchases for a considerable period, had made it difficult for the car-building industry to take advantage of the economies forecast in its new production methods. Thus anticipation of impending increases in certain types of fall and winter traffic was the occasion in 1927 for the placing of an order on short notice which kept the freight-car plants busy overtime, while leaving the passenger-car part of the industry completely idle. Introduction of the 2-class system in 1928, on the other hand, resulted in a sudden need for large numbers (8,000) of the cushion and other types of passenger coaches, and overburdened this portion of the industry, while leaving the freight-car section idle. The effect of such policies was largely to offset the cost advantages accruing from the reorganization—which had by that time largely taken place—and to discourage further effort along these lines.

Many other branches of the machine and engineering industries have more or less similar histories. In some cases it has been possible to carry through reorganization with great speed and to realize therefrom tremendous increases in general plant efficiency.[32] Director Lange of the *VDMA* attributed the increase in efficiency in the engineering field, which he found to be some 28 per cent, or an increase of an average output per worker from 1,090 to 1,500 kg. between the

[32] Thus the RKW *Schriftenreihe* (Berlin), vol. 1, offers the following data on a sewing-machine plant located in Karlsruhe, showing output increases ranging from 40 to 60 per cent over previous practice as a result of introduction of conveyor systems, and general plant reorganization taking place between 1925 and 1926:

	1925	1926
Foremen	97	27
Employees	72	35
Productive workers	684	383
Unproductive workers	451	207
Apprentices	62	15
Productive minutes per unit	1,300	600
Transport workers	87	6
Average wage	0.50 marks	0.70 marks
Maximum wage	1.15 marks	1.75 marks
Units in circulation	60,000	14,000
Time necessary for the production of a unit	90 days	16 days

Cited in B. I. M. I. (September, 1927):12.

Another example is offered in the case of the Deutz Motor Works, where rationalization measures gave the following results:*

1. The experts in the workshop suggested an improvement in the shape of the twin-cylinder casting of a large 20-HP two-stroke motor which resulted in a reduction of the gross weight by 15 per cent and a reduction of the total costs by 45 per cent.
2. The time required for mechanical work in finishing the crank-shaft of a 10-HP motor was reduced by 28 per cent by the application of a multiple lathe (Vielstahlbank) and the conveyor principle.
3. The time needed for the finishing of a 25-HP cylinder was reduced by 42 per cent by the use of special drilling machines and by the application of friction in lieu of grinding.
4. The use of the conveyor for the erection, filling up, and lacquering of the two-stroke motors resulted in savings of 67–80 per cent.
5. The employment of individual control resulted in an improvement of quality which made it possible to reduce the time required for passing the test room by 30–60 per cent.
6. The output per head rose from 24.5-HP in 1914 to 34-HP in 1924 and to 55-HP in 1926.
7. For the production of 1-HP there were needed 84 hours in 1914, 59 hours in 1924, and 38 hours in 1926.
8. The time needed for the complete manufacture of a 600-HP motor which was 6 months in 1925 was reduced to 4 months by the end of 1926. The manufacture of a small motor was completed in 3½ months in the beginning of 1925, in 3 weeks in the beginning of 1926, and even in 10–12 days.

* Source: *ibid.,* and quoted in B. I. M. I. (August, 1927):9.

first quarter of 1925 and the last quarter of 1926, to rationalization in this branch of industry.[33] The accompanying chart, constructed from figures provided by the *VDMA* itself, shows the general progress of the machine industry, taken as a whole, as estimated by the *VDMA*. Whatever reasons may be given for all the increases shown, there can be no question that the greater part is directly traceable to the various reorganization measures described.

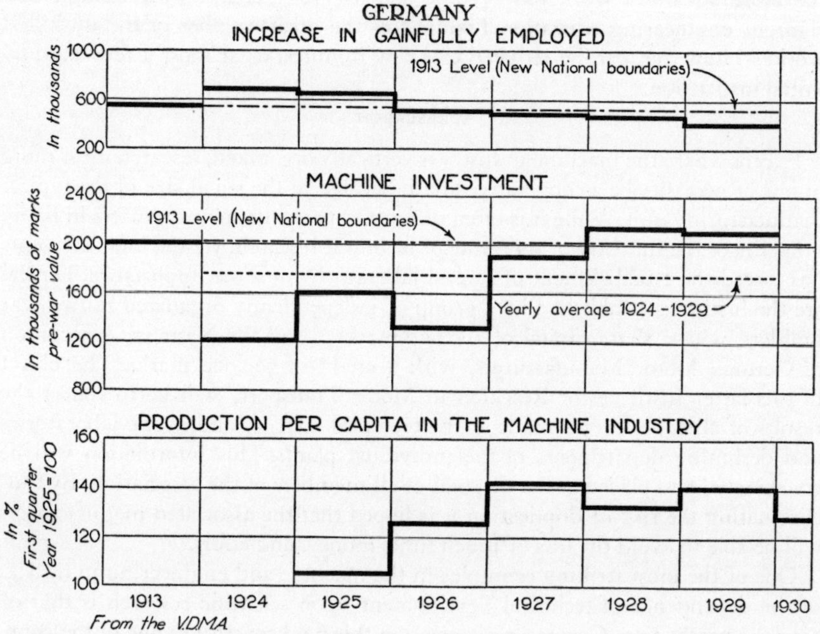

How much the individual changes are responsible for the improvement shown, it is likewise impossible to estimate. The individual changes are so much a part of the whole process of reorganization, and changes made in one phase of plant activity are so closely bound up with the new organic and functional set-up, that it is impossible to isolate the causal efficiency factors, in terms of either physical output or costs, except in certain rather striking examples, and even then only by the use of rather arbitrary criteria.

Particularly is this true as far as training and selection of personnel are concerned. As noted above, there is a tendency for the highly skilled to become more skilled and enter the managerial or engineering ranks, and for the less skilled to gravitate into the unskilled classifications. Apprenticeship has become largely a matter of technical schooling and education in the making and reading of

[33] *Maschinenbau*, VDI, Nr. 7 (Berlin, 1927).

designs and blue-prints, and the acquisition of a certain basic manual dexterity. Some of the machine shops have their own schools, and the larger companies, directly and through the engineering and promotional organizations to which they belong, cooperate very closely with the German Institute for Technical Education and Schooling. While rule-of-thumb methods are being supplanted among the lower skill classifications by systematic training guided by coded practices, the more advanced work has become a matter of increasingly thorough and rigorous engineering education. Training of the great number of the unskilled workers, however, can be reduced to a few minutes, or at most a few days, of initial instruction.

5. RESEARCH

Except where the machine industry is vertically organized, research must more or less of necessity be a cooperative affair, because of the small size of the typical manufacturing unit. While it is often difficult to persuade manufacturers in many branches of the industry of the value of technical research, yet the logic of events has forced the establishment of several laboratories of some importance. Typical are the institutes established by a group of independently organized railway-car builders, with a share capital of 100,000 marks,[34] and the National Association of German Motor Manufacturers, with a credit of 500,000 marks. The object of this latter Institute for Research in Motor Transport, "will be to collect the results of all experiments made at the technical colleges and in the laboratories and designing departments of the individual plants. This information will be coordinated and placed at the disposal of all members of the association. By thus eliminating the risk of duplication it is hoped that the associated manufacturers will be able to avoid the loss of much time, money, and effort."[35]

One of the most striking examples in the machine and engineering industries of the dependence of technical development upon scientific research is that of airplane production. German pioneering in this field constitutes one of the country's most notable contributions to modern industry. Almost from the beginning of the airplane building industry, research, largely because of the strategic, spectacular, and hazardous peculiarities of air transport, has been more or less of a public function. The three more important airplane research institutes, the German Research Institute for Air Transport *(Deutsche Versuchsanstalt für Luftfahrt)*, the Aerodynamic Research Institute at Göttingen *(Aerodynamische Versuchsanstalt zu Göttingen)*, and the Aerodynamic Institute of the Aachen Technical College *(Aerodynamisches Institut der Technischen Hochschule Aachen)*, cooperate very closely with the *Kaiser Wilhelm-Gesellschaft*,[36] and are semi-public in character.

---

[34] *Statist, op. cit.*

[35] VDI *Nachrichten*, cited in B. I. M. I. (December, 1928):235.

[36] The second mentioned institute is associated with the Kaiser Wilhelm Institut für Strömungsforschung at Göttingen.

In management proper, one of the most interesting developments in the machine field has been the development of "Management Research Groups." The first of these was formed by the Association of German Machine Tool Factories *(Verein Deutscher Werkzeugmaschinenfabriken),* under the leadership of Dr. Schoening of the *Raboma* works (radial boring machines). Subsequently several *"Erfa" (Erfahrungs-Austausch*—"exchange of experience") groups have been been formed, and their success has been acclaimed with almost apostolic fervor. With the warning that "business secrecy" is an "economic danger," under the inspiring motto, "All for each and each for all," and with the counsel that "in business life all labor is vain unless inspired with the spirit of mutual effort and fellowship," these merchant knights of St. George have girded their armor and are going boldly forth to slay the dragon of "excessive individualism," and to banish the "pettiness and harmfulness of mutual distrust."[37] A judicious mixture of metaphysical terminology and canny foresight makes it possible for the promoters of this movement to come directly to the real point, viz., that the advantages of pooling information and of breaking ground for the effective abandonment of competitive production are so great that even this highly individualistic industry cannot afford to ignore them longer. Organized in small groups of six to eight among non-competitive firms, the movement has spread into various branches of the machine industry, and more recently groups have been formed to include competitive concerns. At first the programs were rather general and vague, but these have been quickly followed by more definite and practicable plans for action. It has been insisted that "all cards must be laid on the table," and that they must include practically the entire range of managerial and factory problems. The program of the *Erfa* group mentioned above has the following scheme of study:[38]

1. Works management:
   - Objects and methods of the modern type of group work
   - Handling of visitors
   - Apprenticeship
   - Methods of stimulating workers to take pleasure in their jobs
   - Statistics and comparative reports
   - Capital
   - Taxes and depreciation
2. Raw materials:
   - Methods of increasing the output of foundries
   - Laboratories in connection with foundries
   - Testing of materials
   - Physics laboratories
   - Purchasing (cooperative buying)
   - Selection of material

[37] Hermann Schoening, "Geschäftsgeheimnisse—eine wirtschaftliche Gefahr!" *Maschinenbau* (January, 1930).

[38] Ferdinand Lingemeyer, "Der Werksleiter," *Erfahrungsaustausch* (February, 1930).

3. Manufacture:
   - Speeding up of production
   - Practical standardization
   - Flow of material
   - Reduction of immobilized capital
   - Simplification of the production program
   - Transport, railway sidings
   - Wage systems, the Bedaux system

4. Sales organization:
   - Construction of a sales organization
   - Relations with own agents
   - Market analysis and research
   - Exports, opening up new markets, advertising
   - Trade with Russia
   - Index cards and addressing

While it is maintained that these groups are patterned after American practice, their proponents are very careful to differentiate this type of organization from the work "... done in the many hundreds of existing industrial associations in bringing together competing firms with the object of reaching an agreement as to prices, marketing conditions, etc. ...," since the members of these latter are "careful to guard against the giving away of trade secrets,"[39] and thus run counter to the intention of the *Erfa* groups.

Whether these groups, branching out to include competitive concerns, may be preparatory to, or are in fact themselves, communities of interest, and thus first steps in the direction of amalgamation and combination is somewhat of an academic question. They show the admission, however reluctant, that the competitive cell, surrounded as it is with an air of secrecy, is no longer large enough to afford the expense, or comprehensive enough to provide the experience required, in order to solve modern managerial and productive problems on its own account. It has become apparent that systematic, far-sighted, and comprehensive research can no longer be confined within the limits of factory walls even in the more highly specialized fields. These problems reach horizontally out into and affect every single productive unit in the field. Their solutions call for consideration of issues relating to materials, methods of working, personnel, and distribution which must be brought under review in cooperation with industries reaching backward into supply and forward into distribution fields. The major rationalization problems faced by the industry can be handled only through systematic and cooperative labor. Industrial and organizational research is thus placed on precisely the same footing in the machine industry as the standardization movement.

This fact becomes still more apparent upon examination of the forces behind the combination movement in various branches of the machine industry. The problems of machine production cannot be separated in many respects from those

[39] Cited in B. I. M. I. (July, 1930):144–146.

facing the various industries which they supply: textiles, steel, coal mining, chemicals, etc. These technical ties become more binding and coercive with the passage of time. Here, as elsewhere, the same forces making for increasing simplification and standardization of types and component parts and for increasing shop and plant specialization also compel the integration of these processes into the larger "four-dimensional"—horizontal and vertical—set-up.

6. INDUSTRIAL AND INTER-INDUSTRIAL COORDINATION AND INTEGRATION

Enough, perhaps, has been said above to indicate the essentially "service" and feeder rôle which the machine industry plays to other related industries. Whether initiative comes from the side of the raw-materials supply, or the machine-using industries, makes little difference in the long run. In nearly all branches where machinery and auxiliary equipment are highly specialized, the tie-up with machine-using industries is apt to be very close. The textile industry has a very direct interest in all technical changes brought about in textile-machine manufacturing plants looking towards increased efficiency, mechanization, precision in control, and lower costs. The machine plants, on the other hand, have a very direct interest in textile methods, fiber research, textile markets, and other matters conditioning machine requisitions. These ties are becoming closer and more binding in all industries where the technical and organizational problems overlap to a considerable degree. Changes in any such interdependent complex—textiles, chemicals, automobiles, airplanes, locomotives, etc., and their auxiliary machine industries—whether of a purely technical or an organizational character, and wherever originated, affect all other related branches. This is true not only in the general market sense in which all individual economic activities are dependent upon all other economic processes, but also in the sense that they mean direct and significant technical and managerial adjustment through the complex.

A very interesting example is afforded by the shake-up in the locomotive construction industry incident to reorganization of the National Railways. Technical rationalization was held up by a number of factors, foremost among which were excess plant capacity, decline in domestic and foreign orders, and the habit competing firms had of equipping themselves to bid for the construction of nearly every type of locomotive desired at home or abroad. Transfer of the railways from the separate states to the Reich in 1929 accelerated the process of concentration previously under way, eight companies out of 20 having been eliminated by 1930. A series of combinations, quota transfers, and reorganizations resulted in the rise of a small group of powerful concerns, most important of which are *Krupp, Henschel,* and *Schwarzkopf.* With these changes went plant specialization, as in the railway-car-building industry. *Krupp,* for example, in taking over the quota of *Linke-Hofmann-Busch,* ceded to the latter its railway-car quotas. *Borsig* concentrated on the production of small-capacity locomotives. *A. E. G.* utilized its locomotive plant for other purposes, keeping, however, its electric-locomotive works. These changes, brought about in large part by managerial concentration of the railway lines, and under pressure of the latter for cheaper and more efficient locomotives, paved the way for a thorough overhauling of most of the locomotive plants left in the supply field. Mechanization, standardization, simplification of types, and all the attendant changes were forced through with great vigor and thoroughness.

In the main, however, the cases cited can scarcely be held typical of the production side of the German machine industry. Drastic and thorough as the changes have been in certain branches, the industry at large is still mainly small scale, in many respects technically old fashioned and out of date, and is plagued with excess plant capacity. A spirit of conservatism and individualism antithetical to technical reorganization and acceptance of the new organizational configuration, forecast in slowly developing schemes for a systematically planned and functionally integrated economic order, is common to the industry.

With the exception of the vertically integrated concerns, the distribution side of the machine industry is almost as chaotic as blind and unrestricted eighteenth-century laissez faire could make it. The cartels have not improved matters in these respects, although the *Reichsverband der Deutschen Industrie* has been able to regroup the machine cartels into a more or less orderly system. In 1924 a special industry group included 147 machine-building cartels, with 57 cartels being attached to three other special groups which fall under the *VDMA* machine and engineering industry classification.[40] Since that time the picture has shifted considerably, yet the cartels are essentially temporary, the members distrustful of each other, and the objectives are determined by special group interests. There is small reason for regarding them as significant promoters of technical rationalization or as institutions enforcing any considerable order and stability—other than as relates to price maintenance—in the various branches of the industry. The *VDMA* publications emphasize the increasing importance of technical rationalization as an efficient cause leading to and an important effect flowing from the more recent amalgamations. The communities of interest, fusions, and special trade agreements have been turning their attention to these matters much more than formerly.[41] Yet there is little evidence that such changes as have been made have wrought any drastic alterations in the chaotic marketing system that characterizes most branches of the machine industry the world over.

The *VDMA* has been actively working along these lines, as have the various member trade associations. While the number of member companies has increased somewhat, the number of these associations decreased from 108 in 1924

---

40 Max Metzner, *Kartelle und Kartellpolitik*, p. 13.

41 "Die deutsche Maschinenindustrie," *Bericht* des Vereins Deutscher Maschinenbau-Anstalten über die Jahre 1927 und 1928, 35. und 36. Geschäftsjahr, pp. 24–29.

to 80 in 1928, indicating that a good deal of reorganization was going on among these groups.[42] The activities of the *VDMA* and member groups have, meanwhile, been more and more taken up with problems of technical organization, standardization, propaganda and literature on serial and flow production, and closer cooperation with the *RKW* and the Committees on Economic Production (*Ausschuss für Wirtschaftliche Fertigung—AWF*) and Economic Management (*Ausschuss für Wirtschaftliche Verwaltung—AWV*). The *VDMA* has undertaken active promotion of marketing proposals. The agreement made with the steel interests, the so-called *Avi-Abkommen,* whereby machine producers received a reduction in the price of steel ordered for the purpose of machine manufacture for the export trade to the amount bringing such costs down to the level of the prevailing world price, was designed to better the competitive position of the German machine industry in foreign markets. Yet such efforts do not appear to have greatly improved the general distribution mechanisms of the nation's machine industry.

7. SUMMARY

Data obtainable on cost reduction, increased output per worker, and other efficiency checks show that the process of reorganization in some branches of the German machine industry has achieved considerable success. The greatest strides appear to have been made in fields relating to standardization, typification, conditions and terms of delivery, plant and office reorganization, introduction of serial and flow production systems, use of cost-accounting and statistical control methods, plant specialization, and similar technical problems. Both vertical and horizontal integration and coordination have helped to accelerate the adoption of these measures, as they in turn have promoted such amalgamation. Trade associations, cartels, and special federations such as the *VDMA,* the *VDI,* and the *RKW,* have been able measurably to accelerate the adoption of the various rationalization factors relating to research, standardization, scientific management, and systematization through fusion. Inter-industrial integration, particularly in the specialized branches such as machine tools, textile, chemical, shipbuilding and mining machinery, etc., has made considerable headway.

Yet there are many respects in which the whole process, considered either in detail or in terms of the larger organization of the industry, can be said scarcely to have started. Many, if not all, branches of the industry are still faced with (1) excess plant capacity; (2) duplication of productive, and especially distributive, machinery and equipment; (3) ignorance of and indifference or hostility towards the advantages of standards, scientific management, serial and flow production, etc.; (4) badly located and technically obsolete plant; and (5) failure to integrate horizontally and vertically where technique and organization leave no question as to the course that should be pursued.

---

[42] *Ibid.*, p. 24.

There is nothing even roughly equivalent to systematic inter-corporate integration and coordination in any branch of the industry. What progress has been made in the more highly specialized branches has fallen far short of any conceivable type of industrial planning. While the *VDMA* has been able to knit various branches of the industry together for study and general policy-forming purposes, yet it cannot by any stretch of the imagination be called a planning body. Nor is there any indication that such plans are even remotely in prospect. The industry is lacking in organization and efficiency and contains few elements of stability. It has been unable to guarantee either certain returns to owners or security to workers. It has been too disorganized even to attempt to face any of the larger problems of group or social objectives. Except in details—and then only in a rather spotty fashion—rationalization has hardly affected the industry.

Yet the lines of force seem apparent. The coalescing, integrating, and organizing forces have been steadily at work. The logical and organizational implications of the changes already made point to systematic planning as the major alternative to the chaos that has characterized the various branches of the industry throughout the period under review.

CHAPTER VIII

THE ELECTRO-TECHNICAL INDUSTRY

It would be difficult to overestimate the importance of the electrical industry in the whole series of technological and economic ground-swells leading to the outcropping of rationalization as a definite and formally organized movement. The revolution which it has brought about both in detail and in the larger configuration of all branches of industrial activity is still running its course. It is in process of reorganizing many branches of handwork and agriculture. Household techniques—methods of lighting, heating, cooking, cleaning—are being overhauled by the introduction of electric power and electrical equipment. It is an integral part of nearly all problems of plant location, urban planning and decentralization, internal transport, belt and conveyor systems, dust, noise, and health control, and a thousand and one other problems attached to individual process, factory, industrial, urban, and general economic planning.

No less significant are the revolutions brought about by application of electricity to transportation and communication, and the consequent development of rapid-transit networks, the telephone, the telegraph, and finally the radio. So important has electrical development become in these allied fields that the twentieth century has been deservedly called the "electrical age." Electricity holds together and provides the delicate, far-flung, and finely meshed nervous system vital to the systematic organization of markets, exchanges, and production and distribution schedules with all that these mean in a world attuned to mass production, geographical and international specialization, mass distribution, and mass marketing.

The electrical industry divides into two main groupings, the electric machine and equipment producing, or electro-technical, branch, and the electric-current producing, or "power" industry. While the latter was almost from the start a "natural monopoly" industry, the former possessed even more powerful incentives leading to output on a gigantic scale. From its inception, the electro-technical industry was a child of the laboratory. At a very early stage patents assumed an overwhelming importance. At the same time, significant progress was made first in the communication field, where the electro-technical industry was compelled from the beginning to produce for telegraphic and telephonic units of a "natural" monopoly character. The purchasers of equipment—cities, states, and nations, or privately controlled monopolies—were able to buy on a large scale, but were anxious to be guaranteed against faulty and unsatisfactory supplies.

Thus the firms possessing key patents were able to expand their supply business at the expense of companies not so protected. Further, the rapid expansion of the industry called for ability to command large capital investments. The larger and older firms had a very decided advantage in this respect.

When the heavy-current industry came into existence with the development of the electric motor some 30 or 40 years later, the dominant companies were apparently able to expand their activities to include the new field more easily than new companies could be capitalized to compete with them. Had the order been reversed, and the heavy-current industry developed first, it is hard to tell what would have been the story. It would seem, at first glance, that the degree of concentration subsequently developed might have been somewhat less than was actually the case. But this latter branch of the electro-technical industry was also a product of laboratory research, and, like the communications field, has remained dependent upon research ever since. Thus, in contrast to the machine industry, of which the electro-technical industry is, in a sense, a branch, the latter has operated on a large scale throughout its history, and this fact has made it possible for rationalization measures to be introduced systematically somewhat earlier than elsewhere. The war forced further realignment and stimulated the attempt to carry out rationalization to the limits set by scale of production and capital requirements.

TABLE 19

Country	1913			1925		
	Production in million marks	Percentage of total production	Export in million marks	Production in million marks	Percentage of total production	Export in million marks
Germany	1,300	34.9	330.6	2,100	23.3	356.5
United States	1,078	28.9	112.4	4,330	48.1	353.2
England	600	16.0	156.2	1,037	11.5	352.2
All others	756	20.2	89.6	1,527	17.1	241.3
Total	3,734	100.0	688.8	8,994	100.0	1,303.2

Germany was one of the early leaders in the electro-technical field; the growth of this industry practically paralleled the transformation of the country from a technically and economically backward and politically disunited territory to one of the three foremost industrial nations at the outbreak of the war. The relative position of Germany among the three most important electro-technical producing countries is shown in table 19.[1]

[1] *Monograph of the Electrical Industry,* prepared for Committee B of the Preparatory Council of the International Economic Conference of the League of Nations (published by the Zentralverband der Deutschen Elektrotechnischen Industrie; Berlin, October, 1926):18.

The German industry has thus lost its 1913 lead in total production but has regained its position as the largest exporter of electrical goods. In view of the fact that the German industry suffered more acutely than foreign competitors during the war, and of the fact that the post-war settlements deprived it of former foreign holdings, its recent growth may be regarded as phenomenal. By use of appropriate indices which deflate the 1925 figure to pre-war values, it has been shown that the industry registered an increase of 34.7 per cent over 1913 in value of output. Since 1925 German producers have steadily increased their percentage of world export, the value of electro-technical products sent abroad equaling 638.6 million marks, or 27.8 per cent of the world export in 1929.[2] In 1929 the industry provided employment for 351,791 persons.[3]

I. CONCENTRATION OF PRODUCTION

The degree of concentration is shown by the fact that while but 1.9 per cent of the total number of firms fell in the classification of those employing more than 5,000 persons, this group accounted for 66.1 per cent of the total number of persons employed in the industry. On the other hand, 29.8 per cent of the firms employed less than 35 persons and accounted for but 0.8 per cent of the total number attached to the industry.[4]

Geographically the industry is highly concentrated in a few large cities, most important among which are Cologne, Frankfurt, Mannheim, Stuttgart, Nuremberg, and Berlin, the capital city alone accounting for somewhat more than 50 per cent of all the persons employed.[5] Nuremberg is second in importance.

The reason given for concentration of the industry in the large cities is that the great part of electro-technical output requires a high degree of skill and specialization in the various manufacturing stages and processes. Only the large city can supply skilled workers for all the various branches. An additional reason is that the large scale on which manufacturing operations are carried out has necessitated a high degree of mechanization and standardization of routine work. The

[2] *Statistischer Bericht, 1930* (Zentralverband der Deutschen Elektrotechnischen Industrie; Berlin, 1930):9.

[3] *Ibid.*, p. 258. Of this number 71,349 were salaried employees (Angestellte), affording a rough indication of the importance of skilled and specialized persons in the industry.

[4] *Idem.* The figures are as follows:

Size by number of employees	Firms in percentage of total number	Employees in percentage of total number
Under 35	29.8	0.8
35–100	24.2	2.1
100–200	16.3	3.2
200–500	16.0	7.5
500–1,000	6.5	6.2
1,000–3,000	4.2	8.9
3,000–5,000	1.1	5.2
More than 5,000	1.9	66.1

[5] *ETZ* (June, 1930):857.

industry, calling as it does for great precision in the fitting together of many minute parts, and the use of electric power in all phases of manufacture, has created ideal conditions for the employment of large numbers of women; and women, unattached by household duties, particularly in Germany, are to be found in considerable numbers only in the large cities.

A further, and perhaps the most important, reason for the geographical concentration is the dominance of the large concerns. In sharp contrast to the small-scale, and corporately, managerially, and geographically decentralized machine industry, the electro-technical field is almost completely dominated by two gigantic concerns. The combined *Siemens & Halske-Siemens & Schuckertwerke* and the *A. E. G. (Allgemeine Elektrizitäts-Gesellschaft*—called the "German General Electric") control directly about 60 to 65 per cent of the output of the entire industry; through participation in numerous other companies these concerns probably account for about 80 per cent of the total. The headquarters and main manufacturing plants of the two concerns are in Berlin, practically the entire plant of the former being concentrated in Siemensstadt, lying on the outskirts of the city. The former combine is now much the larger of the two, the combined capital of the two branches being 227,090,000 marks, and the number of employees in all plants controlled 100 per cent being 137,000 in 1928–1929.[6] The *A. E. G.* is capitalized at 200,000,000 marks and in 1928–1929 employed 60,107 persons in all plants entirely owned by the concern.[7]

2. ORGANIZATION OF THE BIG COMBINES

These two gigantic combines illustrate very well the two main types of organization evolved in the whole industrial concentration movement. As in the cases of *Ford* in the automobile and *Krupp* in the steel industry, the *Siemens* combine is family owned, has been closely held by the same group from its inception, its directing staff has resisted all attempts at amalgamation with its principal competitor, and its productive and distributive policies have been characterized by "enlightened competition" and a willingness to cooperate with other concerns when it has been manifestly advantageous to do so. Like the *Krupp* concern it was founded by a man of considerable inventive and organizational genius, Werner Siemens, and it has persisted throughout its history in placing emphasis upon the engineering aspect of the industry and the pursuit of conservative corporate policies. As in the case of *Krupp* also, its connections with landed nobility and powerful political parties have been close and intimate throughout.

A. E. G., on the other hand, was founded by an organizational genius of the more purely commercial and entrepreneurial type, Emil Rathenau. The corporation has never lost the original stamp. Its organization more closely approximates

[6] "Der Siemens-Konzern, 1930," *Das Spezial Archiv* (Berlin, 1930):26, 30, 53.

[7] "Der A. E. G.-Konzern, 1930," *Das Spezial Archiv* (Berlin, 1930):27, 29.

that of other large corporations built up more recently in various countries where concentration is more of the fusion than of the expansion type. Analogous are the American Telephone and Telegraph, General Electric, and General Motors corporations in America, and the *Vereinigte Stahlwerke* and *I. G. Farbenindustrie* in Germany. In contrast to the *Siemens* concern, no one family has exercised a dominating control,[8] the plants of the combine are spread over a wide geographic area,[9] plant management has been very greatly decentralized, great emphasis has been placed upon exploitation of foreign markets, and there has been a notable tendency on the part of management to associate itself with more liberal domestic and foreign policies.[10] The *A. E. G.* has usually taken the initiative in promoting fusion of the smaller units, in cooperation with its principal rival, and is unquestionably in favor of combination with the *Siemens* concern.

The *Siemens* concern is divided into two groups, *Siemens & Halske* concentrating upon the light-current, or low-voltage, field—telephone, telegraph, cable, radio, police and railway signal apparatus, etc.—and the *Siemens-Schuckertwerke,* concentrating on the heavy-current, or high-voltage, field—switches, dynamos, motors, cable, transformers, porcelain, etc. Until the entry of the *A. E. G.* into the field more recently, *Siemens & Halske* almost completely dominated the light-current industry. Its contacts with the *Reichspost,* under whose management telephone, telegraph, and most radio transmission systems come, were very close, and the bulk of the local, state, and federal orders for such supplies were given directly to the *Siemens & Halske* concern. In both low and high voltage fields, plants have been highly specialized, internal transportation systems have been installed, overhead conveyor and endless belts have been introduced wherever feasible, and the inter-shop, inter-plant, and inter-process integration has reached a high state of perfection.

Expansion has been in both horizontal and vertical directions, with a tendency to establish separate managerial units, closely controlled by the central office, along both lines. Vertically, there has been a tendency for the company to reach back into the raw-materials field and forward mainly into the power-plant construction and electric-current producing fields. The relations between the concern and the steel industry have always been very close, *Siemens* having taken a leading rôle in the organization of the *Siemens-Rhein-Elbe-Schuckert-Union* during the inflation period. With the collapse of this Stinnes concern, and the subsequent formation of the *Vereinigte Stahlwerke,* the *Siemens* interests were seg-

---

8 Emil Rathenau was, it is true, succeeded by his son, Walter Rathenau. Yet it was less a family affair and more distinctly a transfer of ability than in the case of Siemens. The Rathenau family never owned controlling stock in the A. E. G.

9 While the main plants are in Berlin, the units are smaller than those of the Siemens concern, and the small outside-of-Berlin domestic and foreign plants are much more numerous.

10 Particularly true during the period of control by Walther Rathenau, subsequently asssassinated because of his apparent willingness to compromise with radical and anti-nationalistic elements.

regated and confined more directly to the electro-technical field. Interest in the *Rhein-Elbe-Union* has remained strong, and Carl Friedrich von Siemens, chairman of the board of directors of *Siemens & Halske* and *Siemens-Schuckertwerke,* is a member of the board of directors of the *Vereinigte Stahlwerke,* while Albert Vögler, managing director of the latter concern and of *Ruhrgas,* sits as a member of the board of directors of the *Siemens* combine. In addition, Fritz Thyssen, chairman of the board of directors of *Vereinigte Stahlwerke,* sits with Vögler as a member of the board of directors of the *Siemens-Schuckertwerke.*

The combine possesses in Siemensstadt facilities for refining and drawing imported pig copper for the manufacture of wire, bands, and miscellaneous shapes, plants for the refinement of rubber, the manufacture of porcelain, the weaving of specialized textile fabrics, and the production of other basic supplies. It controls plants, such as those of the *Siemens-Planiawerke,* manufacturing graphite, silicate, carbons, etc., located outside Siemensstadt, which round out the controlled supply system into an almost completely balanced and unified system.

The combine's interests have brought it also into close contact with electric-power production, power-plant construction, and other similar fields. Through the *Elektrizitäts-Aktiengesellschaft, vormals Schuckert & Co.,* the *Elektrische Licht- und Kraftanlagen A. G.,* and other participations, it controls a number of power-production plants, transmission systems, gas plants, and street-car and electric interurban systems. Through *Siemens Bauunion G. m. b. H.,* it engages in construction engineering, its two most notable achievements being supply of the foundation work for the new Danube River bridge built near Belgrade, and the construction of the gigantic Shannon River power plant in Ireland. Construction engineering in the field of high-tension long-distance power transmission, as in the main transmission line of the *Rheinisch-Westfälische Elektrizitätswerke*—"which links up the South German and Alpine hydro-electric stations with those in the North German coal fields"[11]—in which the *Siemens-Schuckertwerke* took a leading rôle, has brought the combine into closer touch with nearly all the major power systems in Germany.

The selling organization ofthe concern has also "been systematically extended hand in hand with the growth of the manufacturing side. Sixty-three branch offices in all the lager and more important towns in Germany are in close contact with the head office; similar branch offices and representatives of the firm are domiciled in Denmark, Sweden, Norway, Finland, England, Ireland, Holland, Belgium, France, Luxemburg, Italy, Poland, Latvia, Spain, Portugal, and Switzerland. The Austrian *Siemens-Schuckert Co.* and *Siemens & Halske* are represented in Austria, Hungary, Czechoslovakia, Roumania, Bulgaria, and Jugoslavia. Resident agents in Esthonia, Lithuania, and Greece take care of the firm's

[11] *From Workshop to Factory-Town; Origin, Development and Structure of the Siemens-Concern* (published by Siemens & Halske):46.

interests in these States. The connection to a large number of overseas countries is upheld by houses affiliated with the Siemens-Concern."[12]

Horizontally, the combine ties together systematic production of a vast range of materials, equipment, and machinery in the same stage of manufacture. It produces every conceivable type of telephonic, telegraphic, and radio transmission apparatus in its low-current plants. It was a pioneer in the field of long-distance telephone and telegraph transmission, having laid the first line connecting England with India, and (through a subsidiary) the first trans-Atlantic telegraph cable. It manufactures and installs all the equipment necessary for telephonic, radio, and telegraphic transmission, including wires, automatic telephone exchanges, receiving and dispatching equipment and sets, television apparatus, and teletypewriter, multiple-telegraphy, electric-signal, clock, and train dispatching systems, etc. Its heavy-current plants produce all types and capacities of dynamos, motors, steam and water turbines, transformers, switches, and miscellaneous tools, fixtures, and apparatus, whether intended for power plants, industrial purposes, or household uses.

While the organization of the concern has been more or less of the "military" type, that is, highly centralized and closely controlled in detail, its evolution has shown appreciation of the need for a considerable degree of managerial decentralization. This has gone hand in hand with plant specialization, a process which has been carried through in a most thorough fashion. As mentioned before, most of the light-current production has been centered in the direct control of the *Siemens & Halske* concern, and in the plants located in Siemensstadt. In 1927 the *Siemens & Halske* railway-signal works, the *Siemens & Halske A. G. Blockwerk*, was separated from the company, united with the *Eisenbahnsignal-Bauanstalten Max Jüdel, Stahmer, Bruchaal A. G.*, and the Railway Signal Department of *A. E. G.*, to form the *Vereinigte Eisenbahn Signalwerke G. m. b. H.* An electro-medical apparatus branch was segregated, combined with four other concerns, and placed under the control of *Siemens-Reiniger-Veifa Gesellschaft für Medizinische Technik m.b.H.* Likewise, the incandescent-lamp works were combined with those of the *A. E. G.* and the *Auer* concern to form *Osram*. Construction and engineering work has been concentrated in the hands of *Siemens-Schuckertwerke* and *Siemens Bauunion*. A similar process of segregation into separate managerial units, and at times cooperation with competing concerns, has been followed in several other fields.

The technical segregation has been even more thoroughly carried out. Separate plants have been erected for the manufacture of cables, airplane engines, rubber products, transformers, meters, porcelain, switch gears, dynamos, small accessories, heating and cooking apparatus, electric motors, etc. At the same time the high degree of specialization has been paralleled with an extraordinarily efficient

[12] *Ibid.*, p. 50.

and smooth-working inter-plant and inter-process integration. Within the individual plants flow-production has been introduced in nearly all manufacturing operations of a repetitive, automatic or semi-automatic, and standardized character. The case of the *Elmo* Works (Electro-Motor Works) is typical. "All machine tools and apparatus are arranged as required by the natural progress of manufacture, all work-places are connected by suitable transport devices, as, for instance, an endless conveyor with hooks and buckets running through 3 stories for a distance of 500 yards. The semi-finished parts are assembled on a long bench the platform of which moves forward at definite intervals from one operative to the next, after which the completed machines pass through the testing station, are painted, pass through a 33-ft. drying stove and are finally delivered either to the packers or the stores."[13] The same process characterizes inter-plant processes so far as technical interdependencies permit. Those plants and buildings most closely related are grouped so as to feed into and take away from flow systems, with the minimum of friction, time loss, waste floor space, transportation equipment, etc. Particularly is this the case with the newer plants. Inter-shop and plant transportation has been mechanized almost completely, flow—i.e., continuous belt and conveyor—systems having been introduced to handle such transport in many cases.

As pointed out above, the *Siemens* combine, while refusing to unite with *A. E. G.,* has on occasion shown its willingness to cooperate with that concern or other companies specializing in some particular field. Exchange of patents agreements have been made, in addition, with several foreign electro-technical companies, most important of which is the American Westinghouse Electric and Manufacturing Company. Through and in cooperation with Westinghouse, the patent exchange agreements extend to and include the Radio Corporation of America, Metropolitan Vickers Co. in England, the *Compagnie Electro-Méchanique* in France, and the *Mitshubishi Deni K. K.* in Japan. Similar agreements have been made with large electrical concerns in Czechoslovakia, Norway, Sweden, and Italy. The agreement with Westinghouse provided for the establishment of non-competitive marketing areas, the United States and Canada being reserved for the American company, and Germany, Austria, Hungary, Danzig, Latvia and Esthonia being reserved for the *Siemens* group.

The post-war development of *A. E. G.* has been in many respects different from that of the *Siemens* group. These differences are in part conditioned upon the pre-war history of the concern. Founded in 1883, 36 years after the inauguration of the *Siemens* company, and at the opening of the heavy-current machinery and power-development era, *A. E. G.* very rapidly expanded its manufacturing and marketing operations, until by the outbreak of the war it was quite the larger of the two concerns. By fusion, the creation of communities of interest, and special patent and trade agreements, it had collected under its control a large number

[13] *Ibid.,* pp. 32, 34.

of plants distributed rather widely over Germany and producing a great variety of equipment. The dominance of the *Siemens* group in the low-current field, and the general strength of that concern in the internal market, were responsible for a general tendency to specialize in the heavy-current field throughout the plants brought under *A. E. G.* control, and for cultivation of the foreign market. The first trend took them into the raw-materials supply field, *A. E. G.* emphasis here always having been greater than with *Siemens*. The second trend resulted in the establishment of hundreds of foreign branches and affiliations, the loss of which during the war caused the tremendous scaling down of the company's post-war capital, number of employees, capacity, and relative importance in the industry.

No fundamental changes have been made in the structure of the *A. E. G.* combine since the war. Although it now faces active competition from the *Siemens* group in the foreign markets, its foreign business is still much the larger of the two concerns, its sales organization including, in 1930, more than 300 separate offices scattered throughout Germany and the rest of the world.

While, as is typical of the industry in general, *A. E. G.* has placed primary emphasis upon horizontal combination, its growth and expansion has been characterized, as above mentioned, by vertical integration as well. By means of separately established plants, fusion with already established companies, or by special participations, agreements, or contracts, the company has extended its control into fields supplying all or a considerable portion of its raw materials. These include such commodities as porcelain, coal, briquets, building stone, lignite, oil (and by-products from lignite), aluminum, foundry and steel products, and gas. The general nature of certain of these affiliations has brought the *A. E. G.*, as in the case of *Siemens*, into rather close contact with the large concerns in the producing field. While the company was never so closely tied up with the large steel interests as was *Siemens*, the working agreements and effective communities of interest must be rather strong. *A. E. G.*, for example, has a direct interest in *Rheinmetall*, which it acquired through a community-of-interest arrangement with *Linke-Hofmann-Lauchhammer*, subsidiary of *Mitteldeutsche Stahlwerke*, which is controlled in turn by *Vereinigte Stahlwerke*. Its interests in the coal-mining industry are centered in the *Grube Leopold A. G.*, Bitterfeld, and in lignite in the *Kohlenveredlung A. G.*, Berlin. These are held through control of a separately organized holding company, the *Bank Elektrischer Werte A. G.*

The company has reached out, on the other hand, into the electric-power producing, building construction, and marketing fields. Through the holding company last mentioned, and the *Elektrizitäts-Lieferungs-Gesellschaft*, Berlin, the concern has extensive holdings in the electric-power field in various parts of Germany and in numerous foreign countries. Its construction work has included such jobs as the construction of the huge Berlin *Klingenberg* power plant, building of electric railroads such as the *Bayerische Zugspitzbahn* and the *Thüringer-*

wald-Bahn in Germany and similar projects in foreign countries. Americans should be interested to learn that two of the most recent *A. E. G.* electric-railway building contracts were given by the Central American states of Guatemala and Costa Rica. Other recent foreign engineering contracts involved the construction of a large steam-power plant, *Krivoj-Rog* in southern Russia, construction of Diesel-motor power plants in Turkey at Angora and Adana, and construction of a large water-power plant in Austria. The concern's extensive domestic and foreign distributing system has previously been mentioned. In connection with its power companies, and through corporate and contractual affiliations, the company has been able to supplement the work of its directly controlled marketing system. Through special publications, such as the "*A. E. G. Mitteilungen*" (technical journal published in German, English, and Spanish), and the "*Spannung, die AEG-Umschau*" (directed primarily to household consumers), and the maintenance of a permanent exhibit in the *Haus der Technik*, located in Berlin, the company is able to supplement and promote its marketing activities.

In the manufacturing field the concern controls plants manufacturing an even greater variety of output than that of the *Siemens* interests. Its high-voltage output includes the entire range of light and heavy power-producing machinery, transmission apparatus, and power-consuming machinery and equipment known to the industry. Through its acquisition of the firm *Mix & Genest A. G.* in 1921 the concern was brought into the low-voltage field and became an extensive manufacturer of telephone, telegraph, and radio apparatus. With the reorganization of this company in 1929, in which the *A. E. G.* pooled its interests with the International Standard Electric Corporation of New York and the *Felton-Guilleaume-Carlswerk A. G.* to form the Standard *Elektrizitäts-Gesellschaft A. G.*, the concern was placed in a strong position in the low-voltage field. The company controls, or owns outright, plants producing cooking apparatus, electric supplies for automobiles (mostly ceded, under special arrangement, to the *Robert Bosch* concern), typewriters, electric trucks and lorries, electric locomotives, cars and trams, radio apparatus, complete "talkie" recording and amplifying equipment, etc.

Internal plant organization has been drastically overhauled and modernized during the post-war period. These changes range all the way from details of internal transportation and introduction of automatic machinery and continuous-flow production methods to reorganization of entire factory layout.

Its plant management, more or less in contrast to that of *Siemens*, is very much decentralized. Each plant constitutes a separate organizational unit which is self-sufficient so far as the conduct of all internal operations is concerned. Reports—daily, weekly, monthly, and annual, so far as these are called for—are made to the central office more or less as though to the board of directors of each unit. Within the confines of the rules laid down by the central office, complete authority over personnel, work methods, design of machinery and equipment, range of productive output, budgetary procedure, and the whole range of plant and office routine resides in the manager of each separate managerial unit.

But the central administration, in thus delegating responsibility to individual plant management, does not by any means withdraw itself from active plant control. The attempt to obtain the maximum of individual initiative and responsibility through managerial decentralization is coupled with rigid insistence upon conformity to the general plans and policies laid down for the integration and coordination of all constituent works. First among these requirements is that of plant specialization. Among plants directly under its control, the concern has regrouped companies and plants so as to avoid as nearly as possible all duplication of facilities and the occurrence of excess or under-capacity at any stage of interdependent manufacturing processes. In all cases emphasis has been placed upon provision of conditions which promote production upon the most efficient mass-output basis possible. Where local conditions, freight charges, or other factors—such as tariff discrimination in foreign fields—have justified, local plants have been established, or communities of interest with local companies have been made with the intent of promoting geographic as well as plant specialization.

Oriented as the concern has been almost from the beginning of its history in the direction of expansion by fusion, its post-war development along these lines has been combined with emphasis upon plant and geographic specialization. Communities of interest, special contracts, and regrouping of products arrangements have been made in many different fields with this object in view. The agreements made with *Siemens* leading to the establishment of jointly-owned and semi-monopolistic companies in the fields of incandescent-lamp and railway-signal apparatus have been previously mentioned. Similar agreements have been made with companies producing electric condensers, copper and brass, automobile accessories, steam and electric locomotives, and various other types of machinery equipment, and supplies. Typical of work along this line were the numerous moves whereby *A. E. G.* combined with *Siemens & Halske,* the *Polyphon-Werke,* and the *Tobis-Konzern* to form the *Klangfilm-Tobis-Gruppe,* which possesses practically a monopoly of "talkie" machinery and equipment in Europe, and is able to compete in the foreign markets with the largest American producers.

The most important *A. E. G.* foreign alliance is with General Electric. The International General Electric, foreign subsidiary of General Electric, concluded in August, 1929, an arrangement with *A. E. G.* calling for exchange of patents, "experience," results of research in their respective scientific laboratories, special study trips for engineers, scientists, and managers of each company to the plants and offices of the other, and (presumably) a certain degree of market delimitation. For certain fields of electro-technical production, this and the arrangement with Westinghouse made by *Siemens* would seem to establish an effective internationalization of patents, research findings, and manufacturing methods as far as the major producing interests in the various important industrial countries are concerned. Westinghouse Electric and General Electric, for example, have pooled patents and research facilities in America in the establishment of Radio Corporation of America. Similar agreements in Germany, especially those relating to the "talkie" machinery and equipment field, when coupled to the American concerns would seem to pool patents and methods for practically the entire industry. The international affiliations of the grouped concerns extend almost indefinitely and include practically all the important companies in the world.[14] Another important international agreement is that made between the German concerns, *Polyphon-Werke A. G.* and *Deutsches Grammaphon A. G.*, with the Brunswick-Balke-Collender Company of Chicago for the introduction of the phonograph electric recording and reproduction method into Germany.

3. STANDARDIZATION

Emphasis upon standards has been characteristic of the industry from its earliest beginnings. It is one of the most interesting facts of the modern industrial system that throughout its history the "mushroom" growth of this industry has depended almost as much upon close and continuous attention to systematic and thoroughgoing standardization as it has upon that laboratory research from which it originally sprang and upon resources of which it has continued to feed. This results, in part at least, from the fact that the industry expanded in the low-voltage field first. It was almost immediately apparent that telephonic and telegraphic communication systems partook, in a unique sense, of the character of "natural monopolies." The original principles and necessary equipment were comparatively simple. A system of intercommunication to be worthy of the name had to be placed on as comprehensive a basis as possible. Hence the early emphasis upon simple, cheap, standard equipment, interchangeable parts, cheap maintenance and repair, readily understandable and standard rules for operation and use, and the largest possible number of subscribers, connections, and users. Early development of inter-district, inter-municipal, and long-distance communication stiffened these rules into unbreakable codes within the confines of which all future expansion and improvement had to take place. Telegraphic service, especially in Europe, was international almost from its inception; telephonic service shortly followed in the same path, and radio transmission of course can scarcely be confined by any means known within national borders.

Emphasis upon cheap, standard, interchangeable equipment in the low-current field provided a technique and an appropriate manufacturing and designing discipline which could easily be imposed upon heavy-current production when it came along. Tendencies in the opposite direction were further curbed in this field

---

[14] See, in particular, an article in *Die Wirtschaftskurve,* 4 (1927):420–432, on "Die internationale Elektrizitätsindustrie und ihre Verflechtung."

by the fact that safety assumed such an important rôle. Many and frequent accidents would have created prejudice against the new power systems which it might have taken years to overcome. Vigorous action by the larger producers and the extremely systematic work of the early engineering societies resulted in the condition that life and fire hazards did not at any time become important deterrents to the industry.

It was also true that the late industrial appearance of electricity as a lighting, power, and heating supply was an advantage from the point of view of standardization. When the electric-manufacturing industry first began, mass production methods of the familiar modern type were being widely introduced in several of the older industries. Long before standardization and simplification had attracted much attention, these new methods had resulted in purchase upon the basis of fairly rigid engineering specifications—specifications in which standards and tolerance limits were becoming more numerous and more rigid with the passage of time.

When the electro-technical industry, particularly in its power phase, put in its appearance, a number of additional factors helped to place output in this field on mass bases and to endow the principal producers with semi-monopolistic powers.

Perhaps the most important of these factors was that the electro-technical industry catered to power producers and distributors who were forced to expand their services on a more or less monopolistic basis. For this situation the power industry had to thank, in part at least, the fact that its expansion was faced from the earliest days by the existence of closely organized and well established competitive energy and lighting systems. A widespread network of coal yards and distributing systems had been built up by the time electric power came on the scene. Gas-supply systems, organized on a municipal basis, and supplying a cheap and efficient light and heating fuel had put in their appearance, and in the early stages expanded much more rapidly than the electric-power systems. The development of the industry was paralleled throughout by still another competitor (potential, if not always actual) in the form of petroleum and its distillates. Hence the power industry was forced, from its cradle days to its emergence as the newest and most powerful of the recent industrial giants, to concentrate on cheap and efficient service. That is to say, it was forced to orient its whole productive mechanism upon a mass-output, or standardization, basis.

It was further true that the electro-technical industry was born of, cradled in, and nurtured by laboratories and laboratory research. Comparatively little except of an experimental nature was known about electrical phenomena even at the time when inventions and improvements made it possible to launch actual production. Contrary to the popular belief, science here as elsewhere developed experimentally in terms of precipitates from reasonable hypotheses, and it couched results reverifiable in the language of working principles and empirically validated "laws." The early scientific findings of immediate moment from the point of view of industrial usage, were relatively simple of comprehension, called for differentiation of design, pattern, and construction only within relatively narrow and fixed margins, and forced the major outlines of both detail and larger configuration into molds and patterns from which the industry has never escaped. On the whole, it seems reasonably consistent with the facts of historical evolution within the industry to say that its scientific foundation was coercive of standardization to an increasing extent, rather than the reverse. The early importance of patents further emphasized this trend. Closely held patents meant that only the owners thereof could exploit the development of the industry. Large-scale operation incident to patent monopoly appears to have markedly encouraged standardization in the development of the industry.

Along this line it was also true that the establishment of manufacture in most lines of the industry required heavy investment, not the least of which was that tied up in scientific equipment, laboratories, and high-priced laboratory and engineering personnel. This factor tended to concentrate production in the hands of the more powerful concerns, hence to promote mass, or standardized, output. The preponderating importance of scientists and engineers in this field unquestionably lent a certain peculiar color to manufacturing emphasis. Concern with industrial exploitation of natural resources, and emphasis upon efficiency and conservation in use, rather tended to promote standardization than the reverse.

Early German expansion in both heavy- and light-voltage fields caused the industries in that country to take an active interest in the standardization movement. Post-war reconstruction placed the industry under handicaps common to industries previously reviewed. The recovery of their position in the world market, and the general advantage of electricity as a power source in most industries faced with the problem of drastically overhauling and rationalizing existing plant and equipment, has brought to the fore and increased emphasis upon the problem of standardization. The various general interest organizations in the field, the *Verein Deutscher Ingenieure,* various groups and committees under the *RKW,* in particular the *Deutscher Normenausschuss,* the *Verband Deutscher Elektrotechniker,* the *Zentralverband Elektrotechnischer Industrie,* the *Vereinigung der Elektrizitätswerke,* the *VDMA,* various government departments, in particular the *Physikalisch-Technische Reichsanstalt* (roughly equivalent to the American Bureau of Standards), and other groups combine with the individual companies in carrying through standardization work. Much of this work, particularly that lying in the field of telephonic-telegraphic, radio, and long-distance power transmission, is carried on in cooperation with international bodies and in collaboration with similar groups in other countries. Nearly all of it is carried on in cooperation between the electro-technical and the power production and distribution, telephone, telegraph, and radio broadcasting interests and authorities.[15]

[15] For a good description of the standards work of the various special-interest associations in Germany devoted to electrical problems, see Paul Meyer, "Organisation und Aufgaben der massgebenden Elektroverbände in Deutschland," *ETZ* (January 15, 1931):69–72.

It would take this discussion altogether too far afield to attempt even an outline of the important developments along this line. German experience differs from that abroad only perhaps in that the movement has been somewhat more systematically organized and carried through in Germany than elsewere. The work ranges from extremely abstract and difficult standardization problems to the establishment of codes for general guidance of consumers using various types of electrical equipment. Thus it includes such things as basic standards of weights, measures, methods of measuring, rating, and controlling; rules for handling machine tools and for controlling output with the maximum emphasis upon standard interchangeable parts; rules for consumer use; standardization of voltages, frequencies, types of current, wiring methods; making provision for interchangeability of plugs, sockets, lamps, cord, and miscellaneous fixtures; coding rules for putting through telephone messages, locating radio stations, making complaints, and paying bills.

Concentration of output in the hands of a few large producers has facilitated the process of standardization and introduction of standards into practice. In most cases standards in this field can be established without the elaborate preparation, detailed procedure, and need of facing objections based upon ignorance and misunderstanding, which are so typical of most standards work. Problems which in other fields would affect hundreds of producers and perhaps several different industries, in the electro-technical industry are matters for inter-plant solution.

4. RESEARCH

As previously stated, standardization and scientific research have gone hand in hand in the development of the electrical field, particularly on the electro-technical side. Most notable are the research facilities of the two large groups. In the case of the *Siemens* combine, "The research laboratory, which serves the common interests of both partners of the concern, is an outcome of the physical-chemical laboratory which Wilhelm von Siemens created for the primary purpose of developing the filament lamp. One of the first problems to be dealt with soon led to an epoch-making practical result: the production of ductile Tantalum metal. The Research Laboratory to-day has a staff of 200 employees and has been housed since 1924 in a building of its own equipped with all modern accessories. To its sphere of work belong in the widest sense all physical and chemical problems in any way connected with the production of the concern. Many an important discovery from the ranks of its workers has been placed in the service of the associated firms or communicated to other industries. Amongst the large number of recent investigations, the following in particular have exerted a definite influence on the development of science: investigations of the technical analysis of gases (flue gas testers); precision speed regulation of large machines; temperature regulation; in the field of electro-acoustics: condensor microphones and Dr. Riegger's system of loud-speakers (*Blatthaller*), submarine signaling apparatus, objective sound analysis of speech and music, traffic noises, and the sounds emitted by the heart in breathing; the development of large amplifier valves; investigation of light metals and magnetic alloys, hard metals, insulating and synthetic materials, and, finally, the development of high-quality spark plugs.

"The majority of the problems investigated are of a fundamental nature, but special investigations are also carried out for the various manufacturing departments in cases where the equipment of the works' laboratory concerned is inadequate. The connecting link between these various works' laboratories and the research laboratory is the Central Scientific and Technical Bureau. The scope of its activities within the concern can be characterized as follows: initiation and supervision of new research work; information and advice on scientific questions, also on such as exceed the limits of the firm's activities; to maintain contact with scientific bodies, academies, research institutes, etc.; to report on contributions of these institutes and bodies; to arrange for scientific lectures and, finally, to edit the 'Scientific Publication of the Siemens-Concern.' "[16]

The *A. E. G.* central research laboratory was founded in 1928, as a special and general research coordinating agency for the various laboratories of the concern. It has branches in the *Kabelwerk Oberspree (Metallographisch-Magnetisches Laboratorium)*, and in the *Isolierstoffabrik Hennigsdorf (Laboratorium für Isolierstoffentwicklung)*. Its work is carried out in seven special laboratories—physics, acoustics, pipe-technique, electro-technique, chemistry, metallography-magnetism, insulation materials-chemistry—and is organized under four headings: (1) pure scientific research, relating to such problems as the nature of the electron, Roentgen rays, gas absorption and gas content of metals, study of gas molecular constitution, etc.; (2) technical research and development, "with the object of bringing to technical fruition ideas which appear first only as possibilities," and including such problems as perfection of the technical possibilities of talking-cinema equipment, loud-speakers, insulation materials, cathode rays, etc.; (3) research in the development of manufacture, i.e., primarily problems relating to manufacture which may at times call for installation of entirely new apparatus, processing methods, and the actual taking over of production by the laboratory staff until particular processes have been worked through; (4) general assistance to the various branches of the *A. E. G.,* as problems arise such as those involved in the handling of the numerous variable factors affecting electrical heating equipment and apparatus.[17]

It would be difficult to find a better example of how both the theoretical problems of the various fields of scientific inquiry, on the one hand, and the various problems of the technique of manufacture on the other, have become common issues to be handled only by the use of elaborate facilities and cooperative effort. The facilities required are necessarily elaborate, expensive, and complicated. The

[16] *From Workshop to Factory-Town,* pp. 51–52.
[17] A. E. G., *Mitteilungen* (February, 1931):48–55.

problems met in the fields of physics, chemistry, and more recently biology have become interrelated, and their solutions point to a common body of interdependent principles and laws. The need for specialization among the scientists has found its counterpart in the need for closer cooperation between disciplines. The problems of technology are tied up more and more intimately with abstruse scientific problems calling for intensive research in less arbitrarily divisible fields. Problems which come to a theoretical or technological focus in the electro-technical industry radiate, in their implications, into allied disciplines on the one hand and into allied industries on the other. Thus the *A. E. G. Forschungs-Institut* has found it necessary on numerous occasions to cooperate very closely with laboratories of the *I. G. Farbenindustrie,* the *Telefunken-Gesellschaft für drahtlose Telegraphie,* the *Klangfilm* company, the *Studiengesellschaft für elektrische Beleuchtung,* the *Kaiser Wilhelm Institut für Metallforschung,* the *Deutsche Versuchsanstalt für Luftfahrt,* the *Heinrich-Hertz Institut,* and the laboratories of various other research institutes and universities.[18]

Nor is it possible, or at the present stage of the game even desirable from a purely capitalistic point of view, to attempt to confine the findings of their laboratories in all cases to the source from which they arose. The members of the research staffs of both *Siemens & Halske* and *A. E. G.* are encouraged to belong to and participate in the deliberations of the various scientific societies, national and international in scope.[19] Findings of a more important theoretical character are regularly published by both companies; the *A. E. G.* publishes, in addition, a Yearbook *(Jahrbuch des Forschungs-Instituts)* containing a collection of the most important discoveries and contributions of its research staff.

Thus every discovery in the electro-technical industry acts as a scientifically and industrially integrating force. As science must be planned, systematically carried out, and cooperatively organized, so its significance for allied industries acts as a force coercive of technological integration. All research in power transmission, production, and consumption, works in the direction of promoting interdependence between the electro-technical and power industries, and the advancement of super-power inter-territorial networks. Every discovery in electric metallurgy, and every changed specification for refined steel, steel, and other metal alloys, brings these industries into closer and more intimate contact with the electro-technical interests; likewise with chemistry, and with other technically related industries. Moreover, an increasing range of processing and manufacturing methods, mechanical, chemical, and human, are being brought under the dominance of the laboratory in this industry.

---

[18] *Idem.*

[19] A. E. G. laboratory people are members and attend the meetings of such societies as the Physikalische Gesellschaft, the Gesellschaft für technische Physik, the Bunsen Gesellschaft, the Gesellschaft für Metallforschung, the Technische Roentgenkunde, etc. Contacts with foreign companies, such as those with Westinghouse Electric and General Electric, supplement and add to the scientific work of these laboratories.

5. SCIENTIFIC MANAGEMENT

Scientific management was tied up with engineering in the electro-technical industry in Germany long before her industrial leaders had ever heard of the American movement. How expansive and inclusive the work of the electro-technical engineer is, and how important his rôle in the industry, is shown by a summary given by a biographer of Emil Rathenau, founder of *A. E. G.:*

"Everything that is essential is engineering work .... the collection of new experiences in processes and the evalution of these as a foundation for new plans and new construction. . . ." A careful eye should be kept fixed at all times on factors of "economy and efficiency of management and the undertaking." To this should be added the propaganda and information activity relating to the "created and the coming, which explains clearly the advantages of progress, opens or closes the way for business," and, through appropriate publications, "announces achievements to acquaint numerous interests with developments without saying too much to competitors."[20]

Activities along these lines are brought to the highest stage of usefulness in the large enterprise, "where much stimulating and expert knowledge can be brought together and unified for adaptation. . . ." "Thus is brought about the great effect which its engineers and business representatives have on the entire world; their knowledge and experience return to the center of the technical network where they can be remanded to and worked into useful new developments according to the planned machinery of the construction division, the laboratory, and the workshop. Innovations will be tried and tested; all flows back to the many business branches, from thence returns to the center of the system; reciprocal clarification will be demanded and connections with other experiences sought, new needs will be known, new tasks will appear, and everything will be bettered.

"Thus the stream of progress flows hither and yon; the immediate living, fructifying connection between the leading office and the factory, the branch plants and the management will be established. Everywhere engineer labor is at work. Outside management and experience fructifies domestic creative power. The earlier oral instruction is supplanted by uniformly patterned reports on progress made, in which facts, numbers, experiences, and promotion will be laid down. . . ."

"Through the activities of this great organization the endlessly numerous achievements of science will be quickly exploited and carried over into other industries. That progress which previously cost a heavy struggle now springs quickly into allied and foreign fields and finds profitable exploitation. The chain of progress is endless; its working links are found everywhere, and these are

[20] A. Riedler, *Emil Rathenau* (1916), quoted in Werner Sombart, *Das Wirtschaftsleben im Zeitalter des Hochkapitalismus* (1929):892–893.

wrought under the hand of the engineer. Great upbuilding is organic, and is brought about through the pooling and fructifying utilization of all knowledge and experience."[21]

This ecstatic version of the dominating rôle of the engineer in the industry, while dedicated to undeviating pursuit of the main-profits chance, has not prevented hard-headed use of all the possible alternatives provided by the development of the scientific management movement. As previously mentioned, flow systems, serial production, plant, office, and process mechanization, and other allied systems have been used by the industry for many years. Experience along the line of personnel selection and training has been more recent. While both the large concerns cooperate closely with *DATSCH,* and apparently with *DINTA,* they appear, on the whole, rather to have taken such matters into their own hands. Both have established, for the testing and selection of workers, psycho-technical laboratories modeled more or less after the plan of Dr. Moede of the *Technische Hochschule* in Charlottenburg, although many of the tests previously made have now been abandoned, and the feeling is now prevalent that much of the psycho-technical testing work has been greatly over-rated on both scientific and practical grounds. All workers, however, are put through those tests which trial and error have demonstrated to be of some value; and there are given to workers, from time to time thereafter, careful instructions, both oral and written, in details of the tasks to be performed and in the methods which past experience has proved to be the most efficient and saving in time, energy, and materials.

More interesting is the attempt to control the entire technical education of skilled workmen and engineers by the establishment of works schools, finishing courses, and special instruction. Both *Siemens & Halske* and *A. E. G.* have extensive facilities dedicated to this purpose. The equipment of the latter is perhaps the more extensive of the two, the facilities now provided by *A. E. G.* including three technical-school workshops and one business and commercial school. The technical schools are elaborately equipped with classrooms, workshops, tools, machine tools, libraries, eating, sport, and recreation rooms, and miscellaneous facilities. The larger of the three technical schools, located in the outskirts of Berlin in Reinickendorf-Ost, is an imposing five-floor structure, and its equipment and layout might be taken as model for establishments of its sort. Including gymnasium and athletic facilities, and the workshops, these three schools occupy some 215,000 square feet of floor space, and provide facilities for an almost complete technical education in nearly every phase and aspect of the electro-technical industry.

Facilities are provided in the technical schools for three types of students, young boys just graduated (around 15 years of age) from the Public Schools *(Volksschulen),* technical probationers *(Technische Praktikanten)* from the intermediate and collegiate technical schools, and engineering probationers *(In-*

[21] *Idem.*

genieur Praktikanten) drawn from the same source. The requirements for entry in all cases call for suitable physical and psychological equipment, although the rules are less rigid with the latter two groups. The young boys, classified as "special-worker apprentices" *(Facharbeiter Lehrlinge)* are selected from children of employees and outsiders upon the basis of ability to pass physical and psychological examinations. Physical testing calls for a good general state of health, normal build and body functioning, physical agility, courage, etc. Psycho-technical testing calls for ability to handle problems and perform tasks designed to test for such things as manual dexterity, rapidity of work, dimensional comprehension, memory, technical and general knowledge, ability to concentrate, reaction timing, ability to differentiate sharply, accuracy of work, and general intelligence. In addition, all persons admitted to the schools are examined with an eye to determination of psychological "twists," general attitude and point of view. Although it is not a part of stated policy, examination is usually made of the political, economic, and religious affiliations and sympathies of the technical novitiate and of his parents, great emphasis also being laid upon "happy," "contented," and "loyal" workmen, engineers, and other specialists.

The apprentices are first advised as to the possibilities and attractive features of the skilled profession which they are about to enter. Encouraged to go forward, they are given work which is divided into that which is basic for all, and that which is essential only for the special technique of interest. In both branches the work is graded from the simple to the complex, the first workshop tasks being taken up with simple operations involved in the making of standard shapes and forms by the use of simple hand tools such as chisels, files, and hammers. From thence the work begins to take on a productive character, graduating from the production of the simpler fine mechanical tools to construction of usable machine tools—fits, gauges, rules, calipers, gears, etc. Classroom work is alternated with shop work and emphasis is laid upon the ability to read and interpret drawings and standard signs and symbols, and to recognize the advantages of various types of tools and machinery for various purposes, standards work, etc. When the schooling has been completed, the apprentices are examined by the joint Testing Commission of the Berlin Handwork Chamber and Association of Berlin Metal Industrialists *(Verband Berliner Metall-Industrieller)*. The advantage of their system is shown, the *A. E. G.* people argue, by the large percentages of their students who pass these examinations with high grades, and by the fact that those who have gone through their system are adapted for the particular type of work of importance to the industry.

Training of the two classes of engineers mentioned above is designed to offer to students enrolled in the regular intermediate and higher technical schools an opportunity to obtain practical work with machinery and manufacturing problems which will supplement the more theoretical instruction given in such schools. Specialists of importance to the industry are thus acquainted with its peculiar problems and are able to become employees upon completion of their training with the technical, scientific, and practical interests and problems of electro-technical production clearly in mind. The business and commercial school is organized along the same general lines. In addition, special language courses are maintained, special lectures are given, and demonstrations held, and educational films are shown both in the regular schools and from time to time in the manufacturing plant to regular employees.[22]

A feature emphasized only in recent years, and now believed to be of great importance, is the provision of special playground, athletic field, gymnasium and sporting equipment. These are provided for all the schools, and in some places for all or nearly all the employees of the various plants. *Siemens & Halske,* apparently under the influence of *DINTA,* perhaps through its connection with the steel interests which control that organization, have laid great emphasis upon this side of the personnel problem. These features, coupled with provision of auditoriums and facilities for performance of plays, orchestra practice, etc., mountain cabins, swimming pools, and company parks for recreation and week-end trip purposes, special sight-seeing trips to shipbuilding, power-plant, and other industrial works, and numerous other plans and programs, show an acute appreciation for the need of combining systematic technical work with more general education, and the importance of emphasis upon physical and psychological aptitudes and loyalties.

Trends along these lines have interesting implications for future development. It is expected that perfection of the methods and greater experience in testing for physiological and psychological aptitudes and proclivities will make it possible for every person to be directed from the the start towards that niche for which he is best adapted. Once so fixed, the life cycle will run its course without change of occupation. Failure of this result will bring charges against the foresight of the tester or the adequacy of the tests. Those scheduled for high places must be trained so as to fill that rôle as efficiently and as early as possible.

Along with developments in the field of personnel relations, and in conformity with the same impelling forces, much work has been done in the electro-technical industry with standardized and systematic cost-control and cost-accounting. It would be impossible even to summarize in a separate chapter the report, instruction, cost-allocation, cost-accounting, statistical summarization, and other methods utilized by these two corporations for purposes of control of costs, prices, and managerial details. The entire round has been standardized and systematized in accordance with plans which bear upon the time factor, long-range expansion and development, and the managerial problem of integrating a host of partly parallel, partly interlocking technical processes. The systematization is not yet complete, nor will it be as long as the industry is expanding rapidly. Yet on the

[22] Most of the above detail on A. E. G. educational programs and equipment was taken from a little pamphlet, published by the concern, entitled *AEG Ausbildungswesen.*

whole it would appear that such plans have been carried through with due regard for the need of maintaining flexibility, the spirit of individual initiative and responsibility among skilled workers and managerial staff, and the need of tying efficient production to innovating scientific discovery.

The position of the rank and file workers is somewhat different. The science of work movement has in most cases not gone beyond establishment of certain differential piece-wage systems and the quite general introduction of chain or gang labor. Time and motion studies have been made, but apparently have not led to any extensive reorganization of work routines. Heating, ventilation, and work places have been placed upon a modern basis throughout. But there is much complaint of labor driving, and considerable evidence of bad labor morale.

6. THE TREND TOWARDS MONOPOLY, AND FURTHER INTER-INDUSTRY INTEGRATION

Many observers are of the opinion that effective competition no longer exists between the *Siemens* and *A. E. G.* concerns. The history of the rise and expansion of the two combines is on the whole remarkably free from underbidding on construction work, cut-throat competition on domestic and foreign markets, and other evidences of uncontrolled competition. There has been keen competition at times, but in the main the lapses have been few and far between; in recent years there has been little, if any, evidence of real struggle. Entry of *Siemens* into the foreign fields and of *A. E. G.* in the low-current industry are scarcely evidence of a significant change of trend. Both corporations are controlled by a comparatively small group of powerful banking and industrial interests and have shown willingness to cooperate whenever the exigencies of current developments have appeared to require. That a certain amount of confusion and overlapping still current in the industry could be eliminated by amalgamation of the two concerns is, of course, obvious. Yet the necessary paring down and reorganization caused by such a change would be much less important than that which would accompany absorption of the smaller concerns specializing in the production of some one good or narrow range of commodities.

The cartels have added little to the systematization of the industry, largely because of the dominating position of the two large combines. Nearly all the attempts to establish cartels in the heavy-voltage field, especially in the branches devoted to turbines, motors, generators, switches, transformers, and power-plant construction, have either failed at the outset or have been of but short duration. Some of the cartels, such as that of the Measuring Instrument Producers *(Verband der Messinstrumentefabriken)* resemble loosely organized trade associations, their cartel functions being limited to such things as price comparison, the gathering of relevant market and other types of statistics, or similar activities. The Meter Cartel *(Verband deutscher Elektrizitätsfabriken),* originally organized more or less as a trade association, has subsequently been reorganized to take over such cartel functions as price regulation, and control of conditions and terms of delivery.

Internationally the situation is somewhat different. After many trials and tribulations the International Incandescent Lamp Cartel was established in 1925 and included the more important electric-globe producers in Germany, England, France, the United States, Japan, Belgium, Italy, and other countries. An interesting feature of this cartel is the pooling of technical information and the granting of preferential rights to representatives of any member concern. Among special privileges accorded each member concern are the following: free access to all patents, production methods, and statistical information of all other members; the privilege of visiting plants of other member companies at any and all times; preferential rights in the home market; the right to establish central sales offices abroad. Details of organization are handled through the *Phoebus* Company at Geneva.

Other cartels exist in both light- and heavy-current branches of the industry, relating, usually, to specialized but standard types of product such as galvanic batteries, porcelain, insulating equipment, transformers, and cable.[23] One of the most recently formed electro-technical cartels is that of the manufacturers of conduits. This cartel *(Vauelfa Vereinigte Leitungsdrahtfabriken G.m.b.H.)* includes the firms *A. E. G., Siemens-Schuckertwerke, Bergmann,* and *Rheinische Draht-u. Kabelwerke,* and constitutes the fifth group in the *Vauelfa Syndikat,* in turn made up of 30 special producers in this field. The association regulates prices, conditions and terms of delivery, and markets. Centralized sales are handled by the *Syndikat,* although not through the first-mentioned auxiliary organization.[24]

The electro-technical producers have also—and of necessity—had a hand in the establishment of international associations to regulate telephone, telegraph, and radio transmission. The oldest of these associations, the Universal Telegraph Union *(L'Union Télégraphique Universelle),* was organized in 1875, with headquarters at the Berne office of the International Telegraph Union. In effect, this system called for systematization within and among the various countries where standardization of parts, equipment, receiving and sending methods, codes and procedure, rates, and all the range of mechanical, organizational, and procedural details, was a basic condition to operation. This in turn called for effective co-operation between the telegraph service and the electro-technical industry on the one hand, and amongst the various concerns in the electro-technical industry itself on the other.

International telephone systems became important at a later date. Nevertheless a meeting of the Telephone Engineers of Europe in 1924 was able to establish the Advisory Technical Committee for Long Distance Telephony *(Comité Con-*

---

[23] See Gottfried Eissfeldt, *Die Kartelisierung der deutschen Elektro-Industrie* (Berlin, 1928).

[24] *Frankfurter Zeitung,* May 23, 1930.

sultatif International de Communications Téléphoniques—abbreviated *CCI*). A body of rules and regulations, built up on the basis of experience in Germany, England, Holland, Sweden, and Switzerland, was established with a view to linking together the networks of the countries of Europe into a unified and uniform European telephone system. The basis was laid for a system of long-distance cables covering the European continent. This system was practically complete by 1927. In 1925 the Universal Telegraph Union and the *CCI* were brought together for purposes of closer cooperation and the pooling of information and experience.

Experience along these lines in Europe has led to the sketching of still more ambitious plans. Plans have been prepared, and webs are being spun which, reaching out from the European continent, will eventually unite the entire world into a single unified, uniform, and closely knit communication system. The basis for this, even more than in the case of telegraphic communication, is standardized equipment, codes, methods, etc., and the elaboration of such a system calls for the closest cooperation between this service and the electro-technical industry, locally, nationally, and internationally.

The case of radio is more interesting still. Originally a matter of wireless transmission of telegraphic messages, the most spectacular feature of which was its use for purposes of transportation and sea navigation, the industry has branched out to include radio telephony, broadcasting, and, more recently, television. Experience accumulated in the development of telephonic and telegraphic communication is being applied to these new systems. The various international wireless and radio conferences have attempted to deal with the problems of transmission, equipment, receiving, wave lengths, etc., and are achieving a degree of order and system in this field comparable to that obtaining in the older communications services. Marine radio service has been brought under the control of the International Telegraph Bureau in Berne. Union with the Universal Telegraph Union is bringing all wire and wireless communications systems together. This development, even more than that of telephonic communication, forces cooperation between transmission systems and the electro-technical supply systems. Patents must be pooled, standards must be established, and regulating codes must be made uniform before this system, which because of its technical nature has been essentially international from the start, can function on the geographic basis for which it is ideally adapted.

This process has been brought to completion in the case of wireless telegraphy. Settlement in 1912 of the patent dispute between the Marconi Wireless Telegraph Company in London and the *Telefunken-Gesellschaft* in Berlin has led to a cartel and pooling arrangement almost as complete as that common to the incandescent-lamp industry. Four companies, the two mentioned above, the Radio Corporation of America, and the *Societé Anonyme Internationale de Télégraphie sans Fil (S. A. I. T.)*, pool all patents and manufacturing experience, fix all standards, divide all markets, and regulate all miscellaneous details so far as their power and influence extends. The process of amalgamation within each individual country is steadily extending the importance and influence of these concerns. Cooperation between these concerns and the important electro-technical concerns in the respective countries is paralleled only by that existing among the various electro-technical companies and the wireless-telegraphy concerns themselves.[25]

Further work along the line of international standards, and international and inter-industry cooperation, has been carried out by the International Electro-technical Commission, and the International Commission on Illumination. The former group has been devoted since its inception at the St. Louis Electrical Congress in 1904 to the task of securing "the cooperation of the technical societies of the world by the appointment of a representative commisssion to consider the question of standardization of nomenclature and rating of electrical apparatus and machinery."[26] The second group was dedicated to the study of "all systems of lighting and technical problems connected therewith." This involved "bringing together for work of common interest the representatives of industries of which not merely the modes of production or manufacture are totally different, but which are in competition commercially."[27]

Aside from the cartels, communities of interest, and special cooperative work in the low-current communications field, the electro-technical industry has been brought into very close contact with a number of industries primarily through its engineering work. This branch of the industry has brought it into very close contact with nearly all other industries through its influence upon plant construction, type of power installations, and even such problems as general location of plants. The electro-technical industry, in fact, has been compelled to act more and more in advisory capacities to all industries faced with the problem of general reorganization prior to or consequent upon electrification. Interesting examples of such relationships are to be found in the electrification of mining operations and rail transportation systems. Similar close engineering cooperation is to be found with shipbuilding in the development of special electric machinery and apparatus, and with the steel, textile, machinery, agricultural, and chemical industries in the shifting of power and prime-mover systems onto an electrical basis.[28]

These various engineering and technical interconnections between the electro-technical industry and nearly all other industries has given to the former a rather unusual function. It has come more and more to take on the character of a gen-

---

[25] *Monograph of the Electrical Industry,* pp. 7–13, 32–36.

[26] *Standards Yearbook* (1928):16.

[27] *Idem.*

[28] The transformation of power systems from steam to electricity, and the introduction of direct electric drive is gradually fusing the machine and electro-technical industries together. Machine "building" or fabrication tends to dominate in both fields, the individual parts supplied to assembly plants being manufactured in highly specialized plants. See, E. A., "Der deutsche Aussenhandel unter der Einwirkung weltwirtschaftlicher Strukturwandlungen," Zweiter Halbband, pp. 41–42.

eral "service" or advisory rôle to transportation and communication, nearly all branches of manufacturing, the handicraft trades, agriculture, trade and commerce, and domestic economy. The industry is in a most unusual position, one which provides a basis for special study of the needs of various industries and comparison and contrast of the strengths and weaknesses of all. It is in a position to act as a major integrating, coordinating, systematizing, and unifying force, not only within individual plants, but also within entire industries and technologically balanced economic areas.

7. SUMMARY

The German electro-technical industry has long been dominated by the *Siemens* and *A. E. G.* combines. During the post-war period their influence in nearly every line of output has been even greater than before. Although the two concerns are competitors, both have shown a general willingness to cooperate whenever circumstances seemed to require. This same cooperative spirit has been extended to include the international field. Patent pooling, marketing, and other agreements have been made with British, French, American, Japanese, and other foreign electro-technical concerns. In most of the foreign countries, one or two large concerns are in a controlling position. Hence, in both domestic and foreign markets there has been relatively little cut-throat competition, and cartels have been unable to exercise a great deal of power.

This might have led to the usual abuses of monopolistic or semi-monopolistic powers, had it not been for several important factors. Especially important were the following: (1) The fact that both light- and heavy-current fields were early placed on a mass-production basis meant that the industry had an unusual incentive for obtaining mass distribution through low prices. (2) The fact that the light-current field was developed first meant that the industry was expanded to supply a natural monopoly service under the control of the state (in Germany). It was a basic requirement for this service that it be widely used, simple to operate, and relatively cheap. That is to say, the equipment had to be highly standardized for both service and cost reasons. This influence was felt when the heavy-current field was first exploited. (3) While the importance of patents prevented the growth of outside competition, the unusually rapid rate of technological change did not allow processes and methods to become stereotyped. (4) Scientific invention has played an unusually important rôle throughout the history of the industry.

Hence, post-war rationalization in this industry was largely a matter of returning to long-familiar techniques of production and methods of organization. This meant (1) increasing emphasis upon (*a*) horizontal and vertical integration, (*b*) strengthening intercorporate ties with supply and marketing concerns, or (*c*) the establishment of jointly owned and highly specialized plants (incandescent lamps and railway signal apparatus); (2) the habit of pooling patents, manufacturing methods, and (in certain special cases) laboratory facilities; (3)

greater dependence upon control methods directly associated with mass production; (4) more reliance upon *(a)* piece wages (individual or gang), bonus schemes and special incentive systems, *(b)* careful selection and training of workmen, *(c)* individual initiative, secured by *(a)* and *(b)* above and by the device of greater decentralization of managerial authority with increasing centralization of coordinating and policy-forming powers; (5) more numerous, more carefully prepared, and more widely applicable standards; (6) more attention to the needs of industries with which the electro-technical industry is technologically related, and to which it has become a sort of general engineering service.

The major trends within the industry, in short, are towards (1) increasing use of science and scientific methods, (2) more cooperative effort, (3) managerial decentralization, (4) central coordination and planning, (5) cheap mass-output methods, and (6) inter-industry integration. It is impossible to measure or evaluate the net effect of all these trends upon efficiency of output. Individual improvements are so numerous, and, in many cases, so striking, that they would unquestionably cumulate to show a remarkable net technical advance for the industry as a whole if the necessary data and the appropriate techniques for totaling were available. There is some evidence that the industry has been suffering from excess plant capacity. Nevertheless, there is little criticism to advance on that account.

The industry has, likewise, probably achieved as much stability as is possible through resources and methods available to it. But it does not seem to have the loyalty of the rank and file of its workers nor to have solved the problem of individual security.

CHAPTER IX

THE POWER INDUSTRY

"IT IS IMPERATIVE," Oskar von Miller[1] writes, "that a general plan for the production and distribution of electric current for the entire Reich be developed as soon as possible. This general plan must, independent of special interests of regional groupings, political parties, and competing companies, be elaborated solely according to the principles of maximum economy and efficiency."[2] Four years previous to publication of this opinion in the report of the *Enquete* Committee, von Miller had expressed this view to Julius Curtius, Federal Minister of Economics. At the latter's request von Miller, utilizing material subsequently collected by the ministry through the circulation of questionnaires to experts in various parts of the Reich, began and brought to completion in May, 1929, the task of sketching such a general plan. This report *(Gutachten über die Reichselektrizitätsversorgung)*,[3] published by the *VDI* in 1930, is a model of clarity and conciseness. Before attempting to evaluate the controversial issues involved in or the implications of the von Miller plan, it will be necessary to obtain a pretty clear picture of the present status of the German power industry.

1. PRODUCTION AND CONSUMPTION OF POWER

While world power production increased between 1925 and 1928 from 184 to 265 billion kilowatt hours, or by some 44 per cent,[4] German output advanced from 20 to 27 billion kilowatt hours, or by about 37 per cent. The advance was maintained throughout 1929 and a part of 1930. A condensed picture of German power development since 1925[5] is offered in tables 20 and 21 (p. 197).

A number of significant changes are brought out in these tables. Per capita consumption, in the first place, has been growing quite rapidly, the 1929 figure showing an increase of nearly 51 per cent over that for 1925. With the exception

[1] Director of the Deutsches Museum, Munich.

[2] "Ausführungen des Sachverständigen Dr. Oskar von Miller über die derzeit wichtigsten Fragen der Elektrizitätswirtschaft," *Enquete Ausschuss,* "Die deutsche Elektrizitätswirtschaft" (Zweite Auflage, Berlin, 1930):145. Referred to hereafter in this chapter as E. A., "Die deutsche Elek."

[3] VDI Verlag G.m.b.H. (Berlin, 1930).

[4] "Zentralverband der deutschen elektrotechnischen Industrie," *Statistischer Bericht* (1930): 261.

[5] *Statistischer Bericht, op. cit.,* p. 284.

TABLE 20

INSTALLED CAPACITY

Year	Public works*			Private works†			All works		
	Number	Capacity in 1000 kw.	Percentage of total capacity	Number	Capacity in 1000 kw.	Percentage of total capacity	Number	Capacity in 1000 kw.	Increase in percentage over previous year
1925	1,370	....	....	6,122	....	....	7,492	8,713	......
1926	1,408	5,171	54.1	6,057	4,384	45.9	7,465	9,555	9.6
1927	1,399	5,728	55.9	6,015	4,515	44.1	7,414	10,243	7.2
1928	1,417	6,297	56.7	5,800	4,805	43.3	7,217	11,102	8.3
1929	1,488	7,495	60.3	5,612	4,921	39.7	7,100	12,416	8.8

* Plants producing current for sale to others. † Plants producing current for self-consumption (industrial plants).

TABLE 21

ELECTRIC POWER PRODUCTION

Year	Public works*			Private works†			All works			
	Number	Production in million kwh.	Percentage of total production	Number	Production in million kwh.	Percentage of total production	Number	Production in million kwh.	Percentage increase over previous year	Production per capita
1925	1,370	9,915	48.8	6,122	10,413	51.2	7,492	20,328	....	325
1926	1,408	10,208	48.1	6,057	11,010	51.9	7,465	21,218	4.4	340
1927	1,399	12,317	49.0	6,015	12,818	51.0	7,414	25,135	18.5	392
1928	1,417	14,146	50.8	5,800	13,725	49.2	7,217	27,871	10.9	442
1929	1,488	16,391	53.4	5,612	14,269	46.6	7,100	30,660	10.0	485
Percentage increase 1929 over 1925:	....	65.3	....	....	37.0	....	....	50.8	....	....

* Plants producing current for sale to others. † Plants producing current for self-consumption (industrial plants).

of countries with water power but no fuel resources (e.g., Switzerland), or countries using large quantities of electric power for certain highly specialized industries (e.g., Norway and Sweden), per capita consumption in Germany stands high among European nations. Abroad, only the United States and Canada have higher consumption levels.[6]

The distribution of power consumption among various classes of consumers differs considerably from country to country, and conditions materially plans for the further expansion and integration of the industry. The importance of industrial consumption has probably not declined considerably since 1925, when the following percentages held:[7]

	Percentage
Industry	80
Railroads	5
Agriculture and auxiliary industry	3
Self-consumption of power plants	3
Miscellaneous users	9

In that year electricity supplied about 67 per cent of the total industrial motive power consumed in Germany. In certain industries the percentage was much higher, as table 22 (p. 199) shows (comparative data are given for England and the United States).[8]

These percentages have undoubtedly been increasing since 1925. As Friedrich has pointed out, a sudden stoppage in the German electric-power industry in 1929 would mean cessation of about four-fifths of the national economic activity. Some of the figures are quite interesting. In that year, about 80 per cent of the motive power of German industry was supplied by electricity. About 80 per cent of all agricultural establishments and about 75 per cent of all domestic households were supplied with electric power. Electricity was practically the sole energy supply in the electro-chemical and metallurgical industries, and in nearly all municipal street, suburban, and rapid transit systems.[9]

[6] Per capita consumption figures for 1928 for the most important countries are as follows:*

	Kilowatt hours		Kilowatt hours
Norway	3,001	Germany	442
Canada	1,794	Austria	358
Switzerland	1,313	Australia	350
United States	940	Great Britain	337
Sweden	724	New Zealand	329
Belgium	466	France	316

* Source: *ibid.*, p. 265.

[7] *Das Spezial Archiv*, "Der AEG-Konzern," p. 9. Miscellaneous consumers include households, street and public lighting, etc.

[8] Klaus Dohrn, "Die Elektrizität im deutschen Wirtschaftskörper," *ETZ* (June, 1930):872.

[9] *Das Spezial Archiv*, "Deutscher Elektrizitäts-Konzern," (1931):10–11.

The most important fields for future expansion lie in railroad electrification, agricultural utilization, and household consumption. While at the beginning of 1930 about 15,558 kilometers of railroad, interurban, and municipal rapid transit lines had been electrified, these made up but 2.9 per cent of the total kilometer network.[10] The possibilities of expansion in this field are, accordingly, very great. The situation is about the same in the agricultural field. Domestic consumption is also quite low. Von Miller estimated in 1926 that the annual electrical requirement for a simple middle-class family of four persons, for lighting, power, cooking, and water-heating purposes, exclusive of room heating, should be about 2,000

TABLE 22

Industries	Germany 1925	England 1924	United States 1925
All industries	67	51	73
Iron and steel	74	42	72
Machine building	93	91	100
Automobile	92	88	44
Textiles	55	....	67
Paper	63	63	62
Chemicals	72	52	63
Stone and pottery	57	....	81

kilowatt hours per annum.[11] In contrast, consumption in that year for all purposes was but 100 kilowatt hours for families of the given size.[12] Another set of figures for the city of Berlin in the year 1928 shows 45 per cent of all households still without electrical connections of any type.[13] Of those connected 44 per cent had no electrical equipment (other than light) of any type, 56 per cent possessed electric irons, 28 per cent vacuum sweepers, 16 per cent heating pads, and the percentages of other household electrical equipment were still lower.[14] New housing projects in such places as Romerstadt and Praunheim by Frankfurt a.M., Elberfeld, Bremen, Schwandorf, Schweinfurth, etc., have introduced the wholesale substitution for gas, coal, and wood, of electrical cooking and water-heating appa-

10 *Statistischer Bericht, op. cit.*, p. 288.

11 *The Electrical World* (August 17, 1929:363) has estimated that the average consumption of electric current per household in the United States with "full electrification" would be about 7,800 kilowatts per annum. In 1928 the average actual consumption was 507 kilowatts.

12 E. A., "Die deutsche Elek.," p. 146.

13 The figure, 45 per cent without electrical connections for Berlin in 1928, may be questioned in view of Friedrich's estimate that 75 per cent of all households in Germany (1929) had such connections.

14 *Das Spezial Archiv,* "Der AEG-Konzern" (1930):9.

ratus.[15] Yet domestic consumption for all purposes is still at a very low level throughout Germany.

A second important fact brought out by the table on page 197 is that the number of power plants has decreased while output has been growing, average output per plant having increased 67 per cent over the five years, or from 2,713,000 kilowatt hours to 4,321,000 kilowatt hours. This advance was shared by both public and private plants, the latter expanding in size somewhat more rapidly than the former. This largely results from the fact that the smaller and less efficient local private plants have been abandoned, and current has been purchased from the large public companies as these have gradually expanded their networks over the country. The private plants left are maintained as reserve capacity, or are kept in operation for a number of technically important reasons. Among these may be: ability to use the power plant continuously at or near to capacity; use of capacity to the full, with peak load supplied by purchase of outside current; possession of large quantities of some low-grade fuel—as in the cases of blast-furnace gas, coal dust, low grades of coal—not otherwise recoverable and not fit for sale on the open market.

For such reasons the load factor tends to be better in the private plants than in the public works, as is shown by the fact that while their total capacity in 1929 constituted 39.7 per cent of the aggregate, output was rated at 46.6 per cent of the kilowatt hours produced. Most of the private works, however, are small. In 1928 89.1 per cent of the plants under 50-kilowatt capacity, and 86.2 per cent of the kilowatt-hour output of such plants, fell into the private works category, while 77.8 per cent of the plants and 85.8 per cent of the kilowatt-hour production of plants of over 100,000 kilowatt capacity, were in the category of public works.[16]

It is interesting, in this connection, to note also that the public works have been gradually gaining the upper hand, in both installed capacity and kilowatt-hour production. This results, of course, primarily from the development of long-distance transmission power systems, and the gradual abandonment of decentral-

[15] Fr. Mortzsch, "Einführung der Elektrowärme im deutschen Haushalt und Gewerbe," *Der Werbeleiter, Monatsschrift für Elektrizitätswerbung* (published by Vereinigung der Elektrizitätswerke, June 25, 1930):124.

[16] The following table for the year 1928 is instructive.*

Size of plant in kilowatts	Percentage of each capacity class (each class = 100)		Percentage of production of each capacity class (each class = 100)	
	Public plants	Private plants	Public plants	Private plants
1 to 50	10.9	89.1	13.8	86.2
51 to 100	16.2	83.8	16.5	83.5
101 to 1,000	22.9	77.1	24.8	75.2
1,001 to 5,000	27.1	72.1	26.4	73.6
5,001 to 10,000	27.2	72.8	28.8	71.2
10,001 to 100,000	58.7	41.3	67.2	32.8
Over 100,000	77.8	22.2	85.8	14.2

* Source: E. A., "Die deutsche Elek.," p. 14.

ized current production. The advantages of large-scale output more than offset the additional costs involved in construction and maintenance of the transmission lines except where circumstances are peculiarly favorable for local plants.[17]

2. SOURCES OF POWER

The rapid rate of growth shown in the table on page 197, and the great importance now being attached to the development of a national electric-power grid, have raised the question of future water and fuel energy resources. At the present time dry fuels are the backbone of power systems, as shown in table 23 (p. 202).[18]

Despite the overwhelming importance of the dry fuels—coal and lignite—the total consumption of the electrical industry, when lignite, briquets, and coke are translated into terms of coal, was but 6.8 per cent of the total internal coal production in 1928.[19] Consequently, dry fuel resources afford possibilities for almost unlimited expansion of the electrical industry in the future. But, while, at present rates of exploitation, exploitable German coal reserves will last for somewhat more than 1,000 years, lignite will be quickly exhausted. Between fifty and eighty years hence, German lignite reserves will have been completely exploited. The importance of this fact for the power industry is to be seen in the large percentage of current output owing its origin to this fuel. In 1929 39.0 per cent of the kilowatt hours produced came from lignite, while 36.7 per cent came from coal.[20]

While methods used in the lignite power industry result in practically no fuel waste at any stage of the process, coal mining has always been attended with certain losses of peculiar importance to the electric-power industry. Much inferior coal is mined for which there is little if any ordinary commercial use. Nearly always a necessary by-product, this fuel has been previously discarded entirely, or used only in very limited quantities. Here is to be found an extremely cheap fuel both for electric power and for long-distance gas supply systems. In addition considerable quantities of high-grade coal have always been lost in the form of the

[17] See the discussion of Professor Walther Windel, "Selbsterzeugung oder Strombezug?" *Technik und Wirtschaft* (VDI Verlag, June, 1930):151–154, and various sections of E. A., "Die deutsche Elek."

[18] *Statistischer Bericht, op. cit.*, p. 284.

[19] Reckoned in the above-mentioned terms, the internal coal consumption of 145 million tons for 1928 was divided as follows:*

	Percentage
Mining industry	20.7
Miscellaneous industry and commerce	27.7
Electric power production	6.8
Gas works	5.0
Railroads	9.9
Shipping	2.2
Total for industry and transportation	72.3
Domestic heating and agriculture	27.7

* Source: Thierbach, "Die Brennstoffe," *ETZ*, p. 848.

[20] *Statistischer Bericht, op. cit.*, p. 283.

TABLE 23

ELECTRICAL PRODUCTION ACCORDING TO POWER SOURCE

Year	Total production in million kwh.	From dry fuels		From water		From oil		From gas		From other sources	
		In million kwh.	Percentage of total production	In million kwh.	Percentage of total production	In million kwh.	Percentage of total production	In million kwh.	Percentage of total production	In million kwh.	Percentage of total production
A. Public Works											
1926	10,208	8,127	79.6	1,988	19.5	76	0.7	17	0.2	0.2	....
1927	12,317	9,849	80.0	2,367	19.2	79	0.6	21	0.2	1	....
1928	14,146	11,797	83.4	2,227	15.7	95	0.7	26	0.2	1	....
1929	16,391	13,965	85.2	2,285	13.9	112	0.7	28	0.2	1	....
B. Private Works											
1926	11,010	7,179	65.2	1,329	12.1	98	0.9	2,359	21.4	45	0.4
1927	12,818	8,338	65.0	1,439	11.2	111	0.9	2,690	21.0	240	1.9
1928	13,725	9,504	69.2	1,339	9.8	116	0.9	2,514	18.3	252	1.8
1929	14,269	9,615	67.5	1,279	9.0	107	0.8	2,995	20.8	273	1.9
C. Public and Private Works											
1925	20,328	15,098	74.2	2,852	14.0	154	0.8	2,186	10.8	38	0.2
1926	21,218	15,306	72.1	3,317	15.6	174	0.8	2,376	11.3	45	0.2
1927	25,135	18,187	72.4	3,806	15.1	190	0.8	2,711	10.8	241	0.9
1928	27,871	21,301	76.4	3,566	12.8	211	0.8	2,540	9.1	253	0.9
1929	30,660	23,580	77.0	3,564	11.7	219	0.7	3,023	9.7	274	0.9

dust incident to mining operations. The more explosives and mechanical devices such as coal cutters and pneumatic hammers are used, the larger the percentage of loss on this account has become. Previously this coal, amounting according to estimate to from 20 to 30 per cent of total output, has been a waste product.[21] The development of coal-dust firing, principally in connection with large-scale power production, has afforded a ready market for this product.

Other fuels, such as peat, oil, and oil shale are to be found in but very limited quantities in Germany. Water-power resources offer important opportunities for development in the future. Of the estimated 5,000,000 kilowatts available in the country, but slightly over 1,000,000, 21.52 per cent of the total, to be exact, had been exploited in 1924.[22] Since that time extensive water-power systems have been constructed, and other plans are in prospect.

Exploitation of total available domestic water-power resources in Germany would not take care of current power demands. It is not, however, the actual amount of water power utilized that is of importance at the present time, so much as it is the problem of securing, through the integration of steam and hydro-electric power systems, the best possible inter-district load equalization. Although such equalization is possible within German borders, the proportioning would of necessity be far from ideal because of natural limitations on resources. Ideally the best equalization would have to be international.

3. THE PROBLEM OF "OFF-PEAK" LOAD[23]

The center of gravity of the problem of technical efficiency in the power industry is bound up with degree of plant utilization. This is because of the dominating rôle of fixed charges in power production. Large hydro-electric and steam generating plants, long-distance transmission systems, and the necessary switching, transforming, and miscellaneous equipment involve the investment of large sums of money under conditions in which expenses vary but little with power output.

---

[21] R. Fischer, "Elektrizitätswirtschaft," *Sammlung Göschen* (Leipzig, 1928):12.

[22] *Ibid.*, p. 19.

[23] It will help to clarify the discussion in this section if the following definitions are kept in mind:

Capacity factor. Ratio of current to rated capacity output for any given time interval. (In this section expressed as total hours per annum that each capacity unit is utilized, the maximum being 8,760 hours per annum. As an average figure, this would be: total units generated divided by sum of the rated capacities of the generating units.)

Diversity factor: Sum of separate maxima loads divided by total maximum load; or, ratio of total of separate peaks (e.g., agricultural and industrial; summer and winter) to combined simultaneous peak.

Load factor: Ratio of kilowatt hours generated to peak demand multiplied by total hours of period (day, month, or year); or, ratio of current to maximum usage for any given time interval.

Operating ratio: Ratio of operating expenses to income from operation.

The Committee of Inquiry *(Enquete Ausschuss)* has estimated the total investment to be, on the average, 1,000 marks per kilowatt capacity for steam plants and 1,600 marks for hydro-electric plants.[24] Total costs for both types, however, tend to be about the same.[25] This is because of the fact that lower initial investment in steam plants necessarily involves construction of less permanent works and equipment than in the hydro-electric plants. While hydro-electric plants are constructed to last for several decades, if not centuries, transmission lines wear out in about 30–50 years, and much of the steam plant and equipment must be replaced at the end of eight or ten years. Labor, materials, and replacement costs with the hydro-electric systems remain approximately the same regardless of the degree of plant utilization. While such is not strictly true of steam generating plants, most of the expenses which would be considered variable in other industries, principally labor and fuel costs, show overhead behavior. That is, they vary per unit of output in nearly all cases inversely rather than directly with increase in plant utilization up to the limit of capacity.[26]

Low kilowatt-hour tariff schedules, which are necessary in order to secure the wide and extensive use of electrical current, are, consequently, themselves determined by costs with levels fixed, in the main, by the degree to which existing plant is utilized. It is impossible, in other words, to get low rates without a high degree of plant efficiency; it is impossible to increase plant efficiency materially without extensive and continuous usage. The problems to be solved here are (1) lowering of the reserve ratio necessitated by adjustment of capacity to maximum or "peak" load, (2) increasing the total number of hours of plant utilization, and (3) distributing these as evenly as possible over the hours of the day, days of the week, and seasons of the year. These problems can be solved, to state the issues in somewhat more technical terms, by securing the best possible (1) capacity, (2) load, and (3) diversity factors.

The electric-power industry is characterized, to an even greater extent than long-distance gas main and other strictly "service" systems, by the fact that its output cannot be produced for storage. Such storage as is made possible—at the present stage of technical development, by the use of batteries, reservoirs, and other devices—is of incidental importance. Electrical current must be used when and as fast as it is generated. Hence generating capacity must be adjusted to the maximum, or "peak" load, demand.

[24] E. A., "Die deutsche Elek.," p. 70.

[25] Beyond a certain point the advantage of hydro-electric power increases almost as fast as load and diversity factors improve. Between a certain minimum and this point, neither of which is always definitely ascertainable, the costs of the two types of service are about the same. Present rates of utilization lie, in most cases, between these two limits.

[26] There are, of course, degrees of "inverse cost behavior." Scarcely any of the operating or capital costs show absolute constancy in direction or rate of change with increased output. But in the power industry only incidental expenses vary directly or more rapidly than output. That is to say, nearly all ordinarily variable costs are inverse to some degree or other in this industry. Neither fuel nor labor is an exception to this rule.

If every kilowatt of installed capacity were used every hour of the day and every day of the year, 8,760 hours, then full capacity utilization would be 8,760 kilowatt hours. If, furthermore, the greater part of the costs of production is overhead, every approximation to this total would mean an increase in efficiency and a lowering of costs. The number of hours of utilization then serves as one important check on power production efficiency. For public and private German plants taken together, the three years 1926, 1927, and 1928 showed capacity factors of 2,220, 2,454, and 2,510 hours respectively.[27] That this general increase went hand in hand with better equalization of load over days, weeks, and seasons, is shown by the fact that reserve capacity (percentage of unused capacity to maximum capacity used) has steadily fallen. While in 1913 reserve capacity amounted to some 42 per cent of the total, it had dropped to approximately 29 per cent in 1928.[28]

Both peak load and degree of plant utilization over the year depend upon a number of variable factors, among which the following are the more important: types of resident industrial occupation; degree of population concentration; diversity and seasonality of industrial activity; relative importance of industrial and domestic consumption; and the geographic scope of the isolated or interconnected transmission system. A few examples will serve to clarify the problem.

An agricultural district possessing 1,000 inhabitants, and consuming 55,531 kilowatt hours per annum, utilized plant, at the maximum, at the rate of 690 hours per annum (capacity factor). An overland transmission system supplying current to 1,000 separate localities with a total of about 1,000,000 inhabitants, showed utilization, at the maximum, of 2,950 hours. A third system, supplying power primarily to large industrial consumers, showed maximum plant utilization at the rate of 6,000 hours. In the first case, peaks were reached on a typical December day at ten o'clock in the morning and three o'clock in the afternoon, with current used but eight and one-half hours per day. In the second case, the annual peak was reached at three o'clock in the afternoon of December 9. The peak on August 11 was about 55 per cent, and on June 2 was about 40 per cent of the December maximum. Plant was utilized to some extent throughout the day, although in June the percentage of annual maximum dropped at five o'clock in the morning to about 15. In the third case, the lowest point amounted to about 62 per cent of the maximum.[29]

The defined conditions for low plant capacity are high daily and seasonal peaks and relatively large percentages of time with no, or only very low, con-

---

27 E. A., "Die deutsche Elek.," p. 21.

28 The above statement may be somewhat misleading. Lowering of the reserve ratio does not mean better load distribution. It could only occur, however, under conditions in which the margin of safety could be lowered because of better load distribution.

29 The charts given on pp. 17–20 in E. A., "Die deutsche Elek.," give a good cross-section of the whole story.

sumption. For this reason the public works (central plants) may have a lower load factor than private plants wherever they serve thinly populated and technically backward rural districts, or mainly domestic consumers.[30] As the public plants expand geographically, however, their load factors tend to rise, and, in so doing, they tend to supplant private plants. This results not only from the fact that the average is brought up by the inclusion of industries with high load factors, but also from the ability of a centralized system to take advantage of different peak demands by dovetailing industrial and domestic, urban and rural, and other peaked usage. In purely urban districts, further improvement may be brought about by diversity between industrial and domestic classes in spite of lower load factor for domestic. Rural territory usually has little industry, hence little diversity of classes of users. By high-voltage transmission, however, rural and urban territory can be interconnected and served by a common system of plants, whose load factor may be improved by diversity between rural and urban demand. Diversity between consumers or classes may be by hours of the day or by seasons of the year; industrial use by day and domestic use at night; dovetailing of seasonal peaks of different industries; dovetailing of farm power in spring, summer, and fall, with domestic lighting in winter, etc.

Thus, production and distribution costs typically decrease (1) the larger the territory, (2) the more diversified the range of different classes of users,[31] and (3) the larger the demand of each class.[32] As these costs decrease the kilowatt-hour rate can fall; as the rate drops both load and diversity factors tend to im-

---

30 The figures for three recent years are*

Year	Public supply systems—hours	Private plants—hours
1926	1,974	2,511
1927	2,150	2,839
1928	2,246	2,856

* Source: *ibid.*, p. 22.

31 How important the inclusion of various types of industries may be on this account is shown by the following table of average capacity factors for various privately owned plants by industries in 1928:*

Industrial group	Rated capacity in kw.	Production 1,000 kwh.	Average capacity factor in hours, 1928	Average capacity factor in hours, 1927
Iron manufacturing	866	3,027	3,495*	3,762
Mining	1,488	3,969	2,667	2,535
Chemical and metallurgical industries	855	3,560	4,164	4,201
Paper and multigraphing industries	328	1,210	3,689	3,556
Iron and metal manufacturing	439	586	1,335	1,387
Textile and clothing industries	365	580	1,588	1,546
Miscellaneous	464	793	1,709	1,937

* Source: *idem.*

32 Other factors, largely dependent upon the character of consumer usage, are important in cost reduction. Thus, a low power factor (ratio of power actually developed by a generating unit to energy apparently developed) is costly to generating plants. But details such as these are largely technical, and are typically of a lower order of importance than the factors discussed in the text.

prove, hence to reduce costs still further. It happens, for example, that the average depreciation and capital charges for all electric-power systems in the Reich, with an average capacity factor of 2,246 hours, was 6.2 pfennigs per kilowatt hour produced. Saxon plants, however, with a capacity factor of 3,630 hours allotted for these purposes 3.9 pfennigs per kilowatt hour, while Schleswig-Holstein plants with capacity factors of 1,380 hours set aside 10.2 pfennigs per kilowatt hour for this purpose.[33] Many other costs vary, with shifts in capacity and load factor, in the same general fashion.

TABLE 24

Installed machine capacity in kw.	Investment, marks per kw. capacity	Capital charges per kw. year at the rate of 12 per cent in marks*
10,000	520	60
20,000	470	55
100,000	325	40
200,000	290	35

* The 12 per cent capital charges include 7 per cent interest on investment, 3 per cent for renewals, and 2 per cent for maintenance.

Equally important is the fact that these more comprehensive systems are able to operate on a large scale. The correlation which usually exists between size of installed capacity and capacity factor[34] results in part from the fact that numerous costs drop with increase in the scale of output, and this makes it possible to solicit the type of trade which raises off-peak loads. Total investment in plant drops markedly with increase in installed capacity, as the estimates, given in table 24, of steam generating plant costs by a German expert show.[35]

---

[33] E. A., "Die deutsche Elek.," p. 73.

[34] The following figures on capacity factor (in hours) of public power plants, arranged according to size, for the years 1927 and 1928, illustrate the point:†

Size of plant in kw. capacity	1927 Hours	1928 Hours
1 to 100	1,927	1,671
101 to 1,000	1,898	1,735
1,001 to 5,000	2,269	2,009
5,001 to 10,000	2,147	1,686
Over 10,000	2,154	2,242*

* 10,001 to 100,000 kw = 1,979 hours; over 100,000 kw. = 3,025 hours.
† Source: *ibid.*, p. 23.

[35] *Ibid.*, p. 220. These figures are given for a "modern steam power plant in which electricity is produced by steam turbines, gas or oil motors," and include costs for the "necessary reserves, building, land, and switching plant." It excludes only "permanent high-tension transformer stations for long-distance transmission" from total plant investment costs. See also pp. 154 and 292. On p. 292 investment per kw. for plants with 1,000 kw. installed capacity is given at 650 marks, for 5,000 kw. 450 marks, for 20,000 kw. 360 marks, and for 50,000 kw. 250 marks.

The same holds, in general, for hydro-electric plants, although additional variable cost factors are to be found here in the height and volume of fall, and the nature of the reservoir system. Investment per installed kilowatt capacity, for example, varies from 750 marks for plants depending upon flowing water having a drop of 75 meters, to 3,000 marks for plants depending upon impounded water falling from comparatively low levels.[36] But for each type of hydro-electric plant, investment costs per unit capacity decline as the size increases.

Transmission costs show a similar behavior. The original investment here is usually several times that required for generating plant—ranging, depending upon the degree of concentration in use and the thickness of population, from three- to sixfold that amount.[37] But the greater the capacity of the transmission lines and the higher the tension (voltage), the lower are the original costs per kilowatt, other factors remaining the same.[38] Increase in the length of the transmission lines for given kilowatt capacity and voltage tension means, of course, increase in invested capital per kilowatt hour for a given load. Yet the facts that the load and diversity factors tend to be better with such systems, and that increase in the length of the lines may not, on account of interconnection between power plants, of necessity mean that current travels a much greater average distance than before, result in lower average costs as high-voltage lines increase in kilometers. Hence, growth of high-tension transmission lines in Germany has been very rapid since the war.[39]

More significant still is the fact that these super-power systems make possible the construction of great works on the coal or lignite site, thus saving freight charges for fuel. Frequently losses incurred as a result of longer power lines are more than offset by this saving alone.

It is further true, as indicated above, that variable expenses per kilowatt hour tend to drop with increase in the size of producing plant. Larger steam plants, for example, have been able to lower materially the fuel consumption per kilowatt produced by utilization of purer coal, higher steam pressures, super-heaters, pre-heating of air, better steam turbines, substitution of turbines for reciprocating engines, and numerous other methods not available to the small plant or involving investment out of reach of the local unit. A conservative estimate has shown that with a load factor of 2,200 hours, plants of 10,000 kilowatt capacity, having capital costs of 3.4 pfennigs per kilowatt produced, required one-tenth of

---

36 *Ibid.*, p. 221. 37 *Ibid.*, p. 293. 38 *Ibid.*, pp. 221–222.

39 The length of high-tension transmission lines has increased since 1910 as indicated in the following table:*

Year	Tension in 1,000-volt units		
	40–60	110	220
1910	88 km.	....	....
1920	3,071 km.	1,020 km.	....
1929	8,180 km.	6,350 km.	1,512 km.

* Source: *ETZ*, *op. cit.*, p. 851.

a pfennig more per kilowatt for fuel (1.5 pfennigs) than plants of 100,000 kilowatt capacity (1.4 pfennigs) having capital charges of 2.3 pfennigs per kilowatt produced.[40] Thus, to savings effected in fuel costs by general improvement of thermal efficiency, amounting in certain cases to well over 100 per cent during the last decade, must be added those incidental to the factor of size of the unit alone.[41] Fuel costs per kilowatt produced at the generating plant have been as low as 0.5 pfennigs where size has been combined with favorable location with respect to type (coal dust in this example) and quantity of fuel supply. Since 1913 the amount of fuel of given caloric value required to produce a kilowatt of electrical energy has been nearly halved[42] in the larger and more efficient plants. Further increases in thermal efficiency of approximately 50 per cent over present practice are now theoretically attainable.[43]

For plant of any given size and with any given technical equipment, thermal efficiencies rise with increase in the load factor; and so do nearly all the ordinary variable expenses, usually. Consequently, such changes make possible sale of current at lower prices with a given load factor, or a lowering of the load factor with given kilowatt tariffs. Should an increase in both load factor and thermal efficiency go together, costs, under appropriate circumstances, may be drastically revised downwards.

Development along these lines in steam-generating plants tends to increase their competitive advantage over hydro-electric plants. Longer transmission lines

---

40 E. A., "Die deutsche Elek.," p. 230.

41 The following figures on heat consumption, in calories, per kilowatt produced at the plant by steam-generating works with a load approximating full utilization of machines and boilers for a ten-hour day in the middle of the year, illustrate the importance of size of the producing unit, all other technical and efficiency factors assumed to remain the same.*

CALORIES PER KWH. PRODUCED AT THE PLANT

Installed capacity in kw.	Lignite of 2,000 calories per kg.	Bituminous coal of 7,200 calories per kg.	Coal dust from bituminous coal or lignite
10,000	6,200	5,300	5,100
28,000	5,900	5,000	4,850
50,000	5,750	4,850	4,650
100,000	5,650	4,750	4,550

* Source: *ibid.*, p. 224.

42 In technically very efficient plants the amount of coal of 7,500 calories per kg. required for the production of one kilowatt was*

In the year	kg.
1913	1.15–1.05
1924–1925	0.8
1926–1927	0.58

* Source: *ibid.*, p. 12.

43 The thermal efficiency, according to another estimate, differing slightly from the figures given for number of kg. of coal of 7,500 calory value in note 42 above, was 10 per cent (of total thermal content) in 1913, 14.5 per cent in 1924–1925, 20.0 per cent in 1926–1927, and will probably be 29 per cent in the newer plants constructed between 1930 and 1935.—*Ibid.*, p. 172.

and more expensive plant tend to force upward the capacity factor necessary before the latter type can compete on an efficiency basis. With a capacity factor of 3,500 hours or over the advantage tends to shift, in Germany at least,[44] quite rapidly to the hydro-electric systems. Other factors—further increase in expense of hydro-electric power plant construction, longer transmission lines, further improvement in steam-generating plants—may force this limit higher still.

It therefore becomes apparent that hydro-electric power must be confined to production for industries operating almost continuously throughout the day and the year, such as the steel-working, chemical, and paper industries, or else it must be used for basic-load purposes in mixed steam- and water-power interconnected systems. Where it is possible for both systems to serve the same general territory, every improvement in steam-generating efficiency will tend to force utilization of water power for the latter purpose. Steam plants in general, and the older plants in particular, can then be used for purposes of covering peak load. It can be demonstrated from the history of such interconnected systems that significant cost reductions are the result of such integration. Lowering the costs, once more, tends to spread the service geographically, diversify the uses of current, aid the dovetailing of peak load demands, and thus to improve the capacity factor of that portion of the system suffering the disadvantage of being used to cover only the variable portion of demand.

Such an interconnection makes feasible the employment of certain other devices for cheapening over-all costs. Technically out-of-date and badly located plants can be used for reserve purposes only, permitting the more efficient works to run continuously. It is at times possible to cover peak loads by utilizing equipment where the cost advantages over alternative systems tend to increase as the capacity factor is lowered. Such is the case with oil motors, particularly with those of the Diesel type. On account of the comparatively low original cost of Diesel motors and auxiliary buildings and equipment, and the fact that expensive fuel means relatively high variable expenses, the advantage of this method of generating power is greatest with capacity factors under 1,000 hours per annum. In connection with water-power systems the economic margin of operation may be considerably higher.[45]

Some experts attach considerable importance to the possibility of utilizing off-peak hours for pumping water from streams or lakes into artificial basins, whence it may be taken during peak hours for emergency generating purposes. Such an arrangement can be utilized with both steam- and water-power systems, although it is generally more feasible with interconnected networks. These plants must be as cheaply constructed as possible, although it is not necessary that they be regarded as temporary in character. They need not be located at or near parent stations, it being possible to construct such stations wherever geographical and

[44] *Ibid.*, pp. 236–239.

[45] E. A., "Die deutsche Elek.," p. 240.

geological conditions permit. Careful study has shown that the advantages of utilization of basic plant to capacity, even though a large portion of the current generated is used for pumping water uphill, is greater than the losses incurred by such a practice—all factors included—if sufficient care and foresight are exercised in the location of the necessary pumping stations and emergency power plants.

There is still another way in which the problem of capacity factor affects the question of interconnection. Development in coal chemistry known as "low temperature coking" *(Tieftemperaturverkokung)* by distillation has made feasible the use of the resultant coke *(Schwelkoks)* for purposes of power generation by direct firing. The additional expenses attached to construction of the necessary buildings, machinery, and equipment for the distillation process mean an increase in overhead costs, per kilowatt year, of approximately one-third. Depending upon the tar or bitumen content of the coal or lignite used for the process, however, by-products, in the form of tar, paraffin, oil, lubricants, etc., will provide enough or more than enough income to compensate for the higher overhead charges. But these income factors, plus the high overhead expenses, tend to lay great emphasis upon continuous production and high capacity factor.[46] To the extent, consequently, that this process is developed in the future, its prospects must depend upon capacity factors approximating those necessary for the larger hydro-electric plants. Thus, this process as and if it develops still further, will lay still greater emphasis upon high capacity factors and the use of special plant and equipment for taking care of peak demands.

The net resultant of the convergence of all these problems upon the central issue of increasing efficiency by lowering the ratio of peak to ordinary load, and the better distribution of daily, weekly, or seasonal current consumption, is to emphasize large-scale output, high-tension long-distance transmission lines, and a grid of ever expanding geographic scope. Certain—and in some networks at least, numerous—additional overhead and variable costs[47] attending such expansion are more than offset by parallel cost reductions. So overwhelming are the favorable cost differentials that the history of the power industry in Germany, as elsewhere, has been marked by almost complete lack of controversy over the advisability of expanding networks. The trend here has been uni-directional, and no apparent reasons exist for expecting any reversal in the future. From every point of view, except, perhaps, that of nationalistic political opportunism, almost the whole argument lies on the side of a single nation-wide network interwoven,

[46] Compare E. A., "Die deutsche Elek.," p. 241.

[47] Highly important is the fact that larger networks and lower rates, while increasing the number of consumers, tend to lower average kwh. consumption, and thus to increase labor, office, and management costs materially. How important a factor this trend may be in the future is indicated by the fact that the average kwh. consumed per meter installed was 240 in 1910, 165 in 1915, 136 in 1924, and 110 in 1926.—Source: *ibid.*, p. 303.

where technical and economic factors determine, with an international system. Such a system calls for the same careful, planned interweaving on a comprehensive scale as that characteristic of telephone and telegraph service, railway and long-distance gas main networks. The larger the geographic area included, the greater is the necessary original investment. The more significant the service supplied in the routine economic life of the population affected, the more imperative it is that enforcing plans be systematic, comprehensive, and farsighted. The evolution and present status of the German power industry show that no other course is possible in the future.

4. PRESENT STATUS OF THE POWER INDUSTRY

The larger power companies in Germany are usually classified as of the following types: (1) Concerns which through direct ownership or inter-corporate participation dominate large unified power-supply districts. Examples of this type among the publicly owned and operated companies are *Elektrowerke* taken jointly with its subsidiary companies; the *Preussen-Elektra* taken jointly with the *Nordwestdeutsche Kraftwerke A. G.*, and the *A. G. Sächsische Werke* taken jointly with the *Elektra A. G.;* among the mixed companies (owned jointly by public and private interests) such concerns as the *RWE (Rheinisch-Westfälisches Elektrizitätswerk A. G.)* working in cooperation with the *VEW (Vereinigte Elektrizitätswerke Westfalens)* and neighboring companies. Privately owned enterprises are sometimes of this type also. (2) Financial and holding companies. These large combines usually dominate a considerable number of geographically scattered, but in some cases large, companies. Examples of this type are the *Gesfürel,* the *Elektrizitäts-Lieferungs-Gesellschaft,* the *Rheinische Elektrizitäts A. G.*, the *Elektrische Licht und Kraftanlagen A. G., Lahmeyer,* and the *Dessauer Gas* and *Thüringer Gas* concerns. Usually this type of concern is privately owned, though a few are of the public-controlled type. (3) Communal works. These may be publicly or privately owned, or of the mixed type. Their field of operation, however, is confined to some particular locality; an example is that of the *Hamburgische Elektrizitätswerke.*[48]

The degree of concentration in the industry is shown in table 25 (p. 213), including the twelve largest German electric power companies delivering over 300,000,000 kwh. of current in 1929.[49]

Six of the largest concerns delivered a total of 8.8 billion kilowatt hours. The author from whom the above figures are taken estimates that, including concern participations, and the *Nordwestdeutsche Kraftwerke A. G.,* affiliated with *Preussische Elektrizitäts A. G.,* "two-thirds of the current production and deliv-

---

[48] *Das Spezial Archiv,* "Deutsche Elektrizitäts-Konzerne" (1931):17.

ery of all German public electrical enterprises (concerns producing power for sale to third parties) are concentrated in the hands of seven concerns." Forty-four concerns delivered over 100 million kilowatt hours each in 1929.[50]

TABLE 25

Name of company	Installed capacity 1,000 kw.	Current production, million kwh.	Current delivery, million kwh.	Population in field of immediate supply in 1,000
Berliner Stadt. Elektrizitäts Werke A. G.	644*	1,118	1,460	3,884
Märkisches Elektrizitätswerk A. G., Berlin	191	443	501	812
Preussische Elektrizitäts A. G.	179	424	467	......
Vereinigte Elektrizitätswerke Westfalens, Dortmund	220	501	567	1,529
A. G. Sächsische Werke	398	914	1,069	713
Unternehmungen des Bayr. Staats†	......	469	654	......
Schlesische Elektrizitäts- u. Gaswerke A. G., Gleiwitz	83	323	355	425
Elektrizitäts-Werk Sachsen-Anhalt A. G., Halle	56	65	354	......
Hamburgische Elektrizitätswerke	226	448	443	1,211
Rheinisches Elektrizitätswerk im Braunkohlenrevier, Köln	174	384	389	‡
Elektrowerke A. G.	736	2,332	......	‡
Rheinisch-Westfälisches Elektrizitätswerk A. G.	770	......	2,782	......

* Including reservoir capacity.

† Walchenseewerk and Mittlere Isar; current delivery through the Bayernwerk.

‡ Delivery only to large consumers (industries, municipalities, etc.).

Of these, "the two largest German electrical undertakings, the *RWE* and the *Elektrowerke,* are the largest on the European continent, and can be favorably compared with the largest in the world. Only three companies in the United States produce more current and supply larger markets. Inclusive of its participations, the *Elektrowerke* produced 3.5 billion kilowatt hours in 1929, while the *RWE,* with its affiliated works *(Mainkraftwerke, Braunkohlen-Industrie A. G. Zukunft, Paderborner Elektrizitäts- und Strassenbahn A. G.,* etc.) delivered a similar amount in the fiscal year 1929–1930. The total delivery of the two concern groupings constituted, consequently, 7 billion kilowatt hours, or more than 40 per cent of the total German public electrical supply. The *RWE* possessed in the middle of 1930 a long-distance network for 100,000 and 220,000 volts tension

[50] *Ibid.,* p. 18.

of 4,300 kilometers; the *Elektrowerke*—exclusive of participations—owned outright over 2,394 kilometers of 100,000 voltage line. These two concerns possess the two largest power plants in Europe. The *RWE* owns the *Goldenberg-Werk* with 500,000, the *Elektro-Werke* the *Goldpa-Zschornewitz* plant with 440,000 kilowatt hours installed capacity. These two plants, constructed for exploitation of lignite deposits, have a load factor twice as high as the average for all German public supply works.

"While the *RWE,* inclusive of the *VEW,* supplies the most of the current for the provinces of Westphalia and the Rhineland, and possesses a transmission network stretching from the Ems district to Vorarlberg, the 100,000-volt lines of the *Elektrowerke* span central Germany and Silesia, and stretch, when all participations are included, from Sachsen-Anhalt and Braunschweig to Upper Silesia."[51]

TABLE 26

Type of plant	Capacity		Production	
	Billion kw.	Percentage of total	Billion kwh.	Percentage of total
Publicly owned	3.720	57.3	8.196	56.6
Privately owned	895	13.8	2.112	14.6
Mixed public and private ownership	1.881	28.9	4.171	28.8
Totals	6.496	100.0	14.479	100.0

The influence of various governmental bodies—municipalities, the various states, and the Reich—is very important in the German power industry. The relative importance of public ownership and control is indicated by table 26 on power plant capacity and output by ownership classification for the year 1928.[52] With expansion of the larger networks there is a tendency for the mixed type to grow in importance.[53] Further, while there has not been apparent—at least up to 1929—any tendency towards further socialization through ownership of electric-power generation and transmission since 1924, growth of the larger regional and national interconnected systems has been accompanied by steady increase in the rigidity and comprehensiveness of governmental regulation and control. Important auxiliary trends were the following: (1) A tendency for both ownership and regulatory authority to shift from the communes and municipalities (except

[51] *Idem.*

[52] E. A., "Die deutsche Elek.," p. 68. The figures for both capacity and output are taken from data of the Vereinigung der Elektrizitätswerke, and, because of inclusion of certain plants usually classified otherwise, are somewhat larger than those given on page 197 for all plants selling current to the public.

[53] *Das Spezial Archiv,* "Deutsche Elektrizitäts-Konzerne" (1931):17.

the larger cities) to the states and the Reich;[54] (2) consolidation, both corporate and technical, within the various geographical regions—Bavaria, Rhineland, Central Germany, Upper Silesia, East Prussia, etc.—constituting more or less "natural" and homogeneous power supply and distribution areas; (3) a tendency for managerial decentralization, partly through separation of publicly owned and operating systems from direct fiscal control of more purely political authorities, to accompany regional consolidation and the elaboration of inter-district networks;[55] (4) a tendency for loose territorial and corporate agreements to resolve themselves into direct managerial control through company consolidation of the corporate *(Aktiengesellschaften)* type;[56] (5) growing emphasis being laid on international[57] interconnections; (6) a tendency for vertical consolidation to accompany horizontal combination as shown in the linking of power production to transmission and distribution on the one hand, and, in the case of the steam generating plants, to fuel supply (coal and lignite mines principally) on the other.[58]

Before the publication of the von Miller plan, the most significant steps in the direction of constructing a national power network had been taken by the west German power interests under the leadership of the *RWE,* and the central German publicly owned power systems under the leadership of the *Elektrowerke.* It is interesting to note here that the technical ties and interconnections have anticipated and prepared the way for the consolidation of ownership and the systematization of management of the larger entities. In this respect systematization within the various geographic regions, and between the two principal working

[54] The division for the publicly owned plants in 1928 was as follows:*

Owner	Capacity million kw.	Production billion kwh.	Purchased current, billion kwh.	Current deliveries, billion kwh.
Reich and states	1.229	3.819	.552	4.035
Cities	1.798	2.918	2.206	4.349
Provinces, districts, communes	.371	.839	.574	1.231
Miscellaneous	.322	.620	.285	.800
Totals	3.720	8.196	3.617	10.415

* Source: E. A., "Die deutsche Elek.," p. 69.

[55] Shown by *(a)* shift in control from local groupings to states and the Reich—in which more purely fiscal motives are usually less important; *(b)* the tendency to separate for managerial purposes the production and distribution of current; and *(c)* the tendency to (1) transfer state-owned properties to private operating groups, or (2) to place state properties on a strictly civil service basis.

[56] Of 118 companies, having installed capacity of 5.7 million kilowatts, (or 90 per cent) of the capacity of the 611 reported by the Vereinigung der Elektrizitätswerke) as public supply companies, 74 were organized as corporate enterprises. The fact that these companies had installed capacity of 3.85 million kilowatts is indicative of the fact that size and this legal type go together in the power industry as elsewhere.—*Ibid.,* p. 68.

[57] Primarily in the south with Switzerland and Austria. See pp. 221 ff.

[58] Nearly all the larger concerns, depending largely upon coal and lignite, own their principal supply outright.

combinations, merely follows the course characteristic of development in the industry from its earliest stages. Technique has blazed and forced the way almost throughout.

In both the cases mentioned in the preceding paragraph, separate corporations have been established for the purpose of carrying through the agreements made among participating companies. In the first case, the *Westdeutsche Elektrizitäts-Wirtschaft A. G.* was established to act as a sort of holding company (*Dachgesellschaft*) uniting the *Rheinisch-Westfälisches Elektrizitätswerk A. G.*, the *Vereinigte Elektrizitätswerke Westfalens G.m.b.H.*, and the *Kommunales Elektrizitätswerk Mark A. G.*, without at the same time depriving any of these companies of its corporate independence. The various plants and transmission lines brought together under the new company unite nearly all the important coal, lignite, and water-power systems of western Germany into a single network stretching north to south from the west-German North Sea coast and the Ruhr district to the Bavarian and Swiss Alps, and east to west from the French, Belgian, Dutch, and Swiss borders to the central German territory dominated by the *Elektrowerke*. With the object of eliminating duplicate generating and distributing facilities, and of raising the efficiency of the included systems to the highest possible point, interconnection—through the construction of new high-power 380-, 220-, and 110-kilovolt lines—has been carried forward rapidly. The Rhineland-Westphalian district has been "ringed" by a 220-kilovolt line, constructed jointly by the *RWE* and the *VEW*. Plans are in prospect for improving the high-tension lines running north and south, and agreements have been made with the *Elektrowerke* and other concerns providing for both demarkation of the field of control and the interchange of power over mutually controlled high-tension lines.[59]

In 1928 the *Elektrowerke* (owned by the Reich), the *Preussische Elektrizitäts A. G.* (owned by the state of Prussia), and the *Bayernwerke A. G.* (owned by the state of Bavaria) founded the *A. G. für Deutsche Elektrizitätswirtschaft*, "for the purpose of friendly cooperation in matters connected with large-scale supply. One of the schemes which this association will study is the construction of 220,000-volt lines from the northeastern part of Germany through Central Germany to Southern Germany. Contracts already exist for exchange of current between a number of great power enterprises during the periods of emergency. Thus, to cite only one example, the *Bayernwerke A. G.* has agreed to transfer, through Aschaffenburg, to the *Preussische Elektrizitäts A. G.* a considerable amount of current to mitigate shortage in Prussia, while the *Bayernwerke* will in turn receive electrical energy from the *Preussische Elektrizitäts A. G.* in times when water conditions are unfavorable or the *Preussische Elektrizitäts A. G.* is not sufficiently occupied. The *Rheinisch-Westfälisches Elektrizitätswerk A. G.*, too, will furnish the *Bayernwerke* with current when the latter is in need—which

[59] See *Das Spezial Archiv*, "Deutsche Elektrizitäts-Konzerne" (1931):24–25.

current is returned as soon as conditions permit."[60] The network thus established extends all the way from the territory dominated by the *Westdeutsche Elektrizitäts-Wirtschaft A. G.* to the Polish border and the Corridor on the east.

While the central German combination is made up of concerns entirely owned by the Reich and the various states, the western combination is largely under the influence of governmental agencies. The dominating concern in the *Westdeutsche Elektrizitäts-Wirtschaft A. G.* is the *RWE,* which is a mixed type. Share capital is held by cities, communes, and the state of Prussia[61] in large enough quantities to assure effective representation of governmental bodies in the determination of all important corporate policies.

5. THE VON MILLER PLAN[62]

While several features of the von Miller plan were already out of date at the time of its publication by reason of the rapid development in the power industry itself, the main outlines are still to be completed. As the plan stands it represents a bold attempt to sketch the outlines of a single national electric-power network covering every section of the German state, with power generation so adjusted as to secure the maximum of efficiency and highest possible load factor, and distribution networks so interwoven and reorganized as to secure the best diversity factor and the lowest possible kilowatt-hour rate for the various types of consumers.

On the basis of detailed study of previous rates of increase in power production and consumption for various classes of consumers in the several power districts, it was estimated that the plan must call for a minimum of 8.5 million kilowatt installed capacity and 34 billion kilowatt[63] output at the time of its completion if it were not to be outdistanced by intermediate secular growth. In the year of its completion—a year which could not be exactly stated inasmuch as it was impossible to estimate accurately the time required to put the plan into effect; it could, however, be taken as after 1935—the plan would permit future expansion to double the stated output without necessitating fundamental alteration of the then existent network. The plan called, in other words, for the construction of a super-power system of 34 billion kilowatt annual capacity which would be capable of expansion to 68 billion kilowatt capacity as growing demands might dic-

---

60 *Statist, op. cit.*

61 Cities, towns, and communes own about 33.2 per cent, the Prussian state, 6.83 per cent, Viag (controlled by the Reich) 1.84 per cent of common, and 3.63 per cent of preferred stock. —*Das Spezial Archiv, op. cit.*, p. 32.

62 Gutachten, *op. cit.*

63 These figures apply only to public utility systems and do not include plants producing power exclusively for their own consumption.

tate. The first figure, which was to be the capacity of the initial year and as close to 1935 as possible, compared with 23 billion kilowatts (not including transmission losses) estimated for that year—under conditions of ordinary growth—from data supplied by experts from the various power districts.

For purposes of detailed study leading up to the plan finally presented, the Reich was divided into a number of main and subsidiary power districts.[64] In each of these districts a study was made of the existing and potential power-generating and transmission capacity, and the trends in consumer usage. Estimates were made of the probable consumption of the most important classes of domestic and industrial users, both agricultural and urban, and these were set against the available domestic power supply when developed according to the minimum required to put the plan into action.[65] With this as a foundation it was possible to determine (1) the amount to be produced, plant capacity, and the direction of current flow for each district and according to each type of generating system ("running-water," impounded-water, pumped-water—i.e., reserve—coal, lignite, peat, gas, oil); (2) the points of maximum concentration in consumer usage; (3) the amount of deficit or surplus for each district; (4) the probable amounts of intra- and inter-district current flow; (5) the quantitative importance of the interchange between districts predominantly relying upon water power and those depending on steam generation for various seasons of the year; (6) the probable importance of international current import and export used for equalization purposes; (7) the capacities and location of the main transmission, primary and secondary distribution systems, transformer and switching stations, etc.; (8) the fixed investment and operating charges for the system taken as a whole and by types of plant, structure, and auxiliary apparatus.

At the heart of the system to be elaborated is a ring made up of 220,000-volt double alternating current transmission lines. The ring is to extend down the

---

[64] I. Bavaria, right of the Rhine
II. Central Germany
a) Mark district (märkisches Gebiet)
b) Saxony-Thüringia
c) Berlin
III. Prussian district
a) Weser district
b) Northwest German district
c) Pomerania
d) East Prussia
IV. Silesia
V. Rhineland-Westphalia
VI. Baden-Württemberg
a) Baden-Rhine Palatinate
b) Württemberg
VII. Hamburg—Schleswig-Holstein

[65] In the case of water power, potential could be accurately estimated; in that of coal and lignite, capacity could be adjusted to the needs of the system as it developed.

Rhine from Cologne over Coblenz, Frankfurt, and Rheinau, to Hoheneck, where it turns eastward over Crailsheim to Nuremberg. At Nuremberg the line turns north to Zschornewitz, passing over Burgk and Bohlen, and thence it returns to Cologne over Harbke, Hanover-Lehrte, Bielefeld, and Hengstey. Reaching out like the arms of an octopus from this central ring, are 220,000-volt lines at various points: Coblenz to Trier; Rheinau to Oberrhein; Hoheneck to Voralberg and the Tyrol; Crailsheim to Landberg; Nuremberg over Regensburg to Passau; Zschornewitz over Berlin to Neustrelitz; Lehrte north to Rendsburg over Hamburg and south to Borken; at Bielefeld a special ring passes north over Ibbenburen and Wesel—with another line running north from Ibbenburen to Farge—and back to Cologne. From this main network, which may be transformed into a 380,000-volt system at will,[66] there stretch out in all directions double and single line primary distribution networks of 110,000 volts, and from both 40,000- to 60,000-volt secondary distribution systems. With the exception of East Prussia, which on account of the unfortunate Corridor is separated from the main body of the country, all Germany is brought into the interconnected system. A separate plan has been elaborated for East Prussia which can be connected with the main network in the event it becomes politically feasible to span the Polish section.

During periods of high water (spring and summer) the principal surplus points would lie in the south where melting snow, heavy rainfall and mountainous territory combine to provide a plentiful supply of hydro-electric power. The power network here combines plants located on the Upper Rhine and in the Bavarian Alps, with supply drawn from Switzerland (over Oberrhein), and the Austrian Alps (Voralberg, the Tyrol, and over Passau from Salzburg and Upper Austria). During periods of water shortage (autumn and winter), current is sent south from the lignite and coal steam-generating works. Much more current would be sent north than south, and, with the exception of the plants at Zschornewitz during the spring and summer, practically no current would ever travel over the main lines from east to west. The net shortage districts lie to the east and north; the surplus districts to the south and west.

Increase in the size and efficiency of generating and transmission plant and equipment, and the ability to dovetail a great number of different types of peak load demand, would lead, von Miller believes, to achievement of a capacity factor

[66] The following figures show the relations existing between voltage and kw. capacity.*

Alternating current voltage	Transmission capacity		Transmission distance, km.	Per cent loss in transmission	Per cent decline in tension
	kw. per system	kw. per double system			
60,000	19,000	38,000	100	10	10
110,000	40,500	81,000	200	10	10.15
220,000	110,000	220,000	400	10	10.2
380,000	550,000	1,100,000	600	10	10.5
380,000	500,000	1,000,000	1,000	15	15.7

* Source: Dr. Walther Windel, *Aufbau und Entwicklungsmöglichkeiten der europäischen Elektrizitätswirtschaft* (Berlin, 1928): 206.

of 3,600 hours for the entire system.[67] Current interchange would make it possible to lower the necessary reserve capacity for peak load purposes, and to divide current production geographically as well as by power source into basic load and auxiliary types. Basic load plants could then be increased to the size dictated by resources (in the case of water power) and the proportioning of factors leading to maximum efficiency and economical production. Certainty that outside power could be substituted immediately would make it possible for each basic load plant to curtail its idle reserve capacity almost to the vanishing point. Auxiliary plants, whether relying mainly on water or steam power, could then be constructed and geographically spaced as the exigencies of topography and fuel determined. Equalization of loads would make it possible, by the law of averages and on the basis of past experience, to isolate daily, weekly, and seasonal peaks so as to bring these plants into operation with the minimum of lost time and effort. Typically, also, such dovetailing should increase the load factors of such plants while affording a basis for construction of the various types of plant best suited and most economically operated with varying loads.

While not definitely stated in the plan, it is apparently expected that lower kilowatt-hour rates would have a tendency both to increase industrial usage and to substitute purchased for self-produced current in all plants where unusually favorable circumstances and the need of large quantities of process steam are lacking. Average consumption per connection would tend to rise for industrial users, thus lowering certain of the more important variable expenses in the distribution network. Growth in average energy consumption for household and agricultural purposes should work even more favorably in this direction. Electrification of the National Railways, which would mean an average power consumption of 430,000 kilowatt hours per kilometer per year, would necessitate an enormous expansion of plant and transmission facilities.[68] All these changes should mean average lower kilowatt-hour rates for all classes of consumers, increase in the demand for electrical energy, and further expansion of the available facilities, thus promoting still lower tariff schedules.

Including costs of power plant, transmission lines, distribution lines, transformer station, office buildings, and all miscellaneous equipment, the total investment required to put the plan into execution was estimated to be 3,663,000,000 marks. The output for the structures to be built with this money would be 22,400 million kilowatts. With estimated operating costs—including (1) depreciation and maintenance, (2) material consumption and the costs of current purchased, (3) service, and (4) management and general costs (taxes, insurance, etc.)—of

[67] This contrasts with estimates of experts of 3,300 hours for 1935, and the figure of 2,900 hours given for 1925. This latter figure is considerably higher than that given for the following year by the Enquete Ausschuss. The source of the discrepancy has not been learned. See Gutachten, *op. cit.,* p. 9.

[68] *Ibid.,* p.6.

365,000,000 marks, expenditure on this account would amount to 1.63 pfennigs per kilowatt hour delivered to the principal distribution centers. If to this amount be added an amount for interest and amortization sufficiently great to earn 8.5 per cent return upon invested capital (or a total of about 300 million marks annually), bringing these costs per kilowatt hour produced to 1.35 pfennigs with 22,400 million kilowatt-hour output, then total costs to the central delivery points would be 3 pfennigs per kilowatt hour. If total costs from this point on were to equal those enumerated for production and transmission—they might be somewhat higher—then current could be delivered under the von Miller plan for an average charge of 6 pfennigs (approximately 1½ cents in American money) per kilowatt hour. In the event that capital charges and high interest rates should be somewhat reduced, and that corresponding improvements could and would be made in local distribution networks, this rate would be still further lowered in the future.

That the von Miller plan will be put into effect in its present form is unlikely even though the necessary funds and executive authority are provided. Such changes as it may be necessary to make in the future, however, should not fundamentally alter the basic outlines of the plan if the full advantages of such a unified power system are to be fully realized. Should the plan, in its present or in some modified form, be fitted into a general European power system the same general advantages flowing from national unification would find international application. Development in transmission technique which now makes it theoretically possible to send current 1,000 kilometers or over by means of 380- to 400-kilovolt lines, and the small size of most European nations, has raised this problem into the sphere of practical politics. An engineer named Oliven[69] presented a European power plan at the World Power Conference held in Berlin, 1930.

6. A UNIFIED CONTINENTAL POWER SYSTEM

At the outset, "we are faced with the practical fact," Oliven argued, "that exchange and equalization of electrical energy has begun to take place over political borders." It is necessary at this point, consequently, "to be perfectly clear that .... this exchange and equalization is a question of the greatest significance for all Europe, and that we have previously done nothing to create the indispensable conditions of organized cooperation between political and economic factors in our portion of the world basic to this development."[70] In order that development be carried out on the most systematic and comprehensive basis possible, he proposed the construction of a Europe-wide interconnected system of high power

[69] Chairman of the Sofina concern.

[70] *Das Spezial Archiv,* "Deutsche Elektrizitäts-Konzerne" (1931):19.

transmission lines, with tensions of 380 to 400 kilovolts, and totaling around 10,000 kilometers, as a backbone for further national and international integration. The main lines were to be the following:[71]

	Kilometers
Paris—Central Germany—Upper Silesia—Warsaw	1,200
Lyons—Alps—Vienna—Bucharest—Odessa—Rostov	3,000
Norway—Sweden—Denmark—Hamburg—Central Germany—Tyrol—Genoa—Rome	3,000
Calais—Paris—Lyons—Madrid—Lisbon	2,100
Upper Silesia—Vienna—Jugoslavia—Albania	1,500

It was estimated that these lines, involving as they would in many cases merely the extension and interconnection of existing systems, could be constructed for approximately two billion marks. This sum would include 25 phase-converter (*Phasenschieberstationen*) and 20 transformer (*Umspannwerke*) stations. Utilization of the capacity of the lines at the rate of 5,000 hours annually would make it possible to transport current over these lines at a transmission cost of 1.1 pfennigs per kilowatt hour.[72] Dovetailing of peak loads, and the practical certainty of current supply over all portions of the network, would have the effect of reducing necessary reserve capacity throughout all parts of the system. With a load factor of 5,000 hours the existing plants and machinery of the various European countries would be able to produce an additional 20 billion kilowatt hours (over present output of 80 billion kilowatt hours) at an all-around cost of 1.5 to 1.6 pfennigs per kilowatt hour.[73]

Technically there is nothing fantastic in the Oliven proposal. Nearly as extensive lines as those proposed by Oliven exist in the United States; the super-power networks projected in Soviet Russia are even more extensive. It has been pointed out that sufficient capital for the plan is to be found in Europe, French investment surplus for export purposes alone averaging around 1½ to 2 billion marks annually. Exclusive of reparations receipts French net surpluses available for this purpose would amount to 1 to 1½ billion marks annually. Such difficulties as are encountered through different types of current and voltage tensions can easily be taken care of by appropriate technical equipment.

The real obstacles are economic and political. Tariff walls, nationalistic economic policies, social cleavages, national and political antipathies, the vested interests of military cliques, and numerous allied forces making for exclusiveness, Balkanization, and the buttressing of decadent European capitalism stand in the way. The projected system is an engineering plan. It proposes to produce and

---

[71] *Ibid.*, p. 20. [72] *Idem.* [73] *Idem.*

deliver current under the most efficient possible conditions and at the lowest possible rate. Low rates would increase the use of electricity and hasten the process of transforming the bulk of domestic, industrial, and agricultural lighting, fuel, and energy requirements onto an electrical basis. Within its entirety the system would have an immense flexibility. Individual stations and segments of transmission lines could be temporarily stopped without damage to either current feed or the efficiency of the functioning dependent establishments and enterprises.

But in order for the entire system to function properly, it is necessary that a high degree of cooperation be assured in advance. For, when geographic is added to industrial specialization, it becomes possible for a major breakdown to throw the whole system out of gear. Centralization of control, combined with decentralization of detail management, calls for a smooth-running adjustment, continuous flow, a neat adjustment of functioning plants, transmission lines, distribution networks, and consuming units. The proposed power network is directly analogous to the existing railroad, telephone, telegraph, vehicular highway, airplane, and radio systems spanning the continent. Because of the instantaneous character of the service, and the fact that storage is practically impossible, any number of events might happen to disrupt the functioning of nearly the entire power network. Such things as strikes, boycotts, national wars, and revolutions, would be capable of bringing the whole nicely balanced system to a standstill. A few well-placed bombs, a little sabotage at strategic points, and the entire functioning complex would come to an immediate and disastrous halt.

Europe is a house divided against itself a dozen different ways. These cleavages are all antithetical to the efficient operation of the various international service industries which are slowly enveloping the continent in their unified webs. Every year these webs, despite the political, national, and other obstacles placed in the way of their further expansion, become more comprehensive, and the logic of their technical and economic power more irresistible. At the same time they become more delicate and fragile. For analogous to all highly rationalized and mechanized plants, swift, smooth, and uninterrupted functioning requires ever closer attention to dovetailing of interdependent machinery and processes. A serious breakdown tends to ramify throughout the entire system. The addition of no type or number of reserve units can ever completely offset this tendency. The very fact of their existence acts as a spur to their elimination, thereby increasing the hazards attendant upon failure of the remaining apparatus. Thus arises the supreme paradox of the rationalization movement in Europe. The necessity of cooperation is paralleled only by the inability to meet the conditions upon which such cooperation is possible. Germany lies at the heart of nearly all the major networks, and Germany is the major danger point in the European picture.

As Oliven stated, export and import of current across national borders are already accomplished facts. Power lines cross nearly all the borders of Germany's immediate neighbors. Perfection of 380–400-kilovolt transmission lines of 1,000-kilometer efficient length or over, will increase the importance of such interchange. It is expected, for example, that technical improvements will shortly justify the laying of under-sea power cables bringing current to Germany from Sweden and Norway. Interchange among German steam plants, and Swiss, Austrian, Italian Alpine, and Carpathian hydro-electric plants is now technically feasible and has already been partly carried through. The larger international corporations, such as the *Elektrobank* (Switzerland), the *Sofina* group (Belgium), the *Gesfürel* concern (Germany), and the *Sidro* group (subsidiary to *Sofina*) have not been able to promote materially a thoroughgoing reorganization and consolidation of the European electric-power systems.[74] The expansion of their control, however, is laying the organizational basis for such an integration in the future. The dominating importance of governmental ownership in various countries, particularly in Germany, would appear to discourage international exchange until political guarantees safeguarding interconnected systems have been given by all participating nations. Efforts along this line, such as the League of Nations convention of 1923, do not appear to have had much effect thus far.

7. INTER-INDUSTRIAL AFFILIATIONS OF THE POWER INDUSTRY

Horizontal combinations between power-generating systems of various types have been paralleled, as previously indicated, by vertical integration of fuel supply (in steam-generating systems), power generation, transmission, and—in many if not most cases—current distribution. The large lignite pits of the Westphalian district are almost exclusively used for electric-power production. In central Germany a very large percentage of the lignite mined is used, either in its original or (more generally) its refined form, for power-generating purposes. Much, and in certain sections nearly all, of the mining by-product coal-dust is used for these purposes. Use of otherwise wasted low-quality by-product coal has further strengthened the interest of mining interests in power production.

The community of technical and economic problems common to electric-power generating and transmission systems and the electro-technical industry has naturally brought these industries into very close contact with each other. The market for heavy-current electro-technical products is not only dominated by requisitions from the power industry but also subject to expansion or contraction according as efficiency, costs, and other factors tend to force kilowatt-hour rates up or down. Low rates mean substitution of other energy, fuel, and lighting equipment by electrical types. Efficiency in energy production, transmission, and consumption are thus electro-technical as well as power problems at the outset.

---

[74] See the article in *Die Wirtschaftskurve,* "Die internationale Elektrizitätsindustrie und ihre Verflechtung," 4(1927):420–432.

The research, standardization, scientific management, and combination problems of the two industries intertwine so closely that they can scarcely be separated at any point. That intercorporate affiliations have not been more extensive is only because of the tremendous rapidity of growth shown by both branches. The scale on which operations in both fields are carried out, however, justifies and necessitates the growing managerial bifurcation.[75] But parallel and complementary to this trend has been the increasingly coercive technical interdependence.

The technical tie-up between power and the machine and engineering industries is nearly as close. Reorientation of machine production onto a power basis has, as in all substitutions of electrical current for other fuel and energy types, meant perfect dovetailing of energy feed with routine machine shop processing. The efficiency requirement of smooth, uninterrupted, and continuous flow of materials, parts, and processes, and of perfect adaptability of volumetric change at any point with volumetric change at all other points is met in the ideal form by electric energy. But aside from this, orientation of increasing portions of industry and transportation upon an electric prime-mover basis has meant the adjustment of more and more types of power-driven machinery to the peculiarities of direct electric-motor drives, and the construction of more and more boiler, superheater, turbine, and auxiliary apparatus to fulfil the efficiency requirements of electric-power production. Except where large quantities of process steam are required, the shift to electric power usually means partial or complete (1) abandonment of steam plant, steam-transmission apparatus, shafting and belt equipment, and belt-driven machinery; (2) the reorganization and rearrangement of machines, floor-spacing, and walls and columns; (3) new layout of shops and factories; (4) and changes in the direction, timing, and speed of flow of individual and dovetailed processes. To these, many other minor and major changes of direct importance to the machine and engineering industries might be added; for example, the tendency to incorporate the motor into the frame of the individual machine, and thus to make one out of two formerly separate units.

Because of the changes indicated, both the electro-technical and the machine industries are coming more and more to act as suppliers of component parts to a synthetic product under conditions in which the synthesis is becoming increasingly technical and calls for ever larger and more sympathetic cooperation in research, standardization, and general problems of shop, factory, and industrial organization. In a very real sense of the term, nearly the entire heavy-current

[75] Directly or indirectly nearly all the large steel, electro-technical, and machine companies are represented on the boards of directors of the large "mixed" power concerns. Vögler, to cite a leading case, already a leading figure in the Vereinigte Stahlwerke, Ruhrgas, DINTA, and member of the boards of Siemens & Halske and A. E. G., is chairman of the Board of RWE, the largest of the "mixed" concerns. The fact that intercorporate relations between electro-technical, machine, and other industries, on the one hand, and the power industry on the other, have been slow to develop is largely due to the preponderating importance of governmental ownership and operation in the latter, particularly in the post-war period.

electro-technical industry has become a "machine industry," and nearly the entire machine-, and much of the engineering industry have become electro-technical in character. At the same time, these changes increase the theoretical, organizational, and direct technical tie-up with the power industry taken as a whole.

It is scarcely necessary to emphasize the importance which attaches to the fact that chemical development has become in large part an elaboration in the application of electrolytic action. Aside from the fact that the handling of materials in the chemical and metallurgical[76] industries (where most processes are, in the final analysis, chemical) has been almost entirely mechanized on an electrical basis, there is a tendency for electricity to be introduced directly as the active force in both chemical decomposition and synthesis. And nearly all chemical processes are continuous in character. Iron, steel, non-ferrous metal, and heavy chemical production are geared to output continuously. In becoming electrical processes, chemical and metallurgical production raises another body of theoretical, technical, and organizational problems of direct interest to both industries, while at the same time increasing the range and coercive strength of the direct technical interconnections existing between them.

The chemical breakup of coal, which promises more or less completely to dominate coal utilization in the future, means, further, the necessity of dovetailing these processes into the requirements of the power industry for dry and liquid fuels. Power production, which will probably come to depend more rather than less upon such fuels in the calculable future, may eventually become a type of "by-product" problem for the chemical industry. If so, it will be impossible, except in a managerial sense, to tell where the chemical industry ends and the power industry begins.

The dominating importance of the steel industry in coal production and (through coking processes) in chemical breakdown of crude fuels promotes still further the linkage between power and the coal, metallurgical, and gas industries. The relationships between steel and gas production have been previously described. Equally intimate have been the relationships between the gas and electrical industries. As pointed out, organization of *Ruhrgas* by the steel interests involved the cession of gas-main holdings by the *RWE* and the *VEW*. From a functional and managerial point of view there was everything to be said for this division, yet it cannot be too strongly emphasized that the separation strengthened rather than weakened the technical and economic ties binding the two industries together. If there be any doubt on that score, it should suffice to point out that the elaboration of long-distance gas-supply systems, begun and carried through by the power companies themselves, provides a basis for bitter competition between the two types of services. While gas is no longer able to compete with electricity for lighting purposes, it is still superior as a source of heat, and is more

76 Particularly in non-ferrous and synthetic metallic products.

than able to hold its own as a source of power in all industries using by-product process steam or requiring direct flame for heat-treating purposes.

A number of rather complicated theoretical and practical issues would be raised, were the two types of service developed and expanded upon somewhat the same mass-output and nation-wide bases. Technical development in the two fields might show that they were non-competitive but complementary services by dividing the field of usage between them according to the technological superiority of each type. Or, again, it might so happen that the net relative advantage of gas for certain specific purposes would not outweigh the cost of construction of a distribution system which would duplicate the power network in all other particulars. Whichever way the weight of technical and cost efficiency factors might point, the fact that there has been little active competition between the two industries affords some evidence that the affected companies realize the necessity of extremely close cooperation. The problems of long-view planning in this general field are extremely technical in part, and call for utilization of all the devices of rationalization of the most comprehensive, thoroughgoing, and scientific character.

One other important issue is raised by the expansion of gas-main and power-transmission networks, and that is their relation to the railroad and waterways transportation systems. Gas pumped through extensive mains, and power relayed over unified transmission networks, will tend more and more to deprive the railroads and river and canal shipping companies of important sources of revenue. In certain areas, particularly in the Ruhr and Upper Silesian districts, coal shipments make up as much as two-thirds of railroad and barge line business. Overhead costs are nearly as important in these industries as they are in power and gas systems. These shipments are needed in order to maintain revenues, and can be taken under existing circumstances at any rate which will meet operating expenses and pay something on overhead if the alternative is loss of the shipments. If this factor is not enough to promote the necessary cooperation, the program for electrification of the railroads, involving as it does enormous increases in overhead charges, should force interested groups to get together in the sketching of long-range and comprehensive plans for the expansion of both systems.

The relationships existing between the power industry and all other productive and distributive operations relying upon interconnected networks are partly of a character analogous to those sketched above. In a general way the same holds for the relation to all households using electricity for light, cooking, heating, and power purposes. No consumer, domestic, industrial, commercial, or municipal, can afford a serious break in the service or a capricious manipulation of service conditions and tariff schedules. Direct interest promotes insistence that the public have a hand in the regulation of the service supplied; the power industry is a *public* utility in the same unique sense that railroads, telephone and telegraph systems, water supply and sewage disposal networks, and similar services fall under that classification.

Finally, mention should be made of the enormously important rôle played by the power industry in the geographic location and relocation of nearly all types of industrial enterprises. As far as fuel and energy are concerned, unified electric-power grids practically free all enterprises oriented on an electric-current basis from the usual geographic localizing and centralizing forces. Electrically driven municipal rapid transit facilities have made it possible for concerns needing great numbers of highly skilled workmen to build factories in suburbs rather than near the center of the large cities.These changes, along with shifts in the configuration and layout of both large and small cities, have been sufficiently spectacular to draw popular attention to city planning projects of one sort or another. City planning commissions, which have become tremendously important in urban development in newer industrial countries such as the United States and (especially) Soviet Russia, owe much of their inspiration to, and are largely guided by the technical and economic forces compelling and expressed through the expansion of power networks. It is no accident that the "power age" is likewise the "city planning age." With the construction of national power networks has come increased emphasis upon the still comparatively novel ideas of district and "national" planning. Expansion of these networks beyond national and political barriers has played its part in raising the problems of "regional" and "international" planning.

8. SUMMARY

The power industry, if properly planned, is able to act as a sponge soaking up all the fuel and natural energy not absolutely necessary for other purposes, and to transport the current generated efficiently, instantaneously, and cheaply to the points where it is needed. It is thus ideally adapted for several of the basic requirements of the rationalization movement. Use of all types of fuels—low-quality as well as the best—and the exploitation of water power and other types of natural energy are measures which will conserve natural and mineralogical resources to the maximum. Large generating units, high-voltage long-distance transmission lines, and the dovetailing of various types of energy source on the one hand, and energy requirements (loads) on the other, make for efficient low-cost operation. High overhead expense and the relatively permanent nature of generating, transmission, and distributing installations require careful long-run planning on a geographic basis as extensive as that covered by the interconnected network and as comprehensive as the industrial, economic, and domestic cross-section of the territory served. Orientation of productive and distributive activities on a power basis requires continuous and unbroken energy feed, and the careful dovetailing of this service with other basic competitive and complementary service networks.

The von Miller plan for Germany proposes to knit the existing systems together in satisfaction of these fundamental technical and economic principles governing the industry. The Oliven plan extends the proposed network on a continental basis. The important technical and purely economic issues involved in both plans have been successfully met in the field of theory. The practical obstacles are of two general types: political and financial. The financial investment would be very great in either or both cases. The necessary funds, however, are to be had in Europe. Political and nationalistic considerations prevent spinning of the Oliven web; regional, ownership, and party cleavages apparently stand in the way of the von Miller plan. Internally, the financial obstacles seem most important; internationally, the political barriers seem insurmountable.

Meanwhile every significant change made in the evolution of the power industry tends to compel fitting, cutting, and shaping of plans to fit in with some such basic patterns. Every step made in these directions seems irretrievable. Once the step is taken it can rarely be recalled. The logic of technical and economic forces compels ever larger units, more comprehensive geographic systems, more closely woven and meticulously detailed webs. With every shift in these directions, industrial interdependence becomes greater, the necessity for cooperation of all interested parties more insistent, the number and importance of interested groupings greater, and the nature of the decisions of the policy-forming control more socially significant. In no other industry are the interdependencies among scientific, technical, economic, political and social forces and factors so coercive and binding; in no other sector is the antithesis between planning and competitive capitalism so clear-cut and decisive. Scarcely a step has been made by even the more capitalistically controlled power units in Germany during the last decade without involving partial or complete abandonment of one or more of the favorite laissez faire tenets. And the end is not yet.

CHAPTER X

THE CHEMICAL AND POTASH INDUSTRIES

THE RATIONALIZATION MOVEMENT has accelerated three major technological changes, namely, mechanization, electrification, and chemicalization. The first means transformation of the tempo and scale of output, and combination of interlocking processes so that units larger than any single machine (factories and perhaps even technically interrelated industries) may function as integrated mechanical systems. The second means a revolution in the energy and fuel requirements of nearly all branches of industry, a radical alteration in the power-transmission and utilization systems of nearly all plants, exploitation of new sources of energy, a complete change in methods of using dry fuels, and a new set of determinants for plant location. The third means an almost indefinite widening of the base of industrial raw materials, a practically unlimited variety of products through synthesis of basic chemicals, and the artificial acceleration of many natural chemical processes.

In some industries these three revolutionizing changes are found to be taking place at the same time.[1] In others, one change comes first and the others follow shortly.[2] In still others, it is not theoretically possible[3] to have change along more than two lines. Usually the spectacular character of mechanization and electrification overshadow the advance of chemical technology. Yet singly or in combination with these changes, chemical analysis of basic raw materials is steadily increasing in importance, and synthesis is penetrating more and more fields of industry.[4] Thus, the rationalization of industrial chemistry, as of the machine industry, is a two-sided problem. On the one hand it means chemicalization of more and more industrial processes; on the other it means modernizing, integrating, and coordinating the chemical-producing industry itself. In both respects rationalization of industrial chemistry represents one of the most important technically cohesive forces in the modern industrial world.

---

[1] E.g., the coke and paper industries with electrically equipped and controlled mechanical handling apparatus; the chemical industry itself, where, in addition to electric machinery, electrolysis is widely used.

[2] E.g., electrolytically produced copper.

[3] E.g., machine making, most woodworking, the building, and other shaping, fashioning, and assembling industries.

[4] The following may be regarded as almost entirely chemical industries: rayon, paper making, coking, sugar refining, leather tanning, perfumery, artificial leather, and paint and varnish making. About 50 per cent of German flour-mill products are chemically treated; nearly all the early stages of ferrous and non-ferrous metal production are chemical, etc. See E. A., *Gesamtbericht,* p. 43.

I. THE MAJOR DIVISIONS OF THE CHEMICAL INDUSTRY

The history of chemical technology has been characterized by three major developments: (1) a significant relative increase in chemical processes *per se;* (2) the gradual transition of manufacture of a particular chemical from a particular raw material—potash from wood ashes, table salt from potash salts, tar from coal, etc.—to chemical transformation, treatment, and exploitation of many or all of the chemical components of given raw materials; and (3) the growing importance of chemical synthesis. As such changes have occurred, it has become increasingly difficult to determine just what is meant by a chemical industry. Definitions such as those of Sombart[5] and the *Enquete* Committee[6] emphasize chemical processes rather than the production of chemical products. But this is altogether too broad a classification; under it the greater number of metallurgical processes would be classified as chemical, as would likewise nearly all operations involving heat or electric-current treatment. Although such a definition might be technically and scientifically accurate, under it examination of rationalization in the chemical industry would mean viewing about half of German industry from this particular angle.

A more useful circumscription is contained in the classification adopted by the *Enquete* Committee itself. According to the committee, the chemical industry proper includes the following branches:[7]

Production of the so-called heavy chemicals: sulphuric acid, hydrochloric acid, soda, carbide, etc.
Manufacture of artificial fertilizers; in particular, those of the nitrogenous and phosphoric types
The aniline dye industry
Production of mineral dyes and lacquers
The explosives industry
Production of pharmaceutical goods
Production of cleaning and polishing materials
Production of ether (vapor) oils, perfumes, and cosmetic supplies
Production of chemical materials for photographic purposes
Production of medicinals for combating disease
Production of artificial cutting- *(Schnitz-)* and shaping-materials *(Formerstoffen):* celluloid, Galalith, artificial resin
The rayon industry

---

[5] According to Sombart all non-organic (non-agricultural), economically significant techniques are divisible into two mutually exclusive classes: "(1) the chemical: artificial transformation (metamorphosis?) of the inner combinations of material substances; (2) the mechanical: artificial alteration of the outer form of material substances."—*Das Wirtschaftsleben im Zeitalter des Hochkapitalismus,* 3(1):102.

[6] "All industrial production takes place either through fashioning or transforming materials. Most industrial production consists in reshaping of crude materials; iron is used for making machines, and textile products are fashioned from animal or plant fibers. In contrast, other industrial branches are characterized by the process of altering substances as such.... consequently, production which involves shaping and fashioning is called mechanical, while those processes which alter the materials themselves are called chemical."—*Enquete Ausschuss,* "Die deutsche Chemische Industrie" (1930):1. (Hereafter referred to as E. A., "Chem. Ind.")

[7] *Idem.*

Even such a classification as this, however, leaves much to be desired. Rayon production, for example, could also be classified among the textile industries. Pharmaceutica includes over 7,000 different commodities, many of which involve chemical processes of only a secondary nature. Several different types of products, such as soaps, cleansing materials, perfumes, and cosmetics, involve combination of materials by mechanical methods. Several of the groups listed by the *Enquete* Committee are scarcely more of a chemical type than the production of such commodities as sugar, rubber, paper, potash salts, and refined petroleum products. Finally, much of the production of nearly all types of chemicals listed above is carried out on a by-product basis in connection with other industries. For example, gas, tar, the sulphates, cement, fertilizers (Thomas meal in particular) are by-products of mining, smelting, coking, and other analogous industrial processes.

Furthermore, among the various branches of the chemical industry as listed above there exist almost as many differences in equipment and processing methods as are to be found in the mechanical industries. Refinement in methods and increase in the scale of operations has come to mean a high degree of specialization in plant, auxiliary machinery, equipment, and methods. Total reorganization of plant would usually be required in order to shift production from one to another chemical type.

2. THE ECONOMIC AND ORGANIZATIONAL STRUCTURE OF THE GERMAN CHEMICAL INDUSTRY

While the chemical industry is represented in nearly every section of Germany, production in the most important branches is concentrated in a few districts. The most important of these are the Rhineland-Main district, the Central German district (centered around Leipzig in the lignite district), Berlin-Brandenburg, Hamburg-Hanover, and Bavaria.[8] This geographic concentration, brought about largely by factors of transportation, energy, and location of raw materials and

[8] The geographic distribution by districts as shown by the 1925 census of professions and establishments was as follows:*

Geographic district	Factories		Employees	
	Number	Percentage of total	Number	Percentage of total
Rhineland-Main	2,099	24	121,845	39
Central Germany	2,016	23	79,664	25
Berlin-Brandenburg	1,142	13	30,762	10
Hamburg-Hanover and Northwest Germany	1,088	12	32,752	10
Bavaria (excluding the Palatinate)	968	11	18,701	6
Württemberg	647	7	10,265	3
East Germany	484	5	12,365	4
Westphalia	288	3	7,969	2

* Source: *ibid.*, p. 29.

technically allied industries,[9] has materially aided corporate concentration in the chemical field. How far this process had gone by 1925 is shown in table 27 (p. 234), by the census figures for that year.[10]

As these data show, 243 concerns employ about 60 per cent of the persons and use about 80 per cent of the installed horsepower attached to the chemical industry. Six firms in the 5,000-employee class hire 18 per cent of the employees and use over a third of the horsepower. All establishments included, there has been a tendency for concentration to continue since 1925.[11] Excluding from the above figures all those branches which do not fall clearly and distinctly under the chemical classification, the relative importance of the various productive classes in 1925 is shown by table 28 (p. 234).[12]

Many of the chemical industries listed are essentially small-scale and local. For the remainder the degree of concentration is much greater than would appear from any of the foregoing data. Among the larger concerns, the *I. G. Farbenin-*

[9] Cosmetics and pharmaceutica are not much affected by geographic considerations. Where electro-chemical processes are key, nearness to hydro-electric power may be important. (This factor has become less important with the construction of interconnected power networks.) Location in the soda industry is usually determined by cheap and plentiful supplies of rock salt, limestone, and coal. Superphosphate production is apt to be concentrated in districts affording cheap water transportation for the bulky raw materials used. Because of the overwhelming importance of raw materials which appear as by-products from coking and other distillation processes, the aniline dye industry is concentrated largely in the Ruhr and Rhineland areas. About 85 per cent of the total number of persons engaged in the aniline dye industy, about 40 per cent of those employed in the "large-scale" (chemische Grossindustrie) branches, and even higher percentages of the employees attached to the pharmaceutical and photographic supply industries are employed in and around Cologne, Mannheim, and Frankfurt a. M. Because of technological interdependencies, large portions of the heavy industrial chemicals, celluloid, lacquers, and explosives industries are domiciled in the same area. The existence of close relationships between dyeing and textile industries has been an added factor making for such localization. Plentiful supplies of cheap power and raw material for chemical manufacture have brought about the location of important branches of the industry in the central German lignite fields. Fertilizer production in this area has the further advantage of being close to the market.

[10] *Ibid.*, p. 31.

[11] The number of establishments and full-time workers for the years 1913, 1924–1929, according to data supplied by the Employers' Liability Associations (Berufsgenossenschaften) is given as follows:†

Year	Number of establishments	Number of full-time workers	Number of establishments	Number of full-time workers
	Uncorrected		Corrected*	
1913	15,042	277,629	....	....
1924	14,357	360,390	6,561	261,978
1925	13,936	371,408	6,118	260,313
1926	14,091	335,918	6,118	244,503
1927	14,377	377,992	6,228	273,612
1928	14,434	398,107	6,165	289,806
1929	14,762	401,659	6,232	289,267

* From the first two columns are subtracted all industries, such as the soap, apothecary, rubber and gutta-percha groups, which do not properly belong to the chemical field, and all those which are contested as border cases—such as manufacture of stearin, wax candles, coal tar distillation, rosin, and pitch. Of the remaining 6,000 (or more) establishments, somewhat more than 3,000 are domestic and trade enterprises.

† Source: *ibid.*, p. 6.

[12] *Ibid.*, p.32.

TABLE 27

Size according to number of employees	Number of establishments	Total number employed in all establishments	Installed motor horsepower
Over 5,000	6	56,568	351,659
2,000–5,000	10	25,994	128,962
1,000–2,000	19	25,303	81,785
500–1,000	40	27,567	81,174
200– 500	168	50,129	91,477
50– 200	650	64,933	111,682
6– 50	3,190	52,754	84,180
1– 5	4,553	10,313	9,648
Totals	8,393	313,561	940,567

TABLE 28

Industrial branch	Establishments	Employees	
		Number	Percentage of total number (313,561)
Combined works in chemical industry	231	110,431	35.0
Large-scale chemical works	299	33,052	10.5
(Lime) Nitrogen and carbide	25	3,033	1.0
Wood distillation	264	3,786	1.0
Aniline dyes—special establishments	20	2,279	1.0
Dye-goods industry	301	4,924	1.5
Mineral and miscellaneous dyes	440	14,074	4.5
Explosives	240	14,085	4.5
Chemical-pharmaceutical supplies	1,240	25,193	8.0
Photochemical industry	90	9,232	3.0
Chemical-technical supplies	1,015	9,172	3.0
Ether oils and perfumes	181	3,697	1.0
Cosmetic preparations	376	3,690	1.0
Glues and gelatine	288	7,550	2.5
Lacquer, putty, and varnish	656	9,106	3.0
Celluloid and artificial bone	289	13,056	4.0
Concentrated and liquefied gases	107	2,443	1.0
Incandescent mantles	61	2,702	1.0
Totals	6,123	271,505	86.5

dustrie A. G. occupies a dominating position. Founded in 1925 by union of six of the largest chemical concerns in Germany,[13] the loose Community of Interests (*Interessengemeinschaft—I. G.*) which had previously held them together was turned into a corporation possessing the largest capital stock of any company in Germany except the *Reichsbahn.* In 1930 the capital stock was 1,100,000,000 RM. Inclusive of *Merseburg, Kalle & Co. A. G.*, and the *A. G. für Stickstoffdünger* (nitrogen fertilizers), the company employed, on January 1, 1930, 74,000 workers and 22,000 salaried employees. If there are added all employees working in mines and other controlled enterprises, the total number of persons on the company's payroll on that date was 130,000.[14] Excluding this latter group, the 96,000 persons employed directly by the *I. G. Farbenindustrie A. G.* constituted over one-third of the total in the chemical industry (proper), while its capital made up about 35 per cent of all money invested in this general field.[15] In the aniline dye field the company holds a monopoly position. It almost completely dominates the nitrogen and explosives industries. It produces very large percentages of German output of pharmaceutical and photographic supplies and all commodities found in the "heavy chemicals" group. It is likewise an important producer of rayon.

According to Ungewitter there are about two dozen companies, next in size after the *I. G. Farbenindustrie A. G.*, possessing capital ranging from 10 to 100 million marks, about the same number with capital ranging from 5 to 10 million marks, about 200 with capital between 1 and 5 million marks, and about 1,000 with capitalization of less than 1 million marks. The remainder, classified by the census as belonging to the chemical industry, are of minor importance. Consequently, while the number of establishments classified as chemical producers is large, the greater part of the chemical output is in the hands of a comparatively small group of gigantic and compactly organized concerns.[16] What technical,

[13] (1) Badische Anilin- & Soda-Fabrik, Ludwigshaven; (2) Farbenfabriken vorm. Friedr. Bayer & Co., Leverküsen; (3) Farbwerke vorm. Meister, Lucius & Brüning, Höchst a. M.; (4) Chemische Fabrik Griesheim-Elektron, Frankfurt a. M.; (5) A. G. für Anilinfabrikation (Agfa), Berlin; (6) Chemische Fabriken vorm. Weiler ter Meer, Uerdingen a. Rhein.

[14] *Das Spezial Archiv*, "Die grossen Chemie-Konzerne Deutschlands" (1931):44 (Hereafter referred to in this chapter as *Das Spezial Archiv.*)

[15] *Ibid.*, p. 11. Including public reserves and convertible bonds the capitalization totals approximately 1,400,000,000 marks.

[16] Other large concerns are the following:*

Firm	Capitalization (marks)	Workers
Kokswerke & Chemische Fabriken A. G.	90,300,000	25,270 (1930)
Schering-Kalbaum A. G.	30,000,000	5,930 (1930)
Rutgerswerke A. G.	80,000,000	3,070 (1930)
Deutsche Solvay-Werke A. G.	75,000,000	6,451 (1930)
E. Merck, Chemische Fabrik	(Family controlled)	3,056 (1930)
Kali-Chemie A. G.	35,000,000	4,395 (1931)
Deutsche Gold- und Silber Scheideanstalt, vormals Roessler	35,600,000	1,968 (1930)

* Source: *Das Spezial Archiv.*

organizational, and economic rationalization has been carried out in the chemical industry has, therefore, been mainly the work of these larger entities. The history of the *I. G. Farbenindustrie A. G.* may be taken as model in these respects.

3. REORGANIZATION: THE CASE OF *I. G. Farbenindustrie A. G.*

That such a few large concerns, led by the gigantic Dye Trust, should dominate a field of production supplying such a bewildering variety of chemical commodities and by-products, and made up of so many individual plants and separate enterprises, is the best proof that could be offered for the validity of the generalizations made regarding the high degree of technical interdependence characteristic of modern chemical industries. Scarcely a discovery has been made or a change brought about in any stage of chemical processing but has tightened the bonds binding the various major and minor branches of the chemical industry together. Nor have these technologically integrating forces ever been in serious conflict with those making for closer commercial cooperation. German producers, never addicted to belief in the indefeasible Smithian competitive formulas, have always been ready to cooperate in promoting the main chance. Cooperation in chemical production necessarily means the pooling of vital patents and processing secrets. Consequently, difficulties have always been faced with agreements which did not carry with them active control or at least participation rights through stock interchange of the companies affected.

There has been a persistent tendency, consequently, for a few large companies to dominate in each of the major branches of the chemical industry, and for their interrelationships to become closer and closer. Patent pooling agreements, arrangements for pooling and exchanging manufacturing and business experience, special community of interest agreements, and, especially, mergers have been of frequent occurrence throughout the modern stage of large-scale production in this industry. Further support was given to the concentration tendency by the fortunes of war. German producers lost important markets and many foreign manufacturing plants.[17] More important, however, was the tremendous expansion of

[17] While various corporations lost large parts of their markets as a result of the war (see testimony of Dr. Bosch of the I. G. Farbenindustrie A. G. in the report of the Enquete Ausschuss, p. 112), German foreign trade in chemicals has not been quite so hard hit as one might be led to suppose. The Enquete report quotes the following figures from the "Verein zur Wahrung der Interessen der chemischen Industrie."*

Year	Export of chemical products			Import of chemical products		
	Million marks	1913 100	Percentage of total German exports	Million marks	1913 100	Percentage of total German imports
1913	915	100	9.1	433	100	4.0
1925	962	105	10.4	185	43	1.5
1926	1,062	116	10.2	177	41	1.8
1927	1,190	130	11.0	285	66	2.0
1928	1,319	144	10.9	303	75	2.2
1929	1,420	155	10.5	297	73	2.2

* Source: E. A., "Die deutsche Chem.," p. 83.

foreign productive capacity during and immediately following the war. For German producers it was a matter of "hanging together or hanging separately."

At the center of the larger corporate complexes stands the *I. G. Farbenindustrie A. G.* Extensive as its corporate holdings are, its control and influence extend far wider than its stock holdings. Through a series of cartels, community of interest agreements, patent pools, market division contracts, and similar methods it has covered the most important European and non-European chemical branches with a network of special interest bonds. Every year these tend to become more numerous, their terms more clear-cut and coercive, their duration longer, and their final evolution into inter-corporate ownership alliances more certain.

The evolution and present organization of the Dye Trust offer a basis for forecasting future developments in the chemical field. This huge concern—engaged in the production and sale of nearly all types of chemical goods for industrial or ultimate consumer usage—is modeled more or less after the type of the General Motors Corporation, the *A. E. G.*, and similar concerns. As with the *Vereinigte Stahlwerke A. G.*, combination made it possible to concentrate production in a few highly specialized plants. Aniline dyes which were formerly produced in eight different places are now concentrated in highly specialized works. Indanthrene dyes are produced only at Ludwigshaven, while wool and silk dyes are concentrated in the Höchst works. The same sort of plant specialization characterizes production of pharmaceutica, the heavy chemicals, rayon, fertilizers, etc. In all cases a systematic attempt has been made to secure the best compromise between the requirements of plant specialization and mass production on the one hand, and complete exploitation of all constituents of the basic organic and inorganic compounds treated on the other.

Somewhat the same type of managerial decentralization and plant autonomy previously noted in the cases of the *A. E. G.* and *Vereinigte Stahlwerke* has been adopted by the Dye Trust. While final authority in all matters of policy is vested in the central management, all routine factory problems are relayed to one of four subsidiary managerial groups. All factories and workshops are divided among these four, each of which enjoys complete autonomy within the rules laid down by the central management. Within each of the major and minor managerial groups, the division of authority and responsibility has been functional. Each producing, distributing, or special staff unit is thus able to specialize on a narrow range of functions, while at the same time it is closely tied in with the larger enterprise. By systematic application of these principles of organization the company has been able to secure a high degree of individual and group responsibility, and a managerial system which is quickly responsive and at all times flexible in the face of either major or minor changes.

It has not been the intention of the company to eliminate completely all elements of competition within its own properties. A measure of competition obtains throughout the various companies, and, within limitations, competitive activity of prescribed types has at all times been encouraged by the central management. In fact, controlled competition is the essence of functional organization, and the company has been aware of the manifold advantages of competitive incentives.

Decentralization has not, however, tolerated maintenance of the usual types of competition. Trade and processing secrets have been pooled without exception. Along with elimination of duplicate plant facilities, relocation and reallocation of plant and productive schedules, and similar changes, has gone reorganization and combination of laboratories. Research in the various fields has been concentrated in a few well-equipped and thoroughly modernized laboratories attached to the larger specialized works in Ludwigshaven, Leverküsen, Höchst, etc. Smaller laboratories have been ruthlessly scrapped in whole or in part wherever unnecessary duplication has been discovered. Those that are left are either concentrating upon some relatively narrow and highly specialized field of research, or—more usually—are maintained primarily for control purposes. Inasmuch as most chemical production under modern conditions is essentially a laboratory process, the control of the laboratory staff must be continuous throughout all stages of manufacture. New discoveries call immediately for perfection of new processing methods, design of new types of receptacles, machinery, and miscellaneous handling equipment, and the establishment of new work routines. Research and control of manufacturing processes come to their natural focus in the laboratory. Concentration and rationalization of the laboratory network within the confines of the company have thus served as major integrative forces. The experience of the Dye Trust in this field may be taken as typical of all the larger chemical concerns.[18]

Marketing organization of the constituent concerns has likewise been pooled and reorganized. A separate sales office or syndicate (*Verkaufsgemeinschaft*) has been established for each of the five main divisions into which the corporation's products fall.[19] All foreign and domestic sales, the control over all advertising

[18] The relative importance of research and technical supervisory staff in large-scale chemical production is shown by the following data:*

Industrial group	Managerial and commercial personnel in percentage of total	Technical, management, and supervisory personnel in percentage of total	Workers in percentage of total
Distribution	37.7	1.0	16.7
Industry and handwork	5.5	3.3	74.1
Industries with over 1,000 employees	5.8	5.9	88.1
Chemical industry	14.0	7.4	74.6
Chemical establishments with over 1,000 employees	10.8	10.6	78.4

* Source: E. A., "Die deutsche Chem., p. 48.

[19] (1) Dyestuffs and organic and inorganic chemicals, with main office in Frankfurt a. M.; (2) pharmaceuticals, fungicides, and insecticides, with headquarters in Leverküsen; (3) photographic materials, rayon, and perfumes, main offices in Berlin; (4) nitrogen products, *(a)* fer-

and marketing policies, the fulfillment of all cartel agreements, conventions, and similar contractual arrangements relating to sale and distribution are brought under their control. Domestic sales, at least so far as industrial consumption and the wholesale trade are concerned, are made through the company's own organization. Branch offices have been established in the various large cities by the several sales syndicates for this purpose. In the foreign markets, sales are made partly through branch offices, partly through special representatives, and partly through the usual commercial channels.[20] Concentration of sales and marketing control in the hands of these specialized sales syndicates has made it possible to simplify greatly the whole commercial end of the chemical industry, and greatly to reduce marketing costs. "In the place of numerous marketing agencies—particularly pronounced in the dyestuffs field—existing side by side in the same localities, at home and abroad, each of which maintained special warehousing facilities, there now exists but one agency and one warehouse."[21]

It would be impossible in less space than a volume to summarize the more important descriptive facts relating to detailed internal reorganization brought about by the changes indicated. Reorganization of production, research, managerial structure, and marketing have not stopped with systematization of the major configuration, but have forced their way down through the vast and bewildering maze of routine productive, distributive, personnel, and organizational processes. Standardization has made considerable headway in equipment, processing methods, nomenclature, and ultimate products.[22] A great deal of attention has been paid to securing greater safety to workers in working and handling various types of chemicals, and to the combatting of chemical poisons.[23] Conditions of work have been materially improved. Better lighting, heating, ventilation, and work places have been provided. Personnel selection and training, and special worker's incentives have been elaborated for the purpose of improving morale

tilizers and *(b)* nitrogen for industrial purposes, with main office in Berlin; (5) synthetic gasoline, with main offices in Berlin.—I. G. Farbenindustrie A. G., *An Outline of its Organization and Products* (published by I. G. Farbenindustrie A. G., 1930):47.

[20] See testimony of Dr. Bosch, *op. cit.*, E. A., "Die deutsche Chem.," pp. 130–131.

[21] *Ibid.*, p.113.

[22] In certain branches, e.g., aniline dyes, the variety and number of types produced have been considerably reduced. There is a tendency to concentrate upon "pure dyes," with tonal effects depending upon combination of basic colors. The same thing is happening in production of the more important basic and combined medicinals, perfumes, cosmetics, fertilizers, etc. Sale of balanced, "full" fertilizers, providing all the chemicals lacking in certain types of soils, does not constitute a reversal, but rather a strengthening of this trend. Equally important are standard processing methods, standard safety devices, standard instructions for use of materials sold, standard equipment and control devices, etc.

[23] Of the 39,400 accidents reported in 1928 for the chemical industry, 6,018 were results of working with specifically chemical equipment or with chemicals, 2,287 were caused by burns from caustic acids, 1,188 by steam and hot fluids, 723 by miscellaneous heated and burning materials, 495 by poisons, 298 by explosions and ignition of dust, vapors, and gases, 185 by direct flames, 149 by contact with explosives, etc. Of the 511 cases officially reported in 1928 under the classification of industrial diseases, 360 were from lead poisoning.

and heightening efficiency.[24] All heavy labor, and every highly repetitive job has been mechanized where feasible from the cost viewpoint. Duplicate facilities have been ruthlessly scrapped wherever found, and every stage and process of manufacture in every field geared to mass output where technical and marketing conditions were at all favorable. All statistical data relating to output, costs, markets, and sales are now centralized in the new and quite magnificent central headquarters office building on the outskirts of Frankfurt a. M. Cost-accounting procedure has been standardized so as to permit statistical treatment and the use of Hollerith and other special machinery in the keeping of accounts.

4. INTER-INDUSTRIAL AFFILIATIONS

The *I. G. Farbenindustrie A. G.* and some of the other large chemical combines are integrated both horizontally and vertically. In most cases the source of the basic raw materials is either owned and operated outright or very closely controlled. The *I. G. Farbenindustrie,* for example, has extensive coal and lignite properties,[25] controls many and in some cases all of the raw materials sources for its fertilizer, rayon, light metal ("electron," aluminum, duralumin), benzol, benzine, sulphuric acid, basic heavy metal, and other branches, and combines in its system nearly all the processes of manufacture and many of the auxiliary services—machine and apparatus construction, power plants, agricultural experiment stations, etc.—from the raw materials to the finished and marketing stages. Some branches of the chemical industry are built up for the purpose of exploiting other-

24 Nearly all hand and "helper" workers are paid on a piece-work basis; most of the skilled and supervisory employees receive bonus wages of some sort or other. In the larger plants—Ludwigshaven, Höchst, Leverküsen, Merseburg, Wolfen—apprentice workshops and, in the last three named, special work schools have been established. Youths, having passed special examinations, are given free instruction preparatory to their subsequent employment in laboratory work. About 10 per cent of the employees live in quarters owned by the corporation. Special hospital and ambulance service is provided for employees affected by industrial diseases. Lunch rooms, restaurants, and casinos are provided for noon-day meals. Showers, bathtubs, gymnasiums, and athletic fields are available for the sport-minded. Alongside the special works schools are provided libraries and reading rooms, special works newspapers, and facilities where lectures, moving picture shows, concerts, and theatrical productions can be given. Hospital and consultation services are provided for expectant and nursing mothers who are employees, wives of employees, or direct family relatives of employees. Household economy schools are available for the daughters. The company estimated its voluntary social expenditures for the year 1929 at 31,043,325 marks, or the equivalent of 8.52 per cent of the wages paid. Adding to this amount 20,570,580 marks required by law, the company paid out 51,613,905 marks or 14.16 per cent of its annual wage bill, for social services. See E. A., "Chem. Ind.," pp. 114–117.

25 Production of coal, lignite, and coke for the years 1927, 1928, and 1929 was as follows in tons:*

	1927	1928	1929
Lignite	18,590,883	22,040,375	20,289,467
Zeche Auguste Viktoria			
Coal	900,427	980,925	1,148,982
Coke	417,845	467,693	508,709

* Source: *Bericht* des Vorstandes und des Aufsichtsrates über das Geschäftsjahr 1929, I G. Farbenindustrie A. G., Frankfurt a. M.

wise waste by-products. Thus *Ruhr-Chemie* and the chemical plants of *"Oberkoks" (Oberschlesische Kokswerke & Chemische Fabriken A. G.)* were established to utilize by-products of the coking process, the *Th. Goldschmidt A. G.* has long specialized on recovery of chloride of tin and scrap iron from by-product sheet waste of the tin-plate industry, and many branches of the chemical industry are based upon recovery of by-products as indicated by the summary of the structure of the industry outlined in the report of the *Enquete* Committee.

The special nature of these contracts and the peculiar industrial rôle of chemistry in general have brought about the extremely close contacts which exist between the various branches of the chemical industry and these other technically related industries. Ownership of coal and lignite mines makes the *I. G. Farbenindustrie A. G.* party to the *Reichskohlensyndikat* and its regional cartels. Ownership of 44.7 per cent of the *Rheinische Stahlwerke* shares brings the corporation into direct ownership relations with the *Vereinigte Stahlwerke*. Production of benzol and other gasoline substitutes, and control of the Bergius hydrogenation process, has brought the corporation into direct contact with the oil industry, and has led to special patent, production, and marketing agreements with the Standard Oil Company of New Jersey.[26] Production of nitrates from coal by-products, potash holdings, and the fixation process has called for internal adjustment within the corporation, active participation in the scientific, productive, and marketing problems of these three branches, and the conclusion of special trade agreements with domestic and foreign producers.[27] Production of balanced fertilizers has brought the industry into close contact with nearly every branch of agriculture, and has caused the establishment of special research laboratories and experiment stations to handle problems of plant and soil chemistry, and the combatting of plant and animal diseases of various types. Manufacture of pharmaceutical goods has brought the industry into extremely close contact with all companies dealing in and handling medical supplies, and with hospitals and the medical profession. Production of dyestuffs is the cause of the close cooperation between various branches of the textile industry and the *I. G. Farbenindustrie A. G.*, which

[26] The Standard I. G., founded jointly by the Standard Oil Co. of New Jersey and the I. G. Farbenindustrie A. G. in 1929, possesses monopoly production and licensing rights for the I. G. hydrogenation process for the whole world, excepting only Germany. In 1930 the Standard I. G. transferred licensing rights within the United States to the Hydro Patents Co. Through purchase of shares this company has become the common property of large oil companies having a nation-wide business and producing three millions of barrels of oil daily. It is expected that the process will find wide application in the near future.—The perfection of a new catalytic process has made it possible to cheapen further the process of producing by this method. See *Frankfurter Zeitung* (July 31, 1931).

[27] The nitrates cartel, which included Chilean, German, American, and other producers, controlled practically the entire world output, and included invested capital to the total of about $2,000,000,000, broke up following failure of negotiations to patch up market, price, and production difficulties. The Chilean producers, dominated by the American Guggenheim interests, withdrew after the German Government imposed a very heavy duty on imported Chilean nitrates.—New York *Times* (July 17, 1931) and *Frankfurter Zeitung* (July 21,1931).

possesses a virtual monopoly in the aniline dye field.[28] The company's control of large rayon manufacturing plants is a further contact with the textile industry. Direct contacts have been established with the photography and film-producing industries through the virtual monopoly which the corporation possesses of the German manufacture of film and photographic supplies. And so one might go through nearly the entire range of chemical production, finding that technical interdependencies have proved coercive in the establishment of ownership, control, or special corporate agreements in nearly all the more important branches of the industry.

Competition in the international markets, and to a lesser degree in the domestic markets,[29] coupled with general overproduction in various branches of the heavy chemicals industries, has provided the stimulus leading to the conclusion of a number of corporate, patent-pooling, and cartel agreements. Some of these have already been mentioned. Others that should be noted are the convention uniting the German explosives industry, the dividend guarantee agreement giving the *I. G. Farbenindustrie A. G.* control of the *Internationale-Gesellschaft für Chemische Unternehmungen,*[30] the founding by the Dye Trust of the American I. G. Chemical Corporation,[31] the agreement reached between the *Agfa* company and the American Ansco photographic supplies manufacturers,[32] the German-Swiss-French aniline dye agreement,[33] and the European nitrates cartel.[34]

---

[28] Concentration of the textile industries in the Rhineland, Bavarian, and Central German (Saxony in particular) districts results chiefly from the location of the dye and dyestuffs industries in those areas. The latter are in turn dependent upon the resident coal, lignite, coking, and steel by-products industries.

[29] Fifty-five per cent of the market of the I. G. Farbenindustrie is foreign, and is thus subject to outside competition directly. On the domestic market foreign competition is severe in certain branches. Among these are the nitrates (Chilean competition), kodak and photographic supplies (Eastman Kodak Co.), perfume (French, Swiss, and Dutch), pharmaceutical (Swiss, French, English, and American), and rayon industries. Fifty per cent of the German rayon market, it is alleged, is in the hands of foreign competitors. See E. A., "Chem. Ind.," pp. 121, 125–126, and following testimony by industrial branches.

[30] The agreement with the above company, usually known as I. G. Chemie, "provides for a dividend guarantee with mutual rights and obligations, whereby I. G. Dyes guarantees to the holders of I. G. Chemie common stock the same dividend as it distributes in gold marks on its own common stock for the year."—I. G. Farbenindustrie A. G., *An Outline of its Organization and Products,* p. 22.

[31] "This company was formed in April, 1929, for the purpose of fostering and financing the development of chemical and allied industries in the United States and elsewhere. In consideration of an option to buy one million common A shares of American I. G. Chemical Corporation, I. G. Dyes has guaranteed principal and interest on this company's $30,000,000 5½ per cent convertible debentures, due 1949."—*Ibid.,* p. 26.

[32] The new firm is known as the Agfa Ansco Corporation, and has the sole right to manufacture and sell in the United States all photographic products developed by the I. G. Dyes.—*Idem.*

[33] Including the agreement with Imperial Chemical Industries Ltd., and other British concerns, the cartel now exercises practically world monopoly powers. American producers export only a very small percentage of their own output, and are not in a position to influence the cartel.—*Frankfurter Zeitung* (November 18, 1931).

[34] The German Nitrates Cartel, and the nitrates convention between the I. G. Farbenindustrie A. G. and Imperial Chemicals Industries Ltd., practically control the European market,

Metzner lists 91 German chemical cartels for the year 1926.[35] Including international agreements, and domestic cartels formed since that date, the number would probably be considerably larger at the end of the period under survey. In some fields the conventions and cartels appear to have brought about considerable improvement in the organization of production and distribution; in other fields, the reverse. Most of the cartels regulate the marketing rather than the producing. Prices, conditions, and terms of sale and delivery, marketing areas, and related issues are usually brought under their control. In some cases the cartels cooperate directly with centralized marketing agencies. Thus the German Nitrates Cartel *(Stickstoff Syndikat G.m.b.H.)*, uniting nearly all the important German producers, sells about 40 per cent of its combined output through the central Purchasing Association of German Agriculturists *(Bezugsvereinigung der deutschen Landwirte G.m.b.H.)*.[36]

The cartels in the chemical industry have the fatal weakness that they concentrate upon only a single commodity or very narrow range of commodities. Chemical production, in contrast, is characterized by multiplicity of types of output. It functions primarily as a method for systematically breaking down certain basic compounds as found in their natural state. Even where synthesis plays an important rôle, combination and recombination of basic chemical elements tend to multiply variety rather than diminish it. Consequently the cartel type of organization is only fitted to those branches where output is highly standardized, and the danger of cut-throat competition is always present. Even in these branches the cartel is at best only a makeshift and temporary device. As mentioned before, patents play a dominating rôle in nearly all branches of the chemical industry. Marketing agreements sooner or later tend to involve problems of production, and thus to raise issues relating to patented products and processing methods. Thus cartels appear in the chemical industry mostly as stages preliminary to more rigid and binding inter-corporate arrangements. The cartel is usually followed by the community of interests, patent-pooling agreements, and finally intercorporate amalgamations. Such has been the history of the *I. G. Farbenindustrie A. G.*, the Imperial Chemicals Industries Ltd., the Du Pont group in America, and other large combines. The net result has been that horizontal combination has gone hand in hand with vertical integration.

While the technologically coercive forces making for vertical organization flow largely from the nature of the chemical industry itself, those forcing through horizontal combination appear largely in the guise of price and cost factors. Costs are at a minimum with mass output, and horizontal combination makes possible plant specialization for the achievement of this objective. But a necessary con-

since a fair degree of harmony exists between these two concerns and other important nitrates producers in Belgium, Holland, Czechoslovakia, Norway, Italy, etc. Chilean competition, however, has largely nullified the effects of these agreements.

[35] Metzner, *op. cit.*, p. 13.

[36] E. A., "Chem. Ind.," *op. cit.*, pp. 167–168.

dition is the pooling of patents and methods which lie at the basis of cut-throat competition among producers in specialized fields and between competing products. This, in turn, makes possible plant specialization, more thorough functional organization, and more systematic and comprehensive coordination. Typically, coordination along horizontal lines in the chemical industry tends shortly to encourage extension of vertical lines of influence, and ultimately vertical integration. The two concentration tendencies act and react upon each other.

To repeat the obvious, concentration in either direction is dependent upon technological and organizational changes of the familiar modern types. Thus, every increase in emphasis upon rigid, costly, and painstaking laboratory research,[37] every pressure towards further standardization and simplification of materials, methods, and products, every trend towards increased mechanization and electrification, every tendency towards more plant specialization, and every shift in the ratio of overhead to variable costs[38] serves, consequently, to promote ever closer coordination and integration in both horizontal and vertical directions.

[37] Aside from the actual expenditure for research purposes—expenditure which admittedly increases steadily from year to year and constitutes one of the most powerful levers of the amalgamation movement in the chemical field—the character of the problems involved calls for ever more consistent, thoroughgoing, and long-run planning. The rapid rate of technical obsolescence with scientific development in various chemical branches requires that experiments carry the technical problems to the theoretical limits before expensive plant is constructed for manufacturing purposes. Many of the experiments take years for completion. "Even in fields such as the production of dyes, in which a proportionately great accumulation of experiences is on record, further development of present productive methods remains in large part so difficult that fifteen to twenty years must ordinarily ensue between the first significant discovery and its subsequent introduction into actual manufacturing practice."—E. A., "Chem. Ind.," p. 93.

[38] ". . . . it is agreed among the overwhelming majority of the chemical producers that the largest part of their costs is for the most part fixed and rigid, and that economical production is dependent on the degree of plant utilization. The share of fixed costs in the total cost structure of the chemical industry is far above the general level, and is considerably greater than that obtaining in most capital intensive industrial branches. This is in large part due to the relatively low value of the basic raw materials and the low ratio which wage expenditures bear to total costs. Total wages in the chemical industry, which constitute from 20 to 25 per cent of total costs, include wage funds disbursed for the rebuilding and enlargement of plant and facilities. . . . . If one neglects this portion of wage costs, the percentage of wages to total costs would fall under 20 per cent of the total." It is pointed out further that permanent structure has a much lower average life, and consequently much higher replacement and maintenance costs, than is usually the case in most industries. Chemical acids, such as sulphuric acid, attack and rapidly destroy all wooden and metal portions of machinery and buildings. Sometimes this process requires but a very few months. How important these factors are in the cost structure of the chemical industry is shown by the following data taken from the reports of the Statistisches Reichsamt on depreciation charges of chemical corporations for various balance reporting days in the third quarter of the year.—E. A., "Chem. Ind.," pp. 92, 103–104, 105.

Year	Number of enterprises	Sum of the Working capital	Investment	Depreciation*	Percentage depreciation is of investment
		in millions of marks			
1926	86	2,138.7	761.3	102.5	13.5
1927	84	2,219.7	782.1	102.2	13.1
1928	72	2,683.4	844.2	102.1	12.1
1929	94	3,036.6	992.6	116.2	11.8

* Includes expenses for renewals.

The semi-monopoly position at present occupied by the Dye Trust provides a nucleus around which further monopoly powers can be concentrated. That the Trust alone, or in combination with a small group of large compactly organized concerns working in close harmony, will ultimately exercise complete monopoly power over all the principal chemical manufacturing branches is but a question of time. It will then be possible to force through the remaining competitive production branches and the whole marketing organization the same principles of action as are now dominant within the confines of the existing corporate structures.

5. THE POTASH INDUSTRY

Technical rationalization in the potash industry has paralleled concentration of plants and corporate enterprises and drastic reorganization of nearly all phases of production in the post-war period. The combined changes have placed potash production on an efficiency level which may be taken as model for German industry. The steps leading to, and the measures utilized to bring about, this resulting efficiency have been so frequently and so adequately reviewed[39] that it suffices here to summarize merely the categories of change.

The potash industry being judged at least partially "ripe" for socialization by the law of 1919, machinery was set up by the state designed to regulate and control (and eventually to own) it. The original law and subsequent legislation forced all producers in the industry into a "forced cartel" *(Zwangskartell)* roughly analogous to that obtaining in the coal industry.[40] Ownership, with the exception of the Preussag *(Preussische Bergwerks- und Hütten-Aktiengesellschaft)* owned by the Prussian state, was left undisturbed, and management by the private corporations has been, on the whole, unabridged by action of the state.[41]

---

[39] See, in particular, George Ward Stocking, *The Potash Industry: a Study in State Control* (New York, 1931).

[40] "The Law for the Regulation of the Potash Industry, enacted April 24, 1929, ... provided for the establishment of the Federal Potash Council and created a Board of Experts which should work out the details of this organization. It also authorized the Government to issue the ordinances necessary to achieve the principles which the law enunciated. The law was followed on July 19, 1919, by a repeal of the Potash Law of 1910, and on July 18 by a detailed set of ordinances issued by the administration to realize in practice the broad provisions of the law of April."—*Ibid.*, fn. p. 153. The central governing body (Reichskalirat) is made up of thirty members, divided as follows: Representatives of the potash producers, five; Syndicate representatives, three; agriculture, four; potash trade, two; chemical industry consuming potash, one; technical employees of potash mines, one; clerical employees of potash industry, one; labor in the chemical industry, one; labor in potash industry, eight; the State, three; potash mining, refining, and research, one expert. Its principal functions were to regulate maximum prices and to prevent the sinking of further shafts. Additional machinery was provided in the Potash Examining Board (Kaliprüfungsstelle), the Potash Board of Appeals (Kaliberufungsstelle), the Potash Wage Examining Board (Kalilohnprüfungsstelle) and the Potash Wage Board of Appeals (Kalilohnberufungsstelle). The first two of these groups handle matters relating to quotas and technical efficiency; the latter two are responsible for the wage provisions of the potash law.

[41] "No longer is the Syndicate a State-controlled syndicate for purely State ends; it is rather a business-controlled syndicate for business ends. Mercantilistic control of potash has surren-

The possession—in combination with French producers—of practically a world monopoly of important potash deposits,[42] provided ample incentive for combination among important producers. The exercise of Syndicate powers and aggressive action on the part of the larger producers speedily brought the old conditions of practically unrestricted competition—carrying with it excessive numbers of small plants, mine openings, and duplicate facilities—to an end. Of the 229 mining establishments listed in 1929, 111 had been closed more or less permanently, 46 were held in reserve, and only 60 were being fully operated. The

TABLE 29

Concerns	Number of works			Proportion of Syndicate participation 1,000 = unity	Capital in 1,000 marks
	Total	Closed down	In reserve		
Wintershall-Kaliindustrie A. G.	94	56	18	385.7804	200
Salzdetfurth-Aschersleben-Westeregeln	49	23	10	216.5850	72.7
Burbach-Gumpel	37	14	9	167.7667	125
Preussag	10	6	1	59.4514	110
Anhaltische Salzwerke	6	3	1	31.1775	....
Mansfeld-Einigkeit	(Transferred)			51.1349	....
Kali-Chemie A. G.	12	8	1	39.5396	35
Dr. W. Sauer-Werke	5	1	3	25.1368	....
Deutsche Solvay-Werke	5	....	3	22.1929	75
Totals	218	111	46	998.7652*	617.7

* The remaining quota has been taken over by the Syndicate.

number of refining plants had been reduced from 71 in 1913 to 31 in 1928.[43] The process of corporate concentration had brought these works under the domination of a small group of compactly organized concerns. Excluding the 11 works of the *Mansfeld-Einigkeit* concern, the industry in 1919 was divided as shown in table 29.[44]

dered to business control; business enterprise has once more triumphed." Thus Stocking (p. 194) summarizes the process of evolution under the potash laws. It should be pointed out, however, that there was comparatively little evidence of genuine desire to socialize the industry at the time when even the first enabling laws were passed. Theoretically the industry has now attained that degree of "ripeness" for socialization which it so conspicuously lacked in 1919.

42 In 1913 Germany produced about 99 per cent of the world output of pure potash salts. In 1928 she produced 75.5 per cent of the total. Other important producers (1928) were France (18.3 per cent of the world total); Poland (1.6 per cent); Spain (0.7 per cent); United States (3.6 per cent). Other deposits are known to exist in India, Palestine, Tripoli, and the U. S. S. R. The scheduled production in Russia for 1933–1934 is 2.2 million tons.—*Das Spezial Archiv*, "Die deutsche Kali-Industrie" (1930):6, 18–19.

43 *Ibid.*, pp. 9–10. 44 *Ibid.*, p. 13.

The corporate concentration is even greater than these figures show. The second, third, seventh, and last-named concerns have organized themselves into a working unit through the founding of the *Vereinigte Kaliwerke G.m.b.H.* (known as *Kaliblock*). Since its organization the group has taken over *Mansfeld-Einigkeit.* More recently a close working alliance has been set up among the first three companies listed. In addition to control of about 77 per cent of the potash syndicate quotas, change in the organization of the Syndicate has made it possible to establish a triumvirate presidency to which Rosterg of *Wintershall,* Korte of *Burbach,* and Zirkler of *Salzdetfurth* were elected.[45] Meanwhile the *Anhaltische Salzwerke* has been taken over by *Preussag.* Thus, while a trust cannot be said to exist in the potash industry as yet, the degree of harmony that prevails among the larger producers, and the forces at work making for combination forecast *de facto* unity at some time not very far in the future.

Meanwhile corporate concentration has promoted, as it has been aided by, concentration of mines and plants, and thoroughgoing overhauling of the technique of production. Mining operations have been mechanized as far as possible in every stage of the extraction, under- and above-ground transportation, refining, and miscellaneous processes. In place of the old rather empirical mining and refining methods, research and engineering have substituted proving, testing, mining, and refining, in keeping with latest developments in engineering technique. An extensive system of machine, tool, process, and safety standards has been worked out. Electricity and electrically driven machinery, trams, elevators, etc., have been introduced wherever possible. Water-pumping, ventilation, lighting, and general conditions of work have been improved and thoroughly modernized. The German Potash Association *(Deutscher Kaliverein e.V.)* has taken the initiative in cooperating with special mining and technical schools, and has promoted a series of special lecture courses dealing with certain phases of potash mining, with particular reference to the training of electrical workers.[46] Methods have been drastically overhauled and placed on a mass output basis throughout the entire concert of mining and refining operations. Introduction of the flow principle[47] and the adjustment of all processes to the tempo of mechanically controlled routines have enormously increased efficiency of production.

---

[45] *Ibid.*, pp. 12–14, and Stocking, *op. cit.*, p. 193.

[46] *Bericht* über das Geschaftsjahr 1929 (Deutscher Kaliverein e. V. zu Berlin):27–49, gives a fairly complete and condensed cross-section of technical rationalization for the entire industry.

[47] "Large-scale production is made possible by and likewise necessitates a coordination of processes—a flow of materials from their raw state to their finished form. The old refining process was characterized by starts and stops; the new, by continuity. At every stage of the refining process lost motion has been eliminated and machines have driven out the hand worker. The old refining process could handle about 3000 dz. of crude salt per day. The newer does the same work in little more than an hour .... numerous economies are reflected in an increase of approximately 1,000 per cent in the capacity of the most approved refining plant. The plant with daily raw salt capacity of from 2,000 to 5,000 dz. has given way to the plant of from 20,000 dz. to 50,000 dz."—Stocking, *op. cit.*, pp. 226–228.

Output per producing mine has increased from an average of 92,000 dz. (*doppelzentner* = 220 pounds) in 1922 and 144,000 dz. in 1925 to 237,000 dz. in 1928. At the same time concentration upon salts containing higher potash content (hartsalz and sylvanite)[48] decreased the percentage of poorer grades mined (carnallite) from 47.3 in 1913 to 16.5 in 1928, while increasing the average percentage of pure potash content from 10.2 to 13.6. While, as a consequence of these changes, output of potash salts increased by 7.6 per cent during this period, pure potash produced increased 27.6 per cent, and the number of laborers decreased 30.4 per cent. Output per worker per shift increased from 159 kg. in 1913 to 417 kg. in 1928. Simultaneously with a total cost reduction of about 22 per cent from 1926 to 1928 went increase in production of 31 per cent. While nominal wage disbursements increased slightly despite labor reduction, total real wages declined considerably. Additional important cost reductions were the following: 54 per cent from closing down pits; 41 per cent of interest on foreign capital; 31 per cent in management costs; 26 per cent on depreciation charges.[49]

Concentration within the industry has necessarily combined both horizontal and vertical integration. Each of the larger concerns is in control of a more or less completely balanced technical unit. But developments within the industry have carried the process of integration further still. Particularly is this true on the chemical side. The entire industry is, in a sense, of the chemical type. Research and technical development have tended to emphasize this side of the industry, partly as a result of attempts to find solutions for the by-products problem, and partly because of the existence of common technical and scientific bonds binding it to various branches of chemical production. Thus the *Anhaltische Salzwerke* has established a community of interest with the *Concordia Chemische Fabrik*, and with the *Stassfurter Chemische Fabrik* for the manufacture of chloride of magnesium, bromine, Epsom salts, chloride of calcium, potash, boracic acid, superphosphates and fertilizers. The *Kaliindustrie A. G.* has teamed with the *Kloecknerwerk* to construct a nitrogen plant in Rauxel. Opposition to the *I. G. Farbenindustrie A. G.*—largest consumer in the world of potash salts for mixed fertilizer manufacture—has given way to agreements providing for close cooperation between it and important potash producers.

The fact that more than nine-tenths of both domestic and foreign consumption of potash is agricultural has caused the industry to pay considerable attention to agricultural technique. An elaborate agricultural research station has been established in Berlin (*Versuchsstation des deutschen Kalisyndikats*) by the Syndicate for purposes of research in soil and plant chemistry. The employment of fer-

[48] The pure potash content of carnallite averages about 9.8 per cent; sylvanite about 17.4 per cent, and hartsalz about 13.0 per cent.

[49] Meanwhile capacity of operated plant was utilized about 40 per cent in 1921, and about 90 per cent in 1928.—*Das Spezial Archiv, op. cit.*, pp. 9–11.

tilizer containing potash has become so general as a result of such propaganda and agricultural experience that the potash industry has become largely independent of cyclical fluctuations. Farmers have been convinced that the soil must be kept in repair if exploitation is to continue in the future. Regardless of the prosperity of agriculture, potash requisitions must be maintained.

Between the Syndicate and agriculture a number of special community of interest compacts have been effected from time to time. Sale of potash in large quantities to such organizations as the *Deutsche Landwirtschaftliche Gesellschaft,* the *Bund der Landwirte,* the *Reichsverband der Deutschen Genossenschaften,* the *Westfälischer Bauernverein,* and the *Raiffeisenverband* have made them practically sales and propaganda agencies for the Syndicate.[50]

The loss of Alsace to France in 1919 transferred important German potash resources to that country. The German Syndicate was not long, however, in coming to an agreement with its new competitors. In December, 1926, an "understanding" was reached with the French group, *Société Commerciale des Potasses d'Alsace,* which included the two most important French producers, the state-controlled *Mines Domaniales de Potasse d'Alsace* and the privately owned *Société de Mines de Kali Sainte Thérèse.* The agreement gave Germany exclusive control of the German market, and the French exclusive sales privileges in France and her colonies and mandated territories. Outside of these areas the German quota was to be 70 per cent and the French 30 per cent of all sales. This compact has practically established a world monopoly of French and German producers in the potash industry.

6. SUMMARY

The chemical and potash industries offer almost the best possible examples of how the scientific, technological, organizational, and economic facets of modern production and distribution hang together in nicely balanced theoretical and administrative wholes. Rationalization of the various branches of the chemical industry has brought many of them into fairly complete harmony with the underlying functional pattern dictated by technological and organizational factors. This is particularly true of the potash branch. Evolution within nearly all branches of the heavy chemical field has gone far enough to show quite clearly the drift of the major lines of force. The outlines within which future development is apt to take place, barring impeding forces, seem fairly clear and distinct.

The impeding forces working against further rationalization of the chemical industry are not dissimilar to those noted in other fields. Some of them are of

[50] The existence of contractual and close working agreements between these organizations and the potash producers has not always acted to the benefit of the agricultural population. It has frequently been contended that their sole effect was to raise prices to the farmer. See Stocking, *op. cit.,* pp. 259–286.

a temporary, others of a more enduring character. They include such factors as nationalistic economic policies, corporate overlapping and resulting managerial confusion, cut-throat competition, conflict between entrepreneurial and ownership groups at the source of managerial authority, and pursuit of narrowly capitalistic principles in a world slowly adapting its ways of thinking and rules of action to non-capitalistic economic and political realities.

The growth of the larger combines has meant gradual subjugation of the most important branches of the industry to orderly control and management. But in most cases rationalization has not seriously affected intercorporate relationships. Important gains have been made, but the contrast between internal order and external chaos is marked. Within the individual concerns there now exists a high degree of internal order, systematic arrangement, long-range planning and technical efficiency. But between individual concerns and technically related industries, wherever formal agreements or tacit understandings are lacking, secrecy, cut-throat competition, national marketing intrigue, and general confusion are the rule. With the partial exception of the potash industry, the products of such a lack of *industrial* and *inter-industrial* coordination have been duplication of facilities,[51] pleas for governmental subventions and protective tariffs,[52] chronic excess plant capacity, lack of manfacturing and geographic specialization, relatively inefficient production and distribution, high costs,[53] high prices, and general disorder. Certain of the heavy chemical industries have been able to eliminate seasonal fluctuations. None have been able to free themselves from cyclical disturbances. In many branches a large percentage of the skilled and salaried

[51] The history of the breakdown of the international nitrates cartel is illuminating in this respect. Here it is a matter of excess and duplicate facilities on an international scale. When it is remembered that approximately one-third of total German chemical production is exported (E. A., "Chem. Ind.," p. 87), the relative significance of the international market for Germany can be appreciated. The following figures give the percentages of sales of principal producing countries on the world market:*

Exporting country	1913	1925	1927	1929
Germany	28.5	23.0	26.0	28.0
Great Britain	15.6	13.6	13.5	14.0
United States	9.7	16.0	15.5	16.0
France	9.7	13.3	12.0	12.0
All others	36.5	34.1	33.0	30.0

* Source: *ibid.*, p. 84.

[52] The testimony of the experts before the Enquete Committee is replete with complaints of discrimination and the throttling effect of high tariffs on German foreign sales. For pharmaceutical goods the tariff of the United States is regarded as prohibitive. Even in England such goods were forced to climb a 33⅓ per cent ad valorem duty wall. Tariff charges for sulphide of sodium constituted the following percentages of sales price in different countries: Czechoslovakia, 142 per cent; Spain 212 per cent; Chile, 201 per cent; Poland, 68 per cent; U. S. A., 40 per cent; Italy, 41 per cent; England, 33⅓ per cent; France, 27 per cent; Japan, 30 per cent.—*Ibid.*, pp. 122–123.

[53] Most chemical production takes place under conditions analogous to those obtaining in the power field, except that the necessity of continuous and unbroken processing is technologically as well as economically coercive.

classes have been given a status which makes them more or less economically secure. The same cannot be said for the larger percentage of the rank and file workers.

In short, rationalization has been carried out with great success in the chemical industry on the internal, structural, and organizational side; but only the first steps have been taken to rationalize the industry as a whole, or to plan its course and development with regard to long-run economic considerations. Social desiderata have played relatively minor rôles. The human factor has been almost completely ignored, in the potash industry in particular.

CHAPTER XI

THE STATUS OF RATIONALIZATION IN OTHER INDUSTRIES

THE PROBLEMS of rationalization in other fields are not fundamentally different from those met with in the industries reviewed. In some fields—notably transportation and communication—the revamping required in attempting to apply the various technical and organizational aspects has been carried through with great skill and thoroughness. In other fields, such as textiles, agriculture, and distribution, only the initial steps have been taken. A rapid summary of rationalization developments in some of these remaining industries may serve to clarify and sharpen some of the more significant issues and organizational implications implied in the new configuration.

1. RATIONALIZATION OF THE GERMAN NATIONAL RAILWAYS (*Reichsbahn*)

Credit for planning and carrying out the first genuine railroad network in Germany (the Leipzig-Dresden railway system) is given to no less a person than Friedrich List.[1] How well his theory that railroads were by their very nature designed as monopolistic and all-inclusive networks has been borne out in practice is shown by the subsequent history of German railroad development. From small local systems the railroads gradually developed into regional networks, and finally, with the passage of the law governing the railroads under the Dawes plan, into a unified national system covering the entire Reich. With the passage of this law, ownership was concentrated in the national state, and management was placed in the hands of a private corporation possessing operating rights for the entire German railway system.

With unification, the German National Railways constitutes the largest railway system in the capitalistic world, and is far in the lead as the largest corporate and managerial entity on the European continent. In 1929 the company operated 53,434 kilometers of standard and narrow gauge lines (121,324 kilometers of track), owned 24,089 locomotives, 66,003 passenger coaches, 21,004 baggage cars, and 647,530 freight cars; employed 713,119 persons, and possessed assets valued at 27,018,800,000 marks ($6,429,474,400). The total capital of the company at the time of the inauguration of the Dawes plan, including the mortgage of 11,000,000,000 marks on reparations account, was 26,000,000,000 marks, of which

[1] Bruno Enderes, "Aus den Kinderjahren der deutschen Lokomotiv-Eisenbahn, Beiträge zur Geschichte der Technik und Industrie," *Jahrbuch des Vereins deutscher Ingenieure* (1929):38.

13,000,000,000 was represented by common shares. By 1929 amortization had reduced the reparations mortgage to 10,731,100,000 marks.[2]

The heavy reparations burden laid on the railways by the Dawes plan (including the transport tax, 38 per cent of the reparations payments in the standard year),[3] and the run-down condition of the system called for a drastic overhauling of the whole complex. Cessions under the Versailles treaty had seriously depleted the rolling stock;[4] the remaining rolling stock, and roadway, terminal, and loading facilities, passenger stations, repair shops, and miscellaneous plant and equipment were in a badly run-down condition. The personnel was larger than that required for efficient operation. Other transport services—canal and river shipping services in particular—had begun to offer the railroads severe competition in the heavier traffic. Lack of national coordination had led to duplication of repair and maintenance shops, bad distribution of rolling stock at certain seasons of the year, excessive bookkeeping, and numerous allied maladjustments.

The problems of reorganization were attacked with great vigor. The rolling stock was rounded out to the total required for handling peak traffic. The costs of freight, passenger, and baggage cars, locomotives and tenders, switching and signalling apparatus, and miscellaneous equipment were considerably reduced by a number of measures. Orders were placed with but a limited number of companies, enabling them to specialize on certain car and locomotive types, or parts, and to produce these under mass production conditions.[5] The number of types of cars and locomotives was reduced. In collaboration with supply companies, the remaining types were simplified and brought into line with latest engineering practice. Auxiliary parts were eliminated wherever possible, and component parts were standardized wherever feasible. The tractive power of locomotives was considerably increased; fuel power per ton-mile was reduced; coal dust and heavy oil fuels were introduced.[6] Larger freight and hopper-bottom cars, with capacities to 50 tons, were introduced for special use in the coal and lignite producing areas.

---

[2] *Statistical Figures of the German National Railroad Company* (prepared by the Chief Administration of the German National Railroad Company; Berlin, 1930):3, 4, 8, 9, 10, 11, 13, 31, 44–47.

[3] Angell, *op. cit.*, pp. 68–69. Angell points out the fact that the German railways were able to discharge pre-war debts by the process of inflation, and that the reparations debt is but two-thirds the size of the pre-war figure, translated into present values.

[4] See p. xiv.

[5] Examples are given by Promnitz and Philipp in "Gemeinschaftsarbeit zwischen Erzeuger und Verbraucher," *Verkehrstechnik* (January, 1930):63–68. As pointed out above (p. 159) the supply companies complain that orders for various types of rolling stock are given by the Reichsbahn at infrequent intervals, more or less as the exigencies of current developments require, and without warning. Thus they find it difficult to keep plants running continuously, and to operate under favorable engineering and cost-accounting conditions. The railroad officials argue, on the other hand, that general shortage of funds and the extraordinarily heavy financial burdens of rehabilitation and reparations have thus far made it practically impossible to "rationalize" requisitions further.

[6] The number of persons transported in 1927 was 19 per cent, the kilometers traveled 23 per cent, the tonnage transported 4 per cent, the kilometer tons 30 per cent higher than in 1914. The

The work of repair and maintenance of rolling stock and operating equipment was centralized in a special department attached to the central management in Berlin. The various work shops were placed under regional directors, with headquarters at Altoona, Berlin, Breslau, Dresden, Munich, Cassel, Cologne, Karlsruhe, Stuttgart, and Königsberg. The main plants and special works sections were geographically and functionally specialized as far as possible. Thus the principal repair shops equipped to handle efficiently heavy freight cars are located in the Ruhr and Upper Silesian districts where such cars are in use in large numbers. Passenger car repair is centralized in Berlin and Altoona so far as possible. Certain establishments concern themselves primarily with problems of labor hygiene, physiology of working conditions, and accident prevention. In many places it has been found possible, through concentration, to dispense with foundries, woodworking shops, switching apparatus departments, and numerous other special shops. Those that remain have been enlarged, mechanized, and thoroughly reorganized along with the works to which they are attached. Savings from these and allied changes have been very great.[7] Along with sci-

number of trains had declined by 14 per cent, while the trainload increased 25 per cent. Locomotive tractive power had increased 42 per cent. Excluding small locomotives, the number in use had declined from 27,000 in 1914 to 22,000 in 1927. The number of super-heated high steam-pressure locomotives had increased from 6,000 to 15,000. Steam pressures of 13 to 14 atmospheres have been replaced by pressures of 60 to 100 atmospheres. New orders placed reduce the number of types of locomotives from 250 to 35–40. Heavy self-dumping freight cars of 50–60 tons have reduced the time required for discharging loads of 1,000 tons from 24 hours to 4 minutes. Empty running time and kilometers have both been cut considerably. The speeds of trains have increased. The through train from Berlin to Cologne covers the distance of 570 kilometers in 7 hours at an average speed of 81.4 (50.5 miles) kilometers per hour. Higher speeds have been achieved in more recent trials. It has been found practicable to maintain speeds of 140 kilometers per hour with four-axle passenger coaches between Magdeburg and Berlin.—*Frankfurter Zeitung* (March 20, 1931). See Dorpmüller, *Rationalisierung bei der Reichsbahn* (lecture given to the Handelshochschule, December 5, 1927, and printed by the Reichsbahn); also Erich Marcus, *Reichsbahnzentrale für den deutschen Reiseverkehr* (mimeographed material). Leibrand estimates that rationalization of locomotive service has effected a clear saving of sixty-four million marks per annum.—*Fortschritte und Probleme in der Rationalisierung des Reichsbahn Betriebes* (Verlag der Verkehrswissenschaftlichen Lehrmittelgesellschaft m.b.H. bei der deutschen Reichsbahn; Berlin, 1930).

[7] The following may be regarded as typical.*

	1925	1929—first half-year
Number of repair shops (Ausbesserungswerke)	97	78
Number of maintenance workshops (Unterhaltungswerkstätten)—		
for locomotives	64	47
for 2- and 4-axle passenger coaches	62	35
for 3-axle compartment and "D" train coaches	34	21
for freight cars	74	49
Number of switch work shops (Weichenwerkstätten)	18	11
Number of iron foundries	11	2
Number of brass foundries	52	16
Number of woodworking work shops	75	24
Number of employees in the repair works and main work shops	94,468	77,337
Number of officials and salaried employees	9,263	8,916

* Source: Kühne, "Sparwirtschaftliche Massnahmen in den Werkstätten der deutschen Reichsbahn," *Verkehrstechnik*, p. 51.

The amount of money tied up in warehoused materials decreased from 112,307,000 marks in January, 1926, to 58,529,000 marks on June 1, 1929.

entific layout of workshops, car barns, switching yards, and repair shops, and with thoroughgoing overhauling of the technical details of construction, maintenance, and repair of rolling stock, roadway, railroad stations and terminal facilities, has gone attention to the selection and training of personnel. Nearly all the various classes of workers—repairmen, engineers, firemen, switchmen, brakemen, conductors, station help and station masters, track foremen and supervisors, etc.—are selected only after painstaking physiological and psycho-technical examination in the various laboratories and testing stations located in Grünewald (Berlin), Altoona, and other places. Subsequent training, except for routine unskilled labor, is quite rigorous and thorough. Advancement has been placed on a quite exacting civil service throughout nearly all phases of the managerial hierarchy.

Final authority in all managerial details lies with the central administration located in Berlin. Management is then functionally divided according to the principal sections under which the work more or less naturally falls—accounting, finance, personnel, maintenance and repair of roadway, passenger service, freight service, work shops, etc. In every department it is a principle of organization that management shall be functionally and geographically decentralized as far as possible.[8] Throughout the various stages of the hierarchy only those questions and problems of policy and organization are passed on to the next higher managerial authority which cannot be decided by the smaller unit because of the limited character of its functions.[9]

Throughout the hierarchy an attempt is made to secure the maximum of flexibility, adjustibility, and personal responsibility by constant propaganda designed to fix attention upon the dual problems of engineering efficiency and cost reduction. Standardization of materials, parts, routines, and tasks, has been paralleled by standardized cost-accounting and the placing of nearly all accounting procedure on a statistical foundation. Blanks, forms, units, and methods of entry, filing methods, and all miscellaneous equipment and processes have been standardized and arranged with an eye to mechanical handling, tabulation, and summarization.[10]

---

[8] A source of considerable friction is found in the desire of every important locality to be represented by a regional office of railroad management, whether factors of efficiency and economy dictate or not. Separation of operation from ownership has made it possible to ignore such local pressure in many cases. It is, however, not always possible to do so. See Dorpmüller, *op. cit.*

[9] See, for example, the discussion of the organization of the repair and maintenance work of the Reichsbahn, in Ernst Spiro, *Rationalisierung im Werkstättenwesen der deutschen Reichsbahn,* VDI Verlag. All advertising is segregated in a separate organization established in 1920 and known as the Reichsbahnzentrale für den deutschen Reiseverkehr. This company takes charge of posters, placards, calendars, and other special advertising material designed to promote travel—in particular, foreign travel—over the Reichsbahn, "sells" Germany to friend and foe, and attempts generally to improve the quality and tone of passenger service. Special folders and booklets deal with life and culture of various parts of the Reich, and "promote" the castles, music, technology, scenery, sports, spas, and other attractions of local significance.

[10] See the summaries of work along this line in Kurt Tecklenburg, *Betriebskostenrechnung und Selbstkostenermittlung bei der deutschen Reichsbahn* (Verlag, Verkehrswissenschaftliche

The major problems of rationalization now facing the directors of the National Railways relate to competition with other types of transportation. In the freight field the most important competitors are water transportation, long-disance trucking services, and gas and electric-power transmission systems. In the passenger branch, competition comes chiefly from bus systems and—more recently—air transport. The *Reichsbahn* losses from the freight competition of trucking companies was reckoned at from 200–210 million marks for the year 1928 upon the basis of 1925 rates. Bus system competition had cost the railway on the same basis about 2,300,000,000 passenger miles, or a revenue of 140–150 million marks.[11] Since the bulk of both passenger and freight transportation expenses is overhead in character, and does not consequently shrink much with fall in business, it has been reckoned that gross revenue losses are reflected in almost equally great net revenue losses.

The *Reichsbahn* has attempted to meet this competition in a number of ways. More efficient handling and special tariff schedules for various classes of heavy goods and for long-distance shipment have done much to counteract price-cutting policies. It has not seemed expedient for the most part to oppose expansion of the extensive canalization and internal waterways systems which have been improved and considerably expanded since the war. It has proved advantageous, however, to cooperate very closely with the Federal Ministry of Transportation *(Reichsverkehrsministerium)* and the special canal and waterways authorities and shipping companies. Through water-rail tariffs have been worked out over a number of routes, particularly in the Rhine territory. In some districts parallel expansion has worked out a fair division of labor between rail and water systems. In other districts the existence of powerful combines and cartels among the river and canal shipping companies has made it possible for them to reduce costs for heavy freight below rail competition points.[12]

Lehrmittelgesellschaft m. b. H.; Berlin, 1930), and Gerhard Sommer, "Selbstkostenermittlung im Verkehrswesen," *Rationalisierung in Verkehrsbetrieben* (Sonderdruck aus der *Verkehrstechnischen Woche,* and published in the Technisch-Wirtschaftliche Bücherei series; Berlin, 1927): 19–42.

[11] *Reichsbahn und Kraftwagenverkehr* (herausgegeben von der deutschen Reichsbahn-Gesellschaft; January, 1930):9–19.

[12] One of these cartels unites practically all the internal waterways shipping companies (excluding motor ships only) operating on the Elbe, the Oder, and the canals and tributary waterways of entire east and central Germany. The object is price and shipping regulation for the whole industry.—*Der Tag* (March 14, 1931). One of the most interesting of the recent emergency decrees is the Decree for Combatting the Distressed Condition of Internal Shipping, of December 23, 1931 (Verordnung zur Bekämpfung der Notlage der Binnenshiffahrt). The decree invests the government with sweeping powers. Under it, the government may compel all shipping companies to enter legally regulated associations, can limit and control the use of all right-of-way and terminal facilities, can control the height of the freight rate, regulate the division of freight between independent and combined shipping rings, and, if necessary, can compel complete elimination of all cut-throat competition, not only between water shipping companies, but also between these and railroads and bus systems. The decree rests upon the functioning of three organizations; with them it is hoped to carry through a thoroughgoing

The railroads very early saw the futility of opposing expansion of long-distance gas and electric-power transmission systems. It is probable that in the long run, excepting such districts as the Ruhr and Upper Silesia, the gains in general productivity incident to industrial substitution of these services for coal and lignite as fuels will more than compensate the railroad through increased shipping for the loss of fuel transport which results from expansion of these systems.

Against competition from trucking and bus systems, however, the company has made a very determined stand. The principal argument advanced by the railroad people is that the new competition means duplication of facilities, high operating ratios for both systems, and, generally speaking, a backward step in the field of improved transport. It is argued that the new services are able to compete over long distance only because they cut prices under the level of costs, and because subventions and special facilities which lower expenses of operation to the disadvantage of the railroads, are provided free of cost.[13] Professor Pirath has shown that trucks are unable to compete on an out-and-out cost basis for distances over 100 kilometers. Railroads, however, have lower all-around costs than shipping over natural waterways up to about 250 kilometers, and over canal shipping up to about 750 kilometers.[14] These estimates are made on the supposition that truck and water shipping facilities should have assessed against them their proportionate share of costs for original construction, and for maintenance and repair of right of way.

The *Reichsbahn* has supplemented its opposition by the positive proposal that legal means be utilized to force specialization and integration of the two services. The trucking and bus systems would then be confined to short distances, and would serve mostly as feeders and distributors for the railroads. Some success has been achieved along this line by the partial integration of rail passenger traffic with the bus service operated by the National Postal Department *(Reichspost)*.

---

overhauling of the entire internal water transport system. The organizations are the Freight Committee, the Associations of Shipping Companies, and the comprehensive Elbe Shipping Federation. See Dr. Robert Platow, "Planwirtschaft in der Binnenschifffahrt auf der Elbe, der Oder, und den märkischen Wasserstrassen," *Der deutsche Oekonomist* (June 10, 1932):754–757.

[13] The motor shipping companies subsequently founded a community of interests (Interessenverband der Privatmotorschiffer e.V.) governing this industry over much the same territory. Doubt has been expressed as to its power to control motor shipping when but 55 out of 180 owners participate in the association. Nevertheless this association indicates once more the general trend.—*Frankfurter Zeitung* (November 3, 1931).

[14] With the exception of certain special loans from the Reich at very low interest rates, the railroads operate entirely "on their own." The internal waterways shipping companies are not compelled, however, to bear the full expense of construction and maintenance of canals, or river and harbor improvement. Total operating costs and interest charges were reduced for this industry by 27–30 million marks in 1927, according to an estimate of the Ministry of Transport. Including loans at low interest rates, returns from mail contracts, and special subventions, the contribution of the state to ocean shipping and air transport is very much greater. They constitute especially important sources of revenue to ocean shipping concerns. See Fritz Neumark, "Verkehrssubventionen," *Die Wirschaftskurve,* Heft 3(1930):273–283, and the estimates of Professor Pirath in *Deutsche Allgemeine Zeitung* (March 12, 1931).

The contract made between the *Reichsbahn* and the *Bahnspedition Schenker & Co. G.m.b.H.,* whereby the latter was given semi-monopolistic rights in the to-and-from-station freight and express business, was an attempt to force the hand of the various trucking and express companies operating over local territory. The existence of a large number of small companies competing for this business has been responsible, the railroad people maintain, for the existence of cut-throat competition among them, for slow and expensive service, and for some of the loss of business to the inter-city and inter-district trucking companies. Little success, however, has thus far been achieved in meeting the competition of the latter group. The vigorous protests lodged against the *Schenker* contract may well forecast a more bitter contest over the more drastic proposal for elimination of trucking and bus lines from long-distance transport.[15]

A fair division of labor has been worked out between the railroads and the quasi-monopoly *Lufthansa* air transport system. Combined air-rail rates for small express package goods and passenger service have been worked out by the two systems. Mail carriage has called for the integration of this new service in the network of the *Reichspost.* Between the *Reichsbahn* and the *Lufthansa* the time schedules, the tariff rates, the division of labor with respect to the type of commodity carried, and numerous other details have been developed with an eye to elimination of duplicate services and facilities, and in order to secure the closest possible cooperation and integration of the two services.[16]

In general, problems of integration and coordination of competing passenger and freight services in Germany have theoretically very simple solutions. Each service can be technically overhauled, internally systematized, and placed on the highest possible level of efficiency. The widest possible latitude can be given for horizontal combination until the effective operating unit is regional, national, or international in scope. Thus the *Reichsbahn* is already a national monopoly in the railroad field; the *Lufthansa* is practically a national, and, in cooperation with foreign companies, an international monopoly in air transport; the *Nord-Deutscher Lloyd* and the *Hamburg-Amerika Linie* have brought together for 50 years about 85 per cent of German-controlled ocean shipping; the national canal and navigable rivers networks are being woven into a single interconnected national system; the public roads are being rounded out in somewhat the same fashion; the auto transport industry is attempting to combine on a nation-wide

[15] Some hope of voluntary cooperation in securing such specialization between rail and auto transport is held out in the organization of the Autotransport Kontor G.m.b.H., to regulate, on a national scale, the smaller trucking companies, and to work in close harmony with the larger concerns organized in the "Deukraft" system. Among other objectives, the reason for such combination was given as "doing away with uneconomic competition with other transport means, and only to compete with the railroads in the future where lower costs and technical superiority made it possible for them to operate at an advantage."—*Frankfurter Zeitung* (April 19, 1931).

[16] *Der Luftfracht Verkehr* (1931) and other publications of the Deutsche Lufthansa A. G.

basis; some of the more important river and canal shipping combines, looking towards an eventual national integration of this type of transport, have been mentioned.

Combination and rationalization in each case have led to or been accompanied by similar action on the part of supply and service construction industries. Locomotive, freight and passenger railroad car, automobile and truck, airplane and dirigible, barge, tug, motorship and shipbuilding,[17] and miscellaneous supply industries have been organized, in each case, in a small number of compactly organized companies, or brought under the control of large combines, cartels, or communities of interest. In cooperation with the industries which they supply, these companies have standardized, simplified, and typified equipment, parts, supplies, and general construction. Dependence upon the service industries for their markets has caused them to work in close contact with those industries on many important projects.

The same efficiency and cost factors leading to internal rationalization, and closer contacts with supply groups have operated to promote specialization, functionalization, and integration between and among complementary systems. The dangers attending unregulated competition, the national scale upon which each operates, and the high overhead costs typical of all transportation systems have led to unusual emphasis upon elimination of duplicate facilities and the dovetailing of service wherever possible. Long-range planning, which is national in scope and inter-industrial and inter-service in character, is thus typical of German transportation systems. The frictions that have developed from time to time serve, among other things, to indicate the coercive power of these integrating forces.

2. THE GERMAN NATIONAL POST *(Reichspost)*

The governmentally owned and operated German National Post is a fitting partner to the *Reichsbahn*. Its size is indicated by the fact that some 356,236 persons were employed in its 15,723 separate establishments in 1926. Plant and equipment, valued in excess of 2,500,000,000 marks in 1930, include the entire post office, parcel post, telephone, telegraph, and a large portion of the radio and bus services of the country.[18]

The strengths and weaknesses of long-range planning should be clearly shown in the organization and managerial history of this gigantic complex. As a publicly owned and managed system its development offers a splendid example for study of the comparative efficiencies of capitalistic and non-capitalistic operating

[17] "Die Konzentration in der deutschen Werftindustrie," *Die Wirtschaftskurve,* Heft 3 (1927):297–301, with accompanying chart.

[18] Most of the material for this section is taken from Willy Muser, "Die Rationalisierungsbestrebungen bei der deutschen Reichspost," *Hamburger wirtschafts- und sozialwissenschaftliche Schriften,* Heft 16 (Rostock, 1930).

methods. Formal combination of a series of nation-wide technically related services into a single functioning unit should make possible some interest in comparisons with looser types of association.

As a matter of fact, the organizational differences between this type of system and those previously examined are less marked than would at first be supposed. The technical problems—standardization, simplification, scientific management, personnel selection and training, the issues of sabotage and bureaucracy—are no different, and their solutions are being sought in much the same manner and by the use of the same methods and institutional aids as those indicated in other industries previously outlined. The problems of the structure of management and the organizational implications of the new configuration are, at bottom, no different in the *Reichspost* from what they are elsewhere. What we may say is merely that the *Reichspost,* including as it does a series of services of a more clearly "natural monopoly" character, took on earlier the definite impress of the "public service" institution, and that it represents more or less the prototype towards which other key industries are developing.

The Weimar Constitution transferred the postal services from the states to the Reich. By special enactment in 1924 *(Reichspostfinanzgesetz)* the *Reichspost* was given fiscal independence from the state and formally established as an "independent enterprise" to be managed according to "business and economic principles" by a National Postal Minister with the advice and counsel of a managing board. That the separation affected was more nominal than real is shown by the fact that the Postal Minister is a political appointee, and by the membership of the Management Board.[19] The intention of the law, however, was to place the various branches of the post office on a fairly rigid civil service basis. In this respect the move appears to have been amply justified by the subsequent development and improvement of the systems controlled.

The 50,000 separate postal units in the Reich are now divided into 45 separate districts, each presided over by an official responsible to the central management. Central management is functionally divided into six sections: (1) postal service; (2) telephone service and telegraph construction; (3) telegraph and radio service; (4) personnel; (5) bookkeeping, accounting, and post office construction; (6) Bavarian postal service.[20] Within each district the Chief Postal Administration *(Oberpostdirektion)* is held responsible for carrying out provisions of the enabling law and miscellaneous decrees, and for supervision of all the various postal services in that area. In all general matters the central administration is the final authority, but the details of management are left largely to the district

[19] The Administration Council now numbers 41 members. Of these the Reichstag appoints 11, the National Council (Reichsrat) 10 (representing the various national administrative areas), the National Finance Minister (Reichsfinanzminister) 7, and general business the remaining 12.—*Ibid.,* p. 12.

[20] *Handwörterbuch der Staatswissenschaften,* 4:909–911.

groups. Operating units are either separate establishments, postal agencies, or postal representative offices *(Posthilfsstelle)*. The former are graded into three classes according to size. Where the volume of traffic is heavy enough to justify, special offices are established for the various services under the administration of special Railroad Postal, Postal Check, Telephone and Telegraph Officers.

Throughout the various services with their pooled and special hierarchies the principle of decentralization and individual responsibility is carried as far as possible. Rights, duties, and obligations of various officials under the law and the administration are detailed at some length in special instruction books. But there is now apparently a tendency to delineate duties less minutely and to permit more latitude and personal initiative in their fulfillment than formerly.

In cooperation with the Federal Statistical Office *(Statistisches Reichsamt)* and the Institute for Business Cycle Research, cost, marketing, and numerous special research projects of an economic character are carried on. Numerous technical committees, and close engineering cooperation with electro-technical and other supply industries, provide means for keeping management at all stages in touch with technical developments of importance to the several branches of the postal service. Research in these fields provides the scientific foundation for the numerous and extensive rationalization measures introduced in recent years. Standardization, simplification, apparatus typification, mechanization, personnel selection and training, and numerous other rationalization features have brought about drastic changes in internal set-up. Automatic stamping, telegraphic transmitting, telephone exchange, and other types of special machinery have been introduced. Component parts of typewriters, transport mechanisms, trucks, autobusses, telephonic and telegraphic sending and receiving apparatus, have been reduced in number and standardized.[21] Envelopes, writing paper, money-order blanks, check and registry forms, filing, bookkeeping, reports, accounting terminology, mail bags, package wrapping, transmitting codes, sending and receiving calls, and a thousand and one other details have been simplified or coded.

Personnel selection and training have long been familiar to the postal service. With the reorganization in 1924 there was a tendency in fact to lay undue emphasis upon these rationalization features. Psycho-technics was regarded as a rigid science. Testing of mail-bus chauffeurs was described as the equivalent of submission to a torture chamber. As a result of much criticism and complaint, consequently, the seven special testing laboratories in existence from 1923–1924 to 1928 were broken up, and their functions taken over by a special Central Psycho-technical Office *(Psychotechnische Zentralstelle)* under the direct control of the central post-office administration. For certain classes of workers, such as telegraph construction apprentices, telegraphic operators, and mail-truck apprentices, testing for physical and mental abilities is indispensable as a prerequisite

[21] Centralized purchase of simplified typewriters brought the Reichspost estimated savings of 45,000 marks in 1924, 34,000 marks in 1925, and 41,000 marks in 1926.—Muser, *op. cit.*, p. 43.

to employment. For other classes of workers the requirements are less rigid. Training is exacting in some fields, less so in others. In more recent years the tendency has been to spread training over a longer period of time and thus make it possible for jobs to be learned as they are worked into. Not a great deal has been done with time and motion studies, since most of the tasks to be performed are not of a highly repetitive character. Considerable changes have been made, however, in general layout of offices, furniture, equipment, work routines and miscellaneous details.

Savings from the more technical features of rationalization are difficult to estimate in many cases. From a pecuniary point of view they have been considerable, as available data indicate. The savings in labor power shown by the discharging of some 92,000 men from those employed in 1923 cannot be taken as indicative of rationalization, since the postal service, in common with the situation existing in nearly all industries during the inflation period, was very much overmanned. Estimated saving of about 16,000 persons since 1924 is not, however, so significant as the increase in traffic per employee. The increased volume of business handled is to be only in part attributed to betterment of personnel. Mechanization, more efficient handling methods, automatic machinery, better arrangement of offices, and similar changes play more important rôles.

Integration among the various services brought under the control of the *Reichspost* is paralleled by close cooperation with technically and commercially related industries. These relations must necessarily be very close with railroad, airplane, omnibus, and other transportation systems serving as mail carriers. The Post owns and operates 3,336 (1928) mail coaches over the railroad system. Special facilities, contracts, and agreements govern mail and package deliveries over all common carriers. In many sections of the country mail busses also carry passengers between outlying districts and railway stations and airports. Technical and commercial contacts are very close between the Post and the various supply industries. The control of the Post over radio distribution has made possible the coordination and systematization of various types of radio broadcasting services.

In nearly every field of effective control, the Post operates on a national and monopolistic basis. The services operated are also, in most cases, of direct and immediate significance internationally. The *Reichspost* is thus party to a number of international agreements and conventions tying together radio, telephone, cable and telegraph transmission services, and dealing with such problems as postal and package marking, and handling, charging, and delivering conditions. These international integrative functions are steadily growing in importance; the *Reichspost* in these respects is coming to take the rôle of an administrative adjunct of a still larger and more comprehensive managerial network.

Here, as elsewhere, the rationalization movement cannot be said to have come to a resting place. The larger organization and configuration of part and entity are tied up with the more detailed routine problems of efficiency. At scarcely any point have these been given thoroughly satisfactory solution. Criticism of bureaucracy and charges of inefficiency have, however, been remarkably few; peculation and corruption have never been problems.

3. THE TEXTILE INDUSTRIES

Rationalization in the textile field, compared with the various industries previously reviewed, has made but little headway since the war. The changes that have been brought about lie largely on the technical side, or in those phases of production in which the textile industries had long enjoyed a high degree of perfection. The more important problems of inter-process and inter-industry integration, excessive plant capacity, market stagnation, geographic specialization, high operating costs, and other more purely organizational phases of textile production and distribution have scarcely been touched.

A number of reasons account for the backwardness of the textile industries in these respects. *(a)* The age of most branches of the industry. Even before the advent of the "Industrial Revolution" fiber preparation, spinning, knitting, weaving, dyeing, and clothes-making had been brought to a fairly high level of technical development. Many of the basic processes were known, and had been tested and refined by millions of workers in every known civilization since long before the dawn of written history. The "Industrial Revolution" introduced mechanization into what was already a large-scale industry.[22] This stage in the history of textile technology was virtually brought to a close by the middle of the nineteenth century. Hence, more recent refinements and improvements—important as they have been in many respects—play a less spectacular rôle than would be the case if the technological base were not already so broad, comprehensive, and mature.

(b) In the course of technological development handicraft skills have played an extremely important rôle. Combined with comparatively slow technical change and a persistent tendency towards technological stagnation, this has made for a widespread spirit of individualism and conservatism in the various branches of the industry.[23] The more modern counteracting influences of mechanization,

[22] Compare, Werner Sombart, *Der moderne Kapitalismus,* 2:766–772.

[23] Otto Pennenkamp summarizes the opposition to rationalization in the textile industry under the following heads: (1) Belief that theory is in large part divorced from knowledge of the special problems of the industry. Proposers of rationalization measures are greeted as fake "wonder doctors." (2) The demands made upon the skilled textile worker are very great. Frequent changes of patterns, with changes in fashion, mean changes in machines—sometimes of a rather radical character, costly stoppages, etc. Competition is keener in retail distribution even than in production. (3) Conditions peculiar to textile production make for a feeling of self-consciousness and self-reliance. Conditions within the same branch of industry are sometimes quite different between companies and different branches of the same company. Much, if not everything at times, depends upon the initiative and ability of the specially trained staff. These are strongly individualistic, and the belief persists that this individuality would be sacri-

automatization, and commercialization have been largely nullified by the growing importance of fashion and the necessity of catering to a fickle buying public.

(c) Trends in the geographic distribution of textile industries, enormously accelerated by the war and the unusual conditions prevailing throughout the world subsequently, have shifted the relative importance of the various countries. While about 80 per cent of world production is confined to eight countries—Germany, Great Britain, France, Italy, Russia, United States, Japan, and India[24]—no country is without its textile industries, and the outlying territories have been rapidly increasing their independence of the older countries.

(d) The comparatively high percentage which raw-materials costs bear to total expenditure mean that the possibilities of cost reduction through technical and commercial reorganization are relatively limited.[25] A large percentage of the remaining expenditures is taken up by wages and salaries of highly skilled workers.[26] The fact that the skilled workers (in Germany at least) are strongly organized and group conscious tends to emphasize the overhead character of disbursements made to them.

(e) The various branches of the industry have long been plagued with excess plant capacity. This excess capacity is to be found in every producing country, every branch of textile production, and in every stage of manufacture and dis-

ficed with rationalization. (4) Rationalization smacks of the schematic. The belief persists that this is antithetical to artistic or creative effort, which is of key importance in the textile industry.—"Die psychologische Wertung von Rationalisierungsfragen in der Textil-Industrie," *Die Gesamte Band-, Spitzen- und Weberei-Industrie,* Nr. 15:7–8 (Leipzig, September 1, 1927).

[24] The Institut für Konjunkturforschung has compiled index numbers for various classes of countries designed to show the significance of the geographic shifts that have taken place since 1913. Index numbers with 1913 as base were constructed for the period 1926–1928 to show the average production by four types of countries. For the older European textile producing countries (with 1913 = 100) the average was 91; for the principle raw materials countries (China, Japan, Australia, New Zealand, British India, South Africa, Brazil, Chile, Mexico) the average was 218; for the countries favored by easy capital markets (Sweden, Norway, Holland, Canada, United States, Belgium) the average was 169; for the countries whose economic activities are shaped and guided by largely non-economic considerations (Roumania, Hungary, Italy, U. S. S. R.), the average was 148.—*Die Welttextilkrise,* Sonderheft 24:13 (Berlin, 1931).

[25] Hellwig and Mackbach have estimated raw-materials costs to constitute the following percentages of total expenses for various branches of the textile industry*

Cotton textiles	50–60
Linen and cotton textiles	55
Cotton and silk textiles	35
Natural silk textiles	54

* Source: Bruno Birnbaum, *Wirtschaftlichkeitsbestrebungen in der Textilindustrie* (Berlin, 1929): 4.

[26] The same authorities estimate wages and salaries to constitute the following percentages of total costs for the same industries respectively (Source, *idem.*):10–15, 17, 40, 30. With utilization of plant to capacity and a high degree of mechanization, it is possible to reduce this percentage to about 10. See Hermann Schaefer, "Rationalisierungsbestrebungen in der Textilwirtschaft," *Die Wirtschaftskurve,* Heft 4 (1926):428–432.

tribution.[27] So serious has the problem of excess capacity become that one author estimates that but for seasonal demand the entire textile industries of Germany, France, and Czechoslovakia could be regarded as superfluous.[28] The rapid rise of the rayon and silk industries in recent years has tended to increase excess in the older textile industries still further.[29]

(f) The relatively small size of the typical enterprise has tended to perpetuate the importance of family ownership.[30] This fact in turn tends to act as a brake on all efforts towards horizontal and vertical integration. This is particularly true in the older branches of the industry, and in those divisions catering to highly specialized markets.

(g) Nearly all branches of the industry are highly sensitive to cyclical fluctuations. Experience has shown that relatively few combinations have been able to last more than three or four years. If to these be added seasonal fluctuations and capricious fashion changes, it will be seen that the industry rests upon a highly unstable market foundation.

(h) Textile manufacture involves so many different processes, so many different types of highly specialized machinery, and the cooperation of so many dif-

---

27 Some check on degree of plant utilization is obtained by the following figures on percentage of persons employed per 100 trade union members (exclusive of short-time work) for the years 1926–1929:*

Year	Silk and rayon	Wool	Cotton	Linen	Jute	Weaving, knitting	Curtain lace	Total textile industry
1926	51.2	57.9	40.3	....	....	49.2	23.1	47.0
1927	91.5	92.2	93.4	....	....	90.9	80.5	92.3
1928	76.7	77.2	67.6	47.0	94.1	87.7	48.8	73.4
1929	74.4	71.9	56.8	47.0	70.4	68.0	48.8	63.9

* Source: *Wirtschafts-Jahrbuch für Industrie und Handel, 1929–1930.*

While output was declining by 5 per cent and consumption by 12½ per cent in rayon during 1930, capacity was steadily increasing. It was estimated in March, 1931, that 50 per cent of world capacity was excess at that time.—*Tageblatt* (March 6, 1931).

28 Georg Müller-Oelinghausen, "Rationalisierung der Textilindustrie," *Die Bedeutung der Rationalisierung für das deutsche Wirtschaftsleben, Industrie- und Handelskammer* (Berlin).

29 The relative importance of the various branches of German textile production is shown in the following table:†

VALUE OF OUTPUT OF IMPORTANT TEXTILE GROUPS (BILLIONS OF MARKS)

Group	1913*	1925	1926	1927	1928
Cotton industry	2.35	5.08	3.39	4.95	4.49
Wool industry	1.72	2.61	2.55	2.92	2.57
Silk and rayon industries	0.49	0.63	0.64	1.04	1.09
Linen industry	0.28	0.31	0.18	0.30	0.22
Jute industry	0.14	0.20	0.13	0.17	0.19
Totals	4.98	8.83	6.89	9.38	8.56

* Pre-war territory.
† Source: Herbern Klebs, "Die deutsche Textilindustrie," *Technik und Wirtschaft* (April, 1930): 85-94.

The post-war figures would not, of course, be nearly so high if rated in terms of a constant monetary unit.

30 The result is that only a small percentage of the textile establishments are incorporated.

ferent institutions, persons, and vested interests that rationalization—technical, industrial, national—is bound to be a very slow process, wherever it may take root.[31]

Despite the number and complexity of the handicaps peculiar to the textile industry (to which must always be added those common to all enterprises, and to enterprises in Germany in particular), important developments along general rationalization lines have taken place. Progress in standardization has been quite noteworthy. Cooperation with agricultural growers of vegetable and animal fibers, and international agreements between manufacturers in various branches of the industry, have brought about a measure of improvement and quality standardization of raw materials,[32] and methods of classifying, testing, and handling raw materials. Basic standards relating to dimensions,[33] color tones, color fastnesses,[34] thread strength, count, and weave for certain staple products,[35] have

[31] The textile industry, taken as a whole, divides into four main groups: (*a*) spinning—carding, combing—flax, hemp, jute, cotton, silk, and rayon spinning; (*b*) weaving and knitting; (*c*) clothing; (*d*) retail and wholesale. The latter two main divisions are usually not included in discussions of problems of the textile industry. Vertical integration, however, necessarily brings them into the picture.

[32] Fairly rigid quality standards and systems of classification have been worked out for flax, cotton, hemp, woolen, and silk fibers. The work of the Japanese government in improvement and standardization of silk fiber is particularly noteworthy.—"Japanische Rohseidenstandards," *Textil Zeitung,* Nr. 63 (March 16, 1927).

[33] German cotton weavers set the web to one-quarter of the French inch but reckon width in centimeters, while the goods are sold by the meter. Sailcloth weavers take the width of the loom in Saxon quarter-ells, and in all other measurements use metric units. In the silk industry two units (Krefelder Feine and Elberfelder Feine) taken from the French inch are used. In the jute industry still another unit (the Porter) is used. The Rheinisch and Berliner inch units are still to be found. The English inch is basic to all imported English textile machinery. See "Die Normung in der Textilindustrie und im Textilmaschinenbau," Vortrag gehalten im Rahmen eines Vortragskurses für die Lehrkräfte an Sächsischen Textilfachschulen, (Dresden, October 5, 1928).

[34] There is a tendency in dye manufacture to produce more concentrated primary colors, leaving tonal effects to be developed as desired according to some more or less standard scheme of color classification and intensity graduation. But to get any particular color tone requires not only that the original dye be color constant, but also that textile fibers be uniform with respect to a number of physical-chemical constants, that methods of mixing, treating, and bleaching be relatively invariable, and that preceding and following processes deviate from fixed patterns by only narrow margins. Depending upon these factors being fixed as rigidly as possible, it is then feasible to attempt drawing of standards and standard methods of test for color resistance to such things as light, washing, heating, water, rubbing, ironing, sulphur, sweat, alkali, street dirt, and possible combinations of these variables. A great deal of work has been done in these fields by various laboratories and special committees, in particular by the Echtheitskommission of the Fachgruppe für Chemie der Farben- und Textilindustrie im Verein deutscher Chemiker. See its publication, *Verfahren Normen und Typen—für die Prüfung der Echtheitseigenschaften von Färbungen auf Baumwolle, Wolle und Seide* (Berlin, 1926).

[35] These variables have been fixed for sailcloth, nearly all types of hospital linen, etc. That the process has great possibilities for producers catering to industrial consumers is shown by the general lack of standards obtaining in textile materials delivered to the latter. There were in 1924, for example, 624 different dimensions for jute sacks to hold rye or wheat flour of one and a half hundredweight, and 360 different dimensions and weights of jute sacks for a hundredweight of cement.—Waldemar Boke, "Die Normalisierung und Typisierung der Juteerzeugnisse," *Der Textil-Markt* (Pössneck, December 22, 1924).

been introduced. Machines, machine tools, and machine parts have been standardized in many cases with considerable success.[36] Finally, it has been possible to introduce commodity standardization into several rather highly specialized branches of textile production. Underclothing (particularly men's wear), shirting, stockings, socks, handkerchiefs, sheeting, sail cloth, and other staple goods have been more or less standardized through combination of conventional selection and formal agreement.[37]

Individual companies, trade associations, municipalities, states, and the Reich have all contributed support and encouragement to textile research in the various laboratories established at Krefeld, Sorau, Dresden, and other places. The work carried out in these laboratories, or in cooperation with other laboratories, concern nearly every phase of textile technology. At Sorau, the laboratory established by the linen manufacturers possesses a special experimental farm, where flax types, soil and climatic conditions, time of cutting, method of treating at various stages before the fiber goes to the spinning mill, and other problems relating to raw materials are carefully examined. The various laboratories combine physical, chemical, botanical, and bacteriological research with careful examination of the various stages of textile production.[38]

Physiological and psycho-technical suitability tests have been rather sparingly used in the textile industries thus far. A few large concerns, such as the *Norddeutsche Wollkämmerei und Kammgarnspinnerei A. G.*, have worked out qualifying tests for reelers, spinners, weavers, and other specialized workers. But on the whole the existence of large numbers of unemployed skilled workers has had the effect of shifting personnel interest to specialized training in textile schools,

[36] A few examples will serve to show possibilities in this field:*

Number of	Before standardization	After standardization
Weft forks (Schusswächtergabeln)	40	3
Filling-fork grates for stationary-reed looms (Schusswächtergitter für Festblattstühle)	20	1
Warp-beam diameters (Kettbaumdurchmesser)	28	7
Large warp-beam rollers (Kettbaumscheiben, grosse)	400	37
Pickers for light overshot looms (according to the lists of one firm)—(Picker für leichte Oberschlagstühle—nach der Liste einer Firma)	2,000	55
Shuttle sizes (Schutzengrössen)	800	50
Loom widths between 75 and 245 cm	51	18

* Source: pamphlet called *Herr Textilfachman!* put out by the special textile committee, Textilnorm, of the Deutscher Normenausschuss.

One author has counted 873 different shuttle dimensions, each to be had in 9 different qualities, thus compelling the supplier to stock 8,000 different sizes and qualities.

[37] Uniforms and costumes of nurses, policemen, soldiers, postal and railroad employees, bus and tram operators, maids, doormen, musicians, mourners, clergymen, priests, nuns, etc., are rigidly standardized. Custom has rendered relatively unchangeable socks, garters, winter and summer underwear, brassieres, men's hats, caps, shirting, neckties, handkerchiefs, tablecloths, sheeting, pillowcases, etc. Fashion fixes, regiments, "freezes" just as much as it liberates and sets free.

[38] See, in particular, publications of Das Forschungs-Institut für Bastfasern in Sorau, and the Textilforschungs-Anstalt, Krefeld, e. V.

betterment and systematization of working environment and labor routines, and improvement of morale by special wage, bonus, and other incentive schemes. Some of the larger concerns have made changes involving time and motion studies, simplified automatic and semi-automatic machinery, better lighting, heating and ventilation, simplified processing methods, more rigid control over rest pauses, closer attention to problems of fatigue, and other features of work involving the human element.[39]

While technical reorganization has been slow, and the level of mechanization—as judged in terms of horsepower consumed per worker,[40] or degree of electrification—is comparatively low for German textile production as a whole, the depressed state of the industry, the general inability to control variable market factors, and the growing importance of overhead costs, has led to considerable emphasis upon unified and standardized cost-accounting systems, and the systematic use of budgetary procedure. Textile manufacturers have participated in committees of the *Reichskuratorium* whose work has been dedicated to the perfection of these techniques.[41]

Hand in hand with these studies have gone efforts to assemble and utilize marketing statistics, and to carry out various special marketing studies. Textile industrialists have been especially interested in business cycle research, and to this end have cooperated at times very closely with the *Statistisches Reichsamt* and the *Institut für Konjunkturforschung*. A good deal of attention has been more recently paid to special training of traveling salesmen, studies of and attempts to control fashion change, group advertising, etc.

While the individually more promising rationalization measures are of a technical character, the more significant possibilities in the textile branches unquestionably lie in the direction of horizontal and vertical amalgamation, and the gradual elimination of large numbers of small, badly located, technically obsolete, and (in many cases) sweated textile establishments. The road leading to combination of either type, however, has been strewn with the corpses of repeated

[39] Birnbaum, *op. cit.*, pp. 8–11.

[40] The Institut für Konjunkturforschung estimates that the United States, with a textile labor force but slightly larger than that of Germany, produces goods with 130 per cent higher value than that of Germany, and about 40 per cent higher than that of Great Britain (whose textile labor force is likewise about the same). Value of product per worker per annum is estimated at 9,000 marks for Germany, while the British figure is 11,000 marks and the American 17,000 marks. "This marked difference," the Institut holds, "is not to be entirely explained by the differences in price levels, but is to be mainly found in the much higher mechanization of American textile industries." While the figures are not exactly comparable, it is believed that the following data on installed horsepower capacity per 10 workers tells the significant story:

Germany (1925)	11 h.p.
Great Britain (1924)	19 h.p.
United States (1925)	32 h.p.

Source: *Die Welttextilkrise*, p. 7.

[41] Birnbaum, *op. cit.*, pp. 22–25.

failure, marked but here and there with an occasional success. These latter have been, as one would naturally suspect, confined largely to the newer branches of the industry, the producers catering largely or exclusively to consumers of staple goods, and to those processes, such as spinning, in which mass production methods have long been basic.

Among the newer branches of textile production the case of rayon is conspicuous. Two firms, *Vereinigte Glanzstoff-Fabriken A. G.* and the *I. P. Bemberg A. G.* practically control the entire German rayon industry. Competition between the former company and the *I. G. Farbenindustrie A. G.* for the control of *Bemberg,* brought about a combine between the two leading concerns, known as *Aku (Algemeine Kunstzijde Unie,* with headquarters in Arnheim). Cooperating in the new combine, aside from the two firms mentioned, were *Courtaulds Ltd.* and *Snia Viscosa.* The first of these two companies is the largest rayon producer in the world, and the second practically controls the entire Italian rayon industry. *Snia Viscosa* and producers of about two-thirds of the American rayon output (American production is the largest in the world) are more or less completely under the joint domination of *Courtaulds* and *Aku.* The *I. G. Farbenindustrie A. G.* is connected with the new combine through *Aceta* (to *Vereinigte Glanzstoff*) and *Holkenseide* (to *Bemberg*). The larger French, American, Japanese, and Belgian producers are either directly or indirectly controlled by the group.[42] Although attempts to establish a world cartel have not thus far met with any considerable success, the dominating importance of the combined concerns is apparently sufficiently great to guarantee effective control of production, marketing, and price at some not very distant time in the future.[43]

A position analogous to *Aku* in the rayon field is occupied by the *Blumenstein* group in German jute production. This group, centered in the *Bank für Textilindustrie A. G.,* controls practically the entire jute industry, and has important holdings in the cotton textile field.[44] In the cotton textile industry several large concerns are to be found. The *Hammersen-Dierig* group controls about 929,000 spindles, nearly 16,000 looms, and invested capital to the amount of 53,199,000 marks.[45] Three mills combined in 1927 to form the *Baumwollindustrie Erlangen-Bamberg A. G.,* which, with about 280,000 spindles, is the largest German manu-

[42] See "Die deutsche Kunstseidenindustrie," *Die Wirtschaftskurve,* Heft 2(1927):198–201; "Die Kunstseidenindustrie der Welt," *ibid.,* Heft 3 (1927):308–320; and "Der neue Kunstseidekonzern," *ibid.,* Heft 3(1929):285–289. The first and third of these articles contain excellent charts showing corporate and inter-corporate relationships. The second contains an appendix giving data on capitalization, yearly production, processing method, and corporate affiliations, in tabular form.

[43] "Die Kunstseide-Politik vor Entscheidungen," *Frankfurter Zeitung* (May 1, 1931).

[44] "Die Blumenstein-Gruppe," *Die Wirtschaftskurve,* Heft 1(1926):67–70, with organization chart.

[45] "Die Hammersen-Dierig-Gruppe," *ibid.,* Heft 2(1925):196–197, with organization chart.

facturer of light cloth.[46] In the wool field, the *Norddeutsche Wollkämmerei und Kammgarnspinnerei A. G.*, owning about 400,000 spindles,[47] held a dominating position until it went bankrupt early in 1931.

The last three companies owed their strength in large part to the fact that they controlled important branches of the spinning industry in their respective fields. Vertical expansion has been severely criticized by authorities on the industry, it being generally maintained that the finishing industries have been too much split up, too badly organized, and too readily affected by highly variable market factors to be suitable fields for combination. The collapse of the last-mentioned concern has been attributed in part to its expansion into the finishing field. Until more orderly conditions obtain in the textile finishing and distributing branches, it would appear that the critics of vertical concentration have the better of the argument. The rise of such large chain firms as *Rudolph Karstadt* and *Leonard Tietz* in the department store field, and of centralized purchasing agencies which have been established by numerous distributing groups,[48] are gradually forcing a somewhat more systematic alignment of textile marketing systems. Attempts by textile manufacturers to take over wholesaling and retailing functions directly have met with practically no success whatever.

Integration with industries supplying materials and equipment has not been carried much further. The fact that most of the raw materials for textile production—excepting rayon—are imported, would react against such integration in Germany even though no other technical and organization factors militated against it. And such factors do, of course, exist even in the countries plentifully supplied with raw materials. The existence of the powerful *I. G. Farbenindustrie* combine in the dye field prevents expansion by textile manufacturers in this direction. What integration has taken place here has been confined to the rayon industry, and has been carried through at the initiative of the dye interests. Standardization and simplification of machines, machine parts, and routine operations has called throughout for very close cooperation between textile manufacturing and machine supply concerns.

What vertical integration has taken place has been almost entirely confined to unification of textile manufacturing processes formerly divided among several different concerns. Carding, spinning, weaving, dyeing, and—in some cases—manufacture of staple goods have been brought together in most of the large establishments. Important as these technical developments have been, however,

---

46 *Statist* (July 5, 1930):10–11.

47 "Der Konzern NWK," *Die Wirtschaftskurve*, Heft 3(1929):290–295, with organization chart.

48 A 1927 canvass showed 40 purchasing associations and 30 purchasing concerns dealing with textile products in Germany. Meanwhile these have apparently increased in number and importance.—"Die Rationalisierung im Textileinzelhandel," *Die Wirtschaftskurve*, Heft 3 (1927):290–293.

they have served primarily to indicate the larger economies to be realized from, and the economic and political importance to be attached to the larger organizational patterns still to be sketched and carried into execution before the German textile industries are brought to that stage of technical and economic perfection which present engineering and economic planning require as a condition to enduring prosperity.

4. THE CASE OF AGRICULTURE

Nearly every difficulty faced by programs for the rationalization of the textile industries is multiplied a hundredfold in agriculture. The unit is typically small; management is primarily a family affair; the prevailing techniques, tools, and auxiliary equipment are grounded in and conditioned by centuries of settled habits and customs; the possible areas of control by man seem relatively fixed and unchangeable; the farmer or peasant is typically backward-looking, typically conservative and suspicious of change in time-honored ideas, institutions, and ways of doing things; the managing authority rarely conceives of farming as either a business or an engineering proposition. The fact that the majority of the agricultural population in most countries is desperately poor, and that rural standards of living are usually far below that of urban and industrial populations, is more apt to make farmers envious than to stimulate them to change their modes of work or their attitudes towards the routines of planting, tending, breeding, feeding, and harvesting. The sons and daughters may drift to the cities, but the residual population remains fixed—even in modern times—to the soil with a tenacity and stubbornness that submits to no other adequate generalization than that their "souls" are rooted to the soil because no other way of life has any genuine substance or meaning for them.

Rationalization, which implies displacing of rule-of-thumb and traditional procedures by scientific criteria and scientific methods of organizing work, and the gradual mechanization (i.e., "industrialization") of all routine processes, is faced with these rigid patterns at the outset. The forces retarding rationalization in agriculture are more rigid and patterned in the older countries than in the newer. The case of German agriculture is typical. Difficulties here have been further accentuated by post-war troubles common to nearly all phases of economic life—shortage of capital, run down plant and equipment, political disturbances, nervous exhaustion.

The depression which has existed in many branches of German agriculture since the stabilization,[49] interrupted only by a slight advance in 1927, has been

[49] While both average yield per hectare for the staple crops and gross income for each of the main agricultural branches have increased since 1924–1925, the farmers are worse off because of higher labor and equipment costs, smaller average holdings, and failure of the gap between agricultural and industrial prices to narrow. There are a few exceptions to this generalization to be found in the more highly specialized dairy, poultry, and animal branches. See *Blätter für landwirtschaftliche Marktforschung* (January-February, 1932):343–344.

so severe that Feiler has compared it, and the agricultural unrest to which it has given rise, to that which brought about the Peasants' Revolt in 1525.[50] The more extreme agricultural position has been painted by novelists and politicians as a revolt against the whole modern "system"—growing strength of the state, urbanization, capitalism, the Roman Catholic Church, the Jews, and modern civilization.[51]

A few figures speak eloquently of the situation at hand. Contrasted with the pre-war period, the number of farms has increased; the percentage of the total area devoted to small-scale farming has grown;[52] yield per acre has fallen off[53] for nearly all the principal crops; the burden of mortgages and indebtedness has

---

50 Arthur Feiler, "Bauernkrieg," *Frankfurter Zeitung* (February 23, 24, and March 2, 1932).

51 *Ibid.* These features of the modern "system," plus the tendency towards socialism, make up the catalogue of demoniacal forces working for the disintegration of "culture" and the substitution therefor of decadent "civilization" in the modern era, according to Spengler. See *Decline of the West,* vol. 2, chaps. IV, X–XIV in particular.

52 Only the census figures for 1907 and 1925 are available. From current comment one would gather that the trends shown by these figures have continued to assert themselves since the latter date. The data are summarized as follows:*

Size of establishment in hectares	1907				1925			
	Number of establishments	Number hectares 1,000	Percentage of establishment	Percentage of area	Number of establishments	Number hectares 1,000	Percentage of establishment	Percentage of area
0.05–2	2,575,925	1,506	55.5	5.5	3,027,431	1,588	59.4	6.2
2–5	886,455	2,917	19.1	10.7	894,454	2,924	17.5	11.4
5–20	930,785	9,075	20.1	33.4	956,155	9,158	18.8	35.8
20–100	228,456	8,091	4.9	29.8	199,825	6,769	3.9	26.4
100 or over	18,933	5,584	.4	20.6	18,668	5,159	.4	20.2
Totals	4,640,554	27,175	100.0	100.0	5,096,533	25,598	100.0	100.0

* Source: *Statistisches Jahrbuch* (1930): 56–57.

The data relate to lands used, i.e., waste is excluded.

53 Angell (*op. cit.,* p. 397) has assembled the following table:

AGRICULTURAL PRODUCTION

(Annual totals in million metric tons; yields per hectare in tons)

Year or average	Rye		Wheat		Barley		Oats		Potatoes		Sugar beets	
	Total	Per hectare	Total	Per hectare	Total	Per hectare	Total	Per hectare	Total	Per hectare	Total	Per hectare
1909–1913	9.6	1.9	3.8	2.3	2.9	2.1	7.7	2.0	38.0	13.8	14.0	30.0
1919	6.1	1.4	2.2	1.7	1.7	1.5	4.5	1.5	21.4	9.9	5.8	19.3
1920	4.9	1.2	2.2	1.7	1.8	1.5	4.8	1.5	27.9	11.5	7.9	24.4
1921	6.8	1.6	2.9	2.0	1.9	1.7	5.0	1.6	26.1	9.9	8.0	20.5
1922	5.2	1.3	2.0	1.4	1.6	......	4.0	1.3	40.7	14.9	10.8	25.9
1923	6.7	1.5	2.9	2.0	2.4	1.8	6.1	1.8	32.6	12.0	8.7	22.7
1924	5.7	1.4	2.4	1.7	2.4	1.7	5.7	1.6	36.4	13.2	10.3	26.0
1925	8.1	1.7	3.2	2.1	2.6	1.8	5.6	1.6	41.7	14.9	10.3	25.6
1926	6.4	1.4	2.6	1.6	2.5	1.7	6.3	1.8	30.0	10.9	10.5	26.1
1927	6.8	1.5	3.3	1.9	2.7	1.9	6.3	1.8	37.6	13.4	10.9	25.0
1928	8.5	1.8	3.9	2.2	3.3	2.2	7.0	2.0	41.3	14.5	11.0	24.2

steadily increased;[54] the number of non-profitable farming enterprises constitutes more than 50 per cent of the total;[55] the discrepancies between prices of farm produce and machinery and products purchased by the farmer have steadily increased;[56] an increasing percentage of farm labor is supplied by the members of the peasant family.[57] Thus conditions amounting to indenture, pauperization, declining soil fertility, and low levels of industrialization have gone together in German agriculture.

The plight of the agricultural interests has received widespread attention[58] in Germany, and has given rise to the usual crop of causal interpretations and proposed remedies. The fault has been variously traced to unusual weather condi-

[54] Until 1929 there had been, however, a tendency for agricultural indebtedness to increase somewhat more slowly from year to year. The totals for the years 1925–1929, as estimated by the Institut für Konjunkturforschung, were as follows:*

AGRICULTURAL CREDIT BURDENS IN MILLIONS OF MARKS

	December 31, 1925	December 31, 1926	December 31, 1927	December 31, 1928
Fixed credit	3,223.2	4,277.3	5,684.6	6,831.1
Estimated floating credit	1,600.0	1,550.0	1,250.0	950.0
Totals	4,823.2	5,827.3	6,934.6	7,781.1

* Source: quoted by Hans Wilbrandt, *Agrarkrise und Rationalisierung*, dissertation (Langensalza, 1930): 10.

It should be noted, however, that the inflation almost completely eliminated all agricultural indebtedness existing at that date—some 16 to 17 billion marks. The new indebtedness has been almost entirely accumulated since 1924.—*Blätter für landwirtschaftliche Marktforschung*, pp. 342–343.

[55] The estimates of Otto Jüngst for the years 1912–1914 show 7 per cent of all agricultural establishments operating at a loss; for 1924–1926 52 per cent fell into this class.—"Planmässige Absatzgestaltung in der Landwirtschaft," RKW *Veröffentlichungen*, Nr. 29:4.

[56] *Ibid.*, pp. 5–6. A wealth of statistical materials is available on this point. Labor costs appear also to have risen somewhat more rapidly than farm prices.

[57] While the number of workers in Germany increased 24 per cent between 1907 and 1925, the number of agricultural workers declined 9.4 per cent. Meanwhile the number of wives, sons, and daughters of peasant proprietors working on the land increased from 3.4 million to 4.8 million.—Feiler, *op. cit.*

[58] Particular attention has been paid to the alarming increase in food imports. Net plant and animal foodstuff imports in 1913 amounted to 1,424,998,000 marks. By 1928 this sum had increased to 2,829,848,000 marks. In terms of constant purchasing power, the net import surplus of foodstuffs for 1926 (the imports continued to increase thereafter) was 448,801,000 marks higher than in 1913. The import surplus is particularly marked in certain lines, as the following index numbers taken with 1913 as base (not deflated for price change) show:

	1925	1926	1927	1928
Wheat	129	157	199	155
Potatoes	337	485	764	379
Fruit and vegetables	168	128	147	192
Eggs and poultry	147	125	147	196
Cheese	412	277	301	276
Butter	315	279	310	369

Source: Jüngst, *op. cit.*, pp. 36–39.

The decline indicated in the above figures for 1928 has, as would be expected, continued since that date. In 1930–1931 grain imports were 10 per cent of total consumption in contrast to 17 per cent in 1928. In 1930–1931 practically no meat whatsoever was imported. Other food imports fell off in proportion. See *Blätter für landwirtschaftliche Marktforschung*, p. 348.

tions prevailing over a long period of time, unusually high interest rates on capital, tariff protection for industrial products, the burdens of high wages, taxes, and social charges, and numerous additional and allied factors. Remedial measures proposed run along somewhat the same lines. In the latter part of the period under consideration, however, there has been a disposition to look more closely into problems of agricultural efficiency. The cumulating body of descriptive and analytical literature dealing with these aspects of the "farm problem" have gradually evolved institutional equipment and concrete proposals for "rationalization" of the various branches of agriculture.

Typical of the German method of approach, a single national body was established to centralize, systematize, and coordinate all institutional effort aimed at improvement of agricultural technique. This body, known as the National Board for Technique in Agriculture (*Reichskuratorium für Technik in der Landwirtschaft,* abbreviated *RKTL*), is, like the *RKW,* with which it is affiliated, a semi-governmental institute, and is charged with the duty of systematically studying, testing, and promoting proposals, methods, and techniques leading to improvement of agricultural technique. It acts as semi-official advisor to the national Ministries of Food and Agriculture, cooperates with the various special research, experimental, and educational schools, farms, and institutes, and gives advice to and collaborates with farm organizations, other governmental bureaus, and distributing agencies dealing with various types of agricultural problems.

The *RKTL* collaborates closely with the various agricultural scientific institutes, most important of which are the National Biological Institute (*Biologische Reichsanstalt*) and the Kaiser Wilhelm Institute for Plant Breeding (*Kaiser Wilhelm Institut für Pflanzenzüchtung*). The former institution is the central scientific institute for plant protection service, being aided and supported in its work by a widespread net of auxiliary experimental and scientific stations covering the entire Reich. The latter institution is engaged in scientific and experimental work in plant breeding, with special reference to types best suited for German soil and climatic conditions and those most resistant to plant diseases.[59]

Since the tradition-bound attitude of the peasant, and his general indifference towards or ignorance of business and engineering facts, have proved the greatest handicaps to introduction of scientific farming methods, a great deal of attention has been paid to agricultural schooling, and to propaganda through farm jour-

[59] Leo Drescher, "Die deutsche Landwirtschaft unter volks- und weltwirtschaftlichen Gesichtspunkten," *Jahrbücher für Nationalökonomie und Statistik,* 137:742–750 (November, 1932). This article is a review of the monumental survey of Max Sering, built upon the exhaustive researches of the Enquete Ausschuss on German agriculture, "Die deutsche Landwirtschaft unter volks- und weltwirtschaftlichen Gesichstpunkten. Dargestellt unter Verwertung und Ergänzung der Arbeiten des Ausschusses zur Untersuchung der Erzeugungs- und Absatzbedingungen der deutschen Wirtschaft," *Berichte über Landwirtschaft* (published by the Reichsministerium für Ernährung und Landwirtschaft, Neue Folge, Sonderheft 50; Berlin, 1932). This book is represented as the most complete and exhaustive survey of the German agricultural system, analytical, historical, and descriptive, which has thus far appeared.

nals, newspapers, and cooperative producing and marketing organizations. According to Wilbrandt, the Prussian agricultural continuation schools increased in number from 6,775 in 1913 to 13,000 in 1928, while the number of persons attending increased from 111,699 to 273,000. Special agricultural schools in Prussia increased from 239 to 392 in number over the same period, while the number of students enrolled increased from 9,903 to 18,380.[60] Spectacular as this increase has been—and the data for the entire Reich do not appear to be dissimilar to those for Prussia—it would still leave over 50 per cent of all peasant proprietors unaided by formal training in the elements of their occupation.[61]

A more direct, and in some respects more effective, attack on peasant inertia has been made through the medium of model farms. This movement, which was first organized on a systematic footing around the period of the currency stabilization, has spread quite rapidly throughout the country. Some 758 of these model farms were to be found in Prussia at the end of 1929.

The proprietors of the farms selected for experimentation were usually guaranteed free artificial fertilizers for the first year on the understanding that the experiment was to continue for three more years under the control of the agronomist in charge. By careful seed selection, better plowing and preparation of the soil, more scientific use of fertilizers, and other means, remarkable increases were made in soil productivity. Output of rye was made to increase from 6–8 and 10 hundredweight (*zentner* = 110 lbs.) to 16 hundredweight and more per *morgen* (nearly an acre); wheat increased from 8–12 to 18–21 hundredweight per *morgen;* hay tonnage increased over 100 per cent, etc.[62]

The reports written on some of these experiments are very interesting. Those experiments which rested upon combination of several different farms into single operating units are particularly significant, for the reason that they strike at the organizational foundation of peasant proprietorship. Since family and traditional attachments to particular pieces of land are so strong among the peasants, it was always necessary to carry out the experiments without in any way offending the ownership sensibilities of the natives. Persons charged with carrying out the experiments were, therefore, chosen as well for their tact and personalities as for their knowledge of agricultural techniques. In most cases, organizers lived directly in the villages, and succeeded in being adopted into the community life. The greatest care was taken that they should not be suspected by the peasant as purveyors of radical ideas.

In a typical case, an experiment was carried on in a village whose occupants possessed some 210 hectares. Cultivated land comprised 144 hectares, field and

[60] Wilbrandt, *op. cit.*, pp. 43–44.

[61] Enrollment in the agricultural colleges has also increased considerably since the war, although these play a less important rôle in the German educational system than they do in that of the United States.

[62] *Ibid.*, p. 46.

meadow 58 hectares, and forest land 8 hectares. The holdings were divided among ten peasant families, and ranged in size from 1 to 38 hectares. Two of the ten decided not to join the experiment. The land had long been divided into many small parcels, as is typical of German agriculture in general, though great care was taken that the experiment be carried out with farm lands not unduly split up in the traditional fashion.

The peasants were gradually persuaded to diminish the number of horses, to pool funds for the purchase of better plows, harrows, and seeding, reaping, threshing and other types of machinery, to sink into the ground their border-line stones (*Grenzsteine*) indicating limits of strip ownership and thus to prepare the soil, sow, and harvest in common, and to reorganize their farming and farm-account methods. Seed selection, better ground preparation, more careful seeding, and improved harvesting, packing, and shipping methods brought about an increased yield per hectare, improved the quality of products, and increased the price for which the goods might be sold. Electric power installations, an electric bakery, and an electric laundry were added.[63]

The changes made required introduction of a high type of farm engineering, *de facto* pooling of the land,[64] standardized raw materials, standardized and graded agricultural products, labor specialization,[65] careful and systematic cost accounts and budgets, mechanization, and other allied changes. Supplementary studies have been made through work with seed selection, soil fertilization, motorization, etc. An intensive survey of eighty-three separate establishments, for example, showed sixty with definite gains through substitution of tractors for horses and oxen. Important savings were effected for each of the four different farm sizes investigated, those for the largest and smallest sized farms being the greater per hectare. The important results of the investigation are summarized in table 30 (p. 277).[66]

The average annual saving of 19.39 marks per hectare, significant as it appears, would be still larger if cultivated area were taken as the denominator instead of total farm area (which includes, in addition to plowed area, meadows and grassland), and the savings of farms showing positive results were taken as the numerator instead of total farms, successful and unsuccessful alike. Of the 60 farms showing gains, 15 were able to pay the entire cost of motorization from savings

63 Unpublished material of the Institut für Wirtschaftslehre des Landbaues, lent to the writer by the RKTL.

64 Never *de jure*. The peasants dread communism as a plague. Hence the truth must never be told, that these farms are being covertly modeled after the Russian collectives.

65 The women, in their turn, insisted upon the right to use the new facilities as they saw fit. Despite the fact that the kilowatt-hour rate was held as low as 4 pfennigs ($.00952), both laundry and bakery expenses remained prohibitively high until the women could be persuaded to specialize the labor among them.

66 Ernst Zander, "Die Motorisierung der Zugkraft in der deutschen Landwirtschaft," Heft 17, RKTL *Schriften* (Berlin, 1930).

in one year; 19 in one and one-half years; 9 in two years; 8 in three years; while 9 required more than three years.[67] Various factors have contributed to the failure of motorization to effect definite savings on the remaining 22 farms. Typically either the attitude of the management was hostile, the farm unit was bad, soil conditions were unfavorable, or the necessary organizational setting was lacking. In most cases it was believed that the controllable factors could be manipulated so as to show a gain could the experiment be continued for a longer period.[68]

TABLE 30

Size of farm, hectares	Number of farms	Total area, hectares	Savings, marks	Losses, marks	Net savings, marks	Savings per hectare, marks
24– 50	14	525.7	19,657.15	2,291.52	17,365.63	33.03
51–100	27	1,899.5	43,387.38	5,954.83	37,432.55	19.71
101–200	21	2,754.1	26,705.19	13,187.81	13,517.38	4.98
Over 200	20	6,366.0	158,104.97	272.26	157,832.71	24.79
Totals	82	11,154.3	245,563.17	21,706.05	223,857.12	Av. savings per hectare =19.39marks

Parallel with introduction of tractors has gone expansion in the use of various types of stationary engines, electrically driven machinery, and improved farm implements and equipment such as plows, diskers, harrows, seeders, mowing machines, hayrakes, tedders, cutters and choppers, reapers, binders, and threshing machines. Such mechanization has of necessity meant increasing emphasis upon simplified machine types, standardization and interchangeability of component parts, and close cooperation between agricultural training schools, research institutes and farmers' cooperatives on the one hand, and machine and equipment

[67] Once the project was well under way, and the principal fears of the peasants had been settled, the main difficulty to be faced was the large number of visitors. These crowded around the machinery, trod over the fields, raised hosts of questions, and vented their curiosity in so many different ways and so continuously and insistently at times as to bring all work to a standstill.

[68] One important factor appears to have been neglected, however: animal fertilizer. Perhaps the economies from motorization, combined with the movement towards mixed farming and more careful crop rotation, would more than offset losses on this account occasioned by the substitution of tractors for draft animals. Whatever be the case, it will not do to ignore this factor, as is shown by the following figures of various fertilizer chemicals supplied by manures and artificial fertilizers used annually by German agriculture.*

	Nitrogen	Phosphoric acid	Potash
Animal manures	1,300,000 tons	780,000 tons	2,400,000 tons
Artificial fertilizers	360,000 tons	420,000 tons	620,000 tons

* Source: "Der Produktionsplan der deutschen Landwirtschaft," *Die Wirtschaftskurve*, Heft 3 (1928): 289–295.

manufacturers and distributors on the other.[69] A special committee for standardization of agricultural machinery and equipment *(Fachnormenausschuss für landwirtschaftliche Maschinen und Geräte)* of the German Standards Committee has been established. By the first of May, 1929, 64 national and agricultural standards, relating principally to simplified machine parts and quality specifications, had been completed or were under consideration.

Little success has thus far been registered in the application of personnel selection to agricultural workers. This results partly from the relative importance of members of families among agricultural laborers. More significant, however, are the small size of the average holding, the hostile attitude of farmers towards "faddist" innovations, and the general diversity of farming operations, which does not permit the degree of labor specialization that is characteristic of routine factory operations. Special training, however, has been on a somewhat different footing. Schools for mechanics operating and repairing agricultural machinery, special agricultural departments in the ordinary schools located in agricultural districts, agricultural continuation schools, experimental farms, governmental propaganda, quasi-technical but popularly written agricultural journals, and other educational means are employed which sooner or later show results attributable to improvement in personal standards.[70]

Relatively few German farmers keep books, compute costs scientifically, or couch the financial aspects of their planning in budgetary terms. Only the larger, better organized, and more definitely specialized farms producing highly standardized goods have been able to carry through this phase of agricultural rationalization with any considerable dispatch and thoroughness. A great deal has been done, however, with standard grading, classification, marking, packing, storing, refrigeration, shipping, and handling. Following American and Danish practice, the National Committee for Conditions and Terms of Delivery *(Reichsausschuss für Lieferbedingungen*—abbreviated *RAL)* has promoted and very actively cooperated with agricultural societies in the establishment of type, quality, marking, and packing standards for eggs, potatoes, cabbage, cheese, etc. Special milk testing stations have been established by several of the large dairy cooperatives for the purpose of hygienic, quality, and delivery control.

Contrary to the situation typical of most of the manufacturing industries, agricultural distribution mechanisms seem to be somewhat more highly developed than the productive. It may not be quite accurate to call the cooperatives distribu-

---

69 See DIN, *Normung der Maschinen und Geräte in der Landwirtschaft* (Berlin, 1929). One difficulty faced by agricultural mechanization has been inability to obtain quick repair service, and this in turn has been caused by the fact that few districts possess enough tractors to justify the establishment of repair shops specializing on such equipment.

70 Wilbrandt, for example, quotes figures indicating that attendance at the agricultural continuation schools resulted in the following increases in hundredweights per morgen for certain Prussian farms investigated; wheat yield increased from 9.97 to 14.09; rye from 9 to 12.6; hay from 9.75 to 14; barley from 9.37 to 13.2; potatoes from 80 to 119.—*Op. cit.*, p. 43.

tive organizations, but their functions have been mainly oriented market-wise rather than production-wise. In any case, their expansion onto a national basis, their highly centralized character, and the steady increase in the range of their interests and the rigidity of their control make them the most powerful single force for constructive effort in this direction. Excluding a few "independent" associations, all German agricultural cooperatives are associated with either the General Association of German Raiffeisen Cooperatives *(Generalverband der deutschen Raiffeisen-Genossenschaften)*, or the National Association of German Agricultural Cooperatives *(Reichsverband der deutschen landwirtschaftlichen Genossenschaften)*. These in turn have combined to form the National Association of German Agricultural Cooperatives—Raiffeisen *(Reichsverband der deutschen landwirtschaftlichen Genossenschaften-Raiffeisen e.V.)*. This latter group had a membership of 36,223 cooperative societies on the first of March, 1930.

The importance of these associations as centralizing agencies is shown by the range of functions for which the separate member cooperative societies were organized. Thus, on the date mentioned above, the membership of the National Association of German Agricultural Cooperatives-Raiffeisen included 19,749 savings and loan cooperatives, 3,753 purchase and sales cooperatives, 3,570 dairy, creamery, and condensary cooperatives, 9,151 cooperatives specializing in cooperative threshing, use of electrical equipment, cattle breeding and grazing, and miscellaneous activities, 37 auditing associations *(Revisionsverbände)*, and 116 central cooperative associations.[71] The purchasing cooperatives are organized for the purpose of centralized buying of fertilizers, feed, seed, machinery and equipment, etc. The selling cooperatives combine sale of such commodities as eggs, milk, potatoes, and grain in the hands of a central agency. Other cooperatives specialize on common purchase and use of steam plows, electric motor-driven equipment, tractors, and other equipment, the establishment of technical advisory bureaus, etc.[72]

The central and regional cooperative societies work—in some cases at least—in close harmony with various special agricultural unions, and the regional Chambers of Agriculture *(Landwirtschaftskammern)*. The latter carry on agitation and promote, among other things, technical rationalization and general reorganization of agricultural production and distribution.[73]

How much overlapping exists between and among the various cooperatives and between the cooperatives and the Unions and Agricultural Chambers would be difficult to say. The consolidation of the Raiffeisen and the National Associa-

---

71 *Statistisches Jahrbuch* (1930):390.

72 *Handwörterbuch der Staatswissenschaften* (Vierte Auflage), 4:178–186.

73 *Ibid.*, pp. 212–220 on "Landwirtschaftliches Vereinswesen," and pp. 220–229 on "Landwirtschaftskammern." See also article on "Genossenschaftswesen," Ergänzungsband, pp. 267–284.

tion took place only after long agitation against the competition between the two organizations which many felt led to duplication of facilities, wasted effort, and a general weakening of the strength of the cooperative movement.[74] From time to time the state has come to the rescue of the cooperatives in their struggle to rationalize agricultural technique and improve marketing methods. Thus the Reichstag placed at the disposal of agricultural interests some 61,000,000 marks for purposes of improving agricultural marketing methods and "rationalization of agricultural cooperatives."[75] Other subsidies have been granted since that date.

Although the various phases of agricultural technique, combination, management, and marketing have been attacked with considerable vigor and in a characteristically thorough and systematic fashion, it does not appear that German agriculture has enjoyed any considerable measure of benefit from the improvements made. The proposals of Jüngst[76] and others for the complete overhauling of agricultural marketing organization on a national scale are proof of the general dissatisfaction with existing machinery.

It is interesting, in this connection, to note that practically none of the writers dealing with phases of the general agricultural depression see much hope in proposals for further tariff protection. Despite the facts that geographic specialization, product standardization, improvement in methods of packing, handling, and transport, and allied changes have made it possible for foreign producers of staple wares—eggs, butter, cheese, fruits, vegetables, grain, etc.—to underbid German producers on their own markets, it is generally held that the disastrous effect of high tariff walls for industrial products affords ample grounds for rejecting the tariff solution to the agricultural situation. In those fields in which German producers have a natural advantage by reason of proximity to markets, and suitable climatic and other factors, it is believed that technical improvements will make it possible to meet the problems of foreign competition. In other fields, it is held that tariff unions which would unite economically interdependent and complementary territories would make it possible at once to secure the advantages of territorial specialization in agriculture, lower the prices of industrial commodities purchased by farmers and held high largely because of industrial tariff protection, and at the same time provide the market stimulus for increased productive and distributive efficiency now lacking in agricultural organization. Thus Hantos believes that Germany, Austria, Hungary, Poland, Roumania, Jugoslavia, and Czechoslovakia constitute a more or less complete and balanced eco-

---

[74] See, in particular, Ergänzungsband, *op. cit.*, article on "Rationalisierung in der Landwirtschaft," pp. 765–795. That the combination between the two central cooperative associations has already borne some fruit is shown by the fact that, while the total number of cooperatives has increased, nevertheless, many of those that were overlapping in the functions of purchasing, selling, savings and loan, etc., have been eliminated.—*Frankfurter Zeitung* (June 15, 1931) and Willy Krebs, "Das Genossenschaftswesen im Jahre 1931," *Jahrbücher,* Heft 4:544–562 (October, 1932).

[75] Ergänzungsband, *op. cit.*, pp. 794–795.

[76] *Op. cit.*, pp. 47–71.

nomic unit. The first two are primarily industrial countries, and are compelled to import large quantities of grain, animal foodstuffs, and other agricultural commodities which the latter four are compelled to export. The reverse holds as far as imports and exports of industrial products are concerned. Thus a tariff union including these countries would constitute a first major step in the direction of solving the related problems of foreign competition, unfavorable balances of trade, and high living costs.[77]

The various international agricultural congresses, conventions, and institutes have not been able to make much headway along these lines. Some effective work has been done in methods of handling and shipping, agricultural standards, marketing research, and the gathering of agricultural statistics on crops, prices, costs, degrees of mechanization, the causal factors lying behind agricultural depressions, and numerous related problems. But the larger marketing and organizational problems—confessedly regional and international in scope—have scarcely been touched at these meetings, and in the work of these institutes.[78]

5. THE MACHINERY OF DISTRIBUTION

Broadly speaking, the German distributive system—jobbing, wholesale, retail—is less advanced than that in the United States, and by contrast to reorganization in German extractive and manufacturing industries at large, rationalization in this field can be said to be only at the beginning of its development. Technically or organizationally considered, the German distributive mechanism is decidedly in arrears. The factors retarding systematization in the various fields of distribution are the same as those found elsewhere, except that, with the possible exception of agriculture, they operate in this field with peculiar force. Among the factors which make rationalization of distribution a very slow and painful process are the following: tradition, vested (in particular, family) interests, the small scale of the holdings, the relative insignificance of overhead expenses, the failure or unwillingness to keep accurate cost accounts, the large number of operating units, the variety of goods sold in each establishment, the custom of catering to a special clientèle, and the unscientific buying habits of retail stores and nearly all ultimate consumers.

Two national organizations have been established in Germany to carry on rationalization work in the distribution field. The first is the special Expert Committee on Commercial Organization *(Fachausschuss für Handelswirtschaft)* of

---

[77] Elemer Hantos, "Das Mitteleuropäische Agrarproblem und seine Lösung," *Mitteleuropäische Wirtschaftsfragen, Schriftenreihe des Mitteleuropa-Instituts zur Förderung der wirtschaftlichen und kulturellen Annäherung* (Vienna and Berlin, 1931):95.

[78] The proceedings of the International Institute of Agriculture (Rome), the International Congresses of Agricultural Engineering, and the informal meetings of agricultural experts held at Devon, England, and Cornell University, United States, have been mainly concerned with statistics and debate.

the Committee for Efficient Business Administration *(Ausschuss für wirtschaftliche Verwaltung)*, which is, in turn, a subcommittee of the *RKW*. The second is the Trade Research Center *(Forschungsstelle für den Handel)* attached to the Berlin College of Commerce *(Handels Hochschule)*. The first is designed to handle primarily the practical, and the second to take care of the theoretical aspects of the various phases of rationalization in the distribution field.[79] Professor Julius Hirsch is at the head of both organizations, and has been quite successful in the attempt to dovetail the research, experimental, and promotional work of the two organizations. Both units cooperate closely with leading wholesale and retail associations, the Government, and the *RKW*.

It is quite unnecessary, for present purposes at least, to go into the detailed accomplishments of these organizations. In general, their work has covered a wide range of problems, dealing with the assembly, analysis, and publication of case studies and statistical materials relating to costs of labor, stock turnover, budgets, sale of standardized and unstandardized goods, office procedure, standardization and mechanization of accounting data, reduction of inventories, store layout, advertising, personnel selection and training, and numerous allied and complementary details of distribution management. The various studies made have attracted widespread attention, and have unquestionably brought about many important changes in numerous stages and branches of retail and wholesale trade.

The major economies to be realized in the distribution field, however, appear to lie in the larger field of organization.[80] If distribution costs are to be reduced very far in Germany, the tremendous duplication of warehouses, stores, shops, restaurants, buying and selling agencies, and the commodity outlets which are typically small and wasteful of capital and labor must be in large part eliminated. While German accomplishments along this line have thus far not been nearly so striking as the American, the will has been expressed, and the foundation has been laid for far-reaching reforms in this field.

---

[79] The objects of the Research Center are given as follows: (1) To ascertain and publish facts which are relevant to commercial organizations and commercial management. (2) To discover the causes of greater or lesser prosperity and so to estimate the amount of what the Americans call waste in distribution, that is, the sources of waste in retail distribution and in the economic system as a whole. (3) To draw attention to the means of eliminating these sources of waste and so to secure greater efficiency in trade, both retail and wholesale. (4) To lay down principles, disseminate knowledge, and train men who will improve the working of this important branch of the economic system, and to inspire such men with the true spirit of efficiency.—RKW *Nachrichten* (April-October and November, 1928).

[80] As proof of the need for rationalization in distribution, one author cites figures showing sales (distribution) costs in typical industries to be as follows: automobile, 35 per cent of total cost; some agricultural machines, 38 per cent; some machines used in the timber trade, 36 per cent; manufacture of various types of instruments, 45 per cent; building materials, 52 per cent.—*Technik und Wirtschaft,* January, 1929, p. 1. Marketing costs in German retail trade in 1927, excluding bread and meat, were, according to Julius Hirsch, 8 billion marks on a turnover of 28 billion marks.—RKW *Nachrichten,* Nr. 3.

In the larger cities, the bigger department stores, and particularly the chain department stores, have developed rapidly since the war. The two largest of these, the firms of *Leonard Tietz* and *Rudolph Karstadt* do a nation-wide business, and have expanded chains which bring together manufacturing (in part), wholesaling, warehousing, and retailing functions into single compact units. The retail outlets sell practically the entire range of commodities purchased by the ultimate consumer, and have more recently added restaurant, tonsorial, repair, and other service departments to their establishments. Five years after its foundation in 1920, the *Karstadt* system possessed 32 retail outlets, was directly interested in the *Althoff* group possessing 13 retail outlets, owned 6 central purchasing and 6 wholesale establishments, and had special pool-purchasing agreements with 47 stores scattered throughout the Reich. Expansion from that time on was steady and rapid. By the first of January, 1931, the company had a common share capitalization of 80,000,000 marks, reserves of 23,420,000 marks, and an annual business turnover of 310,610,000 marks.[81] The *Tietz* department store system is even larger. In 1928 the company possessed 17 department stores (operating on a much larger scale than most of the *Karstadt* stores), and was associated in a community-of-interest arrangement with *M. Conitzer & Sohn* controlling 22 firms located in various parts of Germany. Its turnover of 300,000,000 marks in 1928 had made it by that time the largest wholesale and retail combine in Europe.[82]

Other large department store chains are the *Epa Einheitspreis A. G.* and the *Wertheim* concern. The former has a capital value of 30,000,000 marks and controls some 45 large and 5 small branch stores. The latter is concentrated in Berlin, and among other units operates in the heart of the city what is asserted to be the largest and most modern department store in the world. In the restaurant field such chains as *Kempinski* and *Aschinger* have been expanding rapidly.[83]

[81] *Frankfurter Zeitung* (May 31, 1931). [82] *Industrie-Bibliothek*, 31:5 (Warenhauser, 1928).

[83] Excellent examples of the advantages of large-scale distribution are shown by cost figures for wholesale concerns in the recent American census of distribution, taken in connection with the Fifteenth Decennial Census. ". . . . in California, for example, wholesale establishments in all trades with sales of $25,000 per year or less show a total operating expense figure of 28.1 per cent of net sales. This ratio drops as the average size of business increases until a low of 9.7 per cent for establishments selling in excess of $1,000,000 per year is reached. This indication of a reduction in cost as size of business increases for all wholesale trade is borne out by the grocery trade, where the cost variation ranges from 22.5 per cent for small ($25,000) concerns to 6.4 per cent for large-scale establishments ($1,000,000 or over). In the hardware trade, however, the cost declines from 33.3 per cent for small-scale houses to 12 per cent for businesses with average sales of $250,000 per year. The costs increase thereafter to 17.9 per cent for the large-scale houses with average sales of $1,000,000 or over."—Nathanael H. Engle, *American Economic Review* (September, 1932):550. It is interesting to note, in this connection, that the reports of the Enquete Ausschuss on retail trade showed that, practically without exception, "retail costs increased progressively with the growth of the enterprise," and that this generalization held whether one have in mind operating expenses or savings accruing from large-scale purchase. With each cost and type of enterprise there appeared to be a definite optimum point beyond which further increase in size meant increasing expense per unit volume of business rather than decreasing. See Fritz Redlich, "Wandlungen in der Absatzorganisation," *Jahrbücher*, Heft 2 (August, 1932).

A somewhat more interesting development is that of the consumers' cooperatives. Like the agricultural cooperatives previously mentioned, the consumers' cooperatives were organized in highly centralized systems long before the war. The post-war period saw a consolidation of their forces and further expansion of their activities. Almost all the consumers' cooperatives in Germany have been brought under the control of a central organization known as the Central Union of German Consumer Associations *(Zentralverband deutscher Konsumvereine)*. The growth and relative importance of the consumer cooperative movement and this central organization is shown by the following statistical data, given in table 31, on post-war development:[84]

TABLE 31

Business year	Number of member co-operatives	Number of members, in thousands	Total proceeds in million marks	Value of goods produced in own plants in million marks	Value of goods in stock in million marks	Value of property in million marks	Own, held in trust for members, and outside capital in million marks
1919	1,134	2,309	580.9	105.9	43.9	42.6	170.2
1920	1,293	2,715	417.7	69.3	64.0	16.6	82.2
1924	1,166	3,506	555.5	116.6	69.1	90.1	123.9
1925	1,113	3,383	854.3	205.9	101.8	100.0	177.8
1926	1,093	3,197	1,052.6	240.5	112.9	119.9	274.1
1927	1,109	2,918	1,276.6	313.5	122.8	146.2	404.3

The present structure of the German consumers' cooperative movement represents perhaps the most systematic attempt at organization of distribution on a national scale within capitalist countries to be found to date, excepting perhaps the Cooperative Wholesale Society of Great Britain. Under the *Zentralverband deutscher Konsumvereine* are gathered most of the local cooperative societies, which are brought under the direction of regional Associations of Chartered Accountants *(Revisionsverbände)*, of which there are ten. The latter act as central coordinating agencies for wholesale purchasing and the distribution of goods to the local cooperatives, have charge of the various plants owned by the central association and producing goods for sale through the cooperative system, and supply the organizational coordination necessary to pursuit of common objectives, carrying out of common policies, elimination of excessive and duplicate facilities, plans for expansion, methods of accounting and cost reckoning, and similar details. Purchase is centralized in the Wholesale Purchasing Company of the German Consumers' Cooperatives *(Grosseinkaufs-Gesellschaft Deutscher Konsum-*

84 The figures include data on the Grosseinkaufs-Gesellschaft; Hans Georg Pauls, "Die Grosseinkaufs-Gesellschaft deutscher Konsumvereine," *Die Wirtschaftskurve,* 1(1928):71–79.

vereine m.b.H.) with headquarters in Hamburg. The Wholesale Company is divided into three sections: merchandising, banking, and manufacturing. The first section has control of the various regional warehousing companies located in Hamburg, Breslau, Chemnitz, Magdeburg, Spandau, and other cities throughout the Reich, operates an extensive trucking and delivery system with headquarters in Hamburg, centralizes all purchases from the open market whether domestic or foreign where the advantages of pooled buying power justify such action, and controls some incidental coffee and spice-mixing and grinding mills. The second section acts as central banker for the cooperative system, and more recently has established banking machinery with branches for use of the members of local cooperatives. The third section controls numerous manufacturing and refining plants, including textile weaving and ready-made clothing plants, plants making soap, woodware, brushes, matches, and numerous special establishments—bakeries, cigar and cigarette works, plants putting up conserves, mustard, chicory, sugar and coffee, meat products, etc.[85]

Coordination of distribution on a national scale has been paralleled by internal reorganization and general improvement of stores, goods, retailing methods, and services. Sales and managerial personnel are carefully chosen, and in most cases are systematically schooled in their functions by special courses giving instruction on qualities of commodities sold, warehousing methods, store decoration, store management, purpose and objectives of the cooperative movement, keeping accounts, and other wholesaling and retailing problems. Wages of personnel have been increased, and special incentive systems elaborated for the purpose of keeping efficiency at a high level. Store layouts have been simplified. Package goods have been substituted wherever possible for commodities previously sold in bulk.[86] Refrigerator and other sanitary devices have been widely installed. Goods bearing trade-marks of private concerns have been reduced to but 1 to 2 per cent of total sales, while about 40 per cent of the entire turnover bears cooperative insignia. Quality and quantity standards have been introduced in many commodity lines.

The results of the changes and improvements made are to be seen in more standardized and higher quality goods, lower prices than those obtaining on the open market,[87] better equipped and stocked stores, more members, and higher sales per member. Turnover per member before the war ranged from 181 to 515

[85] These plants are supplementary and complementary to those operated directly by the Zentralverband. A very complete and condensed cross-section of the development, present status, and organization of the German consumers' cooperative movement is to be found in the article in *Die Wirtschaftskurve,* previously cited.

[86] From 50 to 90 per cent of all goods sold are packaged prior to sale. This fact indicates a revolutionary change from pre-war methods, a change which has reached out and affected nearly every phase of distribution in a thousand different ways.

[87] This is attributable in part to greater efficiency and in part to the practice of lower markups. See report of the Enquete Committee, summarized in *Vorwärts* (March 13, 1931).

marks per member; in the post-war period it has ranged from 140 to 763 marks per member.[88] The range of commodities sold has increased considerably, a typical store now selling between 700 and 900 different commodities. The greater number of the members now fall into wage- and salary-worker classifications, these two making up approximately 85 to 90 per cent of the membership.

To the organizational changes made in German distribution previously mentioned, two others should be added. The first of these is the increase in number and expansion in scope of wholesaling and retailing trade associations, special unions, centralized purchasing agencies, and communities of interest. As these have expanded, whether on a national or a regional scale, they have been attached to a central promotional and general interest organization. In the wholesale field the *Reichsverband des Deutschen Gross- und Ueberseehandels* brings together domestic and foreign wholesale interests of every industry into a single national group so far as these are already organized into regional or national trade associations.[89] A similar function is performed in the retail field by the *Hauptgemeinschaft des Deutschen Einzelhandels.*[90] Both these groups, along with similar organizations in other fields, are tied in with the *Zentralausschuss der Unternehmerverbände.*[91]

The second development lies in the field of integration between the raw materials, manufacturing, and distributing branches of economic activity. This trend has been discussed in several places in the foregoing chapters. At times the initiative has come from the production side, at other times from the distribution side. In some cases the integrating force has been corporative in character, and in others it has been primarily associational—cartel, community of interest, or trade association.

In nearly all cases the order of development has been from the more local and loosely organized associational groupings to the national and more compact type. Usually the first step that has been taken has been to organize a local cartel, trade association, or community of interest. These have then expanded into national organizations, or have been absorbed into existing national organizations. While the latter process is going on, there is a tendency for ownership and control to be concentrated in a few large concerns. Sometimes the existence of a national organization tends to restrict such concentration, but typically the reverse is true.

[88] Members increased the percentages of their incomes spent for commodities purchased from the cooperatives by from 30 to 100 over the pre-war period.—*Vorwärts, op. cit.*

[89] This association includes 230 central wholesale organizations, having a membership of 50,000 firms, 10 import and export associations, 34 local and regional associations (with about 6,000 members), and 22 industrial and commercial chambers. A complete membership catalogue is to be found in the *Jahrbuch der Berufsverbände im Deutschen Reiche* (52d Sonderheft zum Reichsarbeitsblatt, 1930):50.

[90] Includes 78 national and regional trade associations, and 43 chambers of commerce.—*Ibid.*, p. 51.

[91] *Ibid.*, p. 43. The charts shown on p. 43 and following give a very excellent picture of the whole centralized business organization of Germany.

Up to this point, concentration usually follows horizontal lines. But both expansion of the looser associations and cartels onto a national scale, and growth of large member corporations, tends to increase emphasis upon vertical integration. This tends in the long run to mean (1) closer coordination between the centralized associations in the various branches of wholesale and retail distribution, and between these two and both manufacturing and raw-materials supply industries (particularly agricultural), and (2) closer working agreements with foreign central distribution agencies. The federations of central associations which arise at this juncture tend, largely because of the fact that their interests cut across industrial, regional, and national lines, and because of the multifarity of their interests and activities, rather to reinforce than to weaken the strength and authority of the various member central associations, unions, cartels, and chambers.

The rationalization problems undergo a gradual change as one goes from the more local and loosely organized associations to either the large compact combine or the national association or federation of associations. Problems of a more purely technical and organizational character tend to fade into the background. Their places are taken by questions of a more distinctly commercial and "business-like" nature. Questions of strategy, price control, duplication of facilities, and general policies become more important. As in all industries, concentration tends to increase emphasis upon administrative problems, and to require more and more administrative training on the part of the controlling officialdom.[92]

Tardy though German development has been along these lines, nevertheless the organizational basis is being laid for further systematization on industrial, regional, national, and inter-industrial bases. Once the structure of events and the will and authority combine, the remaining obstacles to an integrated and coordinated national system may be brushed aside. Developments in German distribution machinery, slow as they have been, are slowly preparing the way for the time when incisive policies may be substituted for vague and empty formulas, and when far-flung, far-sighted and concrete plans can be poured into the molds which have been prepared in anticipation, not of order, but incipient chaos. Meanwhile every step taken to improve the quality of goods, standardize sizes, packing, and marking, introduce scientific cost-accounting and budgeting systems, eliminate excess capacity and duplicate facilities, and better the quality of personnel, dovetails with, reinforces, and is reinforced by structural changes in the larger configuration.

[92] Henri Fayol, the famous French writer on management problems, has attempted to express the changed requirements of the administrative staff as the scale of operations increases. While his tables were intended to apply to *industrial* concerns primarily, he believed them to hold for all types of organized activity. See Appendix B, p. 436.

6. RATIONALIZATION DEVELOPMENTS IN OTHER INDUSTRIES

One is safe in the generalization that practically no branch of German economic activity has remained wholly unaffected by the post-war rationalization movement. To trace through the evolution of all these changes, however, would require the addition of many pages to the outline already given. The reports of the *Enquete* Committee, which deal only incidentally with the rationalization movement, include more than a hundred volumes. The detailed information gathered and published by the *Reichskuratorium für Wirtschaftlichkeit,* the *Verein Deutscher Ingenieure,* the *Reichsverband der Deutschen Industrie,* the *International Management Institute,* and numerous subsidiary and complementary organizations dealing with rationalization of German industry, would fill a good many volumes. In the main, further details need not be added to the outline given. The lines of development, the interdependence between the various aspects and phases of the movement, and the more important handicaps to be overcome are not fundamentally different in these other fields, nor would a fuller picture of the industries sketched add much to an understanding of the problems which rationalization presents, or the prevailing methods by way of which these problems are attacked.

It would be particularly interesting, were the space available, to follow out developments in such fields of economic activity as the handicraft trades, the personal service businesses, banking, the professional trades, and household economy. The national organization of the handicraft trades, and the attention being paid to standardization of tools, equipment, raw materials, and finished products, to division of labor and better marketing organization, to cost-accounting, to technical and economic research, to apprenticeship regulations, and to other details of production and distribution in this field, constitute one of the most interesting developments of the modern era. These changes mean that system and scientific criteria are being substituted for caprice and rule of thumb in regions of human activity long hostile to the disciplines of machine technology. A series of subtle emotional, intellectual, and organizational "climatic" mutations has transformed the citizens of this tradition-bound Erewhon into subjects of the traditionless empire of machine technology, whether or not time-keeping mechanical watches have as yet been given or may ever be given a position of honor.

Equally interesting are the changes wrought in ways of living and in professional life as a result of attempts to introduce the rationale of engineering technology into consumption and professional practice. With characteristic thoroughness the Germans have attacked both problems in systematic fashion. The Household Economy Group of the *RKW (Gruppe Hauswirtschaft beim Reichskuratorium für Wirtschaftlichkeit)* has combined the work of the various national and regional Housewives Organizations, trade unions, wholesale and retail trade, consumers' cooperatives, handicrafts, schools, governmental departments, trade associations, and other groups directly interested in more "rational," less costly, and less time- and labor-consuming houses, apartments, building materials, stoves, heating equipment, linoleums, floor polishes, lighting, washing equipment, bookkeeping, pots and pans, door and window fasteners and fixtures, curtains, window shades, carpets, plumbing equipment, etc.[93] A great deal of work has been done by the special hospital standards committee *(Fachnormenausschuss Krankenhaus)* of the German Standards Committee on standardization of surgical instruments, hospital beds and linen, and numerous other details.[94] The lawyers have recently become interested in reorganization of courtroom procedure, and the standardization of paper sizes for various types of legal documents.[95] The teaching and engineering professions have likewise been drawn into the movement from several different angles. The work of *DATSCH,* the technical universities, and the various engineering societies have already been touched upon in several places.

The other side of rationalization in household economy and in the various professional trades means pooled and institutional living and working. The whole trend away from single-family houses and towards multiple-family and apartment houses, with all that it means by way of scientific organization of labor, better coordination of necessary and auxiliary services—heating, lighting, plumbing, janitor service, cooking, entertainment, laundry—communal living, smaller families, and other alterations in the structure and organization of family life and the "art" of living has been so rapid as to constitute almost a revolution in the most conservative and culturally backward-looking institution of all times. The gradual usurpation by institutionalized sources of learning of the education and habit-forming functions of the family, the gradual shift in emphasis within the schools away from more purely "cultural" studies to problems of scientific and engineering technique, and the subtle transformations wrought in teaching techniques as a result of the slowly cumulating body of scientific and quasi-scientific

---

[93] The *Handbuch der Rationalisierung* has a section devoted to "Rationalisierung in der Hauswirtschaft" (pp. 1032–1053) showing the organization of work in this field, and the great detail into which efforts along this line have already gone.

[94] An article in the VDI *Nachrichten* (October 26, 1927) gives a most interesting cross-section of work in this field. An ingenious Frenchman, Fernand Brochier, has written a book on "Rationalization in Dentistry. How the Principles of Physiology and of Taylor's System help the Elimination of Fatigue."—*L'Organisation du Travail en Dentisterie* (Paris, 1927). Along this same line, "The German Association of Dental Surgeons has made tests of aptitude compulsory for dental apprentices and has set up laboratories for this purpose in all more important towns. The tests cover the following points: (1) Acuity of perceptive faculties, sense of color, sense of touch, sensitiveness of the articulations, sense of smell; (2) manual ability; sureness of the hand, dexterity; (3) general intelligence, perception and observation, memory, logical combination, logical and critical reasoning; (4) practical intelligence, ability to sum up a situation, concrete thinking, ingenuity, technical understanding; (5) attitude towards work: rhythm, method, cleanliness, tidiness, zeal, energy; (6) knowledge, etc.: handwriting, spelling and grammar, ability to express thought in writing."—Summary in *Bulletin* of the International Management Institute (October, 1929):201, of an article in *Industrielle Psychotechnik* (Berlin, July, 1929):239.

[95] *Mitteilungen des deutschen Hauptverbandes der Industrie* (June 13, 1929):488.

information dealing with human types, learning processes, and the graduation of knowledge from the simple to the complex, and other changes in informational data and methods of approach are slowly revolutionizing the whole educational system. Specialization of information along industrial and scientific lines is bringing schools into closer and closer physical contact with the larger industrial enterprises. It is quite conceivable that we are about to witness the transformation of the greater part of the educational plant into industrial enterprise, taking the form of the specialized institutes now so common in Soviet Russia.

Among the medical and dental professions the most important developments along these lines are the rise of state medicine, factory hospitals, and large clinics. The day of the individual doctor, possessing his own office and equipment, developing his own practice, and working entirely separate from all other doctors and hospitals is rapidly passing. Clinical medicine is even more highly developed in Germany than it is in the United States.

Changes analogous to those already mentioned have been made in the financial and banking mechanisms of the country. Technical reorganization has gone hand in hand with combination, centralization of ultimate authority, decentralization of managerial discretion, closer and more intimate working alliances with complementary and functionally related financial and banking institutions, more intimate knowledge of and closer tie-up with industrial and commercial establishments and processes dependent upon the money and credit machinery of the country, functional and geographic specialization of labor, closer working agreements and compacts with foreign financial and banking systems, submission to more exacting and more far-reaching governmental regulation and control, and other allied and complementary changes. There will be occasion later to return to an evaluation of these shifts from the point of view of trends in and the incidence of rationalization upon economic oscillations and governmental control.

Other fields in which rationalization has brought far-reaching changes are the glass-making, brewing, bookbinding, building materials—window frames, sash and door, cement, brick, tile, plumbing, structural steel, porcelain, plaster, architecture, engineering construction, etc.—boot and shoe, leather working, paper, and cigarette industries. Economies brought about and increases in efficiency in these industries as a result of various rationalization measures have been, in some cases, even more striking than in the industries reviewed.

With these facts as a background, it is now possible to turn to the more interesting set of problems associated with the rationalization movement, namely, the incidence and implications of the structural and organizational changes noted in the more tenuous and controversial fields of economic planning and social control. This is marshy and uncertain ground, and it will be necessary to return many times to the descriptive facts lest the delineation of possibilities, weaknesses, and trends depart widely from the patterns being outlined by the underlying drift of events.

PART THREE

The Incidence and Implications of Rationalization

CHAPTER XII

ECONOMIC STABILITY

ECONOMIC STABILITY is nearly always given as one of the principal objectives of rationalization. Yet the period under review was punctuated by two minor "business cycles," and closed with the disastrous breakdown of 1929–1932. In view of the objective, what interpretation is to be given to the actual course of events? Is "rationalization" *per se* causally at fault? Has it been rather the way in which rationalization measures have been introduced and carried out? Has the tempo of change been too rapid as a whole, or perhaps too rapid in certain sectors? Or, to attack the issue from another angle, has it been because rationalization has not been carried far enough? Is blame, if blame is to be assessed at all against the various changes subsumed under the broad rubric of rationalization, to be levied on the count that the full organizational, political, economic, and social implications of the forces set in motion have not been adequately visualized nor made a proper portion of the program which is their matrix?

Finally, two other questions may be raised. First, given the will, the machinery, and the necessary domestic authority for manipulation to the end that fluctuations in economic activity be eliminated, would it have been possible for Germany to have avoided the recessions that did occur within the period under review? Second, given ability to handle the domestic situation in the future, is there any reason to believe that Germany can "rationalize" this phase of her economic life?

These are large questions, and their answers would require a combination of omniscience about the past not yet vouchsafed to any individual and an apocalyptic grip on the future not allowed to members of the human species by the prevailing canons of scientific truth. In the first place—except for daily, weekly, and seasonal fluctuations—a definitive, inclusive, and universally recognized causal interpretation of economic fluctuations has not thus far been articulated. Nor, in the present state of knowledge, is any such rigid and universally valid explanation even remotely in view. It would rather appear that each such fluctuation is in part a law unto itself, and to that extent must be regarded as a phenomenon meriting detailed causal analysis without undue prejudice derived from observation of preceding phenomena of analogous character.

Even then, we have no instruments of precision for measuring the relative force of any one causal factor, or group of causal factors entering into the background of economic change. To this methodological difficulty must further be added the fact that rationalization appears not as a single-plank program but as one involving a multiplicity of dynamic forces bearing in on the structure and functioning of the economic system from several different angles. The component variables in any parallelogram of forces may converge more or less harmoniously, or may so conflict with each other that the parallelogram can scarcely be said to exist. Only on the assumption that the forces and factors reviewed in Part One are at bottom more or less complementary, mutually reinforcing, and unidirectionally inclined, is it possible to weigh "rationalization" in the balance with respect to its bearing upon economic oscillations. And could this assumption be made, a final stumbling-block would seem to offer insuperable difficulties, namely, that the cyclically important resultants of rationalization measures as actually carried out in the period under review most certainly would be different from those which would have ensued had a somewhat more deep-seated philosophy of control, a somewhat more comprehensive, unitary, and far-sighted enforcing plan, and a somewhat more vigorous method of approach been substituted for those used. We are faced at the outset with the Janus-faced problem of what was, and what might have been.

Yet despite these obstacles to scientifically complete analysis, the bearing of various rationalization measures upon economic oscillations are in many respects so obvious and clear-cut that rigorous proof of their incidence can be dispensed with as superfluous. It will not be possible, in the present study, to devote more than passing attention to any one phase of the problem, nor will it be feasible to attempt a complete catalog. The more important conditioning factors, however, may be taken up seriatim.

I. TYPES OF ECONOMIC OSCILLATIONS AFFECTED BY RATIONALIZATION MEASURES AS DEVELOPED IN POST-WAR GERMANY

The effect of rationalization measures upon all economic fluctuations, recurrent or non-recurrent, with the exception of the distinctly cyclic type, can be dealt with in brief space. Diurnal cycles, dependent in large part upon the natural facts of alternating light and dark, waking and sleeping, work and recuperation, represent elements of inefficiency so far as they fail to correspond with coefficients of exploitation of continuous services during the available working period, on the one hand, and, on the other, with continuous use throughout the full twenty-four hours where matters of human convenience are relatively unimportant. Thus, if strictly humanitarian considerations outweigh the possible advantage of continuous usage throughout the full twenty-four hours, economy dictates that usage during the working period should be as uniform and near the maximum as possible. If, on the other hand, the advantages of continuous operation outweigh any possible humanitarian objection to night work, and if the operations be so highly mechanized that work is reduced to inspection and supervision, the same criterion can then be extended to the full twenty-four hours. The higher the ratio of costs of the overhead type to total costs, the more rigorously will these generalizations hold.

Six factors, of importance in the rationalization movement, converge to promote twenty-four hour production schedules: standardization, continuous flow production, mechanization, automatization, chemicalization, and electrification. In combination these *tend* to reduce the direct labor factor to a minimum, and to shift the minimum into the inspection and supervisory classifications. All other labor can then be handled in the regular day shifts. Industries in which these factors have converged in the direction indicated are smelting of ores, certain pig iron and crude metal refining processes, coking, gas production, nearly all the basic heavy chemical processes, electric-power production and transmission, and the railroad, shipping, telephone, telegraph and radio services. Other industries in which full twenty-four hour production schedules are becoming common under "normal" circumstances are brick and tile making, glass manufacture, paper making, printing, rayon production, cotton spinning, and airplane service. In nearly all these the production problem of continuous daily operation has already been solved, or is being solved. Where consumption must synchronize with production—railroad, gas, airplane, telephone and telegraph, radio, power, etc.—the sole obstacle to this end is lack of continuous consumption usage, or "drain." In other industries—paper making, printing, metal refining, chemical production, etc.—the main obstacle is adequate markets for the existing productive capacity.

Whether full utilization on a twenty-four hour or the conventional working day basis be the objective, geographic expansion of interconnected service networks, inclusion of different classes of consumers supplied, and special tariff schedules for off-peak usage will aid in filling up troughs and in dovetailing peak loads. Herein lie the advantages of such developments as moving of long-distance freight at night, and the national power grid of the von Miller type, or the international power hook-up of the Oliven type. Emphasis found throughout rationalization literature on gearing of production to market requirements is at least a partial answer for the second type of more or less continuously operated industry. But there is another and even more important connection between rationalization as traced and these diurnal cycles, namely, the effect of direct engineering linkage between technically related processes where efficiency measures governing one or more operations are superimposed on those with which these are meshed in the concert of production. The best example is afforded by developments in continuous heat treatment whereby blast furnaces and by-product coke ovens, operated continuously through the day and night—as the only alternative to complete stoppage for time intervals of more than one day—are linked directly with steel making and rolling mills, on the one end, and with ore pre-treating plants and coal delivery systems on the other. It is possible to keep the molten metal in warmers over night before sending it to the converters, or to keep the steel ingots heated while the rolls are idle, but it is not economical or efficient to do so. It is also possible to store the coke-oven gas accumulated over night in reservoirs, but the process is not so simple if gas energy is delivered without storage in the form of electric power.

The same general argument holds for most heavy chemical processes such as the refinement of soda and hydrochloric acid, nitrogen fixation, coal hydrogenation, potash extraction, aniline dyes production, and oil distillation. Continuous processing in any one stage tends to draw preceding and following operations into its own dominant pattern. If, as one has reason to expect, mechanization and electrification of these operations continues, pressure in this direction will become more and more insistent.

Weekly cycles are determined almost exclusively by the conventional calendar pattern. Rationalization changes can, consequently, have no effect upon these cycles except so far as factors of convenience combine with disintegration of the mores in undermining mortmain in this sphere. Steady growth of the service-type industry is unquestionably militating against survival of the universal "week-end" tradition, as are the cost and efficiency motives which make for unbroken production in such industries as glass, brick, iron, heavy chemicals, and paper.

Techniques for seasonal regularization of economic activities call for little comment here. This is not because they are considered unimportant, but because most of the methods used and usable are well known.[1] Different industries and different establisments have different seasonal cycles in production and demand, and their own more or less unique methods of meeting them where some degree of control seems at all feasible. Manufacture to stock during off-peak seasons, dovetailing of two or more lines of production having different peaks, filling in of seasonal slack periods by production of standardized commodities and leaving all periods available for production of specialty goods as demand dictates, and other similar methods are well known and frequently used in Germany as elsewhere. One of the most interesting developments along this line is tied up with unified electric-power grids, making possible, geographically, a decentralization of seasonally active industries with peaks which do not coincide with periods of greatest agricultural activity, so that agricultural labor can find employment during its slack period.

Perhaps more important is the development of large, highly mechanized, mixed farms and cooperatively operated farming projects. The amount of labor required on these farms does not vary a great deal the year round. Plowing, harrowing, sowing, cutting, and harvesting do not require a great expansion of

[1] See E. A., *Gesamtbericht,* pp. 44–45. As a result of organized propaganda, special prices, and rebates, the potash industry was able to reduce its percentage of highest monthly to lowest monthly output as follows: 1924, 288; 1925, 184; 1926, 163; 1927, 152; and 1928, 139.—*Idem.*

labor force, and the care and maintenance of herds of cows and sheep, or flocks of chickens, ducks, and turkeys is about the same in winter as in summer. Repair of machinery and equipment, or expansion of building and auxiliary facilities can come, however, entirely at the convenience of the labor force.

Principal interest in this chapter, however, centers in the effect of rationalization upon so-called "business cycles." It will be necessary to discuss this subject under several different heads.

2. QUANTITY AND QUALITY OF STATISTICAL AND OTHER RELEVANT INFORMATION

Considering the complexity of the problem, and the general paucity of reliable data, the establishment of centralized research institutes, such as the *Institut für Konjunkturforschung* and the *Institut für Weltwirtschaft und Seeverkehr,* to deal primarily with collection, analysis, and publication of statistical materials relating to structural and cyclical changes, may be regarded as the most promising development along informational lines in Germany. These institutes, in fact, are sometimes said to be functioning for the purpose of "rationalizing" statistics, statistical methods, and the quantitative side of descriptive information needed for cyclical control purposes.

The *Institut für Konjunkturforschung* stands at the center of a series of dovetailed and comprehensive organizational networks, the segments of which reach out into almost every phase of national economic life. On the one side, it is very closely associated with, and may be regarded as a branch of the National Statistical Office (*Statistisches Reichsamt*). This latter is under the administration of the Ministry of Economics, and to it flow all census data—occupational, population, industrial output, price, etc.—and current statistical materials of a similar character from the various departments, commissions, committees, surveys, councils, and courts under the control of this Ministry, and the federally allied ministries of Labor, Food and Agriculture, Traffic, and other departments. Each of these ministries, and each of their separate departments, divisions, and subdivisions in turn, is organized on a most thoroughgoing basis, and includes in the information gathered practically all data of a quantitative character to be had in its field which is not strictly private and confidential. When it is remembered that governmental control over corporations, cartels, and trade associations is much more rigid and far-reaching in Germany than in the United States, and that the *Reich* and the various states are holders of important industrial properties—railroads, telephone and telegraph, radio, warehousing, mining, hydro- and steam-generated electric power and transmission systems, etc.—the significance of this tie-up can be readily appreciated from a statistical point of view.

Special publications and departmental connections are made available to the *Reich* through the statistical materials collected by the various states, and these materials are in turn gathered in large part from various subsidiary regional groupings and municipalities. Most important for present purposes are the statistics gathered by the state of Prussia. Since Prussia includes practically all northern Germany and the whole Rhineland-Westphalian industrial district, its quantitative data are of tremendous significance as a basis for analysis and control relating to the entire *Reich*.[2]

Associated with and aiding in the support of the *Institut* are to be found most of the important national centralized organizations in trade, commerce, industry, agriculture, handicrafts, banking, and labor.[3] The high degree of centralization characteristic of these organizations makes it possible for them to pool, in each case, information from many industries and from the various branches of each industry in a central office. Data relevant to any particular problem, industry, or policy can be brought together from any number of different angles. The reverse flow of systematically assembled, analyzed, and presented summaries keeps all branches of economic activity in close touch with the larger movements in prices, production, employment, etc.

On the more purely technological and managerial side, the *Institut* is tied up very closely with the *Reichskuratorium für Wirtschaftlichkeit,* of which it is, in in a way, a special sub-organ. Through this contact it is kept in touch with structural, efficiency, and cost changes in the various branches of industry which the various other special sub-organs and sub-committees deal with. The *RKW* is enabled to call on the *Verein Deutscher Ingenieure,* and any of its sub-committees, for further data along any line of investigation it may see fit to enter. Where issues may trace back into more purely scientific fields, another nationally organized and integrated institutional complex is available in the *Kaiser Wilhelm-Gesellschaft.*

Data collected by the *Institut für Weltwirtschaft und Seeverkehr* relate more specifically to the international field. Its comprehensive *Archiv,* however, contains the best general newspaper and periodical clipping file on all matters relat-

---

[2] The quality of materials obtained by the government should typically be higher in fields dominated by a single combine, or a small number of closely organized concerns, as is the case in iron and steel, coal, potash, chemicals, power production and distribution, long-distance gas supply, etc. Where the government is represented on industrial governing boards, as is the case with the "forced cartels" in the potash, lignite, coke, and coal industries, machinery is already available for public assembly and analysis of all relevant statistical material. See Chap. XIV, pp. 372, 386 ff.

[3] "The following organizations are associated in supporting the Institut: the federal government, the Reichsrat, the Reichsbank, the Federal Railway Company, the Federal Postal Service, and the so-called 'leading associations of German business,' consisting of the Deutscher Landwirtschaftsrat; Deutscher Industrie- und Handelstag; Reichsverband der deutschen Industrie; Reichsverband des deutschen Gross- und Ueberseehandels; Hauptgemeinschaft des deutschen Einzelhandels; Zentralverband deutscher Konsumvereine; Zentralverband des deutschen Bank- und Bankiergewerkes; Allgemeiner deutscher Gewerkschaftsbund; Deutscher Gewerkschaftsbund; Gewerkschaftsring deutscher Arbeiter-, Angestellten- und Beamtenverbände; Reichsverband des deutschen Handwerks; Deutscher Sparkassen und Giroverband; Deutscher Städtetag; Deutscher Beamtenbund; Allgemeiner Freier Angestelltenbund."—Carl Theodore Schmidt, *Am. Econ. Rev.* (March, 1931):67.

ing to domestic economic developments to be found in Germany, if not in the entire world. As stated before, the Kiel Institute has been largely responsible for carrying out the labor of assembling, analyzing, and preparing for publication the monumental *Enquete* reports provided for in the law of 1926 (*Gesetz über einen Ausschuss zur Untersuchung der Erzeugungs- und Absatzbedingungen der deutschen Wirtschaft*).[4]

The general rationalization movement has unquestionably had a great deal to do with the development of these organizations and the improvement which is to be noticed in the quality and range of the statistical materials dealt with. Simplification and standardization of terms, basic units, nomenclature, entry forms, methods of entry, records, methods of handling, analysis, summarization, and presentation have immensely facilitated the rapidity with which quantitative materials can be manipulated, while at the same time they have helped to broaden the base of the statistical pyramid. Paralleling in part, but usually preceding these methodological changes, rationalization has greatly simplified the raw materials for statistical analysis through standardization of materials, parts, productive methods and equipment, and products, and the general tendency towards typification of assembled machinery and auxiliary apparatus.

As standardization has improved physical statistical units, so standard cost-accounting has improved the quality of price and profits data, and rendered them comparable. Nearly every committee of the *RKW*, nearly every agricultural and consumers' cooperative, nearly every cartel, trade association, and community of interest, nearly every governmental department, division and publicly operated property, and nearly every large corporation has made some effort to systematize and standardize cost-accounting terminology, classifications, methods of entry, report and summarization, and methods of tracing and allocating expenditures of the overhead type. Standards have been worked out by several of the largest corporations, central association bureaus, and governmental departments with an eye to their statistical manipulation, summarization, and interpretation. Such is the case with the *I. G. Farbenindustrie*, the *Vereinigte Stahlwerke*, the *Reichsbahn*, and similar corporations.

In this general field accountants, managers, and engineering staff must work very closely together. Practical engineers, such as Schulze-Mehrin and Professor Schlesinger, have elaborated and built upon the theoretical systems of such persons as Professor Schmalenbach—one of the great pioneers in this field—and Peiser. Of particular importance in this field has been the work of the *Ausschuss für Wirtschaftliche Verwaltung*, sub-committees of the *RKW*, several groups

[4] This committee, whose work has been previously referred to in several cases, carried out its work in five special sub-committees: (1) General Economic Structure; (2) Agriculture; (3) Industry (Manufacturing, Trade, and Transportation); (4) Labor Efficiency (Effect of labor time and wages upon labor efficiency); (5) Money, Credit, and Finance. See the sketch of its aims and working agenda in the *Handwörterbuch der Staatswissenschaften*, Ergänzungsband, pp. 1093–1098.

associated with the *Verein Deutscher Ingenieure,* and the *Verein Deutscher Maschinenbau-Anstalten.* The first of these groups has worked out Unified Accounting Methods (*Einheitsbuchführung*) for various special industries, such as those for medium-sized iron foundries, textile weaving, internal water transportation, medium-sized machine shops not engaged in serial production, and lignite mining.

This work is tied up very closely with formal standardization of statistical terms, graphic methods, and methods of analysis, as carried out by the *Deutscher Normenausschuss* and the *Institut für Konjunkturforschung,*[5] on the one hand, and the introduction of the budgetary principle on the other. The former paves the way for the statistical treatment and mechanization of cost-accounting procedure—use of Hollerith punching, verifying, sorting, and tabulating machines. The latter orients this information in terms of trends and policies within the corporation and the industry, and relates these in turn to the larger fluctuations in costs, prices, volume of activity, and the general economic outlook as shown by the studies of such centralized statistical agencies as the *Institut für Konjunkturforschung.*

All these trends tend to reinforce each other, and to demonstrate the truth that there is scarcely any direction in which the rationalization movement can not be said to simplify statistical data, broaden their base, increase their intelligibility and ease of interpretation, widen their application, and increase the use made of them. So far as control and manipulation of cyclical fluctuations, whether within special plants and branches of industry, or in the economic system at large, are dependent upon more adequate and reliable quantitative information, the influence of rationalization can be said to be almost wholly positive. This information is given enhanced value by the gradually changing attitude towards business secrets shown in the rise of the *Erfa* (*Erfahrungs-Austausch*) groups, and the increasing ease with which central organizations such as the special committees of the *RKW* are able to obtain data for their various purposes.

3. CORPORATE AND GROUP ADJUSTMENT TO THE CYCLE

One of the major quasi-mechanical difficulties faced in every business cycle is centered around accumulation of stocks at various stages of the productive and distributive process.[6] The facts, the situation that develops around this core, and the explanation of their bearing upon cyclical oscillations are about as follows. Managerial experience determines the ratio that stocks on hand should bear to current sales for each industry and trade. These stock ratios need not be regarded

[5] Of particular importance among the Special Volumes (Sonderhefte) are the following numbers: (4) *Die Analyse von Wirtschaftskurven;* (6) *Die Saisonschwankungen als Problem der Konjunkturforschung;* (9) *Der Trend;* (12) *Russische Arbeiten zur Wirtschaftsforschung.*

[6] A portion of the argument that follows is a summary of that presented by Professor W. C. Mitchell at Columbia University, Winter Session, 1927–1928.

as absolutely fixed for each trade, nor for every phase of the cycle. The ratios will be allowed to fluctuate between minima and maxima, the facts fixing these points being somewhat different for each enterprise in each industry and separate trade. Statistical evidence, however, points to the existence of fairly definite ratios for each type of retailing, wholesaling, manufacturing, and manufacturers' supply industry.

To replenish stocks, retailers purchase from wholesalers, wholesalers from manufacturers, and manufacturers from dealers in manufacturers' supplies. Given stock ratios fixed within fairly definite limits, it can be demonstrated mathematically, or shown by simple illustration that the following are typically the necessary resultants of a change in the rate of increase or decrease in consumers' purchases (increases or decreases in the rate of increase or decrease): (1) The change shown in sales to consumers will be amplified as one goes back through the process; wholesalers' sales will be larger (or smaller) than retailers' sales; manufacturers' sales will be larger (or smaller) than wholesalers' sales; the sales of dealers in manufacturers' supplies will be larger (or smaller) than manufacturers' sales. (2) A change in the rate of increase (or decrease) in consumer purchases (with or without a change in direction) will be reflected (*a*) in actual change of direction of sales at some point removed from the retailer, and (*b*) in a tendency for these changes (in direction of change) to be more numerous as they become further and further removed from the ultimate consumer. (3) These changes tend to date earlier in point of time as one proceeds from retailer to dealer in manufacturers' supplies, and thus tend to precede the cause which brought them about—the result, in other words, appears to precede the efficient cause. Thus it may come about that a decrease in the rate of increase of consumers' purchases will bring about a series of changes, leading to serious decline in volume of sales in the earlier stages of production. Falling off of business activity in these fields will lead to curtailment of production, discharge of workmen, decline in wage disbursements, shortage of consumer purchasing power, and actual decline of consumers' purchases. This actual decline will in turn be amplified throughout the various stages of distribution and production, accelerating further the process of decline.

An allied factor tends still further to reinforce this process in those branches of industry mainly devoted to production of heavy machinery and construction materials used by manufacturing industries. These industries supply a market of which the demand is compounded of renewals at a fairly constant rate and additions for expansion purposes. When the manufacturing industries are operating to or at less than capacity, their requisitions upon the construction industries will be made up solely of orders for replacement and repair of worn-out machinery, buildings and equipment. But when the former begin to expand, the latter will find themselves swamped with orders which may, for some time at least, be mainly placed for expansion rather than replacement purposes. Along towards the close of such a period of expansion, the decline in manufacturers' orders for new and additional equipment will bring about a serious fall in the sales of supply concerns some time before any actual decline in manufacturing activity can be shown at all.[7]

Rationalization affects these two problems—both of which are peculiar to modern technology and the capitalistic order of production—in several different ways. Most important for present purposes are the following: (*a*) It increases the relative importance of those industries—or rather "services"—where storage for any appreciable period is either technologically impossible or financially prohibitive, or both. (*b*) In both its engineering expression, as continuous and unbroken production of simplified and standardized output, and its accounting expression as emphasis upon reduction of all overhead and variable expenses to the minimum, rationalization tends to force reduction of stocks at all stages of production and distribution to the lowest possible levels. (*c*) Horizontal combination, and any step in the direction of the exercise of effective monopolistic or semimonopolistic powers in any individual industry, has the effect of increasing the flexibility and adaptability of productive equipment to unusual demands made upon it up to the limits set by full utilization of all or nearly all the available plant. The same holds for vertical integration, but in a different way and for different reasons. (*d*) There is a persistent tendency in nearly all industries in which rationalization has become significant for important classes of variable expenses, principally labor, to take on overhead characteristics, and as a consequence for policy to shift with an eye to continuous employment for growing percentages of the labor force. These may be taken up in order:

(*a*) From a statistical point of view, growth in the relative importance of the "service" industries may not be strictly demonstrable because of difficulties in definition. In speaking of railroads, tramway and bus systems, water shipping and airplane lines, telephone, telegraph, and radio, and water, sewage, gas, and electric-power systems as "service" industries, however, certain common—though perhaps rather vague—ideas are in mind to mark them off from other industry. Typically these are (1) equal treatment to all comers and general availability of the "service" at all ordinary hours and seasons; (2) direct technical linkage with the consumer, industrial or ultimate, which makes him a distinct part of the system whenever and wherever he may avail himself of the "service"; (3) the "service" cannot be stored, but must be used "at the time produced"; (4) costs of the overhead type predominate; there is a tendency for unit cost to decrease as the reciprocal of rising capacity factors; (5) most "services" tend to become natural monopolies, to be "key" for the industries or territory served. "Service industries," in other words, are typically vested with a public interest in a rather unique way, and almost from the beginning of their institutional existences.

[7] See, in particular, J. M. Clark, *Economics of Overhead Costs,* Chap. XIX, on "Overhead Costs and the Business Cycle."

These industries are unquestionably increasing their importance in the budgets of both industrial and ultimate consumers. Certain of these service industries, while they may bring with them untold economies, represent entirely new charges upon the budget. But the influence of gas and electric-power networks is even more far-reaching. Here a definite, concrete, storable fuel—wood, coal, coke, petroleum—has been replaced by a continuously flowing, non-storable, and highly destructible energy and fuel supply. The rapidity of the change has been so great as to amount to a revolution in this phase of industrial technology. The conquest of the home offers the next great field for the expansion of gas and electrical energy consumption. Important inroads have already been made. The time is probably not far off when practically all industrial and ultimate consumer energy, fuel, and lighting requirements will be met by gas or electric current.

If to these changes be added the growing importance of the technically significant professions—engineering, accountancy, statistics, surgery, dentistry, instruction, etc.—of essentially a "service" character so far as industry is concerned, and the personal "services" such as supplied by friseurs and barbers, entertainment, recreational, and touring "services" and the like, it should be possible to demonstrate statistically that increasing portions of the economic apparatus are shifting to an area where the importance of stock ratios is practically nil. It is also a fact of observation that the major service industries, other than transportation, are not nearly so sensitive to cyclical fluctuations as those industries in which stocks are necessarily high.

(*b*) No single factor receives greater emphasis in argument promoting the advantages of standardization, simplification, scientific organization of factory routines, mechanization, cost-accounting and budgeting than reduction in stocks of raw materials, goods in process of manufacture, and finished or semi-finished commodities. Continuous flow production reduces stocks to a physical minimum; cost-accounting and budgetary practice lay emphasis upon turnover, and a consequent reduction of stock ratios. As stock ratios fall they lose importance as factors making for cyclical irregularity. The fact that rationalization in Germany has not always resulted in lower stocks is no argument to the contrary.[8] As pointed out before, many German industries are afflicted with excess plant capacity, and consequently produce large quantities of goods at all times for which there are rather uncertain markets. The process of reorganization, and of systematically gearing production to distribution requirements, have not been carried far enough where these excessive stocks are to be found.

---

[8] The point is made by a writer in the *Frankfurter Zeitung* that rationalization, particularly as advanced in the paper and glass industries, was followed by increasing stocks of manufactured goods because the new technical set-up, once put in motion, could not easily be stopped. In the wool industry, which is described as being technically backward, such a cumulation of stocks during the depression has not taken place.—*Frankfurter Zeitung* (July 26, 1931). Whatever be the facts, it is not entirely accurate to assess the onus where it has been laid.

(*c*) Increasing flexibility and adjustability of horizontal and vertical combinations and semi-monopolies are propositions which cannot be definitively proved without recourse to involved theoretical considerations and appeal to a considerable range of new facts. In fact, it is customary to find the opposite assertion made. German writers delight in pointing out tendencies to growing rigidity (*Starrheit*) in the industrial system at large contained in various rationalization measures. Besides, combination, even when it takes the loose form of cartel agreements, is rarely free from at least the potential threat of competition. Liefman has dwelt frequently on this theme,[9] and Stocking has shown how this fact is capable of robbing industry of much of even those advantages which are commonly granted to effective monopolies.[10]

But up to the limits of capacity it is possible for adequate organization to increase rather than decrease adjustability of industrial processes so organized. Horizontal combination typically means elimination of excess plant capacity by closing down of badly located and inefficient plants, a high degree of plant specialization, and careful attention to long-run considerations when proposals for expansion are advanced. Unless dismantled, closed-down plants provide a cushion of reserve capacity when unexpectedly large demands are made upon the usual operating facilities. Highly specialized plants may, and in certain lines typically do (in many branches of the machine and engineering industries) mean production of component parts which are common to different types of products, capacity to shift from one type of component part to closely allied types, or ability to add a certain amount of fabrication and assembly as occasion may demand. Anticipation of change makes it possible within the closed system to shift, adjust, and reorganize plants, departments, shops and machinery as the necessity arises without the usual delay and uncertainty experienced by independently operated and corporatively secretive enterprises.

Vertical combination may be brought about by desire to control raw and semi-finished materials supply or distribution facilities on the one hand, or by engineering considerations promoting technological linkage in one or both directions, on the other. A number of factors promote adaptation of managerial policies of combinations brought together for the former reasons to those pursued by management in the latter type of case. And within the confines of such a technically integrated unit, the cumulation of impacts brought about by shifts in consumer purchases simply could not take place. Even where a high degree of managerial decentralization is the rule—and in those cases where engineering ties are rather tenuous—no management would permit pursuit of policies based upon any notion of stock ratios with such dangerous implications for portions of the controlled system as are carried by the analysis indicated above. A drop in output in

[9] In particular, "Kartelle und Konjunkturen," by Robert Liefman, *Kartell Rundschau,* (November, 1929):559–565.

[10] Stocking, *The Potash Industry, loc. cit.*

any one stage *tends* to ramify immediately and in proportion throughout the entire system, or to be ignored, if possible, in the determination of larger policies. The system *tends* to move in a unit, instead of by pieces. If demand for all finished commodities drops by 10 per cent, steel production, and in turn pig iron production, ore mining, coal mining, coke, gas, and chemical by-product output, and other technically integral processes tend to be correspondingly curtailed. So far as this process is coercive it means not less, but greater adaptability to significant changes in economic activity at large.[11]

It is further true that, while highly mechanized individual plants may be run full blast after demand has fallen off for combined cost and competitive reasons, the same policy would probably not be followed by a more or less inclusive combine, whether horizontally or vertically organized. If all manufacturers in a particular line stood ready to make a cut as soon as it was necessary in prices or output, or both, Professor J. M. Clark argues, it probably would not be necessary for any of them to cut very far. It is never a good policy, however, for the individual concern to act for the good of the group; quite the reverse, in fact. But with combination and a measure of unified control all along the line, such unified action is possible, and will be followed out for purely managerial reasons.

Combinations, however, may attempt to shift the burden to other shoulders. Thus it is argued that the quota exemption of the steel companies from coal cartel regulations, because of production for self-consumption purposes, makes it possible for these concerns as a group to shift the burden of cyclical changes to the shoulders of the independents—shortening the commercial market supply when demand is high, and increasing the salable surplus when demand is low.[12] It is also contended that the steel interests exercise monopoly powers to shift the burden of market fluctuations to the small independent dealers in such a way that stocks in the hands of the latter are materially increased at the very time when they are least able to stand the strain.[13] These, however, are problems in manipulation and strategy by powerful capitalistic interests, and have little to do

---

[11] It is interesting to note, in this connection, the results of the exhaustive study by Professor Mills on "Economic Tendencies," where it is shown that industrialization of the United States has meant, almost without exception, relatively greater increase in output, growth of plant, and labor productivity in those fields most sensitive to cyclical changes than in the less sensitive. Similar facts for Germany would undoubtedly show the same trends.—Mills, "Economic Tendencies," *National Bureau of Economic Research* (New York, 1932), 21:1–49, 241–314. This relative broadening in the stream of goods flowing from cyclically sensitive industries does not necessarily mean that the industrial system will experience greater cyclical shocks in the future because of the changes noted. It does mean, however, that the danger of a major economic catastrophe is greater, and that the measures taken to counteract must be more scientifically calculated, more comprehensive in scope, and more adroitly manipulated if greater sensitivity is not to result in greater shocks.

[12] Likewise, industrial price control may shift the burden of depression to the shoulders of agriculture, or labor, or the middle classes. See Dr. Fritz Sternberg, "Die Weltwirtschaftskrise," *Weltwirtschafiliches Archiv*, 36:109–132 (July, 1932).

[13] "Absatzrationalisierung und Lagerhaltung," *Berliner Tageblatt* (August 3, 1927).

directly with rationalization. They are not, that is to say, part of the rationalization movement in any organizational sense.

(*d*) Expenditures for highly skilled and specialized supervisory staff tend to become overhead in nearly all cases with the advance of technical rationalization. Within limitations, careful personnel selection and training of routine workers tends to advance their wage costs into overhead classifications wherever the process involves considerable original cost. For those who are indefinitely displaceable the importance of incentives steadily increases as operating mechanisms become more finely and delicately balanced and adjusted. The capacity for damage through malice or neglect of every worker in the process grows as mechanization increases and as the productive importance of the individual shrinks in the cosmos surrounding him. In becoming a cog in the machine he takes on both analogous anonymity and key importance.

For this reason, while it may be considered largely fortuitous that social insurance is widely developed in Germany, it is no accident that nearly every large corporation, whether located in Germany, the United States, or the U.S.S.R. is paying at least lip service to the notion that provision must be made during times of plenty for income shortage during periods of possible general shortage. Several large corporations in Germany—notably the *I. G. Farbenindustrie A. G.*—claim larger expenditures for "social services" set aside of their own volition than those required by the insurance laws. Pressure is developing in favor of extending these, required or not required by law, to cover more and more aspects of labor as an overhead charge on industry. And, of course, it is scarcely necessary to add that such is the attitude of labor.

So far as pressure along this line is coercive, it combines with tendencies, previously noted, to stabilize the more sensitive manufacturing and construction industries and aids in bolstering up consumer purchasing power. One factor promotes this end by steadying wage disbursements, the other by transferring it from years of relative surplus to those of relative scarcity.[14]

4. TECHNOLOGICAL UNEMPLOYMENT AND THE BUSINESS CYCLE

High wage levels, said to be brought about by relative scarcity of labor, are given as one of the really important reasons for acceleration of rationalization measures of the labor-saving type. Since relative scarcity of labor should appear primarily during a period of intense business activity, any net displacement of labor would assume cyclical significance so far as it led to net decrease in wage disbursements reflected in real decline in consumer purchasing power. Such a lag in the reabsorption capacity of the industrial system, fairly to be termed tech-

[14] The other side of this picture is to be found in the tendency of costs to become rigid and unadjustable; hence, factors tending to perpetuate depressions once prosperity has been interrupted. See Colm, "Deutschland und die Weltkrise," *Schriften des Vereins für Sozialpolitik*, 187:34–51.

nological unemployment if and when unemployment observed can be definitely traced to such a source, could then be assigned as a causally significant factor in bringing about reversal of prosperous conditions.

There do not appear, however, to be any particularly good reasons for confining net labor displacement because of technological changes to periods of relatively active business. At least half of all the rationalization undertaken in German industry calls for little or no additional investment in capital goods. The "slack" observed by so many writers in nearly every phase of production and distribution—because of bad labor morale, bad organization and layout of plants, work routes, and miscellaneous "blue-print" details, duplicate plant, machinery, and supplementary facilities, bad proportioning of technical and labor factors, inexact and misleading cost-accounting systems, failure to plan details and policies in terms of long-run considerations—was unbelievably great. This "slack" can be taken up just as easily—and in some cases more easily—during periods of depression as in more active times. The immediate effect of such changes has been in nearly all cases to curtail the amount of labor required at any given level of output. Thus technological unemployment can be said to exist just as clearly in depression as in "prosperity."

In fact, case records are available by the thousands which justify the belief that such displacement can and does occur throughout all phases of the cycle. It is merely accelerated when plentiful supplies of investment funds and expanding markets permit addition of costly labor-saving rationalization changes to those which may be made at any and all times. But the fact remains that if such net displacement exists it reduces purchasing power in the hands of consumers when circumstances require still further expansion, and contracts such buying capacity at the very time when there is already a plethora of goods on the market and a great scarcity of buyers.

Were unemployment insurance to be paid displaced workers to the full amount of wages formerly received, minus the equivalent of any price reduction brought about by changes incidental to such curtailment of the labor force, the major problem of constant consumer purchases, from a cyclical point of view, would disappear. But this does not happen. Whatever the cause of the unemployment that has existed in Germany during the various periods of the interval 1924–1932, unemployment insurance paid out has never constituted in the aggregate more than a small portion of the wages and salaries ordinarily receivable by workers when normally employed. Hence, technological unemployment, so far as it serves to redistribute income so that the normal direction of consumer purchases is seriously altered, can be said to be uniformly depressive; it has a dampening effect during periods of high activity, and it deepens depression beyond the customary levels.[15]

[15] Contrast: Paul H. Douglas, "Technological Unemployment," *American Federationist* (August, 1930); Alvin Harvey Hansen, *op. cit.*, pp. 161–173; and various papers delivered at

All this, of course, is on the assumption that technological unemployment really exists. Into this discussion it is not necessary to enter. The tremendous volume of material written in Germany on the subject demonstrates the widespread belief that it does exist. The evidence appears, in a good many respects, to justify the contention made. Increased output per worker after 1923 was accompanied in most of the heavy industries, for example, by drastic cuts in total labor force. Subsequently, labor discharged from coal and lignite mining, iron, steel, machine, textile, chemical, electro-technical, and numerous other industries was taken back in such numbers that the employment figures in 1928 were approximately the same as at the beginning of the rationalization period. Yet the existence of a lag in reabsorption is undeniable. Although many displaced laborers were able to find substitute employment during the intervening period, the fact that much unemployment existed throughout the whole period from 1924 to 1929 indicates the presence of chronic maladjustments. Among these technological unemployment may reasonably—though not statistically—be counted constituent.[16]

Despite the apparent soundness of such a conclusion, it still seems ridiculous to assign the cyclically depressing influence of technological unemployment to rationalization *per se*. The fault lies rather with rationalization as carried out—without comprehensive plans, for primarily capitalistic purposes, without regard to social and human considerations. The facts that workers' standards of living in Germany have been typically low, that productive facilities have been idle part of the time, and that human ability, energy, and initiative have not been used to the full, offer sufficient proof that displaced labor might have been thrown into the weaker sectors of the national system, and might have been absorbed into the industrial and commercial mechanism had the process been viewed as a whole, and had change in each segment been dovetailed into a much larger and more comprehensive pattern.

Before leaving this topic, one other aspect should be noted. Cassel believes that cyclical fluctuations are made more acute than would otherwise be the case because of the enormous labor reserves for purposes of expansion in industrial activity to be found in agricultural regions.[17] Surplus agricultural labor can be drawn into industry as economic activity expands, and discharged with relative

the World Social Economic Congress, Amsterdam, August, 1931, and published under the title, *World Social Economic Planning* (Hague, 1932)—in particular those by Dr. Otto Neurath, "Das gegenwärtige Wachstum der Produktionskapazität der Welt," Dr. Max Lazard, "Le Paradoxe de l'Heure Présente—Le Chômage en Plein Progrès Economique," and those of the Soviet delegates, V. Obolensky-Ossinsky, "The Nature and Forms of Economic Planning," S. L. Ronin, "Planned Economy in Operation in the Soviet Union," and I. A. Kraval, "Labour in Soviet Planned Economy."

16 Chronic unemployment, parallel phenomenon to high interest rates in Germany, is coparent to the theory that, Germany being "poor in capital and rich in men," the entire rationalization movement in the future must be oriented on absorption and not displacement of labor power. There is a catch in this theory, however. See comments on DINTA, Chap. XIII.

17 Gustav Cassel, *A Theory of Social Economy* (New York, 1924), Fourth Book, "The Theory of Conjuncture-Movements."

impunity and turned back to the land when contraction takes place. This agricultural labor may be drawn from domestic sources, such as East Prussia and northern Germany, or from adjoining agricultural states, such as Poland, Czechoslovakia, and Hungary.

The technical and organizational changes subsumed under rationalization may affect this situation in several respects. In the first place, rationalization of agriculture—mechanization, scientific farming, mixed agriculture, large-scale production—tends to reduce the necessary labor force and to even the seasonal round of labor duties. Since the bulk of agricultural produce—particularly in Germany—is intended for ultimate consumer uses, and since purchases of basic foods show relatively little cyclical sensitivity, reduction of agricultural labor to the technical minimum should render its supply for industrial usage highly inelastic, temporary surplus on account of meteorological factors excluded. Industrialization of outlying countries, as well as industrialization of agriculture in those areas, should work in the same direction so far as imported labor is concerned.

In the second place, any decentralization of industry that takes place as a result of expansion of electric-power networks would presumably be most marked in those branches where activity peaks dovetail instead of conflicting with agricultural peaks. It is at least possible that this seasonally flattening development would tend, for occupational reasons, to fix geographically a fairly large percentage of the dispensable labor left after the above-mentioned forces had spent their influence.

Set off against changes in elasticity of agricultural labor supply are those in female labor. Urbanization, increase in facilities for efficient performance of household duties, decrease in the size of household units—number of rooms, floor space, location of built-in closets and shelving, etc.—community living, decrease in the number of children per married couple, decrease in percentage of waking hours spent by children at home, delay in marriage, and other factors have increased the number of women available for industrial labor. Mechanization and repetitive operations, on the other hand, increase the number of factory jobs open to women and older children. As rationalization has advanced, the percentage of female labor has increased in nearly every industry. Only after a large proportion of this available supply shall have been absorbed into the industrial system will it lose its elasticity.[18]

[18] From 1907 to 1925 there was an increase of 3.9 million male and 3 million female gainfully employed persons in Germany. Female labor comprised 30.5 per cent of all gainfully employed (8.51 million) persons in 1907; in 1925 the parallel percentage was 35.6 per cent (of 11.47 million gainfully employed). Part of the cause for this increase results from differences in statistical classification, part from decimation of able-bodied males during the war, and part from changes in mode of living. Of the new additions to the gainfully employed from 1925 to 1931 (1.53 million), 77 per cent, however, were male. Percentage gains of female labor are particularly marked in distribution, consumers' goods industries, and large-scale enterprises. See E. A., *Gesamtbericht,* pp. 61–63.

But whether the supply of either female or agricultural labor, or both, becomes more or less elastic as rationalization develops, the effect upon cyclical fluctuations will largely depend upon how labor reserves are managed and how industry is regulated. Both an inexhaustible pool and a rigidly limited supply of labor could be made, under appropriate circumstances, to increase or decrease the amplitude and severity of cyclical oscillations. The intellectual and organizational pressure, however, is towards a lessening of these shocks as far as the labor factor is concerned.

5. RETARDATION IN SECULAR RATES OF CHANGE

Numerous causal explanations of cyclical fluctuations fix upon some phase of secular growth or rates of change in secular trends. Schumpeter[19] and others find the root of the evil in wave-like irregularities in the rate at which significant industrial and commercial innovations are made. Sombart[20] attaches considerable importance to disturbances arising from clashes between the (assumed) dissimilar rhythms of industries dependent upon organic and inorganic materials respectively, the center of gravity shifting towards the latter, which are held to be more sensitive and more adjustable to cyclic change. Mills[21] believes the duration, and perhaps the amplitude, of cycles to be conditioned by general rates of secular change, rapid change shortening and slow change lengthening the cycle. Kuznets[22] finds fairly definite connections between contours of plotted cyclic data and their location with respect to secondary cycles (or trends) and Gompertz type functions which he fits, substituting various constants, to all basic quantitative phenomena characterized by the growth factor.

Without attempting proof or refutation of any of these theories—for which there is neither space nor occasion in the present study—the bearing of rationalization upon the angle of approach to cyclical analysis common to all of them seems, in some respects at least, fairly clear. As pointed out in the Introduction and in various places in Part One of this book, rationalization as a more or less formal, organized, and systematically articulated movement has appeared only after the basic scientific, technological, and organizational arts have become mature. For this reason its emphasis has been primarily organizational. It tends to fix upon those reasonably permanent elements in science and engineering not liable, as a basis upon which to organize productive and distributive networks and processes, to be seriously affected by further improvements within the visible

19 Josef Schumpeter, *Theorie der wirtschaftlichen Entwicklung* (Munich and Leipzig, 1926), Chap. VI.

20 Werner Sombart, "Die Störungen im deutschen Wirtschaftsleben während des Jahres 1900," *Schriften des Vereins für Sozialpolitik* (September, 1903), 113:130–133.

21 Frederick Mills, "An Hypothesis Concerning the Duration of Business Cycles," *Jour. Am. Statis. Assoc.* (December, 1926).

22 Simon Kuznets, *Secular Movement in Production and Prices* (Boston and New York, 1930).

future. From an industrial point of view, the changes that will take place in the future will probably be of a less revolutionary, less drastic, nature than those that have already been made. The organizational networks set up, or forecast by present developments, or theoretically capable of application will probably be but little altered in their major contours by science and invention within the next four or five decades. Infinite change may take place within the confines of these larger patterns, but major operations will probably be less frequent, and the cutting and refashioning which they will compel will probably be less of a shock to the whole interconnected set-up.

To the extent to which technique and science may be considered to have "ripened" within special industries and within the industrial system at large, any perturbations arising from future innovations will probably be of less relative importance than those which have occurred in the past. Even should changes, however, as revolutionary as the development of the steam engine, Faraday's disc, and wireless telegraphy evolve from future laboratories, the organized character of contemporary scientific and engineering research would forecast and prepare the way for introduction of the new improvements long before practical application would be possible. Industrial planning, further, should make it possible to mesh gradually the new technique or techniques into the existing machinery without radically disrupting the existing concerts and routines.

Perhaps even more important is the fact that industrialization of nearly all productive and distributive operations, and urbanization of the conditions of life tend sooner or later to affect the rate of population growth. Nearly all major industrial countries are affected with a declining rate of population increase; nearly all should have stable or even declining populations by the turn of the present century.[23] Great as pressure has been in the past and probably will be in the future towards increased standards of living, it is hardly probable that this factor alone would possess enough buoyancy to prevent continued decrease in the rate of expansion in productive output.

There is, consequently, every reason for believing that output of both producers' and consumers' goods will sooner or later reach a more or less definite plateau.[24] A stable or declining population will probably not continue indefinitely to expand its demands after a certain standard of living, not exactly ascertainable, has been achieved. In the producers' goods field, an increasing percentage of total

[23] See the excellent summary on "The Declining Birth Rate and the Changed Age Distribution," by Professor Hansen, *op. cit.*, pp. 225–238.

[24] ". . . . a growing population has a larger number of workers than the previous generation of workers. A stationary population has the *same* number of workers as the previous generation. The latter has only to replace depreciated capital goods; the former must, in addition, fit out each new working person with a whole new set of capital goods. In a stationary population all this productive effort would be available for other uses. It is reasonable to suppose, therefore, that a stationary society will produce relatively more consumer goods and less producer goods than will a growing society. . . . . In the future productive effort will turn relatively more in the direction of personal services."—*Ibid.*, p. 232.

output should go for repair and maintenance purposes as soon as the rate of industrial expansion drops off. If and when it should reach a plateau, practically all such production would go for these purposes. There would then be less additional construction of new residences, apartment houses, highways, railroad tracks, terminals, telephone lines, factories, steamships, and more repair and replacement of the same.

As effective operating units become larger, and more carefully integrated and controlled, as the corporation or some analogous legal type of enterprise becomes even more common, and as government control becomes more widespread and inclusive, more of this replacement and repair will be budgeted, and conditions will promote greater dovetailing of extensions contemplated into long-range plans. The best that can be said for rationalization is that under these circumstances conditions favoring many and catastrophic cyclical oscillations would have largely disappeared, and that these circumstances provide the setting for, the impulse towards, and the logical answer to rationalization developments as we now see them. The organizational emphasis of the movement provides, in addition, ways and means for direct attack upon the problem which is now, on its more purely structural side, coming to be regarded as an integral part of the larger task of rationalization itself.[25]

6. COMPETITION AND THE PROFITS SYSTEM

Whatever be the nature of the initiating and conditioning factors, business cycles run their course in capitalistically organized countries where ultimate discretionary authority is concentrated in the hands of those persons whose interest in productive and distributive processes terminates with the making of profits. In other words, to employ the *patois,* we are living in a "profits economy." In the final analysis business cycles occur in this system because present and prospective profits alternately increase and decrease. Business activity increases when the

---

[25] Mention should probably be made here of an interesting theory of the cause of business cycles developed by the Russian statistician, Eugen Slutsky, and elaborated in the United States by Simon Kuznets, "Random Events and Cyclical Oscillations," *Jour. Am. Statis. Assoc.* (September, 1929):258–275, and "Equilibrium Economics and Business Cycle Theory," *Quart. Jour. Econ.* (May, 1930):381–415, which is constructed on an analysis of random changes as they bear in upon the economic system, conceived as being normally in a state of equilibrium. According to this theory, random changes may be conceived of as frequency distributions strung out along the line of time. Large deviations will be small, but will occur. Small deviations will be more numerous and large, but may be more numerous and disequilibrating at certain times than others. These form causal nuclei, which radiate unidirectionally along the line of time, i.e., become cumulative. If they come in positive or negative clusters for short periods, they will tend to accentuate the cumulative effects of previous disequilibrating forces. Time builds these unbalancing forces into plateaus by knitting them together into mutually reinforcing complexes. These plateaus upset the round of business processes, and thus bring on business cycles. By eliminating the accidental, the fortuitous, the chance item, rationalization would tend to deflate such random disturbing factors, if and when they could be said to be causally significant. The whole argument, however, may not be able to stand close scrutiny.

greater number of capitalistic enterprises are able to show or to forecast a larger return upon invested capital, and declines when the reverse is the case. The prospects for profits improve (1) when the margin of return or the span between costs and prices widens, turnover being constant; (2) when turnover increases, margins being held constant; (3) when both happen at the same time; (4) when shrinkage in profits margins on sales is more than compensated for by increase in turnover; (5) when decline in turnover is more than compensated for by widening of net return margins on sales.

Nearly every phase of rationalization converges to promote increased turnover. Mechanization, flow production, mass output, cost-accounting, overhead costs—all emphasize increased turnover in production, and in wholesale and retail trade. Typically this is achieved by one or both of two policies; (1) concentrating demand upon a narrow range of highly standardized or typified commodities, and (2) increasing demand as far as possible. The most effective methods for achieving the former are education, conference, and promotion; the latter is advanced most rapidly by price decreases. The tendency is towards lower and lower price mark-ups over all costs, considered either as absolute amounts or as percentages. To the extent to which this is true, it means that price and cost fluctuations necessarily make the conduct of business more and more speculative. A small fluctuation in either price or cost, the other staying constant, or tendencies to converge or diverge, would make possible the reaping of enormous profits or the suffering of serious losses with any given output. Capitalistically conducted business enterprise necessarily becomes much more risky, much more uncertain.

Thus it would appear that considering this factor *alone,* the degree of security to workers and income certainty for owners of industrial equipment would sink with advance along rationalization lines.[26] Both trends would tend to steepen the gradients of change and to increase the amplitude (and perhaps shorten the duration) of cyclical fluctuations.

Following out this trail would lead one far afield. This is particularly true, since at the same time it would be necessary to trace and explain two other related facts of observation, namely, that the preponderance of evidence seems to indicate that the smaller establishments in most industries suffer relatively less than medium and small concerns from most cyclical fluctuations, and that there is fairly clear proof that price fluctuations are decreasing in violence, while the reverse is true for production. This latter point is especially important since it is change in production that mainly determines volume of full-time employment, and, by so doing, controls the larger portion of purchasing power available on the markets where mass-produced goods are sold. Such a shift, in other words, would tend to aggravate cyclical alterations, and its influence would serve to reinforce the tendency noted in the paragraph above. At the same time, it would seem to

[26] The labor side of this argument has been developed by Hero Moeller in "Rationalisierung und Arbeitslosigkeit," *Weltwirtschaftliches Archiv,* 34:387–422 (October, 1931).

be in conflict with the observed fact that the larger enterprises—*by implication* the ones most thoroughly "sold" on rationalization—appear to be less affected so far as net income is concerned by the extremes of cyclic oscillations.

In connection with these problems, the following observations appear to be relevant. *(a)* Hand in hand with the expansion of the rationalization movement has gone an increase (secular) in state ownership, regulation, and control of business enterprise. *Etatisme,* so widespread a phenomenon during and following the war in nearly every major industrial country, can be regarded as a development wholly unrelated to, or as one organically associated with the rationalization movement. If the conviction of the writer that the latter is the fact is correct,[27] then by this route rationalization may be said to have eliminated the profit motive from important segments of the German industrial system, and to have modified very seriously its importance in the conduct of all those sections of the business and industrial system where governmental forces have made their influence felt. Angell estimates that 12 to 15 per cent of the economic activity of all Germany is to be found in the hands of the various governments. This figure would amount to at least 20 per cent, if agriculture were excluded from the total.[28] Mendelsohn placed the total capital invested in German governmentally owned industrial properties to be between 50 and 53 billion Reichsmarks.[29] The total labor force employed is over 2,000,000, and constitutes about 11 per cent of all industrially occupied persons. Outright ownership, or control through ownership by the Reich and political subdivisions, includes the entire railroad, telephone, telegraph, and postal systems, between 65 and 80 per cent of all electric power, about 85 per cent of all gas, practically all water and sewage systems, the whole of the eleborate canal and waterways networks, about 50 per cent of all banking activity, and large operating units in coal and potash mining, street railway enterprises, and other fields of industrial activity.[30]

The policies of managerial decentralization and civil service regulation pursued in many of these governmentally owned systems—of which the most notable example is that of the *Reichsbahn*—have served rather to promote efficiency than to reemphasize profit motives. At the same time, governmental control over corporations and cartels, inadequate and ineffective as it has been in many cases, has promoted considerations of general social policy, the well-being of labor, and the national welfare to positions of importance in the councils of such groups. Had more attention been paid to the counsels of even the capitalistically minded "fathers" of German rationalization, von Moellendorf and Walther Rathenau, the rôle of profits as a determinant of corporate and industrial policies would

[27] This case is argued in Chap. XIV. [28] Angell, *op. cit.*, p. 245.

[29] Kurt Mendelsohn, "Die Wirtschaftsführung öffentlicher Betriebe," *Die Wirtschaftskurve,* Heft 3(1931):281–294. See also Hans Rietschl, *Gemeinwirtschaft und kapitalistische Marktwirtschaft* (Tübingen, 1931):125.

[30] Mendelsohn, *op. cit.*

have been still further reduced. Under the various Emergency Decrees of the Bruening administration, the government has shown its willingness to set aside (laissez faire) capitalistic rules of procedure in any and all branches of business when occasion requires.

(b) Parallel to and perhaps of even greater importance than *Etatisme,* has gone a shift in the location of effective policy-forming power from the owners to the management. This shift in part results from peculiarities of the rationalization movement, and in part from the growing importance of the corporate legal form among the larger concerns. Rationalization elevates the status of the expert, attempts on the personnel side to inculcate professional attitudes and points of view, attaches a great deal of importance to individual and group responsibility and initiative, and promotes formation of policies according to plan rather than as dictated by personal interest or individual caprice. Attempts to develop a high labor morale and to ward off the impending dangers of sabotage and bureaucracy by special incentives systems, systematic good-will propaganda and other methods, necessitate paying at least lip service to the notion that production is a collective enterprise in which labor and management share with the owners the rewards of success and the penalties of failure.

The corporate form, on the other hand, tends to lessen the control of the owners, and to narrow their interests in the conduct of the enterprise. Diffusion of ownership[31] is the essence of division of property claims into numerous small parcels carrying definitely limited rights. In practice the owners of small blocks of stocks rarely attempt to participate in, and usually take an almost completely passive attitude towards, the determination of corporate policy. So far as the run of the stockholders is concerned, interest is centered primarily upon dividend returns and opportunities for speculative profit through stock market operations.

The stockholders' interests, in other words, tend to be short run; the interests of management and personnel long run. Rationalization sharpens this dichotomy by promoting expansion in the size of the corporate unit. Typically such growth in size calls for larger supplies of investment capital, increase in the number of shareholders, and (at the same time) more effective concentration of ultimate managerial authority. Increase in size raises, as previously indicated, a whole series of managerial problems whose solutions call for plans based upon long-run considerations, and for use of incentives which definitely attach more of the supervisory personnel to the fortunes of the enterprise. Measures taken to achieve either object tend to increase the relative final discretionary power of management, and to reduce correspondingly that of stockholders. This is particulary true if at the same time ownership becomes more diffused.

[31] Diffusion does not mean "democratization" of ownership, as is sometimes supposed. It means that typically each holder of corporate rights has diversified his purchases so that he now possesses smaller ownership claims on more corporations. This is not "democratization."

Results of these drifts are to be seen in several directions. Management is typically interested in stabilized production and earnings. Not only does the enterprise run more smoothly under these conditions, but also management avoids a type of criticism during periods of depression which may, under appropriate circumstances, be sufficiently influential to bring about a change in staff. So far as management becomes a professional field, the whole point of view tends to become different. The entrepreneurial drive gives way to motives of workmanlike skill, security, and desire for orderly change. Hence, such efforts as are made within individual factory walls, and such pressure as is brought to bear upon trade associations and other cooperative systems, emanates largely from managerial ranks, not from the legal owners of the properties.

This is nowhere more apparent than in the attitude towards dividend payments. The managerial ranks have been mainly responsible for the various attempts made by large corporations to stabilize dividends. Now stabilization of dividend payments tends to eliminate windfall gains (or losses) to investors through stock market operations. Likewise it reduces the volume of such payments during periods of relatively active business, and increases them (over what they would otherwise be) during reverse periods. Since, despite increasing diffusion of ownership of the shares of any particular corporation, stocks are closely held by a very small class, the bulk of both windfall gains and ordinary dividends would not be currently consumed. The surplus would then either be poured into speculative channels—which is, generally speaking, bad from a cyclical point of view—or into further investment. This would mean, during periods of active business, increase in productive capacity after purchasing power had already declined relatively to the point where goods produced from existing plants could not be sold at the prevailing prices. Hence a policy which tended to eliminate windfall gains and the disbursement of unusually large profits during periods of active business should have a stabilizing effect.

Combined considerations of long-run corporate welfare and desire to be rid of stockholder control has led, however, to use of funds accumulated for purposes of further expansion. "Self-financing," now practiced by nearly all large corporations, when combined with long-range planning and conscious realization of the need to keep overhead expenses down to a minimum, should tend to increase the "plowing in of profits" during periods of off-peak activity. The effect here would tend to reinforce governmental efforts to mitigate cyclical fluctuations by recourse to long-range planning of public works.[32]

---

[32] Of course there is nothing to prevent management from (1) plowing in surplus earnings immediately, thus perhaps unduly expanding plant capacity at the wrong time, or (2) using funds accumulated for speculative purposes. It was because—apparently—both these policies were followed by American corporations in the period prior to 1929 that the panic on the exchanges which followed was of such unusual intensity. "Plowed in" undisbursed corporate income is commonly believed to be one of the most important sources of the widespread Kapitalfehlleitung (misplaced investment) and excess plant capacity in numerous German industries.

The corporate form in Germany, further, carries with it more rigid governmental control than does any other type of business organization. Many of the provisions governing corporate policies contained in the Weimar Constitution and subsequent enabling legislation show evidence of further dilution of profit motives in the manipulation of economic forces.[33] This is true even though their actual administration of the law appears typically to have been somewhat less rigid than the original lawmakers intended.

(c) Rationalization unquestionably implies modification of price and market competition. One need but point to developments commonly cited as examples of rationalization for proof of the widespread belief in Germany that this is the case. Among these are the "forced cartels" in coal, coke, lignite and potash, the unified railroad and communications networks, the rise of super-cartels, trade associations, cooperatives and communities of interest, the pooling of information in such organizations as those attached to the *RKW,* the rise of the *Erfa* groups, the expansion of horizontally and vertically organized combines in coal, steel, electrotechnical, textile, dyes and chemicals, shipping, potash, glass, banking, insurance, and other fields, the extension of effective control of the larger combines and cartels into the international field, and government encouragement (coupled with closer regulation) of the general combination movement.

Free competition and capitalism are not interchangeable terms. One relates to a state, and the other to a system of economic guidance and control. Nor is it possible to relate free competition directly to cyclical oscillations in a capitalistically organized world. Yet nearly all authorities agree that price and market competition sharpen cyclical oscillations in various ways, and that, under given circumstances,[34] its complete or partial elimination would at once do much to mitigate the severity of cyclic change and modify the capitalistic conduct of economic activity.

Price and market competition, for example, is responsible for the bidding up of prices during periods of active business beyond the point where the prices reflect ultimate demand as expressed in purchasing power available for this purpose in the hands of consumers. One result of such competitive bidding is placing of surplus orders in the expectation of being rationed in their fulfillment. The existence of such orders furnishes a false basis for expansion of firms receiving them, and an opportunity for subsequent cancellations in the event general busi-

---

[33] See Chap. XIV.

[34] This is an important reservation, for it is obvious that price fixation by cartels and combines without regard to purchasing power of the community, or the general conditions of domestic and foreign markets, although it most certainly limits and restricts competition, does at the same time tend to increase the structural maladjustments which bring on depression, and, once it has arrived, helps materially to prolong it. See, in particular, *The Course and Phases of the World Economic Depression* (published by the Secretariat of the League of Nations; Geneva, 1931):259–273. The same generalization holds for non-adjustable costs, such as cartel-controlled raw materials, or union-controlled wage scales, which exclude competition, but which are not, at the same time, correlated with other controls designed to aid general stability.

ness prospects have dimmed in the interval between placing and filling of requisitions. The net effect is to advance prices beyond the level justified by sales at one time, and to depress them unduly at a later date.

During periods of depression, competition is apt to take the "cut-throat" form, since excess plant capacity and high overhead costs mean that goods can be sold below cost to an advantage so long as variable expenses can be covered. While the net effect of such policies may be said to depress the market further, there is no particularly good reason for limiting "cut-throat" competition to such periods. In fact, one of the outstanding characteristics of the rationalization movement in Germany has been the existence of excess plant capacity in nearly every major industry. The constant threat of price wars has gnawed at the vitals of every German business man, and he has left little untried which promised discovery of ways and means for ridding business of this disease, without, at the same time, further compromising his own control over economic processes.

It is this phase of competition which has largely brought about most of the cartels, and given rise to the expression that cartels are "children of necessity." The danger has been not only domestic, but also international. In some form or other it touches nearly every product in every industry, and nearly every industry catering to domestic and foreign markets alike. For the same reason, however, nearly all the major combinations and communities of interest in Germany could be called "children of necessity."

One other aspect of competition is of particular interest in the present connection, namely, business secrecy. One of the main drives behind the whole combination movement, the principal justification for the *Erfa* groups, and the tacit assumption underlying the work of the various committees of the *RKW* is the notion that business secrecy and rationalization are necessarily antithetical. It is slowly becoming clear that business secrets, rule of thumb, technical backwardness, and industrial inefficiency usually, and in some cases necessarily, go hand in hand. To a very few writers and industrial leaders it is gradually becoming apparent that the attitudes underlying and the reasons fostering business secrecy are likewise those which promote exclusive patent rights, trade-marks, and competitive advertising.

The tendency towards monopoly—observable in nearly every phase of German economic activity—tends to snuff out competition completely or to transfer it into channels promoting rather than retarding systematic and efficient ordering of industry.[35] At the same time, monopoly or quasi-monopoly places upon the persons or groups exercising executive authority the necessity of making many decisions which, unavoidably, possess political, social, and cultural significance. The power which they possess over the lives of workmen, and the influence

[35] Much use is made of competition between individual workmen, gangs, shops, departments, factories wherever rationalization has been introduced. Such competition has found even more widespread use in the U. S. S. R. than in Germany or the United States. See Chap. XIII.

which they exercise over consumers' habits and in the councils of state turns directors into political potentates, and the enterprises which they dominate into separate principalities—states within a state. Whether they choose so to visualize the rôle which they occupy or not, directors of enterprises which are free in the main from the rules of play of the competitive system grapple with different situations, couch the terms in which they speak in an altered conceptual setting, and make decisions reaching out and affecting different layers of the population in different ways from those typical of the superseded order. Managerial policies relating to more problems must be formulated with an eye to reactions of more special interest groups, and must be carried out by specialists endowed with a sense for the humanly important imponderables. At least lip service must always be paid to "service to the consumer," the welfare and contentment of the employee, and the national well-being. The propaganda literature of the *RKW* and its special sub-committees, the various branches of the *Reichsverband der Deutschen Industrie,* and the various large corporations are so replete with these "theme songs" that one might almost be led to believe that the public welfare was the sole care of the business community standing behind rationalization.

Few readers will require a reminder that such is not the fact. German business leaders not talking for publication rarely resort to subterfuge. The primary object of rationalization in a capitalistic economy, whether under monopolistic or competitive conditions, is the making of profits. Yet the conditions under which profits are made have shifted, and the attainment of these where rationalization is in mind and monopoly prevails, calls for attention to details and policies looking towards variable factors in the current social and political setup, and outlined with regard to longer run considerations than formerly obtained. The shift in emphasis, while not revolutionary,[36] is certainly very important.

Emphasis has largely been placed, thus far, upon price stabilization, because prices, under prevailing conditions, are more easily stabilized than production, and price-controlling mechanisms are more easily established and regulated than output and efficiency control systems. Where monopoly or quasi-monopoly organizations are found in states committed to the pursuit of mercantilistic national policies, price control is the more easily obtained of the two. Such a situation exists in Germany. There cartels and trade associations, in addition to the large combines, have been able to stabilize prices more effectively than in any other capitalistically organized country.[37] Production control, on the other hand, has not met with any considerable measure of success.

[36] To the contrary see writings and speeches of Ford, Willard, Filene, Dennison, Köttgen, Werner von Siemens, Vögler, Walther Rathenau, and other industrial leaders. See in particular B. Josephy, "Die stabilisierenden Kräfte in der gegenwärtigen Wirtschaft," *Annalen der Betriebswirtschaft und Arbeitsforschung,* 4:427–465.

[37] According to the Institut für Konjunkturforschung, cartel prices in the post-war period have shown practically no fluctuation at all. See *Vierteljahreshefte zur Konjunkturforschung,* Heft 2, Teil A, pp. 62–63 (Berlin, 1930).

It is difficult to evaluate such increase in price rigidity. The League of Nations Report on the Course and Phases of the World Economic Depression[38] finds it to be a widespread phenomenon of the post-war period, but has difficulty in estimating its importance. Taken by itself—and price stabilization has in the main been unaccompanied by significant constructive measures in the production field[39]—price fixation does little more than merely transfer the burden of cyclic change to other shoulders. The more price control is limited to a narrow range of commodities, or to a small number of industrial groupings, the more this generalization holds.[40]

If price stabilization by "sectors" does more than transfer cyclical risks, its effect is probably to make the general instability characteristic of capitalism worse rather than better. While this cannot be statistically demonstrated in any given case, for obvious reasons, there exists ample theoretical justification for the generalization. Most important is the general rule that flexibility of the price system is absolutely indispensable to the competitive system; this rule carries with it the corollary that retreat from laissez faire must be orderly if it is not to be turned into a rout. The failure of the various stabilization measures aimed at price alone—Brazilian coffee valorization, Federal Farm Board, Stevenson rubber plan, world potash cartel, Copper Incorporated—show what happens when production is neglected.[41] Possession of monopolistic powers over internal markets, such as exercised by some of the larger German cartels, has not shown better results, however, on this account. Cartel prices have been held so high in some fields as to raise costs for other industries to the point where they are prohibitive. Fixed prices which affect ultimate consumers have raised costs of living as the general price level has fallen and as unemployment has increased. Meanwhile, the decline in volume of business experienced by some of the cartels has probably more than compensated for the gains achieved on account of the price-cost spread incident to price stabilization under such conditions. Whether or not this be the case, however, there is practically no descriptive evidence nor analytical proof capable of demonstrating that price stabilization in isolated businesses, for a narrow range

---

38 *Op. cit.*

39 Cartels, it is quite usually argued, have precisely the opposite emphasis—retardation of technical progress. How little of a positive character has been accomplished along rationalization lines is indicated by the scanty evidence used to back the claim of the cartels for public support because of their interest in technical progress. See, in particular, "Kartelle als Produktionsförderer," Nr. 4 (January, 1928), and "Produktionsförderung durch Kartelle," Nr. 5 (December, 1929), in *Schriften der Kartellstelle des Reichsverbandes der deutschen Industrie.*

40 See "The Course and Phases of the World Economic Depression," *op. cit.,* Dr. Alexander Mahr, "Monopolistische Preispolitik in der Depression," *Weltwirtschaftliches Archiv,* 35:386–418 (April, 1932), and Hansen, *op. cit.,* pp. 358–380. Exactly the same argument applies to uncoordinated and unplanned governmental intervention in the affairs of private enterprise. See Colm, *op. cit.*

41 Compare Dr. Max Lazard, "Le Paradoxe de l'Heure Présente—le Chômage en Plein Progrès Economique," *World Social Economic Planning,* 1:83–103.

no ideological applicat° of Sc Mgmt

of commodities, and unaccompanied by attempts at production control and employment stabilization, is capable of reducing either the severity or the frequency of cyclical fluctuations. The least that we can say safely is that all phases of the problem must be attacked at once, and with an eye to the same ultimate objective. Partial measures will never reach very far anyway; it is at least debatable that they do not always make the situation worse. At any rate, skepticism is justified so long as we are dealing with cartel price control.[42]

7. LONG-RANGE PLANNING

Limitations of space prevent consideration of other aspects of the bearing of rationalization upon cyclical fluctuations, for the above outline by no means exhausts the subject; it merely indicates a few of the more important aspects of the problem. An exhaustive treament of even these would require at least a volume, if not a whole library.

But in a very real sense the foregoing sketch merely begs the question. For if it is a part of the rationalization movement to eliminate cyclical fluctuations, then their occurrence is prima facie evidence of failure on this count, and nothing more need be said about it except to inscribe the epitaph. Business cycles have occurred in post-war German national economy, and the present depression has reached hitherto unplumbed depths. None of the measures described above, and none of the structural changes incident to the rationalization movement, seem to have been able to stem these tidal sweeps. It is not even certain that their combined influence has not served to hasten these breaks in the rhythm of national life, and to deepen and widen their negative influence once the change in direction has occurred.

It is more accurate, however, to say that in the main no serious attempts have been made in Germany to cope with the problem of business cycles as such. Rationalization emphasis has been largely technological, intra-plant, and intra-industry. It is only in these spheres that its many organizational features have received systematic analysis and application.

The period under review has been essentially transitional in character. In many branches the old competitive and unregulated capitalistic order has been definitely left behind, or so seriously modified in outline and in principle that it is fair to say that the Smithian system has been clearly abandoned. Yet the future is less certain for the changes that have been made, inevitable as these may have been from a historical point of view. The drift of events has presented to the Germans—as to most other capitalistically organized industrial countries—a problem which they appear unable to solve. They cannot turn back to the old

[42] Professor Bonn is most emphatic in his belief that cartels, in addition to being anti-rationalization and anti-efficiency, are likewise the promoters of technical stagnation and business disorganization. "The organizations (cartels) have not eliminated chaos, but have highly organized it."—*Das Schicksal des deutschen Kapitalismus,* pp. 73–95; 106.

order; yet they seem to lack the social philosophy, the singleness of purpose, and the will to take the next step.[43] Every development in the rationalization movement has called for more comprehensive and far-sighted social and economic planning; yet every year appears to have passed with a deepening confusion as to objectives and methods.

There is a certain truth in the contention that cyclical oscillations are merely temporary phenomena in an economic order where self-equilibrating forces can be said to lurk constantly in the background of economic change. In tampering with that order it is necessary that something be supplied in the place of these self-equilibrating forces, whatever they may have been. Otherwise, the situation must of necessity become worse when changes take place which would ordinarily be met by the system's capacity to heal itself.

Capitalistic economy has been called "unplanned," and indeed it is when considered as a whole. Yet the individual capitalistic cell—the business enterprise—has been characterized from the beginning by its systematic organization for the purpose of achieving a simple and clear-cut objective. It has, so to speak, been uniquely characterized by the dominance which planning has exercised in the conduct of its affairs. "In the last resort," Weber states, "the factor which produced capitalism is the rational permanent enterprise, rational accounting, rational technology and rational law, but again not these alone. Necessary complementary factors were the rational spirit, the rationalization of the conduct of life in general, and a rationalistic economic ethic.[44] In a similar mood, Sombart is thinking of the capitalistic economic order when he writes: "Rationalization is in thorough keeping with the trend of modern times; in it we have one of the most significant series of developments and tendencies of modern history. It is not necessary (in this connection) to point out that this rationalization trend is everywhere observable. It extends from the reaches of philosophy to the subject of shoe-blacking; in the most general and significant sense of the word, it is coterminous with *Intellectualization*. A German term has been fitly used to characterize this process, *Entzauberung der Welt,* (world disenchantment, disillusionment, secularization, 'sobering'). This great process of rationalization, in the midst of which we stand at the present time, is synonymous with this trend

---

[43] Professor Hansen writes: "Once human beings have set out on a certain course of economic evolution and development, it is not possible to turn back." Viewing the trends of the modern period he concludes, in summary: "On the whole the conclusion here reached is essentially a pessimistic one. A controlled economy is less flexible, less adaptable, less capable of finding adjustments to disturbing changes, than a free-market economy. *Yet we are moving in that direction.*" (Italics mine.)—*Op. cit.*, pp. 141 and 194. It seems to the writer that, without accepting the pessimistic conclusions of Professor Hansen, his summary must of necessity be the point of departure for all speculation about trends in the future. History is irreversible. It never repeats itself. The age of planning and control is here. The human race may bungle at this stage of development worse than ever before. But if so, bungle it will. There is no turning back—at least, not for many generations to come.

[44] Max Weber, *General Economic History,* (New York, 1927):354.

towards *Entzauberung der Welt*."[45] It is not lack of planning in the individual capitalistic enterprise against which Marx gathered evidence for his terrific attack upon the existing economic order, but rather the singleness of purpose and diabolical efficiency with which objectives laid down were pursued in these units.[46]

The system which has prevailed within individual enterprises has found its complete antithesis in the anarchy typical of the capitalistic world at large. "In detail .... economic activity is planned and directed with skill; but in the large there is neither general plan nor central direction .... coordination among independent enterprises cannot be said to be planned at all."[47] Yet, while we can accept the statement that, "So long as free enterprise prevails on a competitive basis, there cannot be a stable adjustment of supply to demand,"[48] we have small warrant—in view of the historical facts—for assuming that partial abandonment of economic anarchy would bring with it proportional relief from cyclic disturbances. Such measures as have been utilized in the past, and such as are being currently applied, have apparently not had the slightest favorable effect upon either the severity or the duration of business cycles. There are excellent reasons for holding that they have made the general situation considerably worse than it would have been had such attempts not been made at all.

At any rate, this much seems reasonably clear: the principal choice before the various industrial countries lies between comprehensive, far-sighted, and all-inclusive economic plans, and the constant risk of breakdown in the whole economic system. These plans call for regulation of production, distribution, markets, costs, finances, investments, expansion, and all the other related technological, commercial, social, and political factors of moment in the conduct of an integrated and coordinated economic system. Production plans must be accompanied by and coordinated with cost plans, financial plans, marketing plans, and control over distribution of wealth and income if the system is to be kept on even keel. Centralization of information, and the elaboration of the larger horizontally and vertically combined trusts have prepared the way in Germany for the production plans. The close tie-up which exists there between the larger enterprises and the equally highly centralized banking system have aided systematization of this side of the problem. The gradual seepage of government influence into various branches of industry is slowly preparing the ground for exercise of effective discretionary authority once public opinion has crystallized enough to lend force and direction to governmental policy. The weight of rationalization, exercised through cost factors and technological change, is almost entirely on one

[45] W. Sombart, *Die Rationalisierung in der Wirtschaft* (Düsseldorf, 1927):11. See also pp. 594–940 in *Das Wirtschaftsleben im Zeitalter des Hochkapitalismus,* by the same author.

[46] Both the Communist Manifesto and the famous chapter on "The General Law of Capitalist Accumulation" (Chap. XXV, *Kapital,* vol. 1) are in perfect agreement with the comments quoted from Weber and Sombart. The interpretation, however, is radically different.

[47] W. C. Mitchell, *Business Cycles: the Problem and its Setting* (New York, 1927):172.

[48] *Ibid.,* p. 156.

economic plans

side of the picture. Rationalization has sharpened the issues and perfected the machinery for social planning and control. In every case the advantages of the new techniques, when used in conformity with the lines of force which have brought them to the surface, are paralleled only by the disaster which they imply when directed to particularistic ends.

Thus the various changes wrought by rationalization and discussed in the preceding pages of this chapter can in nearly every case be found to worsen cyclic fluctuations, or, when woven into some comprehensive plan, to bear in exactly the opposite direction. There is a growing appreciation among German industrial and political leaders of the paradoxical position in this respect of the rationalization movement. Even a cursory examination of the tremendous volume of rationalization literature published during the period under review will show how definite the shift in opinion has become. Recent literature emphasizes more and more the necessity of dovetailing detailed rationalization measures into plans which embrace the entire national economy.

This shift in opinion has served to throw one major difficulty into sharp relief, namely, that Germany is not self-sufficient. In no way is she a self-contained economic unit. Unified plans, to be effective, must be international in scope. Here, consequently, lies the supreme paradox of the German rationalization movement. To be effective in salvaging the economic life of the country, rationalization must be carried out in the higher organizational sphere. But the unit of organization is larger in nearly every case—in nearly every respect—than Germany. Rationalization of production and marketing in such industries as coal, steel, lignite, potash, machines, electro-technical, transportation and communication should be Europe-wide at least.[49] Inter-industrial coordination and integration double the emphasis on this aspect of the problem. Yet it is precisely in the international sphere that rationalization has the least chance of successful application as long as European nationalism survives in its present form. If business cycles are thought of as functionally dependent upon capitalistic economic organization, it is also true that their elimination must be effected through measures whose field of application is as broad as the phenomenon itself. Measures applied on a national scale can be no more effective than the range of control. Germany cannot long remain a closed economic system; international action is thus far out of the question. There will be occasion to return shortly to the reasons for this latter situation, and the bearing of rationalization upon it.

---

[49] It cannot be too strongly emphasized that the rise of the "new mercantilism" is far more than a mere recrudescence of post-war "nationalism." It represents an attempt to control industry and trade by setting up a series of water-tight compartments simply because there is no other clear alternative to complete surrender to uncontrolled world production and price changes. See, in particular, Dr. Max Victor, "Das sogenannte Gesetz der abnehmenden Aussenhandelsbedeutung," *Weltwirtschaftliches Archiv,* 36:59–85, and the two monumental summary volumes of the Enquete Ausschuss dealing with foreign trade, "Der deutsche Aussenhandel unter der Einwirkung weltwirtschaftlicher Strukturwandlungen," (Berlin, 1932).

Taylore

CHAPTER XIII

THE ATTITUDE OF LABOR

I. RATIONALIZATION FOR WHAT PURPOSE?

"ALL EMPLOYEES should bear in mind that each shop exists, first, last, and all the time, for the purpose of paying dividends to its owners."[1] Thus the "father" of Scientific Management, and hence one of the recognized forebears of the rationalization movement, brought the philosophy of science in industry to its capitalistically significant focus. While labor might—and to Taylor's credit it must be added that he believed it should—gain from the new techniques through better wages, shorter hours, and improved working conditions, these must be made subsidiary to the main objective. Since to his mind reason and science were necessarily synonymous with justice and equality, and since labor organized only to protect itself from unjust treatment at the hands of employers, he held that introduction of Scientific Management would at the same time automatically provide the universal solvent for all industrial antagonisms. Strikes, lockouts, and labor unions would simply disappear. Except for chronic malcontents, universal peace and harmony would then prevail.[2]

The German employer's point of view has not departed very widely from Taylor's position. Rationalization to them is merely the industrial extension, perfection, and adaptation of scientific methods and points of view first heralded in the Scientific Management movement. As indicated in an earlier chapter,[3] there does not seem to be a great deal of confusion among employers as to the real objectives of rationalization. With few exceptions these can be summarized in a single word: profits. And, "if here and there social and ethical considerations appear as the basis for decisions and policies, so these must soon drop into the

[1] Frederick Winslow Taylor, *Shop Management* (New York and London, 1919):143.

[2] "There has never been a strike by men working under this system, although it has been applied at the Midvale Steel Works for the past ten years; and the steel business has proved during this period the most fruitful field for labor organizations and strikes. And this notwithstanding the fact that the Midvale Company has never prevented its men from joining any labor organization. All of the best men in the company saw clearly that the success of a labor organization meant the lowering of their wages in order that the inferior men might earn more, and, of course, could not be persuaded to join."—*Ibid.*, p. 183. Again, "The opportunity which each man should have of airing his mind freely, and having it out with his employers, is a safety valve; and if the superintendents are reasonable men, and listen and treat with respect what their men have to say, *there is absolutely no reason for labor unions and strikes.*" (Italics mine.) —*Ibid.*, p. 184.

[3] Chap. III.

background . . . . singly and solely to increase dividends should be the purpose of every larger measure, and consequently must be the basis for the rationalization of every enterprise."[4] As a Ruhr mine owner expressed it, rationalization "aims solely at the increase of productivity and profitability by the reduction of working costs, with prices remaining at the same level, or actually falling."[5]

If this be the position of the employers, then left-wing writers can scarcely be blamed for regarding rationalization as synonymous with capitalistic exploitation of the workers. The farther one travels to the left, the more explicit and emphatic the exploitation argument becomes. Thus a writer in the *Communist Labor Monthly* asserts that the "phenomenon itself is of ancient lineage. Rationalization in its broader sense means a redistribution of the total profits of capitalist society in favor of those sections carrying out the process of rationalization. Rationalization in its narrower sense means an increase in the rate of surplus value, and a decrease in the workers' share of the product."[6] Along the same line another writer holds rationalization to be ". . . . only a wholesale attempt by the capitalists to force all producers and consumers into a state of economic subservience, in order to be able to profit, at an ever-mounting rate, at their expense." And again, "Rationalization is the systematically and deliberately forced competition between machines made out of flesh and blood and machines made out of steel and iron, in order that the cumulating return shall fall singly and solely into the lap of the entrepreneur."[7]

The two extremes rest on common ground. Only the descriptive terms applied are different. Hence, to the Communist writers, capitalistic rationalization means a war to the finish. Triumph of capital means slavery for the workers, a new type of industrial feudalism, perhaps Fascism. Triumph of labor would mean, on the other hand, abolition of the capitalistic system.

Most of the organized German working class is non-Communist, and is therefore officially opposed to the Communist postion. The largest of the central trade union associations, the General Union of German Trade Unions (*Allgemeiner Deutscher Gewerkschaftsbund*—abbreviated *ADGB*) is unable, either through its own officials or through its political representatives in the Social Democratic Party, to cooperate with the Communist leadership. Yet, so far as the rationalization movement is concerned, the ultimate objectives of the two groups do not appear to be very far apart. The *ADGB* has always been a socialist organization. In detail and at large it is committed to permanent struggle with the capitalistic system. Ultimate success will crown its efforts only when capitalism has been

[4] R. v. Holzer, *Systematische Fabriksrationalisierung*, p. 1.

[5] Quoted by Walter Meakin, *The New Industrial Revolution*, p. 16.

[6] *Ibid.*, p. 14.

[7] Quoted by Julius Hirsch in "Rationalisierung und Arbeitslosigkeit," *Die Bedeutung der Rationalisierung für das deutsche Wirtschaftsleben* (published by the Berlin Chamber of Industry and Trade; Berlin, 1928):53.

abolished and the proletarian state has been established. According to Socialist theory, one of the principal features of such a state would be the universal application of scientific principles to all phases of production and distribution. That is to say, the *ADGB* would favor even more rationalization of industry than has already taken place in any economic order in which it possessed the power to dictate.

The same thing is true of the Communist position—despite the foregoing quotations—for the contexts from which these quotations are taken leave perfectly clear that emphasis in condemnation is upon *capitalism,* and not upon rationalization. If there be any doubt in the mind of readers on this score, conviction will come with perusal of details of the Five Year Plan in the U. S. S. R., or the arguments advanced by both the official and the unofficial Soviet press. In such books as those of Ermanski[8] and Grinko,[9] or the collected papers presented by the Soviet delegates at the International Congress of the History of Science and Technology held in London in the summer of 1931,[10] rationalization is raised to the level of a program capable of completely abolishing poverty and of assuring the enduring prosperity of a classless society.

The most important difference in the attitude of the two groups is that the *ADGB* workers are gradualists while the Communists are revolutionists. The latter believe that all attempts to cooperate with employers and the existing capitalistically controlled state are futile, and therefore that such efforts constitute betrayals of the working-class struggle for industrial freedom. The former believe it possible to wring concession after concession from capital, and in the process to prepare and educate the workers for intelligent control of the state which they can and will establish as soon as the educational program has had its effect upon the slowly crystallizing proletarian point of view. To them the Communists are scatter-brained folk whose haste slows progress and tends to confuse issues among the rank and file.

The *ADGB* and other meliorist labor union groups, however, have not always been consistent in their attitude towards rationalization. While the subject has given rise to an amazing quantity of written material in labor papers, journals, yearbooks, labor convention reports, and miscellaneous publications, it is difficult to show therefrom any consistent attitude towards any particular phase of the movement, or towards the movement as a whole. In any attempt at synthesis of opinion, one is faced at the outset with the fact that these unions have never developed an official policy on rationalization, nor have they at any time elaborated programs for incorporating rationalization into the mechanism of the

[8] J. Ermanski, *Wissenschaftliche Betriebsorganisation und Taylor-System* (Berlin, 1925), and *Theorie und Praxis der Rationalisierung* (Berlin, 1928).

[9] Grinko, *Der Fünfjahrplan der Sowjetunion* (Vienna and Berlin, 1930).

[10] *Science at the Cross Roads* (London, 1931).

state which they apparently believe they are about to establish.[11] For this reason the less radical labor unions have lost much ground to the Communists during the latter part of the period under review.

In a general way it can be said that the German trade unions were distinctly hostile to rationalization during the first two or three years after the stabilization. As conditions grew better and unemployment fell off, the attitude was modified to one of general approval, with reservations as to details. But, with the coming of the depression in 1929, opinion seems to have returned to the earlier position. As the depression continued the mood tended once more to become distinctly hostile. Yet with comparatively few exceptions the charges brought against rationalization have had to do not with the movement as such[12] but with its use for purposes of exploitation of the laboring class.[13] Rationalization that lightens and simplifies labor, increases its productivity, grants to labor a hand in manage-

[11] The nearest approach to such a labor program is to be found in an Austrian trade union publication, "Grundlagen und Richtlinien Gewerkschaftlicher Rationalisierungspolitik, Arbeitsergebnis des Ausschusses für gewerkschaftliche Rationalisierungspolitik der AFAB im Bunde der Industrieangestellten Oesterreichs," *Schriftenreihe des Bundes der Industrieangestellten Oesterreichs,* Heft 10 (Vienna, 1929). This publication, however, is so complete, is so frequently quoted in German trade-union literature, and so adequately expresses the German labor point of view that it can be freely used as a source book for the German as well as the Austrian labor attitude towards rationalization. Hereafter it will be referred to as "Grundlagen und Richtlinien."

[12] Thus a German trade unionist, Eggert, believes rationalization to be merely the "practical application of technical achievement and organizational knowledge to the labor process." "We recognize immediately," he argues, "that there is nothing fundamentally new in the concept of rationalization. Since men first accustomed themselves to construct their productive equipment with deliberate intent, they have striven towards discovery of new and better methods of work, towards their steady perfection, and towards a higher state of planned coordination in the economic world. This ambition of the human species to contrive instruments, equipment, and machines, to search into the secrets of nature, and to gather together and control natural energy in the service of economic progress, is to be found as a more or less powerful drive in every historical epoch."—Quoted by Elisabeth Schalldach, *Rationalisierungsmassnahmen der Nachinflationszeit im Urteil der deutschen freien Gewerkschaften* (Jena, 1930):17.

"In September, 1928, the Congress of the International Federation of Private Employees, held at Dresden, adopted a resolution on the question of 'rationalization and salaried employees,' stating that 'by increasing the output for human work, rationalization creates the conditions requisite for a rise in the standard of living of both manual workers and salaried employes.' "—Quoted in the *Social Aspects of Rationalisation* (publication of the International Labour Office, ser. B, No. 18:229 (Geneva, 1931).

[13] "Our objective is to influence technical progress and fight against the greater exploitation of labour through false methods of rationalization; to increase the consumption of the surplus products of industry by raising real wages; and to prevent the working class from being plunged into the miseries of unemployment, in consequence of the appropriation of the fruits of rationalization by the minority that controls the means of production."—*Idem,* quoted from the resolutions of the Fourth Congress of the International Federation of Factory Workers, held in Hanover, July, 1929. "The rationalization policy of the labor unionists must center around the attempt, by direct and indirect means, to influence the leadership of economic affairs so that the damages, caused by capitalistic rationalization or by omissions of socialized rationalization, to the physical, psychical, and moral personality and the economic and social status of individual workers and the class to which they belong, can be averted, and in their place substituted the greatest possible improvement in the [workers'] economic, hygienic, and cultural class conditions."—"Grundlagen und Richtlinien," *op. cit.,* p. 31

ment, shortens hours, increases wages and purchasing power, and betters the status of the workers has been approved almost without exception. But rationalization which supplants and renders superfluous large numbers of workmen, decreases security in the job, speeds up work routines, deprives labor of all initiative and personal incentives, renders labor repetitious and monotonous, lengthens the hours of work, increases mechanical hazards to life and limb, and generally speaking lowers the status of workers has been most vigorously opposed. The reaction varies with different phases of the movement, and with the methods and results flowing from their introduction.

2. ATTITUDE TOWARDS THE MORE PURELY TECHNOLOGICAL ASPECTS OF RATIONALIZATION

Mechanization which results in the use of machines for the performance of heavy and arduous labor has been enthusiastically endorsed. The machine in this rôle is viewed by German labor as the great emancipator, raising man from the status of servant and slave to that of overseer and master. Enthusiasm for mechanization which serves such purposes knows no bounds. The machine is seen to be the concrete and physical embodiment of science dragooned into the service of mankind; it liberates labor from its ancient bondage, multiplies its power a hundredfold, and makes possible the abolition of poverty and the enjoyment by the working masses of standards of living formerly vouchsafed only to princes and prelates.[14] The labor union attitude here is diametrically opposed to that of the founders of *DINTA,* who argue that Germany's wealth lies in men, not in capital goods or raw materials—of both of which she possesses a shortage as contrasted to the United States, France, and the U. S. S. R. For this reason, *DINTA* opposes further substitution of labor-saving devices as long as large numbers of men are available as cheap labor. The labor unions argue, on the contrary, that in many cases mechanization has not been carried far enough. The cartels are generally charged, for example, with deliberately attempting to slow up the rate of technical change.[15]

[14] Under capitalism, according to Marx, man is slave to the machine. Socialism, he held, must and will reverse the order. The Socialist and Communist unions in Germany both pay tribute to this idea. It is the theme that runs like a golden thread through all the literature on the Five Year Plan in Russia. "The prognosis of Marx and Engels rises more and more clearly, that of the passing of humanity from the reign of necessity into the reign of liberty, where not the machine nor the product governs the man, but the man governs the machine and the product. There is still a difficult road ahead, it will still require a good deal of struggle and many sacrifices, but there is no other way, and overcoming all the obstacles and difficulties, the human race will enter into this world of free and joyous labour by the aid of the subdued forces of nature and of its steel slaves—machines."—M. Rubinstein, *Science at the Cross Roads,* p. 24. The German trade unionists of all shades of opinion would find themselves in perfect agreement with this argument. See Schalldach, *op. cit.*

[15] Schalldach, *op. cit.,* pp. 54, 85–86.

The attitude is also uniformly friendly to attempts at bettering working conditions in general. In nearly all cases labor has actively cooperated to aid improvement of work places, stools and benches, arrangement of materials on work tables, protection from gears and other dangerous machine parts, elimination of dust and noise, better ventilation, heating, and lighting, and other similar changes.

Much skepticism, on the other hand, has been expressed on the Taylor system. *Taylorismus* was first opposed as a new method of capitalist exploitation, the effect of which would be to depress further the professional and economic status of the worker, and correspondingly expand the power of the master class.[16] But inability to prevent introduction of Taylor methods shortly led to reconsideration of the earlier position. Many held that it was possible to pull out the "poisonous teeth" carried by the monster imported from America, and to turn its powers of destruction into service of the common weal.[17] In this act the labor unions look for guidance from sympathetically conducted research in the physiology and psychology of work. Leipart, chairman of the *ADGB,* and a local representative from Dortmund are members of the managerial board of the Kaiser Wilhelm Institute for Labor Physiology *(Kaiser Wilhelm Institut für Arbeitsphysiologie)* located in Dortmund and presided over by the famous research specialist, Dr. Edgar Atzler.

Atzler has attempted substitution of more rigidly scientific and objective tests than those used by Taylor and his followers. The latter were primarily interested in analysis of work from the point of view of highest level of output. The result has been, laborers have argued, to speed up and overdrive workers to the point where fatigue tends to become cumulative, accidents due to the human equation increase, and premature old age becomes the rule instead of the exception.[18] Atzler has approached the subject from both sides. On the one side, work is analyzed with an eye to maximum economy of effort in the performance of

---

16 *Ibid.*, pp. 36–39.

17 ". . . . when the democratization of Germany assures the laboring class of sufficient economic influence, the objections (based upon the fears of laborers that not they, but the capitalist will reap the harvest of changed working methods) will not only disappear, but all rationalization possibilities, inclusive of those relating to human labor, will be changed into labor's greatest opportunities. . . . . From this point of view the Taylor system will gain a significance not yet sufficiently appreciated, namely, when it is in the hands of a democratized and well defined socialist state. . . . . In agreement with the National Ministry of Economics, I am of the opinion that the question of the Taylor system, in particular from the standpoint of the labor interests, requires testing."—National Minister of Labor, Bauer. Quoted in Schalldach, *op. cit.*, pp. 36–37.

18 It is conventional to classify accidents according as they are traceable to environmental factors not directly subject to workers' control, and as resulting from the human equation. In nearly all cases, the latter account for much the larger number. Yet examination of the facts leads to the conclusion that speeding up and fatigue account for much the larger portion of those accidents which are traceable to the human equation, and that, therefore, responsibility lies elsewhere. See pp. 346 ff.

various types of work. This involves time and motion studies, the use of special stop-watch methods of examining labor routines, and the breaking down of labor processes into their lowest possible units for representation in cyclographs and other ways. On the other side, methods have been worked out for testing the effects of various types of labor—heavy, repetitive, performed in various postures—lighting, ventilation, rest pauses, and other environmental factors in the performance of work, upon the nervous and muscular systems of various types of male and female workers.[19]

Gearing labor to performance levels such that fatigue does not become cumulative makes possible scientific labor according to the principle of "optimum" instead of "maximum" results. According to Ermanski and others,[20] the latter abstracts the ultimate effort from the labor; the former requires attention that the normal life cycle of each type of individual shall not be disturbed. Fatigue becomes cumulative whenever physiological tests show failure of anabolism to offset katabolism as indicated by amounts of carbon dioxide expelled from the lungs, blood and urine counts, and other criteria. The most efficient labor is that which, given proper physical environment and the most efficient machines and tools to work with, keeps energy output within the limits set by cumulative fatigue. Fatigue may also result from peripheral nerve and muscular weariness, or from strain on the central nervous system.[21]

Since fatigue from either physical or nervous sources, but in particular the latter, involves psychic factors, it is necessary that this work be tied up very closely with psycho-technical research. Münsterberg was the great pioneer in this field, and subsequent experimenters have never lost the original optimism which he possessed for the results of such research.[22] The work of Atzler, Moede, Kraepe-

---

[19] Both DINTA and the trade unionists, though from entirely different angles, have condemned Atzler and the Kaiser Wilhelm Institut für Arbeitsphysiologie for carrying out its work in an academic and unrealistic atmosphere. In most of the experimental work carried on in the Institut, only the crudest approximation is made to actual working conditions; in many cases no attempt to duplicate such conditions in the laboratory is made at all. Many of the Institut's publications constitute ponderous and labored adumbrations of the obvious; many of its experiments do not relate directly to the science of work; many of the most pressing and vital problems have not even been attacked. Precious little of immediate value to either labor or capital has thus far come from what appears on paper to have been highly significant experimentation.

[20] This is the basis of Ermanski's differentiation between scientific management under capitalism and socialism. See in particular pp. 1–71 in *Theorie und Praxis der Rationalisierung.*

[21] See in particular the *Handbuch Psychotechnischer Eignungsprüfungen* (1925), vol. 4, and "Anatomie und Physiologie der Arbeit," by Dr. Edgar Atzler and Dr. Gunther Lehman, of the *Handbuch der Arbeitswissenschaft,* 3, Teil I (1930), edited by Dr. Fritz Giese, Halle, and the collection of essays edited by F. Ludwig called "Der Mensch im Fabrikbetrieb," and published in the series, *Schriften der Arbeitsgemeinschaft deutscher Betriebsingenieure* (Berlin, 1930), vol. 3.

[22] "The economic experimental psychology offers no more inspiring idea than this adjustment of work and psyche by which mental dissatisfaction in the work, mental depression and discouragement, may be replaced in our social community by overflowing joy and perfect inner harmony."—Closing words in Hugo Münsterberg, *Psychology and Industrial Efficiency* (Boston and New York, 1913).

lin, and others has attracted a great deal of attention among the labor unions. Their attitude towards such scientific work appears to have been uniformly favorable. If anything, there has been a tendency to overestimate the advantages to labor and the community at large from the general application of psychotechnics to all labor processes.[23]

Psycho-technical work leads directly to attempts at scientific personnel selection and training. In so doing, it immediately loses much of its abstract and impersonal character, and becomes tied up with criteria for selection and methods of training which are distinctly unscientific, or, at least, definitely controversial. The employers have a tendency to scoff at attempts to apply to factory conditions the findings of experimenters working in specially equipped laboratories.[24] Laborers, on the other hand, complain that science is used as a guise under which to weed out radical workers and agitators, and to establish, as normal, standards of work which only unusual men can satisfy. The professional selection tests of the *Vereinigte Stahlwerke* were described as a species of "vivisection."[25] The railroad workers strenuously opposed introduction of psycho-technical tests by the *Reichsbahn* directorate.[26] Opposition to the new methods was so widespread among the workers that the directors of *Osram* finally set up a governing committee, with the function of supervising the tests, to which the workers were asked to appoint representatives.[27]

In general, however, it may be said that German labor no longer opposes even this aspect of Scientific Management where it is given a hand in the control of the methods used.[28] In theory it is now definitely committed to endorsement. In

[23] See Schalldach, *op. cit.*, p. 42.

[24] Even though Vögler, directing genius of the Vereinigte Stahlwerke, is a member of the directing staff of the Kaiser Wilhelm Institut für Arbeitsphysiologie, it is believed by employers that the work of the Institut has been unfriendly to their interests. DINTA, of which Vögler is also president, is especially critical of Atzler's work, and—it must be added—with good reason, for that organization is dedicated to building up a strong and employer-loyal staff of anti-union workers and directors. Atzler to them is a heretic; even some of the Communists approve him. What could be worse?

[25] *Metallarbeiterzeitung,* as quoted in Schalldach, *op. cit.*, p. 43.

[26] *Ibid.*, pp. 144–152.

[27] "Die Bedeutung der psychologischen Eignungsprüfung für die Angestellten," *Afa Bundes Zeitung,* Nr. 6 (June, 1929).

[28] Schalldach, *op. cit.*, p. 42. Labor cooperation with the Institut für Angewandte Psychologie, and its criticisms of the "Refakalkulation" (standards of the Reichsausschuss für Arbeitszeitermittlung, established by the Gesamtverband deutscher Metallindustrieller and the Arbeitsgemeinschaft deutscher Betriebsingenieure—Schalldach, pp. 44–45) and the Reichskuratorium für Wirtschaftlichkeit, show no indication of doubt concerning the value of psycho-technical work as such. Dr. Otto Suhr (*Die Arbeit,* 7:454–464 [July, 1930]) criticizes the RKW for ignoring the human equation—the effects of accelerated labor tempo, problems of fatigue and monotony, the matter of loss of craftsmanlike skill, etc. The RKW is accused of taking a patriarchal attitude towards labor; few of its committees have labor representatives, despite the fact that nearly all deal with problems which are of vital importance to labor. Meanwhile, the RKW has published the first volume of a work dealing with this phase of the subject, *Der Mensch und die Rationalisierung* (Jena, 1931). In general, labor appears thoroughly convinced of the usefulness of scientific management. See the first section of "The Social Aspects of Rationalisation" previously cited.

no place in the world, as a matter of fact, has psycho-technical research received such enthusiastic support as in the Soviet Union,[28a] where the conditions demanded by German labor would be considered ideal in this respect.

The reception given to flow, serial, and chain work—or *Fordismus*—has had a slightly different history. At first these methods were heralded as the real secret of the new economic wonder, America, where worker standards of living were higher than in any other country or during any previous epoch in human history.[29] Seventeen German trade union leaders made a trip to the United States in 1925 with the intention of looking more carefully into this aspect of the American scene. While their report[30] was tempered by many doubts as to the Ford mass-production system, Tarnow and others remained hopeful that Ford had shown the way to a new economic order, in which mass production was tied to high wages and mass consumption in a single and unbroken chain of cause and effect.[31] Others were able to endorse mechanization, while insisting that the chain work in the Ford plant drove workers at an inhuman pace, increased labor turnover, heightened the accident rate, and ruthlessly discarded the men as rapidly as it wore them down to the point where they could no longer keep up.[32]

These charges have been subsequently repeated in connection with introduction of such methods in various German industries. The effects of monotonous

[28a] Noteworthy are the following psycho-technical institutes located in Moscow: The Institute of Labor, The Institute for the Defense of Labor, and the special laboratories of the Transportation Trust. The Soviet plan for organizing such work in a Republic-wide network of specialized and generalized, but cooperative and integrated, laboratories dealing with every phase of the subject meets perfectly the complaint of Woldt that German efforts in the psycho-technical field are largely wasted because of lack of organization on a national scale. See Schalldach, *op. cit.*, p. 43.

[29] That level is by no means as high as is ordinarily believed by either European or American workers. Professor Hansen points out that, "Three factors of the highest significance are too frequently overlooked with respect to the so-called American standard of living: (1) the vast number of unskilled laborers working at low wages; (2) the low level of wages in the Southern States; (3) the lack in the United States of any social protection against sickness, unemployment, and old age." While, all factors included, "on the average, the purchasing power of wages is higher in America, *one cannot say that the standard of living is higher*."—Alvin Harvey Hansen, *Economic Stabilization in an Unbalanced World,* pp. 258–267.

[30] *Amerikareise deutscher Gewerkschaftsführer* (Berlin, 1926).

[31] "The center of gravity in the modern productive system lies in mass output, and the transition from unitary to serial manufacture is responsible for the wonder of unlimited development in productivity. This transition is not only socially, but even more technically conditioned; that is, even if capitalistic leadership desires no relations which bring it into dependence upon the purchasing power of the masses, it will nevertheless be compelled to do so by the coercive force of technical development. This is the new side of social class relationships, that alongside the dependence of wage labor on capital, there goes increasing dependence of capital on the labor consuming class."—F. Tarnow, *Warum Arm Sein?*, p. 70.

[32] Citations in Schalldach, p. 57. Fritz Kummer, a German worker who spent some time as an employee at the Ford plant in Detroit, speaks about the seamy side of the new economic wonder, but "Who cares about the victims? Detroit grows. In its hurry and speed there is no social side. It is the undisguised music of the capitalist spirit. But the directing spirits smile superior to their creations, the soaring skyscrapers."

and repetitive labor have been particularly emphasized, and the voluminous case records setting forth the complaints of labor on these counts are filled with weariness, despair, and disillusionment. "Eight hours long," writes a German female textile worker, "from seven o'clock in the morning to five-thirty in the evening, I stand fixed on the same place, the upper part of the body bent over and nearly motionless. Only the hands move, making forever the same motions—pressing the stamp on the goods, and the brain counts from one to twelve again and again, eight hours long."[33] Another writes, "My work is not so difficult, but it is so monotonous that it kills nerves. Year in and year out the same grasp of the hands without ever a change. This monotony cannot be overcome."[34] Literally thousands of such testimonials are strewn through labor literature, scarcely a magazine, yearbook, or brochure which does not offer some case material along this line. It is the picture of Sombart's depersonalized worker, caught in the network of a mechanically integrated, externally controlled, amoral, and humanly "soulless" factory system. In this view man has become the slave, a cog in the machine —"only a number to be thrown out like a piece of waste iron when he has been used up and no longer possesses value." Joy in work, workmanlike pride, a sense of human worth and dignity—these are taken from the job, and as routines are stepped up to a killing pace, nervous tension and slowly cumulating physical exhaustion make rest and relaxation impossible. The life cycle stretches out under a graying dawn, with weariness dogging the worker every day of his life, and despair serving as the only fitting partner of his misery. It is a picture not unlike, in many respects, those given by the Hammonds in their three memorable volumes on the beginning of the English factory system; a system which was made the center of Ruskin's smashing indictment of machine industry, and the withering attack of Marx and Engels on industrial capitalism.

Yet there is another side to the picture. It has been pointed out that many workers do not object to monotonous and repetitive labor at all. Some even prefer this type of work, and most laborers will put up with it so long as they are rewarded by higher wages or shorter hours, or both.[35] In a good many cases there is considerable doubt whether mechanization has increased the importance of

---

[33] From the story of one of the 150 female textile workers brought together in the volume, *Mein Arbeitstag—mein Wochenende* (Berlin, 1931). This volume created somewhat of a sensation when first published, being reviewed at some length in nearly all the important German periodicals and daily papers. See, for example, the very sympathetic review of Arthur Feiler, *Frankfurter Zeitung* (October 9, 1931).

[34] Dr. L. Imhof, "Arbeiterschaft und technischer Fortschritt," *Der deutsche Metallarbeiter* (May 11, 1929).

[35] "My work is truly monotonous. But I am satisfied with it, since I am happy at work." "Some monotony is to be found in nearly all factory work. I work, however, with joy and gusto, and then monotony disappears in the background." "I am satisfied with my work, when I make more money." "The work is not monotonous, because I work on a piece-rate basis, and therefore make more money." These, and many others like them, are cited by Imhof, *op. cit.*, among replies to a questionnaire on monotonous labor sent around by the Christlicher Metallarbeiterverband.

repetitive labor at all. Machinery typically takes over the heaviest and most monotonous jobs. Technical development has devised machines to tend machines where the element of personal judgment can be largely eliminated, and the possibilities in this direction have by no means been exhausted. Workers are thereby raised to the status of machine drivers and supervisors almost as often as they are shifted from skilled to unskilled classifications.[36] Even then, many jobs performed from time immemorial without the use of machines—digging ditches, cutting hay by hand, spinning, weaving, etc.—are so highly repetitive and standardized that it requires much more romance and ignorance than appreciation of hard facts to enlist sympathy in campaigns directed against their conquest by machines.

In the main, the attitude of German workers has been friendlier to *Fordismus* than to Scientific Management. If this new wonder-child of science possesses a seamy side, German labor holds that this is only because mass output has been directed solely in the service of an exploiting class. While occasional voices are raised against standardization, typification, mechanization, and flow or gang labor as such, on the whole the attitude is definitely favorable. These changes, in combination with concentration and the general enlistment of science in the service of industry, are regarded as preparatory steps in the social evolution whose end product is of necessity the socialist state.[37]

[36] In industries formerly requiring high levels of craftsmanlike skill the decline in skilled workers, as mechanization advances, has been most striking. Tarnow cites the following cases from the wood-turning industry: ". . . . in 1913 83 per cent of the workers in a Berlin furniture factory were skilled, in 1929 only 37 per cent; in a furniture plant in Brandenburg 92 per cent of the workers were skilled in 1913, in 1924 72 per cent, and in 1929 only 46 per cent; in a bedroom furniture factory located in Radeberg the percentage of skilled workers decreased from 59 in 1924 to 34 in 1929; in Eilenberg from 81 in 1913 to 35 in 1929; in a bedroom furniture factory in Stadthagen from 63 to 33; in a furniture factory in Olderburg from 50 to 27; in a small furniture factory in Finsterwalde from 61 to 13; in a Cologne kitchen furniture factory from 80 to 25."—Quoted in "Tatsachen und Probleme der Rationalisierung," *Gewerkschafts-zeitung* (December 20, 1930).

[37] To Taylorismus and Fordismus should be added "Fayolismus" and "Bataismus." Fayolismus represents for the German worker a type of high-class benevolent industrial feudalism. Worked out first in the French Commentry Collieries under the management of Fayol, this system adds to Fordismus an industrial paternalism, cemented to a flexible hierarchy of administration, which takes class status and the capitalistic system for granted. It appears to resemble DINTA, yet at the same time to be more generous and less "hard-boiled" than that organization. Bataismus, on the other hand, is the system worked out by Bata at his gigantic shoemaking plant at Zlin, Czechoslovakia. It attempts to make a "petit capitaliste" out of every worker by making him strictly accountable for every item chargeable to him, and for crediting him with every good or part of good produced. Individual and gang records are kept, and every attempt is made to induce in workers the sentiments and points of view, not only of general administrator and business man, but also of owner of resources and maker of profits. The system is distrusted as readily by all good trade unionists as Fayolismus.—There is a considerable literature dealing with both systems, and their application to various European industries. See various issues of the *Bulletin* of the International Management Institute, and, in particular, "Industrial and General Administration," by Henri Fayol, *op. cit.*, and "Working Conditions in a Rationalised Undertaking: The Bata System and its Social Consequences," *International Labour Review*, 21, Nos. 1 and 2 (January and February, 1930).

3. ATTITUDE TOWARDS INDUSTRIAL CONCENTRATION

Subscription to Marxian doctrine compels German trade unionists to endorse the concentration movement in industry, although it is also a part of the Marxian position that labor must bear the brunt of the burden which this transition entails for the non-capitalist class. "The labor unions," the German Metal Workers Union states, ". . . . do not oppose the conscious merging of similar industrial establishments, under the stress of technical progress, into concerns and super-state organization, since these are preparatory steps to the coming socialistic communal economy."[38] In principle such concentration merits all labor support.

But the birth of the new order finds no end of outcry from those compelled by their unfortunate status to suffer the pangs of delivery. The concentration movement is viewed as a struggle of giants for control of economic power in a system rapidly being liquidated by virtue of the corrosive influence of paradoxes inherent in it. According to socialist theory the "law of the jungle" has characterized capitalism from its inception. It pits man against man, machines against workers, centralized power against the individual, profits against life. It knows and cares nothing for human suffering; compassion is mixed with its policies to its eternal detriment. Hence, in this last Herculean struggle all scruples are thrown to the wind, and its ruthlessness knows no bounds.

Accusations against the concentration movement are particularly bitter on two counts. The first of these relates to the "closing down" (*Stillegung*) process involved in combination and technical reorganization. This process, as noted in the descriptive chapters, has been of particular importance in the coal, coke, potash, iron ore, iron, steel, and metal-working industries. The labor unions contend that speculative, not efficiency, motives are responsible for a large percentage of the closures. In many cases the way has been prepared for abandonment by deliberately manipulating accounts so as to show unprofitable exploitation.[39] In other cases such closures have been unaccompanied by effective measures for prevention of new expansions—opening of new pits, construction of new factories—when temporary market and price conditions permit.[40] Closure not infrequently

---

[38] Quoted by Schalldach, *op. cit.*, p. 131.

[39] Schalldach, p. 112. This general contention is particularly well brought out in labor union protests over the closing of certain mines, among which were the Alter Hase, Glückauf-Segen, Freie Vögel, Margarethe in Sölde, Rottenbach, Grube Rechlinghausen (state owned), and Johann Deimelsberg (state owned).—*Ibid.*, pp. 113–114.

[40] As Liefman, *op. cit.*, insists, few of the major combines enjoy real monopoly powers. While the Vereinigte Stahlwerke and the I. G. Fabenindustrie A. G. may be able to carry through systematic reorganization within the confines of the portions of the industries which they control, there is no guarantee that a favorable price and market development would not call into existence another mushroom crop of badly located and poorly equipped enterprises, which would later require elimination when circumstances required a new reorganization of the industry taken as a whole. The results of the quota struggles in the coal, steel, chemical, potash, and other industries organized along cartel lines are no more encouraging.

means permanent loss of valuable natural resources.[41] But most important is the effect upon the workers themselves. Establishments closed down in numerous localities mean not only loss of jobs to the workers, but also no opportunity for new employment without change of residence. Homes must be given up, new occupations found, and in some cases entire towns must be abandoned.[42] Workers are left stranded; savings of an entire lifetime, when invested in local property, must be lost. In some cases, notably those which affect miners, new jobs are found only with the greatest difficulty. The miner is highly specialized; he has learned how to do one very difficult and hazardous job. When this is gone he is left to shift for himself in a world where his low powers of adaptation place him at a marked disadvantage.[43]

The labor unions insist that the government take action designed to place upon any enterprise, or government department, the burden of proving why any particular plant or mine should be abandoned.[44] They feel that the government should see that books are properly kept, profitability correctly defined, the future of national resources taken care of, and that labor displaced by closures, if and when permitted, shall have its interests fully safeguarded. In no case should consideration of corporate strategy, and personal or group lust for power, be allowed to pauperize workers and impoverish entire communities.

The second major indictment is leveled against cartels. As previously indicated, labor pressure was behind the socialization laws which set up the governmentally controlled coal, lignite, coke, and potash cartels. They are largely responsible for the famous cartel law, established in 1923 (*Verordnung über den Missbrauch wirtschaftlicher Machtstellung*), and subsequent legislation increasing the rigidity of governmental control over cartels, combines, various legal entities of an economic character, and, in particular, for that portion of the regulatory laws relating to the corporation (*Aktiensgesellschaft*). Both the government

---

41 Mines extracting low-grade ores and coal, from thin seams, or under unfavorable geological conditions, once abandoned, are frequently lost for good. The costs of reopening them, pumping out the water, and competing with the hazards incident to prior exploitation of better seams above and below (as frequently happens) would be prohibitive under almost any degree of scarcity.

42 This problem was met in abandonment of certain ore workings in the Siegerland district, and in numerous places where potash and coal pits have been closed down. Some of the larger companies, notably the Vereinigte Stahlwerke, the I. G. Farbenindustrie A. G., and the Reichsbahn, assert that they have accompanied such closures by special aid to former employees, thereby transferring the risks of the change almost entirely to the companies in question. The writer has not been able to go into this matter very deeply.

43 This is given as one of the reasons why so few of the miners' sons are staying with the industry. The mine owners, in certain districts, have become quite alarmed by the situation.

44 See the proposal, quoted in Schalldach, *op. cit.*, pp. 110–111, of the labor unions for establishment of a regulatory body to handle such matters. The Prussian government, and the governmentally controlled Reichsbahn, have been accused of tactics as bad as those pursued by the privately controlled concerns.

and labor seem to have lost ground in the forced cartels.[45] Labor representatives in the councils of the various syndicates set up under these laws wield no real positive or negative power, little influence, and are completely ignored—in the final analysis—when all decisions of importance are made. But wherever they have possessed power there has been very little relaxation of the labor drive for closer governmental control in these and other fields.

The cartels are accused of holding prices high, of working to undo and break down the power of organized labor, and of holding back technical progress. High prices increase the cost of living; when held rigid, they decrease the flexibility of the economic system, and, generally speaking, they run counter to the universal tendency of rationalization to cheapen production and to lower prices. In increasing the cost of living they decrease the purchasing power of the masses, and make worse the dangers inherent in inability to sell the volume of goods produced on account of the existing bad distribution of income in capitalist society.[46]

Allied to the charges brought against the cartels and the policy of closing down "profitless" (*unrentabel*) plants,[47] is the contention that capitalist rationalization, whether accompanied by concentration or not, affects adversely only the rank and file of salaried and day laborers. A writer in the *Berliner Tageblatt* cites with approval the statement that, "while since 1880 the population of the United States has doubled, the professional class (excluding agriculture) has more than tripled, and the number engaged in managerial labors has increased seventeen-fold. Italiener writes,[48] 'The proportions in Germany are doubtless quite similar. It is especially true here, that the technical rationalization of great industrial concerns often appears to have created as a by-product an official hierarchy which nullified the savings obtained from the technical change,' "[49] Peter Grassman, a chairman of the *ADGB,* cites trustworthy sources to the effect that comparative material relating to 604 enterprises shows total increases between 1913 and 1926 of 499 high administrative officials (from 1,329 to 1,828), and 1,692 members of boards of directors (from 3,895 to 5,587). At the same time

[45] See, e.g., Stocking, *op. cit.,* Chap. VII, "The Triumph of Business Enterprise."

[46] See, e.g., the vigorous indictment of Bonn, in *Das Schicksal des deutschen Kapitalismus,* pp. 94–132. See also pp. 362 ff. Only limitations of space prevented inclusion of this subject in the previous chapter, where it rightly belongs. The labor unions, particularly those with more radical programs, have never deviated from the basic criticism, that all capitalistic rationalization has the ultimate effect of decreasing the relative size of labor income.

[47] Schalldach, *op. cit.,* p. 112.

[48] Dr. Robert Weiss, *Berliner Tageblatt* (May 17, 1927).

[49] *Ibid.,* quoted from an article by Karl Italiener in the *Zeitschrift der Gesellschaft für Organisation.*

workers and salaried employees decreased about 45 per cent in these companies.[50] The *Leipziger Neueste Nachrichten* found that ten Saxon companies required 20 managers and 50 board of director members in 1913; by 1926 these had increased to 30 and 74 respectively.[51]

The various reports of the *Enquete* Committee lend ample support to these labor union contentions. The summary volume finds that not only has the number of salaried employees, general administrators, and directing personnel increased for practically all branches of industry, and in particular for all the larger concerns, but also that the increases shown seem to be out of all proportion to the requirements of the various industries. The result has been a steady tendency towards bureaucratization of management, pauperization of the smaller proprietors (especially hand-work masters and farmers), and mounting costs. In summary it finds that, "In all branches of economic activity the investigation has shown that, beyond peradventure of a doubt, the increasing managerial labor has, throughout the post-war period, proportionately decreased the profitability of individual businesses, burdened the undertaking with mounting costs, and, through the increased expenditure for officials and managerial employees, decreased the 'wage fund' of laborers immediately engaged in the enterprises."[52] Nearly all expenses of a non-productive character have grown in proportion. More money is spent on lawyers, for promotion, for personnel hired to manage cartels, pooling agreements, trade association details, and so forth. The overhead for these latter purposes must be, in the aggregate, very great. For example, in 1930 there were no less than 1,476 national associations and 2,157 regional associations of business men in Germany.[53]

It is not the actual figures that are important, the unions argue. One may grant a certain amount of shifting between numbers of managerial and routine employees as an incident in rationalization. Nearly all the original studies by Taylor, for example, showed actual increase in supervisory personnel to be an inevitable

[50] Peter Grassman, "Warum Wirtschaftsdemokratie," *Wirtschaftsdienst,* 2:43 (January 14, 1927). The following figures, undoubtedly relating to the same group of concerns, are given by the A. F. A. *Bundeszeitung,* and are cited in the *Bulletin* of the International Management Institute (June, 1928). (The figures relate to "600 firms."):

Industries	Number of salaried employees to 100 wage earners		Number of leading executives to 100 wage earners	
	1913	1926	1913	1926
Iron and steel industries	8	10.6	0.8	1.5
Metal construction (bridges, etc.)	10	20.5	1.3	2.7
Shipbuilding	7	16.9	1.1	3.2
Rolling stock	7.7	12.9	0.9	1.8
Motor industry	9.9	18.2	....	....
Mechanical engineering	13.5	20.1	1.4	2.8
Wholesale distribution	....	....	9.2	19.0
Insurance	....	....	6.6	11.1
Paper industry and press	....	....	4.6	6.8
Transport	....	....	4.8	7.9

[51] Grassman, *op. cit.*

[52] E. A., *Gesamtbericht*, p. 69.

[53] *Ibid.*, p. 70.

accompaniment to the new methods. The development of rationalization has shown a similar movement, and there is no reason for supposing that purely engineering considerations would materially reverse the trend. Yet the organizational requirements of rationalized industry certainly do not justify increases of the order cited. These are to be traced—especially the ones relating to the higher managerial and directing staffs—in large part to the way in which, and the motives for which, concentration is brought about under capitalism. The unions charge that the usual provision for former owners and managers is to absorb them in the staffs of the new units, whether important posts exist for them to fill or not. If no posts exist for this purpose, they will either be created, or the dispossessed persons will be added to managerial and directing boards without functions other than the right to draw handsome salaries. Thus topheavy, bureaucratically-minded, and expensive[54] managerial groups are placed at the heads of enterprises formally combined with the object, among others, of reducing costs to a minimum. This de-rationalization, however, is but part and parcel of the general policy or policies leading to misuse of capital funds, overinvestment in various fields, duplication of facilities, and allied shortcomings of an economic order which has already outlived its usefulness. German labor believes that reversal of these trends can only come with a socialist state and a planned economy.

4. WAGES AND HOURS

The study made by the International Labour Office on the relationships between rationalization and wages is fairly exhaustive.[55] It demonstrates that on a *case basis* increased productivity in rationalized undertakings is nearly always accompanied by wage-rate advancement. This is true whether one has in mind the measures relating to the more purely technological side of rationalization, or those affecting personnel directly—selection and training of workers, working methods, methods of remuneration, incentive systems, and other like measures. Thus, for example, all the various systems of remuneration—Halsey, Bedaux, Piece Wages, Rowan, Taylor "differential piece rates," Gantt, Emerson, 100 per cent premium, group bonus—show parallel improvements in productivity and wage payments to the workers.

---

[54] "The Director of the Steel Works Association (Stahlwerksverband) receives 180,000 marks per year, of the Pipe and Tubing Association (Röhrenverband) 110,000 marks per year; every inactive titular director (stellvertretende Titulardirektor) 75,000 marks per year. Every member of the Board of Directors of the Dye Trust received 38,000 marks during the past year; in the case of the Wintershall-Konzern they received from 10,000 to 20,000 marks each. These sums take on greater significance when they are compared with the total wage and salaried payments. Sixty salaried employees in a South German industrial establishment receive a total of 144,000 marks; the three directors 150,000 plus 144,000 marks in royalties. Twenty-four employees in an Augsburg establishment receive a total of 57,000 marks, the one director 60,000 marks."—Data taken from the *Leipziger Neueste Nachrichten,* and cited in Schalldach, *op. cit.,* pp. 165–166.

[55] *The Social Aspects of Rationalisation,* Part III, pp. 157–230.

Taking the period under review as a whole, there seems likewise no reason for questioning the usual conclusion that nominal (i.e., tariff) wages and wages actually paid increased steadily up to the time of the depression. This is shown by studies of wage rates contained in the various volumes of the *Enquete* Committee reports,[56] by data gathered and analyzed by the *Institut für Konjunkturforschung,* and by various special studies made by various persons and institutes. So far as changes in wage rates during this period can be traced to rationalization, the conclusion is fully justified: rationalization has as one of its typical results increase in nominal wages.

But with this statement agreement ceases. Employers are wont to argue that labor-union pressure, coupled with governmental regulation of wage terms and conditions favorable to labor, has brought production costs to the point where reorganization involving large expenditure for labor-saving devices has been absolutely necessary. There is usually implied in this argument, if not frankly alleged, that such pressure gave to labor a larger distributive share in the total proceeds of industry. As productivity increased this trend would necessarily mean further advance in real wages until the point was reached where further labor-saving substitutions would have to be made. Labor is thus accused of "muscling in" at the same time that its tactics provide one of the important causal factors leading to rationalization.

While willing to take a certain amount of credit for initiating rationalization, German labor unions are emphatic in their denial that they receive the gains attributed to them by the employers. They insist that the employers have intentionally confused the real issues in two ways; first, by not discriminating between nominal and real wages, and second, by not differentiating between wage rates and annual earnings. When these factors are taken into consideration it is doubtful whether labor has really gained anything substantial from rationalization.

The mass of literature on this controversial subject leaves the facts in doubt. Since comprehensive and satisfactory statistical materials are not to be had it is impossible for even the expert to strike a balance. As usual, even where statistics are concerned, there are plenty of facts to go around. Careful selection of materials will prove either case to the satisfaction of respective proponents, and still leave a plentiful supply of unused facts so that independent investigators may "rigidly" prove their respective theses to their hearts' desire.

In support of the thesis that capitalistic rationalization means systematic exploitation of workers at accelerated speeds, left-wing writers adduce evidence to prove that the movement has had that necessary effect. The most telling case along this line has been developed by Jürgen and Marguerite Kuczynski[57] in a

[56] A typical statement: "Dr. Vögler, Chairman of the Board of Directors of the United Steel Works, states that the average monthly wage rose from 160 marks in April, 1925, to 231 marks in May, 1927."—*Ibid.,* p. 184.

[57] Referred to by the Communist press as "bourgeois."—See *Rationalisierung und Wirtschaftskrise* (Berlin):16.

statistical study of conditions of German industrial workers.[58] In order better to evaluate the wage status of various classes of industrial labor they make a number of statistical corrections in the official data given out by the government. First among these are corrections for amount of time lost per annum through full-time and part-time unemployment, expressed as percentages of trade union membership. Tariff (officially established) wages are then revised by additions for extra hours, special wage concessions, etc., and this sum is then checked for labor losses resulting from payments made by labor for social burdens and taxes. The residual is then divided through by the official cost-of-living index used by the government. Although the cost-of-living index is held to be much too low—and therefore tends to show higher real wages than the facts justify[59]—the final results show a decrease in real wages since 1924 in nearly all cases. The summary table for all classes of labor is as follows:[60]

REAL WAGES, 1913–1914 AND 1924–1930 (1927 = 100)

Year	Index of labor income (1)	Index of cost of living (2)	Index of real wages (1÷2)
1913–1914	69.3	67.8	102.3
1924	65.4	86.5	75.6
1925	87.7	94.7	92.6
1926	83.6	95.7	87.4
1927	100.0	100.0	100.0
1928	105.2	102.8	102.4
1929	104.0	104.2	99.8
1930	91.1	99.8	91.3

When the purchasing power of industrial workers is set off against per capita (consumer) production, one obtains a picture of the relative standing of labor. Using 1913–1914 as a basis, the authors find the index number of labor's relative standing (secured by dividing an index of labor purchasing-power by an index of per capita production) to be 59 in 1924, 72 in 1925, 76 in 1926, 74 in 1927,

[58] *Die Lage des deutschen Industrie-Arbeiters* (Berlin, 1931).

[59] The government cost-of-living index is criticized on two grounds. First, it is held to be inaccurate. Foodstuffs are weighted about 55 per cent of the total, a weighting which, it is held, would be valid only for Chinese coolies and primitive peoples. The foodstuffs are in turn very heavily weighted by cheap commodities like bread and potatoes; very little weight is put on vegetables, and none on fruit. Educational and recreational needs are almost entirely ignored. In the second place, the index is criticized as an example of class ideology, items being excluded which are permitted to landlords and dividend clippers, but not to labor.—*Ibid.*, pp. 18, 25.

[60] *Ibid.*, p. 19.

67 in 1928, 69 in 1929, and 76 in 1930.[61] Thus the conclusion is reached that taking the last seven years as an average, labor has been pauperized about 30 per cent.[62]

With the general tenor of this argument the regular trade unions appear to be in agreement. Without subscribing to the Communist argument that the interests of capital and labor are necessarily antipathetic in all cases, it is usually held that labor gains have either been comparatively small or actually non-existent. Thus a writer in *Vorwärts*[63] cites as typical of capitalistic rationalization a case in which, despite nominal increases in wages paid to workers remaining on the staff, total wage disbursements declined by nearly one-half while prices of finished products remained about the same.[64] To workers as a class, decrease in employment would rarely make up for any increase in rates paid to those remaining. Consequently, analysis shows that "previously employers have used rationalization only against the workers. The entrepreneurs use their positions as controllers of the means of production to sharpen the class struggle. . . . ." In this view labor will only gain its due and be avenged for its sufferings when it rises, embittered, in mass revolt against the poverty that has been imposed upon it.[65]

It is still more difficult to evaluate labor's charge that rationalization has resulted in the reaping of enormous profits by the owners of productive equipment. Dividends are notoriously unreliable as an index of profitability. Stated return upon invested capital, whether disbursed or not, is not much better. The unions charge that many of the large concerns are overcapitalized, that large sums of money have been paid (and charged as a cost) for plants subsequently closed down, that depreciation and maintenance charges have been unduly high, that salaries paid to the higher managerial staff and the inactive directorates have been exorbitant,[66] that prices have been arbitrarily fixed at unjustifiably high levels, and that mismanagement of capital funds has been widespread and scandalously close to graft and peculation in many cases.

---

[61] *Ibid.*, p. 20.

[62] *Ibid.*, p. 25. Which leads them to the conclusion: "Perhaps at no time in its history has the German industrial worker been impoverished relatively and absolutely with such rapidity and to such an extent as during the period 1913–1914 to date, 1930. This tempo of pauperization, however, is not an isolated phenomenon, but is a portion of a process which will not cease until Socialism has taken the place of Capitalism."

[63] Official organ of the Social Democratic Party; hence the mouthpiece of the ADGB.

[64] "Rationalisierung und Arbeitslohn, Warum die Rationalisierung nicht neue Arbeitsmöglichkeiten schafft," *Vorwärts* (July 28, 1926).

[65] *Ibid.* The index numbers of real wages for German skilled and unskilled workers, given by the International Labour Office in the study previously cited, show, with 1927–1929 as base, increases for the former from 88.0 in April, 1925, to 109.9 in September, 1930; for the latter, the corresponding figures are 86.5 and 110.4. These data, however, are based on "Weekly Earnings, According to Collective Agreements," and are deflated by the use of the above-mentioned cost-of-living index, and therefore do not meet the objections of the Kuczynskis.—*Social Aspects of Rationalisation, op. cit.*, p. 205.

[66] See p. 352, this chapter.

That profits have been high among some of the larger companies is undeniable, even though dividend declarations cannot be made to show it.[67] Others have not fared so well. In general it would appear that those concerns and those industries which have been most thoroughly overhauled and vitally affected by the rationalization movement were not very prosperous at the beginning of the period under review.[68] Rationalization in most cases involved large capital investments which could be (capitalistically) justified only on the ground that the alterations made would insure profitability in the future. The measures taken were beginning to show results in corporate balances before the depression began in 1928–1929. After the latter date the picture is less clear, and serious doubts are once more expressed as to the value of the whole preceding rationalization movement. During the period of rationalization itself, expenditures for the changes made were so great that net returns, on the average, were apparently not very large.[69] A great deal depends, of course, upon whether payments made out of current receipts—although such payments constituted only a small percentage of the total capital required for the changes made—can be considered as legitimate costs, and not as "plowed in" profits. At any rate, it would appear that the labor contention has significance primarily when related to prospective profits. The companies which had rationalized their plants and administrative systems were prepared to reap handsome returns from the changes that had been made, and probably would have been successful in their endeavors had the depression not occurred.

[67] The following data on dividends of various large corporations previously mentioned may be taken as typical:*

Company	1924	1925	1926	1927	1928	1929
Vereinigte Stahlwerke A. G.	....	....	3	6	6	6
Fried. Krupp A. G.	0	0	0	0	0	0
I. G. Farbenindustrie A. G.	....	10	10	12	12	12
Oberschlesische Kokswerke & Chemische A. G.	6	0	0	6	7	8
Kali-Chemie A. G.	....	5	5	5	7	9
Allgemeine Elektrizitäts-Gesellschaft	6	7	8	8	9	....
Siemens & Halske A. G.	6	10	12	14	14	....
Siemens-Schuckertwerke A. G.	6	8½	9	10	10	....
Rheinisch-Westfälisches Electrizitätswerk	12	12	15	9	10	10
Elektrowerke A. G.	7	8	8	8	8	8
Wintershall A. G.	0	12	12	12	12	12

* Source: various publications, previously cited, of *Das Spezial Archiv.* Note: When the data refer to fiscal years, then they are entered under the latter of the two calendar years noted. In all the entries they are given for common stock only.

[68] Previous dividend declarations do not show this. But reserves had been depleted, plants were technically obsolete, and the beginning of foreign competition, after stabilization of the currency, showed the position of many of the larger concerns to be dangerously close to bankruptcy. Witness the crash of the spectacular Stinnes combine.

[69] This is shown, as far as dividends are concerned, by comparison between the declarations of the larger concerns and the run of corporations in all lines of business activity. Thus, out of 7,586 corporations operating in all fields, 2,753 declared dividends in the fiscal year 1928–1929, with an average of 6.3 per cent return on invested capital. For the following fiscal year, despite the depression, the comparative figures were 2,428 and 5.8 per cent—*Berliner Tageblatt* (March 7, 1931).

This general conclusion, however, does not refute the charges made by the labor unions. These related in the main to specific changes made in specific plants, at definite times, and maintained that each change as it occurred tended to redound primarily to the advantage of the employer. As cumulated, labor believed that the more important differential gains must have accrued to the capitalist class. Support has been given to this contention by statistical data, such as cited above, showing that labor gains have not kept up with increase in productivity,[70] and by numerous theoretical considerations. Most important among the latter is the notion commonly held in all labor-union camps that, aside from the characteristics of the capitalist system itself, the depression was brought about by shortage of purchasing power in the masses of the people.[71]

The labor-union solution has been simple and to the point: rationalization must increase efficiency, and at the same time increase the purchasing power in the hands of workers who buy the goods produced by rationalized plants. Otherwise the circle of production, distribution, and consumption is broken, and stoppage is the inevitable result. It makes no particular difference in the long run how the desired change is brought about. If prices fall as efficiency increases, all consumers gain alike. If wages rise as rationalization develops, prices being held constant, a differential gain is scored by those affected by the wage advancement. The smaller and more individualistically inclined labor unions favor the latter policy. There is a tendency, however, to insist that both wage increase and price reduction should go hand in hand as rationalization develops, although it is generally felt that labor influence on the former is much greater than on the latter.[72]

Reduction in working hours through rationalization is always claimed as the laborers' right. Whether taken as cause, effect, or coincidence, the two have gone together, as shown in table 32 (p. 346) by *ADGB* estimates of percentages of its membership working 48 hours or less at different times since 1923.[73]

Acceleration of and improvement in working processes opens up unlimited possibilities here. The labor program is clear: the eight-hour day is not to be taken as the objective. A seven-hour or even shorter working day[74] is altogether

[70] None of the statistical data is above question. On the whole, however, there seems to be fairly clear evidence that wages lagged behind productivity from 1925 to 1928—in the sense indicated above—not only in Germany, but in nearly every major industrial country.

[71] Woytinski estimated productivity to have increased by 11 per cent and real wages by 8–9 per cent from 1927 to 1929. Had wages increased by 11 per cent the main cause of the depression would have been eliminated, he feels.—*Gewerkschaftszeitung* (March 1, 1930).

[72] Schalldach, *op. cit.*, pp. 26, 76–78. See also "Grundlagen und Richtlinien," *op. cit.*, pp. 234–251.

[73] Quoted from the *Jahrbuch* of the ADGB, p. 221, by Jürgen and Marguerite Kuczynski, *op. cit.*, p. 27. See in particular the summary in *Enquete Ausschuss*, "Die Ergebnisse der Arbeiten des Arbeitsleistungsausschusses."

[74] A few of the more hopeful writers are inclined to look forward to four- and five-hour days as genuine possibilities when rationalization has been systematically introduced in all phases of industry and then socially tamed. Charles P. Steinmetz has argued this case in the United States. See his book, *America and the New Epoch*.

possible, and should be incorporated into the platform of labor's program for rationalized industry.[75] This change is felt to be necessary not only because it frees labor from the rigors of its age-old bondage to the necessity of making a living by long working hours, but also because the new labor tempos and the accelerated pace of work are physically and nervously exhausting and therefore require compensation in shorter hours.[76]

TABLE 32

Time	Percentage working 48 hours or less	Percentage working over 48 hours
3–8 November, 1924	50	50
25–30 April, 1927	49½	50½
24–29 October, 1927	56½	43½
1–6 October, 1928	70	30
10–15 February, 1930	77½	22½

At the same time, the unions have demanded abolition of extra-time work so long as thousands of men and women are unemployed. Extra hours are apt to exhaust workers prematurely, while they prevent other men from receiving incomes so long as labor is a drug on the market. Unemployment is properly regarded as a type of enforced leisure which is wasteful of productive power, and therefore irreconcilable with rationalization except in a strictly profits economy.

5. HAZARDS TO LIFE, LIMB, AND WORKING TENURE

Labor expressions of opinion on these problems have been particularly outspoken, critical, and bitter. Mechanization and speeding of work routines are held to have increased fatal, major, and minor accidents and the number of persons suffering from industrial diseases. It is asserted that speeds are adjusted without regard to cumulative fatigue, and that the killing pace which workers must keep shortens their life cycles and throws them into the discard at an early age. Rationalization has rendered much work monotonous, repetitive, and deadening to all sense of craftsmanlike skill, and joy in work and living. At the same time it has undermined all remaining sense of security in the job. Not only may reorganization throw countless numbers of men on the streets without warning, but rationalization eats like a subtle poison at the foundations of professional status. A technical change may almost at a moment's notice destroy the economic

[75] "According to my point of view, the eight-hour day and the forty-eight hour week are not to be taken as the lowest limits of labor time in a rationalized economic system."—Quoted from Eggert by Schalldach, *op. cit.*, p. 26.

[76] *Idem.*

justification for any particular skill or professional occupation. It has done this so frequently, and in many cases so unexpectedly, that no man can be certain that technology will not find a way of reducing him to the status of an unskilled and low-paid workman.

Needless to say, enthusiastic proponents of rationalization as it has occurred take the categorically opposite position. To cases that are cited by labor in support of its various criticisms, similar cases are cited in proof of exactly the opposite conclusions. Statistics are freely used to buttress the respective cases.

Without attempting to pass judgment on these issues, a few of the statistics adduced by radical writers may be of interest. Jürgen and Marguerite Kuczynski appear to have gone into this matter much more systematically than other left-wing authorities. On the basis of data given out by the National Ministry of Economics on accidents per thousand full-time workers, they have computed the accident rates, given in table 33, for workers coming under the Professional (Liability) Insurance Association:[77]

TABLE 33

Year	Injured per hundred	Compensated per thousand	Killed per ten thousand	Output per worker (1924=100)*
1924	6	5	5	100
1925	7	6	5	116
1926	9	7	6	125
1927	10	6	5	133
1928	10	7	5	132
1929	10	7	5	140

* Jürgen Kuczynski, "Die Unfall-Häufigkeit," *Finanzpolitische Korrespondenz* (January 16, 1931), Jahrgang XII, No. 2.

Thus, according to this reckoning,[78] injuries reported have steadily increased as output per worker, indicating greater productivity through rationalization, has risen. The 1929 rate is regarded as particularly alarming. Jürgen Kuczynski, in another connection, has estimated the number of times workers would be injured in an active lifetime of forty years, if available figures were applied to the rates reported by the various special Liability Insurance Associations for 1929.[79] These estimates are given in table 34 (p. 348).

At this rate, roughly 55 per cent of the first two, 50 per cent of the third, and 45 per cent of the remaining classes would be severely injured at some time in the 40 years. While this rate may be unusually high—the figures relate to 1.8

[77] Jürgen and Marguerite Kuczynski, *op. cit.*, p. 32.

[78] Part of this increase may result from inclusion of types of accidents formerly not reported.

[79] *Ibid.*

TABLE 34

Liability insurance group (Berufsgenossenschaften)	Number of accidents reported per 100 workers in 1929	Number of times a worker would be injured at the 1929 rate in 40 years of active work *
Excavation and construction engineering..	24	10
Mining	20	8
Quarrying	19	8
Brewing	19	8
Building industry (Bavaria)	17	7
Iron and steel industry (Silesia)	17	7
Iron and steel industry (South Germany)..	16	6
Vehicular repair	15	6

* These accidents are said to be "severe" because they result in partial inactivity, or compel change or loss of professions.—*Idem.*

million workers and therefore are not representative of all industry—they afford some insight into the labor case against rationalization and large-scale industry. The figures adduced for fatal accidents are even more gruesome. Kuczynski estimated that within a period of 40 years of professional life the following percentage of all persons employed would be fatally injured for the specified industries:[80]

Ocean shipping	about 9
Internal water transport (western Germany)	about 8
Shipping on the Elbe	about 8
Mining	about 7
Internal water transport (eastern Germany)	about 6
Industrial vehicular repair	about 5
Quarrying	about 5
Excavation and construction engineering	about 4

Data from various sources might be used to check these figures. Aside from the official source materials, which are themselves subject to interpretation,[81] most such data refer either to special industries or special districts or plants. The *Enquete* Reports have taken up the matter in numerous of their special industry studies. While in nearly all cases accident rates have increased since the pre-war period, in the main their data do not show any very decided changes during the

80 *Idem.* He concludes: "These fatal accident rates are truly monstrous. Of every eleven young men who go to sea, one will lose his life. Of fifteen young workers first entering a mine, one will meet with the misfortune of fatal accident. Of twenty-five apprentices in excavation and construction engineering, one will be struck down by accident."

81 The data given by both industrial and professional classifications in the *Statistisches Jahrbuch* show, in nearly all cases, increases in accident rates between 1927 and 1928. Estimates for 1929 are still higher. In all cases the post-war figures are much larger than those for 1913.

post-war period.[82] Increase in accidents as shown in the case of the chemical industry from 1921 to 1927 cannot be said to possess particular significance, since the period is altogether too short to justify generalizations as to trends.[83] Nor can much confidence be placed in broad conclusions drawn from such data as adduced by specialists to show that fatal accidents in the Dortmund coal area have decreased from 1,144 in 1920 to 800 in 1927,[84] or those adduced by the trade unionist, Olk, for various mining concerns.[85] The former show one trend, the latter another.

The very fact, however, that improvement along this line is so hard to show offers considerable support for the labor-union contention that this side of the rationalization movement has not received the attention it deserves. With the exception of the very interesting work of the Union of German Professional (Liability) Insurance Associations *(Verband der Deutschen Berufsgenossenschaften)*,[86] accident prevention has played a relatively minor rôle in rationalization. Certain of the scientific societies, such as the German Society for Industrial Hygiene *(Deutsche-Gesellschaft für Gewerbehygiene)* and the German Technical Lighting Society *(Deutsche Beleuchtungstechnische-Gesellschaft)*, have done useful work. Certain of the physiological and psycho-technical institutes have attempted to cope with accidents resulting from the human equation, since

---

[82] E.g., the previously cited reports on the coal and steel industries. The number of years for which data are given is too short, in most cases, to justify generalizations as to trend. Thus the number of sicknesses and accidents reported for the iron and steel industry was 177 per 1,000 insured persons for both 1927 and 1929, while the number of cases reported for the first time as entitled to sickness and/or accident indemnity was 1,669 in 1927 and 1,776 (1,951 in 1928). E.A., *Gesamtbericht, op. cit.*, p. 59.

[83] Accidents reported according to paragraph 1552 of the Reichsversicherungsordnung, and industrial diseases, totaled, per 1,000 insured persons in the chemical industry, 89.40 in 1927 and 100.31 in 1928. See E.A., "Die deutsche Chem.," *op. cit.*, p. 62.

[84] ADB, "Mitteilungen des Ausschusses deutscher Betriebsingenieure," *Maschinenbau* (Berlin, January 3, 1929):27.

[85] The ratios given for percentages of working shifts lost through sickness to total working-shift time for the various works of the Preussag-Konzern show marked increases. E.g., Ibbenbüren 1913 : 1925 : 1926 = 2.85 per cent : 4.21 per cent : 6.20 per cent; Hindenburg 2.49 per cent : 3.49 per cent : 4.59 per cent; Loderburg 2.96 per cent : 4.68 per cent : 7.61 per cent, etc. "For the year 1926 the figures of the Hibernia-Konzern showed that the percentage of workers absent on account of sickness increased from January to September from 5.6 per cent to 9 per cent, while output per capita per shift in the Ruhr district increased from 1,065 kg. to 1,138 kg. (period of the English miners' strike)."—Schalldach, *op. cit.*, p. 166. The miners assert that the machines used in the pits create so much noise that they are prevented from hearing sounds which warn them of explosion, earth pressure, water leakage, and other hazards, and that many of the more recent mine disasters are directly traceable to failure to hear these warnings in time to protect themselves by fleeing to specially prepared shelters and using other safety measures long familiar to the underground worker.

[86] This society has put out a very complete list of accident prevention posters and pamphlets under the title, *Unfallverhütung durch das Bild*, which are specialized according to industries, and which have been worked out in cooperation with various special industry committees. They are published by the Unfallverhütungsbild G.m.b.H., and distributed through the agency of the Beuth-Verlag G.m.b.H., Berlin. See also, *Handbuch der Rationalisierung*, pp. 402–403, and other places.

statistics show that in most accidents the partial or complete failure of the human agent is the cause, and that these failures are definitely associated with physical and nervous weaknesses on the one hand and with fatigue on the other. The fairly rigorous control exercised by the Government over industrial practices through its system of regulations dealing with collection and disbursement of accident and sickness benefits has unquestionably helped to depress the accident rates.[87] Yet despite all such work and pressure there has been little evidence of improvement in general, and alarming indications of failure in particular industries.[88]

The labor case relative to insecurity of tenure is more convincing than those advanced regarding premature discarding of workers, the psychological effects of repetitive labor, and the loss of skills. It is extremely difficult, for example, to isolate any generally valid and consistent trend in age groupings from the reports of the *Enquete* Committee. Not only is the period covered too short, but a considerable number of factors make it practically impossible to interpret and causally assign the responsibility for any change indicated.[89] Thus far the psychological effects of repetitive labor are not quantitatively measurable, and the available evidence fails to support complaints that they are, *per se,*[90] emotionally or intel-

87 See the full discussion of accident statistics and accident insurance measures in the *Handwörterbuch der Staatswissenschaften,* 8:400–410 and 410–452 respectively.

88 In many cases, increases result from failure to realize that new technical conditions have made old accident-prevention measures necessarily obsolete. Thus, mining at lower levels always increases water, gas, and earth pressure, and other hazards. Use of gas as domestic and industrial fuel increases explosion dangers. High-speed transportation systems increase danger to life and limb of all travelers. Substitution of direct electric-power drive for belting systems, and similar changes, however, have a reverse effect. In this connection it is worth while to point out that payments for sickness and accident insurance have increased, from 1924 to 1929, from one to two billion marks, or at the rate of about 200,000,000 marks annually. While this may in part result from greater liberality in payments and more inclusive classifications of workers entitled to the benefits, there is still plenty of room for the contention that such increases indicate growing sickness and accident hazards in rationalized industry. By the spring of 1930 social insurance contributions of workers constituted 16 per cent of wages paid.—*Lokal-Anzeiger* (December 28, 1930).

89 Among these are: peculiar age groupings due to the war (older average age of German population in general, and special provisions for various classes of war veterans); laws preventing youths from working in various dangerous occupations (mining); increase in number of female workers; desire of parents to have children follow other and more satisfactory occupations than their own (mining in particular); lack of knowledge as to causes of morbidity and other relevant rates; preference shown to older, more experienced, and married employees when unemployment is high (sometimes each of these is reversed); increased average years of schooling, etc.

90 Where associated with labor-sweating, such may be the fact. But, excepting certain emotional and nervous types, repetitive labor seems to be well adapted to peculiarities of the human species. Most hand work is distinctly repetitive, and while the tempo of sowing, cutting, reaping, hammering, digging, spinning, rowing, and other hand operations may not be mechanically set, they offer relatively little play to imagination or opportunity for the expression of personality. They are highly repetitive, and their performance chains man to fairly rigid patterns and routines—patterns and routines which are blood brothers to endless belts and uniformly repeated motions on the assembly line. Sombart and others have been guilty of a lot of romantic

lectually deadening. Statistical and other evidence likewise fails to show that rationalization typically means small percentages of highly skilled workers. In certain industries, and as far as certain rationalization measures—mechanization, introduction of flow labor, etc.—are concerned, this may be the result. But in other industries, and with other rationalization measures, the reverse is the case.[91]

But that security in the pursuit of any particular profession or skilled trade, in any particular industry, has been threatened is beyond question. Aside from the effect on labor status of growing insecurity in the industrial system at large,[92] rationalization bears down with cruel force on this side of the worker's existence. A writer in *Wirtschaftsdienst* states that by the time of writing (1927) conservative estimates show that "more than 400,000 workers and at least 100,000 salaried employees were thrown out of work by Rationalization."[93] If one could assume that these persons would be reabsorbed by subsequent expansion in industrial activity incidental to increased efficiency, lower prices, and consequently larger or more effective markets, these figures would serve only as watermarks of a rising tide of national prosperity. But rationalization has not yet graduated to the status of comprehensive economic and social planning, and its piecemeal measures have provided no effective offset for the "automatic" mechanisms of the superseded Manchesterian order which it has helped to banish. Reabsorption in detail, but not in the large, has been the story of the post-war German rationalization era. Unemployment seems to have become an enduring phenomenon, an integral part of the contemporary economic order. At no time since the stabilization has Germany had fewer than 1,000,000 unemployed workers, and the totals have run from that amount to nearly 7,000,000 in the spring of 1932. Unemployment insurance is, as Bandman has pointed out, no longer a temporary palliative, but a sort of permanent relief from which government insurance systems no longer expect to be relieved.[94]

While this situation may result not from actual rationalization, but from failure to carry rationalization far enough, or to realize the full organizational, economic, and social implications (whatever these may be) of the steps already taken, these facts do not lighten the force of the labor indictment since they fit neatly into the socialist argument that rationalization without comprehensive economic planning is necessarily bad in the long run. Nor is there, apparently,

---

nonsense along this line. Six weeks' hard work using the cradle in cutting grain, or the shovel in digging ditches would do much to disabuse these romantics of the notion that modern factory labor is, on this side, particularly and uniquely "soulless" and depersonalizing.

[91] See, e.g., Dr. Berger, Ministerialrat in the Reichsarbeitsministerium, on this question, "Wirtschaftsrationalisierung und Facharbeiterfrage," *Reichsarbeitsblatt* (Berlin, July 1, 1926).

[92] See the following chapter, this study.

[93] Ernst Lemmer (Generalsekretär der Gewerkschaften), "Rationalisierung und Arbeitnehmerschaft," *Wirtschaftsdienst*, 12, Nr. 2:45–47 (January 14, 1927).

[94] Egon Bandman, "Arbeitslosigkeit als Dauerzustand?" *Wirtschaftsdienst*, 12, Nr. 15:545–546 (April 15, 1927).

any effective answer to the charge that rationalization, whether under capitalism or socialism, necessarily decreases professional security.[95] Many workers reject all attempts at rationalization on this account. It is small consolation to the individual to know that statistics show that rationalization does not decrease the proportions of skilled to unskilled workers. Little, if any, provision has been made for this aspect of the movement.

6. INCENTIVE SYSTEMS

The labor unions have expressed no consistent objection to piece-work systems as such, but they have on numerous occasions registered emphatic disapproval of various "patented" types. Among these the Bedaux system[96] has been the object of particularly bitter attacks. The grounds on which the system has been rejected are particularly interesting, since they indicate the general labor attitude towards the whole subject of incentive wages and the task and time studies which lie at their foundation. Following a detailed analysis, Dr. Bramsfeld, lecturer at the *Technische Hochschule* in Darmstadt, has outlined ten points which he considers must be observed in the taking of unobjectionable time studies. Against these he compares the shortcomings of the Bedaux system, on the following grounds:

(1) They pay no attention to the special nature of processes and labor jobs, and make no effort to improve working environment. They do not exclude use of false methods and positions, and do not genuinely enter into labor processes.

(2) They neglect many material and all personal auxiliary factors. No attention is paid to labor types (suitability, age, experience, personal tempo as a characteristic of special methods of work, unusual conscientiousness, etc.).

(3) They introduce the subjective judgment of the engineer making the basic time studies; work tempos are estimated and reckoned on such a basis as a factor in task time; special cases (not representative) are chosen according to personal judgment.[97]

While such charges cannot justly be brought against all time and motion studies, or all wage systems resting on such quasi-scientific information, they show clearly the basis upon which labor is willing to cooperate. They must have a hand in all such studies, and must be assured in advance that the principal gains flowing from the new methods are theirs.[98] The same might be said for

[95] This result, in fact, is directly implied in labor-union endorsement of mechanization, and technological changes which necessarily undermine certain skilled occupations. Rationalization of industry under the Soviet assumes that this will happen. The main problem is not Will it happen? but If and when it happens what will be done about it? The labor unions expect little relief along this line under capitalism. See also Hermann Bente, *Organisierte Unwirtschaftlichkeit* (Jena, 1929).

[96] This system, imported from America, has a patented process which it sells to factories, supplying its own engineers to make the studies and introduce the methods. These involve establishment of standard "B" time, labor, time-cost, and other units as the basis for wage payments. See E. Bramesfeld, "Das Bedaux-Prinzip," *Die Betriebswirtschaft*, Nr. 12 (Stuttgart, December, 1930).

[97] Cited in the *Deutsche Bergwerkszeitung* (Düsseldorf, December 28, 1929).

[98] See Schalldach, *op. cit.*, pp. 87–90.

labor participation in all bonus systems and in all matters of working environment which are perfected with the idea, among others, of increasing the willingness of workers to give their best.[99]

The attitude towards non-commercial incentive systems is a little more difficult to evaluate. It is safe to say that in nearly all cases such devices are regarded with suspicion, if not openly rejected, at first. The *ADGB,* for example, has flatly rejected *DINTA,* and refuses to cooperate with it under any circumstances.[100] Aside from the charge that such methods are distinctly paternalistic,[101] the unions have usually questioned the sincerity of the persons advancing the new proposals. For what purpose do employers provide lunch room facilities, music halls, athletic fields, gymnasiums and athletic equipment, parks and playgrounds, vacation resorts, prizes and medals for fast and high-quality work, and numerous other attractive features if not to smash the solidarity of labor, and to prepare the way for more consistent exploitation in the future?[102] Capital's alleged solicitude for labor, the unions argue, is given the lie by both the trend of events and the professed objective of rationalization in capitalistic society.

This attitude is significant, so far as it has received articulate expression, largely because of the extent to which such systems have been used, not only in Germany but all over the world where rationalization measures have been introduced. These systems are indicative of the changed status of labor in the new technological set-up. As previously noted in several different places, the problems of bureaucracy and sabotage have grown with the complexity of organization. As tasks become more definitely circumscribed, as the range of discretion becomes more narrow and specialized, and as responsibility becomes more nearly a function of position in fixed hierarchies of command and subordination, the necessity becomes greater of finding new methods of attaching worker loyalties to the enterprise, and of offsetting the growing danger of fixity, lack of flexibility, lack of initiative, and lack of interest in the larger "organism" of which each job is a functioning cell.

The larger and more complex a managerial unit becomes, the more difficult it is to detect sabotage or evidence of bureaucratic tendencies. At the same time the

[99] See *The Social Aspects of Rationalisation,* Chap. V. [100] Schalldach, *op. cit.,* p. 90.

[101] See the sections in previous chapters on incentive systems employed in various industries. Note the tenor of the following: "Far more important than any achievement in the psychotechnological field is the task of affording the worker relief from the worries and repressions which are rooted in his family life and haunt him in the factory. On these grounds, Arnhold considers that the arrangements originally made in a great many factories for social motives, and generally alluded to as welfare work (advice to mothers, housewives' courses, care of infants, legal advice, etc.) are essentially features of scientific management, their object being to smooth out a large part of the worker's troubles and so to make him more efficient and more eager to work."—B.I.M.I., 3, Nr. 12:33 (February, 1929).

[102] The promoters of DINTA, for example, do not oppose labor unions directly, but expect to build up a strong corps of loyal workers who will side with them in future struggles with the unions.

capacity of every individual, working in a functionally interdependent system, for damage through neglect or malice rises as the inverse of his submission to the rôle of cog. Thus, failure of the human agent at any single point may hold up an entire assembly line. Neglect at a critical moment may spoil a whole batch of steel, wreck a power plant, or cut off an entire city from gas and light. Rigid adherence to a particular system or technique may be scientifically defensible today; tomorrow, earlier practices may be followed blindly as rule of thumb; and the day following, adherence to these methods may act as definite brakes on technical progress. Because of ill will a hammer may drop into a piece of flying machinery, an antagonistic idea may be germinated, a resentment harbored. The result of such a hostile or negative attitude may be factory closure for repairs for an hour or a week, reorganization of an entire shop, factory, or industry, and even a strike which will paralyze all manufacturing activity dependent upon a key process.

Thus it is that the inability to trace costs specifically to any one point, the rise of gang and group labor, the sinking of the individual into a more or less rigidly controlled and mechanically regulated series of interlocking processes and functions, and the tendency for administration to phrase objectives in terms connoting respect for and interest in community welfare, find their counterparts in the necessity of seeing that routine workers identify their interests with their fellows and the system which they serve. That is to say, rationalization which promotes the aforementioned tendencies—quite aside from the mere matter of efficiency—necessarily dedicates itself to apotheosis of non-commercial incentives. This is true whether one have in mind rationalization under capitalism or under socialism.

It is no accident, but rather a fact of industrial evolution and modern economic organization, that the greater number of routine incentive systems in force in Soviet Russia do not differ markedly from those in force in Germany, the United States, England, and other industrial countries. Piece-work wages; group bonus schemes; prizes and medals for rapid and high-quality work; competition between individuals and gangs; pitting shop and factory records of today against those of last week, and of a year ago; special lunch rooms, gymnasiums, and entertainment facilities; day nurseries for children of female workers; medical care and hospital treatment; parks and vacation facilities; factory newspapers; rewards for ideas and suggestions for improving working methods and saving of time, money, and materials; educational opportunities; free lectures; autonomous or semi-autonomous shop government with respect to conduct of routine details—these and many other devices are used in Soviet Russia even more freely than in other industrial countries.

The major difference between ideas of socialists and capitalist entrepreneurs lies in the objectives for which all the various incentive systems are introduced. In the U. S. S. R. these are openly stated to center on bettering the status of the working personnel to the end that their standards of living may be increased and their working hours more pleasurably and profitably spent. In Germany employers are frank to state (though usually not for publication) that all rationalization measures—and of necessity incentive systems among them—are intended singly and solely to increase the profitability of companies employing them. That questions may be and have been raised on the singleness of purpose with which both stated objectives have been pursued, cannot obscure the fact that a fundamental and unbridgeable difference lies between them. Without anywhere or at any time committing themselves to the unforgivable heresy of endorsing the U. S. S. R., the greater number of the more important German trade unions hold at bottom the above-outlined position on this aspect of rationalization.

7. SUMMARY

The German trade unionists—so far as they have become articulate in these respects—find themselves, in other words, at the close of a period of transition, the beginning of which was heralded by the first signs of disintegration in nineteenth-century capitalism, and the end of which spells some type of socialist state. They hold that rationalization is the technological and organizational expression of evolution from the old to the new order, and that its inevitable product is comprehensive economic planning. According to this doctrine, socialism and economic planning are the two halves which make a humanly and institutionally satisfactory whole. Hence, to German labor, economic planning is unthinkable without socialism; without socialism rationalization is devoid of meaning, content, and direction.

But the German trade unionists are, in the main, meliorists. They hope to arrive at the goal by gradual stages, and the final assault upon capitalist fortresses would leave them, in a sense, with a hollow victory, for the significant gains would already have been made. What was already *de facto* would then be made *de jure*. Hence, from this angle it is possible to cooperate with capital in promoting rationalization measures, while aligning themselves against those who would attempt to reap the major portion of the gains without contributing the labor of body or mind. This is the key to the gradualist, and dominating, labor-union attitude towards rationalization in Germany.[103]

importance of socialism

[103] It is necessary to guard against the conclusion that there is practically complete unanimity of opinion. As Schalldach has pointed out, it is extremely difficult to summarize German labor-union sentiment, largely because the central organizations, such as the ADGB, the Deutscher Gewerkschaftsbund, and others have dealt so little with rationalization, in general or in particular, in their official literature. Between the ADGB and other moderate central trade-union associations and the Bund Revolutionärer Industrieverbände (Communist) there has been open animostiy. Yet, all things considered, and speaking in terms of the "drift of opinion," it is believed that a careful, systematic, and relatively objective canvass of the German organized working-man viewpoint will justify the outline given above, in general and in detail. See in particular "Grundlagen und Richtlinien."

CHAPTER XIV

THE ROLE OF POLITICS AND THE STATE

1. THE PROBLEM OF ECONOMIC SECURITY

ECONOMIC SECURITY, Wiedenfeld argues, has been seriously undermined in the contemporary economic order.[1] The reasons for this fact are many and complicated. They reach deep into the structure and peculiarities of both the capitalist order and machine technology, and are rooted firmly in features basic to world economy and contemporary economic points of view. The new insecurity, however, plays no favorites. All are affected by it, whether one examine the changing fortunes of labor or capital, stock broker or scullery maid.

Analytically, part of the blame is to be assigned to rationalization. Rationalization typically shifts cost ratios, so that overhead expenses come to play more and more important parts in the determination of prices at which goods can be sold at a profit. Broadly speaking, that is to say, rationalization tends to make dispensable costs less important, tends to lessen the ease with which costs can be adjusted to variations in markets and prices. The range of discretion permitted to the entrepreneur or manager on the cost side is consequently narrowed; judgments passed with respect to lowering and raising costs are surrounded with more danger signals which must be strictly heeded.

Rationalization likewise nearly always favors mass output, whether this means perfecting and accelerating older mass-production systems, or placing older techniques on a mass output basis. With high overhead expenses, the truism that cheapest production is that which is closest to the capacity maximum takes on a new significance. Because it is necessary to reduce prices to achieve capacity output, it is believed that profit margins on sales will be found smaller and smaller as mass-production methods progress. If this is true, then given percentages of change in costs or prices would necessarily make the conduct of business more speculative as rationalization advances. A relatively slight favorable spread would mean unusually large net percentage returns on invested capital; an opposite development, convergence, could on short notice eliminate profits completely.

Now it is a further characteristic of rationalization, that it tends to force nearly every (competitive) industry which it affects to sell its output, whether on domestic or international markets, at world prices. In simplifying, perfecting, inte-

[1] Kurt Wiedenfeld, *Kapitalismus und Beamtentum: Produzententum und Konsumententum in der Weltmarkt-Wirtschaft* (Berlin and Leipzig, 1932).

grating, coordinating, cheapening, and expanding transportation and communication techniques it perfects the foundation for centralized and interconnected commodity exchanges. In standardizing, simplifying, and typifying raw, semi-manufactured, and finished commodities it expands the area over which such commodities can be traded. Standards for most basic commodities very shortly take on international significance; they become the joint product of systematically cooperating national and international standards bodies. The perfection of grading, packing, storage, canning, refrigeration, and shipping techniques increases the number of commodities which can be sold on international markets. Apples, pears, oranges, lemons, grapefruit, grapes, prunes, various types of staple vegetables, potatoes, dairy produce, meats, and numerous other types of agricultural produce have international markets, and are in large part subject to world price factors. Geographic specialization and mass output, made possible by the aforementioned technical changes, force ever increasing quantities of goods onto markets where quotations are fixed by world-wide price determining factors.

For the individual manufacturer, or the nationally organized combine or cartel,[2] these world prices are uniquely unpredictable and highly capricious. The number of commodities now sold on these markets, the relationships existing between them, the bearing upon them of financial factors,[3] political developments, structural changes—these and other variable factors are so numerous, so complicated in their behavior, and so apparently unstable in their directional changes that price control seems fantastic. The base from which present action proceeds is altogether too small to be effective.

Since *(a)* present and prospective profits dominate productive schedules in capitalistically organized society, *(b)* the number and importance of industries sensitive to world price are steadily increasing, and *(c)* all economic processes are, under modern conditions, so closely tied together by technological, marketing, and financial bonds that any major impulse emanating from any sector of

[2] "Free competition was mainly conceived in classical economics as a non-encroachment of public authority, the absence of deliberate organisation and regulated co-operation."—Gustav Cassel, *A Theory of Social Economy* (1924):119.

[3] These factors, and others to which they are related (in particular Reparations and Inter-Allied Debts), taken together help to explain the peculiar importance which short-term credits now play on the international market. More and more short-term funds are used for investment purposes—readily marketable stocks, early maturing bonds, renewable floating debts. This dangerous practice tends to add a considerable portion of investment capital to commercial capital used in international trade, and to increase the quickly withdrawable total to which the exchanges of every country are subject, since it is typically true that, as international trade expands and the volume of funds available for international investment grows, the possible short-term gap between visible and (certain) invisible imports and exports tends to bear an ever larger ratio to the normal gold stocks of every industrial country, and therefore tends to increase the danger that any country may be forced off its gold standard with but little warning. This fact, coupled to the close relationship between monetary standards and fiscal (budgetary) policies, and the bearing of political developments (war, radical movements, government regulation) upon these latter, further increases the uncertainty which is the source of the change noted.

the economic system will quickly affect all other sectors, it necessarily holds that world price fluctuations introduce elements of uncertainty into all phases of national economic life. Not only is every business enterprise affected, but, at some remove, nearly all classes of income receivers dependent upon monetary income are cast under an ominous shadow of uncertainty. No mind seems capable of grasping all the causal, complementary and conditioning factors bringing about changes in this world economy. World depressions seem to appear suddenly on the horizon without any apparent rhyme or reason. The attitude of the average man towards them is like that towards "acts of God"—the unreasoning wastes of war, the sourge of an unknown plague, the parching desolation of a cloud of locusts—something to be endured and cursed, but not to be accounted for.

But it is precisely this situation, Wiedenfeld believes, which has caused all consciously and compactly organized groups to seek ways and means for insuring themselves against the uncertainties which threaten all alike. Owners of industrial shares "spread" their risks, and utilize stock exchange machinery to protect themselves from violent and catastrophic changes. Directors of industrial plants and business enterprises take new measures to insure the solvency of the concerns under their control, and the income which they receive from the fortunes of their undertakings. Employees, managerial, salaried, skilled and unskilled workers follow suit with methods appropriate to their peculiar problems.

Nearly every one of the measures taken separately, however, tends to increase the general uncertainty for all, while aiming to better the status of each. Spreading risks means a large volume of funds on the stock, bond, and commodity markets, and these funds are subject to speculative manipulation, and can be readily transferred from one industry, or one country, to another. Insuring solvency by disbursement of only a portion of earnings during good times tends to encourage self-financing and expansion without regard to market needs and considerations, and to furnish funds for short-time loans on stock and commodity markets which cannot be controlled through the ordinary banking and financial machinery. Payment of salaries to directors, and the substitution of paid managers for independent entrepreneurs (with the growth of corporations) tends to substitute a more or less irreducible cost in the place of proportional participating rights in business gains, if and when these might be realized. But even more important is the fact that the growth of labor unions, and of associations of salaried and professional workers, makes it possible for employees to bring to bear upon entrepreneurs forces which make their costs to the latter less and less flexible. Among these are: fixed salary and wage schedules which cannot be easily altered without further collective and time-consuming bargaining; pressure through the instrumentality of the government to prevent (1) price increases in basic commodity lines, and (2) arbitrary cuts in wage and salary tariffs in the heavy, key, and public service industries; sickness, accident, old age, unemployment and other insurance schemes which must be paid in large part by the business enterprise, and cannot be reduced or eliminated at the discretion of any business manager. Tendencies along this line are further reinforced by attention given to publicity showing the productive possibilities in the newer rationalization methods, and the rise of the concept of minimum standards of living.

The greater the uncertainty, the more insistent each group becomes in its quest for institutional aids to protect it from the fluctuations of income and employment which threaten its standards of living. Thus arises a subtle, far-reaching, and immensely significant drift in the institutional attitudes of all classes of the population. The overwhelming importance of individual and group insurance, in all its highly varied and almost infinitely elaborated manifestations, is but a reflection of the growing uncertainties and risks incident to the contemporary technological and world-economic posture of affairs. Its individual expression is found in the desire to insure oneself against loss of a socially established, and monetarily measurable, standard of living. Its emphasis is upon consumption (to the neglect of production), stability, order. Its reliance is upon group action and, to an increasing extent, the state.[4] It is, in a sense, forcing a sort of economic and political "transvaluation of all values" which, Wiedenfeld urges, compels all classes of persons affected by the drift to adopt the attitude of the "functionary" (*Beamte*).[5]

The attitudes and value systems of the governmental "functionary," Wiedenfeld argues, have long been characterized by attachment to group interests, and by submission of personal initiative to orderly performance of duties circumscribed and fixed in a hierarchically patterned system. When the round of duties

[4] Tariffs, subsidies, subventions, most-favored nation treaties, commercial conventions and agreements between governments, patent rules, and other state actions are enthusiastically endorsed by the very business interests which damn governmental regulation of wages and working conditions as reckless contraventions of sacred rights and natural law. Yet these measures, and the mercantilistic state which they promote and fortify, are rooted in the same economic complex—whatever form of analysis may uncover its inner workings—which gives rise to state interference in wage contracts and fixation of cost-of-living variables. Professor Bonn's remarks in this connection are interesting. "The animosity of German capitalism against the state does not rest upon fundamental theoretical foundations, but upon purely opportunistic considerations. It is opposed to the state when state control is in the hands of a political majority whose permanent good will it doubts. Then it becomes excited about the idea of liberal Manchesterianism, and promotes a policy of laisser faire, laisser aller." But, "The new Manchesterianism, which German capitalism has occasionally blazoned forth, does not seek to destroy an old feudalism, but to create a new one..... German capitalism, which would like to be freed of the power of the state, and which seeks to push back state intervention as far as possible, is constructed exclusively upon the most thorough intervention of the state." He cites, as particular examples, the attempts of nearly all capitalist groups to secure high tariff protection, and the nearly universal desire that the state should aid cartels, trade associations, and other groupings to stamp out effective competition—the leitmotif of the whole capitalist system.—*Das Schicksal des deutschen Kapitalismus*, pp. 95–96, 98.

[5] A number of terms employed by the Germans cannot be accurately translated into English. Technically, a "Beamte" is an official, but "Beamtentum" does not mean "official" in the usual sense of the term, but refers both to the body of governmental functionaries and to their point of view with respect to performance of their delegated functions. It should not be translated "bureaucracy," or to imply bureaucratic methods or points of view, as is sometimes done.

associated with the job has been completed, personal responsibility ceases. The duties are woven into a graduated pattern the ultimate objective of which is to promote the common good, regardless of the limits to which this end may demand personal sacrifice. The language in which the "functionary" couches his generalization bespeaks his conception of the rôle which he fills and the ends which he serves. The terms are typically abstract, generalized, vague, and anti-individualistic. "Patriotism," the "common weal," "public service," the "people," "justice," "equality," "fairness," and similar terms are woven into the texture of law, the mode of speech, and the habits of thought. Position in the hierarchy of command and subordination determines, in large part, social status. Within each class there is a measure of rest, fixity, and order. Advancement, when it comes, rests in large part upon non-commercial and non-pecuniary qualities, and the new level of living is more a matter of status than of range of goods and services.[6]

At the same time, the borrowing of ideas, attitudes, and habits of thought is not uni-directional. The very fact that the government takes a more active interest in all phases of industrial and commercial activities—regardless of the reasons that may be given for such an interest—tends to condition the attitude of the "functionary" rank and file which comes into contact with the new problems. Governmental ownership and regulation place new burdens on the machinery of state, and compel adaptation to different working rules. If it be a part of governmental duty that it own and operate, or at least regulate, industries "affected with a public interest," it is no less a part of that public interest that service be cheap and efficient. The evolution of publicly owned and operated industries has built up a number of working rules which the state appears to have borrowed directly from the capitalistic economic order.

Efficiency demands maximum flexibility in the technological and personnel organization of industrial processes. The technological side must be kept abreast of the latest scientific and organizational arts. And since the various aspects of the problem of efficiency are those upon which the techniques of rationalization are brought to bear, all governmental contact with industry—whether in promotional, regulatory, or ownership capacities—forces the "functionary" to adapt his habits of thought and working disciplines to these vitalizing environmental forces. Private enterprise thus becomes, in the words of Norden, the instructress for public management.[7] The ideas and methods borrowed affect the whole range of governmental activities, and run the full gamut of rationalization techniques. Emphasis upon research, standardization, scientific management, personnel selec-

---

[6] This paraphrased (and somewhat altered) sketch of Wiedenfeld's characterization of the "Beamte" point of view is subject to attack on the ground that all governments serve special or class interests. In this connection, it is interesting to note that the expression "class" assumes, as usually used, a solidarity on the part of the capitalist group which is apparently contrary to the left-wing argument that capitalism is essentially atomistic, anarchistic, and individualistic.

[7] Walter Norden, "Verwaltungsbehörde und Unternehmung, Organisation und Personal." *Zeitschrift für die Gesamte Staatswissenschaft,* 92:238–249 (March, 1932).

tion and training, horizontal and vertical combination, mechanization, and allied technical and organizational aspects of management are accompanied by emphasis upon managerial decentralization, individual initiative, personal responsibility, competition between individuals and groups, rewards and punishments in both monetary and non-monetary terms, and, last but not least, by accounting systems designed to summarize input-output ratios with the idea of showing net gains where possible, and minimizing losses where net receipts are obviously impossible.[8]

The "functionary" is thereby compelled to follow routines and assume responsibilities more closely approximating those long familiar in the field of private enterprise. Elements of uncertainty respecting tenure, standards of living, and professional standing enter into the complex of forces determining his points of view, his value systems, and the objectives for which he labors. This trend tends to eliminate barriers which formerly existed between the "public servant" as a type, and the capitalistically hired worker as a type, and, taken with the shift in the point of view of the latter previously noted, creates a certain community of interests between the two classes of workers which increases the popularity of and prepares the way for even closer identity between government (representing consumer interests) and industry (representing income and productive interests).[9]

An attitude receptive to increased governmental influence and control in the affairs of production and distribution is thus created which unites with other—and more commonly appreciated—forces having the same directional bent. For rationalization accelerates and lends emphasis to all those developments out of which has come the submergence of individual into group interests. It weakens the individual worker on the labor market, and compels him, under pain of economic extinction, to identify his bargaining efforts with those of his fellows. It weakens the individual business man, and drives him to join cartels, trade associations, and other special interest groupings. Technology and commerce, in decreasing the relative importance of the individual and in elevating the significance of group activities and policies, help to apotheosize corporative ideas and

[8] There is scarcely a government department in Germany, including such departments as Health, Education, Parks, Justice, Consular Service, which has been unaffected by efforts to standardize, concentrate, coordinate, eliminate red tape, utilize mechanical equipment, simplify, and in general "rationalize" its theoretical, structural, and procedural apparatus and methods. See the excellent theoretical summary of the evolving functions of government by Herbert Gross, "Moderne Probleme der öffentlichen Unternehmung," *Finanzarchiv*, 1:155–168 (1932).

[9] Wiedenfeld warns against interpretation of all phases of economic activity in terms of trends characteristic of the larger corporations, such as those dealt with in the preceding descriptive chapters of this work. Data collected by the Bank für Deutsche Industrie-Obligationen show that, when all small establishments not included among those responsible under the Dawes plan for reparations payments are left out (all firms with assets under 20,000 marks), the small concerns (Kleinbetriebe—with assets under 100,000 marks) constituted 70 per cent of all establishments in 1929, while the large concerns (Grossbetriebe—with assets of 5 million marks or more) made up only 8 per cent of the total. The average assets of all concerns was only 340,000 marks.—Bank für Industrie-Obligationen, *Zahlen aus Deutschlands Wirtschaft* (Berlin, 1931).

institutions, and merge every matter of detail into a matrix which is essentially political and social. One of the most significant aspects of the "mental revolution," which Taylor characterized as the main feature in the conduct of industrial processes brought under the impersonal domination of scientific methods, is that it everywhere rivets attention upon problems of power. In the final analysis, this means exercise of the functions of the state. If the state by neglect permits, or chooses to delegate to other units the exercise of corporative powers—trade associations, cartels, trade unions—the facts are in no wise altered. But, in the main, forces in technology, finance, and world markets seem to be steadily widening the geographic scope and power spheres appropriate to these various groupings organized along special interest and corporative lines. The only major equalizing force in the whole picture is the state—at the present time, unfortunately, organized almost exclusively on a national basis.

2. STATES WITHIN AND AMONG STATES

Capitalism and state laissez faire policies brought an end to both the corporatively[10] organized and "closed" medieval economic systems, and their immediate successors in the mercantilistic and cameralistic[11] systems of the late eighteenth and early nineteenth centuries. But the microcosmic and self-sufficient economic cells of the capitalistic style could not long remain in isolation. They began very early to cluster under a number of legal and extra-legal forms as the forces of machine technology and expanding markets became more and more coercive. The results of these coalescent forces during the evolution of capitalism in the more highly industrialized nations are matters of common notoriety. Once more the greater part of economic activity has been brought under the immediate or proximate control of series of interlocking special group-interest organizations or "corporations," the structure and objectives of which are (in many respects) distinctly reminiscent of the medieval system, and their methods and operating rules disruptive of the economic order which gave them birth. German writers refer to this contemporary set-up as an Associational Economy (*Verbandswirtschaft*), or a Confederational Economy (*Verbundene Wirtschaft*), or, again, as a Corporational Economy (*Korporative Wirtschaft*).[12]

[10] The word "corporation" is used in its canonical, not its legal sense, to mean organizations of persons by merchant, craft, residence, belief (ecclesiastical), status or other special interest attachments, either by free choice or by prescription, to serve the interests of members, represent them in the hierarchy to which they may be members, and to compel individual members to subordinate their activities to the codes and working rules of the group. The medieval craft and merchant guilds are the best examples.

[11] A type of mercantilism, primarily associated with Germany from the beginning of the sixteenth to the end of the eighteenth century, in which all economic activity is subordinated to the policy of service to the dynastic state. See the article, "Kameralismus," in the *Handwörterbuch der Staatswissenschaften,* 5:573–576.

[12] German usage differs somewhat from that of the Italian Fascist writers. See the interesting papers of Professors Alberto de' Stefani and Luigi Amorosco in the report of the Milan confer-

With the exception of more purely scientific and cultural associations, the organizations characteristic of this highly modified capitalism fall broadly under three main types: (1) the cartel; (2) *Kammern*—associations, unions, chambers—in agriculture, industry, trade and commerce, handicrafts, among consumers, and among various classes of workers; and (3) trusts or combines. To these should be added certain mixed types, such as various types of producers' and consumers' cooperatives, syndicates,[13] "forced cartels," and communities of interest.

While, with the exception of the combines, the members of these larger organizations maintain their legal independence, they are all compelled, in the act of joining, to subscribe to rules which modify and limit their former freedom of action. How important this change may be depends largely upon the nature of the organization. Members of trade and employers' associations, and trade unions, agree to live up to certain economic codes, and bind themselves not to pursue their respective ends by resort to such practices as "spoiling the market," "dumping" goods in competitors' territory, paying more than tariff rates (wages), "scabbing," and giving away the secrets of the group. To promote the ends of the group, members are usually compelled to pay dues and to perform specified duties. Loss of status or expulsion from the organization may carry serious implications for the individual or enterprise. Thus, if employer morale is good, an expelled member may find it difficult to buy or sell his goods, or to obtain good quality of labor, even though overt action is not taken against him. Likewise, a worker who has lost caste with his fellows may find it impossible to find work in his usual occupation.

As one passes on from these simpler and looser types to the more compact and class-conscious trade unions, and to various types of cooperative societies and cartels, the control of the group over members increases in rigor and in the range of its authority. Frequently, and with certain types always, formal codes are supplemented by contractual obligations legally enforcible in the civil courts. Where this is the case, the association is usually required to take on a legal form permitting it to sue and be sued.

There is a great deal of variety here among the different types of cartels. The *Konditionenkartell* (much the more numerous at the present time) confines its activity to fixing and regulating standard sales conditions.[14] The *Kalkulationskartell* members agree on price lists, but limit their activities to establishment of standards for the determination of unit costs, while the *Submissionskartell* con-

ence on "The State and Economic Life with Special Reference to International Economic and Political Relations, A Record of the First International Study Conference, League of Nations" (published by the International Institute of Intellectual Cooperation; Paris, 1932).

[13] Differentiated from cartels by centralization of selling and marketing in a single place.

[14] Because this type has no monopolistic objectives, Liefman prefers to name this, and the two following types, Associations (Verbände) instead of cartels.—*Kartelle, Konzerne und Trusts* (Stuttgart, 1927):41–49.

trols only the matter of bidding for orders. The *Preiskartell* goes one step further, its activities concentrating on the fixing and regulation of prices. A variant on this type, the *Gebietskartell,* controls the division of markets and selling areas. The *Kontingentierungskartell,* or quota cartel, regulates and limits the output of its members with an eye to prevention of overproduction. Actual cartels frequently combine several of these (and perhaps other) features. Thus, cartels which have centralized their selling and marketing, or *syndicates,* may, in addition to combining control over price and production, regulate market areas, quotas, conditions of sale and delivery, bidding, and other aspects of the conduct of business.

The "forced cartels" and communities of interest exercise even more rigid control over their constituent enterprises. Whether the Reich or the more powerful members in the former come to dominate, the powers of the respective cartels have expanded to the point where they may be classed with communities of interest as forerunners of combination. With formal amalgamation, whether by exchange of shares or by actual reorganization and merger of properties, enterprises lose all independence except such as may be delegated to them by the central management.

While, with the exception of the "forced cartels" and communities of interest, none of the various types of associations mentioned can be considered as historically or logically necessary forerunners of any other type, the origin and organizational justification for them all can be found in the same general series of economic trends. And these, in particular mass-production technology[15] and constantly expanding markets, set in action currents which increase the interdependence between the various groupings mentioned. Although the "cartel of cartels" (*Dachkartell*) such as the *Stahlwerks-Verband A. G.* and the *Reichskohlensyndikat* is to be found only in the unusual case, there is a tendency for cartels organized in the same general field to work more and more closely together. The like holds for the more loosely organized trade associations, and between trade associations and cartels. An example where such developments have resulted in central organizations including practically the entirety of given industries is to be found in the *Verein Deutscher Maschinenbau-Anstalten.* The *Reichsverband der Deutschen Industrie,* on the other hand, serves as the central agency for all trade associations and cartel cooperative action in all branches of German industrial activity. Similar functions are performed in the wholesale and export field by the *Reichsverband des Deutschen Gross- und Ueberseehandels,* in the retail field by the *Hauptgemeinschaft des Deutschen Einzelhandels,* and in the handicrafts industries by the *Reichsverband des Deutschen Handwerks.* The Federation of German Employers' Associations (*Vereinigung der Deutschen Arbeitgeberverbände*), which parallels the aforementioned central associations, and

[15] See Liefman, *op. cit.,* and Metzner, *Kartelle und Kartellpolitik* (Berlin, 1926).

serves as the headquarters for all entrepreneurial interests before labor and the state, includes the following central cartel associations (*Kartellverbände*) in its membership:[16]

Reichsverband der Deutschen Land- und Forstwirtschaftlichen Arbeitgebervereinigungen
Vereinigung der Arbeitgeberverbände in der Freien Stadt Danzig
Reichsverband des Deutschen Handwerks
Vereinigung der Arbeitgeberverbände des Deutschen Grosshandels
Hauptgemeinschaft des Deutschen Einzelhandels
Reichsverband der Bankleitungen
Arbeitgeberverband für das Deutsche Zeitungsgewerbe
Arbeitgeberverband Deutscher Versicherungsunternehmungen

As previously mentioned in the descriptive chapters of Part Two, these various central organizations are banded along industrial, trade, employer, and other special interest lines. Almost without exception, a national organization exists to represent every special interest grouping. Thus the agricultural cooperatives are nearly all included (about 91 per cent) in the *Reichsverband der Deutschen Landwirtschaftlichen Genossenschaften—Raiffeisen—e.V.*, the chemical industry is united in the *Verein zur Wahrung der Interessen der Chemischen Industrie*, and so on throughout the whole range.

Opposed to the entrepreneurial and employer central associations are those of workers, salaried employees, and officials (state employees). Of these the most important are:[17]

Allgemeiner Deutscher Gewerkschaftsbund (ADGB)—(31 unions and 4,866,926 members, beginning of 1929)
Allgemeiner Freier Angestelltenbund—(14 unions and 421,106 members, beginning of 1929)
Allgemeiner Deutscher Beamtenbund—(20 unions and 177,070 members, beginning of 1930)
Gesamtverband der Christlichen Gewerkschaften—(19 unions and 763,843 members, beginning of 1929)
Gesamtverband Deutscher Angestellten-Gewerkschaften (Gedag)—(12 unions and 501,635 members, beginning of 1929)
Verband der Deutschen Gewerkvereine H.-D.—(22 unions and 168,726 members)

The objectives of the central associations are similar to those of member associations which are organized along trade (cartels and trade associations) and regional lines, namely, consolidation of forces in pursuit of gain to the individual members. While, as most authors insist, this means—particularly among entrepreneurial associations and combines—that ultimate authority rests with the individual member or enterprise, it does not follow that these groupings do not

[16] "Jahrbuch der Berufsverbände im Deutschen Reiche," 52 Sonderheft zum *Reichsarbeitsblatt,* Bearbeitet im Statistischen Reichsamt (Ausgabe 1930):45. See the outline in Appendix C, pp. 448–449.

[17] *Ibid.,* pp. 59–62. To these should be added the German Communist representative of the Third International, and the central organization of Professional Associations (Reichsbund der höheren Beamten, with 100,000 members).—*Ibid.,* p. 64.

involve any serious compromise with the conditions of free competition. Quite the reverse is the fact. The struggle of the cartel leadership with the government over Paragraph 8 of the Cartel Law of 1923—which permits members to withdraw without warning for "reasons of weight"—indicates the extent to which the contractual obligations of the membership have gone as interpreted by the cartels themselves.[18] The same is true of the ultimate objective, the making of profits (among business federations). Because each member company will bring its influence to bear upon the group to advance its own interest in the making of money, it does not follow that capitalism of the Smithian order still reigns supreme.

In fact, what we are dealing with here, whether one turn to the relations between central associations and their members, between these and the general public, or those existing among the associations themselves, tends to fall more and more under the head of exercise of political power. It is no accident that nearly every German book written since the war on the development, functions, and policies of cartels, trusts, trade associations, unions, syndicates, and other types of corporative enterprise has been largely concerned with the problem of *Politik*—a term which combines the meaning of *policy* and *political*. This is the burden of Metzner's book, *Kartelle und Kartellpolitik,* Tschierschky's work on *Kartellpolitik,* Vogelstein on *Probleme der Monopolpolitik,* and Wiedenfeld on *Gewerbepolitik*.

While unable to stamp out competition—even the "forced cartels" have been unable to do this—the cartels wield important powers with which to compel internal (among members) and external compliance with their wishes. In either case the weapons used are both positive and negative. In the former, the customary devices are use of black lists, boycotts, appeals to the Cartel Court, suits under contractual obligations, and so forth. Compulsion upon outsiders or competitors is exercised through the use of price-war schedules, purchase of outside interests, prevention of materials purchases, credit stoppage, denial of transportation facilities and labor force, and the devices of exclusive contracts, "loyalty" rebates, exclusive right clauses, etc.[19]

But the *Machtpolitik* (power politics) of the various types of associations, concerns, and combines reaches even further than one might be led to believe by mere examination of formal machinery. The forces of public opinion organized along special interest lines are brought to a focus and given articulate expression in the more loosely organized trade associations and federations. But the cartels go further. Liefman, the foremost German authority on cartels, defines them as "associations between independent enterprises of the same type for the purpose of securing monopolistic control of the market."[20] While there has been a great

[18] See pp. 381–382.

[19] Jakob Herle and Max Metzner, *Neue Beiträge zum Kartellproblem* (Berlin, 1929):73–87.

[20] Liefman, *op. cit.,* p. 10.

deal of dispute over this definition because of the introduction of the phrase "*monopolistic* control of the market," most writers leave their readers in no doubt as to the fact that cartels set themselves no limits in this respect. It is only by failure of strength, and because governmental control has intervened, that the cartels have not achieved the objective stated by Liefman. This is what Tschierschky has in mind in his definition:[21] "Cartels are organizations resting on the contractual agreements of independent entrepreneurs (enterprises) of the same industry for the purpose of raising and insuring the economic success (*Erfolg*) of its members by means of arbitrary regulation of markets."[22]

The communities of interest and larger combines carry cartel objectives one point further. While none of the combines in coal, steel, potash, chemicals, electro-technical, textile, and machine production exercises exclusive monopoly powers, their influence is in many cases greater than if they were limited to mere exercises of such control within such narrowly defined fields. As previously indicated, technological, organizational, financial, and marketing interdependencies are almost as great among several of these industries as within the confines of the industries themselves. The forces making for vertical and horizontal combination are paralleled by those which bind together the coal mining, coking, chemical and gas production, iron ore extraction, smelting and steel making, electric power, machine, electro-technical and other allied industries. When combined with the tendency towards managerial decentralization—a tendency which Dobretsberger[23] believes to be characteristic of corporational or "bounded" economy—and the adoption of the legal device of the Corporation (*Aktiensgesellschaft*) or the Limited Liability Company (*Gesellschaft mit beschränkter Haftung*), these forces can be seen at work in nearly every phase of German economic life.

The more powerful cartels, communities of interest, and combines, frequently organized, as we have already seen, on an international basis, are small empires in themselves. The conduct of their industrial and business affairs affects thousands of persons, and often involves the making of decisions of greater importance than those of such countries as Denmark, Hungary, and Portugal. They possess a strict discipline, exercise police powers on their extensive properties, and control the working hours of armies of men and women, skilled and unskilled workers. During these working hours professions are learned, skills are acquired, and lifelong habits of work are instilled into the rank and file. The conditions of work and the amount of earnings received will largely determine political and social points of view, group affiliations, and the ways in which leisure time is

---

[21] S. Tschierschky, *Kartellpolitik* (Berlin, 1930):3.

[22] Paragraph 1 of the Cartel Law (Kartellverordnung) defines cartels as "Agreements and resolutions which contain obligations over the manipulation of production or markets, the application of (special) business terms and arrangements, the manner of fixing prices or the demanding of prices. . . . ." quoted in Herle and Metzner, *op. cit.*, p. 23.

[23] Josef Dobretsberger, "Korporative Wirtschaft," *Schmollers Jahrbuch für Gesetzgebung*, 56:1 (1932), pp. 7–26.

spent. These economic empires also possess and exercise powers over life and death. They control the conditions of safety to life and limb, the duration of the average life cycle, and (in large part) the security of workers when accident, sickness, and old age have robbed them of their normal earned incomes.

There is scarcely an aspect of the normal functions of the state—protection, education, social welfare, general subordination of the interests of the individual to those of the entire public—which these economic entities do not possess to some degree, or have not arrogated in some wise to themselves. The most important aspect of protection in the modern world is that associated with the job and income. The same is true of education. Nearly all industries and trades requiring specialized and skilled workers—and this is particularly the case with nearly all the larger combines—are directly interested in apprenticeship regulations and technical schooling. The rise of special technical schools located on or in close proximity to the industrial premises is a phenomenon to be found in nearly every branch of industry and commerce. The attempt of *DINTA* to control the schooling of its future managerial and skilled worker class from the primary grades on is no radical departure from common practice. The underlying idea—borrowed from Soviet Russia and turned on its institutional head—is that the practical and theoretical work can be best combined in close touch with the field of application. Since attitudes are an important part of such training, the desire has arisen to control the entire education of as many workers as possible. Ultimately the Soviet system of technical institutes, where education is combined with earning and practical application after the primary years have been passed, would become the foundation of the educational system at large. General intermediate and advanced technical schools would then either lose their independence entirely, or would be brought under the domination of series of interlocking special-interest industrial and commercial groups. Much this sort of thing has already happened, in fact, among the technical schools of Germany.[24] The same holds true for the general field of industrial and commercial research.[25]

Social welfare work has, likewise, been largely centered in the business enterprise in Germany. The funds for the support of such work, made up partly of obligatory and partly of voluntary payments, come jointly from workers and employers. Where "voluntary"—that is to say, incentive—payments are large, the management possesses a powerful lever for influencing the daily lives of its work-

[24] The various Technical and Commercial Colleges (Technische und Handels Hochschulen) are largely under the domination of industrial and commercial interests, the students being trained for definite work in definite places—frequently spending a large part of their spare time in the laboratories and work shops of such industrial establishments—and the professors acting in engineering and advisory capacities in the same places during their spare hours. The Technische Hochschule in Berlin is largely a training school for the Siemens and A.E.G. electrotechnical combines. The various mining schools scattered throughout the west and south of Germany are even more closely attached to the mining interests of these regions.

[25] This is even true of the Kaiser Wilhelm-Gesellschaft. See, e.g., the lists of directors in the various branches of this Society in the *Handbuch der Kaiser Wilhelm-Gesellschaft*.

ers and their families. The services provided constitute further invasion of the normal functions of the state, and go a long way towards the determination of worker loyalties, attitudes, and points of view.[26]

But most important of all, these corporational units are the source from which springs the power and the desire of small vested minority groups to influence, guide, and control the affairs of the state to which they are, at least nominally, subject. Much has been written, and a great deal remains to be said, about the lust for power on the part of industrial, commercial, and banking magnates. They stand at the head of immense properties—factories, offices, warehouses, banks, transportation systems, gas and electric-power networks. The management of these properties affects directly the lives and fortunes of thousands of workers and their families, the prosperity of villages, cities, and sometimes entire states. The limits of their control occasionally reach to the ends of the earth.

The great magnates have, therefore, become important political figures. Their support is sought in the waging of political campaigns as financial "anchor men" and as spokesmen for "substantial" elements in the communities in which they live. They are appointed to serve as economic advisors on governmental committees and commissions, and they are the real representatives of capitalism behind the throne when tariff schedules are drawn, commercial and trading agreements made, and socially significant policies adopted. In Germany, although perhaps not to the extent found in the United States, real government is to be found in managing boards, committees, commissions, and lobbies. In all these the heads or representatives of the great corporations, cartels, trade associations, chambers of commerce and industry, and financial consortiums exercise important, and in many cases dominant, influence. In many respects their power is so overwhelming in the councils of state that all the remaining political machinery—caucuses, party conventions, elections, parliamentary debates and resolutions, official seals—are relegated to mere claptrap for the amusement of professional politicians and the solemn loyalties of ignorant and naïve persons.

At the same time, it is necessary to avoid certain possible, but quite erroneous, interpretations of these trends. Perhaps most important is the frequently expressed notion that these corporate groupings and economic magnates always know, to employ the patois, "what they are about," and that if they do know, their objectives are necessarily the same. To the extent that they have anything in common, it centers around the pursuit of profits, and perhaps the acquisition of power for its own sake. But profits in a capitalistic society are frequently differential gains—gains which represent definite losses to other persons and groups. While nearly all employers can get together on the matter of wage and labor policies, all business men cannot agree on tariffs, the exercise of monopoly pow-

[26] See, e.g., the description of the social service and incentive systems of the various industries as reviewed in Part Two, in particular those of the mining, steel, electro-technical, and chemical concerns.

ers, or the price, production, and marketing policies of cartels and trade associations. Gain to one group frequently constitutes loss to another. Tariffs benefit manufacturers and agricultural interests catering to home markets, but harm importers and (in the long run) exporters. Tying contracts damage competitors in the same line of business. Price and market control tend to damage purchasers in different lines of business.[27]

The best that can be said along this line is that technological, marketing, and financial forces have tended to consolidate interests within each industrial branch, and to establish inter-industry communities of interest where such interdependencies have become more or less coercive. Frequently the line of group interest is much more important between the same industries operating in different countries than it is between different industries operating in the same country. This is most certainly the case with the transportation, communication, power, and electro-technical industries. To a lesser extent the same is true for important branches of the machine, coal, steel, and textile (rayon) industries. But in any case, the tendency in consolidation, wherever it takes place and so far as it extends, is to run along industrial lines, and to include increasing portions of the total range of business activity. As these more or less compactly organized industrial groupings acquire political influence, and come to wield political powers, we are able to discern a major structural change in the whole political set-up. The real basis of politics has shifted from geographic, regional, cultural, ethnic, and similar foundations to industrial, commercial, and financial spheres of influence.

Within these spheres, the boundaries of which are in large part set by technological and organizational factors, there tends to be unified control. The problems of coordination and integration, in a word, the problems of long-range planning, call for the exercise of centralized and dictatorial powers. The problems of management call for a maximum of decentralization within the limits determined by the requirements of unified planning. Within this framework, the problems of management reach out into nearly every phase and aspect of human existence. These spheres are, in a sense, bounded cultural entities as well as more or less homogeneous and balanced economic and organizational units. The development of rationalization has strengthened and enormously accelerated these trends, even though Germany may be said, in many respects, to be only at the beginning of these newer developments.

[27] If so, how do tariffs and price-control measures ever come into existence? How does it not happen that these contradictory forces do not cancel each other? Why do vested interests whose business is tied up with free trade permit tariffs to be established, cartels to be organized, discriminatory practices to be enforced? These are partly questions of shifts in the balance of power, but even more of the essentially anarchistic attitude of each grouping, regardless of the corporational form which it has taken. Until the shoe pinches they are indifferent. When the toes begin to hurt they turn to the use of exactly the same tactics by way of retaliation, whether this means government interference in private enterprise or not. Most business men are in favor of such interference—on their side always! See Bonn, *op. cit.*

Within these spheres, also, the consolidation and unification of opinion and points of view tend to grow apace. Correlative with the crystallization of entrepreneurial and employer points of view, and general disposition to cooperate in the pursuit of common ends, is the unification of labor. In fact, labor began to organize and to acquire a definite social philosophy long before business men became interested in such matters. At any rate, the trend in class sentiment is even more pronounced among German labor ranks than within the owning and managing circles. This in large part results, in all probability, from the fact that cooperation and unification among employers seriously alter the remaining free initiative and openly competitive rules, modify the objectives for which business strives, and call for the construction of philosophies of management which serve, at least in the transitional stages, merely to confuse the group objectives. The reverse is the case with labor. Nearly every step in mechanization, coordination and integration, and expansion in the geographical and organizational scope of the industries with which they are associated, solidifies their ranks, causes them to make common cause among themselves, and sharpens their social philosophies.[28] Just as with capital, so labor becomes definitely international. The more class-conscious it grows, the further it swings to the left, and the more pronounced the international emphasis.[29]

In the struggle for control within each of the spheres, labor resorts to aid of the state as freely as does capital. It tends to be as frank as any group of industrial magnates in demanding the support of the state in furtherance of special economic interests on all important issues. On the whole, labor does not care very much about a hand in the details of management other than as provided by the system of decentralized control in operation. Labor wishes control, wherever it has given articulate expression to its group desires, not of portions of the productive machinery, but of its entirety. Democratic ideas *per se* have largely lost caste. Once control over industry is secured, there is no reason to believe that dictatorial machinery or practices will be abandoned. Coordination of the finely adjusted and closely meshed technological and organizational systems characteristic of rationalized industries does not well subject itself to rules of democracy. The general vagueness of labor along this line might be interpreted as a sort of intuitive recognition of this fact. Certainly, if the system in vogue in Soviet Russia

[28] This is a dangerous generalization. Readers will immediately point to American workmen inured to mass-production methods par excellence, yet politically, organizationally, and philosophically the most confused and amorphous mass of workers in the contemporary industrial world. There is a complicated, but fairly satisfactory answer to this objection found in the general background of the American workers and American industrial and commercial history. The peculiar combination of factors in the American scene—too numerous even to mention here—accounts for the situation, however, without invalidating the argument advanced above. If these lines of force are present and have already made themselves felt in other industrial countries, they will sooner or later assert themselves in the United States.

[29] The war period showed a reversal of trend in the recrudescence of national unionism. Since the war there has been a pronounced tendency to return to the earlier position.

can be taken as an example of what labor will do when the opportunity is provided, there would be small talk of the conventional type of industrial democracy. So long as labor controlled the formation of policies and the general objectives, its representatives who managed the industrial complexes would, under such a system, be permitted a free hand in all details.

But in any case, labor is appealing directly to the state. As it consolidates its ranks under the impulse of the struggle for power in these more or less homogeneous industrial and economic units, it helps once more to shift the balance of power along lines where the effective basis of representation is industrial and professional. In this respect its influence is in no wise contradictory to that of capital. Whether labor or capital wins out in the long run, or whether the present system in these respects stays the same, the really effective political units will probably be industrial and commercial (or trading and financial). It is in all probability within these spheres that programs will be formulated, policies will be tried out, and group interests will come to their significant focus.[30]

3. CONTROL, REGULATION, AND OWNERSHIP BY THE EXISTING NATIONAL STATE

A

In a very real sense, the Reich, like all other nationally organized states, has become the football of the "pressure politics" of the more group-conscious, compactly organized and powerful corporational entities. Trends which lend accuracy to these descriptive terms have, at the same time, caused each group to concentrate its energies in this internal struggle for the balance of power upon the task of turning the machinery and agencies of the state to its own uses. In the beginning of the Republican period, labor held the upper hand. After the establishment of the Weimar Constitution (1919) and the passage of a number of "socialization laws," most important among which were those establishing the "forced cartels," labor union and socialist influence suffered a marked decline. The close of the period under survey has seen an important revival of socialist ideas, and a reintroduction of socialist machinery and plans into the affairs of the Reich.

---

30 It is no argument to the contrary to insist that important sections of economic activity are, and probably always will be, operated on a small, perhaps craft, basis—possessing little more than local significance, and producing or distributing goods for and in highly localized markets. In nearly all cases, these segments are being organized into special-interest associations along national or international lines, and have come, therefore, to take on rôles and functions similar to those of the larger industrial and commercial groupings. But even more significant is the fact that these smaller units perform each their round of functions in an institutional setting dominated by the larger and more important trusts, combines, cartels, trade associations, unions, etc. These latter are the center of gravity in the whole modern economic order; no individual or enterprise in any field can be walled off from the changes they make and the forces they set in motion.

The Weimar Constitution was very much a compromise solution. While labor held the balance of power, radical left-wing sentiment, the centrists, and the labor right were at loggerheads on almost every important issue. The Communists wished to establish a proletarian dictatorship immediately and join forces with the U.S.S.R. The Social Democrats, divided in their councils, possessed no unifying social philosophy capable of welding opinion and bringing it to focus in a coherent and comprehensive plan. Between the gradualists of the right and the revolutionists of the left ranged nearly every possible creed, but at no point a plan. Nearly all socialist groupings subscribed to the notion that all the key industries should be nationalized at some time or other, but there was little agreement on those that were "ripe" for the change, nor on the ways and means by which desired ends were to be encompassed.

The machinery of state thus set up resembled, consequently, a coat of many colors. As with the socialization laws—which it is not necessary to discuss again—the Constitution is philosophically, and to a certain extent organizationally, lacking in "character." Compromise parties came to compromise solutions on the details of organization and the social, economic, and political objectives of a compromise state.[31] The product of these compromises is in no place shown more clearly than in Article 165 of the Constitution, providing for the establishment of what appeared at first to be one of the most promising innovations of the new Republican régime, a National Economic Council. It is worth quoting at some length:[32]

> The workers and employees, in order to guard their social and economic interests, shall receive legal representation in occupational councils, as well as in district workers' councils, organized according to economic districts, and in a National Workers' Council.
>
> For the purpose of fulfilling all economic functions, and of cooperating in the execution of the socialization laws, the district workers' councils and the National Workers' Council shall meet with the representatives of the entrepreneurs and other interested groups of people, as district economic councils and a National Economic Council. The district economic councils and the National Economic Council are to be so organized that all important occupational groups are represented therein according to their economic and social significance.
>
> Before bills of fundamental importance from the standpoint of social and economic policy are introduced, the national cabinet shall submit them to the National Economic Council for its opinion. The National Economic Council has the right to propose such bills itself. If the National Cabinet does not agree to them, it must nevertheless introduce the bills into the Reichstag, with a statement of its own viewpoint. The National Economic Council can have the bill represented before the Reichstag by one of its members.

---

[31] The whole setting, of course, was unfavorable. Throughout the period when the National Assembly (elected in January, 1919) was engaged in its deliberations the Versailles negotiations were in progress (April, May, and June—the treaty being signed June 28, 1919; the Constitution was adopted July 31, and proclaimed August 11, 1919), the economic life of the country had been paralyzed by the cessions already made to the Allies, revolutions were constantly being prophesied and in some quarters being daily expected, and nobody knew to what length French and Polish military leaders might not go in further assault upon the defenseless country.

[32] Blachley and Oatman, *The Government and Administration of Germany* (Baltimore, 1928):593–594.

Functions of control and administration can be transferred to the workers' councils and economic councils with the districts assigned to them.
To regulate the establishment and the duties of the workers' councils and the economic councils, as well as their relationship to other social self-administering bodies, is exclusively a function of the Reich.

The National Economic Council was not to be a state planning commission—no provision being made in the Constitution for such a body—but at the best a sort of industrial parliament such as visualized by late nineteenth-century social reformers. Being purely advisory in character,[33] it did not possess even the significance, as a planning body, of the Guild Socialist industrial congress. Like the Constitution, and the duly constituted economic machinery of state which that document established, the National Economic Council is weak. A product of the general confusion and disorder of the time of its origin, it was at best a compromise solution. It requires a considerable stretch of the imagination to visualize this institution, or any portion of the governmental machinery established at the time it was drafted, as a product, as Professor Bonn appears to believe,[34] of the essential sanity, understanding, and balance of the Teutonic stock. Administratively, the Council has remained without functions, authority, or influence. Although, as Blachley and Oatman[35] summarize, "Like certain other constitutional arrangements, the National Economic Council remains a tool lying in the chest, ready for use, but as yet scarcely tested," it could never be mistaken for a planning body under the most favorable circumstances. And the climate of the following period was never favorable.[36]

Many of the powers, however, that might have been delegated to a central planning and coordinating commission were parceled out among the various ministries. Under the stress of circumstances these ministries have been compelled to utilize most of the powers delegated to them by the constitution and subsequent enabling legislation. In the final analysis, their power and influence reach into almost every phase and aspect of German economic and social life. A certain amount of coordination within and among the various ministries has been necessary as the forces of change have gradually deepened and widened trends along these lines. At the same time, their influence has been brought to bear upon similar trends found throughout industry and commerce. They have, that is to

---

33 The right to propose bills was more negative than positive; the Council was intended to give advice on bills, not to initiate. It possessed no real administrative powers in any respect whatsoever.

34 M. J. Bonn, *Das Schicksal des deutschen Kapitalismus* (Berlin, 1930).

35 *Op. cit.*, p. 594.

36 Lorwin, *Advisory Economic Councils* (The Brookings Institution Pamphlet Series, No. 9, Washington, 1931), is more optimistic. Yet his survey of the history and functions of the Council does not shake the judgment of Blachley and Oatman. Step by step the Council has lost power and prestige both in the councils of state and in the eyes of the populace. Long before Chancellor Bruening deprived it of its last vestigial functions, the Council had been reduced to the status of chance advisor on mainly unimportant types of technical legislation. See Lorwin, pp. 12–30.

say, been directly concerned in the development of industrial and commercial rationalization in nearly every field and in nearly every phase of the social, economic, and political problems its advance has raised.

B

Powers and functions involving rationalization and planning have been largely concentrated in the portfolios of four ministries: *(a)* the Ministry of Traffic; *(b)* the Ministry of Labor; *(c)* the Ministry of Food and Agriculture; and *(d)* the Ministry of Economics. A brief outline of the functions of these ministries will serve to indicate their importance for the general topic in hand.

(a) The functions of the Ministry of Traffic are:[37]

(1) The administration of the *waterways of general traffic* which have been taken over by the Reich; protection of the national waters; care of sea signals and supply of pilots; handling of matters of internal navigation and of traffic on the water courses; development of water craft.
(2) *Aviation:* Legislation regulating aviation; regulation of aerial traffic; development of lines of aerial traffic; licensing, inspecting of planes and aviators; security of airplanes; supervision of aerodromes; examination of technical and industrial matters; compilation of statistics; administration of national property.
(3) *Automobile traffic* and other *street traffic:* Legislation concerning commerce in motor fuels; technical competitions; automobile associations; questions of raw materials for motor fuels; regulation of general traffic by driving and cycling; highway construction and maintenance.
(4) *Railways:* Administration of functions bestowed upon the Cabinet by the Railway Law (RGBI, 1924, II, p. 272, section 31), (supervision of the German Railway Association; administration of the national railway property; representation of the affairs of the railways before the Reichstag and before foreign countries); exercise of the right of eminent domain bestowed on the railways; railway legislation; supervision of private railways for general traffic according to articles 90, 91, and 95 of the Constitution.

In addition, the Ministry of Traffic publishes a map of the navigable waterways in Germany; an occasional gazette concerned with traffic on waterways, by airplane, and by motor vehicles; and a weekly bulletin of information for airplane travelers. The Ministry is headed by a Federal Minister of Transportation *(Reichsverkehrsminister)*, with ministerial directors and councilors in charge of the various departments. The following advisory councils have been appointed to assist in various capacities in the work of the Ministry:

(1) Advisory council on waterways (Constitution, article 98).
(2) Advisory council on airplane and motor vehicle traffic.
(3) National Railway Council (Constitution, article 93; executory ordinance RGBI, 1921, II, p. 77) with a standing committee. Advises on railway matters and rates.
(4) Technical-industrial council.

The Ministry of Traffic, thus, serves the function of a central coordinating agency for all the various transportation networks in the entire country. While actual management is restricted to care and maintenance of rivers, harbors, canal systems, streets and highways, its statistical, advisory, and regulatory authority

[37] This summary, slightly rephrased, is that of Blachley and Oatman, *op. cit.*

covers practically the entire field of transportation. The railroads are operated by a private company, the *Deutsche Reichsbahn Gesellschaft,* but are under the control of the Ministry of Traffic as far as all matters of national policy and the execution of regulatory legislation are concerned. It has lacked the necessary authority, the comprehensive plans, and the financial backing for thoroughgoing coordination of all the networks under its general supervision. Yet the railroads are woven into a single system, the internal waterways networks have been outlined with a considerable degree of care, and a fair portion of the system of interconnected canals has been completed, the airplane industry is under the semi-monopolistic control of compactly organized and cooperatively administered companies, and the main lines have been laid down for some of the more important regional highway lanes. Interconnection and integration of passenger and freight services has been carried through within limits by and with the advice and aid of the Ministry. The information and the machinery are available for further coordination along these lines in the future.

(b) The general duties of the Ministry of Labor[38] are the enforcement and administration of labor laws in general, including special laws for the protection of labor; arbitration of labor disputes; administration of unemployment relief; administration of pension systems and care for those injured in the war, and the widows and orphans of veterans, etc.; administration of social insurance and social aid; supervision of housing and worker settlements.

The work of the Ministry of Labor is divided as follows:

- Division I.
  - General matters; administration of the department and of the subordinate offices.
    - Subdivision I*a*.
      - General business and administration not handled by subdivision I*b*; personnel, budget, economic questions, organization.
    - Subdivision I*b*.
      - Medical questions, especially medical care.
- Division II.
  - Social insurance.
- Division III.
  - Labor legislation, protection of labor, wages policy and general questions of social policy.
    - Subdivision III*a*.
      - Law of labor contracts; labor organization; adjudication of labor cases; adjustments.
    - Subdivision III*b*.
      - Labor code; protection of labor; general questions of social policy; international labor legislation.
    - Subdivision III*c*.
      - Wages policy.
- Division IV.
  - The labor market; arbitration; labor supply, unemployment insurance; unemployment relief.
- Division V.
  - Welfare work; social aid; housing settlements.
- Division VI.
  - Charities legislation.

---

38 *Ibid.*, pp. 166–176. (Slightly rephrased.)

Six related agencies are attached to the Ministry:

(1) Labor Law Committee.
(2) National Committee for Physicians and Hospitals.
(3) Standing Committee for Municipal Housing.
 Subcommittees:
 (*a*) Real Estate Credit.
 (*b*) Questions of Organization and Technical Construction.
 (*c*) Rent Law.
(4) Standing Committee for State Settlements.
(5) Permanent Council on Homesteads.
(6) National Committee for the Care of the War Wounded.

To these should be added a number of subordinate authorities:

(1) *The National Insurance Office* (RGBI, 1911, p. 509; 1924, I, p. 779) is the highest authority for supervising, deciding, and passing upon appeals in the domain of national insurance against accident, disability, and illness; it is the final authority for making decisions and passing on appeals in the domain of employees' and mine workers' insurance; Division I handles matters of accident insurance; Division II, employment insurance, and accident disability insurance.
(2) *The National Court for Social Aid* (RGBI, 1922, I, p. 59) is the highest court of appeals in cases of social aid and relief. Its decisions are published from time to time in *Entscheidungen des Reichsversorgungsgerichts.*
(3) *The National Labor Administration,* together with the related National Office for Labor Arbitration, administers such matters as labor information, decisions upon appeals, and functions bestowed upon it by law in the domain of the labor market for subsidized and productive unemployment relief agencies. Its rates division makes decisions as to the enforcement of rates agreements. Its functions include matters of safety protection, hygienic conditions of labor, the work of children, youths, and women, the apprentice system, domestic labor, the supervision of labor, and the observance of labor restrictions. It maintains an exhibit on safety and hygienic conditions. It participates in the publication of the National Labor Gazette (*Reichsarbeitsblatt*) and its various supplements, and to the weekly Labor Market Advertiser (*Arbeitsmarktanzeiger*).

Related agencies are:

 (*a*) The Administrative Council of the National Service for Labor Arbitration.
 (*b*) Committee on the Severely Injured.
 (*c*) Central Supervisory Office for the Manufacture of Explosives and Munitions.
 (*d*) Advisory Council of the Permanent Exhibit for the Welfare of Labor.

(4) The *National Insurance Institute for Employees.*
(5) The *National Labor Fund* acts as the general disbursing and accounting agency for the National Ministry of Labor, the National Labor Administration, the National Insurance Office, and the National Court for Social Aid. It is also the central treasury for social aid in the Reich.
(6) The *German Agent for Labor Questions in Upper Silesia.*
(7) The *Permanent Adjustment Agents* are appointed for districts and are delegated to decide important controversies as to wages and rates; they also decide whether settlements made by adjustment committees are binding.
(8) *Authorities and Offices of National Social Aid,* of which there are fourteen (head offices) with subordinate offices added thereto, provide social aid, including orthopedic and medical treatment.

The Ministry of Labor is thus charged with the duty of caring for, administering, coordinating, and planning all problems having to do with labor, labor organization, and labor status. Most important among these are problems relating to security, wages, hours, working conditions, and standards of living. In the final analysis the functions performed by this Ministry reach out into problems of city planning (housing, workers' settlements, etc.), health and education (technical), recreation and amusement, the social habits and the emotional temper of all classes of workers. The spheres of its influence include, whether the Ministry is willing to admit it or not, planning of the income side of consumption, and, within important fields, disbursement in maintenance of standards of living.

All these problems involve social objectives and a philosophy of social control. These have been largely lacking in the Ministry itself; there has been little unidirectional pressure brought to bear from without upon it to cut and shape its policies along definite lines. Yet the machinery is in existence for such comprehensive planning and coordination once the necessary power can be used to set it working.

(c) The *Ministry of Food and Agriculture*[39] handles all matters affecting agriculture, food, forests, and fishing. It publishes occasional studies dealing with aspects of national food supply and nourishment, and with various problems of agriculture. Its work is organized in two main divisions:

Division I.

Deals with general questions of agricultural production and of food; price fixing; cartels (affecting agriculture); problems in the production of cereals, potatoes, sugar, malt, yeast, spirits, fruit wine, cattle breeding, meat, tallow, dairying; fertilizers and care of soils; problems of general horticulture, war against pests; agrarian statistics; agricultural labor problems; agricultural tax questions; forestry and timber.

Division II.

Deals with policies of customs authorities and trade agreements; agricultural occupational representation; agricultural associations and credits; rural improvement and betterment; the occupied territories; carrying out of the peace treaty; fodders; fishing.

A number of special organizations are affiliated with this ministry:

(1) German Scientific Commission for Sea Investigation.
(2) Expert Council on Fodders.
(3) Commission to Judge Fodder Mixtures.
(4) Special Scientific Commission for Fodder Mixtures.
(5) National Committee for the Development of Scientific Fertilizers.
(6) National Committee for the Application of Lime to the Soil.
(7) National Committee for Technique and Agriculture.
(8) National Committee for the Cultivation of Swamp Lands and the Reclamation of Waste Land.
(9) National Committee for Food Investigation.
(10) Council for Wine Production and Wine Trade.
(11) Council for the Producton of Fruit and Vegetables.
(12) National Council on Forestry.
(13) National Committee on the Timber Trade, the Sawmill, and the Paper Pulp Industry.
(14) National Board of Guardians of the Stations for Dairy Husbandry.

---

39 *Ibid.*, pp. 176 ff. (Somewhat altered in phrasing.)

The following institutions are also placed under this Ministry:

(1) The *National Biological Institute for Agriculture and Forestry* is engaged in scientific experimentation in fields of research which promise practical results for the development and improvement of agriculture and forestry, particularly horticulture, plant protection, and soil bacteriology. It publishes, in addition to occasional pamphlets and leaflets, the *Nachrichtenblatt für den deutschen Pflanzenschutzdienst,* and the following reports:
Nachrichtenblatt für den Pflanzendienst (monthly).
Bibliographie der Pflanzschutzliteratur (yearly).

(2) *Research Institute for Farms and Settlements.*

(3) A special *Organization of War and Reconstruction Economics* supervises the trade in fertilizers that contain ammonia and phosphoric acid (RGBI, 1917, p. 427; 1918, p. 474).

As this list of offices, divisions, and functions shows, the Ministry of Food and Agriculture serves this field of economic activity in what is known in industry as a "staff capacity." That is to say, its work has little to do, in the main, with administration of properties or regulation of economic processes. Its work is largely scientific and advisory; it is a sort of national coordinating body for the gathering and supply of data and advice to the various fields of agriculture. To this end it cooperates with the various agricultural schools and the *Reichskuratorium für Technik in der Landwirtschaft.*[40] It possesses the relevant information, and the technical ability to plan agricultural production, distribution, and marketing by regions, by types of industry, and for the entire country. Practically nothing has been done, however, beyond scattered propaganda and disconnected advice.

(d) The *Ministry of Economics*[41] comes closer to being a central national coordinating bureau than any other governmental body mentioned. This can be readily seen from a perusal of its organization and functions. In general, it deals with all those economic matters which are not handled by such special departments as the Ministry of Food and Agriculture, the Ministry of Traffic, and the Ministry of Labor. The head of this department *(Reichswirtschaftsminister)* is assisted by a secretary of state, a ministerial bureau director, and a number of directors, managers and referees. Two ministerial councilors are made the heads of services that deal respectively with: (1) matters that concern the industrial and middle classes, handwork (handicraft industries), the individual dealer, industry, and industrial associations; and (2) such general matters as the budget, personnel and organization of the ministry and the authorities subordinate to it.

The functions of the Ministry are brought together under two main divisions, aided and supported by a number of affiliated organizations. The functions of the two divisions are as follows:

Division I.

Problems and associations of occupational groupings; cartel systems; costs of production; price policies; users' and consumers' associations fund for the assistance of industrial enterprises; private insurance systems; systems of weights and measures; questions of standards and values; money, banking, exchange; general questions of the money market and of the credit needs of business; general questions of evaluation; financial relations to foreign coun-

---

[40] See Chap. XI.

[41] Blachley and Oatman, *op. cit.*, pp. 160–166. (Somewhat altered.)

tries; tax questions (national, state, and municipal) including participation in the drafting of new bills, and constant observation of the influence of the formal and material aspects of tax legislation upon general economic developments; gathering and analysis of economic statistics; economic questions of the Versailles treaty and of the international agreements for its fulfillment; Swiss gold securities; economic questions of the occupied Rhineland and of the Saar territory (the former function has ceased with the final withdrawal of foreign troops); supply of general economic information; the press.

Division II.

Trade and customs; ocean travel. Under this division the following publications are issued:

Deutsches Handels-Archiv—German Trade Archives, a journal of trade and industry issued fortnightly.

Handbuch für die deutsche Handels Marine, containing shipping laws, lists of shipping authorities, lists of ships, charts, agreements.

Entscheidungen des Oberseeamts und der Seeämter des Deutschen Reichs.

Nautisches Jahrbuch.

The following special offices, agencies, and services are connected with the Ministry of Economics:

(1) The *National Statistical Service* is assisted by a Council for Trade Statistics, composed of experts in agricultural economics, industry, and trade, and is the national headquarters for the assembly, analysis, and dissemination of all types of population, occupational, economic, social, and other types of statistics. Its publications are as follows:

Statistik des Deutschen Reichs, a publication which has appeared at irregular intervals, issued in separate volumes, since 1873. In it are assembled census and other types of statistical data.

The *Statistisches Jahrbuch für das Deutsche Reich* provides an annual summary of all important statistical data dealing with economic matters, population, agriculture, commerce and trade, prices, salaries, labor markets, credit system, insurance, finance, educational, administration of justice, army, navy, elections, etc. An annex entitled "International Surveys" (*Internationale Uebersichten*) contains summaries of economic conditions abroad.

The *Vierteljahreshefte zur Statistik des Deutschen Reichs* contains extracts and provisional information for the *Statistik des Deutschen Reichs* publications.

The *Monatlicher Nachweiser über den Auswärtigen Handel Deutschlands* contains monthly statements regarding the foreign trade of Germany.

Wirtschaft und Statistik, published monthly, contains current statistical data dealing with domestic economic conditions and German foreign trade.

The *Statistik der Güterbewegung auf Deutschen Eisenbahnen* publishes data concerning freight traffic within the Reich and with reference to certain traffic districts abroad.

(2) The *National Service for Survey of Ships.*

(3) The *National Supervisory Service for Private Insurance.*

(4) The *National Economic Court*[42] decides economic questions arising from the Versailles treaty in certain classes of cases, and cases arising from the public regulation of economic matters such as forfeiture of goods illegally imported, complaints against administrative measures which are taken in connection with the trade in base metals, and issues concerning the extent and obligation of the forwarding of mail. The president and the two senate presidents of the National Economic Court are also members of the elections court for the temporary National Economic Council. The decisions of the court are published in a series of volumes, *Entscheidungen des Reichswirtschaftsgerichts und des Kartellgerichts.*

---

[42] Established by ordinance, RGBI, 1920, p. 1167, and amended by ordinance, RGBI, 1921, p. 1046 and 1924, I, p. 155. See Klinger, *Zuständigkeitsgebiet des Reichswirtschaftsberichts und des Kartellgerichts* (Berlin).

(5) The *Cartel Court* (RGBI, 1923, I, p. 1067) is connected with the National Economic Court, having the same president and some of the same members. Its function is to prevent the "misuse of situations of economic power." The principal classes of questions which it decides are as follows:

Upon motion of the Minister of Economics or the Minister of Food and Agriculture:

Whether a contract or decision of a cartel is to be declared invalid because it endangers the general economic situation or the common welfare, or whether a specific method of executing such a contract or decision is to be prohibited (see *Kartellverordnung, Reichsgesetzblatt,* 1923, I, p. 1067).

Whether contracting parties are to be permitted the general right to withdraw from contracts if these contracts have been made on the basis of trade agreements, or kinds of price fixing by enterprises or associations, which are likely to endanger the general economic situation or the common welfare by utilizing the advantages of a situation of economic power.

Upon motion of the party concerned:

Whether the notice (*Kartellverordnung,* par. 8) given by a member of a cartel under Paragraph 8 (the right to withdraw for reasons of weight upon giving notice) was permissible.

(6) The *National Superior Sea Service* is the highest deciding authority for cases arising from disasters at sea.

(7) The *National Commissioners for the Sea Service* possess chiefly advisory functions.

(8) The *National Inspectors for Examinations* (sailors, pilots, etc.).

(9) *Technical Commission for Sea Navigation and Expert Committee for the Technical Education of Seamen.*

(10) The *Stock Exchange Committee* is an advisory committee chosen by the *Reichsrat.*

(11) *Appeal Chamber for Cases from the Stock Exchange Court.*

(12) *Appeal Commission Concerning Fines for Prohibited Trading in Options.*

(13) *National Commissioner for Permits for Exports and Imports: Settlement Office.*

(14) The *National Commissioner for Coal Distribution* has charge of the production, distribution and use of coal, gas, electricity, steam, hot water, and water supplies.

(15) *National Commissioner for Handwork* (Handcraft trades) *and Small-scale Industry.*

The Ministry of Economics also has charge of a number of self-administering bodies. These are:

(1) The National Coal Council.[43]

(2) The National Coal Association.[43]

(3) The National Potash Council.[44]

(4) The Potash Examining Office and the Potash Examining Office of First Instance.[44]

(5) The Potash Appeal Office and Examining Office of Second Instance for the Income from Potash.[44]

(6) Agricultural-Technical Potash Office.[44]

Returning to the Cartel Court, and its general relationship to the regulatory and administrative powers of the Ministry of Economics, Blachley and Oatman write:[45]

"This court was established in connection with the National Economic Council, by the ordinance of November 2, 1923, 'Against the Misuse of Situations of Economic Power.' The ordinance requires that agreements and decisions as to production, sales, trade conditions, price fixing, and the like, must be in writing; and provides that they may be invalidated by the Cartel Court upon application

[43] See Chap. V. [44] See Chap. XI. [45] Blachley and Oatman, *op. cit.,* pp. 586–587.

by the national Minister of Economics, if they are found to be inimical to the general economic life or the public welfare. Such a system, in which a special court is provided, certainly gives to the national administration a more direct and speedy method of 'controlling big business' than is provided in the United States in the enforcement of the Sherman Act by the ordinary judicial courts, even allowing for the requirement in that act that cases involving questions of monopoly which are of general public importance shall be expedited. It is noteworthy, also, that no special agency outside of the regular administrative departments is employed in Germany for the prevention of abuses by cartels and syndicates. This work is entrusted to a Minister, and thus comes under Cabinet control to a certain extent. It is consequently knit up at every moment with the general economic policy of the administration in power.

"Enforcement of legal or quasi-legal regulations by the courts, either ordinary or special, is not, however, the only method by which business and economic activities are controlled and regulated by the Reich. There is much direct administrative regulation which in the ordinary course of events requires no judicial interference. A survey of the numerous economic functions and controls placed under the administrative authority of the various national departments corroborates the statement made in an important German study, that the economic authorities of the Reich include not only the Ministries of Economics, Labor, and Food and Agriculture, but also those of Finance, Justice, Traffic, and the Post. (De Grais, *Handbuch der Verfassung und Verwaltung*, 1926 edition, revised by Peters and others, pp. 536 ff. Pp. 566 ff. of this book give an excellent brief account of the regulation of business as well as citations of laws and ordinances governing.)

"Exchanges, or bourses, are under the general supervision of the national Minister of Economics, although each bourse is established separately by the state government and directly supervised by it. Chambers of commerce and industry share in the supervision to some extent, through public commissioners. Certain matters connected with bourses are decided by the Reichsrat, which has established an advisory council of experts for its assistance.

"This type of administration is interesting because of the various authorities concerned in it. National, state, and private business are all represented in control over the bourses, and the advisory council system, so frequently employed in Germany, is used here very appropriately."

C

As the foregoing general outline of the functions of the various departments of the German national government shows, some provision has been made, and at least a portion of the machinery has been established by the state for dealing with nearly every phase of the various problems of rationalization and economic planning.[46] It may be worth while to reconsider briefly the extent to which provision has been made for the more important problems raised.

(a) Information. All writers on the more detailed and more purely organizational and technological aspects of rationalization, and on the general problems of industrial, economic, and social planning, agree that accurate, comprehensive, scientific, and timely information is the very beginning of wisdom for constructive work. Much of such information is of necessity highly specialized, and its field of application may be localized to single industries, individual plants, or even to detailed processes unique to small manufacturing cells. Whatever the range of application may be, there is an appropriate field marked off for intensive study of problems unique to that area. The more general the problems, the more centralized and comprehensive the investigatory and informational body may be.

Thus the organization of research and the supply of information must combine two seemingly contradictory features—features common to nearly all phases and aspects of industrial, commercial, financial, social, and economic planning, coordination, administration, and control—*centralization* and *decentralization*. In a sense, the importance of the latter is even greater in the field of research than in any other field of human endeavor for the simple reason that it subjects itself less readily to schematization and rigid delimitation of function and range of inquiry. Yet order and cooperation are also of the essence of nearly all modern scientific research, in both the natural and the social sciences, and in both "pure" and applied branches. Interdependencies among the various fields of research, as previously pointed out,[47] in problem-matter, content and methodology, strengthen tendencies along these lines. Science, in other words, must be planned in order to be in keeping with its own laws of development, and with the institutional (productive, consumptive, equipment) setting in which it unfolds its complexes of laws, theories, hypotheses, discoveries and inventions. As a corollary, its "line" function requires autonomous or semi-autonomous status in general, by special fields, and with respect to special types of problems.

In Germany important steps have been taken along both lines, and for research in both the natural and the social sciences. The *Kaiser Wilhelm-Gesellschaft* is a semi-autonomous centralizing agency, being supported and governed in part by representatives of the state, the engineering and scientific professions, and various branches of industry. As far as the government is concerned, the *Physikalisch-Technische Reichsanstalt* can be considered an essential unit of the system. The same cannot be said, except to a rather limited extent, for the big private industrial, trade-association, and cartel laboratories. The private and capitalistic character of the controlling enterprises keeps these laboratories sealed off from the main body of scientific work. The compartments are not, of course, water-tight;

[46] It should now be possible to use these words together, or, with some mental reservations, more or less interchangeably, without danger of confusion.

[47] See Chap. I.

there is constant seepage of ideas, methods, and information between the public and the private institutions. Yet by so much, industry at large and the public are deprived of the benefits flowing from the constant and free interchange which would take place were no such barriers existent. The barriers can no longer be defended on the grounds that they aid and stimulate scientific effort; exactly the opposite is the fact, as appears from almost every consideration of the case.

Under the *Kaiser Wilhelm-Gesellschaft* the state has had even less success in promotion of centralized semi-autonomous industrial research agencies. Something of the sort is to be found, it is true, for coal between the *Kaiser Wilhelm Institut für Chemie,* the *Kaiser Wilhelm Institut für Kohlenforschung, Mülheim-Ruhr,* and the *Schlesisches Kohlenforschungs Institut der Kaiser Wilhelm-Gesellschaft in Breslau,* for chemistry in the first-mentioned Institut, for the iron and steel industry in the *Kaiser Wilhelm Institut für physikalische Chemie und Elektrochemie,* the *Kaiser Wilhelm Institut für Physik,* and the *Kaiser Wilhelm Institut für Eisenforschung,* and for other industries in such institutes as the *Kaiser Wilhelm Institut für Lederforschung* (leather research), the *Kaiser Wilhelm Institut für Silikatforschung* (glass and silicates research), and the *Kaiser Wilhelm Institut für Faserstoffchemie* (textile fiber research). The borrowing of ideas between these Institutes and the various private laboratories, and the industrial utilization of practical findings is no doubt great, yet there is considerable evidence of overlapping, lack of cooperation, and lack of organization. This is much more the case in most other fields of industrial research. In some fields, no such thing as a central scientific institute can be said to exist. This is true for agriculture, despite the fact that the work of the entire Ministry of Food and Agriculture is largely devoted to investigation and promotion of research in this field. The National Biological Institute for Agriculture and Forestry goes a long way towards this end, but it is no more a central coordinating research agency for agriculture than the *Kaiser Wilhelm Institut für Arbeitsphysiologie* is for work physiology and psycho-technical research.

A somewhat higher degree of coordination is evidenced in the work and organization of the *Institut für Konjunkturforschung.* Although an organizational offshoot of the *Statistisches Reichsamt,* it functions as a semi-autonomous body, and covers, in its researches and publications, practically the entire economic field. The *Statistisches Reichsamt* is, in the first place, a "staff" institution which coordinates all governmental statistical services and supplies every department of the government, as well as business and the general public, with carefully assembled, well presented and comprehensive statistical data. The *Institut für Konjunkturforschung* carries this work one step further. The Institut, however, has not the power, any more than any other research organization, to command all the really significant information which it should possess in order to give either a statistically accurate picture of economic trends, or to supply the basis for intelligent economic and social planning. Its information on such matters as new investment in various industries, degrees of excess plant capacity, quantity of materials in various stages of production and distribution, real wages and the cost of living in different sections of the country and for different classes of workers, and the general subject of overhead and variable costs ratios, is sketchy and inadequate, to say the least. It has gathered relatively little reliable and comprehensive information on industrial accidents, relation between accident and industrial sickness rates and technological change, the problem of technological unemployment, housing conditions, occupational shifts, retirement and average age of employees, and numerous other aspects of the technological and organizational changes falling under the head of rationalization. Much, and in some cases all, of the relevant data is locked up in the secret files of trade associations, cartels, combines, and fraternal organizations.

The same general picture holds for the third and perhaps most important central and semi-autonomous informational and research body, the *Reichskuratorium für Wirtschaftlichkeit.* This organization, which combines in its activities the staff rôle of supplying information and the "line" function of promotion and propaganda, covers nearly all fields of industrial, commercial, agricultural, financial, and consumption activity. It receives money from the government, and cooperates very closely with several government departments, as it does with the various private and professional societies, associations and companies.[48] Yet, with the partial exception of special committees such as the *Deutscher Normenausschuss*[49] and other groups more or less directly under the control of members of the *Verein Deutscher Ingenieure,* there is considerable overlapping among its various committees and subcommittees,[50] few of its committees are nationally organized functional agencies except on paper, in scarcely a single field do its committees possess the power or the will to command the information and examine systematically into many of the more important problems with which they come in contact, it does not command either the confidence or the cooperation of the powerful groups operating in some of the fields with which its committees deal, and it is usually either unable or unwilling, or both, to supply information except on the more technical and restricted aspects of its work. On the informational side, the *RKW* is capable of developing into a central planning body. Instead of that it has confined its attentions to supplying information, in the main, to vested interest groups which are systematically engaged in pursuit of the main chance.[51]

---

[48] See Chap. II.

[49] Even the work of the Deutscher Normenausschuss is quite deficient in several respects. Their work on component parts has made relatively little headway; in certain industrial branches—e.g., agricultural machinery and branches of the textile industry—they have only begun to develop standards.

[50] See its *Handbuch,* pp. 6–53, with particular reference to such things as heat economy and the various aspects of scientific management.

[51] Its leaders and directors are, as in the case of the work of the American Bureau of Standards, and Department of Commerce, committed to the Smithian proposition that gains to busi-

Curiously enough, the one organization that appears to come closer to filling the rôle of a central coordinating agency is the entirely independent professional and engineering society, the *Verein Deutscher Ingenieure.* Its membership reaches out into almost every field of engineering, and into several of the more directly technological professional groupings not ordinarily included under that head. Its various committees seem to have been constituted with an eye to longer run considerations, with closer attention to interrelationships between technical fields, and with a more acute appreciation of the interdependencies existing between science and technology, than is the case with the other central informational organizations mentioned. Its deliberations and printed material have an appearance of detachment, compactness, and thoroughness which indicate that research, propaganda, systematic work, and comprehensiveness can go hand in hand. To all intents and purposes the *Verein Deutscher Ingenieure* comes closer than any other to being the integrating and coordinating force between the various central organizations previously mentioned. Other than the cement provided by the range of its interests and the makeup of its membership, no real central coordinating body for research and information can be said to exist in Germany. The *RKW* might have served this purpose, but it has thus far failed to do so.

Turning the question around the other way, central bodies exist capable of being quickly adapted to provide comprehensive and accurate information for planning purposes on the various phases of rationalization. With the exception of the engineering societies, the government has a direct hand in the administration of each of these groups. In natural science research and its technological adaptations the government connections are primarily through the *Kaiser Wilhelm-Gesellschaft* and the Ministry of Food and Agriculture; in economic research its contact is through the *Institut für Konjunkturforschung;* in standardization it works through the *Deutscher Normenausschuss;* in the general field of scientific management it works through the *RKW* and its various sub-committees; and in the field of horizontal and vertical concentration and combination it gathers its information through the Cartel Court, the National Economic Court, and its various subsidiary regulatory committees and commissions. The powers of each of these bodies might be strengthened, the range of their functions broadened, and the management of their operation systematized to the point where they would be capable of supplying the proper stimuli for accelerating the rate of orderly change, and the foundation for guiding these into channels determined by well-knit economic plans.

(b) Objectives. If the "pressure-politics" of the various powerful special-interest groupings could be said to possess a common set of objectives, with differences only as to details and for comparatively short-run periods, then the state, in its

ness are *ipso facto* gains to the general public, competitive conditions being assumed. Enough competition exists under the present scheme of things, they believe, to warrant that assumption at the present time.

passive rôles as arbitrator, policeman, and compromise court, would of necessity underwrite and promote those ends. If no such common set of objectives exists, then the state must either abandon its passive rôle and enter actively into regulation with an eye to subordinating individual and corporational interests to the specifically defined welfare of the whole group, or abandon the scene of battle to the mercy of the more powerful contestants.

Republican Germany has been no more able and willing to accept the full political and economic implications of Manchesterian doctrine than was the pre-war dynastic and paternalistic German state. From the formative years under the domination of Bismarck, through the war, and down to the present time, the state has entered actively into the control and guidance of economic forces. Before the war, all things were subordinated to the dynastic, imperialistic, and diplomatic objectives of a state which had never fully thrown off the mercantilistic doctrines of early German cameralism. After the war and the revolution, all economic developments were compelled, nominally at least, to expand within the limits set down by the dual objectives, satisfaction of the war claims of the victorious allies, and rehabilitation to the end that the underlying mass of the population might enjoy security and high standards of living.

The radical flavor of the Weimar Constitution, the various socialization laws, the establishment of the National Economic Council, the National Economic Court, and the Cartel Court, the expansion of certain of the functions of the various federal ministries sketched above, and the general temper of state legislation and municipal ordinances show the strength which the new currents possessed in the determination of national policies. Yet, as pointed out above, disunion in the ranks of labor and the return of more stable and prosperous times, shortly reversed the trend. Up to the end of 1929 the tide of reaction was unchecked. The *RKW,* though nominally committed to advancement of rationalization for the purpose of raising the standard of living of the mass of the people, bent its efforts almost from the start primarily to the giving of aid and advice to business men interested in the making of profits. The Cartel Court began to work closely with the *Reichsverband der Deutschen Industrie* in a "helpful way." The "forced cartels" were gradually transformed, and their socialistic features were emasculated step by step. The whole rationalization movement began to take on that curiously bombastic, cocksure, and Rotarian flavor, so familiar to Americans in the great days of the "New Era" of 1926–1929. Writers, politicians, and newspapers[52] whose doctrinal roots and institutional interests were allied to capitalism, began to pour out a flood of literature condemning state interference and extolling the virtues of unregulated competition.

Then, as is well known, the coming of the depression brought a new change of direction. The national state returned, under the guise of meeting a purely

[52] See, in particular, the very interesting "Festausgabe" of the *Frankfurter Zeitung,* called "Nachkrieg Kapitalismus," published in October, 1931.

emergency situation, to rigid governmental control. Slowly the power of the government has been extended as emergency decree followed emergency decree, until Germany can be taken as the closest approximation to the Marxian theoretical state outside of the U. S. S. R.

In a period so confused, and so rocked by the force of contradictory currents, it is difficult to abstract any picture showing consistent adherence by the state to any set of long-run economic and social objectives. Yet the implications of structural change—at the center of which stands the whole rationalization movement—have received at least partial recognition from all contending parties. No political party in Germany, for example, will be able for a long time in the future to repudiate the steps taken thus far to guarantee security to workers in the event of accident, sickness, death, and unemployment. To repudiate the various insurance laws would be political suicide, and the Reich is historically committed to their preservation, and probably to their continued extension.

Somewhat the same generalization will unquestionably hold for maintenance and bettering of the standards of living of the rank and file of the laboring class. The state and politicians of all social persuasions are nominally committed to this objective so far that retreat is impossible. It is the principal burden of the Ministry of Labor; it is the primary aim of the Ministry of Food and Agriculture; it is the goal around which the labor of many of the committees and commissions of the Ministry of Economics gravitate; it is the popular justification for the socialization laws, the Cartel Court, and numerous other regulatory acts and machinery. Lip service to general betterment of worker standards of living and the improvement of national prosperity are indispensable prerequisites in the appeals of nearly all private, autonomous, and semi-autonomous bodies for public support, worker loyalties, and the receipt of state aid. These arguments run through nearly all the cartel and trade association literature, dominate propaganda in support of the big combines and the general concentration movement, and flavor the promotional work of the *RKW*, and *VDI*, the *Kaiser Wilhelm-Gesellschaft*, and similar bodies.[53]

The objectives of *security* and *high standards of living*—which might be broken down into specific programs for shorter working hours, better working conditions, higher wages, various types of insurance for different classes of workers, elimination of seasonal and cyclical fluctuations in business, equating of production and consumption, etc.—have never, however, been the cores around which political parties have centered their activities, nor on which public sentiment has been brought to a clear focus.[54] The rôle of the state here has been

[53] Resort is not made alone, even by the most ardent supporters of laissez faire and "free" competition, to arguments based upon the logic of that order. The literature of the RKW is particularly interesting in this respect.

[54] A distinct exception will have to be made of the Communists, and, although to a lesser extent, of the Social Democratic Party.

almost entirely passive. Many factors have served to confuse the issues, with the result that the struggle over policies has always taken place in a curious twilight zone of uncertainty—uncertainty as to trends, social philosophies, and the outcome of the numerous and kaleidoscopic changes in party groupings. Long-run changes have destroyed the culturally conserving and backward looking foundation of the pre-war generation. The "liquidation" of the church, the army, the dynastic state, and the family, while by no means complete, has gone far enough to have shaken all layers of the German population to their cultural foundations. Official policies have reflected this general confusion; indorsement of rationalization, which of necessity involves long-range planning, has, consequently, been unaccompanied by the general fixation of objectives without which planning loses all meaning.[55]

(c) Administration. If, under the stress of structural changes analyzed, the attitude of the numerically more important layers of the German population towards the state is undergoing a sort of climatic change, and if the various corporational groupings have taken over so many political powers and prerogatives that they tend to become actual states within states,[56] then the regulatory rôle of the national state, as at present constituted, at least, is in process of drastic and far-reaching readjusment. *Etatisme* is coming to acquire a new significance. The state is gradually taking over the functions of central coordination and policy determination for managerially decentralized and organizationally autonomous or semi-autonomous industrial and commercial activities. Steady increase in the range of state administration with full managerial autonomy[57] seems to be the more or less inevitable product of these changes.[58]

Fundamentally the patterns of organization are no different for publicly and privately owned and operated industrial networks. Both are faced with the growing danger of technological stagnation, with rigidity and lack of flexibility in the organization of offices, factories, productive capacity, and the general structure

[55] See Chaps. IV and XV. [56] See par. 1 and 2, this chapter.

[57] See, especially, Gross, *op. cit.,* and Gross, Hoffman, Elsas, Napp-Zinn, and others in "Moderne Organisationsformen der öffentlichen Unternehmung," *Schriften des Vereins für Sozialpolitik,* 176, I and II.

[58] It is interesting to note in this connection that Adolf Wagner, writing in 1891, believed this tendency not only universally applicable in all highly developed capitalistic states, but also so organically related to the course and phases of such development as to constitute a trend with the force of "law." "Extensive comparison of historically (temporally) and geographically different countries shows that all progressive cultures (capitalistic) .... show a steady increase in the activities of the state and the public managerially-autonomous bodies which parallel its work. This is shown in both extensive and intensive ways: the state and these bodies take over more and more activities, and they carry out the old and the new activities ever more fully and completely. In this fashion more and more of the economic requirements of the population, especially group needs, are more adequately cared for by the state and these bodies..... Facts of production technique lead to a steady increase in the activities of the state, local authorities, etc., ... even in the sphere of material and individual requirements."—Adolf Wagner, *Grundlegung,* Book 6, Chap. III (ed. 3; 1891), quoted in Sombart, *Das Wirtschaftsleben im Zeitalter des Hochkapitalismus,* p. 484.

and functioning of parts and the whole, and with the corroding poison of sabotage and bureaucracy in relatively stable hierarchies of command and subordination. The more complex the organization, the greater and more insistent the danger of this hardening of the industrial arteries. Regardless of the location of ownership and final authority, the only methods for combating this tendency are to be found in systematic introduction of science and scientific methods on the one hand, and in incentive systems on the other. The personnel side of the problem is of paramount importance. It can be met by use of (largely) non-commercial competition, emphasis upon individual initiative and the personal equation, wage differentials, and other means. But only a thorough grasp of the key importance of this peculiarly modern problem will show why it is that all phases and aspects of rationalization, in a technologically interlocking, commercially interdependent, and financially unified economic order, comprise a balanced system of problems and historically possible solutions, and why it is that the higher coordination necessarily carries with it exercise of administrative and policy-forming powers. On the organizational side, it is scientific management carried over into the fields of industrial coordination, and thence into the general social and economic field. It is the structural and functioning side of economic planning.

In the long run such central coordination will probably mean transfer of ownership rights either to the central government, or to regional groupings such as communities of workmen, or to various types of producers' and consumers' cooperatives. It is difficult, for example, to see any way in which capitalism can serve any useful purpose as rationalization springs the boundaries of the individual establishment; it is even more difficult to see how it can possibly survive under these circumstances as a system of ownership carrying power to manage and decide policies to the benefit of any special-interest group.

It is interesting, in this connection, to notice the criteria accepted by conservative writers for the legitimate field of governmental ownership and operation, and the bearing that some of the more important rationalization changes have upon their interpretation. Professor Herbert von Beckerath in a general discussion of the subject finds publicly owned and operated systems to be typically limited to industries having (1) the character of natural monopolies, (2) very high overhead costs, or (3) peculiar significance in the welfare work of the state. The first two characteristics are typical of railroads, street car systems, telephone and telegraph systems, electric-power and gas networks, water supply and sewage disposal, and, in a word, of all *service systems*. Because of the third criterion, slaughter houses, educational institutions, informational services, and similar functions and industrially significant institutions properly belong to the state.[59]

But few writers, apparently, have noticed that identically the same criteria would bring omnibus, radio, airplane, and similar services, most of the heavy

---

[59] Herbert von Beckerath, *Der moderne Industrialismus* (Jena, 1930):349–416.

industries, and many of the manufacturing industries into the governmental fold. Government control of power-generating and transmission systems carries it into coal and lignite production and chemical by-product utilization. Gas production on a large scale—with long-distance gas distribution in particular—involves direct linkage with coal mining, coking, chemical by-product utilization, and, in many cases, iron, steel, and machine construction industries. As pointed out in the foregoing descriptive chapters, the interdependencies between various groups of industries on account of supply of materials and equipment and the introduction of large-scale continuous processing methods are frequently so numerous and so organizationally binding that it is nearly impossible, whether for descriptive or analytic purposes, to tell where one industry ends and another industry begins. It is also true that nearly every step in the direction of further rationalization tends to increase these interdependencies, and deepens the absurdity of attempts to cut out particular segments to be earmarked as being peculiarly affected with a public interest. Thus the advance of rationalization means that the whole system, or complex of interrelated and dovetailed systems, undergoes a series of interconnected metamorphoses which break down, step by step, the traditional boundaries separating the so-called "service" industries from all others—overhead costs rise, continuous flow production becomes the rule, stocks of materials and goods are cut to a minimum in all stages of production, the managerial unit tends to take on the character of a natural monopoly, the organizational form becomes corporational, associational, or both, the pace of work and the volume of output in every segment are fixed in the matrix of a mechanically integrated sequence, etc.

Added to these trends in Germany are the peculiarities of her problem of natural resources. Practically without petroleum, with her lignite deposits rapidly vanishing, and with but scanty resources in ferrous and non-ferrous metals, the whole problem of conservation has become a matter of the greatest public concern. The power and fuel resources of Germany will depend mainly on coal in the future. All firing is being gradually transformed onto either a coal-dust or a coal by-product basis. The coal industry is becoming a chemical industry; the chemical industry is becoming a power industry; these and all other industries are erected on the bony structure of steel, and are based on the energy source of electrical current. Every transportation and communication system, every handicraftsman and every shopkeeper, every farmer, and every consumer is directly affected by the functioning of these complexes, not only as they bear in upon the national prosperity, but also as they supply each with the direct services which are indispensable conditions to work, wealth, and leisure in the modern industrial world.

The distinctions made between fields appropriate to governmental and private ownership and operation are, consequently, in large part without difference. The problems of technology, organization, finance, management, and personnel are fundamentally the same, and are being met with the same general solutions. There is little convincing evidence in Germany to support the common claim that governmentally owned and operated systems are any less efficiently organized and operated than private systems, unless one compare failures and shortcomings in the first to the exclusion of successes, with successes in the latter to the exclusion of equally significant failures.[60]

The basic administrative principle, evolved by long experimentation in the field of scientific management, of centralized coordination and integration with managerial decentralization, has been adopted in nearly all the larger governmental undertakings. As shown before, it is typical of the organization of the *Reichsbahn,* the various services of the *Reichspost,* the directly controlled and operated electric-power companies, and the various miscellaneous industrial enterprises in the control of the Reich, the several states, and numerous municipalities and communes.[61] Inefficiency and bureaucracy are to be found in many enterprises under the control of the latter two groupings, and much capital has been made of these facts to discredit public ownership. The *Ruhrgas* long-distance gas-supply system, for example, found political favoritism, nepotism, bureaucracy, technological backwardness, and other faults to be characteristic of the locally controlled networks with which they came into direct competition. Yet such facts as could be brought to light failed to justify the charge that those which were communally owned and operated were worse as a class than those

[60] "The public enterprises show, at the present time, in their technical upbuilding as well as in all their managerial policies, a thoroughly modern picture, and one which is on at least as high a technical level as that found in private industry. The commercial organization (Durchorganisierung) in the central transportation systems and in most of the public corporations has kept pace throughout with technical development. . . . ." Dr. Kurt Mendelsohn, "Die Wirtschaftsführung öffentlicher Betriebe," *Die Wirtschaftskurve,* Heft 3 (1931):294. Dr. Mendelsohn, in drawing this conclusion at the close of his article, points out that many public enterprises keep their books in such a way that it is very difficult to evaluate their technical and commercial status, but that this is not unique to the public undertaking. See also Gross, *op. cit.*

[61] Public enterprises produced the following percentages of various types of industrial products in 1925, according to material cited by von Beckerath, *op. cit.,* p. 354: coal, 10 per cent, and in Prussia 8 per cent of the coke and 5 per cent of the coke by-products; 5½–6 per cent of potash and stone salt; 18 per cent of iron ore mined; 1 per cent of pig iron; 3.85 per cent of lead ore; 35 per cent of lead production; 74 per cent of aluminum; 1.65 per cent of foundry output; smaller percentages of machine production and shipbuilding; 8.16 per cent of nitrogen chalk (1924). These proportions have probably changed a good deal since 1925, even if these "estimates" be taken at their face value. Including all properties, it was estimated (Julius Hirsch) that the ownership of governmental bodies included about 50 billion marks, or about one-fifth of the national total, in 1926. Naphtali has estimated the total contribution of all governmental bodies to the national income to approximate 10 to 12 billion marks annually—about one-fifth of the national income. This sum is the equivalent of the contribution of the combined heavy industries, the machinery industry, and the electro-technical industry; it is approximately the same as the total contribution of agriculture. See Hans Ritschl, *Gemeinwirtschaft und kapitalistische Marktwirtschaft* (Tübingen, 1931):125; Julius Hirsch, "Polizei und Wirtschaft," in the collection, *Die Polizei in Einzeldarstellungen* (Berlin, 1926):53; F. Naphtali, *Wirtschaftsdemokratie, ihr Wesen, Weg und Ziel* (Berlin, 1928); M. Saitzew, *Die öffentliche Unternehmung der Gegenwart* (Tübingen, 1930); also the *Schriften, op. cit.*

privately controlled. The worst that could be said about these enterprises was that they had failed to keep pace, as have the greater number of private concerns, with latest developments in technique and the arts of organization. Most important among the shortcomings has been failure to take advantage of methods of functional organization and managerial decentralization.

In the planning departments of governmental enterprises there has been evidenced lively appreciation of the interrelations between technological, financial, and investment aspects of operation and expansion. In no important respect are the methods of accounting, budgeting, financing, and management essentially different from those in use among the larger private corporations. Uniform cost-accounting and bookkeeping methods are in use in the *Reichsbahn,* the *Reichspost,* and in many of the large electric light, gas, water-works, and similar systems. Self-financing, by the plowing in of a portion of earnings, is widely used. About 40 per cent of the funds for expansion purposes used by the *Reichsbahn* come from this source, while about 60 per cent is the parallel figure for the *Reichspost.*[62] In general, expansion beyond the needs of the market is less marked among public than among private enterprises. While this may result in part from the monopoly or semi-monopoly character of the former, or from the general tendency, as Wiedenfeld believes,[63] for all government enterprises to be more definitely "consumer oriented" than the private, both conditions tend to approximate those which are coming to be characteristic of the dominant industrial patterns of modern Germany.

There is plenty of evidence, however, of government failure in the management of business enterprises—failure that extends far beyond details of mechanical and personnel efficiency. Only the first and very hesitating steps have been taken to integrate the technically interrelated canal, railroad, and truck transportation services. These systems, in certain areas in particular, also come into direct competition with long-distance gas supply and electric-power transmission networks. The importance of development of the latter for transportation service is especially great, since it is generally believed that it will result not only in the shipment of fuel and energy by wire, but also in a quite different geographic distribution of both population and industry. Typically, development will be, it is held, towards decentralization. The population drift towards the cities will be reversed. Industries will domicile more and more in smaller towns and urban communities. With industrialization and electrification of agriculture will go an attempt to dovetail seasonal peaks in these districts, and—what is much more important—a tendency towards a somewhat greater degree of local self-sufficiency.

Such developments might or might not decrease the volume of railroad and other types of shipping. Of greater moment is the necessity of long-range planning between and among the various complementary services, and their integra-

[62] Mendelsohn, *op. cit.,* p. 283.

[63] *Op. cit.*

tion into unified plans for entire regional areas. As they promote, so they are constituent parts of town, city, and regional planning, and failure to tie them together into balanced and interdependent networks means inefficiency, working to cross purposes, excess capacity, and a general deepening of the disorder and confusion characteristic, in particular, of contemporary urban and industrial centers.

Even greater failure has been registered in government regulation of the "forced cartels." The reasons for the general confusion which has prevailed in the coal and potash industries since, as well as before the World War, have been reviewed above. Contrary to accepted opinion in many quarters, there is little evidence that government regulation as such has been at fault. It is rather that the regulatory machinery has been too weak, that it was based on no well-thought-out plan, and lacked strength and vigor through absence of any consistent philosophy of social control. The underlying laws were the product of confusion as to purpose, vacillation as to policies, and lack of understanding as to organization. The history of these cartels affords classic illustrations of the danger of halfway measures, even if these be viewed primarily as transitional. It would have been better, in all probability, to have left the coal and potash industries to the tender mercies of the big combines than to have superimposed upon them the blankets of inconsistencies which have gone under the name of government regulation.

Not much happier is the picture of regulation of cartels and combines in general. In the main, the assertion of the *Reichsverband der Deutschen Industrie* that enough "common sense" had been beaten into the Cartel Court and similar bodies to cause them to adopt policies helpful to the cartels would seem to be justified by the descriptive facts. What government regulation has meant for the national prosperity is quite different. Regulation, to be effective along these lines, must be based upon full appreciation of technological, commercial, and organizational lines of force. Without such an understanding, regulation is apt to become confusion worse confounded, and such understanding has been, in the main, lacking in Germany.

4. RATIONALIZATION, PLANNING, AND INTERNATIONALISM

In searching into the background for the general ineptitude of governmental control in Germany, one is immediately struck by a number of comparisons and contrasts between conditions there and in the United States. The effort to blend effective regulatory power of compactly organized and semi-monopolistic economic empires with laws of competition rooted in the archaic economic conditions of the late eighteenth and early nineteenth centuries has borne fruit, in both countries, in tactics of circumvention and emasculation. The Germans have been more ready to perceive the drift of events, however, and more adroit in meeting the emergencies as they have arisen. Nothing quite so absurd, from modern technological and organizational points of view, as the Anti-Trust Laws and the

Interstate Commerce Commission has been tolerated in Germany.[64] In almost every case, the German government, before and after its first bath of meliorist socialism, has conceded the essentially unitary and integrative character of the key industries and the major transportation and communication services. As other corporational and associational groupings have been organized on a national basis, the government has been able, in some cases, to recognize the character of their origins and the logic of their growth. Such freedom of action as it has guaranteed to individual members, and such competition as it has helped to preserve have largely resulted from the essentially small scale upon which many industrial and most distributive and commercial processes have been carried out up to the present time, the exigencies of the post-war situation, and certain facts of cultural lag. Yet the drift is unmistakably in the direction of the *verbundene Wirtschaft,* and governmental parties have not been the last to appreciate these facts.

The confusion in policies and programs is partly a product of the internal struggle for the balance of power over slowly congealing and gradually unifying industrial, commercial, and financial systems. Victory to capital means a type of industrial, and perhaps nationally unified Fascism. Victory to labor means some system of socialistic or communistic planned and integrated economy. According to the respective proponents, the superficial likeness between the two systems, organizationally, would be very great. But the struggle for control—particularly when the issues are being confused by problems of racial hegemony, treaty obligations, nationalistic policies, disagreement and confusion as to details within the ranks of the major contending forces, sudden emergencies such as unemployment, reparations payments, and financial prostration—has made it impossible for any one party, or any coalition of parties, to hew to any straight line.

But overshadowing these domestic difficulties, in the problem of higher integration and control, is the simple fact that *national* regulation is largely, and in some cases completely, ineffective in the modern world. In scarcely a single respect is Germany a balanced economic unit; few of her industries can be effectively regulated along national lines. Considered from purely technological and organizational points of view, coordination and integration of the following branches of economic activity (to take but a few outstanding examples) on a national basis in Europe is a contradiction in terms: coal, lignite, coke, gas (long-distance—West Germany, Saar, Belgium, Holland, France, etc.), chemicals, power, railroads, internal water transport networks (in part, as far as Germany is concerned), oceanic shipping, telephones, telegraph, radio, airplane, highways and highway traffic, potash, iron, steel, steel products, copper, lead, zinc, alumi-

[64] The Anti-Trust Laws have completely lost any usefulness they may ever have had, since they were based upon a wholly mistaken notion of the organizational requirements for modern large-scale enterprises. The Interstate Commerce Commission in losing its power to compel combination has sunk to the level of (a not too efficient) policeman.

num, rayon, cotton, wool, silk, insurance, banking, finance, etc. It is just as senseless to try to integrate and coordinate, i.e., to rationalize and plan, these industries and services on a national basis in Europe as it would be on a state basis in the United States. One can well imagine the futility of trying to solve any of the organizational and marketing problems in the American steel industry by limiting activity to Pennsylvania, in coal by limiting control to West Virginia, in textiles by attempting to isolate New England. Yet this is precisely parallel to what happens when Germany, without regard to Czechoslovakia, England, France, Poland, Italy, Russia, and other affected countries, attempts to regulate and control any one of these industries.

That is to prove, that so far as coordination and planning within any single branch of industry is concerned, the effective unit is rarely national in extent, but usually European when not world-wide. International cartels, communities of interest, and combines, and the international affiliations of such concerns as the *I. G. Farbenindustrie A. G.*, the *Siemens & Halske-Siemens & Schuckertwerke,* the *Allgemeine Elektrizitäts-Gesellschaft,* and others, are the natural product of this economic, technological, and financial internationalism.[65]

The inadequacy of the national system is even more marked in the service industries. The railroad, telephone, telegraph, radio, and similar networks are essentially European and in many respects world-wide in scope. Power transmission networks, combining hydro-electric with steam-generated current, are essentially international. Even before the drafting of the von Miller plan, this was true as far as Germany was concerned. Lines crossed into Switzerland and Austria to the south, Czechoslovakia to the south and southeast, Poland to the east, Denmark to the north, and Holland, Belgium, France, and the Saar to the west. The von Miller plan made these connections integral portions of the national network. And these plans had scarcely been drawn before the Oliven plan had superseded it in respect to international hook-ups.

When it comes to the matter of inter-industry integration, and general economic planning, the inadequacy of the European state system becomes even more apparent. Proposals which have emanated from the various chancelleries of Europe—the "Green International," the Little Entente, the Danubian Union, the United States of Europe, the various tariff reciprocity agreements sketched, such as the customs union between Germany and Austria, various *Anschluss* proposals—have been guided in part by the underlying facts of technology, finance, and organization. If these forces were permitted to shape political boundaries, the boundaries would be almost entirely eliminated. Natural economic frontiers are now almost entirely continental. Only by chance do factors of natural resources and geographic distribution of industries coincide with national, ethnic,

---

[65] The invaluable handbooks on this subject are the works of Horst Wagenführ, *Kartelle in Europa; Deutsche, Ausländische und Internationale Kartellverträge;* and *Kartelle in Deutschland.* The last-named is particularly full and comprehensive.

cultural, or even geographic boundaries. Europe, in other words, is an effective basis for control of the major industries, where Germany, England, France, and other politically water-tight compartments are not. Many of the major industries require coordination and integration on an even larger scale.[66]

The facts adduced in this study show that in a world where the problems of science, technology, commerce, and finance are fundamentally international in scope, the national state operates almost entirely by way of lag, leak, and friction. It is a historical anachronism which stands in the way of realization of the economies of mass production, geographic specialization, and comprehensive local, regional, continental, and world planning. Because these forces transcend the spatial and organizational limitations of the national state, ownership and control from the latter base introduces about as much confusion as any other single factor that can be mentioned. From an economic point of view, the national state casts problems into an unreal and fantastic mold, subjugates control to achievement of economically preposterous ends, and institutes practices which jam up economic machinery, and spread organizational waste, confusion, and antagonism over a potentially symmetric landscape. Wars, reparations, inter-allied debts, tariff policies,[67] boycotts, racial and cultural antagonisms, political ambitions—these are its stock in trade, and they shoulder up out of the past to the eternal detriment of the more virile forces dwelling in scientific achievement and the organizational arts.

As these latter forces assert themselves, they will tend to lend even greater emphasis to the development of horizontally and vertically integrated, closed, and internationally functioning economic empires. These units are in large part already independent, or largely independent, of local political control, just as the American Telephone and Telegraph company is (in reality) independent of municipal and the railroads of state control in the United States. Interdependencies among them are becoming more and more matters of financial control, intrigue, and economic statecraft. The center of gravity is definitely tending to become financial. It is extremely doubtful whether the German government, or any government so constituted, can long hope to control any isolated portion of the anatomy of these huge international combines and spheres of influence.

---

[66] See in particular the two studies by Elemer Hantos, "Das mitteleuropäische Agrarproblem und seine Lösung" and "Die Rationalisierung der Weltwirtschaft."

[67] Rühl has shown in his interesting study of American imports for the year 1927 that only 10.7 per cent of the total may be regarded as made up of commodities which really compete with domestic production. Doubtless the same relative proportions would hold for the United States for the years immediately preceding and following. Somewhat the same proportions would most probably hold for Germany and most of the European countries. Alfred Rühl, "Zur Frage der internationalen Arbeitsteilung, Eine statistische Studie auf Grund der Einfuhr der Vereinigten Staaten von Amerika," *Vierteljahreshefte zur Konjunkturforschung,* Sonderheft 25. See also, E. A., "Der deutsche Aussenhandel unter der Einwirkung weltwirtschaftlicher Strukturwandlungen."

International agreements and conventions, semi-political in character, such as those governing postal shipments and rates, telephone and telegraph service, radio transmission, railroad and oceanic shipping rules, schedules, and services, and tariff reciprocity, have made important steps along these lines. Financial and corporate alliances and compacts on the capitalistic side, and the slow consolidation of labor-union sentiment on the worker and proletarian side, have done much to undermine the solidarity of the national state.

Yet progress has been unbelievably slow. This is partly because coordination and integration on this larger basis tends to increase the importance of the social problems involved, and, in so doing, to raise to the pinnacle of importance problems of objectives. Internationally there is less agreement here than nationally, just as there is less agreement on a national than on a local, and less on a local than on a local special-interest scale. Tangibility, definiteness, and agreement tend to proceed in inverse proportion to industrial and geographic scope, and to the range of special-interest groups included.

In the main, it seems to the writer that the one principal cohesive force internationally is to be found in the ranks of labor. Underneath the verbiage of disagreement, the drive seems to be fundamentally unidirectional and uniformly the same: the subjugation of economic processes to the achievement of security and higher standards of living. Both, in the modern world at least, are problems which must, in the main, be solved with reference to a world-wide axis of reference if solved at all. One is a problem of coordination and planning so that the greater security to all because of world interdependence shall be the indefeasible property of each; the other is a problem of coordination and planning so that the advantages of inter-regional specialization shall be added to the techniques of routine organization in the guaranty, at once, of the most extensive possible markets and the highest possible level of material welfare to the rank and file. Politically these mean that the sweep of economic forces, expressed through rationalization and economic planning, are driving power into the hands of the left wing, and away from the national state.

5. SUMMARY

Two facts stand out as of paramount importance. First, the desire to go back to a "freely competitive" capitalistic economic system is almost completely gone in Germany. Second, the possibility of such a return has been almost completely eliminated. What lies ahead?

Prophecy does not fit in with the tone and purpose of this study. Yet each future depends upon the living past that preceded it, and some bolder person may find it possible to forecast shrewdly on the cross-section which has been provided. Why are the two above generalizations stated as facts?

Wiedenfeld provides an answer to the question on the first "fact." Bonn supports this argument on every page of his searching and brilliant essay. There are relatively few reputable German economists who will contest the thesis in entirety. That thesis is that the country is finished with the old Manchesterian system. It is desired by neither labor nor capital, industry nor commerce, trade nor agriculture, consumer nor producer. This renunciation, rendered easier in Germany than it would be in the United States or England by virtue of facts of economic, political, and cultural development, has become more complete with changes in the post-war period. The attitudes and the norms of the functionary have penetrated into nearly every layer of the population. All persons seek high income levels, security, and general stability.

They do this partly because the society in which they live has deprived the individual of a great deal of his freedom of choice, and freedom in the exercise of his judgment and authority. In nearly every respect rationalization sinks the individual into the group. The whole movement, in both its technological and organizational aspects, is built on cooperative effort and pooled labor. The individual becomes attached to a union, an association, a combine, a state enterprise, or some other major administrative unit endowed with real policy-forming powers. For reasons of technology and organization these tend to be built along economic lines, with each unit functionally separated but all-inclusive for each field.

These units organized by industries—steel, coal, chemicals, railroads, communication, shipping, machinery, electro-technical products, etc.—or fields, tend to acquire powers and exercise functions of a non-economic character—social, political, cultural. In so doing, they tend to become states within states, new politico-economic units within the shell of outmoded national systems.

There are no good reasons for believing that such tendencies will be reversed in the near future. The changes are rooted too deeply in facts of organization and technology for that. The changes mean that the way is closed to any return to the previous system until an entirely new technology arises to displace that which is now dominant.

But still another factor has intervened to close the way to return—the intervention of the existing state. How far that intervention has gone has been shown in the foregoing chapters. When the pressure towards intervention from socialism began to wane, that of capital appeared in its place. The power and authority of the state now reaches into nearly every phase of German economic life, and touches nearly every aspect of the nation's social and cultural activity. Gradually this expansion of authority has led to taking the first steps in the determination of larger social objectives. Any further rationalization of the organization and machinery of either governmentally owned and administered properties or of the regulatory system of the state must inevitably drive the government farther in this direction.

Can it control the large industrial, commercial, and financial systems which have grown up within the shell of the old national system? It is highly doubtful, and for a number of reasons. Perhaps most important of these is the simple fact that the new economic empires are definitely international. In a very real sense of the term many of them are above and beyond the control of the German state. "Having gone so far in the attempt to shape economic affairs—why should we not attempt to do so according to a rational plan?" writes Professor Lederer.[68] Quite so; but that plan must be worked out on a new resource, geographic, economic, and social scale.

---

[68] Emil Lederer, *Planwirtschaft* (Tübingen, 1932):48.

CHAPTER XV

THE CULTURAL IMPLICATIONS

Rationalization affects the cultural life of the community, but it does so primarily by way of accelerating trends inherent in this side of the modern industrial system. Hence, discussion of the cultural implications of the changes reviewed can add little that is new. It should be possible to pass over this subject on the grounds that it involved only an undue elaboration of the obvious. Yet there is a tremendous German literature written on this phase of rationalization. Much of it is contentious and bitter; much of it is buoyant and optimistic. Nearly all that has been said can be summed up as interpretation of four well-recognized trends: secularization, urbanization, cosmopolitanism, and mass culture.

1. SECULARIZATION

The rationalization movement has been throughout essentially secular. Its intellectual roots are imbedded in the natural and experimental sciences of the times; its philosophical foundations are grounded on the radical empiricism and pragmatic viewpoints of machine technology. Its emphasis is essentially worldly, material—"practical." While connected by right of descent with the "age of enlightenment," industrial rationalization has lost much of the poetry of expression and the imagery of rights, duties, and obligations which characterized even that period. It possesses no Swedenborg capable of backsliding from mineralogy and blast-furnace technique to the Trinity and the New Jerusalem, no Kant to identify "pure reason" with the God-like perfection of the universal ground-plan, and no Goethe to attach reason in the form of Faust to the devil who tempts to win. The light of its inspiration is essentially dry by comparison; reason could scarcely be enthroned nowadays, but the scientist, the engineer, and the industrial magnate can receive medals and be elevated to the newspaper headlines. In rationalization there is less emphasis upon the perfection of nature, and more on the fruitfulness of science; less attention is paid to harmony and more to system and plan; there is less interest in the goodness of law, and more in the productivity of technology. In the place of abstract appeals to justice, beauty, and truth has come emphasis upon comfort, plenty, and security. Instead of proclaiming the high principles of liberty, equality, and fraternity, the proponents of rationalization set themselves to propagandize for a rising tide of prosperity, and strive to make the new disciplines palatable to the man in the street.

And it is important that rationalization be palatable to the man in the street. Its progress depends upon general willingness and ability of the masses of the people to submit to its workaday disciplines on the one hand, and the adoption of a set of life values which find expression in high material standards of living on the other. Mass production and mass consumption are the two inseparable halves of the rationalization whole, and all virtue complexes, ethical systems, and value criteria which stand in the way of the latter are pitted directly against the whole rationalization movement.

That rationalization has had but little organized opposition in Germany results largely from the fact that the ground was well prepared. In the *cliché* of the historian, the "time was ripe." The backward-looking and culture-conserving institutions had been seriously undermined even before the war. The disillusionments of the ensuing years provided fertile soil for the germination of new ideas and renewed attacks upon the old. With the decay of the authority of the traditional family, institutionalized religion, and the national state, went changed points of view. Loyalty, patriotism, piety, and duty were shorn of much of their institutional underpinnings, or attached to secular and material enterprises. The size of the family has steadily decreased, the marriage age has been postponed, women have won a new independence, the domestic establishment has lost many if not all of its economic functions, and the training of children has been taken over more and more by public schools, radio, newspapers, and the movies. The church has lost much of its clientele and even more of its prescriptive authority in the lives of the German people.The generalization holds for both Catholic and Protestant sects. Membership has declined and attendance even more so; many churches have been abandoned, and more manage to survive only with scanty audiences. Masses go unattended; religious festivals are curiosities; Oberammergau has become a huge business proposition advertised by central travel agencies in the interest of profits and the German balance of trade. Public piety has lost its meaning; half the members of a recent Reichstag had no religious affiliations, and a smaller percentage attended church regularly.

The setting up of the Republic loosed the loyalties to the emperor reigning by divine right, and the state possessing superior rights of existence ascribed to it by von Treitschke, Houston Stewart Chamberlain, and their contemporaries. The state became the football of partisan politics largely centered around the struggle of special-interest groups for control to achieve their own ends. The disintegration of the military freed German youth of the intellectual strait-jacket which had dominated the younger generation since the time of Frederick the Great. The recrudescence of extreme German nationalism under the Hitlerites is to bc interpreted more as a reaction against the impossible terms of the Versailles treaty and the economic prostration of the country following the breakdown in 1928–1929 than as significant renewal of the old systems of loyalties.

Nor has Germany been free from the corrosive skepticism which has marked the advance of science in all the great industrial countries. According to the findings of science, the earth is no longer the center of the universe, and man's well-being is no longer the principal concern of a deity ruling an infinitely elaborated cosmos. It is easy for the simple mind to see divine forces at work in the blossoming of spring; but it requires a tenuous and difficult metaphysics to trace the hand of God in the test tube. The "wonders" of science stand in simpler and more direct relation to the genius of the human species than they do to the unfolding of transcendental forces. With the advance of rationalization, the facts of technology and science tend to draw closer, to become more directly related to the round of work and leisure, and to diminish the amount of time and effort expended in submission and supplication to unknown forces.

In the deflation of the Deity, as Veblen would say, by "obsolescence through disuse," science has also done much to deflate the stature of man. He has lost much of that "soul" which German philosophers have honored to the tune of so many heavy tomes. From a self-directing, willing, and cosmically independent entity the researches of biology have reduced him to a tangle of bones, muscles, veins, and ganglia, while the psychologists have found him to be the more or less complete creature of "mechanical" stimulus and response—powerless to alter his destiny except, perhaps, within the most minute frontiers. He has complexes, libidos, and suppressed desires, but little of those divine qualities which the great German romantic, Winckelmann, gave to the Greeks of the Periclean period.

To this depersonalization of science, the discipline of the modern factory lends its compelling support. The operative is a functioning datum fitted, much as any other piece of machinery, into a mechanically controlled and regulated routine of interlocking mechanical and chemical processes. Personal contact between man and man, whether equal or superior, is either lost entirely or reduced to rest pauses, explanation of instruction sheets, or leisure hours. The goods turned out are typically standardized and uniform, and bear few if any marks of craftsmanlike skill. Workmanlike pride in the job as such is largely gone. Often the operative knows nothing of the other processes which go to make up the finished product, and little concerning the source of the materials or the destination of the finished goods. Typically he has even less of a hand in control over any phase of the functioning complex which he serves. Under highly standardized production methods, he tends to become as readily displaceable as any other component part. Training, even up through some of the more skilled and directing staff, tends to be short, formal, schematized, and standard. Any individual is easily displaced; factors of personality have relatively little to do with performance, given willingness to work and the necessary adeptness.[1]

[1] This is particularly true in Germany among the higher managerial and engineering ranks, largely because of the tremendous surplus of candidates for positions turned out by the technical schools and universities.

There are a number of ways in which the highly mechanized plant serves as a prototype for all economic activities affected by rationalization. In field, factory, handicraftsman's shop, transportation, distribution, and even the home, nearly every routine and repetitive operation is sooner or later taken over by a machine. The spirit that adjusts the control equipment on the lathe to the height of the workman also sets up quality specifications for household china, makes bowls and lids of pots and pans interchangeable, provides plans for economical layout of kitchens, bathrooms, and living-rooms, and shows the housewife how to use simplified and electrically driven washing-machines to the maximum advantage and with the minimum expenditure of time and energy.[2] Industrialization of agriculture, mechanization of handwork, and schematization of office and store layout, functions, and duties receive about as much space in the regular publications of the *RKW* as the details of organization and procedure relating to the heavy industries. Plan and order, and scientifically defensible patterns of organization and procedure are the essence of rationalization, regardless of the field of human activity which it touches. The human equation and the elements of personal judgment, individual taste, and caprice are ruled out and set aside as these changes are made. Rationalization on the human side is practically synonymous with impersonalization, and, under modern conditions, with secularization.

It would require an entire volume to describe the major changes that the environmental influence of rationalization has wrought on German standards of living. The trail would lead from the influence of the new factory environment—acceleration of the pace of work, mechanization, placing of every operation and process on an efficiency and mass-output basis, impersonalization—through the surrounding institutional set-up of urban and institutionalized existence, and to the expression of life values in the conduct of leisure hours and the purchase and enjoyment of goods and services. Throughout would be found a change towards uniformity, standardization, institutionalization, and the quantitative aspect of existence. Some German writers vilify these changes by warning against the cultural degeneration of Americanization; others see in them the promise of a new and happier era; both understand that further expansion of these forces means seepage of ideas into all layers of the population which will profoundly change the entire cultural outlook. Community singing, folk dances, the classical opera, and the formal theater are all yielding ground. Fewer German workers, if we can believe critics, sing at their work; fewer youths learn to play musical instruments; fewer girls learn and subsequently practice the more ancient domestic arts of good cooking, child rearing, and clothes making. With the disappearance of the German *Hausfrau* goes decline in emphasis upon *Kinder,*

[2] The Reichskuratorium für Wirtschaftlichkeit has a special Gruppe Hauswirtschaft, to deal with rationalization of all details of household layout, equipment, and technique. See, in particular, the various numbers of the RKW *Nachrichten,* published monthly by the RKW.

Kirche, und Kuchen, or, as Louis Untermeyer translates them, "Children, Church, and Cookies," and increased attention to schools and the cinema, the public forum, and institutionalized eating, drinking, and living.

Some of these changes can be shown by statistical tables, others cannot. As in the United States, there is a tendency for consumption of such heavy foods as rye, wheat, potatoes, and herring to decrease, while butter, eggs, sugar, cocoa, and southern fruits are more widely used. Cotton clothes are apparently giving way, in part at least, to rayon fabrics. More electric light and electric fixtures are used, more people go to hospitals, and more students to college.[3] More important than the actual increase in levels of consumption is the popularization of the notion of minimum standards of health and comfort. While not as widely known in Germany as in the United States, the notion is gradually making its way into all layers of the population and all working and professional classes. Science makes known to all the riches of the earth, and, through the thaumaturgy of technology, promises them the fulness thereof.

In all those fields in which the techniques of rationalization emphasize the service character of industrial and distributive processes, the mass of consumers is tied in with technology in an endless round of production and use. The more gas, electricity, water, and similar services used, the cheaper the rate. The cheaper

[3] The following data, taken from *Deutschlands wirtschaftliche Lage an der Jahreswende, 1929–1930* (published by the Reichs-Kredit-Gesellschaft; Berlin, 1930):29, shows some of the general trends:

CONSUMPTION UNDER THE PRE-WAR LEVEL

Year	Foodstuffs								Clothing	Comforts
	Rye*	Wheat*	Potatoes*	Herring†	Beer‡	Alcoholic drinks‡	Coffee†	Spices†	Cotton	Gas mantels
	Per capita consumption in percentages of 1913									
1913	100.0	100.0	100.0	100.0	100.0	100.0	100.0	100.0	100.0	100.0
1925	74.8	74.8	83.1	72.7	64.4	46.0	54.4	77.3	81.6	42.9
1926	63.5	80.0	54.4	64.6	64.9	48.8	63.2	78.8	64.7	38.0
1927	67.2	89.7	69.8	69.6	68.9	62.2	73.9	83.7	98.8	40.9
1928	....	....	....	70.7	73.1	66.6	81.6	90.1	74.4	35.1
1929	....	....	....	....	74.2	....	....	....	....	....

CONSUMPTION OVER THE PRE-WAR LEVEL

Year	Foodstuffs					Clothing	Comforts	Hygiene		Education
	Butter	Eggs	Sugar	Cocoa	Southern fruits	Rayon	Incandescent electric light globes	Hospital beds	Practicing physicians	Students in college
	Per capita consumption in percentages of 1913							Expenditure per capita in percentages of 1913		
1913	100.0	100.0	100.0	100.0	100.0	100.0	100.0	100.0	100.0	100.0
1925	116.0	92.3	106.4	166.3	137.2	252.6	154.1	114.0	141.5	107.0
1926	115.3	94.2	108.0	127.3	139.6	344.5	180.4	117.3	....	116.3
1927	120.9	106.9	114.3	145.5	151.4	545.1	221.6	121.0	152.1	128.5
1928	121.5	108.8	121.2	157.2	180.2	599.5	227.1	....	159.6	146.8
1929	....	....	125.6	....	....	....	....	....	....	....

* Harvest year; e.g., 1913 = July–June, 1913–1914.

† Per capita of the meat-eating population, which includes about the same group as that consuming herring, coffee, and spices.

‡ Per capita of the alcohol-consuming population.

the rate, the more will be produced. Even among those industries, as previously pointed out, which cannot be placed under the service classification by any stretch of definition, the same rules hold. Elimination of stocks, maximum turnover, continuous production and selling, standardized goods, low prices, large potential markets, and mass purchasing power go hand in hand. These factors are of increasing importance for every raw-materials industry, manufacturing plant, handicraftsman's shop, agricultural enterprise, and wholesale and retail establishment affected by the rationalization movement.

Industrial rationalization, to make a long story short, thrives in an essentially secular, worldly, materialistic, impersonal, and quantitatively minded world. In turn it lends the dynamic of its forces and the logic of its organization and structure to the reinforcement of these features of contemporary existence. It elevates the material level of living of the masses of the people as a condition to its continued existence; their interest in its techniques gradually carries its secularizing influence into every nook and cranny of national life.

2. URBANIZATION

The industrialization of agriculture and the decentralization of industry as electrification networks expand are to be added to earlier changes in technology and organization working to break down the age-old cultural dichotomy between city and country. Through good roads, automobiles, railroads, boat excursion services, and—in Germany and Europe in general—the bicycle, endless crowds of city people are debouched on the countryside on week ends, holidays, and leisure work-day hours, while there takes place a reverse flow of country folk into the city. Periodicals, newspapers, the cinema, and the radio are completing the process. Country and city are merging, until only features of landscape and town organization separate the two. The attitudes, the points of view, and the economically and culturally significant value systems of urban and rural dwellers are slowly becoming the same. Differences in manners and morals are disappearing. Rules governing the routine of work and the spending of leisure time are becoming the same.

While cultural uniformity has never been so pronounced in Germany as in the United States, the trends are unmistakable. There is perhaps even less difference between the various sections of Germany in respect to foodstuffs than in the United States. Clothing of men and women show somewhat greater variation. Yet the *Volkstracht* of Bavaria, the Black Forest, and even the Spreewald areas of Germany are nearly as much items of curiosity to the average German as they are to visiting Americans. With the exception of the hiking costumes and the "clothes-brush" hats and caps of the Bavarians, native clothes are rarely seen on the street. In the Black Forest, native costumes are to be seen only on holidays and festive occasions. Even then, their presentation has somewhat the musty air of an American costume party or a George Washington's Birthday celebration.[4]

In the changes that are taking place, the cultural center of gravity is shifting to the cities. Because of the rural custom of living in villages and towns rather than on scattered farm sites, this transition would naturally cause less of a break with the past in Germany than in the United States. But the shift to living conditions and points of view characteristic of the big cities involves, nevertheless, many and far-reaching changes. The living quarters tend to become typically smaller; there are fewer rooms, and less space in most rooms and hallways than is the case in the rural districts. As in America, the parlor or living-room tends to disappear. Kitchen and bathroom equipment and conveniences, and the accompanying ideas of bathing, shaving, personal cleanliness, and hygiene tend to become standard, uniform, and typically high grade. The family, at the same time, shrinks in size on the average. There are fewer children, and these remain single for a longer period. Children spend less and less time at home; more of the waking hours are spent in schools, on sight-seeing trips, on playgrounds, and—more recently, though the shift is quite slow—in the cinema and other public amusement places. Parents spend less time with their children, know less about their activities, and have less control in the shaping and guiding of younger-generation points of view. Women spend, likewise, less time in the home. More of them are engaged in income-receiving activities, though the common practice of peasant women working in the fields means that urbanization probably decreases the average number of hours spent in labor outside the household. Both working and leisure-hour time are, in short, spent in the city in ways different from those of the old peasant villages, and the generalization holds for both sexes, and all ages.

As soon as one moves from these descriptive facts to a consideration of the social, intellectual, and moral implications of the changes in view, one steps onto treacherous ground. A mass of silly literature has appeared on various phases of the subject—literature ranging from superficial impressions of literal and narrow-minded *Kultur* protagonists to labored excogitations written by humorless philosophers and solemn college professors. Spengler has written a heavy adumbra

[4] There was more uniformity in German national life at the advent of the rationalization era than many German writers are willing to admit. *Kaffee* and *Brötchen* were already the standardized breakfast; in-between-meal lunches, the noonday meal, and the evening supper were eaten, each at fairly regular hours, and were highly standardized in ritual and content. The same holds for the standard articles of clothing, furniture, heating and lighting equipment, the places of amusement and ways of utilizing leisure time. The creed, ritual, and sheaves of doctrine of the various churches were uniform and rigid. From a military point of view, the most highly "regimentized" person in the world was the German. The click of the heels, the stiff bow, the greeting were as standard as if the race were one of robots. And so on throughout the customs, conventions, traditions, and many phases of German material culture. The common German belief that his kind, in contrast to other peoples, insists upon more change, variety, and individuality in the daily complement of goods and services will not stand close examination.

tion in which he classes urbanization with the semi-organic complex of institutionalized forces and habits of mind characteristic, at once, of *civilization* as differentiated from *culture,* and sterile decadence as contrasted to fructifying growth:

"Now the old mature cities with their Gothic nucleus of cathedral, town-hall, and high-gabled streets, with their old walls, towers, and gates, ringed about by the Baroque growth of brighter and more elegant patricians' houses, palaces, and hall-churches, begin to overflow in all directions in formless masses, to eat into the decaying country-side with their multiplied barrack-tenements and utility buildings, and to destroy the noble aspect of the old times by clearances and rebuildings. Looking down from one of the old towers upon the sea of houses, we perceive in this petrification of a historic being the exact epoch that marks the end of organic growth and the beginning of an inorganic and therefore unrestrained process of massing without limit. And now, too, appears that artificial, mathematical, utterly land-alien product of a pure intellectual satisfaction in the appropriate, the city of the city-architect. In all Civilizations alike, these cities aim at the chessboard form, which is the symbol of soullessness.[5]

". . . . But no wretchedness, no compulsion, not even a clear vision of the madness of this development, avails to neutralize the attractive force of these daemonic creations. The wheel of Destiny rolls on to its end; the birth of the City entails its death. Beginning and end, a peasant cottage and a tenement-block are related to one another as soul and intellect, as blood and stone. But 'Time' is no abstract phrase, but a name for the actuality of Irreversibility. Here there is only forward, never back. Long, long ago the country bore the country-town and nourished it with her best blood. Now the giant city sucks the country dry, insatiably and incessantly demanding and devouring fresh streams of men, till it wearies and dies in the midst of an almost uninhabited waste of country. Once the full sinful beauty of this last marvel of history has captured a victim, it never lets him go. Primitive folk can loose themselves from the soil and wander, but the intellectual nomad never. Homesickness for the great city is keener than any other nostalgia. Home is for him any one of these giant cities, but even the nearest village is alien territory. He would sooner die upon the pavement than go 'back' to the land. Even disgust at this pretentiousness, weariness of the thousand-hued glitter, the *taedium vitae* that in the end overcomes many, does not set them free. They take the City with them into the mountains or on the sea. They have lost the country within themselves and will never regain it outside."[6]

Culture, to Spengler, is associated with rural life, aristocracy built up on a peasant or slave foundation, mystic attachment of all classes of the population to spiritual institutions, intellectual and emotional primacy of tradition, close associ-

[5] Examples are Babylon, Tenochtitlan, Thurii, Prience, Rhodes, Alexandria, Bagdad, Samarra, Washington, Philadelphia, Karlsruhe, Mannheim, and nearly all the newer American and Russian towns and villages.—Spengler, *Decline of the West,* 2:100.

[6] *Ibid.,* p. 102.

ation with the moods, caprice, and fortunes of nature, and with constantly and qualitatively changing art forms—music, plastic arts, literature, sartorial and living modes. *Civilization,* on the other hand, is the complex of moods, institutions, and ways of life of city peoples. It is essentially egalitarian, scientific, utilitarian, technological. Under its influence the aristocracy of rights and privileges is worn down, and the proletariat is slowly elevated to dominating control. The new (decadent) emphasis is upon plan, order, arrangement. Life and existence become a complex of problems—the problem of being born, of rearing, of marrying, of dying. Eating, sleeping, work, leisure, art, literature, politics, economics, philosophy—all are cast into the context of problems which demand solution according to the methods of the laboratory, the morals of the counting house, and the techniques of the factory. To this, he maintains, is added boredom, *taedium vitae,* the jaded appetite, tired sophistication. Because the problems relating to vital processes of living, thinking, hoping, and dreaming are insoluble, the cycle of existence itself loses significance. Lacking deeper criteria of worthwhileness, and finding no satisfactory answers to the value problems that disembodied intellect puts to the world of feeling, the product is sterility. Biological sterility is the race suicide of despair. Cultural sterility is the emotional product of the weariness, disillusionment, and frustration fostered by intellectualization, and is cradled in the utilitarian ethic of a decadent urban mode of life. As other cultures have merged into civilization—Babylonian, Egyptian, Indian, Chinese, Aztec, Classical—and thereby erected splendid urban mausoleums to their refined crassness and sterile futility, so Western (Faustian, "Modern") civilization is taking the inevitable "metaphysical turn towards death" that marks its return towards the kind bucolic mother earth which first nourished the frail roots of its slow beginning.

Even this much of the Spenglerian indictment against the Western World would be unnecessary in the present context, were it not for the fact that his doctrines, while repudiated by professional historians and philosophers for their rigidity, cyclic character, and the amazing egotism of the author, are nevertheless echoed in whole or in part by numerous critics of the rationalization movement. Neither a satisfactory nor a complete answer is possible here. Perhaps it will suffice to comment that for every pessimistic note of Spengler's, other writers are able to distil from the same stream of events an optimistic forecast. It is not necessary to side with either party. Careful selection of factors for interpretation, and a sufficiently clever capacity for generalization, will convince the naïve inclined to either pole.

It can be granted that rationalization, intellectualization, urbanization, city planning, utilitarianism, secularization, high material standards of living and comfort, egalitarian doctrines and institutions, the rise of the proletariat, standardization in work routines, uniformity in the basic requirements of existence, and similar cultural changes go hand in hand, and are significant features of modern trends, without granting even Spengler's descriptive conclusions. Electrification, for example, should mean a reversal of the population drift to the large cities with (in the calculable future) "ten to twenty million inhabitants, spread over enormous areas of country-side, with buildings that will dwarf the biggest of today's and notions of traffic and communication that we should regard as fantastic to the point of madness."[7] Relatively stable populations should be achieved in most industrial countries by the turn of the present century, but it is quite another matter to argue that this is biological suicide. Even were the population to decrease for several decades, such a conclusion would not be warranted, though a host of prophets would immediately rise to proclaim and enjoy such gloomy forecasts. High material standards of living, with a fairly high degree of uniformity in the equipment and paraphernalia thereof, might as readily serve as indications for the same sanguine hopes for the masses of the people as Spengler and others reserve for the elect of the past. One thing science has done is to cast doubt upon the alleged biological, intellectual, and emotional superiority of the upper classes of the past. It recognizes differences of endowment, without at the same time granting that prescriptive rights allied to particular sets of capabilities and faculties provide a better foundation for conclusions as to inherent superiority than any other set of arbitrary criteria that might be set up.

Nor does the economic and social emancipation of women, and the growing importance of the younger generation in modern cultural life necessarily imply a soft, effeminate, naïve, and childlike age. One can readily grant Sombart's characterization of the modern business man,[8] without drawing the conclusion that the childishness to which he refers is any more typical of the modern than any other period. The present is, perhaps in a rather unique sense, a *"streamlined" age*. The pace of existence seems to have been quickened over that of all other periods. Speed, kaleidoscopic change, size, color, variation—these are the other side, perhaps the infantile side, of uniformity and standardization typical of the modern discipline. The growing superficiality of contemporary higher educational systems—a trend from which the German universities are no more free than the American—is probably the inevitable counterpart of the rigorous specialization and acute analysis typical of scientific labor in field and laboratory.

How one balances up the complex of variable factors and dynamic changes to arrive at a philosophy of contemporary history depends on how far one is willing to look, and how strongly one desires to prove rather than understand. The domination of fashion, for example, has no end of detractors. It fits into the mosaic of modern existence without bringing a single element of tonal jar with it. It applies to clothes, architecture, food, habits, and beliefs, and it is of a piece with the iconoclasm of science, the dynamic character of modern technology, and

[7] *Ibid.*, p. 101.

[8] Werner Sombart, *The Quintessence of Capitalism* (New York, 1915):168–189.

the mass market requirements of contemporary industrial machinery. It affects all layers and classes of the population, old and young alike. At no time in the history of the world could *vanitas vanitatum, omnium vanitas* be written across the skyline with such (superficial) appropriateness, nor to such sweeping damnation of a way of life. Yet all such charges are based upon either a romantic and naïve view of the past, or some one past epoch, on the one hand, or a lack of understanding of the present period, on the other.

Whatever else the modern period may be, it is transitional. The generalization, of course, holds in a broad way for all periods in human history, but it is peculiarly appropriate to the contemporary world. The old molds are smashing up with amazing rapidity. Technologically, institutionally, intellectually, and philosophically nearly all is a state of flux. It is particularly easy, under these circumstances, to cut and hew available facts to fit in with the pattern of one's own preconceived notions—one's *Weltanschauung*. It is likewise easy to trace a causal nexus, linking disliked possibilities with appropriately detested changes, or connecting achievable objectives with fortuitously converging parallelograms of forces.

Rationalization, in fine, can be viewed as an agent of destruction, laying waste to leisure, the creative faculties, the powers of contemplation, and the beauty, simplicity, and quiet tranquillity of a less complicated mode of existence, or it can be understood as the perfection of a tremendously complicated but equally powerful system for producing the goods and services necessary to emancipate the species from the curse of Adam, and capable thereby of opening up entirely new vistas for the play of human fancy and the expression of the infinitely varied genius of the race. Urbanization, as cause or consequence, will be judged by the same bundle of prejudices which elevates or condemns rationalization without regard to differentiation between what it is, and what it might be if somewhat different backgrounds were provided and somewhat altered philosophies of control were to guide the hand that sketched the enforcing plans.

3. COSMOPOLITANISM

While perfecting the technical equipment which has annihilated age-old physical barriers of time and space, rationalization has placed new emphasis upon a series of interdependencies and interrelationships which destroy localism, abolish cultural isolation, and seriously alter the patterns of racial, linguistic, political, and national difference. Aside from the immense labors of ethnologists, anthropologists, sociologists, geographers, geologists, historians, and other learned men in the study, classification, and analysis of native customs, habits, conventions, tabus, social structure, local topography, mineralogy, and so forth, powerful economic forces have served to familiarize the world with the facts of cultural difference, and to provide media for cultural borrowing which scatter the facts and artifacts of each to the ends of the world. In almost every conceivable respect, rationalization means internationalism and cosmopolitanism—megalopolitanism is the Spenglerian term—with a vengeance. And as with urbanization, so the possibilities of interpretation are as varied as the stretches of the human imagination permit.

Broadly speaking, such interpretations deserve the same general answers as those relating to the trend towards urbanization. Native cultures, with their peculiarities of language, nuances of speech and expression, unique philosophical, religious, social and other institutions, and appropriately patterned material culture, represent the factors of diversity in human existence. They represent, in the patterns of contemporary institutions, though in a less organic sense, the qualitative differences found in vertical cross-sections of the history of any civilization. They are pitted against the leveling tendencies of the machine age—tendencies towards uniformity and standardization. The clothes of the Kaffir and the Igorote, the New Yorker and the Cantonese, tend to be the same. The triumph of the machine age means the universalization of the automobile, good roads, the telephone, the telegraph, and the radio. And so on throughout the range of human achievement, thought, and institutions. The story has been so frequently elaborated of late that it requires no repetition here. There is no end to the lamentations over the disappearance of the native arts and crafts and the decadence of deep-rooted traditions. Some of the elegies are incredibly jejune, and are rooted in a happy combination of profound ignorance and silly romance. Others are based on sympathetic understanding, and a genuine feeling that the changes in view mean permanent loss of exquisitely beautiful products of the more pleasant and engaging aspects of cultural evolution.

So far as rationalization is concerned—and the impelling forces behind it appear to be driving it into every phase of the material side of existence—it would appear that the truth lies somewhere in between. Its benevolent side is found in the assembly of all the known facts of observation which bear upon the problems of production, and bringing them to focus in accelerating the rate of output of those goods and services which lie at the basis of high material standards of living. As such, it is no respecter of persons or cultures. Every artifact run through the technique of production which it constructs, will be turned out in an endless stream. Its thaumaturgy lies in the capacity to spawn millions of identical objects from a single pattern. Every object so produced will be sold to the ends of the earth, regardless of its origin, its original symbolic or cultural significance, or the *cheapness* with which the machinery imitates the product of craftsmanlike skill. So far as such standardization of the material objects of existence carries with it standardization of attitudes, points of view, and life values, rationalization means "one dead level."

Yet it is worth while to recall that Brahms, Richard Strauss, Kreisler, and Rachmaninoff, to take but a few outstanding names, did exactly the same thing when they remodeled folk songs in the pattern of point counterpoint and made the fruits of their labor available to all races and creeds. The phonograph record has immortalized the artists who excelled in rendition, just as the original musical notations have perpetuated the genius of those who preyed upon the native arts for the source of their inspiration. Where mass output has lowered the quality of the musical instruments which translate the records into sound, there are, in nearly all cases, known methods for reversing such a trend. Few artists have objected because violins, pianos, harps, and the various musical instruments are standardized, and relatively fixed in contruction and tonal qualities, or because skill in playing them has sprung the place of cultural origin.

The same generalization holds for such things as Dresden china, Black Forest wood carvings, Nuremberg clocks, and other artistic contributions of the German cultural hinterland. In exchange, those from all other parts of the world come into Germany. Such interchange means an immense profusion, a luxuriance of forms, styles, and modes hitherto unparalleled in the history of the world. This becomes the possible technological heritage of every part of the globe, of every race, and every people. If, given the facts of tremendous dynamic change in the nature of modern technology itself, and the manifold diversity in backgrounds, points of view, capacities, and interests, of the various peoples, the evolution of such a material culture produces a stuffy "one dead level" within the next thousand years, the historian of the future will have more occasion for rating high the passion and the genius of the human species for uniformity than the accumulated facts of observation permit at the present time.

In fact, there is much reason for believing that the pressure will tend to turn in the opposite direction once certain minimum levels of comfort have been reached. In Soviet Russia, where people are usually—and by contrast quite mistakenly—credited with the greatest of all human passions for uniformity, emphasis upon conserving the native arts, traditions, and literature has been perhaps greater than in any other place in the world. As decentralization has been the organizational counterpart to industrial coordination and planning, so cultural diversity is looked upon as the institutional counterpart to thoroughgoing internationalism. A certain leveling tendency with respect to beliefs, codes, and philosophies is inevitable. Yet the rise of associational groupings may be merely the new form in which old cultural interests will survive. In all modern industrial countries these are to be found in great profusion. They include all the professions and all the special-interest groupings outside as well as in the economic field. As in other cases, they promise for the future just exactly what the individual and collective endowments of the species permit.

4. MASS CULTURE

Rationalization is linked through science to a secular *Weltanschauung,* and through technology to mass output. The secular point of view eats like a powerful chemical acid at the foundations of all prescriptive rights, traditional hierarchies of class excellence, and bundles of prejudices, rights, and obligations whose sole sanction is that they are deeply rooted in the "cake of custom." Mass output is unthinkable without mass distribution and consumption, and these are impossible without high material standards of living and extensive purchasing power in the hands of the mass of the people. Furthermore, a worldly-minded civilization, the technology of which must of necessity cater in large part to the mass of the population, cannot possibly avoid building up a mass culture. Hence, rationalization tends to underwrite this solely and uniquely modern phenomenon.

It is also true, as pointed out above, that rationalization relates to the structure and functioning of systems of production and distribution which are definitely international in scope and are rapidly eliminating the cultural dichotomy between city and country. Hence, its influence is at once industrializing, urbanizing, and internationalizing. The mass culture tends to overflow national boundaries, and to escape the limits that might have been placed upon it by fundamentally different economic relationships.

At the same time, rationalization aids and promotes integration and coordination in every phase and aspect of the economic machinery of every industry and the industries of every geographic area. Typically this means at one and the same time (1) centralization of the executive power to make final decisions, (2) decentralization of all administrative routine, (3) centralization of policy-forming authority, (4) long-range planning, and (5) the admixture of non-economic—political, social, cultural—planning objectives with the economic.

Descriptively, then, rationalization tends to underwrite a scientifically organized, technologically efficient, secularly minded, centrally controlled, internationally extensive, and highly urbanized mass culture. Now this might very well mean an absolute leveling out of all differences in language, customs, systems of ethics, individual preferences, and individual and group leisure-time interests if the human race were made of robots, or if it were a part of the passion for coordinated direction that human and cultural differences should be ruthlessly stamped out. The answers on both counts are easy. The observed facts of psychology, biology, and human experience tell us that human beings are not robots, and the trend to date in the major attempts at centralized coordination reveal no passion for the repression of the factors of human and cultural difference. With increasing factory and plant centralization has come increasing emphasis upon the human variable and upon decentralization of administrative control. The same has been true of all the larger combines which cover all or the major portion of particular industrial fields. The same managerially decentralizing emphasis is to be found in all plans for national or international planning, and in the workaday functioning of the various Soviet state trusts.

It is only a step from this principle in factory, industrial, and economic organization, to the notion of cultural decentralization. That is what lies behind the recent Spanish grant of cultural autonomy to Catalonia, and the Soviet official recognition of the several hundred separate languages, religions, and cultural systems of the racial and cultural polyglot which makes up the U.S.S.R. No plan for the "United States of Europe" has a chance which does not recognize the same principle.

It is quite possible that the future may see in this trend the "rationalization of culture": the problems of income and security taken care of by an immense, closely organized, administratively decentralized and internationally inclusive system, and the problems of leisure time and cultural life "solved" by maximum emphasis placed upon differences in human endowment and capacities, and upon richness, profusion, variation, and the infinite nuances of feeling and interpretation which may be expressed through any of the existing art mediums, or even other vehicles of expression still locked up in the womb of nature.

CHAPTER XVI

RETROSPECT AND PROSPECT

An attempt has been made in the foregoing pages to trace the origin, nature, and implications of the German rationalization movement. It was shown that while the movement arose to satisfy immediate and pressing needs of the moment, it was also in thorough keeping with evolutionary trends in science, industrial technology, and modern economic organization. In the descriptive sections it was necessary to point out the limitations of the movement in actual application, and to show wherein failure to grasp the full meaning of rationalization resulted in only partial success, or general breakdown in the new techniques of organization. And, finally, the implications of rationalization were analyzed for the purpose of evaluating the general organizational, economic, and social significance of the various aspects of the movement.

In summary it seems perfectly plain that the revolutionary character of rationalization cannot fully be appreciated until the movement is visualized as a whole. Only then will it become clear that the techniques, ideas, points of view, methods, and objectives involve a radical departure from past procedure. Under its complete domination nothing would be left to chance, for it substitutes conscious control for automaticity, ordered discipline for caprice, systematically articulated plans for chance coordination. It represents the bold attempt to bring all phases of economically significant human activity under the direct management of the human agent.

But it is more than an expression of the human "will to power." Rationalization of the modern type has been made possible only because of the maturation of the basic natural science disciplines. In their present stage these sciences have a technical foundation and a set of criteria which render them capable of dominating the entire range of organized human effort. The *Durchrationalisierung* (permeation of rationalization) of all economic activity is coexistent with *Verwissenschaftlichung* ("scientification") of all techniques and methods.

German experience has demonstrated that this is possible only when cooperatively carried out. Cooperation is as essential to rationalization as to organized science. This is true regardless of whether one have in mind only the local plant or the industry at large, the organization of science itself, the construction of a system of standards, or the planning of an entire economic and social system. It means the pooling of all relevant information, consultation with all interested parties, and the united effort of all those groups which are directly or indirectly concerned with the changes contemplated.

But cooperation is not possible without a common set of objectives. A fundamental condition is clear definition of aims and purposes. It breaks down when these are absent; it has a genuine function to perform when they are present. This feature of rationalization becomes even more important when it is realized that all the facts of engineering change, cost construction, and commercial and financial organization related to the movement call for careful and systematic planning. The dominating plans must be social in character, otherwise the cooperation required in order to achieve the objectives would be lacking.

Of perhaps even greater importance is the fact that all phases of the rationalization movement are interrelated so closely that its growth and expansion compel the adjusting of all detailed changes to the larger objectives. Thus, standards and scientific management, in detail and in general, are closely tied to all problems of technical efficiency and most problems of mass output. These in turn are closely associated with the whole industrial, commercial, and financial concentration movement. The interdependencies are of a quasi-organic character. Change in one direction and one field necessitates changes in other directions and other fields; these bring about still further changes in more remote fields, and so on. The problems of rationalization, in fine, are bound up in a theoretically, technologically, and organizationally balanced system. Such things as standards and time and motion studies are becoming just as much vested with public interest as the whole concentration movement.

An attempt to think through the nature and implications of rationalization makes abundantly clear the reasons for occasional successes and repeated failures in German post-war experience. It also provides a basis for gauging the possible success of similar measures in the future so long as certain factors remain constant. Thus, at the very best, detailed rationalization in the German coal and steel industries will be of doubtful value to the national economic system until solutions are found for such difficulties as the problem of quotas, the chaotic distribution machinery, the frequent lack of managerial coordination with technically related industries, and the intense animosity between managerial and owning groups on the one hand, and organized labor on the other. Likewise, rationalization can make little real progress in agriculture and distribution as long as private ownership is permitted to divide each field into multitudinous, small-sized, poorly equipped, badly proportioned, highly inefficient, and managerially uncoordinated units.

By the same token, rationalization will be retarded in Germany as long as national, political, social, and other barriers stand in the way of technological and economic forces. In many fields the German nation is smaller than the geographically significant unit. In other fields local political differences within the German Reich prevent further rationalization. In nearly all fields some form of centralized organization exists for the express purpose of pursuing anti-rationalization policies. This is particularly true of certain of the cartels and of some of the trade associations. It is usually true of the labor unions only when labor feels that it is being compelled to bear the full burden of the changes made, or when programs are inaugurated for scientifically beating down trade-union opposition.

There are definite limits set to rationalization and economic planning so long as Germany remains a house divided against itself—so long as Catholic Bavaria is pitted against Protestant Prussia, the right against the left, the industrialists against the agriculturalists, the urban against the rural districts, the cartels against consumers, the states against the Reich. The struggle of these various groups for political power is mostly grounded in vested economic interests. These conflicts betray, as they help still further to accentuate, the confusion of doctrines, the cross-currents of interest, and the lack of common objectives, characteristic of post-war Germany.

This confusion has been rather deepened than simplified with the passage of time since 1924. The Allied governments added to the political and social instability of the country so long as they insisted upon payment of reparations. They likewise tended to drain the country of the surplus investment funds required in order to carry through the various rationalization measures. Rationalization was, consequently, carried into effect in a piecemeal fashion, and under the handicap of practically complete lack of well defined aims and objectives. In this fashion, it probably increased rather than lessened the forces making for general instability and ultimate collapse.

The collapse, when it came, was so disastrous and far-reaching that it has unquestionably crippled the capacity of the country to reorganize its industrial and economic life for many years to come. Even worse, it has served to discredit the very rationalization movement itself. Because of the confusion that existed earlier, nearly everything of a positive character that was accomplished has been more recently questioned as contributory to the troubles that followed. Some look upon rationalization as indicative of a decadent civilization. Others regard it as an instrument for exploitation. Still other, and perhaps calmer, critics believe that it was largely the cause of certain of the serious maladjustments—unemployment in particular—which made the collapse inevitable.

Furthermore, the depression showed clearly and decisively that German prosperity was bound up with world prosperity. It finally became quite plain that no nation could be linked with world economic developments by a thousand ties, and at the same time attempt to cut and hew its domestic affairs along any particular line irrespective of the trend of international affairs. The failure of any degree of "rationalization" in international developments, particularly in Europe, meant the partial or complete negation of the advantages of many of the various technological and organizational changes in even the more specialized segments of the German economic system. Hence the big gains to be made in the future unquestionably lie largely in the international field. It is no accident that the depression has brought out such an immense literature in world economic and social planning, nor is it improbable that the future will see the whole problem of rationalization shifted so as to emphasize primarily the larger aspects of international economic coordination and integration.

At any rate, the rationalization movement will unquestionably lose its more purely technological characteristics in the future. Not that the problems of technique will not receive continued, and most probably increased, emphasis, but rather that the larger problems of coordination and planning will overshadow them in importance. If this happens, then the social and political implications of rationalization will most certainly grow in importance in a sort of geometric ratio.

APPENDIX A

THE STRUCTURE AND FUNCTIONS OF THE MORE IMPORTANT GERMAN CENTRAL RATIONALIZATION BODIES

1. The National Board for Economy and Efficiency *(Reichskuratorium für Wirtschaftlichkeit—RKW)* was first set up in 1921 on the joint initiative of the Ministry of Economics and the Federation of Technical and Scientific Associations. It was reorganized in 1925, and, as at present constituted, is a semi-autonomous body, receiving financial aid from the Reich and other constituent bodies. It is charged with the duty of promoting rationalization in all fields of organized economic activity, and to this end cooperates very closely with various national and regional scientific and technical "general" and "special purpose" institutes, associations, and study groups. As the recognized central headquarters for rationalization effort, it is enabled to plan, integrate, and coordinate effort within and between special fields of study, to subsidize work that especially merits attention, and to eliminate duplicate effort and working to cross-purposes. The range of its interests extends from technical and basic standards through the whole round of production in mining, manufacturing, and handicraft fields, and includes fields of research, study, and promotion involving such problems as packing and warehousing, time and motion studies, technical education, heat economy, cost-accounting, budgeting, factory organization, and household economy. It publishes a monthly bulletin, the *RKW-Nachrichten,* giving in clear and non-technical language details on the progress of rationalization work in the various fields. It has issued a monumental Handbook *(Handbuch der Rationalisierung),* now published in a two-volume third edition, giving a complete cross-section of the structure, functions, and progress of the work of the various rationalization bodies. From time to time it publishes special studies dealing with miscellaneous problems *(RKW-Veröffentlichungen);* among these are to be found the annual Yearbook. Its headquarters are in Berlin at the address, NW 6, Luisenstrasse 58/59.

2. The National Board for Agricultural Technique *(Reichskuratorium für Technik in der Landwirtschaft—RKTL)* was established in 1927 by the Federal Ministry of Food and Agriculture as a semi-autonomous body to take over and separately administer research, investigation, and promotion in the field of agricultural technique formerly carried out under the direct auspices of the Ministry. It is a registered association *(eingetragener Verein),* carrying out its work in close cooperation with scientific institutes, agricultural and technical organizations, and special committees. It works very closely with the National Board for Economy and Efficiency, and the various committees and sub-bodies attached to that organization. It is charged with the duty of advising the Ministry of Food and Agriculture on any technical problem with which that body may be faced, and, in general, of promoting the development, expansion, and utilization of all technical equipment, processes, and auxiliary aids to the increase in the economy and efficiency of production in agriculture and forestry—including gardening, fruit and wine culture, and similar fields. It has published a number of miscellaneous studies in its series, *Schriften des Reichskuratoriums für Technik in der Landwirtschaft.* Address: Berlin SW 11, Bernburgerstrasse 14.

3. The German Standards Committee *(Deutscher Normenausschuss—DIN)* was originally established in 1917 as a Standards Committee for the Machine Construction Industry, for the purpose of facilitating war supplies. It was reorganized in the latter part of 1917 to become the central standards body for all branches of German industry. Its legal status as a registered association is without significance. The functions of the Standards Committee have been very broadly conceived. Through the central office, and the various special committees, organized mainly along industrial lines, it has taken up standards work relating to practically every industry in the country. On its governing and main committees sit representatives of producers and consumers, commerce, engineering bodies, governmental officials, and scientific organizations. It has developed an elaborate and exacting machinery for satisfying its dicta that standards shall be economically useful, scientifically defensible, continuously flexible, uniformly applicable

(within the proper field), and, in all cases, the product of the freely pooled labor of all directly interested parties. It develops German General Standards *(DIN-Normen)* and German (Industry) Standards *(DIN-Fachnormen)*. The former are of more general use, applying to nearly every industry using machinery and auxiliary mechanical equipment; the latter are primarily of use within special industrial fields. (See the tables in Appendix B for details on the number and types of standards established.) The Committee publishes its final standards on standard size sheets, with standard format and set-up, as *Normblätter*. These may be given out individually or included with other standards in Standards Books *(Dinbücher)*. The Standards Books may be of regular or pocket size *(Dintaschenbücher)*. The individual sheets may also be obtained in large format for display on factory bulletin boards *(Din-Wandtafeln)*. From time to time the Committee publishes propaganda sheets, booklets, and pamphlets designed to familiarize engineers, business men, and the public with the advantages of its standards, and the progress of its standards work. It holds meetings at infrequent intervals at various places in the Reich to discover the extent to which standards have been introduced into practice. The Committee participates in international standards conferences, and works in close cooperation with the Federation of German Engineers *(Verein Deutscher Ingenieure)* and the National Board for Economy and Efficiency. Address: Berlin, NW 7, Dorotheenstrasse 47.

4. The National Committee for Conditions and Terms of Delivery *(Reichsausschuss für Lieferbedingungen—RAL)* is a special committee of the National Board for Economy and Efficiency. It was established in 1925 to carry on systematic work along the lines of the Standards Committee and in the field indicated by its title. It is, in a sense, a standards body for commerce analogous to the German Standards Committee for industry, though it is perhaps more appropriately described as a body for simplifying, systematizing, and codifying commercial rules and procedures. The rules established apply not only to terms of contract, shipment, delivery, and similar matters, but also to methods of manufacturing (types, formulae, classification, terminology), packing, handling, warehousing, and marking. It works in close cooperation with the Standards Committee, the Federation of German Engineers, and other general- and special-purpose organizations. Its standards or codified practices are issued with the *DIN-RAL* stamp, and are printed and distributed in much the same way as the German General Standards. Address: Berlin, NW 6, Luisenstrasse 58/59.

5. The Committee for Economical Production *(Ausschuss für Wirtschaftliche Fertigung—AWF)* is a special committee of the National Board for Economy and Efficiency; it was organized in 1918, and was affiliated with the National Board when the latter was founded. It is the central German body dealing with all technical problems of production in the fields of industry and the handicraft trades not specifically allocated to such bodies as the German Standards Committee and the National Committee for Conditions and Terms of Delivery. In organization, methods of procedure, and working rules it is similar to these organizations. Specifically, its work deals with the rationalization of auxiliary scientific methods and equipment (graphic computations, gear and driving mechanisms), technical methods (work and work-route preparation, flow of labor, labor processes), and the general field of factory and production efficiency (energy feed, transport equipment, factory layout, etc.). Research work is carried out on the various problems that come before the Committee, and the results of its studies are made available through the publications of the National Board of Economy and Efficiency, special lecture series, films, lantern slides, etc. Address: Berlin, NW 6, Luisenstrasse 58/59.

6. The Committee for Economical Management *(Ausschuss für Wirtschaftliche Verwaltung—AWV)* was organized in 1925 as a special committee of the National Board for Economy and Efficiency, as a registered association to act as the central body for rationalization problems in the general field of business administration and accounting. Its work is carried out by a series of special committees dealing with office organization, working techniques, accounting, business rules, purchase and warehousing problems, banking, selling problems, business terminology, industrial budgets, and trade and business literature. One of its most important tasks has been to aid in the carrying out of a nation-wide locality number system. Its work in the field of cost-accounting and budgeting has been carried out on a wide front, and has laid the foundations for extremely significant future work in this field. It works in close harmony with the various other committees of the National Board for Economy and Efficiency. Its publications appear principally as contributions to the media of that body. Address: Berlin, NW 6, Luisenstrasse 58/59.

7. The Research Bureau for Commerce *(Forschungsstelle für den Handel)* was established as a registered association in 1928 to carry on technical research and propaganda in the field of retail and wholesale trade. Its program of work includes the following: research on costs, size of warehouses, and fluctuations of turnover in retail and wholesale trade; monthly and yearly comparisons in retail and wholesale business in connection with special committees of the National Board for Economy and Efficiency; scientific preparatory work prior to taking of the German commercial census; research on credit and financing methods and problems of retail and wholesale trade; research on types of retail and wholesale trade; research on advertising and market analysis; research on market organization; research on the development of public requisition systems and governmental enterprises; development of an *Archiv* with all trade and commercial problems of domestic and foreign traffic; publication of results of research; problems of schooling for the special problems of commerce; furtherance and improvement of the practical business knowledge of merchants and academics. Address: Berlin, C 2, Spandauerstrasse 42.

8. The Institute for Business Cycle Research *(Institut für Konjunkturforschung)*, organized in 1925, has been described adequately in the text (see pp. 297–299). It works in close cooperation with the National Board for Economy and Efficiency, the various governmental departments, in particular the National Statistical Office *(Statistisches Reichsamt)*, the National Federation of German Industry *(Reichsverband der Deutschen Industrie)*, and similar bodies. Address: Berlin, W 15, Kurfürstendamm 193/194.

9. The German Committee for Technical Education *(Deutscher Ausschuss für Technisches Schulwesen—DATSCH)* was organized in 1908 by the Federation of German Engineers and the Federation of German Machine Building Associations *(Verein Deutscher Maschinenbau-Anstalten)* for the purpose of systematizing, improving, and propagandizing new and scientifically tested methods of teaching technical subjects in schools ranging from the grades through the technical colleges. It prepares slides, instruction sheets, booklets, charts and graphs, tools and equipment, standard methods and procedural rules, etc., for teaching the various subjects in the different grades. Its purpose is given as that of providing a way in which business men, engineers, and industrialists can properly influence the training and education of the younger generation in their chosen specialities. About fifty of the most important national German federations and associations are directly interested in its work. Address: Berlin, W 35, Potsdamerstrasse 119B.

10. The German Institute for the Technical Schooling of Labor *(Deutsches Institut für Technische Arbeitsschulung—DINTA)* has been adequately described in the text (see pp. 82, 101). The Institute operates an extensive experimental laboratory in Düsseldorf, publishes *Arbeitsschulung, Jugendland,* and miscellaneous brochures. Its factory units are scattered rather liberally throughout the iron, coal, and steel districts of western Germany. Address: Düsseldorf.

11. The Federation of German Engineers *(Verein Deutscher Ingenieure—VDI)* has also been adequately described in the text (see pp. 18–19). Some of its important subcommittees, each nationally organized and working in close cooperation with other rationalization agencies previously outlined, are the following:

German Society for Metallography *(Deutsche Gesellschaft für Metallkunde)*

Special Committee for Painting Technique *(Fachausschuss für Anstrichtechnik)*

Special Committee for Welding Technique *(Fachausschuss für Schweisstechnik)*

Working Association of German Management Engineers *(Arbeitsgemeinschaft Deutscher Betriebsingenieure)*

Headquarters of the Federation are in Berlin, NW 7, Friedrich-Ebert-Strasse 27.

12. Some of the other more important national rationalization organizations dealing with special fields of research, investigation, and propaganda are the following:

German Association for Testing of Materials *(Deutscher Verband für Materialprufüngen der Technik)*

Working Association for Fuel Economy *(Arbeitsgemeinschaft für Brennstoffersparnis)*

German Society for Construction Engineering *(Deutsche Gesellschaft für Bauingenieurwesen)*

German Society for Rational Painting Methods *(Deutsche Gesellschaft für Rationelle Malverfahren)*

German Bureau for Dye Technology *(Deutsche Werkstelle für Farbkunde)*

Central Bureau for Heat Economy *(Hauptstelle für Wärmewirtschaft)*

Heat Technical Headquarters for the Furnace Installation Industry *(Heiztechnische Zentrale für das Ofensetzergewerbe)*

National Committee for Time Study *(Reichsausschuss für Arbeitszeitermittlung)*

Heat Technique Advisory Office of the German Glass Industry *(Wärmetechnische Beratungsstelle der Deutschen Glasindustrie)*

Society for Organization *(Gesellschaft für Organisation)*

German Institute for Economy in Working Methods in Public Administration *(Deutsches Institut für Wirtschaftliche Arbeit in der Oeffentlichen Verwaltung)*

Central Working Association of German Retail Trade *(Hauptgemeinschaft des Deutschen Einzelhandels)*

Central Bureau for Technical and Scientific Educational Materials *(Technisch-Wissenschaftliche Lehrmittelzentrale)*

German Handicrafts Institute *(Deutsches Handwerksinstitut)*

Household Economy Group *(Gruppe Hauswirtschaft)*

13. The Kaiser Wilhelm Society for the Promotion of Science *(Kaiser Wilhelm-Gesellschaft zur Förderung der Wissenschaften)* has been adequately described in the text (see pp. 16–17). Its special research institutes are grouped as follows:

A. Chemical, Physical, and Technological Research Institutes:

1. The Kaiser Wilhelm Institute for Chemistry
2. The Kaiser Wilhelm Institute for Physical and Electro-Chemistry
3. The Kaiser Wilhelm Institute for Physics
4. The Kaiser Wilhelm Institute for Coal Research (Mülheim-Ruhr)
5. The Silesian Institute for Coal Research of the Kaiser Wilhelm Society in Breslau
6. The Kaiser Wilhelm Institute for Iron Research in Düsseldorf
7. The Kaiser Wilhelm Institute for Metallography
8. The Kaiser Wilhelm Institute for Textile Fiber Chemistry
9. The Kaiser Wilhelm Institute for Leather Research in Dresden
10. The Kaiser Wilhelm Institute for Silicate Research
11. The Kaiser Wilhelm Institute for Air Current Research in connection with the Aerodynamic Research Institute in Göttingen
12. The Research Institute for Hydraulic Structures and Water Power of the Kaiser Wilhelm Society in Munich
13. The Observatories on the *Hohen Sonnblick* and the *Obir* in Austria

B. Biological, Anthropological, and Zoological Institutes:

14. The Kaiser Wilhelm Institute for Biology
15. The Kaiser Wilhelm Institute for Bio-chemistry (with a division for Tobacco Research)
16. Physiological Research carried out by Professor Abderhalden, Halle, supported by the Kaiser Wilhelm Society
17. The Research Bureau for Micro-biology of the Kaiser Wilhelm Society in San Paulo (Brazil)
18. The Kaiser Wilhelm Society for Anthropology, Human Inheritance, and Eugenics
19. The Kaiser Wilhelm Institute for Brain Research
20. The German Psychiatric Research Institute in Munich
21. The Kaiser Wilhelm Institute for the Physiology of Labor

22. The Hydro-biological Institute of the Kaiser Wilhelm Society in Plön (Holstein)
23. The Biological Station in Lunz
24. The German Entomological Museum of the Kaiser Wilhelm Society
25. The Rossiten Ornithological Observatory of the Kaiser Wilhelm Society
26. The Kaiser Wilhelm Institute for Research on Breeding

C. Social Science Institutes:

27. The Kaiser Wilhelm Institute for German History
28. The Institute for Foreign Public Law and National Law of the Kaiser Wilhelm Society
29. The Institute for Foreign and International Private Law of the Kaiser Wilhelm Society
30. The Institute "Bibliotheca Hertziana" of the Kaiser Wilhelm Society in the Palazzo Zuccari in Rome
31. The Kaiser Wilhelm Institute for Medicinal Research in Heidelberg
32. The Institute for Foreign Visitors (Harnack House)
33. The Zoological Station in Rovigno

APPENDIX B

TABLE 1

German (DIN-) and Special Industry (FACH-) Standards Proposed (and Under Consideration) and Established by the Deutscher Normenausschuss and Affiliated Industrial Groups by Years, 1918–1930*

Year	German (DIN) standards		Special (FACH) industry standards		Totals	
	Proposed	Established	Proposed	Established	Proposed	Established
1918	20	6	......	......	20	6
1919	60	35	......	......	60	35
1920	120	110	......	......	120	110
1921	180	235	......	......	180	235
1922	277	216	92	119	369	335
1923	375	389	120	182	495	571
1924	551	526	151	222	702	748
1925	520	830	78	405	598	908
1926	522	1,101	262	608	784	1,709
1927	515	1,384	312	809	827	2,193
1928	536	1,657	369	1,155	905	2,812
1929	475	1,650	616	1,304	1,091	2,954
1930	522	1,792	508	1,544	1,030	3,336

* Material supplied by the Deutscher Norme nausschuss, Berlin.

TABLE 2

NUMBER OF GERMAN GENERAL STANDARDS *(Dinormen)* IN COURSE OF DEVELOPMENT AND FINALLY APPROVED BY THE DEUTSCHER NORMENAUSSCHUSS, 1929 AND 1930*

Field	In the course of development		Finally approved and in effect	
	1929	1930	1929	1930
1. General basic standards and technical basic standards	18	22	297	321
2. Valves and fittings	88	91	34	49
3. Autogenous industry	....	....	14	14
4. Building industry	68	73	332	352
5. Libraries	....	1	4	4
6. Office and drafting equipment	3	3	....	....
7. Steam boilers	1	1	3	3
8. Railroads	4	2	27	30
9. Bottles	3	3	....	3
10. Conveyors	....	....	1	1
11. Foundry practice	5	5	2	2
12. Home economics	16	10	52	65
13. Hoisting machinery	2	2	16	16
14. Trunks	1	....	....	1
15. Capacity and acceptance tests	....	....	1	2
16. Furniture	2	2	3	3
17. Sewing machines	1	2	6	6
18. Photography	3	3	4	4
19. Piano industry	3	3	2	2
20. Pipe lines	81	82	127	128
21. Typewriters	3	3	26	26
22. Welding	....	....	5	5
23. Materials	15	18	86	117
24. Shoe industry	....	....	8	8
25. Street railways	50	43	1	9
26. Mechanical power transmission	3	3	24	25
27. Weighing and testing machines	1	1	1	1
28. Hydraulic turbines	....	....	5	5
29. Tools	59	75†	207	222†
30. Machine tools	14	17	36	36
31. Machine industry: general	30	35	326	332
32. Heating plants	1	5	....	....
33. Breathing apparatus	....	3	....	....
34. Undertaker's profession	....	1	....	....
35. Horticulture	....	5	....	....
36. Optics	....	4	....	....
37. Foundation engineering	....	4	....	....
Total	475	522	1,650	1,792

* Material supplied by the Deutscher Normenausschuss, Berlin.

† Including jigs and fixtures and hand tools.

TABLE 3

GERMAN STANDARDS FOR SPECIAL INDUSTRIES (*Din-Fachnormen*): NUMBER IN COURSE OF DEVELOPMENT BY THE DEUTSCHER NORMENAUSSCHUSS AND NUMBER FINALLY APPROVED AND IN EFFECT* 1929 AND 1930

Field	In the course of development		Finally approved and in effect	
	1929	1930	1929	1930
1. Mining	103	92	134	171
2. Chemical apparatus	7	4	67	70
3. Printing industry	1	....	5	6
4. Railway car building	12	7	64	71
5. Electrical engineering	89	40	267	337
6. Bicycle manufacture	21	....	17	44
7. Fire fighting technique	25	25	19	19
8. Butcher shop machinery	....	....	10	10
9. Woodworking machinery	14	14	10	10
10. Moving picture technique	....	....	7	7
11. Automotive industry	31	53	218	210
12. Hospitals	45	36	14	26
13. Agriculture	54	50	19	32
14. Locomotives	118	78	371	416
15. Aeronautics	12	18	33	41
16. Testing materials	18	22	12	16
17. National purchase specifications	....	....	2	3
18. Textile industry	56	61	35	53
19. Surveying technique	8	8	....	....
20. X-Ray technique	2	....	....	2
Total	616	508	1,304	1,544

* Material supplied by the Deutscher Normenausschuss, Berlin.

TABLE 4

BITUMINOUS COAL MINING, 1913–1929*

Year	Establishments	Employed persons	Employed persons per establishment (3÷2)	Wages and salaries in 1,000 marks	Average annual wage in marks (5÷3)
1	2	3	4	5	6
1913†	350	654,017	1,868.6	1,094,703	1,673.8
1913‡	285	490,709	1,721.8	869,967	1,772.9
1925	343	557,087	1,624.2	1,101,987	1,978.1
1926	314	514,807	1,639.5	1,124,652	2,184.6
1927	303	542,062	1,789.0	1,235,354	2,279.0
1928	294	517,642	1,760.7	1,239,220	2,394.0
1929§	266	517,401	1,945.1	1,316,557	2,545.0

Year	Production			Value of output in 1,000 marks	Value of output per ton in marks (10÷7)	Value of output per establishment in marks (10÷2)	Value of output per employee in marks (10÷3)	Ratio of average income per employee to average value of output per employee (13÷6)
	Quantity in 1,000 tons	Output per worker in tons (7÷3)	Output per establishment in tons (7÷2)					
	7	8	9	10	11	12	13	14
1913†	190,109.4	290.7	543,170.0	2,135,978	11.24	6,102,794	3,265.9	.513
1913‡	140,753.2	286.8	493,870.8	1,640,848	11.66	5,757,361	3,343.8	.530
1925	132,622.1	238.1	386,653.3	1,903,463	14.35	5,549,454	3,416.8	.579
1926	145,295.7	282.2	462,725.1	2,038,901	14.03	6,493,315	3,960.5	.552
1927	153,599.4	283.4	506,928.7	2,205,041	14.36	7,277,363	4,067.9	.560
1928	150,860.6	291.4	513,131.2	2,220,170	14.72	7,551,598	4,289.0	.558
1929§	163,440.6	315.9	614,438.3	2,480,485	15.18	9,325,131	4,794.1	.531

* *Statistisches Jahrbuch für das Deutsche Reich*, 1930:104. † Pre-war territory. ‡ Present territory. § Estimated figures.

TABLE 5

LIGNITE MINING, 1913–1929*

Year	Establishments	Employed persons	Employed persons per establishment (3÷2)	Wages and salaries in 1,000 marks	Average annual wage in marks (5÷3)
1	2	3	4	5	6
1913†	465	58,958	126.8	79,607	1,350.2
1913‡	464	58,947	127.0	79,596	1,350.3
1925	404	82,023	203.0	153,565	1,872.2
1926	364	76,688	210.7	150,246	1,959.2
1927	338	72,324	214.0	149,273	2,063.9
1928	312	72,589	232.7	168,133	2,316.2
1929§	293	73,610	251.2	176,656	2,400.0

Year	Production			Value of ouptut in 1,000 marks	Value of output per ton in marks (10÷7)	Value of output per establishment in marks (10÷2)	Value of output per employee in marks (10÷3)	Ratio of average income per employee to average value of output per employee (13÷6)
	Quantity in 1,000 tons	Output per worker in tons (7÷3)	Output per establishment in tons (7÷2)					
	7	8	9	10	11	12	13	14
1913†	87,233.1	1,479.6	187,598.1	191,920	2.20	412,731.1	3,255.2	.415
1913‡	87,228.1	1,479.8	187,991.6	191,902	2.20	413,581.9	3,255.5	.415
1925	139,724.6	1,703.5	345,852.9	389,377	2.78	963,804.4	4,747.2	.394
1926	139,150.6	1,814.5	382,281.8	387,794	2.89	1,065,368.1	5,056.8	.387
1927	150,503.9	2,081.0	445,277.8	423,900	2.82	1,254,142.0	5,861.1	.352
1928	165,588.1	2,281.2	530,731.1	468,603	2.83	1,501,932.7	6,455.6	.359
1929§	174,454.0	2,370.0	595,406.1	496,294	2.85	1,693,836.1	6,742.2	.356

* *Stat. Jahrbuch*, 1930:104. † Pre-war territory. ‡ Present territory. § Estimated figures.

TABLE 6

HORSEPOWER EMPLOYED IN GERMAN INDUSTRIES, 1907 AND 1925*

Industrial groups	1925		1907†		Percentage increase	
	Primary	Electric	Primary	Electric	Primary	Electric
Mining	4,266,788	2,614,268	1,091,311	240,555	291.0	986.8
Stone and clay products	627,003	608,711	481,394	117,217	30.2	419.3
Production of iron and other metals	2,435,394	3,178,163	867,290	224,564	180.8	1,315.3
Iron, steel, and other metal products	360,063	564,890	261,535	91,195	37.7	519.4
Machinery, except electric	683,695	1,456,727	333,879	158,748	104.8	817.6
Electro-technical	200,861	489,141	55,331	52,080	263.0	839.2
Chemical	1,118,825	898,545	212,395	74,232	426.8	1,110.5
Textile	1,217,459	809,116	795,745	94,028	53.0	760.5
Paper and printing	881,310	678,390	435,973	122,359	102.1	454.4
Leather and linoleum	118,998	134,328	56,025	19,649	112.4	583.6
Rubber and asbestos	50,526	79,999	22,113	5,552	128.5	1,340.9
Wood and wood products	589,547	662,393	383,590	98,602	53.7	571.8
Musical instruments and toys	20,161	37,321	11,569	6,557	74.3	469.2
Foods and beverages	1,467,952	1,168,591	996,338	173,965	47.3	571.7
Clothing	57,911	119,903	42,925	20,784	34.9	476.9
Construction	310,023	261,719	134,826	24,012	129.9	990.0
Water, gas, and electricity	6,776,879	439,681	997,806	110,454	579.2	298.1
All industries	21,183,395	14,201,886	7,180,045	1,634,553	195.0	768.9

* *Stat. Jahrbuch* 1930:89. † Present territory.

TABLE 7

ELECTRIC POWER PRODUCTION OF PRINCIPAL PRODUCING COUNTRIES,* 1913, 1920, 1925 AND 1929†
(in billions of kilowatt hours)

Country	1913	1920	1925	1929
Germany	7.5	13.0	20.3	30.7
Great Britain	6.0	8.8	11.8	16.3
France	3.5	6.8	10.2	14.3
Italy	2.5	4.5	7.4	12.2
Russia	1.9	2.3	5.2	6.5
United States	17.5	52.3	81.8	125.0
Totals	38.9	87.7	136.7	205.0
Index	*100*	*225*	*351*	*527*

* In plants producing current for sale to the public and for their own consumption.
† E. A., *Der deutsche Aussenhandel . . . . Strukturwandlungen*, I: 292.

TABLE 8

INSTALLED CAPACITY OF ELECTRIC MOTORS AND GENERATORS IN IMPORTANT INDUSTRIAL COUNTRIES, 1907 AND 1925*

Country	Electric motors			Electric generators		
	1907	1925		1907	1925	
	1,000 kw.		1907=100	1,000 kw.		1907=100
Germany	1,500	11,446	*763*	1,000	9,979	*998*
France	300	4,875	*1,625*	600	6,000	*1,000*
Great Britain	800	6,000	*750*	1,750	7,090	*405*
Italy	250	2,403	*961*	500	2,688	*538*
United States	3,000	26,250	*875*	6,500	30,400	*468*
Totals	5,850	50,974	*871*	10,350	56,157	*543*

* E. A., *Der deutsche Aussenhandel . . . . Strukturwandlungen*, I: 294.

TABLE 9

PRODUCTION OF RAW MATERIALS IN GERMANY IN 1913
EARLIER AND PRESENT BOUNDARIES*

Raw materials	Earlier	Present	Loss	
	Tariff boundaries			
	1,000 tons			Per cent
Coal	190,109	140,753	49,356	*26*
Coke	34,630	31,668	2,962	*9*
Lignite	87,233	87,228	5	*0*
Petroleum	121	71	50	*41*
Iron ore	35,941	7,309	28,632	*80*
Zinc ore†	299	120	179	*60*
Lead ore†	100	61	39	*39*
Pig iron	19,312	10,916	8,396	*43*
Fluid and cast steel	18,697	11,916	6,781	*36*
Lead	188	148	40	*21*
Zinc‡	279	111	168	*60*
Potash	11,957	11,607	350	*3*
Thomas slag	2,280	1,317	963	*42*

* E. A., *Der deutsche Aussenhandel . . . . Strukturwandlungen*, I: 329.
† Metallic content. ‡ Crude and refined.

TABLE 10

ABILITY, TRAINING, AND FUNCTION REQUIRED OF THE STAFF OF DIFFERENT SIZES AND TYPES OF UNDERTAKING—AS SUPPOSED BY HENRI FAYOL*

Staff of the Technical Function of a Big Concern

Class of employee	Characteristics or special abilities						Total value percentage
	Administrative percentage	Technical percentage	Commercial percentage	Financial percentage	Security percentage	Accounting percentage	
Big establishments							
Workmen	5	85	....	....	5	5	100
Foreman	15	60	5	....	10	10	100
Shop manager	25	45	5	....	10	15	100
Head of division	30	30	5	5	10	20	100
Head of technical department	35	30	10	5	10	10	100
Manager	40	15	15	10	10	10	100
Several establishments							
General manager	50	10	10	10	10	10	100
State industry							
Minister	50	10	10	10	10	10	100
Head of state department	60	8	8	8	8	8	100
Heads of Industrial Concerns of all Sizes							
Elementary undertaking	15	40	20	10	5	10	100
Small firm	25	30	15	10	10	10	100
Medium-sized firm	30	25	15	10	10	10	100
Large firm	40	15	15	10	10	10	100
Very large firm	50	10	10	10	10	10	100
State undertaking	60	8	8	8	8	8	100

* Henri Fayol, *Industrial and General Administration* (published by the International Management Institute, Geneva), p. 11.

TABLE 11

FATAL ACCIDENTS IN THE RUHR COAL-MINING DISTRICT*

Year	Absolute number	Number per 100 employees	Number per 10,000 working shifts	Number per 10,000 tons production
1912	1,068	2.894	....	0.105
1913	1,089	2.664	0.084	0.095
1914	1,005	2.616	0.086	0.102
1915	1,003	3.405	0.104	0.116
1916	1,218	3.865	0.103	0.129
1917	1,551	4.459	0.120	0.156
1918	1,327	3.809	0.105	0.138
1919	1,116	2.789	0.097	0.157
1920	1,176	2.500	0.078	0.133
1921	1,128	2.171	0.070	0.119
1922	1,093	2.072	0.066	0.112
1923	678	1.288	....	0.161
1924	902	2.304	0.076	0.095
1925	1,128	2.870	0.095	0.108
1926	850	2.297	0.079	0.075
1927	838	2.180	0.075	0.071
1928	688	1.929	0.067	0.060
1929	716	1.912	0.069	0.058

* *Jahresbericht des Vereins für die bergbaulichen Interessen* (Essen, 1929), p. 84.

TABLE 12

AGE DISTRIBUTION OF COAL WORKERS IN THE RUHR DISTRICT FOR VARIOUS YEARS*

Ages	1893		1902		1905		1909		1927		1928	
	Number	Per cent of total	Number	Per cent of total	Number	Per cent of total	Number	Per cent of total	Number	Per cent of total	Number	Per cent of total
15	4,738	2.99	9,572	3.84	9,145	3.39	11,636	3.34	1,445	0.37	1,659	0.43
16	....	....	....	....	....	....	....	....	3,040	0.77	3,393	0.89
17	....	....	....	....	....	....	....	....	4,657	1.18	4,758	1.24
18	....	....	....	....	....	....	....	....	7,116	1.80	6,019	1.57
19	....	....	....	....	....	....	....	....	10,804	2.74	8,414	2.20
20	....	....	....	....	....	....	....	....	12,267	3.10	10,958	2.87
15–20	33,166	20.94	46,800	18.89	48,218	17.88	60,170	17.27	39,329	9.96	35,201	9.20
21–25	24,984	15.78	41,261	16.66	41,096	15.24	52,787	15.15	79,491	20.13	72,954	19.05
26–30	27,818	17.57	50,523	20.39	54,290	20.13	64,994	18.66	73,849	18.70	48,303	19.86
31–35	22,075	13.94	36,742	14.84	43,141	16.00	58,359	16.75	46,296	11.72	38,299	12.64
36–40	16,908	10.69	29,019	11.71	32,636	12.10	40,672	11.67	39,347	9.96	37,652	10.01
41–45	14,089	8.90	19,991	9.07	22,949	8.51	31,303	8.99	37,709	9.55	32,831	9.84
46–50	8,832	5.58	11,995	4.84	14,543	5.39	20,619	5.92	34,015	8.61	22,572	8.58
51–55	5,918	3.74	6,971	2.81	7,886	2.92	11,110	3.19	24,984	6.33	22,572	5.90
56–60	2,925	1.85	3,033	1.23	3,462	1.28	5,757	1.65	13,024	3.30	11,685	3.05
61–65	1,112	0.70	1,029	0.42	1,146	0.42	1,935	0.56	5,597	1.42	5,519	1.44
66–70	443	0.28	298	0.12	290	0.11	572	0.16	1,039	0.26	1,425	0.37
Over 70	100	0.06	45	0.02	42	0.02	111	0.03	247	0.06	229	0.06
Total	158,368	100	247,707	100	269,699	100	248,389	100	394,927	100	382,524	100
Average age	30.5		30.6		31.0		32.0		33.9		34.0	

* *Glückauf*, No. 5, 1929, p. 182.

… BY BRANCH OF INDUSTRY AND TYPE OF ACTIVITY, 1928*

Branch of industry	Employer organizations			Type of activity							
	National	State and regional		Economic problems				Labor problems		Both economic and labor problems	
				Total		Special activities					
		Total	Affiliated with national organization	National	Local	National	Local	National	Local	National	Local
1. Agriculture, Horticulture, and Animal husbandry	45	218	207	41	8	....	....	1	1	3	2
2. Forestry, fishing	10	.....	.....	6	....	1	....	....	....	4	....
3. Mining	15	46	12	11	16	5	7	2	8	2	10
4. Stone and clay products	68	45	....	49	14	17	6	5	7	14	24
5. Iron and metals mining	44	17	12	42	3	27	2	....	1	2	1
6. Iron and metal products	120	117	85	105	18	56	6	1	9	14	5
7. Machine and vehicle manufacture	123	2	....	121	2	58	....	....	....	2	....
8. Electro-technical industry	36	63	55	32	1	9	....	....	5	4	2
9. Chemical industry	62	40	34	57	2	25	2	2	....	3	4
10. Textile industry	124	142	82	113	39	60	21	2	10	9	11
11. Paper industry and multigraphing	65	37	18	47	15	28	3	2	....	16	4
12. Leather and linoleum industry	20	30	26	14	2	5	1	2	2	4	....
13. Rubber and asbestos industry	6	....	....	4	....	1	....	....	....	2	....
14. Wood	66	127	89	44	18	10	1	2	10	20	10
15. Musical instruments and toys	20	15	10	16	3	2	....	1	1	3	1
16. Foodstuffs	115	181	157	90	8	21	1	4	3	21	13
17. Clothing industry	64	111	88	37	7	12	....	8	9	19	7
18. Building industry	27	164	155	9	1	....	1	1	1	17	7
19. Water, gas, and electricity distribution	9	19	19	8	....	3	....	1	....	....	....
20. Commercial enterprises	297	404	280	255	72	69	19	9	16	33	36
21. Insurance	36	30	27	28	....	6	....	2	....	6	3
22. Transportation	35	101	75	27	10	8	....	2	6	6	10
23. Hotels and restaurants	10	26	23	6	2	3	....	....	1	4	....
24. Public administration	25	41	37	13	2	4	....	3	1	9	1
25. Industries devoted to health and hygiene	10	....	....	8	....	1	....	....	....	2	....
26. Household science	3	37	36	....	....	....	....	....	....	3	1
Total	1,455	2,013	1,527	1,183	243	431	70	50	91	222	152

* *Stat. Jahrbuch*, 1930: 575.

TABLE 14

LABOR UNION RATE OF WAGES*

AVERAGE HOURLY AND WEEKLY WAGES OF SKILLED AND UNSKILLED WORKERS, 1925–1929

Year	Hourly wage rate†				Weekly wages‡			
	Skilled workers		Unskilled workers		Skilled workers		Unskilled workers	
	Pfennigs	Percentage of average 1927-1929	Pfennigs	Percentage of average 1927-1929	Marks	Percentage of average 1927-1929	Marks	Percentage of average 1927-1929
1925	86.2	82.2	61.8	79.6	42.13	82.9	31.86	81.9
1926	93.1	88.8	66.6	85.7	45.49	89.4	34.25	88.0
1927	98.4	93.8	71.5	92.0	47.70	93.8	36.21	93.1
1928	105.8	100.8	78.6	101.1	51.26	100.9	39.18	100.7
1929	110.6	105.4	83.0	106.8	53.53	105.3	41.31	106.2

* *Stat. Jahrbuch*, 1930: 299.

† The figures are averages of the monthly figures given in the *Jahrbuch*. The monthly figures are weighted averages of the union wage rates for full-time workers in the highest age class in 12 industries. In general the data are time rates; when piece rates are given the earnings for average efficiency are taken.

‡ Wages for regular weekly working period, usually 48 hours, but from 46.5 to 48 hours in construction, from 46 to 48 in lumber, from 48 to 52 in metal industry, from 51 in national railways, and 54 hours for surface workers in mining.

TABLE 15

INDEX NUMBERS OF WHOLESALE PRICES OF FINISHED GOODS (1913=100)
YEARLY AVERAGES, 1924–1929*

	1924	1925	1926	1927	1928	1929
Consumption Group						
Agriculture†	129.4	133.8	132.9	133.3	139.4	141.3
Industry‡	128.2	136.4	132.5	129.7	136.6	138.1
Household:						
Household furnishings§	171.3	164.2	156.9	154.5	168.1	165.7
Clothing‖	181.6	181.0	165.1	163.2	178.6	174.9
Production Group						
Machines:						
Agricultural machines ¶	129.2	124.5	125.2	124.7	126.8	127.0
Industrial machines ¶	128.2	138.0	139.7	139.5	144.8	147.8
All machines	127.7	135.1	136.3	135.8	140.9	143.8
Small iron ware:						
Tools	134.4	134.4	129.6	118.8	125.6	124.9
Household utensils	166.6	155.1	149.2	145.0	155.3	155.4
All small iron ware	138.7	138.5	134.1	124.6	132.4	132.4
Transport equipment:						
Trucks ¶	93.2	87.7	74.0	66.0	65.7	65.8
Automobiles ¶	114.4	99.4	78.3	67.7	63.3	61.6
Furniture	....	....	144.2	147.1	163.4	159.3
Textile products	189.4	188.2	170.5	167.6	181.7	180.1
Shoes	133.6	137.2	132.1	136.8	159.6	142.6
All finished goods	156.2	156.7	149.5	147.3	158.6	157.4

* *Stat. Jahrbuch,* 1930: 279.
† Dead stock.
‡ Industrial equipment.
§ Includes house linen and bedding.
‖ Textile products and shoes.
¶ Index number is based on consumer price.

TABLE 16

INDEX NUMBERS OF WHOLESALE PRICES (1913=100)
YEARLY AVERAGES, 1924–1929*

	1924	1925	1926	1927	1928	1929
Farm products						
Plant foods	115.1	127.1	130.5	153.8	142.2	126.3
Animals	102.1	120.2	120.9	111.5	111.3	126.6
Animal products	155.3	162.2	145.7	142.9	144.0	142.1
Feed	104.3	122.4	114.6	146.1	147.4	125.9
All farm products	119.6	133.0	129.3	137.8	134.3	130.2
Groceries	131.0	135.8	131.5	129.2	132.8	125.2
Raw materials and semi-manufactured products						
Coal	150.3	128.7	127.8	129.2	132.3	137.3
Iron ore and iron	122.9	128.7	124.2	125.0	127.5	129.5
Other metals	110.9	122.6	117.0	107.5	105.5	118.4
Textiles	208.3	190.8	150.4	153.1	159.4	140.6
Hides and leather	124.9	124.7	114.8	133.6	152.8	124.5
Chemicals	130.3	127.3	123.0	124.2	126.3	126.8
Artificial fertilizers	90.9	88.3	86.3	83.3	81.8	84.5
Fats and oils	131.7	138.0	131.1	125.8	120.6	128.0
Rubber	34.5	93.9	62.7	47.1	29.6	28.4
Paper and pulp	140.1	158.6	151.5	150.1	150.4	151.2
Building materials	143.7	153.0	144.6	158.0	159.1	158.9
All raw materials and semi-manufactures	142.0	141.0	129.7	131.9	134.1	131.9
Manufactures						
Producers' goods	128.5	135.9	132.5	130.2	137.0	138.6
Consumers' goods	177.1	172.4	162.2	160.2	174.9	171.6
All manufactures	156.2	156.7	149.5	147.3	158.6	157.4
All commodities	137.3	141.8	134.4	137.6	140.0	137.2

* *Stat. Jahrbuch*, 1930: 278.

TABLE 17

National Cost of Living Index Number
Yearly Averages, 1925–1929*

	1925	1926	1927	1928	1929
Total cost of living†	139.8	141.2	147.6	151.7	153.8
Total expenditure, exclusive of housing	154.5	151.6	155.8	158.3	160.8
Food	147.8	144.4	151.9	152.3	154.5
Housing	81.5	99.9	115.1	125.7	126.2
Heating and lighting	139.8	142.3	143.8	146.4	151.1
Clothing	173.2	163.6	158.6	170.1	171.8
Miscellaneous, including transportation	183.1	187.1	183.7	187.9	191.9
Food, housing, heating and lighting, clothing	135.3	136.5	143.9	148.0	149.9

* *Stat. Jahrbuch*, 1930: 275. The index is a percentage of monthly expenditure of a worker's family of five members for a fixed budget, to pre-war expenditure. Yearly indexes are averages of monthly indexes.

† Food, housing, heating and lighting, clothing, miscellaneous, and transportation (taxes and social expenditures excluded).

TABLE 18

Unemployment and Part-Time Work*
Average Per Cent of Total Membership of Reporting Labor Unions Unemployed or Working Part Time, 1924–1929

Year	Unemployed: Per cent of total membership			Part-time workers: Per cent of total membership		
	Male	Female	Total	Male	Female	Total
1924	14.7	9.3	13.5	14.9	16.4	15.3
1925	7.1	5.5	6.7	7.6	11.9	8.6
1926	18.3	16.7	18.0	13.3	26.9	16.0
1927	9.1	6.7	8.7	2.8	5.9	3.4
1928	8.8	7.7	8.6	4.3	12.8	5.7
1929	13.6	11.2	13.2	5.8	15.9	7.5

* *Stat. Jahrbuch*, 1930: 320.

TABLE 19

GROWTH OF THE COOPERATIVE MOVEMENT

Purchasing Cooperatives of the Handicraft Trades*

Year	Total number of cooperative societies	Number of reporting cooperative societies	Total turnover in 1,000 marks
1913	323	247	37,833
1925	859	592	246,648
1926	831	589	248,368
1927	893	626	299,607
1928	854	614	299,192
1929	793	606	296,085

Purchasing Cooperatives of the Retail Trade*

Year	Total number of purchasing cooperatives	Number of reporting cooperative societies	Total turnover in 1,000 marks
1913	39	32	17,066
1925	605	407	480,357
1926	580	361	406,488
1927	592	378	393,566
1928	591	381	454,015
1929	584	424	546,110

Turnover of the Central Storage Institutions of the Supply and Marketing Cooperatives attached to the National Federation of German Agricultrual Cooperatives—Raiffeisen*

Year	Total turnover in 1,000 marks	Turnover in 1,000 marks			
		Grain	Potatoes	Fertilizer	Fuels
1913	407,122	130,454	?	120,108	20,257
1925	808,741	273,027	15,795	254,991	29,344
1926	744,647	257,544	10,942	240,051	30,164
1927	815,333	245,212	13,715	254,939	30,337
1928	807,961	256,398	10,699	242,618	45,509
1929	866,504	280,503	10,204	272,474	43,883
1930	841,007	296,564	6,714	271,416	38,105

Turnover of the Consumers' Cooperatives (including Wholesale Deliveries) of the Member Associations of the two Central Consumers' Cooperative Societies.*†

Year	Turnover in 1,000 marks	Year	Turnover in 1,000 marks
1913	634,700	1928	1,235,414
1925	732,863	1929	1,382,659
1926	879,848	1930	1,454,217
1927	1,052,590		

* Taken from R. Schleifenbaum, "Der Grosshandel in de ıdeutschen Wirtschaft, vornehmlich dargestellt an Hand des Enqueteberichts," *Zeitschrift für Handelswissenschaftliche Forschung*, 26. Jahrgang, 8. Heft, August, 1932, pp. 403-422.

† These figures differ slightly from those given in the text (pp. 279, 284) for the earlier years; the differences seem to be due to methods of classifying the cooperative societies.

TABLE 21

NUMBER OF GERMAN CORPORATIONS OPERATING DECEMBER 31, 1929
CLASSIFIED BY AMOUNT OF CAPITAL*

Business group	Share capital† (Nominal capital in millions of marks)													
	5,000 to 50,000 marks		50,000 to 100,000 marks		100,000 to 500,000 marks		500,000 to 1 million marks		1 million to 5 million marks		5 million to 20 million marks		Over 20 million marks	
	Number	Nominal capital	Number	Nominal capital	Number	Nominal capital	Number	Nominal capital	Number	Nominal capital	Number	Nominal capital	Number	Nominal capital
Basic materials	97	1.86	69	4.4	264	63.3	112	73.9	232	510	67	638	54	3,732
Manufacturing‡	465	9.02	480	29.0	1,958	466.3	881	577.5	1,262	2,551	246	2,090	45	3,120
Water, gas, electricity	22	0.53	15	1.0	67	14.0	9	6.0	78	186	56	521	27	1,402
Commercial trade§	885	14.01	518	29.2	805	164.3	199	121.9	219	377	36	294	2	117
Banks and other exchange business‖	94	1.31	52	3.0	170	36.2	84	46.4	142	254	56	513	18	978
Holding companies	18	0.25	6	0.4	19	4.5	14	9.1	33	63	25	253	16	1,338
Insurance	40	0.53	21	1.1	36	8.0	9	5.3	161	343	28	204	4	125
Transport ¶	29	0.48	24	1.5	96	24.2	72	50.2	171	351	54	451	10	1,015
Miscellaneous	142	2.93	93	5.4	244	54.1	73	49.2	101	197	15	118	4	107
Total	1,792	30.92	1,278	75.0	3,659	834.9	1,453	939.5	2,399	4,832	583	5,082	180	11,934

* *Stat. Jahrbuch*, 1930: 381.
† Not including 31 corporations whose share capital is not expressed in Reichsmarks.
‡ Excluding building materials industries.
§ Excluding banks and holding companies, but including books and publishing.
‖ Excluding Reichsbank, Deutsche Rentenbank, and Deutsche Rentenbank Kredit Anstalt.
¶ Excluding German National Railways.

APPENDIX C

CHARTS 1 TO 6

These charts have all been taken from the *Jahrbuch der Berufsverbände im deutschen Reiche* (herausgegeben vom Reichsarbeitsministerium), Sonderheft zum *Arbeitsblatt*, 52, Ausgabe 1930:43.

CHART 1

Central Committee of German Employers' Associations

A National Committee of German Agriculture
- *1* 20 National Associations

B National Federation of German Industry
- *2* 28 Special Groups
- *3* 1,320 Special Associations
- *4* 21 Agricultural Associations
- *5* 87 Local and General Associations
- *6* 72 Commercial and Industrial Chambers

C Union of German Employers' Associations
- *7* 49 National Special Associations
- *8* 33 District Special Associations
- *9* 7 Local Special Associations
- *10* 21 Mixed Industrial, Agricultural, and District Associations
- *11* 70 Mixed Local Associations and 2,820 Subsidiary Associations

D National Association of German Handicrafts
- *12* German Handicraft and Chamber of Commerce Congress
- *13* 47 Special Associations
- *14* German Cooperatives Association
- *15* Federation of German Business Associations and Handicrafts Unions
- *16* Group for Economic Organization
- *17* Association of Insurance Institutions for Independent Handicrafts and Tradesmen of Germany
- *18* 11 Handicraftsmen's Leagues

E National Association of German Transportation
- *19* National Association of German Air Transport
- *20* National Association of the German Automobile Industry
- *21* Association of German Transportation Management
- *22* Employers' Association of German Street Railway, Narrow Gauge, and Private Railway Companies
- *23* Association of German Expressmen
- *24* National Association of German Drayage Companies
- *25* German Rate Broadcasting

F Employers' Association for the German Newspaper Industry (1,800 members)

G Hansa League for Trade, Commerce, and Industry (323,200 members)

H Central Federation of German Retail Trade
- *26* 46 National Parent Associations
- *27* 5 Economic Associations
- *28* 27 Rural and District Associations
- *29* 43 Industrial and Commercial Chambers

I National Association of German Wholesale and Overseas Trade
- *30* 230 Special Associations
- *31* 22 Industrial and Commercial Chambers
- *32* 10 Import and Export Associations
- *33* 34 Local and District Groups (with 6,000 individual members)

J Federation of Wholesale Trade Employers' Associations
- *34* 9 Local Associations

K National Association of Bank Managers
- *35* 34 District = 18 Local Associations

(Continued on second page following)

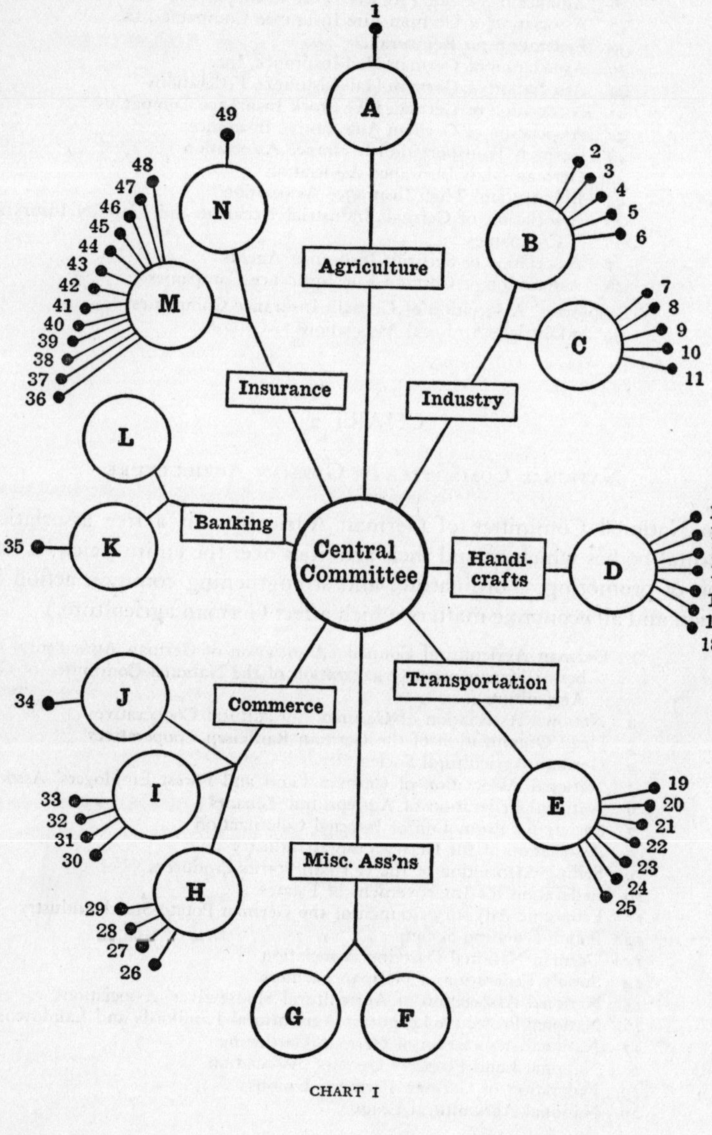
Central Committee
Agriculture
Industry
Handi-crafts
Transportation
Misc. Ass'ns
Commerce
Banking
Insurance
A
B
C
D
E
F
G
H
I
J
K
L
M
N
1
2
3
4
5
6
7
8
9
10
11
12
13
14
15
16
17
18
19
20
21
22
23
24
25
26
27
28
29
30
31
32
33
34
35
36
37
38
39
40
41
42
43
44
45
46
47
48
49

CHART I

L Central Association of German Banks and Banking (1,500 members)
M National Association of Private Insurance
36 Alliance of Private Fire Insurance Companies of Germany
37 Association of German Fire Insurance Companies, Inc.
38 Federation for Reinsurance
39 Association of German Hail Insurance, Inc.
40 Association of German Hail Insurance Federations
41 Association of German Live Stock Insurance Companies
42 Association of German Automotive Insurance
43 German Transportation Insurance Association
44 German Glass Insurance Association
45 Robbery and Theft Insurance Association
46 Association of German Industrial Accident and Liability Insurance Companies
47 Association of Security Insurance Agents
48 Association of German Life Insurance Companies
N Employers' Association of German Insurance Companies
49 7 District = 10 Local Associations

CHART 2

National Committee of German Agriculture

(The National Committee of German Agriculture is a free association of agricultural bodies which extend their activities over the entire Reich; it has the function of promoting, coordinating, and strengthening common action in all legislation and all economic matters which affect German agriculture.)

1 German Agricultural Council (Association of German Agricultural Chambers): Management Organization of the National Committee of German Agriculture
2 National Association of German Agricultural Cooperatives
3 Head Organization of the German Raiffeisen Cooperatives
4 German Agricultural Society
5 National Association of German Land and Forest Employers' Associations
6 National Federation of Agricultural Tenants
7 Society for Promotion of Internal Colonization
8 Association of the German Sugar Industry
9 Selling Association of the German Spirits Producers
10 Federation for Improvement of Estates
11 Economic Advisory Council of the German Potato-Starch Industry
12 Potato Growing Society
13 German National Dairying Association
14 Supply Federation of German Farmers
15 National Association of Agricultural Housewives' Associations
16 National Protective League of Agricultural Landlords and Landowners
17 National Association of German Gardening
18 National Land Property Owners' Association
19 Federation of German Farmers' Unions
20 National Agricultural League

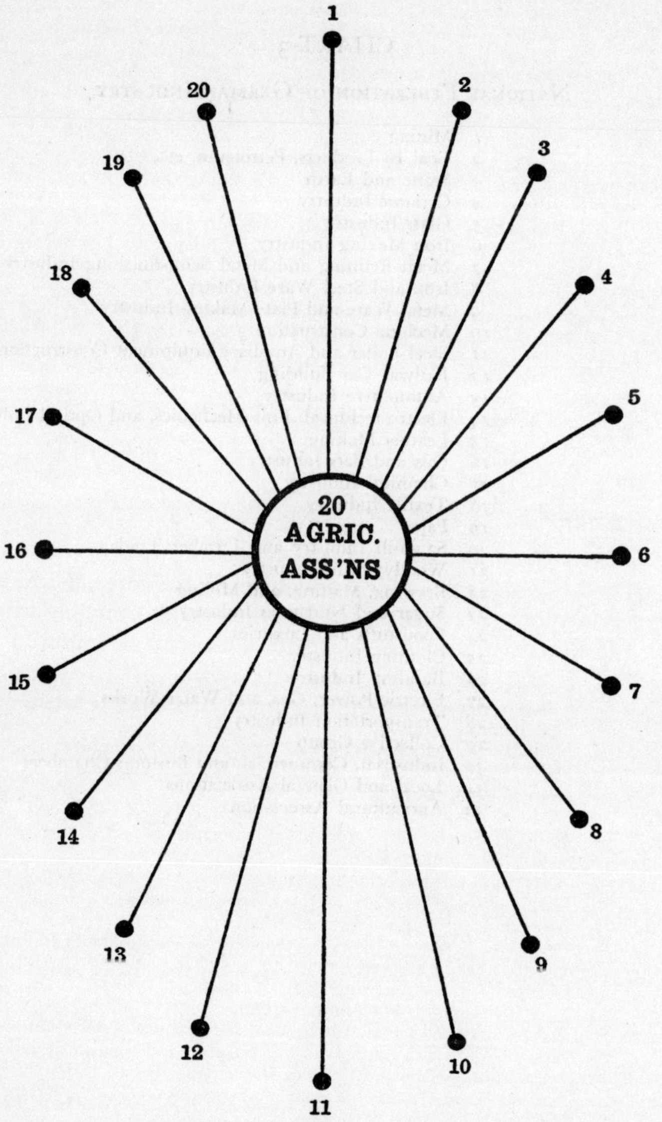

CHART 2

CHART 3

National Federation of German Industry

1 Mining
2 Coal By-Products, Petroleum, etc.
3 Stone and Earth
4 Ceramic Industry
5 Glass Industry
6 Iron Making Industry
7 Metal Refining and Metal Semi-finishing Industry
8 Iron and Steel Ware Industry
9 Metal Ware and Plate Making Industry
10 Machine Construction
11 Steel Boiler and Auxiliary Equipment Construction
12 Railway Car Building
13 Automotive Industry
14 Electro-technical, Fine Mechanics, and Optical Industries
15 Leather Making
16 Oils and Fats Industry
17 Chemical Industry
18 Textile Industry
19 Paper
20 Sawmill Industry and Lumber Trade
21 Woodworking Industry
22 Brewing, Malting, and Milling
23 Sugar and Nutritives Industry
24 Foodstuffs and Luxuries
25 Clothing Industry
26 Building Industry
27 Electric Power, Gas, and Water Works
28 Transportation Industry
29 Collective Group
30 Industrial, Commercial, and Business Chambers
31 Local and General Associations
32 Agricultural Associations

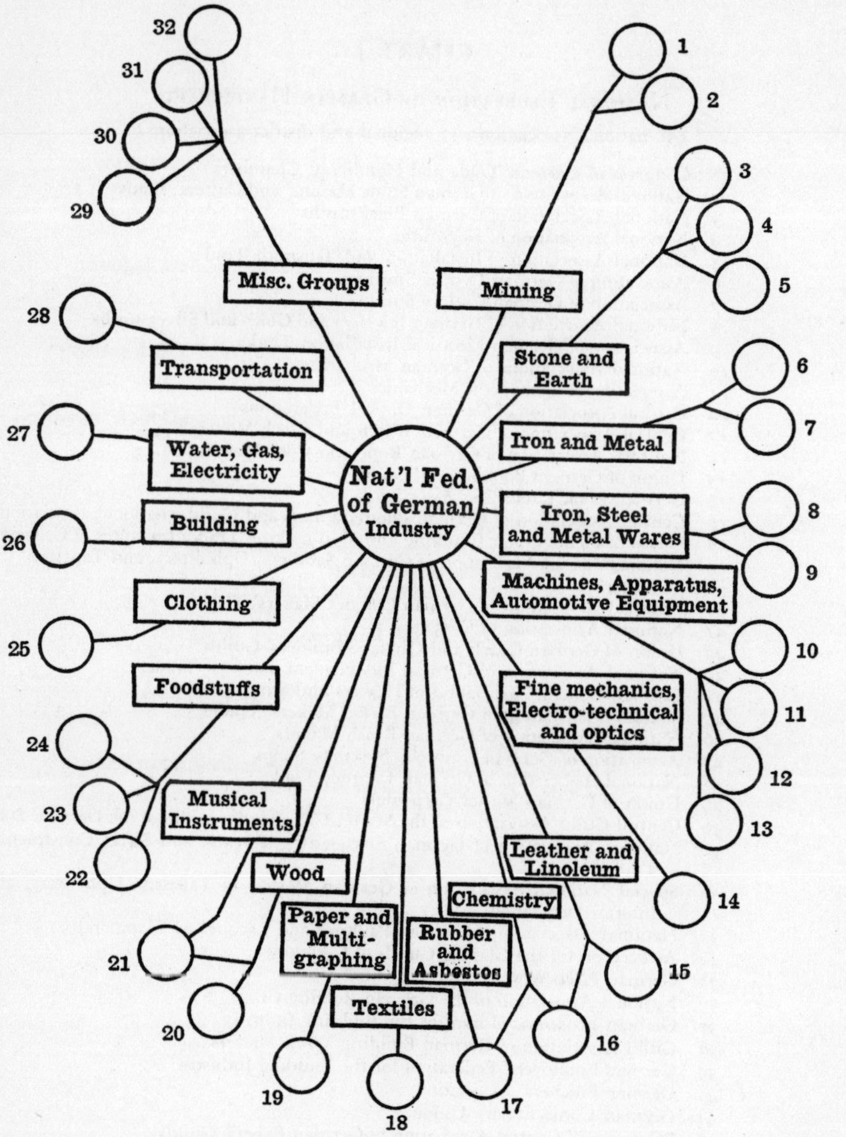
Nat'l Fed. of German Industry
Mining
Stone and Earth
Iron and Metal
Iron, Steel and Metal Wares
Machines, Apparatus, Automotive Equipment
Fine mechanics, Electro-technical and optics
Leather and Linoleum
Chemistry
Rubber and Asbestos
Textiles
Paper and Multi-graphing
Wood
Musical Instruments
Foodstuffs
Clothing
Building
Water, Gas, Electricity
Transportation
Misc. Groups
1
2
3
4
5
6
7
8
9
10
11
12
13
14
15
16
17
18
19
20
21
22
23
24
25
26
27
28
29
30
31
32

CHART 3

CHART 4

National Federation of German Handicrafts

(51 national associations, 11 regional and district associations)

1 Congress of German Trade and Handicraft Chambers
2 National Association of German Stone Masons' and Cutters' Trades
3 National Association of German Blacksmiths
4 National Association of Keysmiths
5 National Association of Installation and Tinsmith Trades
6 Association of German Copper Smithies
7 Association of German Cutlery Smithies
8 National Association of German Jewelers and Gold- and Silversmiths
9 Association of German Electrical Installation Trades
10 National Associations of German Mechanics
11 Association of Orthopedic Mechanics
12 Central Association of German Optical Federations
13 Central Association of German Watch and Clock Makers
14 National Association of German Rope and Cord Makers
15 Union of German Bookbinders' Guilds
16 German Book Publishing Association
17 Central Association of German Photographers and Guilds (national association)
18 Union of Heliographic Caulking and Map-making Trades Institutes of Germany
19 National Special Association of German Saddlery, Upholstery, and Tapestry Masters
20 National Association of German Cabinet Makers' Trades
21 National Association of Coopers
22 Union of German Coach and Carriage Builders' Guilds
23 National Association of German Independent Turners' Trades
24 German General Association of Hewers and Stonemasons
25 National Association of German Basket Makers' Trades
26 National Association of German Brush Makers
27 Association of German Umbrella Specialty Shops
28 National Association of German Lacquer Trades
29 Union of German Master Carpenters
30 Central Guild Association of the Master Chimney Sweepers of the German State
31 National Association of German Stonesetting, Paving, and Street Construction Trades
32 Special National Association of German Masters of Tapestry, Upholstery, and Interior Decoration
33 National Association of German Painting and Lacquering Handicrafts
34 Association for the Glazing Guilds of Germany
35 German Piece-Work Union
36 National Association of the German Roofing Crafts
37 German Economic Union for the Building Industry
38 Guild Association of German Building Work Masters
39 German Employers' Federation for the Building Industry
40 German Butchers' Association
41 German Confectionary Union
42 "Germania" Central Association of German Bakers' Guilds
43 German Milling Federation
44 National Association of German Furriers

(Continued on second page following)

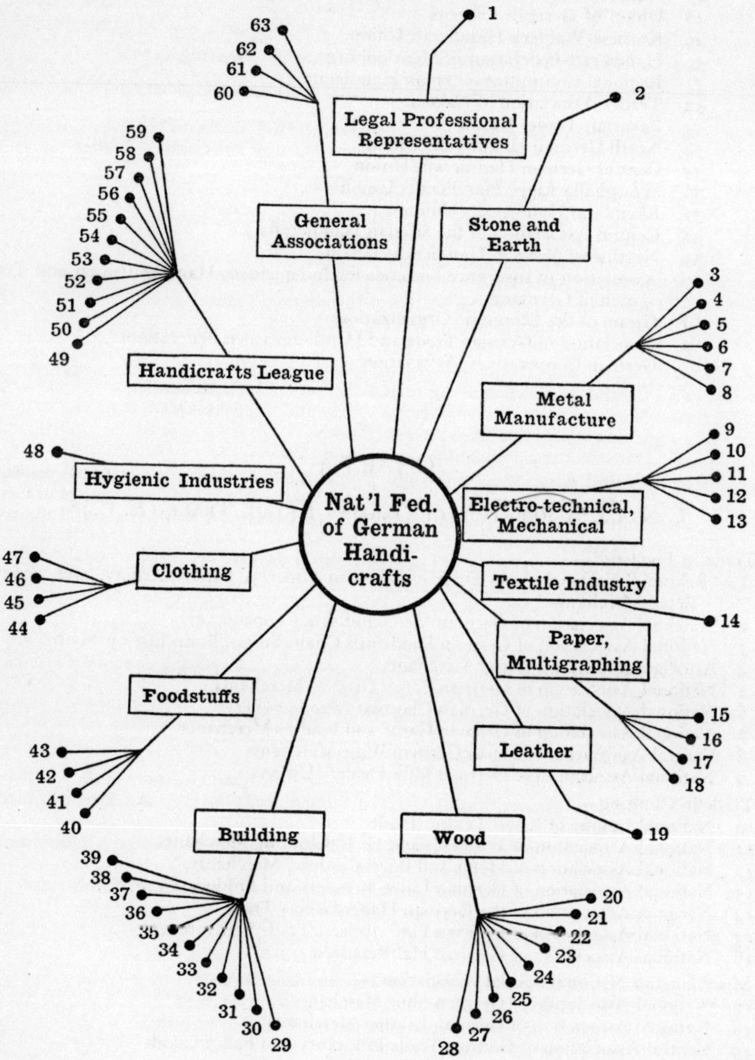
Nat'l Fed. of German Handicrafts
Legal Professional Representatives
General Associations
Stone and Earth
Handicrafts League
Metal Manufacture
Hygienic Industries
Electro-technical, Mechanical
Clothing
Textile Industry
Paper, Multigraphing
Foodstuffs
Leather
Building
Wood
1
2
3
4
5
6
7
8
9
10
11
12
13
14
15
16
17
18
19
20
21
22
23
24
25
26
27
28
29
30
31
32
33
34
35
36
37
38
39
40
41
42
43
44
45
46
47
48
49
50
51
52
53
54
55
56
57
58
59
60
61
62
63

CHART 4

45 National Association of German Craft Shoemakers
46 National Association of the Guilds for the Women's Dressmaking Trades
47 National Association of the German Tailoring Trades
48 Union of German Friseurs
49 Kurhess-Waldeck Handicraft Union
50 Handicraft Federation of Mecklenburg
51 Regional Committee of Saxon Handicrafts
52 Trades Association of Nassau
53 Bavarian Trades Union
54 North German Handicrafts Union
55 Central German Handicrafts Union
56 Westphalia-Lippe Handicrafts Union
57 Rheinland Handicrafts Union
58 Central Association of the Silesian Handicrafts
59 Northwest German Handicrafts Union
60 Association of Insurance Societies for Independent Handicraftsmen and Tradesmen of Germany
61 Group of the Economic Organizations
62 Association of German Trade and Handicraftsmen Federations
63 German Cooperatives' Association

CHART 5

Central Association of German Retail Trade (*E. V.*)*

A Trade in Foodstuffs—
1 "Rekofei," National Association of German Grocery, Fancy Grocery, and Foodstuffs Retail Merchants
2 "Edeka," Association of German Merchandising Cooperatives
3 National Association of German Foodstuffs Chain-Stores, Frankfurt-on-Main†
4 Association of Berlin Butter Merchants
5 National Association of German Fancy Grocery Merchants
6 National Association of German Chocolate Shop Owners
7 National Association of German Game and Poultry Merchants
8 Central Association of North German Wine Merchants
9 National Association of German Milk Dealers' Unions

B Trade in Clothing—
10 National League of Retail Textile Trade
11 National Association of Women's and Girls' Clothing Merchants
12 National Association of Men's and Boys' Clothing Merchants
13 National Association of German Linen Retailers and Producers
14 National Association of the German Haberdashery Trade
15 National Association of German Fine Apparel Trade Federations
16 National Association of German Hat Retailers

C Miscellaneous National Special Associations—
17 National Association of German Shoe Merchants
18 National Association of German Leather Merchants
19 Central Association of German Trade in Luxury and Fancy Goods
20 German Special Furniture Association
21 Association of German Hardware Merchants

(Continued on second page following)

* E. V. = Eingetragener Verein = Registered Association.
† The few associations that are not registered are marked with the dagger.

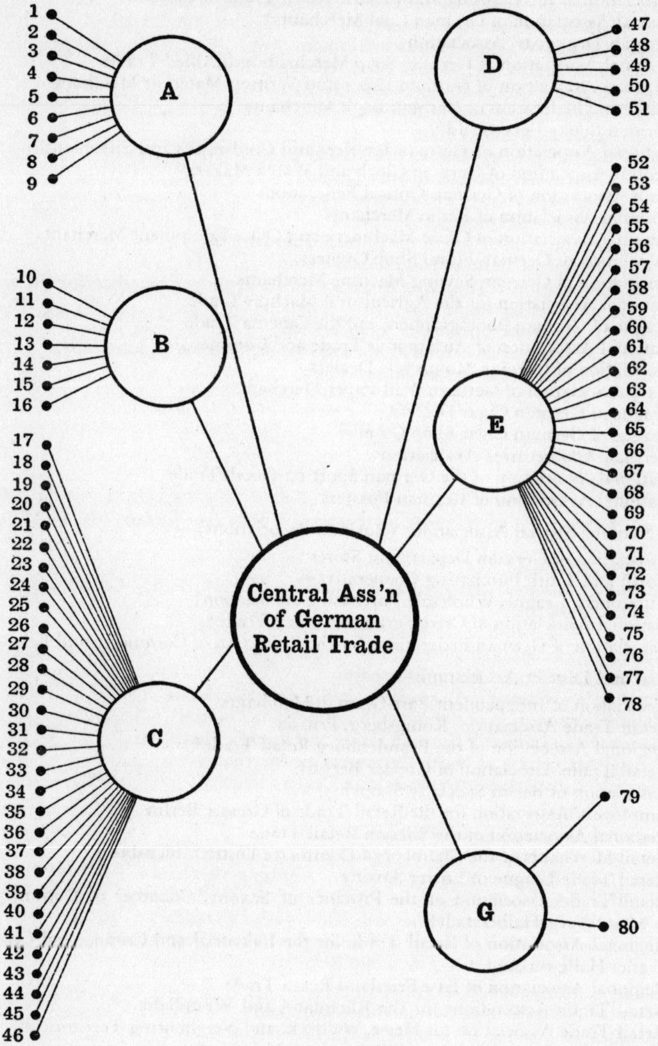
Central Ass'n of German Retail Trade
A
B
C
D
E
G
1
2
3
4
5
6
7
8
9
10
11
12
13
14
15
16
17
18
19
20
21
22
23
24
25
26
27
28
29
30
31
32
33
34
35
36
37
38
39
40
41
42
43
44
45
46
47
48
49
50
51
52
53
54
55
56
57
58
59
60
61
62
63
64
65
66
67
68
69
70
71
72
73
74
75
76
77
78
79
80

CHART 5

22 National Association of German Special Dealers in Porcelain, Glass, Household, and Cooking Apparatus
23 Association of the Lighting and Electric Retail Trade of Germany
24 Central Association of German Coal Merchants†
25 German Druggists' Association
26 National Association of German Soap Merchants and Allied Trades
27 National Association of German Paper and Writing Materials Merchants
28 Marketing Federation of German Book Merchants
29 German Booksellers' Guild†
30 National Association of German Jewelers and Goldsmiths and Silversmiths
31 Central Association of German Clock and Watch Makers
32 Main Association of German Optical Federations
33 National Association of Radio Merchants
34 National Association of Office Machinery and Office Equipment Merchants
35 Association of German Floral Shop Owners
36 Association of German Sewing Machine Merchants
37 National Association for the Agricultural Machine Trade
38 League of German Photographers and the Cinema Trade
39 National Association of Automotive Trade and Commerce
40 Association of German Motorcycle Dealers
41 Main Association of German Wall-Paper Merchants
42 League of German Cigar Dealers
43 League of German Cigar Shop Owners
44 German Apothecaries' Association
45 National Association of the German Sporting-Goods Trade
46 National Association of German Furriers

D Other National Special Associations (Business Associations)—

47 Association of German Department Stores
48 North and South Purchasing Cooperatives†
49 Nuremberg League, Wholesale Purchasing Association†
50 National Association of Credit-granting Retail Trade†
51 Association of German Federations for the Protection of Commerce and Rebates†

E Regional and District Associations—

52 Association of Independent East-German Merchants
53 Retail Trade Association, Königsberg, Prussia
54 Regional Association of the Brandenburg Retail Trade†
55 Retail Trade Association of Greater Berlin†
56 Association of Berlin Specialty Shops†
57 Employers' Association for the Retail Trade of Greater Berlin
58 Regional Association of the Silesian Retail Trade
59 Retail Merchants of the Chamber of Commerce District, Flensburg
60 Retail Trade League of Lower Saxony
61 Retail Trade Association of the Province of Saxony, Chamber of Commerce, District Magdeburg-Halberstadt†
62 Regional Association of Retail Trade for the Industrial and Commercial Chamber, District Halle-on-Saale†
63 Regional Association of East Friesland Retail Trade
64 Retail Trade Associations for the Rheinland and Westphalia
65 Retail Trade Association for Hesse, Waldeck, and Neighboring Territories†
66 Association of Retail Trade of Frankfurt-on-Main†
67 Working Association of the Bavarian Retail Trade
68 Commercial Protective Association of the Palatinate
69 Saxon Retail Trade Federation†
70 Leipzig Association of Retail Trade

† The few associations that are not registered are marked with the dagger.

71 Working Association of the Württemberg Retail Trade
72 Regional Headquarters of the Baden Retail Trade
73 Retail Trade Association of Thuringia
74 Regional Association of the Hessian Retail Trade
75 Regional Association of the Anhalt Retail and Wholesale Trade
76 Working Association of the Retail Trade of Greater Hamburg
77 Regional Association of the Bremen Retail Trade
78 Association of Lübeck Retail Trade Federations†

F Chambers of Commerce—
79 Chamber of the Hamburg Retailers†
80 Chambers of Industry and Commerce and Chambers of Commerce: Breslau, Hirschberg Kottbus, Sagan, Görlitz, Liegnitz, Oppeln, Königsberg, Osnabrück, Münster in Westphalia, Arnsberg (for southeastern Westphalia), Hagen in Westphalia (Southwest Industrial and Commercial Chamber of Commerce), Essen, Düsseldorf, Krefeld, Coblenz, Cologne, Bonn, Munich, Gladbach, Aachen, Stolberg (Rhineland), Oldenburg, Emden, Gera, Weimar, Sonneberg, Frankfurt-on-Main, Wiesbaden, Karlsruhe, Lahr in Baden, Heidelberg‡, Constance‡, Mannheim, Ludwigshafen‡, Schopfheim‡, Pforzheim‡, Augsburg, Nuremburg, Harburg-Wilhelmsburg, Altona, Kiel, and the Retail Trade Chamber of Bremen.

---

† The few associations that are not registered are marked with the dagger.
‡ H. K. = Chamber of Commerce.

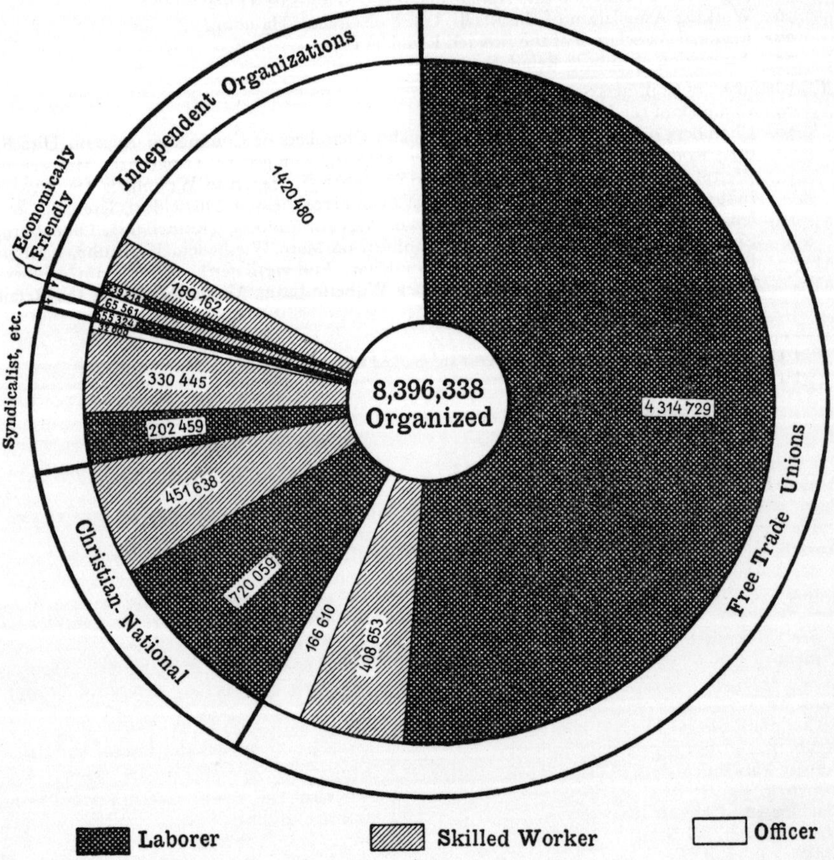
Independent Organizations
1 420 480
Economically Friendly
189 162
65 561
55 324
Syndicalist, etc.
330 445
202 459
451 638
720 059
Christian-National
166 610
408 653
8,396,338 Organized
4 314 729
Free Trade Unions
Laborer
Skilled Worker
Officer

CHART 6

INDEX